D0702059

SQL:1999

Understanding Relational Language Components

The Morgan Kaufmann Series in Data Management Systems

Series Editor: Jim Gray, Microsoft Research

SQL:1999: Understanding Relational Language Components
Jim Melton and Alan R. Simon

Information Visualization in Data Mining and Knowledge Discovery
Edited by Usama Fayyad, Georges G. Grinstein, and Andreas Wierse

Transactional Information Systems: Theory, Algorithms, and the Practice of Concurrency Control and Recovery
Gerhard Weikum and Gottfried Vossen

Spatial Databases: With Application to GIS
Philippe Rigaux, Michel Scholl, and Agnes Voisard

Information Modeling and Relational Databases: From Conceptual Analysis to Logical Design
Terry Halpin

Component Database Systems
Edited by Klaus R. Dittrich and Andreas Geppert

Managing Reference Data in Enterprise Databases: Binding Corporate Data to the Wider World
Malcolm Chisholm

Data Mining: Concepts and Techniques
Jiawei Han and Micheline Kamber

Understanding SQL and Java Together: A Guide to SQLJ, JDBC, and Related Technologies
Jim Melton and Andrew Eisenberg

Database: Principles, Programming, and Performance, Second Edition
Patrick and Elizabeth O'Neil

The Object Data Standard: ODMG 3.0
Edited by R. G. G. Cattell and Douglas K. Barry

Data on the Web: From Relations to Semistructured Data and XML
Serge Abiteboul, Peter Buneman, Dan Suciu

Data Mining: Practical Machine Learning Tools and Techniques with Java Implementations
Ian Witten and Eibe Frank

Joe Celko's SQL for Smarties: Advanced SQL Programming, Second Edition
Joe Celko

Joe Celko's Data and Databases: Concepts in Practice
Joe Celko

Developing Time-Oriented Database Applications in SQL
Richard T. Snodgrass

Web Farming for the Data Warehouse
Richard D. Hackathorn

Database Modeling and Design, Third Edition
Toby J. Teorey

Management of Heterogeneous and Autonomous Database Systems
Edited by Ahmed Elmagarmid, Marek Rusinkiewicz, and Amit Sheth

Object-Relational DBMSs: Tracking the Next Great Wave, Second Edition
Michael Stonebraker and Paul Brown with Dorothy Moore

A Complete Guide to DB2 Universal Database
Don Chamberlin

Universal Database Management: A Guide to Object/Relational Technology
Cynthia Maro Saracco

Readings in Database Systems, Third Edition
Edited by Michael Stonebraker and Joseph M. Hellerstein

Understanding SQL's Stored Procedures: A Complete Guide to SQL/PSM
Jim Melton

Principles of Multimedia Database Systems
V. S. Subrahmanian

Principles of Database Query Processing for Advanced Applications
Clement T. Yu and Weiyi Meng

Advanced Database Systems
Carlo Zaniolo, Stefano Ceri, Christos Faloutsos, Richard T. Snodgrass, V. S. Subrahmanian, and Roberto Zicari

Principles of Transaction Processing
Philip A. Bernstein and Eric Newcomer

Using the New DB2: IBM's Object-Relational Database System
Don Chamberlin

Distributed Algorithms
Nancy A. Lynch

Active Database Systems: Triggers and Rules for Advanced Database Processing
Edited by Jennifer Widom and Stefano Ceri

Migrating Legacy Systems: Gateways, Interfaces, and the Incremental Approach
Michael L. Brodie and Michael Stonebraker

Atomic Transactions
Nancy Lynch, Michael Merritt, William Weihl, and Alan Fekete

Query Processing for Advanced Database Systems
Edited by Johann Christoph Freytag, David Maier, and Gottfried Vossen

Transaction Processing: Concepts and Techniques
Jim Gray and Andreas Reuter

Building an Object-Oriented Database System: The Story of O_2
Edited by François Bancilhon, Claude Delobel, and Paris Kanellakis

Database Transaction Models for Advanced Applications
Edited by Ahmed K. Elmagarmid

A Guide to Developing Client/Server SQL Applications
Setrag Khoshafian, Arvola Chan, Anna Wong, and Harry K. T. Wong

The Benchmark Handbook for Database and Transaction Processing Systems, Second Edition
Edited by Jim Gray

Camelot and Avalon: A Distributed Transaction Facility
Edited by Jeffrey L. Eppinger, Lily B. Mummert, and Alfred Z. Spector

Readings in Object-Oriented Database Systems
Edited by Stanley B. Zdonik and David Maier

SQL:1999

Understanding Relational Language Components

Jim Melton
Oracle Corporation

Alan R. Simon

MORGAN KAUFMANN PUBLISHERS

AN IMPRINT OF ACADEMIC PRESS
A Harcourt Science and Technology Company
SAN FRANCISCO   SAN DIEGO   NEW YORK   BOSTON
LONDON   SYDNEY   TOKYO

Executive Editor	Diane D. Cerra
Publishing Services Manager	Scott Norton
Production Editor	Howard Severson
Assistant Editor	Belinda Breyer
Production Assistant	Mei Levenson
Cover Design	Ross Carron
Cover Image	NASA/JPL/University of Arizona
Text Design, Composition, and Illustration	Rebecca Evans
Copyeditor	Carol Leyba
Proofreader	Ken DellaPenta
Indexer	Steve Rath
Printer	Courier Corporation

Designations used by companies to distinguish their products are often claimed as trademarks or registered trademarks. In all instances in which Morgan Kaufmann Publishers is aware of a claim, the product names appear in initial capital or all capital letters. Readers, however, should contact the appropriate companies for more complete information regarding trademarks and registration.

Morgan Kaufmann Publishers
340 Pine Street, Sixth Floor, San Francisco, CA 94104-3205, USA
http://www.mkp.com

ACADEMIC PRESS
A Harcourt Science and Technology Company
525 B Street, Suite 1900, San Diego, CA 92101-4495, USA
http://www.academicpress.com

Academic Press
Harcourt Place, 32 Jamestown Road, London NW1 7BY, United Kingdom
http://www.academicpress.com

© 2002 by Academic Press
All rights reserved
Printed in the United States of America

06 05 04 03 02   5 4 3 2 1

No part of this publication may be reproduced, stored in a retrieval system, or transmitted in any form or by any means—electronic, mechanical, photocopying, or otherwise—without the prior written permission of the publisher.

Library of Congress Cataloging-in-Publication Data is available for this book.

ISBN 1-55860-456-1

This book has been printed on acid-free paper.

To the teachers and mentors who gave so much of themselves to ensure that I learned how to learn. They include:

> Miriam Darnall, who tried with some success to teach me to play the piano, but taught me that honesty, ethical behaviors, and perseverance are values in every endeavor.

> Perry Dennis, band director *par excellence,* who never allowed his students to give less than their best and taught us never to give in to mediocrity.

> Gloria Wegener, who taught me how to enjoy literature and that it is possible for me to write.

> Barry "The Buddha" Rubinson, who believed in me and helped me into and through my first database architecture assignments.

> Don Deutsch, a friend and mentor who chairs NCITS H2 and keeps me focused on the really important goals.

This book would not have been possible without them.

Jim

Dedicated to all those who have supported me throughout my writing career.

Al

Foreword

Jim Gray
Microsoft Research

The database community labored for most of a decade to produce the SQL:1999 standard, which is now the vendor-independent definition of the SQL language. Now that it is approved, database vendors are evolving their products to align with this new standard. The new standard improved existing features while unifying and generalizing them. There were major advances in security, active databases, relational operators, and datatypes. For me, the most significant improvement is the addition of table-references, which can be the basis for nested relations and for an object-oriented approach to data representation.

This book, along with the forthcoming companion volume, gives a very readable tour of the standard, presented from the perspective of someone who wants to use the language. It is not an SQL tutorial—an earlier book by Melton and Simon fills that role. Nor is it an SQL implementer's guide—the standard does that. Rather, this is a guide for the SQL user who wants to understand the full breadth of the SQL:1999 language. The book presents the ideas and the language in an understandable format, and it illustrates the ideas with extensive examples. While this volume presents the "basic" SQL:1999 features, the companion volume will cover more advanced topics.

Jim Melton has been the editor of the SQL standard for more than a decade. He knows it better than anyone else, and he knows why the standard is the way it is. This book is his opportunity to present the SQL:1999 standard in a format readable for a much wider audience by organizing it in a progression of ideas, and by illustrating the ideas with examples.

Alan Simon has worked on SQL implementations but now focuses primarily on the way SQL is used in practice. He and Jim Melton cowrote an excellent SQL tutorial. Alan brings the user's perspective to this work. Together Melton and Simon have done an excellent job of making the standard accessible to the rest of us.

Contents

Chapter 6   **Advanced Value Expressions: CASE, CAST, and Row Value Expressions**   **165**

Chapter 18   Dynamic SQL   569

Preface

A Word About SQL, Databases, and Programmers

SQL is undoubtedly the most accepted and implemented interface language for relational database systems. Michael Stonebraker has referred to SQL as "intergalactic dataspeak" (a fact that served as the inspiration for our cover). Indeed, like Fortran, C, and COBOL, SQL may be among the most widely used and understood computer languages around.

The fourth revision of the ANSI and ISO standard for SQL has now been published, and all programmers concerned with relational database applications will be affected by it. Because of the influence of the relational model of data, few programmers are unaware of relational database systems and many use them daily. Even programmers who use PC database systems like dBASE, Paradox, and other "Xbase" systems, as well as Microsoft's Access, will be affected by SQL:1999.

Why We Wrote This Book

Most of the books on SQL with which we are familiar are either oriented toward end users who might type queries into an interactive terminal or they are critiques of the language. Neither approach is really adequate for the broad variety of use that now characterizes SQL programming. Moreover, with the increasing use of SQL, many people are learning SQL without the benefit (or disadvantage) of knowing the earlier SQL-86, SQL-89, or SQL-92. We believe that there is a need for a book that presents the entire SQL language from the novice level through the expert level. In taking such an approach, we wanted to focus not on interactive SQL use, but primarily on the ways in which real applications will use the language.

Who Should Read It

Because of the orientation and style chosen for the book, we believe that it will be useful to a broad range of readers. Application programmers are our primary audience, but we have also kept in mind the needs of database administrators and designers as well as system analysts.

We hope that our book will be a helpful resource to programmers at every level. In addition, system designers and implementors can benefit from knowing the design rationale and choices represented in the standard. We have even included some fairly esoteric material from the SQL:1999 standard with the intent to present it more clearly than the standard does. This may be of help to engineers building the SQL DBMS systems that implement SQL:1999.

How This Book Is Organized

SQL is a large and complex language. No linear treatment of it can ever succeed completely. Printed books, unfortunately, are inherently linear. We have tried to organize the book so that you can read it cover to cover if you are so inclined. However, we know that most readers don't approach technical books like this. Instead, you might prefer to skip around and first read certain chapters or sections that are of particular interest to you, or that contain information required for your current projects. Both the amount of material in each chapter and the structure of the discussions are intended to facilitate this kind of "real-world" use.

We start off with basic concepts, move into foundation material, proceed through some rather complex areas related to all aspects of the language, and then spend quite a lot of the book presenting many different areas of SQL:1999. In all cases, when a particularly important concept is used, we give you a cross-reference to the location where it is discussed in detail.

Conformance to the SQL-92 standard was based on three "levels" of the language, ranging from features used in older systems to those that may never be widely implemented. SQL:1999, by contrast, requires implementation of a single set of features—called *Core SQL*—in order for conformance to be claimed. The majority of SQL:1999's features are not included in Core SQL; however, a number of them are grouped into *packages* to which conformance may be claimed once Core SQL:1999 is done.

This book is meant to be used in place of the standard and is not merely a rehash of the standard. While the standard is designed to tell vendors how to write an SQL DBMS, this book is intended to tell application writers how to *use* such a DBMS. If you are interested in the details of the language specification,

Appendix D, "Relevant Standards Bodies," tells you how to buy a copy of the standard for your own use.

However, this book is not a substitute for product documentation. It discusses the entire SQL:1999 language, not only those parts implemented by a specific vendor or at any specific point in time. You will frequently need documentation for your specific products to write your applications. On the other hand, it may also give you some idea of what your system may be capable of in future incarnations.

Examples

One feature that should distinguish this book from most others is the nature of the example application. The great majority of database books seem to choose one of two example applications that they use to illustrate language features—a payroll application and a parts database. We have long since tired of these applications and tried to find something that would be a bit more fun. We are both big cinema fans, so we decided to build a database of movie information and write our sample code to extract information from and manipulate data in that database. Appendix B, "A Complete SQL:1999 Example," presents the database definition (schema) and the data that we used for this application.

Anybody who has ever read a programming language manual or text knows that the authors always have to present the syntax of the language elements (the statements, for example) in *some* form. One of the most common techniques for this is the use of Backus-Naur Form (BNF), which is used extensively in this book.

We use two different styles when we give you the syntax of various parts of the SQL language. One form is the more formal BNF that is actually used in the SQL standard itself. It is distinguished from the other forms in its use of angle brackets (< and >) to identify nonterminal symbols of the grammar. (A nonterminal symbol is one that is further resolved in the grammar; a terminal symbol is one that has no further breakdown.) This more formal notation is usually quite complete, filling out every detail of the syntax. For example, let's consider here a short, hypothetical example of our more formal notation (for a USA-style mailing address):

```
<mailing address> ::=
 <street number> <street name> [ <street type> ]
 <city name> <state code> <zip code>

<street number> ::= <digit>... [ <letter> ]
```

```
<street name> ::= <character string>

<street type> ::=
  Street
  | Avenue
  | Lane

<city name> ::= <character string>

<state code> ::=
  'AK'
  | !! 49 codes omitted here
  | 'WY'

<zip code> ::=
  <digit> <digit> <digit> <digit> <digit>
  [ <digit> <digit> <digit> <digit> ]
```

That bit of syntax provides several pieces of information. First, it says that a
<mailing address> (a BNF nonterminal symbol) is made up of two mandatory
pieces of syntax followed by an optional one, which is followed in turn by three
more mandatory ones. It allows the (mandatory) <street number> to be an arbitrary number of digits, optionally followed by a single letter. We allow a <street
type> to be one of exactly three alternatives. We also used a notation used by the
SQL standard for a BNF comment—the two consecutive exclamation points (!!).
Note also that we did *not* tell you (in this BNF excerpt) what a <digit> is or what a
<character string> is, even though a complete language syntax specification
would have to do so.

The other, more casual form doesn't use the angle brackets, but depends on a
(natural language) interpretation of the various terms used in the syntax being
described. The same (USA-style mailing address) example expressed using the
more casual style would look like this:

```
mailing-address ::=
  street-number street-name [ street-type ]
  city-name state-code zip-code

street-number ::= digit... [ letter ]

street-name ::= character string
```

```
street-type ::=
 Street
 | Avenue
 | Lane

city-name ::= character string

state-code ::= !! one of the 51 codes approved by the postal service

zip-code ::=
 5-digit-code [ 4-digit-extension ]
```

This casual style includes almost the same information as the formal style, but we take for granted a lot more of your ability to intuitively understand our meaning.

In a few cases, where we think that different alternatives for one piece of syntax deserve to be considered almost as though they were complete separate entities, we use bullets to break up the syntax, like this:

```
<mailing address> ::=
 <USA mailing address>
 | <Canada mailing address>
 | <Japan mailing address>
```

- `<USA mailing address> ::= ...`

- `<Canada mailing address> ::= ...`

- `<Japan mailing address> ::= ...`

The bullets have no intrinsic meaning for BNF purposes; they are used strictly to help you visually distinguish among several alternatives easily.

Additional Resources

Many vendors of SQL database management systems allow their products to be downloaded from their Web sites, usually allowing use in a limited situation, most often for a limited time period. The documentation for such products is almost always available on the companies' Web sites as well, often without even requiring you to download and install the products themselves. While no vendor has made a formal claim (as of the time we write these words) of Core SQL:1999 conformance, it may be very helpful to use those products while you learn SQL:1999.

As you will see in Appendix D, "Relevant Standard Bodies," it is possible to purchase copies of the various documents that make up SQL:1999 by visiting certain Web sites. It may also be possible (but will certainly be more expensive if it is possible) to purchase copies of these documents in hardcopy form.

Relevant Products

No known SQL DBMS conforms to Core SQL:1999 at the time we went to press with this book, but a number of vendors are known to be pursuing conformance. The vendors that we believe are actively pursuing conformance, or are likely to be doing so even though we may not have concrete knowledge of it, include

- Hitachi
- IBM
- Informix
- Microsoft
- Mimer
- Oracle
- Sybase

There may be others—in fact, there almost certainly are—but we have little or no awareness of them.

Conventions

A quick note on the typographical conventions used in the book:

- Type in this font (Stone Serif) is used for all ordinary text.
- *Type in this font (Stone Serif Italic) is used for terms that we define or for emphasis.*
- `Type in this font (Letter Gothic) is used for all the examples, syntax presentations, SQL keywords, and identifiers that appear in ordinary text.`

Syntax of the SQL Language

In the previous edition of this book, we provided the entire syntax of the SQL-92 language in an appendix. Feedback from our readers subsequently indicated that providing (only) the printed version of the SQL-92 BNF was less useful than a machine-readable version would have been. The SQL:1999 syntax is significantly larger than the SQL-92 syntax was, and correspondingly less useful in printed form. Instead of printing the BNF for SQL:1999 in this book, we have chosen to provide the BNF on the Morgan Kaufmann Web site for you to access in machine-readable form when you need it. You can find this material at *www.mkp. com/sql99*.

Acknowledgments

This is the second book that we have written together, and both of us hope that it won't be the last. We enjoy working together and may well find future projects that we can divide equitably between ourselves. But the costs of writing a book are high, in terms of energy, time spent researching and writing, and time lost from other parts of our lives.

Writing this book, like writing any book, is a labor of love—with the emphasis all too often on "labor." It's hard, even though the end result is usually quite rewarding (not financially, in most cases!). It's exceedingly rare to do it alone— the assistance of others is necessary and certainly invaluable: for reviews, for trying out ideas and phraseology, and just for offering encouragement. We cannot fail to acknowledge and thank the wonderful and talented people who reviewed this book and offered help throughout the process. We especially want to thank the following people (alphabetized by last name) for their extensive reviews, which heavily influenced the content and accuracy of this book:

- Christopher Farrar, a long-time participant in the United States committee responsible for SQL (NCITS H2) and an acknowledged expert in many aspects of the standard (as well as other data management technologies, such as Java). Christopher is currently working on other projects for IBM, and his absence from H2 is keenly felt.

- Keith Hare, another long-time participant in H2, first representing DECUS (the Digital Equipment Corporation Users' Society) and then JCC Consulting, of which he is a principal. Keith is widely respected for the depth and breadth of his experience in actually using database systems in practical, demanding environments; as a consequence, he gives the user community an extremely effective voice in the standardization process.

- Bryan Higgs, who develops database systems and the suites of tools that help users deal with them, is currently at Oracle (having joined when Digital Equipment Corporation exited the database business). Bryan not only knows database systems inside and out, he teaches others how to use databases, programming languages, and the tools that help users survive in the real world.

- Fred Zemke, Oracle's formal member of H2 and a regular USA delegate to the corresponding ISO committee (JTC1/SC32/WG3). Fred is an expert on more aspects of the SQL standard than most people ever read, and he is one of the most focused people we know.

Of course, all errors that remain in the book (and we have no illusions that we were able to find and eliminate all errors in a topic this complex) are our sole responsibility.

We'd also like to thank Diane Cerra, Belinda Breyer, Howard Severson, and others at Morgan Kaufmann Publishers for their outstanding support during the conception, writing, and production of this book. Whenever asked, Diane provided us with feedback and suggestions about the content and style of the book (and was amazingly tolerant when we missed deadlines). Belinda was always there to answer our questions, always found time to track down information that we'd misplaced, and ensured that our chapters were quickly reviewed. Finally, Howard Severson truly worked miracles during the production process, minimizing the inevitable confusion during the copyedit and final production activities. To these and others, we are most grateful.

As with any large project—of which writing a book is among the larger—other aspects of life are sorely neglected. We are enormously grateful to our Significant Others, Barbara Edelberg and Ann Mergo, for keeping our lives on track and for tolerating our virtual absence from daily life while the more difficult parts of the book were in progress. It may or may not be true that we couldn't have done it without their help, but there's no doubt at all that it would have been vastly more difficult and not nearly as much fun. Thanks!

Chapter

1

Database and Technology Foundations

1.1 Introduction

The decade of the 1990s was notable for many significant occurrences in many different areas of information technology: client/server computing; the evolution of the Internet from an academic and research network into the foundation of e-commerce and e-business; the growth of business intelligence and data warehousing; the widespread adoption of packaged software for enterprise applications, call center management, and sales force automation; and many other advances that have made information technology, circa 2000, exponentially more pervasive in business and society than only a decade earlier.

One common component of all of the above occurrences is relational database technology with database management system (DBMS) products based on SQL. Although today it seems a foregone conclusion that nearly every new application will be built on top of a relational database and that access to that database's contents will be through a dialect of SQL, barely a decade ago relational database technology was just maturing enough to the point where production-quality, high-data-volume applications could be built and deployed by IT organizations and vendors with enough confidence that those applications wouldn't crumble because of the pressures and demands of industrial-strength information systems. So even though SQL had already established its dominance in the relational database world by the early 1990s, there were still plenty of doubters among data center managers, information systems strategists, and "old world" application developers who questioned whether relational DBMSs—and, by extension, SQL—would ever extend beyond the departmental computing dominated by minicomputers and early client/server systems.

But what a difference a decade makes. Today, existing applications that are built on older database technology or file systems are dismissingly referred to as "legacy applications," the inference being that they not only feature older, antiquated technologies and capabilities, but that they are significantly less valuable to an organization than their more modern counterparts. And it is difficult to imagine any new application, on any size platform, that wouldn't be built using SQL and a relational DBMS.

In 1999, work was completed on the latest version of the SQL standard, known as SQL:1999. This book, and its forthcoming companion volume, will teach you what you need and want to know about the SQL language and about the 1999 standard. First, however, we introduce the subject of database management systems and associated concepts. Readers who have experience working with database technology may wish to briefly skim this chapter and skip ahead to Chapter 2, where we introduce SQL:1999.

1.2 | Introduction to Database Technology

In this section, we briefly define the concepts of a database and of a database management system, often abbreviated as DBMS. Within the scope of interest of this book, we will discuss some of the principal characteristics of databases and DBMSs.

1.2.1 Database Concepts

In the most general sense, a database is a collection of data, usually pertaining to some reasonably well-defined purpose. One example of this broad definition might be the collection of data related to music CDs, videotapes, DVDs, computer CD-ROMs, and other entertainment-related media. Let's say an Internet-based retailer ("e-tailer") collected such data and stored it in a computer in some form in support of their business-to-consumer ("B2C") operations. If this data were transformed into a database, it would likely be of the type that we mean to discuss here.

When discussing databases stored on computer systems, we have to get a little more particular about how the data is stored, interrelated, and so on. A computer system "flat file" containing entertainment media data as in our example might be loosely said to constitute a database, but most IT professionals would not think of it as such. Instead, data has to be stored in a way that lends it certain characteristics before most computer-literate people would say that it constituted a database.[1]

In order to say that data has been stored in a database (as opposed to just being stored), certain conditions must be satisfied.

- The data must have a known format (that is, the format of the data must be well defined to the computer system, not just to application programs that use it). This format is defined by the *metadata,* or data about data.
- The data should be stored, retrieved, and modified only by a special type of computer program—the database management system.
- The data should be under transaction control. That is, a formal set of rules and guidelines must ensure that integrity is maintained during and after operations on data. This is especially important when multiple users and applications are simultaneously accessing the data.

If the music and video information in our example were stored in a manner consistent with these characteristics, then it would probably be recognized as having been stored in a database.

1.2.2 Database Management Systems (DBMSs)

A database management system (DBMS) is a special computer program built to store data into, retrieve data from, and modify data stored in a database. In general, DBMSs require that the user (some user, at least) define the format of the data very specifically. At a minimum, this requires that the user define the number of data items, the data types of those items, and how the items are related to one another. The user may be required to specify how the data items are physically stored on the computer's disks or how the data can be located quickly.

One of the most significant advantages of a DBMS is that it protects the data from many sorts of ill-formed operations. Consider a sequence of operations that make changes to a database of bank accounts (to use an example so trite as to be a cliché): one common sequence is the transferral of money from one account to

---

[1] When large amounts of data were first being collected and made available for access, the term *data bank* was often used to refer to the data collection. The terms *database* and *data bank* were used more or less interchangeably in those early days. It was only later that formal characteristics were ascribed to databases, while data banks remained somewhat of a generic concept. Later in this chapter we mention Dr. E. F. Codd's landmark 1970 paper that introduced the relational model; it was entitled "A Relational Model of Data for Large Shared Data Banks."

another. A typical sequence of operations is to subtract the transfer amount from one account and then add it to the other. If the operations were to be interrupted for any reason after the subtraction but before the addition, then the money would have simply disappeared! A DBMS cannot allow this to happen. To protect against this sort of problem, the DBMS applies transaction semantics to the operations.

A DBMS keeps information pertaining to the format of the data it manages. This information is often called metadata, or data about data. In the context of an SQL database management system, which we will explore shortly, metadata looks a lot like data. The metadata of a database describes the data that the database contains. It is often also self-describing; that is, it describes the metadata itself as well as the user data.

Database systems have to maintain the metadata as well as the user data. There are often specific interfaces, such as special statements, used for metadata maintenance. SQL database systems have such special statements, usually called DDL (data definition language), although we shall see later that *definition* is only part of the function of these special statements. (SQL:1999 calls such statements SML, or Schema Manipulation Language.)

1.2.3 The Relational Model

In June 1970, the Association for Computing Machinery published a paper in its journal, *Communications of the ACM,* by Dr. E. F. Codd, then of the IBM Research Laboratory (IBM Corporation) in San Jose, California. This paper, entitled "A Relational Model of Data for Large Shared Data Banks," was the first hint that many people had of a new model for databases: the relational model.

As defined by Dr. Codd in this seminal paper, the relational model of data provided a number of important characteristics that made database management and use relatively easy, error-resistant, and predictable. Most important, the relational model

- describes data with its *natural* structure, without introducing any additional structure for machine representation or implementation purposes;

- provides a mathematical basis for the treatment of derivability, redundancy, and consistency of relations;

- provides independence of the data from the physical representation of the data, of the relationships between the data, and of implementation considerations related to efficiency and like concerns.

The article contrasted this *relational view of data* with previous methods of data management, most notably the then-popular CODASYL database methodology that is briefly discussed later in this chapter. (CODASYL, the Committee for Data System Languages, developed COBOL as well as a specification for the network database model.)

Tables, Columns, and Rows (or Relations, Attributes, and Tuples)

The basic unit of data is the *relation* (the *table* in SQL, with the primary difference that a relation can never have duplicate rows, while a table can). A relation is made up of one or more *attributes* (*columns* in SQL). Each column (we will use the SQL terminology here to avoid confusion) has associated with it a data type. You already know what a data type is: It's the characteristic of a piece of data that says it is a character string, an integer, a floating-point number, or whatever. Data is stored in a table in *tuples* (*rows* in SQL). As a result, a table looks a bit like a matrix, with the columns identifying the individual data elements (by name, usually, as well as by data type) and the rows representing *records* of related data.

We've also heard an analogy drawn with a check register, with its Check Number, To, and Amount columns and the individual checks (too many, in our case!) acting like rows. Or, getting back to our example, a table might look like a CD distributor's account sheet, as in Table 1-1.

Table 1-1 *Distributor's Account Sheet*

Customer	CD	Cost	# Ordered
Zip's Records and Video	Supernatural	5.99	25
OnlineEntertainment.com	Mirrorball	6.25	10
ClickNMortarMedia.com	Millennium	5.99	35

Here, we can see that this table has four columns and three rows. The first column is named Customer and appears to have a data type of *character string*. The second is named CD and also has a data type of character string. The third column is called Cost and has a data type of decimal. The fourth column is called # Ordered (although, as we shall see, that's not a proper SQL name) and is an integer.

The rows obviously relate to three different customers and specific CD orders. The entire contents of one row relate to one and only one customer order for a given CD. By contrast, the entire contents of one column—a vertical slice—deal with a single attribute or property (such as cost) for all rows in the table.

Something important to note is that even though the rows and columns of a table constitute a matrix on the horizontal and vertical axes, the rows and columns are not equivalent entities. That is, there are important differences between rows and columns with respect to the following characteristics:

- *Volatility:* The number of rows in a table will typically change far more frequently than the number of columns. Rows are often added or deleted as, for example, new CDs come into stock or discontinued albums are omitted. In contrast, the number of columns will change only when we discover a need to record more (or less) information in every row.

- *Complexity of change:* When rows are added or deleted or a data value is modified, no metadata change is necessary (although a specific DBMS implementation may contain pseudo-metadata with row counts within a table, etc.). When columns are added to, deleted from, or modified within a table, however, metadata change is necessary. Depending on the complexity of your specific database—the types of key and referential integrity constraints, the privilege model, and the like—this metadata change may be somewhat complex.

- *Homogeneity:* In a column, viewed as a slice of a table, all elements are the same data type. In a row, on the other hand, the elements need not be the same data type (and usually aren't). Note that this is the characteristic difference between arrays and records in most common application programming languages.

Primitive Data Types

In the relational model of data management, there is the concept of a primitive data type, but only because there are rules in the model that describe how to deal with data of different types. For example, some operations in the relational model (such as the comparison of two data items) require that the data types be the same (at a high level, that is) for two or more items. However, the model does not prescribe what these data types are. Of course, SQL does, as we shall see in the following sections.

Nevertheless, the relational model does tell us something about the characteristics of the data types. The most important of these characteristics is *atomicity,* which means that the individual data items of each data type are *indivisible* and must be treated as a unit.[2]

---

2   Later in this chapter, we'll talk about atomicity in the context of the transaction model and the ACID principles. For the sake of clarification, these two types of atomicity are not identical. Data item atomicity is of a spatial nature, whereas transaction atomicity is temporal in nature.

Most of us have no difficulty grasping this concept when we're talking about integers. Some of us might think that a floating-point number can be broken into its mantissa and exponent, but it's really just a single number when the database is dealing with it. Many of us (okay, C and Pascal programmers, raise your hands) often think of a character string as an array of characters, but the relational model encourages us to treat a character string as an atomic unit.

Relational Operations

The relational model also defines a number of specific operations that can be performed on tables, on rows, and on individual data elements. Let's explore these briefly.

The most important operation is *selection,* or identifying a specific row (or rows) in a table. Selection is normally done by specifying one or more predicates that are used to filter a table to identify the rows for which the predicate is true. (A *predicate* is really nothing more than a question asked about the truth of something, or a statement about that truth; the *value* of a predicate is normally either *true* or *false,* although it can sometimes be *unknown* because insufficient information is available to determine the answer reliably.)

Another operation in the relational model is the *union.* It often happens that two tables have the same structure. Consider a database with one table of VHS cassette tapes and another of laserdisc movies. The chances are high that the structure of the two tables is the same. (Why, you ask, wouldn't we put them into the same table with an additional column to capture the format? Well, we might, but some people might not, and it's not our place to tell people how they have to write their applications!) If we needed to produce a report that combined information about the two tables at the same time, we could combine these tables into a single *virtual* table (one that doesn't physically exist but is materialized only as required) containing the rows of both tables. Let's look at an example. Consider Table 1-2 and Table 1-3.

Table 1-2 *VHS Tapes*

TITLE	COST	STOCK QTY
Payback	15.95	6
Pretty Woman	14.95	18
Runaway Bride	14.95	9
Rocky Horror Picture Show	99.99	1
A Night at the Opera	14.95	5

Table 1-3 *DVDs*

TITLE	COST	STOCK QTY
Pretty Woman	8.95	30
The Sixth Sense	28.95	2
The Thomas Crown Affair	29.95	0

You might actually wish to find out the total number of copies of *Pretty Woman,* regardless of the format. The union of these two tables is the way to go; the tables have the same format, so they may be joined in union.

Table 1-4 *Unnamed Virtual Table*

TITLE	COST	STOCK QTY
Payback	15.95	6
Pretty Woman	14.95	18
Runaway Bride	14.95	9
Rocky Horror Picture Show	99.99	1
A Night at the Opera	14.95	5
Pretty Woman	8.95	30
The Sixth Sense	28.95	2
The Thomas Crown Affair	29.95	0

The order of the rows is not important in the relational model. In many situations, applications don't care about the order of rows; for example, if all you're doing is adding up a column of numbers, it doesn't matter in which order you see the numbers. In other situations, applications do care and they must instruct the database system to sort the rows.

In our example, the union operation causes no ordering to take place, so the fact that the rows appear in Table 1-4 in the order that they appeared in the two source tables is accidental (although rather probable in real implementations).

Another operation is called the *join.* A join operation is a way of combining data from two tables based (usually, at least) on the relationships between the data in those tables. Let's look at another example. Consider Table 1-5 and Table 1-6.

Table 1-5 *VHS Tapes*

NUMBER	TITLE	COST	STOCK QTY
285B	Payback	15.95	6
101J	Pretty Woman	14.95	18
092R	Runaway Bride	14.95	9
588M	Rocky Horror Picture Show	99.99	1
288C	A Night at the Opera	14.95	5

Table 1-6 *Miscellaneous Information*

NUMBER	RATING	CATEGORY
588M	R	Cult
092R	PG-13	Romance
101J	PG-13	Romance
288C	G	Comedy
285B	R	Action

If we wished to learn the rating of a film costing less than $15.00, we would have to combine information from these two tables, because the information cannot be obtained from either table alone. However, if we join the two tables based on the values of the NUMBER column (which the tables have in common), we can get a virtual table that looks like Table 1-7.

Table 1-7 *Another Unnamed Virtual Table*

NUMBER	TITLE	COST	STOCK QTY	RATING	CATEGORY
101J	Pretty Woman	14.95	18	PG-13	Romance
092R	Runaway Bride	14.95	9	PG-13	Romance
288C	A Night at the Opera	14.95	5	G	Comedy
285B	Payback	15.95	6	R	Adventure
588M	Rocky Horror Picture Show	99.99	1	R	Cult

From this virtual table, we can now get the information that we need.

Mathematical Foundations

The mathematical foundations of the relational model provide an interesting and important characteristic: closure. The basic element in the relational model is the relation. All relational operations on relations produce relations! This closure makes it feasible to prove the correctness of many manipulation operations. The various operators that have been defined on relations have precise mathematical characteristics; for example, some are commutative, some are distributive, and some are associative. These characteristics can be used, by optimizers in production-quality products, for instance, to determine faster and more effective methods of data manipulation.

For most people, the usual visualization of a relation takes the form of a table. A table, as we are used to it in other contexts, has rows and columns. The columns of a relation correspond to the *data items* for each of the *records* that are represented by the rows of the relation. Table 1-8 illustrates this point.

Table 1-8 *Movie Titles (Name of Relation)*

Title	Type of Movie	Our Cost	Current Sales Price
Lethal Weapon 4	Action	$23.95	$25.99
Batman Returns	Action	$25.95	$27.99
Antz	Animated	$23.95	$31.99
. . . and so on.			

The simple tabular form of the data is easy for most people to grasp. The relational model represents all data (conceptually, of course) in this form. The relational model has many other important characteristics that we will discuss in detail in Chapter 2, "Introduction to SQL:1999."

In the relational model, there are two different means by which data may be manipulated and managed. One form—the simpler of the two—is known as *relational algebra.* The foundations of relational algebra are built around operations such as the following:

- SELECT: Choosing particular records (formally known in the relational model as *tuples*), possibly based on criteria such as the values in one or more columns

- PROJECT: Choosing only selected columns from a relation

- JOIN: Combining aspects of two or more relations

As we go through our discussion and examples throughout this book, you'll see how features of SQL align with these various relational algebra operations, so you needn't focus too much on understanding relational algebra. And, not to complicate matters too much, the other means by which relational data is managed is known as *relational calculus,* which is a more complex set of mathematical expressions and operations.

In actuality, SQL is a mix of relational algebra and relational calculus, which is one of the reasons that "database purists" have long been critical of the language as not being totally faithful to the mathematical nature of the relational model. From a real-world perspective, however, those involved in defining SQL features—either on a vendor-specific, product-specific basis or through the standards committees—have tried to balance the theoretical and mathematical aspects of the relational model with constraints—and opportunities—presented by the evolution of database technology in the 30 years since the relational model was first presented.

Normal Forms

A final topic with regard to the relational model that we need to discuss is that of normal forms, or *normalization*. Even though the table-and-column structure of a relational database is highly flexible with regard to what content you might wish to store as part of any given table's rows, there are some guidelines that should be followed to help preserve the integrity of the data stored within the database. In this section, we'll briefly discuss normalization—and its counterforce, *denormalization*—to provide some context for the examples we'll provide throughout this book.

The original relational model presented three normal forms by which the design of a relational database's tables should be governed. These are as follows:

- First normal form (1NF): No repeating groups are permitted
- Second normal form (2NF): No partial key dependencies are permitted
- Third normal form (3NF): No nonkey dependencies are permitted

With regard to first normal form, consider the following simple (and commonly used) example. Assume you wish to store information about people—customers, for example—within a database. You might create a table called customers and, within that table, create columns for customer_ID, customer_name, customer_address, customer_city, and so on. But how about telephone numbers? Typically a customer would have more than one telephone number (even excluding additional numbers for fax, mobile phone, etc.). If you were designing this database in a *conceptual* manner, that is, using semantics and design constructs that closely mirror the real-world concepts the database is intended to represent, you would likely model *telephone number* as a *multivalued attribute*, or an attribute that (as you might guess from its name) can have more than one value. That is, unlike the customer's name, address, city, and other fields (columns) in which there is one and only one value, each customer could have two, three, or possibly more telephone numbers. So how would this be handled in a database? Most likely by creating a separate table called `customer_telephone` or something like that, in which `customer_ID` and `customer_telephone_number` are stored. At the point you would wish to present all information about a customer—address, city, state, zip code, and all telephone numbers—a runtime *join* operation combining information from the two tables would need to be performed. Very inefficient, we realize, but should you strictly adhere to the normalization rules of the relational model, that's what you would have to do.

In the world of conceptual database design, multivalued attributes are a highly valuable construct for representing data; however, the concept is a definite no-no in the relational model because of the first normal form rule. (However, as we'll discuss later in this section, SQL:1999 introduces a "wildcard" with regard to adherence to first normal form rules.)

The second normal form (2NF) rule comes into play when a database table has a *combination key* (or *composite key*), meaning that two or more columns are needed together to uniquely identify any given row within that table. For example, assume that a database table contains total sales dollars, organized by a company's regions and by month. The combination of both (1) some type of region name or ID, and (2) a month (the name of the month or a value between 1 and 12—either would work for this example) will determine that some sales dollar value applies to a region and month combination. Again, region + month is the combination key.

Second normal form means that only columns such as `total_dollars` should be stored in that particular database table, keyed by the combination of region + month. What should *not* be stored in that table are columns that are dependent on only part of the key. For example, if a region ID is used in the table, then that table should *not* contain data for the region's name, who the regional manager is, how many salespeople work in that region, and so on. Instead, that information should be stored in another table in which *only* the region ID is the key.

Finally, third normal form means that only columns that are dependent on the key of the table—whether it's a combination key or not—should be part of that table. For example, if a `customer` table has `customer_ID` as the key, then only information about customers should be stored within that table; there should be nothing about employees, regions, and so on.

The above examples are, to be honest, somewhat of an oversimplification. The actual rules of normalization are more complex—at least in how they are specified—but for purposes of our discussion in this book, the above should suffice. It's also important to note that there are additional forms of normalization that were identified after the first three normal forms: Boyce-Codd Normal Form (BCNF), fourth normal form (4NF), and fifth normal form (5NF). These are rarely used, however, so we won't discuss them here.

As mentioned above, it's important to note that whereas normalization is the key principle of the relational model, it is very common to deliberately violate normalization rules, particularly second and third normal forms, when designing and implementing a relational database, primarily for performance reasons. Performing join operations (SQL joins are discussed in Chapter 8, "Working with Multiple Tables: The Relational Operators") has always been a performance-intensive action with regard to the impact on relational database management system products. It is a common practice to denormalize a database design—again, that means to deliberately violate second and/or third normal form by introducing partial key dependencies or nonkey dependencies into a database's schema structure—to help reduce the number of runtime join operations that need to be performed.

Finally, the inclusion of array data types in SQL:1999 introduces the possibility now of denormalization with the intention of violating first normal form. Recalling our multiple telephone number discussion above, you could create an array data type for telephone number in the customers table and, instead of having to join information from two tables as discussed above, a single table could now be used.

In general, normalization is a good database design practice, but experience will reveal times when careful denormalization can provide benefits, primarily in data retrieval performance.

1.2.4 Object-Oriented Databases

During the mid- and late 1980s, even as the relational model was taking hold and commercial RDBMS products were beginning to be commonly used, many technology planners and implementers were quick to point out the deficiencies of the relational model in the context of "real-world" applications. Specifically, it was noted that neither complex nor user-defined data types could be easily supported using the available numeric, character string, and date-oriented data types available within SQL or the other commonly available relational languages. (Nor did the rigid mathematical foundations of the relational model support the extensibility needed for applications such as computer-aided design [CAD] or computer-aided manufacturing [CAM], for example.)

A divide emerged between two competing "camps"—those who insisted that the relational model was *the* future of database technology, no questions asked, versus others who insisted that the relational model was proving to be increasingly unsuitable for "modern" applications. At that time, object-oriented languages were coming into vogue, and the principles of object orientation were quickly carried over into the world of databases.

Unlike for the relational model, with its rigid mathematical precision and formal definition (although, as we noted, RDBMS products have always taken liberties with the underlying foundations), there is no standard definition for what object orientation is—or isn't. Volume 2 of this book will discuss the principles of object orientation in more detail, particularly as they apply to SQL:1999.[3]

It is important to note, though, that before this convergence of the relational and object-oriented worlds, the prevailing sentiment within the database world was "relational versus object-oriented," with proponents of each model claiming the superiority of their preferred approach along with the shortcomings of the alternative model.

1.2.5 Extending the Relational Model with Object-Oriented Capabilities

The rigidity of the relational model with its mathematical underpinnings (discussed in Section 1.2.3) made it impossible to include complex user-defined data types, methods, encapsulation, and all the other aspects of object orientation . . . right?

Not exactly, as it turned out. As time slipped away from the 1970 publication of Dr. Codd's paper describing the relational model, many database product strategists and technologists increasingly questioned the merits of trying to adhere strictly to the core relational model in the face of increasingly complex applications, dramatic advances in hardware and software technology, and an ever-more competitive product landscape.

As a result, commercial products have been developed that are primarily relational in their respective foundations—that is, they are built around a table-and-column structure—but at the same time are augmented with the capabilities and structures (user-defined data types, encapsulation, etc.) found in commercial object-oriented database management systems (ODBMSs) since the late 1980s. Many believe that these products, commonly referred to as *extended relational,* or *object-relational,* database management systems (that is, their core capabilities are extended with those from the object-oriented world), combine the best of both worlds.

Not everyone agrees with this trend and the results, however. Many relational "purists" decry the ever-continuing move away from the rigid foundations of the relational model. Regardless, the world of extended relational DBMS products is here to stay, and the publication of the SQL:1999 standard with its object-oriented extensions has codified and formalized this technology direction.

---

3 Jim Melton, *Advanced SQL:1999—Understanding Object-Relational and Other Advanced Features* (San Francisco: Morgan Kaufmann, in press.)

1.2.6 Other Database Models

There are many other data models that have been used over the years for database management. Some readers might choose to skim over this section, or perhaps skip it entirely; those interested in learning about SQL in a broader historical context might find the following paragraphs of interest.

We have already briefly mentioned the CODASYL network data model. A network model database has several (often many) *record types* that contain data of some specific format. The relationships between records of different types are formed by means of explicit pointers that are stored in individual records of data. For example, a record representing a specific department in a company would contain a pointer to the record representing some employee who works for that department. The record for that employee, in turn, contains a pointer to the record for some other employee working for the same department. The remaining employees working for that department are similarly "linked" together. These pointers are often in the form of *disk addresses* or other similar physical pointers that must be maintained by the application program. The dependence of the data on the physical structure is easy to see. In the 1970s and 1980s there were countless (Dare we say arguments? We dare!) arguments on the topic of whether network database technology is more or less efficient than other models. We do not wish to revisit those discussions here, particularly since (as noted at the outset of this chapter) the decade of the 1990s saw tremendous strides in relational databases and almost universal acceptance of RDBMSs and SQL as the technologies of choice throughout most areas of information systems.

Another model that has been widely used is the *hierarchical model*. One of the most popular implementations of this model is IBM's IMS product, which uses a language called DL/I (Data Language One). The distinguishing characteristic of the hierarchical model (vis-à-vis the network model) is that the parent-child record structure resembles an inverted tree—a hierarchy—rather than a multiple path network topology. Some critics consider this a limitation that makes the model unsuitable for many applications, but most implementations of the hierarchical model have introduced "work-arounds" that avoid the difficulties associated with the restriction. Considering the thousands of IMS applications residing on IBM mainframes around the world, it's obvious that IMS and the hierarchical model have their uses. One characteristic of the hierarchical model, as shown by Date's Universal Data Language (UDL),[4] is that the hierarchical addressing mechanism is generally much simpler than that of the network mechanism. This fact is probably responsible for the success of the hierarchical model.

---

4   C. J. Date, *An Introduction to Database Systems*, vol. 1, 5th ed. (Reading, MA: Addison-Wesley, 1990).

Hierarchical and network databases are still commonly found in most established companies as the data management foundation of their so-called legacy systems. Increasingly, there is a need for interoperability and information exchange between these legacy systems and newly developed applications, meaning that SQL developers often need to have at least some understanding of the structures found in those older models and of how the data relationships are represented.

Throughout the years, many other database models have been used, including a variation of the network model (but non-CODASYL) that was part of the TOTAL product; Computer Corporation of America's Model 204, occasionally still found in older military applications; and System 2000, a variation of the hierarchical model that was different from IBM's IMS. Quasi-relational products were frequently found in the early days of microcomputers and throughout the 1980s, with many of them based on the language foundation first widely used in Ashton-Tate's (later Borland's) dBASE product family (dBASE II, dBASE III, dBASE III+, etc.). By the mid-1990s, most of these products had been supplanted in the PC world by Microsoft's Access database system.

These sort-of-relational products were built using a table-and-column structure similar to that found in "real" relational DBMSs, but typically lacked the "heavy lifting" capabilities such as transaction management and security. By the early 1990s, most of these "Xbase" products such as Computer Associates' Clipper and Microsoft's FoxPro were equipped with SQL interfaces, enabling interoperability between the programmatic features of those languages and an underlying SQL database such as Microsoft's SQL Server.

1.3 | Database Languages

The sections below describe the fundamental characteristics of database languages and provide you with a foundation upon which our subsequent discussion of SQL:1999 is based.

1.3.1   Data Sublanguages Versus Applications Languages

As the name suggests, a *data sublanguage* is one that is used in association with another language for the specialized purpose of accessing data. The sort of programming languages with which most people are familiar includes COBOL, Fortran, and C (and increasingly Java and C++). These languages were designed to allow application programmers to express their computational requirements efficiently. Fortran was designed primarily to support application programmers interested in building numeric or engineering applications, while COBOL is generally felt to be more suitable for writing business-oriented applications, and C is often cited as being well-designed for systems programming applications. Languages such as LISP and Prolog, which perhaps are less well known, were designed for other classes of applications—primarily for building certain classes of artificial intelligence systems.

None of these languages was designed specifically for manipulating data stored under the control of database management systems. It has been found that specialized languages for this purpose are very useful because they permit application writers to express accurately (and often concisely) the data management requirements of the application and get the desired results.

However, a data language by itself is usually insufficient for writing real applications. In almost all cases, an application has a mixture of requirements: perform some calculations, manipulate some information, and manage some data. In this common sort of application, it is usually helpful if the application writer can build the calculation or manipulation portions of the application by using a language well-suited for the purpose, reverting to a specialized data language only for those parts of the application that require it. In this way, the data language is often viewed as (and called) a *data sublanguage* with respect to the *primary programming language*, or *host language*.

As noted in the opening paragraphs of this chapter, barely a decade ago one might have been asked about relational data sublanguages and have mentioned SQL as but one of several that were pervasive in late 1980s-era relational DBMS products. The Ingres product, which has been owned by several different product vendors in its life (currently Computer Associates, but previously ASK and Relational Technology, Inc.) featured the QUEL language in addition to its later adoption of SQL. Digital Equipment Corporation's Rdb/VMS product (now owned by Oracle Corporation) supported RDML in addition to SQL.

It is undoubtedly true that over the years other relational languages have had similar expressive power and that at least some have been more faithful to the relational model, but SQL has the distinct advantage of being nearly universally implemented and used. This, more than anything else, is the reason SQL was selected for standardization and that database product vendors still devote such high levels of energy to the standardization effort.

One final observation about data sublanguages that should be made in this section is in regard to XML, the Extensible Markup Language. An XML standard was published in 1998 by the World Wide Web Consortium (W3C), with the objective of providing a mechanism through which Internet "content providers" could add tags to text to indicate the intrinsic meaning of that text—sort of a colocated metadata scheme that might look like the following example:

```
<vehicle vehicle_type = "Minivan">
  <color> Charcoal Gray </color>
  <price> $30,000 </price>
  <manufacturer> Daimler Chrysler </manufacturer>
  <doors> 5 </doors>
</vehicle>
```

The idea is that you could use an Internet search engine to ask for all Web pages based on specified criteria—for example, all Daimler Chrysler minivans—and receive information from auto buying services, evaluation services, and the like.

It is still uncertain how the relationship between XML and SQL will evolve over the next few years. Some strategists with a "Web-centric" philosophy might see XML, or its query-oriented variants, as a successor—or at least a competitor—to SQL, possibly envisioning a day when XML-based data representation will become the default for internal IT applications as well as those intended for Internet deployment and extra-enterprise environments. Others might see a hybrid model where core data-management functions—not only data definition and access, but other functions such as transaction management and security, as we'll discuss in this book—are handled through SQL, with applicable gateways in place for publishing SQL-managed content for use through XML facilities.

What will happen over the next few years is still to be determined, but is also beyond the scope of this book. We make mention of this particular facet of data management languages to ease the minds of any readers who might be wondering if the investment of their time and energies in mastering SQL might be wasted if that language were to fade away as did QUEL, RDML, or other now-forgotten languages. We don't see that happening. What is likely to occur, though, is that when you're manipulating XML within your application, you'll use some form of a data sublanguage, possibly even an extended version of SQL.

1.3.2 Procedural Versus Nonprocedural Languages

Another useful classification for computer programming languages is the degree of procedural support provided within the language's programming constructs, that is, within the basic building blocks inherent in most application programming languages. Constructs such as IF-THEN-ELSE, DO WHILE, DO UNTIL, CASE, and even the much-maligned GO TO all deal primarily with *how* application functions should be performed. The order in which operations are to be performed is rigidly specified and created by the programmer.

Nonprocedural languages, on the other hand, are oriented more toward the results of certain operations, leaving the *how* aspects to the "black box"—the underlying software environment. The approach of nonprocedural languages tends to be more of a hands-off, goals-oriented boss approach, as contrasted with the former model, which might represent the ultimate micromanager. Basically, a nonprocedural language says, "Look through this stuff and get me something based on certain criteria; I don't care how you do it, just do it."

SQL is heavily oriented toward a nonprocedural model, whereas C, COBOL, Visual Basic, Java, and most other application languages tend to be procedural in nature. There are, however, dialects of SQL within leading products that feature procedural constructs. Examples include

- Transact/SQL (Sybase and Microsoft SQL/Server)
- PL/SQL (Oracle)
- SPL (Informix)

Leading RDBMS vendors have been adding procedural capabilities ("stored procedures") to their products since the late 1980s, despite previous versions of the SQL standard not addressing this particular area of standardization (thus leading to the many different dialects). In 1996, though, the SQL/PSM portion of the SQL:1999 standard[5] was published. A complete discussion of SQL/PSM can be found in another work authored by one of the authors of this book.[6]

1.4 The Transaction Model

No one needs the power of a DBMS to manage small amounts of noncritical data. Your personal pasta recipes, for example, can probably be managed with index cards. On the other hand, there are many applications in which the data has significant financial (or other) value. For example, an entertainment distributor that ships compact discs, videotapes, DVDs, and CD-ROMs to retail outlets—both physical stores and "e-tailers" on the Internet—may be dealing with millions of dollars of inventory. If records of the inventory, shipments, payments owed, and so forth were lost or damaged, the distributor could very well be driven into bankruptcy. It is extremely important that the data be protected against a wide range of potential problems. Of course, some problems are beyond the scope of a DBMS, such as the physical security of the computer

---

5 Then referred to as SQL3, given the uncertainty of when the complete standard would be approved.

6 Jim Melton, *Understanding SQL's Stored Procedures: A Complete Guide to SQL/PSM* (San Francisco: Morgan Kaufmann Publishers, 1998).

systems or protection against natural disasters. But some problems are well within the DBMS's scope, and these should be addressed.

One problem that plagued application writers for years prior to the development of the DBMS was that of interrupted operations: an application begins to update the data and fails before it makes a complete update. This can be catastrophic. Consider the following sequence of events:

- The application is told to process an order for 10,000 CDs for a "brick-and-mortar" retailer.

- The application looks up the information about all the CDs in the database and finds that they're all available (a very efficient supply chain, obviously!).

- The application then subtracts the quantity of each CD ordered from the inventory quantity.

- The application generates a shipping order record in the database. (Later, when all outstanding shipping orders are printed, this will trigger the loading of the CDs onto a truck and delivery to the retailer's warehouse location.)

- Meanwhile, before the application can generate a billing record that would later be printed and sent to the store, the system crashes!

At this point, the inventory shows that the CDs have been shipped, and the trucking foreman loads the CDs onto a truck and drives away—but the retailer is never billed for the CDs! The distributor now has a major problem: they have shipped 10,000 CDs and might never get paid for them. Of course, we could assume that the store owner is probably honest and will eventually call the distributor to ask why he hasn't received a bill. But the distributor will encounter delays in getting his money, and there will be the added expense of tracking the situation to determine what happened. Some people might consider the reverse situation even worse: if the bill were sent to the retailer but the CDs were never shipped, the distributor might be accused of fraud. Situations like this make it clear that there is often no safe sequence in which to do the operations to ensure against system problems.

The solution lies in a DBMS feature called the *transaction*. A transaction is an *atomic* unit of work (indeed, some DBMS systems use the phrase *unit of work* instead of transaction), meaning it either completely succeeds or has no effect at all (more about this shortly). Returning to the previous example, we might want to redefine the sequence as a transaction.

1. Look up the information about the CDs in the database.

2. If they're all available, then subtract the quantity ordered from the inventory quantity.

3. Generate a shipping order record

4. Generate a billing record.

5. Update the accounts receivable to reflect the billing record.

6. Generate a reorder record to be printed later, so that replacements can be reordered from the CD manufacturers.

7. Instruct the DBMS to make all actions final.

Presumably, at the end of the day or at various points during the day, all the shipping order records will be printed (and deleted) to trigger the loading of trucks; all the billing records will be printed (and deleted) to be sent to the stores; and so forth.

If at any point anything goes wrong, the entire transaction is *rolled back,* or aborted. This means that *all* actions performed on behalf of the transaction are undone in the database; specifically, the quantity isn't subtracted from the inventory, the shipping order record isn't preserved, the billing record isn't preserved, accounts receivable are not updated, and the reorder record isn't preserved. If nothing goes awry, the database remains updated and all the follow-up actions are performed at the appropriate time.

Given this model, you can see that both the store and the distributor are protected, because any one database update occurs only if they are all successfully executed; if anything prevents the transaction from completing normally, then it is as though the transaction had never been started.

In recent years, transaction theory has taken quite a few steps forward. Numerous papers and books have advanced the understanding of transactions and helped implementors of DBMSs to build reliable systems. Much recent literature describes transactions as having ACID properties. (No, this doesn't mean that the transaction eats the flesh off your database, nor that it's of the 1960s psychedelic variety, either!) The acronym ACID stands for

Atomic, Consistent, Isolated, and Durable.

In the classic text *Transaction Processing: Concepts and Techniques* by Jim Gray and Andreas Reuter.[7] we learn the following about the ACID properties of transactions:

---

7   Jim Gray and Andreas Reuter, *Transaction Processing: Concepts and Techniques* (San Mateo, CA: Morgan Kaufmann Publishers, 1993).

- *Atomicity:* The transaction consists of a collection of actions. The system provides the all-or-nothing illusion that either all these operations are performed or none of them are performed; the transaction either commits or aborts.

- *Consistency:* Transactions are assumed to perform correct transformations of the abstract system state. The transaction concept allows the programmer to declare such consistency points and allows the system to validate them by application-supplied checks.

- *Isolation:* While a transaction is updating shared data, that data may be temporarily inconsistent. Such inconsistent data must not be exposed to other transactions until the updater commits. [Authors' Note: This means until all modifications are officially completed.] The system must give each transaction the illusion that it is running in isolation; that is, it appears that all other transactions either ran previous to the start of this transaction or ran subsequent to its commit.

- *Durability:* Once a transaction commits, its updates must be durable. The new state of all objects it updated will be preserved, even in case of hardware or software failures.

By using a DBMS that implements the ACID properties of transactions, your database operations and the data stored in that database will be protected against the sort of situations that a DBMS can handle. Now all you have to worry about is getting your transactions right.

1.5 | Chapter Summary

In this introductory chapter, we have provided readers who might be unfamiliar with database technology with the foundation upon which our discussion of SQL:1999 is based. As we've discussed, understanding the relational model is very important given that (1) databases built upon the foundations of that model dominate the information systems world today, and (2) SQL is the dominant language for the relational model.

In Chapter 2, we will introduce you to the history and background of SQL, as well as to basic SQL concepts.

Chapter

2

Introduction to SQL:1999

2.1 Introduction

This chapter introduces SQL:1999, starting first with the history and background of the language and then continuing on to discuss the most significant architectural aspects of the language, such as key concepts, data types, and execution models.

2.2 SQL History and Background

The following sections briefly detail how the SQL language has evolved over the last quarter of a century, leading to the SQL:1999 standard. We discuss the history of the SQL standardization process in detail in Appendix F, "The SQL Standardization Process," and we shall survey efforts to further improve the language in Chapter 23, "A Look to the Future."

2.2.1 SQL Versus Competing Relational Languages

After Dr. Codd published his seminal paper on the relational model, research began at the IBM San Jose Research Laboratory on a language to implement that model; the language was called SEQUEL for Structured English Query Language. As part of a project called System R, IBM developed a research database system, also called System R. SEQUEL was the application program interface (API) to System R. This language was first implemented in a prototype, again called SEQUEL, between 1974 and 1975. In the next couple of years, a revised version called SEQUEL/2 was defined; the name of this version was later changed to SQL. (No doubt, this is the source of the popular belief that SQL stands for Structured Query Language and is pronounced "sequel.") The System R project ran from 1971 to 1979 and eventually evolved into a distributed database project called System R* (pronounced "are star").

In the late 1970s, it became common knowledge that IBM was going to develop a relational database product based on the SQL language. Consequently, other vendors began to build and market their own products. At least one, from Relational Software, Inc. (the current Oracle Corporation), beat IBM's product to market. IBM's first product, introduced in 1981, was known as SQL/DS. In 1983, IBM released the first version of its DB2 product.

SQL also became a de jure standard in 1986 with the publication of an American National Standards Institute (ANSI) standard for that language (SQL-86). A follow-on standard was published in 1989 (SQL-89), and another version—a major revision—in 1992 (SQL-92).

Other relational languages have been defined and implemented. Some of these have been commercial successes, but none of them have had as wide a following as SQL. A company called Relational Technology, Incorporated (RTI), later called Ingres Corporation and currently CA/Ingres, sold many copies of a database system called Ingres (initially developed at the University of California at Berkeley by Michael Stonebraker, Eugene Wong, and others). The data sublanguage of Ingres was QUEL, or Query Language. Digital Equipment Corporation's Rdb/VMS and Rdb/ELN relational database products provided a data sublanguage called RDML (called RDO by some). Both of these languages were quite popular with users of those vendors' products, but neither attracted a wide following among competing vendors (although each had other implementations from competitors).

Is the success and de facto standardization of SQL due to its excellence as a data sublanguage? Well, you will have to judge that for yourself as you go through this book and as you use SQL products. However, we can say that IBM's original influence and marketing savvy certainly didn't hurt SQL's acceptance, nor did Oracle's early adaptation of SQL and that company's subsequent leadership in the RDBMS marketplace. The fact that SQL was the basis for early, not entirely successful, formal standardization also sent a signal to vendors that it would be relatively safe to bet on SQL. Like most languages, SQL has had, through its evolution, some very strong points and some very weak ones. SQL-92 resolved many of the weak points found in earlier versions of the SQL standard, but it was far from perfect; the subsequent work that was incorporated into SQL:1999 goes further in bringing the SQL standard in line with real-world database capabilities and user needs.

2.2.2 CLI-95, PSM-96, and OLB-98

During the seven years between the time that the SQL-92 standard was published and the subsequent publication of SQL:1999, it was determined that "interim" publication of various aspects of SQL3 work (again, the standardization effort that would become SQL:1999) would occur.

The first of these publications was for the SQL/CLI (CLI = Call-Level Interface), which became known as CLI-95. The best-known implementation of CLI-95 is the Open Database Connectivity (ODBC) standard, which was championed primarily by Microsoft.

The following year, SQL/PSM (PSM = Persistent Stored Modules) was published. PSM-96, as the standard was known, specifies syntax for procedural logic of SQL-server modules. Leading relational database management systems had long been equipped with "stored procedure" capabilities by their vendors, but with nowhere near the standardization that was inherent in their adoption of the SQL standard in other parts of their respective products. PSM-96 specified a standard toward which vendors could migrate their products or, for new RDBMS products, a standardized syntax that could—or should—be used.

In 1998, the Object Language Bindings—SQL/OLB, or OLB-98—became the next part of SQL3 work to be published. SQL/OLB provides the ability to embed SQL statements in Java programs and is based on the JDBC paradigm/model, using strongly typed iterators instead of cursors and providing implementation-defined "customizations" for better alignment between the standard and products.[1]

2.2.3 SQL:1999, The Latest Revision

Finally, in 1999, the SQL3 standard was accepted and published. Before discussing SQL:1999, we want to address a question that we expect many readers will be asking themselves, and maddeningly wondering why we haven't addressed that question: the naming convention of this latest standard. As discussed earlier, previous versions of the SQL standard were labeled SQL-86, SQL-89, and

---

1 SQL/OLB is discussed at length in another book by Jim Melton and Andrew Eisenberg: *Understanding SQL and Java Together: A Guide to SQLJ, JDBC, and Related Technologies* (San Francisco: Morgan Kaufmann, 2000).

SQL-92, and the incremental parts of SQL-92 were labeled CLI-95, PSM-96, and OLB-98. And so there are *two* significant changes in the naming convention for this latest SQL standard:

- adding "19" to the date ("1999" instead of "99"), and
- changing the hyphen (-) to a colon (:).

The reason for the first change should come as no surprise to anyone in the information systems profession—actually, make that anyone in the world—given the sensitivity throughout the information systems profession business—actually, make that throughout the world—to Y2K (the "Year 2000 computer problem") and the impact of dropping the century indicator from dates. In the interest of correctness (and to ensure proper sort order for the SQL:1999 standard and its subsequent 21st century successors), a date of 1999 instead of the short-hand "99" was used.

(Note that when the previous version of the standard was published in 1992, there was little or no visibility to the upcoming Y2K problem, and the 1980s shorthand-based naming convention used in SQL-86 and SQL-89 was retained, even though Y2K was right around the corner.)

The second change—using a colon instead of a hyphen—was made to align with the conventions of the International Organization for Standardization (ISO), which separates its standards identifications from the year of publication with a colon, rather than that used by the American National Standards Institute (ANSI), which uses a hyphen for the same purpose. This reflects the increasingly international character of SQL standards development.

The following sections present a preview of SQL:1999 and further set the stage for what you can expect from the contents of this book.

2.3 | SQL Concepts

As we've discussed, SQL is based on the relational model, but it is not a perfect implementation of that model. The most important difference, at least from the viewpoint of theory, is that SQL's basic data object is the table and not the relation.

If you've a mathematical leaning, this analogy will help. A relation is mathematically equivalent to a set. You'll recall that a set is a collection of unique objects, allowing no duplicates. By contrast, a table is equivalent to a *multiset,* which is defined to be set-like, *but with duplicates permitted.* (A lot of recent literature has taken to using the unfortunate term *bag* for this concept, but we continue to prefer multiset.)

SQL has a number of other concepts; some of these have direct analogs in the relational model, while others do not. Some of these analogs are listed below; however, we don't attempt to distinguish among them because, after all, our intent is to learn SQL:

- views
- schemas
- catalogs
- users
- privileges
- domains
- connections
- sessions
- transactions
- routines
- paths

2.3.1 Views

One important capability that SQL provides is the ability to define a virtual table (well, "define the derivation of the virtual table" is probably more accurate) and save that definition in the database (as metadata, of course) with a user-defined name. The object formed by this operation is called a *view*.

A view is an example of a virtual table. That is, it is generally not physically materialized anywhere until it is needed—when some SQL statement references it, for instance. The metadata about the view (including the name of the view, the names and data types of each column, and the way in which the rows are to be derived) is stored persistently in the database's metadata, but the actual data that you will *see* in the view aren't physically stored anywhere in association with the derived table. Rather, the data is stored in base tables (*persistent base tables* in SQL) from which the view's rows are derived.

In general, operations can be performed against views just as they can be performed against persistent base tables. The major exception to this rule is that some virtual tables, including views, cannot be updated directly. The reasons for this can be found in relational theory and in much of the relational literature, but let's summarize it here: If you cannot determine uniquely the row (or rows) of the base table (or base tables) to update, then you cannot update the view.

Views are a very helpful mechanism for using a database. For example, you can define complex queries once and use them repeatedly without having to reinvent them over and over. Furthermore, views can be used to enhance the security of your database, as we shall see.

2.3.2 Users and Privileges

An important component of any computer system is the user. Okay, we're being a little tongue-in-cheek, but the point is important, especially when you are concerned about the security of your data. If you don't know who's there, you don't know who's reading—or changing—your data.

Let's consider our entertainment distributor from a few pages back. We doubt that he or she would want just anybody to be allowed to request a shipment of 10,000 CDs to a store or an entertainment e-tailer. It's likely that there will be restrictions on such activity. For example, only sales personnel would be allowed to start such a transaction, while only shipping clerks could cause the shipping orders to be printed and deleted.

In SQL, the concept of a user is captured by an *authorization identifier*. Every operation in an SQL system is validated according to the authorization identifier that attempts to invoke the operation. Now, the details of authorization identifiers (authIDs for brevity) are strictly left up to implementations. After all, a PC implementation of SQL has different requirements than a mainframe implementation. In some systems (this seems to be most common on Unix implementations), the user's logon ID is used for his SQL authID; in others, entire groups of users might be given the same authID.

As we shall see in detail later, SQL requires an appropriate privilege for every sort of operation that can be performed on the database. For example, the SELECT privilege is required for a user to retrieve information from a table. Some privileges are granted on an entire table, while others may be granted on the entire table or only on selected columns of the table. (More on this in Chapter 13, "Privileges, Users, and Security.")

Prior to SQL:1999, privileges were managed on an individual-by-individual basis using authIDs. As you might imagine, though, for large user communities, that model could become quite cumbersome and labor intensive. With SQL:1999, the concept of *roles* has been introduced to facilitate the management of privileges. Privileges can now be assigned not only to individual authIDs, but also to roles. The sequence would look something like this:

- A role is created, representing the individuals who share some commonality in job function, security clearance level, or other attribute by which they may be considered to be part of some group.

- Necessary privileges would then be assigned to that role, as determined by the reason the individuals were assigned to that role (job function, etc.).

- The role is assigned to one or more authIDs as required, thus allowing the individuals represented by those authIDs to fulfill the duties of the role granted to them.

- While additional privileges may be granted to any of the individual authIDs to which a role has been assigned, those privileges have no effect on the actions that can be performed under the authority granted to the role. That is, SQL statements may be executed using the privileges of a role or of an authID, but not both at the same time.

2.3.3 Schemas and Catalogs

As we have already seen in our examples, very few applications are likely to be satisfied with only one table. Most applications require multiple tables, and most implementations are probably going to support many applications, each with its own set of tables. What happens if two applications happen to choose the same name for one of their tables? Well, there are a couple of possible solutions: either absolutely prohibit the possibility (sometimes called the *single namespace solution*) or provide a way to qualify the names with some higher order name (often called the *partitioned namespace solution*).

SQL has always provided the partitioned namespace solution. Tables exist in the context of a higher-level object called a *schema*. This use of the word may confuse you if you are a data modeling expert, because it doesn't mean quite the same thing in SQL as it does in that domain. In SQL, a schema is simply the collection of all objects (e.g., tables and views) that share a namespace. Schemas have names and those names can be used to qualify the names of the objects contained within that schema. You might have movie titles that are members of the Warehouse schema; you can always refer to the table as Warehouse Movie Titles. (No, this isn't the right syntax; we'll get to that later. This section is called concepts, remember?)

During the infancy of SQL database systems, it was very common for an SQL DBMS to support only a very few schemas (some commercially important systems have sometimes supported only one schema for an entire installation), so the names of the schemas were rarely duplicated at any given installation. However, as widely distributed databases are supported by some products and required by some users, the probability that two users will select the same name for their schemas increases. To address this problem, SQL-92 adopted a convention of collecting schemas together into a unit called a *catalog*. A catalog provides a mechanism for qualifying the schema names to avoid name conflicts; it is also the conceptual repository for the metadata of all schemas *in* that catalog. Many people envision a catalog as the unit of management of a DBMS installation, although the SQL standard doesn't make that restriction.

What's to prevent duplicate catalog names? Nothing, really. It's going to happen. However, SQL:1999 defines catalog names in a way that encourages implementations of SQL DBMSs to use a very large namespace (such as that provided by a network naming and directory management service like X.500 or LDAP) for catalog names. This reduces the probability of duplicate catalog names. Since no naming scheme can ever completely eliminate the possibility, SQL:1999 stops there. If duplicate catalog names become a problem, the people administering the database system will simply have to resolve it themselves. We believe that many implementations will provide facilities to aid this administration problem, such as the ability to use a sort of alias to substitute for one of the duplicate catalog names. This escape hatch is not part of the SQL:1999 standard, though.

Caution: Many DBMS products don't implement catalog names, so expect to find a variance between DBMSs you use and the SQL:1999 standard.

2.3.4 Connections, Sessions, and Transactions

Concepts important for understanding the flow of SQL statements, and the relationships among those statements, include

- connections
- sessions
- transactions

First, the definitions:

A *connection*—more formally referred to as an *SQL-connection*—is an association between an SQL-client and an SQL-server. You can think of basic client/ server computing concepts as the framework for understanding SQL-clients and SQL-servers: the client side is the portion that is "user facing" or "application facing" and is the interface point through which statements are issued and to which results are returned. The SQL-server (the term is a generic one in this context, not to be confused with Microsoft's or Sybase's respective SQL Server products) is the environment in which SQL statements are executed and from which results are returned to the client.

A *session*—as with connections, the formal term is *SQL-session*—is the context in which a single user ("user" being a person or an application) executes a sequence of SQL statements through a single connection.

Finally, a *transaction* (or, as you might guess, *SQL-transaction*) is a sequence of SQL statements that is (from the SQL standard) "atomic with respect to recovery." Chapter 15, "Transaction Management," discusses transactions in detail; for our purposes in this chapter, consider that the execution of a series of SQL statements within a session and over a connection occurs, but the results of that sequence of statements isn't "official" until the transaction is successfully concluded.

You should note that even though the terminology for connections and sessions seems to imply some form of networked connectivity among computers, in fact no network need exist, nor does there need to be a physical separation between SQL-clients and SQL-servers. Indeed, the terms indicate the *logical* relationship among components in an SQL system rather than any type of physical topology or architecture.

2.3.5 Routines and Paths

Some additional concepts that should be understood are those relating to routines and paths.

A *routine* is an SQL:1999 procedure, function, or method that is invoked from SQL. A procedure is invoked using an SQL CALL statement and can include both input and output parameters. A function permits only input parameters, with the result being returned as a "value" of the function; it is invoked using functional notation (as contrasted with the CALL statement that is used for a procedure). Finally, a method is a "special case" of a function for use in the object-oriented paradigm; this will be discussed further in Volume 2 of this book.

An embedded SQL host program (see Chapter 12, "Accessing SQL from the Real World") is equivalent to a host language program with a "call" to an externally-invoked procedure in SQL. An SQL-invoked routine—which could be a procedure, a function, or a method—can be written in SQL (in which case it is termed an SQL *routine)* or in an external host language (termed an *external routine*).

A distinction needs to be made between SQL-invoked routines and externally-invoked routines, as well as between external routines and SQL routines. Table 2-1 provides an overview of the relationship between these various types of routines and the ways in which they may, or may *not*, be invoked.[2]

---

2 Table from J. Melton, *Understanding SQL's Stored Procedures: A Complete Guide to SQL/PSM* (San Francisco: Morgan Kaufmann Publishers, 1998), 40; extensive detail about routines can be found in this reference.

Table 2-1 *Relationship of Routine Types*

	Externally-Invoked Routine	SQL-Invoked Routine	External Routine	SQL Routine
Can be written in SQL?	Yes	Yes	No	Yes
Can be written in another language?	No	Yes	Yes	No
Invoked from host program?	Yes	No	No	No
Invoked from SQL code?	No	Yes	Yes	Yes
Can be contained in SQL-client module?	Yes	No	No	Yes
Can be contained in SQL-server module?	No	Yes	Yes ("registered")	Yes
Procedures?	Yes	Yes	Yes	Yes
Functions?	No	Yes	Yes	Yes

A *path* (more formally referred to as an *SQL-path*) is a list of one or more schemas that determine the search order for where an invocation of a routine might find the "subject routine" it needs, *if* the name of the routine being invoked doesn't contain a "hard-coded" schema name. Those readers who have worked in complex production application environments are aware of the need for multiple schemas for testing, quality assurance (QA), and production versions. By using SQL's facility for path specification and management, the need to continuously modify hard-coded schema names in routine invocations is alleviated, resulting in a more professional approach to version control and release management.

2.4 | SQL Data Types

The following sections introduce the data types supported by SQL:1999. Among the enhancements to SQL:1999 over its predecessor SQL-92 version are several new data types; these are discussed below in addition to those that already existed in the prior version of the standard.

2.4.1 Exact Numerics

The exact numeric data types in SQL are those that can represent a value exactly. One category of these is the *true* integers, which are represented in SQL by INTEGER (it is permitted to abbreviate this as INT) and SMALLINT. The other category is intended to permit fractional components, but still provide an exact representation. This latter category consists of the DECIMAL and NUMERIC data types. Each of these data types deserves a closer look.

- INTEGER: This data type represents an integer value (a *counting number,* like the number of pieces of something). Its precision (the number of decimal digits or bits that can be stored, with the implementation choosing whether the precision of INTEGER is in terms of digits or bits) is implementation-defined, if only because the standard must be implementable on many different hardware architectures. When you want to declare some column to use this data type, you simply specify INTEGER; there are no parameters.

- SMALLINT: This data type also represents an integer value. Its precision is also implementation-defined but is no greater than the precision of INTEGER. This allows an implementation to provide a certain amount of storage optimization if the application knows that larger numbers are not required. The precision must be in the same terms (digits or bits) as for INTEGER. Just as with INTEGER, there are no optional parameters on this data type, so you simply specify SMALLINT. (Caution: A popular misconception, especially among C programmers, is that INTEGER is a 4-byte twos-complement number and SMALLINT is a 2-byte twos-complement number. These assumptions are incorrect, since the decision about specific precisions may vary between implementations.)

- NUMERIC: This data type has both a precision and a scale (the number of digits of the fractional component). The scale cannot be negative or larger than the precision, and the implementation will give you exactly the precision and scale that you request. When you want to specify this data type for some SQL object, you may simply specify NUMERIC and accept the default precision for the implementation with a scale of 0. Alternatively, you can specify either NUMERIC(p), where p is a precision value within the range supported by the implementation, or NUMERIC(p,s), where s is a scale value within the implementation's range. This data type is used for numbers with fractional components but exact precision, such as money.

- DECIMAL: This data type also has both a precision and a scale. In this case, though, the precision supplied by the implementation may be greater than the precision that you specify; larger precisions are acceptable, but smaller ones are not. The scale will always be exactly what you requested. As with NUMERIC, you can specify this data type as DECIMAL, DECIMAL(p), or DECIMAL(p,s).

2.4.2 Approximate Numerics

The approximate numeric data types in SQL also represent numbers but only (as you might expect from the term) approximately! In most implementations, you can expect these to be provided by floating-point numbers. While it's possible with the exact numeric types to specify precisely the data values that they support—that is, you can easily specify the exact largest and smallest values— it's not quite that easy with the approximate numerics.

Okay, it *is* that easy, because computer systems are finite state machines and there are a finite number of bits that can be supported. However, the way that floating-point numbers are represented in most computer systems makes it rather awkward to say that exactly *this* list of values is representable. Instead, the nature of the floating-point hardware makes the precision more or less variable, depending on the range being represented. We don't want to spend a lot of time on that—there are lots of good references about this elsewhere. Just remember that SQL supports approximate numeric data as having both a mantissa (the significant digits) and an exponent (to derive the actual size of the number), just like floating-point numbers.

There are three variations of approximate numeric data in SQL. They are used for data whose values have an extremely wide range and whose precision need not be absolute. Let's examine each of these data types in turn:

- REAL: This data type allows you to request a single-precision floating-point data item. The precision is chosen by the implementation, but it's normally the default single-precision data type on the hardware platform. There are no options, so you simply specify REAL.

- DOUBLE PRECISION: This data type also has an implementation-defined precision, but that precision must be greater than the precision of REAL. (Contrast this with INTEGER, which must have a precision *at least as great as* SMALLINT.) This usually translates to a double-precision floating-point data item on your hardware. With no options, you specify only DOUBLE PRECISION.

- FLOAT: This data type allows you to specify the precision that you want. The resulting precision must be at least as large as the precision you request. This could be used, for example, for a portable application; if you request a precision of some value *p,* it might be honored by a single-precision on one platform and a double-precision on another. Because there's an option, you can specify either FLOAT or FLOAT(p) when you want this data type.

2.4.3 Character Strings (Including CLOBs)

There are, depending on how you want to count, either three or six character string data types in SQL:1999 (SQL-89 had only one, while SQL-92 had two). The three basic ones are

- CHARACTER (which you can abbreviate as CHAR)
- CHARACTER VARYING (which can be abbreviated as either CHAR VARYING or VARCHAR)

- CHARACTER LARGE OBJECT (which can be abbreviated as CLOB): CLOBs are new to SQL:1999.

So why do we say that there are either three or six SQL:1999 character string data types? Because SQL:1999 also provides NATIONAL CHARACTER, NATIONAL CHARACTER VARYING, and NATIONAL CHARACTER LARGE OBJECT. We will discuss the implications and semantics of NATIONAL CHARACTER and internationalization in general in Chapter 21, "Internationalization Aspects of SQL:1999." For purposes of this chapter, though, we will mention that a number of abbreviations also exist within SQL for these various NATIONAL CHARACTER data types, just as with the basic character string data types, but beware that with the last of the three, NATIONAL CHARACTER LARGE OBJECT, the abbreviations follow a different pattern than with the other two. These are shown in Table 2-2.

Table 2-2 *Abbreviations for NATIONAL CHARACTER Data Types*

Data Type	*Abbreviation(s)*
NATIONAL CHARACTER	NATIONAL CHAR
	NCHAR
NATIONAL CHARACTER VARYING	NATIONAL CHAR VARYING
	NCHAR VARYING
NATIONAL CHARACTER LARGE OBJECT	NCHAR LARGE OBJECT
	NCLOB

Let's take a close look at the three basic character data types:

- CHARACTER: This data type contains character strings. The specific character sets that can be stored in one of these are defined by your implementation, but it's probably going to include something like ASCII or Latin-1 for compatibility with earlier implementations. You can specify this as either CHARACTER or CHARACTER(x), where x is the number of characters that you want to store. If you specify only CHARACTER, it's equivalent to specifying CHARACTER(1). If you try to store, say, 5 characters into a column specified as CHARACTER(10), then you will still have 10 characters stored; the last 5 characters will be spaces.
- CHARACTER VARYING: If you don't want to blank-pad your character strings (in some applications, blanks have significance, so you can't afford to add them whether you need them or not), then you will want to use CHARACTER VARYING. This data type allows you to store exactly the number of characters

that you have in your data. You must specify `CHARACTER VARYING(x)`; there is no default of 1 (or anything else) as there is for `CHARACTER`.

- `CHARACTER LARGE OBJECT`: Together with the `BINARY LARGE OBJECT` data type (discussed in the next section), this data type is referred to as a *large object string type*. This data type is used for large, variably sized groups of characters—narrative documents (possible encoded in XML) embedded within a database row, for example—and gives the user the ability to specify the maximum size of column in number of characters rather than having to specify the column in number of bits and then performing the necessary calculations to convert the character size to an equivalent number of bits.

In all three cases, each implementation will have an upper limit on the maximum value of the length. In some implementations, the limit might be fairly small (we know of at least one implementation that limited character strings to 240 characters until quite recently), while in others the limits might be extremely large (we have heard of one implementation that supports character strings of over 4 billion characters). You can count on many implementations supporting something in the range of 32,000 or 64,000 characters.

Note that a new feature in SQL:1999 that applies to both types of large object data types—character and binary—is to be able to specify the size in a "shorthand" notation using K, M, or G for kilo-, mega-, or giga-, respectively, rather than having to use actual numbers as part of the data type definition. In SQL:1999, the use of K (kilo) means 1024, M (mega) means 1,048,576 (that is, 1024 times 1024), and G (giga) means 1,073,741,824 (that is, 1024^3).

2.4.4 Bit Strings and Binary Strings (Including BLOBs)

Characters have certain semantics associated with them, and those semantics are normally those associated with written, natural language or something similar. If your application requires the ability to store arbitrary bit (or byte) strings, then `CHARACTER` isn't the appropriate data type to use.

Note that before SQL-92, SQL implementations had no other choice, so `CHARACTER` (or some variation, such as `VARCHAR` or `LARGE VARCHAR`) was often used for this purpose. To resolve that misuse of `CHARACTER`, SQL-92 provided two additional data types that are continued in SQL:1999. Additionally, as mentioned in section 2.4.3, a new data type for large numbers of bits, `BINARY LARGE OBJECT`s, or `BLOB`s, has been added to SQL:1999. Let's look at these:

- BIT: This data type allows your application to store arbitrary bit strings, unconstrained by character semantics. If you need to store only a single bit (for example, if you use "flags" in your data), then you can specify only BIT; if you want more, then you must specify BIT(x), where x specifies how many bits (not bytes or anything else) you want. Fixed-length bit strings have a default length of 1, just like fixed-length character strings.

- BIT VARYING: If your application wants to store one number of bits on one occasion and a different number at other times, this data type should be considered. Specified only as BIT VARYING(x) (there aren't any abbreviations in the SQL standard, although some implementations may use one, such as VARBIT), this type will give you a bit string that allows you to store any number of bits up to x. Variable-length bit strings have no default number of bits, so you must specify the desired maximum length.

- BINARY LARGE OBJECT, or BLOB: As with CLOBs (see section 2.4.3), a "natural" means for handling very large strings of bytes (*octets* in SQL:1999 terms) is now supported in SQL—for example, to embed a large image file within a database row. BLOBs are specified with some size: BLOB(x). As with CLOBs, the size of a column with a BLOB data type can be specified using K, M, or G (kilo-, mega-, or giga-, respectively)—for example,

    EMPLOYEE_PHOTO   BLOB (50K).

Implementations will have limits on the size of x. Those limits will probably be fairly large—at least 32,000 bits and perhaps as many as 4 billion bits or bytes.

2.4.5 Datetimes

Since the very earliest days of computers, applications have had a need to represent dates and times in stored data and to manipulate that information. Many approaches have been taken, but one characteristic was shared by all of them: they weren't standardized. Instead, every computer system or software system invented its own conventions for handling this sort of data. Anyone in the IT profession—actually, anyone in society in general—who was exposed to the consternation and concern over the Year 2000 (Y2K) computer problem in the latter years of the 1990s is well aware of the importance of date representation within computer applications and databases.

This traditional variability is clearly unacceptable. One frequent request received by participants in the SQL standardization efforts was to add a datetime data type. The only problem was deciding how to add that support without locking implementations into a specific implementation technique. The chosen approach expresses the datetime data types in a canonical form and defines the operations supported by SQL.

SQL:1999 times are specified with a relationship to UTC, or *universal coordinated time* (previously called GMT, or *Greenwich mean time*). Different places on the surface of the earth experience different sun times, or sidereal times, because of their relative positions to the sun. Until the middle 1800s, individual communities kept their own time based on solar measurements; this posed an intolerable burden to railroad timekeepers in the large North American continent, so a system of time zones was instituted to place entire strips of the earth into specific time zones, with every community in one strip keeping the same time. This system was very popular and was quickly endorsed by the rest of the world. However, as with all reforms, this one was subject to political manipulation.

Some changes were very sensible: it would have caused much hardship if a city that happened to straddle an arbitrary strip boundary were forced to keep two different times. Other changes were more political: Nepal keeps time that is 15 minutes different from that of India as an expression of independence.

Still other changes are almost arbitrary. Many locales in the world advance their clocks by one hour in the summer and turn them back in the winter. This summer time is perceived as beneficial because daylight lasts until later and more outdoors work can be done. However, there are few standards related to this, and different countries change their clocks on different days. Therefore, the offset from UTC of a given community's time will vary during the year, but not all communities change and those that do may not change on the same day. This further complicates time processing in SQL. SQL:1999 requires that every SQL session have associated with it a default offset from UTC that is used for the duration of the session or until explicitly changed by the user.

As a result, the language defines three specific forms of date and time and two variations on these. Let's examine each of them.

- DATE: This variation stores the year, month, and day values of a date. The year value is exactly 4 digits and can represent the years 0001 through 9999 (that's C.E. 1, or A.D. 1).[3] The month value is exactly 2 digits and is limited to values 01 through 12. The day value is also exactly 2 digits and is limited to values 01 through 31, although the month value can apply additional restrictions to a maximum of 28, 29, or 30.

---

3   Unfortunately, SQL: 1999's date capability cannot handle B.C.E. or B.C. (before the Common Era or before Christ) dates due to a lack of general agreement over issues such as how to handle the year 0, how far back to go (the pyramids? dinosaurs? Big Bang?), and the like. We believe that many products will support such dates, but they may do so in a variety of ways.

The length of a DATE is said to be 10 *positions;* in this way, SQL:1999 does not appear to prescribe—or proscribe—implementations that use character strings, packed decimal, or any other form internally.

You specify a date data type by simply using DATE.

- TIME: This variation stores the hour, minute, and second values of a time. The hour value is exactly 2 digits and can represent the hours 00 through 23. The minutes value is also exactly 2 digits and can represent 00 through 59. The seconds value is again 2 digits, but a fractional value is optional. The seconds value is restricted to 00 through 61.999 . . . . Why 61 instead of the expected 59? Simply because of the phenomenon known as *leap seconds:* occasionally, the earth's official timekeepers will add one or two seconds to a minute to keep clocks synchronized with sidereal time. Support for leap seconds is implementation-defined.

  The maximum number of fractional digits is defined by your implementation, but the standard requires that it support at least 6 digits. If you don't specify a number when you are defining your data types, you'll get no fractional digits. The length of a TIME value is 8 positions; if there are any fractional digits, then the length is 9 plus the number of fractional digits. (The extra position is to account for the period that separates the integer seconds value from the fractional digits.)

  You specify a time data type by either specifying TIME or by specifying TIME(p). The value of p must not be negative, of course, and the maximum value is determined by your implementation.

- TIMESTAMP: This variation stores the year, month, and day values of a date as well as the hour, minute, and second values of a time. The lengths and the restrictions on the values correspond to those in the DATE and TIME data types. The only real difference is the default number of fractional digits. In TIME, the default is 0, but in TIMESTAMP, the default is 6 digits.

  Therefore, the length of a TIMESTAMP is 19 positions. If any fractional digits are specified, then the length is 20 positions plus the number of fractional digits (again, the extra position is to account for that period).

  You specify a timestamp data type by specifying either TIMESTAMP or TIMESTAMP(p). The value of p must not be negative, of course, and the maximum value is determined by your implementation.

- TIME WITH TIME ZONE: This data type is exactly like the TIME data type except that it also includes additional information about the offset from UTC of the time specified. This offset is represented as an INTERVAL HOUR TO MINUTE (see section 2.4.6) that is permitted to contain values ranging from –12:59

to +13:00. (You might expect the range to be from –11:59 to +12:00, but the summer time problem requires the wider range.) This added information requires an additional 6 positions, so the length of a TIME WITH TIME ZONE is 14. If fractional digits are specified, then the length is 15 plus the number of fractional digits.

- TIMESTAMP WITH TIME ZONE: This data type is exactly like TIMESTAMP with the addition of the UTC offset information. The additional information means that the length of TIMESTAMP WITH TIME ZONE is 25. If fractional digits are specified, then the length is 26 plus the number of fractional digits.

2.4.6 Intervals

Closely tied to the issue of storing and processing dates and times is the question of intervals. An *interval* is broadly defined as the difference between two dates or times. SQL:1999 defines two categories of interval: year-month intervals and day-time intervals. The two cannot be mixed in any expression. (We note in passing that SQL's intervals are *unanchored intervals,* meaning they describe only a duration of time without an express starting or ending time; by contrast, *anchored intervals* describe a specific timespan with a known start and/or finish. Anchored intervals are sometimes called *periods,* but that term is not defined or used in SQL:1999.)

The reason for this differentiation is subtle, but important. A year-month interval can only express an interval in terms of years and an integral number of months. We always know (in the Gregorian calendar, at least) that a year has exactly 12 months. A day-time interval can express an interval in terms of days, hours, minutes, and seconds, because we know exactly how many hours there are in a day, minutes in an hour, and (barring the anomaly of leap seconds) seconds in a minute. However, we do not know exactly how many days are in a month, unless we know the month we're talking about in advance.

Therefore, answers to a question like, "What is the result of 1 year, 3 months, 19 days divided by 3?" cannot be determined unless we know the dates spanned by that interval. To avoid the anomalies associated with these problems, SQL:1999 simply makes the restriction that intervals come in two, unmixable classes.

Intervals in SQL:1999 always have a *datetime qualifier* associated with them. This qualifier specifies the class of the interval and the exact precision of the interval. The precision has two components: the leading field can have 1 or more digits and the seconds value (if part of the interval) can have a fractional component.

- *Year-month intervals:* This class of intervals can contain only a year value, only a month value, or both. When you specify a year-month interval, the interval qualifier will specify the maximum number of digits in the *leading* or *only* field. Therefore, you can specify INTERVAL YEAR, INTERVAL YEAR(p), INTERVAL MONTH, INTERVAL MONTH(p), INTERVAL YEAR TO MONTH, or INTERVAL YEAR(p) TO MONTH. In all cases, if you don't specify *p,* the leading field precision defaults to 2 digits.

The length of a year-month interval is either the length of the year field, the length of the month field, or 3 digits more than the length of the year field (year field plus one for the hyphen separator, plus two for the month field).

- *Day-time intervals:* This class of intervals can contain only a day value, an hour value, a minute value, and/or a second value. If it contains two or more of them, it must contain both the leading field, the trailing field, and all fields that are logically between them. For the leading field, you may specify the precision; if you don't, it defaults to 2 digits. If the trailing field is seconds, then you may specify a precision for that, too. If you don't, then 6 digits is the default, which means that your implementation must support at least 6 digits, but it might support more.

Examples of specifying correct day-time interval: INTERVAL DAY TO HOUR, INTERVAL DAY(6) TO MINUTE, INTERVAL SECOND(7), INTERVAL DAY(5) TO SECOND(10), or INTERVAL MINUTE(3) TO SECOND(4).

The length of a day-time interval is computed as the length of the leading field plus the lengths of each other field (if any), plus the number of other fields; if the trailing field is SECOND and there's a fractional second precision, then the length is increased by 1 to account for the period.

Intervals and datetimes can be manipulated together. In fact, it's hard to completely separate these two data types. Sure, you can store dates or times without worrying about intervals, but if you ever want to subtract two times, you've got to have intervals!

Basically, you can subtract two dates or times to get an interval; you can subtract an interval from a datetime to get a datetime; you can add an interval to a datetime (or add a datetime to an interval) to get a datetime; or you can multiply or divide an interval by a scalar numeric value (or multiply a scalar numeric value by an interval) to get a new interval.

2.4.7 Booleans

It might come as a surprise to long-time software developers that until SQL:1999, the SQL standard did *not* have a Boolean data type.

Finally, though, SQL:1999 includes this data type by which a "natural" representation of true-or-false values can be specified rather than, for example, having to specify a CHARACTER(1) data type with permissible values of "T" or "F." Actually, the BOOLEAN data type can have one of three different "Boolean literal" values:

- TRUE
- FALSE
- UNKNOWN

Now it's possible in SQL:1999 to use common programming phrases such as "IS NOT FALSE" or "COLUMN1 AND (COLUMN2 OR NOT COLUMN3) IS TRUE." See section 2.5 for further discussion of application logic, an important consideration for the use of Boolean data types.

2.4.8 Collection (or Array) Types

In addition to the rather more traditional atomic (or primitive) data types (see section 1.2.3, subsection "Primitive Data Types") that SQL has always supported, SQL:1999 now supports several data types that can hold multiple values. One of these is the *array* type, which allows applications to store several values (of the same underlying type) into a single cell of a table. In SQL:1999, the array type is called a *type constructor,* because you use it to construct a complete type (a constructed type) by providing additional information—namely, the type of the array's elements.

Other collection types are possible, such as set, multiset, or list. Indeed, those types were considered for inclusion in SQL:1999, but were ultimately omitted. (We believe they were omitted largely because of certain problems with their specifications that were discovered too late in the standardization process for adequate resolution; perhaps they will be included in a future generation of the language. See Chapter 23, "A Look to the Future," for more information.) However, SQL:1999's designers believe that most application requirements for collections can be met, perhaps with some awkwardness, by the array type.

An array is defined like this:

dt ARRAY [*mc*]

where *dt* is some SQL:1999 data type (other than an array type!) and *mc* is a literal that specifies the maximum cardinality of the array. Naturally, the data type of *mc* has to be fixed numeric with scale zero (that is, no fractional values) and its value has to be greater than zero. Note that SQL:1999 does not provide multi-dimensional arrays; nor does it allow definition of arrays of arrays. These facilities might be added in the next generation of the SQL standard, but until that event you might prefer to think of this type as a "vector."

SQL:1999's arrays are a little different in their behaviors than arrays in many other programming languages, such as C or Fortran. Most (but not all) languages' array types are fixed in size: if you declare a C array to hold 10 elements, then it must always contain 10 elements. However, the array type provided by SQL:1999 is a little bit more flexible: an array declared with a size of 10 elements may hold *up to* 10 elements, but might hold fewer elements at any instant in time. In many ways, this is analogous to SQL's CHARACTER VARYING data type, in that a maximum length is declared and specific values can be of any length from zero up to that maximum. That maximum length is (perhaps obviously) called the array's *maximum cardinality*; the number of elements it contains at any instant is its *current cardinality*.

The ordinal position of each element, called its *index*, is always between one and the maximum cardinality, inclusive. If you assign a value to an element whose index is greater than the current cardinality of the array (but, naturally, less than its maximum cardinality), the current cardinality of the array is increased to be the index to which you just assigned a value. That behavior leaves an interesting question to be answered: Suppose you have an array declared to be INTEGER ARRAY[10] and, before doing anything else with the array, execute a statement that assigns the value 100 to element [5]. What are the values of elements [1] through [4]? Obviously, *some* value has to be assigned to those elements, and SQL:1999 has chosen the null value for that purpose (see section 2.5).

There are essentially three operations you can perform on arrays. You can retrieve the value of some element of the array, you can change the value of some element of the array or of the entire array, and you can concatenate two arrays together to get a new (longer) array. To be fair, you can also determine the cardinality of an array, which many users would consider an operation on an array.

2.4.9 Anonymous Row Types

Another type constructor in SQL:1999's palette is the *anonymous row type*, usually just called *row type*. SQL has, of course, always had a row type—after all, the most fundamental operations in SQL manipulate rows in tables. However, until SQL:1999, it has not been possible to create variables or parameters whose types were rows. With the addition of an explicit row type, you can now create variables and parameters with complex structure. Perhaps even better, you can create tables with columns having complex structure.

You construct a row type by specifying

```
ROW ( fld₁, fld₂, ... , fldₙ )
```

where each *fld$_i$* defines a field of the row, specified like this:

```
fldname fldtype fldoptions
```

Here, *fldname* is simply an identifier that names the field in the row type, and *fldtype* is a data type specification. Row types can contain fields whose data types are any SQL type, including other row types. Of course, since we have called this an anonymous row type, you will recognize that these types don't have persistent definitions (that is, their definitions are not stored in the database anywhere), and you can't "reference" a row type by name to use it multiple times; instead, you have to repeat the definition wherever you need it (using good old cut-and-paste or some similar technique). Don't worry too much about *fldoptions* just now. There are two options for field definitions, one of which is the default collation of the field (only permitted if the data type of the field is a character string type) and the other is allowed (and required) only if the data type of the field is a reference type (see section 2.4.11). An example of a row type is as follows:

```
ROW ( street CHARACTER VARYING (30),
      city   CHARACTER VARYING (25),
      state  CHARACTER (2) )
```

Row types have a *degree,* which is defined as the number of fields in the row type. The analog to the number of columns in a table (and in that table's rows) is obvious. If it were permitted to define a *named* row type (we've already said that it isn't), then it would be possible to define a table using that named row type; the columns of the table would naturally be taken from the fields of the row type. This facility was considered for SQL:1999 but was ultimately rejected on the grounds that it's not very often that you want to create more than one table with a given "shape" and, when you do, SQL:1999 already provides another feature that allows you to define one table "just like" another. In addition, SQL:1999's user-defined structured types (see section 2.4.10) provide a capability very similar to that provided by named row types. Therefore, this capability would be redundant.

2.4.10 User-Defined Types

Because SQL:1999 was in development for such a long time, many people in the computer industry became aware of the plans to add object technology to the language. These plans were ultimately manifested through the specification of user-defined types, of which there are two variations.

Structured Types (Very Briefly)

The more complex variant of the user-defined type is the *structured type.* We're not going to address structured types in detail in this volume, but we suggest that you refer to Volume 2 of this book for comprehensive treatment of the subject. Still, a brief summary is appropriate, if only for completeness.

SQL:1999's structured types permit the creation of persistent, named types (meaning that their definitions are stored in the database metadata) that have one or more attributes, each of which can be of any SQL type (other than the type being defined or a type based on the type being defined—which could occur if you were concurrently defining two types A and B, each of which used the other type in its definition). The attributes can be given data types that are other structured types, array types, row types, and so forth. This is an arbitrarily complex structure, although implementations will certainly have some limits on complexity. In addition to stored data represented as attributes, structured types have behaviors provided by the type definer using methods, ordinary functions, and procedures (see Chapter 17, "Routines and Routine Invocation: Functions and Procedures"). It is primarily through the use of structured types and related facilities that applications access object technology in SQL.

Distinct Types

The less complex sort of user-defined type is the *distinct type,* which is also a persistent named type. A distinct type is defined as a single, primitive type instead of a structure of one or more attributes. For example, in our music and video store, we might choose to define a distinct type called PRICE that is based on DECIMAL(5,2). All values whose type is PRICE would have the same internal representation as values whose type is DECIMAL(5,2). So far, this probably doesn't seem very useful, does it?

The value that distinct types add to SQL:1999 applications is the ability to enforce strong typing among application data. Specifically, an expression that would (say) add a value whose type is DECIMAL(5,2) to another value whose type is PRICE, which is based on DECIMAL(5,2), would be identified as a syntax error. In fact, you would not even be permitted to multiply a PRICE value by the value 0.065 to compute sales tax! Possibly even more surprising, you cannot simply add two PRICE values together: the arithmetic operator + is defined only for numeric types and not for PRICE types. (This, we hasten to add, is recognized as inconvenient to application developers and a relaxation of this restriction might surface in the next generation of the SQL standard.)

SQL:1999 does, however, provide applications with the ability to overcome those apparent limitations. For example, you are given the ability to convert PRICE values into values of its underlying type, DECIMAL(5,2), and then manipulate that value as you need to (such as adding it to another numeric value, or multiplying it by some numeric value); you also have the ability to convert a DECIMAL(5,2) value into a PRICE value, so the results of your manipulation can be represented as a PRICE when you're done.

In fact, SQL:1999 allows you to define any number of methods, ordinary functions, and procedures (see Chapter 17, "Routines and Routine Invocation (Functions and Procedures)") that have one or more parameters whose type is a distinct type. Through careful selection and definition of the routines for a distinct type, you can provide whatever functionality your users need, and you can control that functionality to minimize inappropriate uses. Some people might argue that this ability to specify the semantics of distinct types through the definition of various routines gives it much of the capabilities for which people use object technology. However, we disagree with that assertion, since SQL:1999's distinct types do not have several characteristics that we would find mandatory, such as type hierarchies and inheritance. (For more information, please refer to Volume 2 of this book.)

2.4.11   Reference Types

SQL:1999 has one more type constructor in its repertoire—the *reference type*. One feature of structured types (about which you can learn in Volume 2 of this book) is that they can be used as the type of certain sorts of tables (called, logically enough, *typed tables*); the effect of this use is that the rows of such typed tables are effectively values of that structured type! Having a typed table allows us to access attributes of the type's values directly through the columns of the table.

SQL:1999 goes further: each row in a typed table is given a unique value (a sort of primary key that can be assigned by the database system or by the application) that can be used in methods defined on the type of the table to uniquely identify the instance of the type that is the row. The unique values that identify rows of typed tables are called *reference values* and their type is a reference type.

In SQL:1999, a reference type is strongly typed, meaning that it can contain only values that reference instances of a specified type (equivalently, rows of typed tables whose type is that specified type).

Reference types are not further addressed in this volume; for more information, you'll have to turn to Volume 2.

2.4.12 Locators

In sections 2.4.3 and 2.4.4, we introduced you to the two large object types that SQL:1999 provides. As you know from reading those two sections, and can infer from the types' names, the value of the large object types can be . . . well, large. SQL:1999 puts no limits on their sizes, although implementations certainly do; we are aware of implementations that allow large objects to be longer than 4,000,000,000 octets (4 gigabytes). If you consider that SQL:1999 allows you to create arrays of large objects (and structured types having attributes whose types are large object types), it becomes evident that you can have some incredibly large values hanging around in columns of your tables.

Whenever you manage data that has the potential to be that large, you naturally want to minimize the number of times that any value has to be transferred across the boundary between the SQL system and your application programs—especially if there happens to be a network connection involved. To minimize the number of times when it is necessary to transfer large data items across that boundary, SQL:1999 provides a new data type, valid only on the client side of the interface, that can act as a sort of surrogate for values of certain types. This new data type is called a *locator type* and comes in several varieties: large object locators, user-defined type locators, and collection locators. (Once you learn more about locators, you'll almost certainly wonder why they weren't called "handles," since most programmers would have been very comfortable using that word for this concept. The reason is simple, if a bit subtle: the word "handle" was already in use for a somewhat different concept in the Call-Level Interface, and it seemed inappropriate to overload the term by using it for this purpose, too.)

While locators are valid only in the context of non-SQL code (that is, they cannot be used within the SQL system itself, such as in a stored SQL routine, but they can be used in a stored external routine, as you'll learn in Chapter 17, "Routines and Routine Invocation (Functions and Procedures)"), they are created by the SQL system and returned to an application as part of the response to a retrieval operation. Similarly, they are passed into the SQL system as an argument to some SQL operation, such as an SQL statement that operates on a large object column, a structured type column, or an array column. It is extremely important to note, however, that locators are never stored in the database. No column can have a locator as its data type; neither can any attribute of a structured type. And the element type of an array cannot be a locator unless the array is a parameter of a module-language routine invoked directly from your client code or an argument to a host language stored routine.

Locator types are declared like this:

```
dt AS LOCATOR
```

where *dt* is a data type specification and can be a large object data type specification, a structured type name, or an array specification. For example, the following three lines illustrate locator type declarations:

```
BINARY LARGE OBJECT (25M) AS LOCATOR
employee_type AS LOCATOR
REAL ARRAY[1000] AS LOCATOR
```

In SQL:1999, locator values are either valid or invalid. A locator value is created whenever a value of the large object, user-defined type, or array is assigned to a locator of the appropriate type; when it is created, the locator value is valid (wouldn't you be surprised if it weren't?). Locator values are defined in SQL:1999 to be four-octet, nonzero integers, which makes it easy to know just how to allocate a corresponding variable in your host-language code.

A locator can be marked as a holdable locator (by the execution of a HOLD LOCATOR statement that specifies the locator). A locator remains valid until it is invalidated by any of the following events: a ROLLBACK, a ROLLBACK to a savepoint (but only if the locator was created after that savepoint was established), a FREE LOCATOR statement that explicitly releases the locator, a COMMIT (if the locator is not holdable), or the end of the SQL-session in which the locator was created. See Chapter 15, "Transaction Management," and Chapter 16, "Connections and Remote Database Access," for information about those actions. A non-holdable locator is always made invalid whenever the transaction in which it was created is committed. By contrast, a holdable locator may remain valid even across multiple transactions, until one of the events mentioned above occurs.

2.4.13 Sites

In SQL-86, SQL-89, and even SQL-92, there were only a very small number of environmental objects that could be given a data type. The list was pretty much limited to columns of base tables, parameters of externally-invoked procedures (that is, module language procedures), and the equivalent host variables. PSM-

96 added more possibilities, including SQL variables and parameters of (stored) routines written in SQL and in various host languages.

SQL:1999 adds still more: attributes of structured types, fields of row types, elements of array types, and so forth. With this proliferation of things for which a data type can be specified, and to which values can be assigned, it has become important to create a new term to identify all of those environmental objects. The word chosen in SQL:1999 is *site*.

A site is defined in SQL:1999 as "a place occupied by an instance of a value of some specified data type." This might include entire base tables (although SQL:1999 is not specific about this), a row of a table, a column of a row of a table (that is, a cell of a table), a parameter, an SQL variable, a field of a row type, an attribute of a structured type, an element of an array type, and so forth. Some sites are persistent, such as base tables and their rows and cells. Other sites are temporary because they cease to exist at the end of an SQL statement, a transaction, or a session; these include SQL variables and temporary tables. Still other sites are transient and exist only as long as required to hold an argument value for a routine invocation or the value returned by a routine invocation.

Many sites are referenced by their names; base tables are a good example of this. Other sites are referenced by a reference value (see section 2.4.11 for some information and Volume 2 of this book for more details). Still others are referenced by other mechanisms; for example an array element is referenced by the number representing its index within the array.

The value stored at a site can often be changed by assigning a new value to it. However, the manner in which that value is changed varies according to the type of site. The value stored in an SQL variable may be changed by execution of a SET statement or by retrieving a column value into the variable. The value stored in a base table (that is, its multiset of rows) can be changed by execution of a DELETE statement, an INSERT statement, or an UPDATE statement that identifies the table.

Some sites are nullable (see section 2.5, and Chapter 10, "Constraints, Assertions, and Referential Integrity," for more information); others are not. A base table is never nullable, although it might contain no rows at some moment in time. Most other sites are specified to be nullable or not nullable by explicit (or implicit) declarations.

2.5 | Logic and Null Values

In what usually passes for real life, we don't always know all the answers when we need to know them. In fact, we often encounter situations in which we'd like to know certain information, but it's either not yet available or not applicable to the specific subject.

The same applies in business situations (which, after all, we should consider since few of us would ever have used a computer system otherwise, at least until quite recently). If we're capturing information about people, for instance, we might need to record the maiden names of married women who take their husbands' names, but this is not applicable to single women or to men.

For many years, computerized applications took care of this by trying to use a value of the appropriate type that normally wouldn't be a valid value. For example, they might use blanks or the phrase "Not Applicable" for the MAIDEN NAME field, or the value –1 for the SALARY field. But, in many cases, there are no invalid values, so applications were forced to use more awkward mechanisms. Furthermore, different application programmers found different mechanisms and invalid values. Some programmers would use blanks and others the phrase "Not Applicable" or "Not Specified" or a string of asterisks. When one program stored data and another program read it, the use of different conventions could have results ranging from interesting to costly. (Have you ever received mail addressed something like "Joe N/A Smith"?)

To many people, the solution is obvious: require the data manager to consistently apply some rule that allows a distinction between real values and other situations (such as Not Applicable, Not Given, or whatever). In SQL, the solution has been to store a sort of flag along with every data item (well, almost every data item; as we shall see later, some items can never be unspecified and therefore do not need this flag) to indicate whether or not the data item has a real value. When the flag is set to indicate that no real value is provided, we say that the data item has the null value. This phrase is probably a bit misleading, because null means that there is no "real" value at all; nevertheless, it's a convenient shorthand that you will often find in use.

The existence of null values leads to a further complication: three-valued logic. You may recall from logic classes that there is a system of logic that assumes all questions can be answered as True or False. Consequently, you can combine questions with "and" or "or" to discover more complex information.

For example, you could ask, "Did Mr. Big receive a stock option grant in 2000 greater than one million dollars?" and expect to get an answer of "True, the value of his 2000 stock option grant is greater than one million dollars." Similarly, you could ask, "Is Mr. Big's title 'President'?" and expect an answer of "True, his title is 'President'." You can combine these into a single question in two ways: "Is Mr. Big's 2000 stock option grant value greater than one million dollars and his title 'President'?"; or "Is Mr. Big's 2000 stock option grant value greater than one million dollars or his title 'President'?". You can easily see that these two complex questions are very different. The first asks if both facts are true, while the second asks if at least one of them is true.

In normal two-valued logic (the two values being True and False), combining two questions with "and" means that both have to be true for the result to be true; if either is false, then the result is false. If you combine the questions with "or," then the result is true if either is true; the result is false only if both are false. This is fairly obvious, because we deal with it in everyday life.

However, if we add a third possibility to the various questions, we get a more complex situation. If the answer to the salary question, the title question, or both can be "I Don't Know" or "Unknown," we must define the logical results. SQL:1999 uses two sorts of *truth table,* shown here as Table 2-3 and Table 2-4, to express these rules.

Table 2-3 *Truth Table for AND*

AND	True	False	Unknown
True	True	False	Unknown
False	False	False	False
Unknown	Unknown	False	Unknown

Table 2-4 *Truth Table for OR*

OR	True	False	Unknown
True	True	True	True
False	True	False	Unknown
Unknown	True	Unknown	Unknown

Let's try this out with our Mr. Big example. Suppose the answer to the stock option value question is "I Don't Know" because the value of the STOCK_OPTION_VALUE field for Mr. Big is null. The result of the title question is True, because we know that his title is President. Therefore, the answer to the questions combined with "and" is Unknown AND True, which the table says is Unknown. That makes sense, because the combined question can be True only if the answer to each part is True, but a False result is possible only if the answer to either part is False. We know that one part is True, but we don't know whether the other part is True or False, so we don't know the answer of the result.

If we combine the questions with "or," the result is True. Why? Well, because the result of an "or" combination is True if either one is True alone. In this case, Mr. Big does have the title President, so that part is True. Therefore, it doesn't matter whether the answer to his stock option value question is True or False—or Unknown; the answer to the combined question is always True.

Three-valued logic (True, False, and Unknown) is a very powerful tool for querying data. Like any tool, though, it can be misused. Some of SQL's predicates (a *predicate* is a clause that expresses a possible truth about something) use three-valued logic in ways that may not be intuitively obvious. Our advice is to take care that you use the SQL definition of a word rather than the standard English definition. We'll cover SQL predicates in detail in Chapter 7, "Predicates."

We note almost in passing that not everyone approves of three-valued logic. Some notable database personalities have strongly urged the SQL standards committees to abandon the notion of null values in favor of default values. The standards bodies have resisted such suggestions because of years (even decades) of experience with the problems of using only default values. By contrast, other database personalities have suggested that two null values are required and that a four-valued logic is "the answer." To complicate this issue, a group called the DataBase Systems Study Group, or DBSSG, produced a study a number of years ago that identified as many as 29 possible meanings for a null indicator.

The concept of Unknown came about as the result of testing a value that was null; for example, if X is null, then the predicate "X=2" evaluates to Unknown. With SQL:1999's BOOLEAN data type, however, a more natural approach to handling Unknowns, as well as True or False determination, can be supported because one of the three permissible values for a BOOLEAN data type is Unknown (see section 2.4.7).

2.6 | Data Conversions

SQL has long been thought to have *strong typing*. That is, you could mix only operands of the same type in expressions. Now, SQL was never as rigid about its typing as languages like Pascal and Ada, because you could, for example, add an INTEGER to a SMALLINT. However, unlike languages such as PL/I, you could not add an INTEGER to a CHARACTER string, even if the CHARACTER string contained only digits.

In real applications, however, situations often arise where you must somehow add an INTEGER value to the integer value of some digits stored in a CHARACTER value. Before SQL-92, you were required to retrieve the character string containing the digits into your application program, use some application-specific mechanism to convert those digits to an integer, and then feed that integer value back into the database to be added to the INTEGER value. In SQL-92, however, you were able to specify certain conversions right in your SQL statements.

SQL:1999 continues the conversion capabilities of SQL-92 by defining two sorts of data conversions: *implicit* and *explicit*. Implicit conversions continue to be fairly restricted, although not quite as much as in earlier versions of the standard. For example, you can still add an INTEGER to a REAL if your application requires it. However, if you want something a little more exotic, you must use the CAST function (see Chapter 6, "Advanced Value Expressions: CASE, CAST, and Row Value Expressions") to explicitly convert one type to another type that is compatible with the operation you want to perform. For example, if you happened to have a CHARACTER string that you know (through some application knowledge) contains only digits that can represent an integer value, then you can CAST that CHARACTER string to INTEGER; this will provide you with an integer value that you can add to your existing INTEGER. Of course, if you were wrong—the string contained some characters other than digits, say the letter *X*—you will get an error.

As you'll see in Chapter 8, "Working with Multiple Tables: The Relational Operators," the UNION set operator requires two tables that are identical in structure. If you need to combine two tables that are not quite identical in structure in a union type of operation, then you have to somehow force the structure of the two tables to be the same. Consider a table with columns TITLE, MOVIE TYPE, and OUR COST, and a second table with columns TITLE, MOVIE TYPE, and RATING. To form a union of these two tables, we somehow have to accommodate the OUR COST and RATING columns. One way to do this is to force rows from each table to have four columns: TITLE, MOVIE TYPE, OUR COST, and RATING. Of course, OUR COST is meaningless to rows coming from the second table, just as RATING is meaningless to rows from the first table. The way this is done is to "fill in" the rows coming from the first table to add a new column corresponding to RATING in the second table and to force the values of that new column to be null for every row coming from that first table (and perform the analogous operation for rows coming from the second table). While SQL provides the keyword NULL to represent a null value in an SQL statement, the keyword does not associate a data type with the null value, so SQL provides a syntactic ability to associate a data type with a null value when you need to do so:

```
CAST (NULL AS datatype)
```

This syntactic phrase avoids the necessity of defining a NULL keyword for every possible data type.

Thus far, we've learned about SQL data types and how we can use them as well as how we deal with their absence. Next, we examine how SQL lets you access your database.

2.7 | SQL Statements

SQL causes things to happen by the execution of SQL statements. You can embed SQL statements into conventional third-generation programming languages, you can write SQL-only modules containing procedures that you call from your 3GL programs, or you can invoke SQL statements directly. In each case, your actions or those of your 3GL program cause SQL statements to be executed.

SQL statements come in several categories: data manipulation statements, data definition statements, and management statements. Data manipulation statements, like the ones we will illustrate in Chapter 3, "Basic Table Creation and Data Manipulation," retrieve, store, delete, or update data in the database. Data definition statements allow you to define your database or to modify the definition of your database. Management statements allow you to control the database aspects of your application, such as the termination of transactions or the establishment of certain parameters that affect other statements.

Some statements must execute in the context of a transaction; if no transaction is active, then executing such statements causes a transaction to be started. Other statements must have no transaction active. Some statements require that a session be active; if you don't have a session going, they will cause a default session to be established. Other statements establish sessions. All this will be made clear as we discuss the individual statements throughout the rest of the book.

2.8 | Static Versus Dynamic Execution

SQL statements that are known when you write your application can be embedded directly into your application programs or written directly as modules and procedures. If you do this, you would normally precompile those embedded programs, which, conceptually (implementations differ widely in detail), separates the programs into an SQL part and a 3GL part. The SQL part may be compiled, just as you'd compile a module in an implementation that provided this facility, or it may be handled directly by the precompiler. The 3GL part may be compiled with the compiler for that language, or the precompiler might take care of that, too.

Regardless of the details, the fact that you knew the exact text of your SQL statements at the time you wrote your application means you can direct the SQL implementation (including the precompilers, compilers, and database system) to process the statements long before you have to execute your application. This paradigm is often called *static SQL* because the source text of the statements does not change while your application is running.

However, in many situations, you do not know the precise text of the statements when you write your application. Many so-called 4GL (fourth-generation language) products have this limitation (or strength, depending on your point of view). These products generate the SQL statements while the application is running, as the end user performs various actions at his or her workstation. Because the text of the SQL statement is not known (or not fully known) at the time the application is written, the application programmer cannot direct the implementation to process the statements in advance. They must be processed (compiled or optimized, for example) during program execution. This paradigm is called *dynamic SQL*.

Dynamic SQL has many complicated implications for application programmers as well as for implementations. In many cases, the performance of dynamic SQL is lower than that of static SQL; you can see that doing all of the processing during the execution of your application is bound to use more system resources than merely executing statements, most of which were processed earlier. Furthermore, because you don't know the text of the statements in advance, you don't always know how much data the statements will require from the application program or how much they'll return. These issues are covered thoroughly in Chapter 18, "Dynamic SQL."

Also, as we discuss in Chapter 19, "Call-Level Interface (CLI)," SQL/CLI gives the equivalent of dynamic execution in a manner generally considered very friendly to application programmers.

2.9 | Conforming to SQL:1999

In several places earlier in this chapter, we've made reference to the fact that there is no such thing as a "perfect match" between the SQL standard and the features and syntax of a commercial DBMS product—make that *any* commercial RDBMS product. How, then, does one know whether or not a DBMS product conforms to the SQL standard?

2.9.1 Core SQL

Conformance to Core SQL means that a DBMS product contains all of Entry SQL-92, plus much of Intermediate SQL-92 and some of Full SQL-92, plus a few new SQL:1999 features. Appendix C.5 discusses exactly what capabilities are included as part of Core SQL.

2.9.2 Packages

In addition to Core SQL conformance, there are *packages* of features of the SQL language that vendors may choose to implement within their respective products. These packages, and a brief description of their contents, are shown in Table 2-5.

Table 2-5 *SQL Conformance Packages*

	Package ID	Package Description
1	PKG001	Enhanced datetime facilities
2	PKG002	Enhanced integrity management
3	PKG003	OLAP facilities
4	PKG004	PSM
5	PKG005	CLI
6	PKG006	Basic object support
7	PKG007	Enhanced object support
8	PKG008	Active database
9	PKG009	SQL/MM support*

*"MM" stands for "multimedia," and SQL/MM is itself a multipart standard addressing various aspects of multimedia content. Volume 2 of this book will (briefly) address SQL/MM.

2.10 | Relationship to Products

A final note about relational database management system products for this chapter, following up on the discussion in some of the above paragraphs:

Today (early 2001), the "Big 5" of DBMS products includes the following, all of which are fully based on SQL:

- Oracle
- Microsoft SQL/Server
- IBM DB2

- Sybase

- Informix

Additionally, other relational products that may not be quite as prominent as they once were, but are still being used, include

- CA/Ingres

- Oracle RDB (formerly Rdb/VMS)

- SQL/Base

- Interbase

All of these products have, over the years, closed the gap between their respective syntactical constructs and that contained in the SQL standard. It is still important to note, though, that there is not—nor will there ever likely be—a perfect match between the syntax of any of these products and that contained in the SQL standard. Therefore, it is important for database programmers, administrators, and others involved in relational data management to understand the syntax and behavior of *both* the SQL standard and material found in the reference manuals of the product(s) with which they will work.

2.11 | Identifiers

SQL provides two types of identifiers that you can use to name your database objects. One type, called *regular identifiers* for lack of a better name, corresponds to the identifiers that you have encountered in many other programming languages. Regular identifiers in SQL are not case sensitive—that is, you can spell a name as either TITLES, titles, Titles, or even TiTlEs, and they all mean the same thing: TITLES. In effect, SQL:1999 changes all lowercase letters in regular identifiers to their uppercase-equivalent letters. This is especially important for identifiers that are stored as data values in the views of the Information Schema (see Chapter 22, "Information Schema"). Regular identifiers can contain only letters (in any alphabet, not just the Latin alphabet), syllables (as in the Japanese Hiragana syllabary), ideographs (as in Chinese), decimal digits, and underscores; they cannot begin with a digit or an underscore, however. Chapter 21, "Internationalization Aspects of SQL:1999," describes how non-Latin letters, syllables, and ideographs can be used in identifiers.

However, the designers of SQL:1999 recognized that not all requirements were met by regular identifiers. C and Unix programmers are more comfortable with case-sensitive identifiers, COBOL programmers are used to using hyphens in their identifiers, and there is a fairly large demand for the ability to use special characters (such as spaces, number signs, or hash marks, and so forth) in identifiers. The solution is something called a *delimited identifier*. Delimited identifiers are strings of characters that appear inside double quotation marks. For example, "titles" is a delimited identifier and is different from TITLES and from "TITLES".

You can think of a delimited identifier as being just like a regular identifier except that SQL:1999 does not automatically change its lowercase letters to uppercase ones and all sorts of special characters are allowed in any position. When a delimited identifier is stored into the views of the Information Schema, the double quotes are not stored, but all the other characters are, just as they appeared in the delimited identifier. Therefore, the regular identifier TITLES and the delimited identifier "TITLES" are stored identically and are therefore completely equivalent. However, the regular identifier titles and the delimited identifier "titles" are different. Why? Because titles is effectively changed by SQL:1999 to TITLES, while "titles" is not changed at all.

By the way, since SQL is insensitive to the case of regular identifiers and of keywords, it's not especially important to the language that you write the identifiers in your SQL code with any particular case convention. However, it may well be important to your fellow programmers—the people who have to debug and maintain code you write—so we urge you to adopt a convention and stick to it whenever possible. Throughout this book, we've generally used a convention of using lowercase letters for identifiers (in code examples, that is; in ordinary text, we usually write them in uppercase letters for clarity) and uppercase letters for SQL's keywords; however, we have sometimes used uppercase letters for identifiers, too, either to illustrate some particular issue or just because it seemed appropriate in context. (OK, perhaps we were careless once or twice, too, and just didn't follow our own rules!)

2.12 Chapter Summary

This chapter has presented the foundation upon which discussion about SQL:1999 in subsequent chapters is based. We've covered topics from the background and history of SQL to the fundamental architectural and syntactical constructs. In Chapter 3, we shift our discussion to the hands-on aspects, beginning with the basic ways in which you can retrieve and manipulate data using SQL facilities.

Chapter

3

Basic Table Creation and Data Manipulation

3.1 Introduction

Like any language that interfaces with a database management system, SQL has many important and valuable features. The most basic facilities in any database system are the retrieval, creation, deletion, and modification of data. SQL accomplishes these functions with four basic data manipulation statements: SELECT, INSERT, DELETE, and UPDATE. In our first look at these statements, we explore only their most basic capabilities. In later chapters, we will investigate in detail the more advanced aspects of the statements.

In this chapter we learn how to perform the following functions with SQL:

- retrieve all the rows in a table
- retrieve all nonduplicate rows in a table
- retrieve rows based on simple criteria, such as the value within a particular column
- retrieve only selected columns from a table (as compared to all columns)
- update some or all rows, such as multiplying a particular column's value by, say, 75% (perhaps to put all movies on sale, for example)

- insert new rows—and appropriate values—into a table
- delete some or all rows from a table

   Again, the statements we discuss in this chapter should be viewed for now as standalone. That is, the statements are issued and a certain set of actions occurs. In reality, your own applications will likely contain a mixture of SQL and some host language (as we discussed in Chapter 2, "Introduction to SQL:1999"), and the SQL may be static or dynamic, embedded or module-based. For now, though, we concentrate on the basic functions of the statements themselves, rather than on their role in an overall information system.

   We also see how to create simple SQL tables as a way of helping you to understand the data objects on which the four basic statements (SELECT, INSERT, DELETE, and UPDATE) operate. In Chapter 4, "Basic Data Definition Language (DDL)," we will discuss table creation in much more detail. Initially, however, we concentrate on basic table creation without all of the powerful features SQL provides.

   By the way, in this chapter, you get your first real look at the details of our sample application: the music and video store introduced in Chapter 1, "Database and Technology Foundations." Don't forget that we introduce this application incrementally: as we introduce a new concept, we show how it enhances the application.

3.2 | Our Example

We've hinted that the examples in this book will deal with the sale of music and movie content. There will be the occasional need to provide rather dry examples to explain a given topic, but for the most part we offer examples that fall within our sample application environment. In an earlier edition of this work, published in 1993 and discussing the SQL-92 standard, we focused on a traditional music and video retailer—what today is referred to (sometimes dismissively) as a "brick-and-mortar" retailer. Updating this example to the late 1990s and beyond, we decided to retain the music and video retail flavor, but with a "new economy" twist: an Internet-based e-tailer of entertainment content, including (as we've mentioned) CDs, DVDs, "old-fashioned" videotapes, CD-ROMs, and other entertainment media. The idea of an online e-tailer will be especially applicable in Volume 2 and in the discussion of object-oriented features of SQL:1999; examples will include requesting and receiving content (e.g., MP3-

formatted music) over the Internet, with that content managed by an SQL:1999-compliant DBMS.

We do need to provide one caution relative to our example. As we introduce new SQL principles and syntax, we occasionally modify one or more table definitions specified in a previous chapter, introduce new tables for the duration of a single example, or make some assumptions. Don't be concerned; even though our overall sample application will be consistent throughout the book, the many examples stand alone and do not rely on syntax, sample data, or other examples from previous chapters. We will explicitly give you all you need to understand each example, including table definitions and assumptions, sample data, or both.

In addition to the SQL:1999 syntax examples—and our consolidation of these examples in Appendix B, "A Complete SQL:1999 Example"—you may wish to review Appendix A, "Designing SQL:1999 Databases,"in which we *briefly* discuss the principles of data modeling and database design. You may wonder, for example, why we use multiple tables to store information about movies instead of consolidating the information into a single table. The answer—*normalization*—was discussed earlier in Chapter 1, "Database and Technology Foundations." Many of you will already be intimately familiar with database design principles, but those of you who haven't been exposed to this subject will find a concise discussion to help you decipher some of the *whys* behind our example.

3.3 | Basic Table Creation

As we discussed in Chapter 2, "Introduction to SQL:1999,"relational databases are organized around tables, columns, and rows. All SQL:1999 data manipulation statements must operate on tables that have been created by you or someone else at some prior time. (Technically, that's not quite accurate. Because of SQL:1999's ability to represent tables as table value constructors [seen in Chapter 9, "Advanced SQL Query Expressions"], many SQL:1999 data manipulation statements can operate on tables in that form instead of on only those tables stored in the database.)

SQL:1999 tables are created through the CREATE TABLE statement. The basic CREATE TABLE statement requires a list of the names of the columns being created, the data types, and, if applicable, sizes of values within each column, in addition to other related aspects (such as whether or not null values are permitted). We'll explore the many alternatives of CREATE TABLE and other aspects of data definition in Chapter 4, "Basic Data Definition Language (DDL)"; our purpose here is to create several simple tables with which we can examine the effects of basic data manipulation statements.

A quick word on SQL:1999 syntax: In general, SQL:1999 is a free-format language. Statements may be divided among multiple lines for readability, spaces may be used liberally to offset words from one another, and the use of uppercase or lowercase letters is normally not significant (but there are exceptions covered elsewhere in this book); parentheses may often be used as well to improve understanding of, and sometimes control, the order in which portions of a statement are grouped and processed.

In our sample database application, there are several tables that deal with videotapes and DVDs. For example, our main table that maintains inventory and revenue data might be created as shown in Example 3-1.[1]

Example 3-1 *Creating the MOVIE_TITLES Table*

```
CREATE TABLE movie_titles (
    title                       CHARACTER ( 30 ) NOT NULL,
    year_released               DATE,
    our_tape_cost               DECIMAL ( 5,2 ),
    our_dvd_cost                DECIMAL ( 5,2 ),
    regular_tape_sale_price     DECIMAL ( 5,2 ),
    current_tape_sale_price     DECIMAL ( 5,2 ),
    regular_dvd_sale_price      DECIMAL ( 5,2 ),
    current_dvd_sale_price      DECIMAL ( 5,2 ),
    part_of_series              CHARACTER ( 3 ),
    movie_type                  CHARACTER ( 10 ),
    tapes_owned                 INTEGER,
    dvds_owned                  INTEGER,
    tapes_in_stock              INTEGER,
    dvds_in_stock               INTEGER,
    total_tape_units_sold       INTEGER,
    total_dvd_units_sold        INTEGER,
    total_tape_sales_revenue    DECIMAL ( 9,2 ),
    total_dvd_sales_revenue     DECIMAL ( 9,2 ) ) ;
```

---

1   Readers who are experienced database developers may note that the movie_titles table in this example is highly denormalized (see Chapter 1 for a discussion of normalization and denormalization), and in a real-world application would likely be subject to update anomalies. We deliberately structured the table this way for ease of understanding the basic SQL statements we introduce in this chapter, rather than complicate our examples by using multiple normalized tables that need to be combined (joined)—a concept we don't introduce until Chapter 8, "Working with Multiple Tables: The Relational Operators."

The `movie_titles` table contains a number of columns having different data types: `INTEGER`, `DECIMAL`, `CHARACTER`, and `DATE`. (Each of these data types and their variations was discussed in Chapter 2, "Introduction to SQL:1999.")

Another table that contains related information can also be created as illustrated in Example 3-2.

Example 3-2 *Creating the MOVIES_STARS Table*

```
CREATE TABLE movies_stars (
    movie_title                CHARACTER ( 30 ) NOT NULL,
    year_released              DATE NOT NULL,
    actor_last_name            CHARACTER ( 35 ) NOT NULL,
    actor_first_name           CHARACTER ( 25 ),
    actor_middle_name          CHARACTER ( 25 ) ) ;
```

In creating each of these tables, the NOT NULL clause is used to indicate that no row within that table is permitted to have a null value for that column's value. That is, the `movie_titles` table must not have any rows with an empty `title`; this makes a great deal of sense, since the rest of the columns are meaningless without a specific `title` to which they relate. NOT NULL is a simple example of a *constraint*. We'll discuss other constraints in Chapter 10, "Constraints, Assertions, and Referential Integrity".

We should note that in our sample, we assume that the combination of a movie's title and the year it was released will be sufficient to uniquely identify a given movie. For example, movies such as *The Ten Commandments, A Star Is Born,* and *Dr. Doolittle* have been remade several times. For the purposes of our database, we'll assume that no two movies of the same title were released in the same year.

The `actor_first_name` column, however, is permitted to have null values to allow for one-name stars such as Cher, Sting, and Madonna (their respective names will be stored as `actor_last_name`) or for group stars such as The Marx Brothers or Monty Python. And while most actors' and actresses' middle names are of little importance, some—James Earl Jones, for example—do use their middle names professionally, and their identity is somewhat dependent on the combination of first, middle, and last names. For others, however, `actor_middle_name` is permitted to have null values.

Another brief syntactic note: At first, we will show all SQL statements ending with a semicolon (;). Later, when we discuss embedded SQL, we will show how some languages use a semicolon to terminate an SQL statement, while other languages use other conventions.

Let's look at how the rows of data might look in the `movies_stars` table, Table 3-1 (disregarding for now the year the movie was released).

Table 3-1 *MOVIES_STARS*

MOVIE_TITLE	ACTOR_ LAST_NAME	ACTOR_ FIRST_NAME	ACTOR_ MIDDLE_NAME
The Way We Were	Redford	Robert	
The Way We Were	Streisand	Barbra	
The Thin Red Line	Nolte	Nick	
The Thin Red Line	Penn	Sean	
The Hunt for Red October	Jones	James	Earl
The Hunt for Red October	Connery	Sean	
A League of Their Own	Madonna		
48 Hours	Nolte	Nick	
48 Hours	Murphy	Eddie	
A Star Is Born	Kristofferson	Kris	
A Star Is Born	Streisand	Barbra	
Another 48 Hours	Murphy	Eddie	
Another 48 Hours	Nolte	Nick	
Beverly Hills Cop	Murphy	Eddie	
Beverly Hills Cop	Reinhold	Judge	
Beverly Hills Cop II	Murphy	Eddie	
Beverly Hills Cop II	Reinhold	Judge	
Pretty Woman	Roberts	Julia	
Pretty Woman	Gere	Richard	
Runaway Bride	Roberts	Julia	
Runaway Bridge	Gere	Richard	
The Sixth Sense	Willis	Bruce	
Three Kings	Clooney	George	
Raising Arizona	Cage	Nicholas	
Raising Arizona	Hunter	Holly	
The Outlaw Josey Wales	Eastwood	Clint	
The Outlaw Josey Wales	Locke	Sondra	
Duck Soup	Marx Brothers		
A Night at the Opera	Marx Brothers		

In actuality, of course, any sizable video store would have a database of thousands of movie titles, and we know that e-tailers mostly advertise that they sell even more titles than any physical store location might carry. For obvious reasons of space (and tedium), in this book we will present only portions of tables rather than entire lists of thousands of movies And remember, we are also dealing with an e-tailer that sells other types of entertainment (e.g., music and computer games), so we have thousands of other titles as well (examples in subsequent chapters will make use of other media types).

This self-imposed writing restriction *does* present a problem in certain circumstances, such as when we introduce expressions like COUNT. In these instances, we will make the obviously faulty assumption that the respective segments we present for our examples represent the entire table. The important thing is that you understand the concepts presented in each example, and not whether your favorite Harvey Keitel title is included! Okay, back to SQL.

Because most of SQL's data manipulation statements are set-oriented, the order in which the rows are processed is not significant. There are, of course, situations in which the order of rows is important (such as retrieving rows to be displayed on a terminal or report); SQL's cursors (see Chapter 13, "Cursors") provide an ordering facility for that requirement. Your implementation will likely have some hidden order to rows, such as the order in which they are physically stored in the database, but that is unimportant to SQL.

3.4 | Set Orientation

As we discussed in Chapter 1, "Database and Technology Foundations," SQL is a set-oriented language. This means that most of the SQL statements that operate on data don't do so one row at a time, but deal with entire groups of rows at once. Sometimes, these groups of rows are entire tables; in other cases, the group of rows is identified by the statement to be a part of a table or even rows from more than one table.

There are two primary models through which data is managed in database and file environments. The first, which many users of COBOL, Ada, and other third-generation programming languages (3GLs) will find familiar, is on a single-instance basis. That is, a particular record of a file or row of a relational database is accessed, examined, and manipulated according to some procedural logic, which is usually encoded in a programming language of some sort. SQL:1999 contains facilities, called *cursors*, to manage single-instance processing requirements; cursors are discussed in subsequent chapters (primarily in Chapter 13, "Cursors").

The alternative processing model, and the one we explore through most of this chapter's statements, is set-oriented; that is (in the case of SQL databases), one or more tables are managed as a whole. Based on rules provided for the entire set of data being considered, data are retrieved from, updated within, or deleted from the specified table(s), without the need to process each row individually in an application program. For those unfamiliar with set-oriented processing, the process will be second nature by the conclusion of this chapter.

3.5 Basic Data Retrieval

Given Table 3-1, let's look at some sample data manipulation statements. The basic retrieval method is through the SELECT statement. The basic syntax of the SELECT statement is

```
SELECT columns
FROM tables
WHERE (conditions)
```

The complete syntax for a SELECT statement is more complicated, but this is sufficient to introduce the statement for now. Syntax 3-1 shows what the limited statement looks like in BNF form.

Syntax 3-1 *Syntax of the SELECT Statement*

```
SELECT columns FROM tables [ WHERE predicates ]
```

Depending on your predicates, or search criteria, the specified column(s) will be retrieved from some or all rows in the table. For example, to retrieve a list of the movie titles stored in the MOVIES_STARS table (of which Table 3-1 is a portion), you would issue the following statement (which contains no search criteria):

```
SELECT movie_title
FROM movies_stars ;
```

which would yield the result shown in Results 3-1.

Result 3-1 *Movie Title Result*

MOVIE_TITLE

The Way We Were
The Way We Were
The Thin Red Line
The Thin Red Line
The Hunt for Red October
The Hunt for Red October
A League of Their Own
48 Hours
|
|
|
Duck Soup
A Night at the Opera

3.5.1 DISTINCT

Since most of the movie titles are stored more than once in the MOVIES_STARS table, based on the fact that there is usually more than one star in that movie, a great deal of redundant information is retrieved in the form of duplicate movie titles. To eliminate the duplicate titles, the DISTINCT clause may be used as part of the SELECT statement:

```
SELECT DISTINCT MOVIE_TITLE
FROM MOVIES_STARS ;
```

which would yield the result shown in Result 3-2.

Result 3-2 *DISTINCT Movie Titles*

MOVIE_TITLE

The Way We Were
The Thin Red Line
The Hunt for Red October
A League of Their Own
48 Hours

(Continued)

Result 3-2 *Continued*

MOVIE_TITLE

A Star Is Born
Another 48 Hours
Beverly Hills Cop
|
|

3.5.2 Inside the SELECT Statement

At this point, it's time for us to talk a little bit about what the term *SELECT state-ment* really means. SQL has two distinct uses of the word SELECT. One of these is, in fact, to initiate a SELECT statement. The other is to define a table-valued expression (often called a *query expression*), which can appear in many places in the language. In fact, almost anywhere that you can use a table, you can use one of these table-valued expressions.

In *direct invocation* of SQL (usually interpreted to mean *interactive* SQL), we can use a SELECT statement that retrieves multiple rows from a table. This is possible because the rows are merely displayed on your terminal or on your printer. However, if you write an application program using SQL statements that interact with a 3GL program, you cannot use a multiple-row SELECT statement because it could retrieve an arbitrary number of rows and 3GLs cannot deal with that sort of uncertainty. In embedded SQL, the SELECT statement can return (at most) one row; if it attempts to return more than one row, you will get an error.

Although we often use the SELECT statement in this book to illustrate the contents of a table or to demonstrate the result of some feature, you must understand that the actual SELECT statement of embedded SQL does not have this behavior.

Similarly, the SELECT statement (or query expression) in SQL cannot use the ORDER BY clause except in direct invocation. Cursors can be defined with an ORDER BY clause, as we will see in Chapter 13, "Cursors."

In Section 9.2.2, "Table Expressions," we'll elaborate quite a bit on the under-lying model of the part of the SELECT statement that starts at the FROM keyword (that is, the *table expression* within the statement). As you'll see when you get to that discussion, the clauses of the table expression behave a lot like operators that take tables as input and produce tables as output. The tables they produce are always virtual tables, and the virtual table produced by one of those clauses is the input to the next clause. Well, in the context of the SELECT statement, the virtual table that is produced by the last clause in the table expression is used as input to the SELECT clause itself. This is because the columns to be selected cannot be known until all the other operations have been performed, so the selection of columns is the last operation.

As with all rules, there is an exception to this one, which we cover next. The ORDER BY clause is actually evaluated after the columns have been selected, but, then again, the ORDER BY clause isn't part of the table expression—it's used only for the direct invocation SELECT statement and for cursors.

3.5.3 ORDER BY

To receive the same result we saw with SELECT, but in alphabetical order, the ORDER BY clause may be added to the statement:

```
SELECT DISTINCT movie_title
FROM movies_stars
ORDER BY movie_title ASC ;
```

In this example, only one column is used for the ordering. ASC indicates ascending order, as opposed to DESC for descending order. The statement yields the result shown in Result 3-3. (Remember, our example is predicated on a working database that contains thousands of movie titles, only a few of which can be shown in any given table segment used in this book. Accordingly, some titles are seen here that did not appear in the earlier *unordered* segment, as seen in Table 3-1.)

Result 3-3 *Ordered Movie Titles*

MOVIE_TITLE

48 Hours
A Night at the Opera
A Star Is Born
About Last Night
Animal House
Another 48 Hours
The Way We Were
Yentl
Zorro

3.5.4 WHERE and *

The WHERE clause is the primary vehicle by which retrieval of certain rows that meet a particular set of conditions is accomplished. For example, to answer the question, "What movies do we carry that star Eddie Murphy?" you might issue the following statement:

```
SELECT *
FROM movies_stars
WHERE actor_last_name = 'Murphy' ;
```

The WHERE clause requires a search condition (one or more predicates combined with AND, OR, and NOT) to specify the conditions under which you want rows to be chosen for inclusion in your set of data. We'll learn more about the WHERE clause in Chapter 9, "Advanced SQL Query Expressions."

Result 3-4 *Result of SELECT * FROM MOVIES_STARS*

MOVIE_TITLE	YEAR_ RELEASED	ACTOR_ LAST_NAME	ACTOR_ FIRST_NAME
48 Hours	1982	Murphy	Eddie
Another 48 Hours	1990	Murphy	Eddie
Beverly Hills Cop	1984	Murphy	Eddie
Beverly Hills Cop II	1987	Murphy	Eddie
Beverly Hills Cop III	1994	Murphy	Eddie
Bowfinger	1999	Murphy	Eddie
Coming to America	1988	Murphy	Eddie
Doctor Doolittle	1998	Murphy	Eddie
The Nutty Professor	1996	Murphy	Eddie
|			
Eddie Murphy Raw	1987	Murphy	Eddie

The asterisk (*) means "give me all columns" (unlike our previous examples, where only one column, movie_title, was specified). Result 3-4 shows the answer SQL:1999 will yield for our SELECT * statement with WHERE clause. (Note that not all rows of the result are illustrated, as indicated by the vertical bar (|)in the next-to-last row of the result table.) However—a *big* caution here—the use of the asterisk is not necessarily a good idea. You should be extremely careful when you choose to write SELECT *. In earlier versions of the SQL standard, like SQL-89, the structure of a database couldn't be changed by an application, so the meaning of SELECT * never varied. However, starting with SQL-92, you are able to add columns to or drop columns from your tables (as you have been able to do with real products in use for many years now); this capability (naturally) remains in SQL:1999. That makes the meaning of SELECT * variable; at one point, it might mean "get me columns A, B, and C from Table X," while after a structural change, it might mean "get me columns A, B, D, and F from Table X."

If you are using direct invocation of SQL at your terminal, the effect is merely more or fewer columns being displayed on the screen (and, of course, it is a tremendous shortcut compared with having to explicitly and repeatedly type in a long list of column names). However, if you are writing an embedded SQL program, the entire program can start returning errors related to an improper number of columns or data type mismatch. Therefore, excepting direct invocation, we recommend that you avoid using SELECT * in favor of explicitly coding the exact list of columns that you want to retrieve. It takes a bit more typing when you are developing your programs, but the good programming concept of avoiding system-provided default values and actions directly applies to this recommended explicitness. At some points in this book, we will use an asterisk as a space saver in our examples; in practice, we would explicitly list the column names.

Speaking of explicitly stating the actions you wish to occur: the same generalization can be applied to selection parameters. Let's see how predicates sometimes (often, actually) have to be coupled together in order to achieve the desired results.

3.5.5 Search Conditions Using AND, OR

Note the result (Result 3-5) yielded by the following SELECT statement. To receive a list of movies that star Demi Moore, the following statement does *not* yield the correct result:

```
SELECT movie_title, actor_last_name, actor_first_name, actor_middle_name
FROM movies_stars
WHERE actor_last_name = 'Moore' ;
```

Result 3-5 *Retrieving Specific Columns*

MOVIE_TITLE	ACTOR_ LAST_NAME	ACTOR_ FIRST_NAME	ACTOR_ MIDDLE_NAME
About Last Night	Moore	Demi	
G.I. Jane	Moore	Demi	
Foul Play	Moore	Dudley	
Ten	Moore	Dudley	
Ordinary People	Moore	Mary	Tyler

In this case, our request must be more specific. Use of the AND operator will satisfy our needs (see Result 3-6).

```
SELECT movie_title, actor_last_name, actor_first_name
FROM movies_stars
WHERE actor_last_name = 'Moore'
  AND actor_first_name = 'Demi' ;
```

Result 3-6 *Filtering the Rows to Be Retrieved*

MOVIE_TITLE	ACTOR_ LAST_NAME	ACTOR_ FIRST_NAME
About Last Night	Moore	Demi
G.I. Jane	Moore	Demi
Indecent Proposal	Moore	Demi
. . .		

The first example in section 3.5.6 shows how OR is used, and in Chapter 5, "Values, Basic Functions, and Expressions," we'll discuss the use of AND, OR, and other search condition operators in more detail.

3.5.6 More SELECT Statements

Let's look at our MOVIE_TITLES table (Table 3-2, again, just a small portion of the database) to examine some other forms of the SELECT statement.

Table 3-2 *MOVIE_TITLES Table Contents*

TITLE	REGULAR_ TAPE_ SALE_PRICE	CURRENT_ TAPE_ SALE_PRICE	REGULAR_ DVD_ SALE_PRICE	CURRENT_ DVD_ SALE_PRICE
The Sixth Sense	19.95	19.95	29.95	29.95
Three Kings	15.95	15.95	25.95	22.95
The Thomas Crown Affair	14.95	11.95	24.95	22.95
The 13th Warrior	19.95	19.95	29.95	29.95
The Matrix	18.95	18.95	28.95	28.95
Runaway Bride	19.95	17.95	29.95	27.95
Austin Powers	18.95	17.95	28.95	27.95
Austin Powers: The Spy Who Shagged Me	18.95	18.95	28.95	28.95
Notting Hill	16.95	16.95	26.95	26.95
Big Daddy	19.95	15.95	29.95	29.95
The Waterboy	19.95	15.95	29.95	29.95
Bowfinger	19.95	19.95	29.95	29.95
Man on the Moon	19.95	19.95	29.95	25.95

Perhaps we are interested in listing all movies that are on sale, in *either* DVD or tape format. We can find these by comparing the current sale prices for both formats with their respective regular prices (see Table 3-2). If either is less than the corresponding regular price, the movie is on sale. To accomplish this, we introduce two new aspects to the SELECT statement: the OR operator (as compared with the AND operator just covered) and the use of a comparison operator; in this case, the less than (<) sign.

To avoid any possibility of misunderstanding between you and your DBMS (or, for that matter, between you and the people who will maintain your programs years from now), you might want to use parentheses whenever you combine multiple predicates to ensure that the intended results are obtained.

```
SELECT title, regular_tape_sale_price,
       current_tape_sale_price, regular_dvd_sale_price,
       current_dvd_sale_price
FROM movie_titles
WHERE ( ( current_tape_sale_price < regular_tape_sale_price ) OR
        ( current_dvd_sale_price < regular_dvd_sale_price ) );
```

Result 3-7 *Result of Careful Use of Parentheses*

TITLE	REGULAR_ TAPE_ SALE_PRICE	CURRENT_ TAPE_ SALE_PRICE	REGULAR_ DVD_ SALE_PRICE	CURRENT_ DVD_ SALE_PRICE
Three Kings	15.95	15.95	25.95	22.95
The Thomas Crown Affair	14.95	11.95	24.95	22.95
Runaway Bride	19.95	17.95	29.95	27.95
Austin Powers	18.95	17.95	28.95	27.95
Big Daddy	19.95	15.95	29.95	25.95
The Waterboy	19.95	15.95	29.95	25.95
Man on the Moon	19.95	19.95	29.95	25.95

You can also use expressions in your select lists, perhaps to compute a value that is not actually stored in a table. For example, suppose you want to see the total number of units, both tape and DVD, that have been sold for each movie in stock. We might use the table shown in Table 3-3 to start.

Table 3-3 *Total Units for Each Movie*

TITLE	TOTAL_TAPE_ UNITS_SOLD	TOTAL_DVD_ UNITS_SOLD
Arlington Road	23	8
Bowfinger	98	21
The Seven Samurai	24	12
Shakespeare in Love	456	98
Casablanca	134	32
Ishtar	234	210
Any Given Sunday	122	18

Then we could use the query:

```
SELECT title, total_tape_units_sold,
       total_dvd_units_sold,
       total_tape_units_sold + total_dvd_units_sold
FROM movie_titles;
```

which yields the result shown in Result 3-8.

Result 3-8 *Using Computed Columns*

TITLE	TOTAL_TAPE_ UNITS_SOLD	TOTAL_DVD_ UNITS_SOLD	
Arlington Road	23	8	31
Bowfinger	98	21	119
The Seven Samurai	24	12	36
Shakespeare in Love	456	98	554
Casablanca	134	32	166

In later chapters, we'll discuss additional forms of data manipulation as well as advanced forms of the SELECT statement.

3.6 Updating Information

It's obviously not sufficient merely to be able to retrieve information from your database; data modifications are required as part of most transactional applications (as contrasted with informational applications, such as data warehousing, that *do* tend to be retrieve-only for most end users). The SQL UPDATE statement is used to modify the values of one or more columns in one or more rows, according to the search conditions you specify. The format of the UPDATE statement is shown in Syntax 3-2.

Syntax 3-2 *UPDATE Statement Syntax*

```
UPDATE <target table>
  SET <set clause list>
[ WHERE <search condition> ]
```

Suppose that the site is running a special weekend promotion, and all movies will be on sale for $12.99 for that weekend only. The following statement can be used to adjust all current sales prices to the new sale price:

```
UPDATE movie_titles
  SET current_tape_sale_price = 12.99 ;
```

The omission of the WHERE clause instructs the database system to update *all rows* in the movie_titles table.

Suppose we want to reduce the current sale price of all tapes by $1.00 except for those tapes that currently sell for less than $16.00. The following statement would accomplish this change for the titles in Table 3-4.

Table 3-4 *Regular and Current Videotape Sales Prices before Applying Discount*

TITLE	REGULAR_TAPE_ SALE_PRICE	CURRENT_TAPE_ SALE_PRICE
The Sixth Sense	19.95	19.95
Three Kings	15.95	15.95
The Thomas Crown Affair	14.95	11.95
The 13th Warrior	19.95	19.95
The Matrix	18.95	18.95
Runaway Bride	19.95	17.95
Austin Powers	18.95	17.95
Austin Powers: The Spy Who Shagged Me	18.95	18.95
Notting Hill	16.95	16.95
Big Daddy	19.95	15.95
The Waterboy	19.95	15.95

Example 3-3 *Updating MOVIE_TITLES*

```
UPDATE movie_titles
   SET current_tape_sale_price =
       ( current_tape_sale_price - 1.00 )
WHERE current_tape_sale_price >= 16.00 ;
```

Result 3-9 is the result.

Result 3-9 *Results of Selective Update to Apply Discount*

TITLE	REGULAR_TAPE_ SALE_PRICE	CURRENT_TAPE_ SALE_PRICE
The Sixth Sense	19.95	18.95
Three Kings	15.95	15.95
The Thomas Crown Affair	14.95	11.95
The 13th Warrior	19.95	18.95

(Continued)

Result 3-9 *Continued*

TITLE	REGULAR_TAPE_ SALE_PRICE	CURRENT_TAPE_ SALE_PRICE
The Matrix	18.95	17.95
Runaway Bride	19.95	16.95
Austin Powers	18.95	16.95
Austin Powers: The Spy Who Shagged Me	18.95	17.95
Notting Hill	16.95	15.95
Big Daddy	19.95	15.95
The Waterboy	19.95	15.95

Let's go back to our earlier example of listing movies currently on sale, either in DVD or tape format (see Table 3-2). Suppose the online retailer decides that all movies currently on sale in tape format but that *aren't* currently on sale in DVD format will now have a current DVD sale price that is $2.00 less than the regular DVD sale price, the idea being to test the relationship between current DVD and videotape prices to further understand customer buying patterns. We can accomplish this by issuing

```
UPDATE movie_titles
   SET current_dvd_sale_price = ( regular_dvd_sale_price - 2.00 )
 WHERE ( current_tape_sale_price < regular_tape_sale_price )
   AND ( current_dvd_sale_price = regular_dvd_sale_price ) ;
```

which yields Result 3-10. The two rows in this subset of movie titles whose current DVD prices are changed as a result of the above statement—those for *Big Daddy* and *The Waterboy*—are highlighted for ease of reference.

Result 3-10 *More Careful Selection*

TITLE	REGULAR_ TAPE_ SALE_PRICE	CURRENT_ TAPE_ SALE_PRICE	REGULAR_ DVD_ SALE_PRICE	CURRENT_ DVD_ SALE_PRICE
The Sixth Sense	19.95	19.95	29.95	29.95
Three Kings	15.95	15.95	25.95	22.95
The Thomas Crown Affair	14.95	11.95	24.95	22.95
The 13th Warrior	19.95	19.95	29.95	29.95
The Matrix	18.95	18.95	28.95	28.95

(Continued)

Result 3-10 *Continued*

TITLE	REGULAR_ TAPE_ SALE_PRICE	CURRENT_ TAPE_ SALE_PRICE	REGULAR_ DVD_ SALE_PRICE	CURRENT_ DVD_ SALE_PRICE
Runaway Bride	19.95	17.95	29.95	27.95
Austin Powers	18.95	17.95	28.95	27.95
Austin Powers: The Spy Who Shagged Me	18.95	18.95	28.95	28.95
Notting Hill	16.95	16.95	26.95	26.95
Big Daddy	19.95	15.95	29.95	27.95
The Waterboy	19.95	15.95	29.95	27.95
Bowfinger	19.95	19.95	29.95	29.95
Man on the Moon	19.95	19.95	29.95	25.95

You can change multiple column values in the same UPDATE statement. Assume that our sole distributor reduces our cost on every DVD format movie by exactly $1.00 and, correspondingly, we want to reduce the regular sale price as well as the current sale price for all DVDs by $1.00. You could use the following UPDATE statement:

```
UPDATE movie_titles
  SET our_dvd_cost = ( our_dvd_cost - 1.00 ),
      regular_dvd_sale_price = ( regular_dvd_sale_price - 1.00 ),
      current_dvd_sale_price = ( current_dvd_sale_price - 1.00 ) ;
```

To take this example a bit further, let's do the price reduction for all movies except for that incredibly popular movie *Ishtar*.

```
UPDATE movie_titles
  SET our_dvd_cost = ( our_dvd_cost - 1.00 ),
      regular_dvd_sale_price = ( regular_dvd_sale_price - 1.00 ),
      current_dvd_sale_price = ( current_dvd_sale_price - 1.00 ),
  WHERE title <> 'Ishtar' ;
```

Note that the symbol < > means "not equal to."

Inserting Information

The way that data is put into a table so that it can later be retrieved or modified is with an INSERT statement. There are several variations of the SQL:1999 INSERT statement. In the simplest instance, a list of values is provided (as part of the statement) that provides each column of the new row in the order specified at the time the table was defined (or subsequently altered).

Syntax 3-3 *INSERT Statement, Alternative 1*

```
INSERT INTO table
    VALUES ( value-1, value-2,..., value-n ) ;
```

For example, the following statements add new rows to the movies_stars table.

```
INSERT INTO movies_stars
    VALUES ( 'Rocky Horror Picture Show',
             1977,
             'Curry',
             'Tim',
             '' ) ;

INSERT INTO movies_stars
    VALUES ( 'Rocky Horror Picture Show',
             1977,
             'Bostwick',
             'Barry',
             '' ) ;

INSERT INTO movies_stars
    VALUES ( 'Rocky Horror Picture Show',
             1977,
             'Loaf',
             'Meat',
             '' ) ;
```

(Okay, so the last one might be stretching things a bit . . .)

An alternative form of the INSERT statement is useful for "wide" tables (meaning a large number of defined columns), particularly when only some columns will have data entered initially. In fact, we find this form to be preferable to the one we just saw because of the self-documenting nature of the format:

Syntax 3-4 *INSERT Statement, Alternative 2*

```
INSERT INTO table ( column-1, column-2,..., column-n )
   VALUES ( value-1, value-2,..., value-n ) ;
```

The columns specified as part of the INSERT statement needn't be in any specific order as long as the orders of the column and value lists match with one another. For example, the following statement will add a new row to the movie_titles table with partially complete information.

```
INSERT INTO movie_titles
   ( title, year_produced, our_tape_cost, our_dvd_cost,
     regular_tape_sale_price, current_tape_sale_price,
     regular_dvd_sale_price, current_dvd_sale_price  )
 VALUES (
    'Rocky Horror Picture Show', 1977, 10.95, 19.95,
    15.95, 15.95, 24.95, 24.95 ) ;
```

We were afraid that the preceding example would be, shall we say, a bit forward-looking. However, we got a pleasant surprise when we learned that the *Rocky Horror Picture Show* was finally released on DVD!

The resulting table *may* look like Result 3-11.

Result 3-11 *Possible Result*

TITLE	OUR_ TAPE_ COST	OUR_ DVD_ COST	REGULAR_ TAPE_ SALE_PRICE	CURRENT_ TAPE_ SALE_PRICE	REGULAR_ DVD_ SALE_PRICE	CURRENT_ DVD_ SALE_PRICE
Predator	9.95	18.95	14.95	13.95	22.95	21.95
|						
|						
|						
|						
True Lies	10.95	19.95	14.95	14.95	24.95	22.95
Last Action Hero	11.95	19.95	15.95	15.95	23.95	23.95
Rocky Horror Picture Show	10.95	19.95	15.95	15.95	24.95	24.95

Why do we say that the table *may* look like Result 3-11? In the above case, the new row is inserted at the end of the table. Placement of new rows is an implementation-specific issue. Since any order-specific processing is handled through the ORDER BY clause, physical placement is not an issue for most casual users.

In fact, the SQL language provides no mechanism at all for users to control the physical placement of a row in a table. If your implementation uses the value of some column or the sequence in which rows were added as a physical placement criterion, then the behavior may be predictable. However, the standard leaves such behavior strictly to the implementor's decision.

In general, we recommend that column names be specified even if every column in the new row will be assigned a value, using the syntax shown in Syntax 3-4. This protects against adds and drops of the table's columns or other unforeseen problems.

3.8 | Deleting Information

The DELETE statement operates in somewhat the same way as the SELECT statement, with the primary distinction that rows meeting specified criteria are deleted rather than retrieved. Syntax 3-5 illustrates the syntax of the DELETE statement.

Syntax 3-5 *DELETE Statement Syntax*

```
DELETE FROM <target table>
[ WHERE <search conditior> ]
```

For example, the following statements will delete all rows in both of our database tables for the movie *The Waterboy* if we decide, in the interest of culture, to no longer sell this particular title:

```
DELETE FROM movie_titles
WHERE title = 'The Waterboy' ;

DELETE FROM movies_stars
WHERE title = 'The Waterboy' ;
```

In Chapter 10, "Constraints, Assertions, and Referential Integrity," we'll discuss how the concept of referential integrity can be applied to ensure that rows from multiple tables that are related to one another can be protected from deletion of information from one table but not another. With the previous deletion statement sequence, you are forced to remember all of the tables in which relevant data might appear.

To delete all rows from a given table, the following statement would be used.

```
DELETE FROM movies_stars ;
```

Note that, in all forms of the DELETE statement, no column names are specified; entire rows are deleted rather than individual columns. To "delete" information from a specific column in one or more rows, while still maintaining the rows' existence in the database, the UPDATE statement would be used to set the value of the column to null. (As we will see in Chapter 4, "Basic Data Definition Language (DDL)," it is also possible to completely eliminate all data and metadata for a column from a table.)

3.9 | Chapter Summary

In this chapter, we looked at basic SQL:1999 operations: creating simple tables, retrieving information, and updating tables through update, deletion, and insertion operations. We discussed how you can retrieve one or more rows and/or retrieve one or more columns from a single table. We also saw how you can "blindly" retrieve all rows regardless of their contents.

We discussed how you can use WHERE to specify many different varieties of selection criteria: equality to a specific value, having a value greater than or less than some other value, and combining selection criteria by using AND and OR.

Further, we saw that information access is not limited to retrieval. Data may be inserted into, updated within, or deleted from any given table through statements analogous to the basic SELECT statement.

Those readers unfamiliar with previous versions of SQL should now have a basic understanding of the types of functionality supported by the language and are ready to move ahead to the more advanced facilities of SQL:1999.

Chapter

4

Basic Data Definition Language (DDL)

4.1 Introduction

In the previous chapter, we looked briefly at how tables and columns are created in SQL. As you might expect from the syntax, the CREATE TABLE statement is used to create tables. Because a table contains at least one column, and every column has a set of properties (primarily a data type and size), the process of creating a table also involves creating columns and their properties.

In Chapter 2, "Introduction to SQL:1999," we talked about a number of other database objects: schemas, catalogs, views, and others. As we learn in this chapter, SQL's Data Definition Language (DDL) has facilities through which you can define not only tables and columns but also other database objects. Additionally, we discuss how you can modify and delete these objects through DDL (many SQL experts refer to this function as Schema Manipulation Language, or SML, even though that term isn't defined or used in the SQL standard).

4.2 Data Definition Fundamentals

Tables are the basic unit of data management that you will encounter in SQL. Before we can make much progress in our investigation of tables and how they

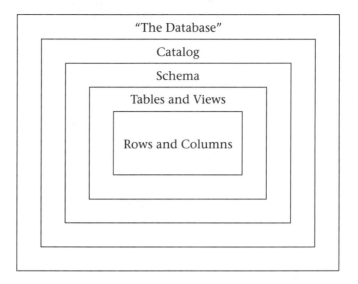

Figure 4-1   Abstraction in the SQL Database Environment

are created and destroyed, we need to understand the structure in which tables are embedded. Tables are embedded in a nested structure of increasing abstractions (remember that tables themselves are composed of rows and columns). Figure 4-1 illustrates the relationship between the data objects we discuss in this chapter; specifically, it shows how collections of columns (tables) are contained within collections of tables (schemas), which are further contained within collections of schemas (catalogs).

Finally, an SQL:1999 database consists of all data described by schemas under the control of a given DBMS at any one time. It corresponds directly to a "group of catalogs." (In point of fact, the SQL standard shrinks from actually using or defining the word *database,* presumably because the word already carries a variety of meanings among different vendors and users. Instead, it uses the term *SQL-data* to refer to the data and *schema* to refer to metadata.)

Let's look a little more closely at some of the data objects summarized in Figure 4-1. We introduced many of them in Chapter 2, "Introduction to SQL:1999"; in the sections that follow, we give an SQL perspective to the generic concepts.

4.2.1 Schema Concepts

We can think of tables as being *contained* in a higher-level construct called a *schema.* We use the idea of containment in many places when discussing relationships between database objects. This usage doesn't imply any sort of physical storage containment or proximity. Instead, it simply means that the containing object has a hierarchical relationship to the contained object; for example, for each schema, there are zero or more tables, and for each table, there is exactly one schema to which it belongs.

We can think of a schema as a place where tables and related objects can be collected together under one qualifying name. In fact, a schema name provides a *namespace* for the names of the objects in that schema. SQL:1999 provides statements for creating and destroying schemas, too, as we shall see later in this chapter. Perhaps an analogy would be helpful: the relationship between a schema and its tables is similar to that of an operating system file directory and the files contained within that directory.

Schemas were originally designed (in SQL-86, for instance) as *containers* for tables that allowed a specific user, identified by an authorization identifier, to be able to create his or her own tables without the concern of choosing the same table name as some other user. In SQL-86 and SQL-89, the name of a schema was identical to the authorization identifier of the user who created—and owned—the schema. In SQL-92, however, this tight coupling between schemas and users was eliminated in recognition of many users' need to create multiple schemas; this approach continues in SQL:1999. SQL:1999 adds the ability for schemas and the objects they contain (such as tables) to be owned by *roles* in addition to individual users. You will learn more about roles in Chapter 14, "Privileges, Users, and Security."

As long as schema names and authorization identifiers had a one-to-one correspondence, there was no problem with having duplicate schema names. After all, a given authorization identifier must be unique within the system. However, with the freedom of a single user to create and own multiple schemas comes the possibility that two or more users would want to use the same name for their schemas, a complicating factor should DBMSs begin moving more rapidly toward distributed environments.

All objects contained in a schema are owned by the same authorization identifier that owns the schema itself. A schema is usually created via a CREATE SCHEMA statement (not all current implementations support this) and can subsequently be modified by using some of the statements described later in this chapter, such as ALTER.

4.2.2 Catalog Concepts

Catalogs are named collections of schemas in an SQL environment. An SQL environment contains zero or more catalogs, and a catalog contains one or more schemas. Every catalog contains a schema named INFORMATION_SCHEMA that contains the views of the information schema, or *system tables*. (See Chapter 22, "Information Schema," for further details on the information schema.) The creation and destruction of catalogs is implementation-defined; that is, SQL provides no facilities for this. The set of catalogs that can be referenced in any SQL statement, during any particular transaction or during the course of an SQL session, is also implementation-defined. (We note that few implementations support catalogs at present.)

The full names of schema objects have three components: the catalog name, the schema name, and the object name. Using a table as the object, the three components would be specified in the order:

```
catalog name . schema name . table name
```

Components are separated by periods when more than one is used. For example, if you have a catalog named movie_catalog and it contains a schema named media, which in turn contains a table named movie_titles, then you can refer to that table as movie_titles, as media.movie_titles, or as movie_catalog. media.movie_titles. If there is any chance of ambiguity (for example, if you are trying to define a view in schema business that references a table in schema media), you must *qualify* the table name (that is, explicitly state the name of the schema to which you are referring). If you write your table names without specifying a schema name (or with a schema name but not a catalog name), a default schema name (and catalog name) is supplied by the system for you. This default depends on several factors, but you can sometimes govern the default by the way in which you write your programs (Chapter 12, "Accessing SQL from the Real World," provides more information on customizing your programs).

4.2.3 Tables

Let's discuss tables themselves a bit further now. SQL provides several types of tables. To better understand the entire repertoire of table types with which you have to work, it's helpful to look back to SQL-89, which provided three types of tables.

- persistent base tables (usually referred to as *base tables*)
- viewed tables (or *views*)
- derived tables

For relatively simple applications, these three types were perfectly adequate; however, more complex applications, such as those that successively refine their information, demand additional types of tables within each of the above categories, as discussed in this section.

First, the official-style wording. A table is a *multiset* of rows. (In Chapter 2, "Introduction to SQL:1999," we discussed the concept of a multiset.) A row is a nonempty sequence of values. This means that a row has to have at least one column, and the order among columns is the same for all rows within a table. Referring back to Example 3-1 and the movie_titles table, you would never find title before our_dvd_cost in one row but following it in another. Every row of the same table has the same number of columns and contains a value (possibly null) for every column of that table. So the fifth value in every row of a table is the value of the fifth column of that table. A row is the smallest unit of data that can be inserted into a table or deleted from a table.

The *degree* of a table is the number of columns in that table, and the *cardinality* of a table is the number of rows it contains. At any instant in time, the degree of a table is the same as the degree of each of its rows, and the cardinality of a table is the same as the cardinality of each of its columns. A table whose cardinality is zero is said to be *empty*.

A table is either

- a base table,
- a viewed table, or
- a derived table.

Furthermore, a base table is either

- a persistent base table,
- a global temporary table,
- a created local temporary table or
- a declared local temporary table.

(More detail on all of the above will be provided shortly.)

A base table is a table whose data is actually stored somewhere—either on disk or in memory—and is either a *schema object* (i.e., it is contained within a schema) or a *module object* (contained within a module). Contrast this with a virtual table, whose data is derived as it is requested by an application: basically, the virtual table isn't persistent in the sense of existing outside the application. Of course, the data visible in a virtual table must have originated in one or more base tables, but it may have been transformed in the process. Some virtual tables exist only for the duration of an SQL statement (see Chapter 9, "Advanced SQL Query Expressions," for information on query expressions), whereas others are specified in the metadata of your database and have some level of persistence to them.

Virtual tables with persistent metadata are known as *views* or *viewed tables.* (There isn't a special name for the other sort of virtual table—those without persistent metadata—so most people refer to these by the generic phrase: *virtual tables.*)

The SQL standard, by the way, defines a number of additional terms for certain types of tables that it uses internally to discuss various operations and other semantics. We will introduce some of those terms in this book, but only as we need them to make ourselves clear when we're explaining some aspect of SQL:1999 that you may use in your applications. Otherwise, we'll try to avoid introducing or using terms that are most likely to add confusion.

Base Tables

Let's look at the types of base tables:

- *Persistent base table:* A named table defined by a CREATE TABLE statement that does *not* specify TEMPORARY.

- *Global temporary table:* A named table defined by a CREATE TABLE statement that specifies GLOBAL TEMPORARY.

- *Created local temporary table:* A named table defined by a CREATE TABLE statement that specifies LOCAL TEMPORARY.

- *Declared local temporary table:* A named table that is declared as a component of a module.

Temporary Table Rules and Characteristics

Global temporary tables and created local temporary tables are a bit like persistent base tables because their definitions are in a schema and stay there until explicitly removed. However, they differ from persistent base tables because their physical existence (their *extension,* if you prefer that terminology) is effectively materialized *only* when they are referenced in an SQL session.

Every module or embedded SQL program in every SQL session that references a created local temporary table causes a distinct instance of that created local temporary table to be materialized. That is, the contents of a created local temporary table (or a *global* temporary table) *cannot* be shared between SQL sessions like the contents of a persistent base table (Figure 4-2). In addition, the contents of a created *local* temporary table cannot be shared between modules or embedded SQL programs in a single SQL session.

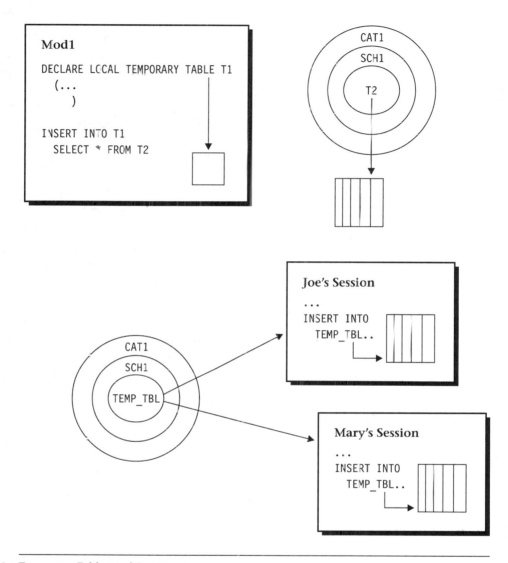

Figure 4-2   Temporary Tables and Sessions

In the SQL language, the name and the scope of the name of a global temporary table or of a created local temporary table are indistinguishable from those of a persistent base table. The contents of these table types vary in their distinction.

- Global temporary table contents are distinct within SQL sessions.
- Created local temporary tables are distinct within modules and within embedded SQL programs within SQL sessions.

A declared local temporary table manifests itself the first time any procedure is executed in the module (or embedded SQL program) that contains the temporary table declaration. To put this another way, a declared local temporary table is accessible only by the execution of procedures within the module (or SQL statements in the embedded SQL program) that contains the temporary table declaration. All references to a declared local temporary table are prefixed by the special name MODULE.

Let's look at a few examples of temporary tables. If you create a temporary table with

```
CREATE GLOBAL TEMPORARY TABLE gtt (...)
```

then you can insert rows in it and share the data among all your modules or embedded SQL programs (in the same session!) as shown in Example 4-1.

Example 4-1 *Using a Global Temporary Table*

```
INSERT INTO myschema.gtt VALUES (...)
SELECT * FROM gtt....
```

The same is true for local temporary tables except that you cannot share data between modules or embedded programs in your session.

Declared local temporary tables are declared with

```
DECLARE LOCAL TEMPORARY TABLE MODULE.dltt (...)
```

This declaration allows you to access the table from the same module or embedded program in which it was declared (see Example 4-2).

Example 4-2 *Using a Local Temporary Table*

```
INSERT INTO MODULE.dltt VALUES (...)
SELECT * FROM MODULE.dltt WHERE...
```

The materialization of a temporary table does not persist beyond the end of the SQL session in which the table was materialized. Temporary tables are effectively empty at the start of an SQL session. Depending on how they were defined, their contents may be cleared whenever a transaction is committed or rolled back, or the contents may be carried forward into the next transaction.

If you define your temporary tables (any type) using the clause ON COMMIT PRESERVE ROWS, then the rows are kept there until (1) you delete them with a DELETE statement, (2) you DROP the entire table, or (3) your session ends. If you define it using `ON COMMIT DELETE ROWS`, all rows in the table are automatically deleted at the end of every transaction that's terminated with a `COMMIT` statement (or committed by an external agent, as discussed in Chapter 15, "Transaction Management").

So what use are temporary tables? There may be occasions when you wish to store some temporary results within the course of your application and, depending on some condition, possibly external to your database, take a given course of action with your temporary results. Temporary tables are a means to accomplish this without having to explicitly destroy (`DROP`) tables after each usage. You can draw an analogy between temporary tables and the local variables in your favorite programming language: they're great for intermediate results and working storage, but they don't allow you to save their data until some future execution of your application.

The use of temporary tables offers a few additional advantages worth mentioning. Since the data in temporary tables are private to an SQL session (perhaps even to a module), there are no problems of interaction with other users. This means that no locking is required and performance may improve over that of persistent tables, which are open to shared access. Furthermore, if you specify `ON COMMIT DELETE ROWS`, the DBMS needn't log your updates to the table because they aren't intended to survive transactions—even in the result of a crash. Again, better performance may result.

Derived and Viewed Tables

A *derived* table is one obtained directly or indirectly from one or more other tables through the evaluation of a query expression. The values of a derived table are derived from the values of the underlying tables when the query expression is evaluated.

A viewed table is a named derived table defined by a `CREATE VIEW` statement, and a viewed table is called a *view*; see section 4.3.8 for further details and examples.

While all base tables are automatically updatable, you may define derived tables that are either updatable or read-only. The operations `INSERT`, `UPDATE`, and `DELETE` are permitted for updatable tables, subject to the appropriate privileges. The operations `INSERT`, `UPDATE`, and `DELETE` are not allowed for read-only tables.

4.2.4 Columns

Every column has a column name. A value of a column is the smallest unit of data that can be selected from a table and the smallest unit of data that can be updated. Additionally, all values of a column in a table have the same data type.

Every column also has a nullability characteristic of *known not nullable* or *possibly nullable*. A column that is possibly nullable has the potential to be set to the null value by an SQL statement. Even if it is possibly nullable, however, other factors may prevent it from taking the null value at any given time. Only if the DBMS can determine for certain (according to SQL:1999 rules) that a column can never become null is the column said to be known not nullable.

Every column also has a default value. The default value of a column is the value that is stored into that column in a row when the row is inserted into the table without specifying a value for the column. If a column doesn't have an explicit default value, then the default value will be the null value. If the column also specifies NOT NULL, then you *must* specify a value for the column whenever you INSERT a row into the table; otherwise, the NOT NULL constraint will be violated, which will cause the INSERT to fail.

4.3 | Basic DDL Statements

In Chapter 3, "Basic Table Creation and Data Manipulation," we discussed a trio of data manipulation statements that can modify the given state of data in one or more tables: INSERT, UPDATE, and DELETE. However, when manipulating the tables themselves—as well as columns, schemas, and the other data definition components discussed herein—these three statements are not used. That is, in order to end the existence of a table itself, not just the rows within it, you do not DELETE the table, you DROP it. Similarly, to modify the definition of a table by adding, changing, or deleting one or more columns, you ALTER the table definition rather than UPDATE it. Therefore, the CREATE, ALTER, and DROP statements are DDL analogs of the manipulation statements INSERT, UPDATE, and DELETE. Note, however, that the SELECT statement is used to "get information about something" in both data manipulation and data definition. Table 4-1 summarizes this correspondence.

Table 4-1 *Correspondence between DML and DDL Statements*

Function	*Data Manipulation*	*Data Definition*
Bringing something into existence	INSERT	CREATE
Modifying something	UPDATE	ALTER
Getting rid of something	DELETE	DROP
Getting information about something	SELECT	SELECT

Note that the metadata for SQL tables, columns, and the rest of the objects is not directly modifiable through these statements; the DBMS itself handles this function within the information schema (see Chapter 22, "Information Schema") as a result of your statements. You could say that your data definition statements effect behind-the-scenes data manipulation actions on the metadata. We'll look more closely at examples of these statements throughout this chapter.

4.3.1 SQL Syntax for Tables and Columns

In Chapter 3, "Basic Table Creation and Data Manipulation," we introduced a simple version of the CREATE TABLE statement to set the foundation for the data manipulation examples we presented. This statement, as should be obvious, causes the creation of a table and column structure that matches that specified in the particular case. Columns can be specified to take on several properties, including data types and collations (and, in most cases, sizes), default values, permissibility of null values (nullability), and specific character sets.

Data Types

In Chapter 2, "Introduction to SQL:1999," we discussed the data types supported by SQL:1999. Table 4-2 summarizes these data types.

Table 4-2 *SQL:1999 Built-In Data Types*

SQL:1999 Data Type	Usage Example(s)	
CHARACTER, CHAR	cd_title	CHAR (25)
CHARACTER VARYING, VARCHAR, CHAR VARYING	artist_name	VARCHAR (20)
CHARACTER LARGE OBJECT, CHAR LARGE OBJECT, CLOB	track_1	CLOB (100K)
NATIONAL CHARACTER, NCHAR, and NATIONAL CHAR	city_released_in	NCHAR (15)
NATIONAL CHARACTER VARYING, NCHAR VARYING, and NATIONAL CHAR VARYING	next_tour_city	NCHAR VARYING (20)
NATIONAL CHARACTER LARGE OBJECT, NCHAR LARGE OBJECT, NCLOB	dvd_chapter_2	NCLOB (200m)

(Continued)

Table 4.2 *Continued*

SQL:1999 Data Type	Usage Example(s)	
INTEGER and INT	dvds_on_hand	INTEGER
SMALLINT	number_employees	SMALLINT
NUMERIC	our_cost	NUMERIC (7,2)
	tapes_revenue	NUMERIC (9)
DECIMAL and DEC	current_price	DECIMAL (6,2)
	bonus	DEC(7,2)
FLOAT	radius	FLOAT (23)
	distance	FLOAT
REAL	width	REAL
DOUBLE PRECISION	volume	DOUBLE PRECISION
BIT	flag_field	BIT
	flag_field2	BIT (100)
BIT VARYING	flag_field_3	BIT VARYING (25)
BINARY LARGE OBJECT, BLOB	cover_photo	BLOB (75K)
DATE	date_released	DATE
TIME	time_of_transaction	TIME
TIMESTAMP	time_row_accessed	TIMESTAMP
TIME WITH TIME ZONE	international_chain_time	TIME WITH TIME ZONE
TIMESTAMP WITH TIME ZONE	worldwide_record_access_time	TIMESTAMP WITH TIME ZONE
INTERVAL	how_long_an_employee	INTERVAL YEAR TO MONTH
	time_to_approve_credit_card	INTERVAL HOUR TO SECOND
BOOLEAN	bought_online_before	BOOLEAN
ARRAY	december_dvd_units_sold_per_day	INTEGER ARRAY [31]
ROW	ROW (given_name	CHARACTER(10),
	family_name	CHARACTER(20))

Default Value

When you create a column in a table, you can specify the default value for the column (for example, in inserted rows when you don't specify a real value for the column). You can specify that the default value is a literal value (of the

appropriate data type, of course), one of the datetime value functions (CURRENT_
DATE, CURRENT_TIME, CURRENT_TIMESTAMP, LOCALTIME, LOCALTIMESTAMP), a user value
(CURRENT_ USER, SESSION_USER, or SYSTEM_USER), or NULL. The datetime and user
values are evaluated when the default value is put into the row in the database.
The syntax for specifying default values is shown in Syntax 4-2.

Null Values

As we discussed in Chapter 2, "Introduction to SQL:1999," SQL:1999 null values
are used to represent information that is essentially out of bounds, that is, not
part of a legitimate range or set of values. The use of null values alleviates the
need to use blanks, 0, –1, or some other flag to indicate *not available, not applicable,* or *unknown.*[1] Most SQL:1999 data elements (such as columns, host variables, and value expressions) are permitted to be given the null value.

It is sometimes desirable to prevent the setting of a column or variable to a
null value. For example, the statement shown in Example 4-3 must be prevented.

Example 4-3 *An SQL Statement to Be Prevented*

```
INSERT INTO movie_titles
  ( our_dvd_cost, regular_dvd_sale_price, current_dvd_sale_price )
  VALUES (18.99, 24.99, 23.99) ;
```

Following execution of this statement, a row will exist in the movie_titles
table with some values for the columns specified, but without a movie title; that
is, the absence of an explicit value for the title column will insert a null value
into that column in the new row. We now have a meaningless row in our table,
and we've compromised the integrity of the data within that table.

This type of problem can be prevented by specifying, at creation time, that a
particular column cannot take on the null value. This is done by using the NOT
NULL clause, as shown in Example 4-4.

Example 4-4 *A Table Definition to Prevent Certain Null Values*

```
CREATE TABLE movie_titles (
  title char (30) NOT NULL,
  |
  | )
```

---

1 Refer to Chapter 2, "Introduction to SQL:1999," for a complete discussion of null values.

It is important to remember that a null value is different from any valid value for a data type. That is, null is not the same as zero, blanks, or any other user-chosen designator.

Be careful about using (and overusing) NOT NULL. It might be tempting to define most or all columns as NOT NULL—say, for price and quantity information (we have to have that information, do we not?)—but at points in your applications this information may simply be temporarily unknown. NOT NULL forces a non-null value to be always present, and overusing this can cause unnecessary headaches.

The NOT NULL clause is really something called a *column constraint*. A constraint is an application rule (sometimes called a *business rule*) that the DBMS enforces for you. You would specify constraints (and there are three types: column constraints, table constraints, and assertions) in your database definitions to express rules that must always be enforced in your business. The DBMS will ensure that they are never violated, and you cannot commit a transaction if any constraints are violated.

In Chapter 10, "Constraints, Assertions, and Referential Integrity," we will discuss the CHECK constraint, a multipurpose clause through which many different types of constraints can be expressed. As a preview, we will tell you that the NOT NULL constraint is equivalent to the following CHECK constraint:

```
CHECK (column-name IS NOT NULL)
```

Now that we've seen the various components of a column definition, let's put it together with the aid of Syntax 4-1.

Syntax 4-1 *Column Definition Syntax*

```
<column definition> ::=
  <column name>
  { <data type> | <domain name> }
  [ <reference scope check> ]
  [ <default clause> ]
  [ <column constraint definition>... ]
  [ <collate clause> ]

<column constraint definition> ::=
  [ <constraint name definition> ]
  <column constraint> [ <constraint characteristics> ]
```

```
<column constraint> ::=
    NOT NULL
  | <unique specification>
  | <references specification>
  | <check constraint definition>

<reference scope check> ::=
    REFERENCES ARE [ NOT ] CHECKED
    [ ON DELETE <reference scope check action> ]

<reference scope check action> ::=
    <referential action>
```

Don't worry about all of those BNF nonterminal symbols at this point; we've given you the entire syntax here for completeness, but some of it won't become relevant until later in the book. (In fact, the optional <reference scope check> and <reference scope check action> won't be addressed in this volume at all; it is covered in Volume 2 of this book.) For example, <column constraint definition> and <column constraint> are addressed in Chapter 10, "Constraints, Assertions, and Referential Integrity," while <collate clause> is covered in Chapter 21, "Internationalization Aspects of SQL:1999."

On the other hand, <default clause> isn't really addressed anywhere else, so we'll show you the syntax for that item right now; see Syntax 4-2.

Syntax 4-2 *Default Clause Syntax*

```
<default clause> ::=
    DEFAULT <default option>

<default option> ::=
    <literal>
  | <datetime value function>
  | USER
  | CURRENT_USER
  | CURRENT_ROLE
  | SESSION_USER
  | SYSTEM_USER
  | CURRENT_PATH
  | <implicitly typed value specification>
```

We'll cover all of those options at the appropriate places in the book.

4.3.2 Domains

A domain is a sort of *macro* that you can define to pull together a specific data type (and, if applicable, size), as well as some characteristics we'll discuss later in the book: defaults, constraints, and collations. You can then use the name of the domain to define columns that inherit the data type (and other characteristics) of the domain.

For example, you might want to ensure that all columns that deal with some form of titles (movie, music CD, CD-ROM, etc.) have a data type of CHARACTER VARYING, are no more than 35 characters in length, and do not permit insertion of null values. The CREATE DOMAIN statement can be used to create a specific domain that is used subsequently in CREATE TABLE statements.

```
CREATE DOMAIN title_type VARCHAR (35)
  CHECK (VALUE IS NOT NULL);
|
|


CREATE TABLE movie_titles (
  title title_type,
  |
  | ) ;
```

The column title inherits from the domain title_type the data type and size specification, as well as the specification that null values are not permissible.

When you create a domain, you specify the data type; you can also specify a default value, CHECK constraints, and so forth. These characteristics are all given to any column based on the domain. However, columns can override the default value and (if applicable) the collation of the domain. Also, the columns can add constraints in addition to those of the domain. In a domain constraint (which can only be a CHECK constraint), the keyword VALUE is used to represent the value of the column defined on the domain.

We were once fans of SQL's domain capabilities. However, they have proved to be less useful than originally hoped, and future editions of the SQL standard may actually delete the facility entirely. For this reason, we do not spend much energy in this book explaining domains, nor do we recommend that you use them—even if you happen to use one of the few SQL products that have implemented them.

4.3.3 Character Sets

A quick note: Throughout most of this book, we will stick to familiar Latin characters, the only type of characters supported by most computer systems until very recently. Later, in Chapter 21, "Internationalization Aspects of SQL:1999," we'll show you how to use character sets other than Latin (to write applications that will support users in Japan or Israel, for example).

Note also that in SQL:1999, Unicode[2] has been selected as the underlying character model; this will be further discussed in Chapter 21, "Internationalization Aspects of SQL:1999."

4.3.4 Distinct Types

In addition to the new built-in data types and data type constructors, such as BOOLEAN, BLOB and CLOB, ARRAY, and ROW, that we've already mentioned (see section 2.4, "SQL Data Types," and Table 4-2), SQL:1999 added two sorts of *user-defined data type*.

The simpler of these goes by the name *distinct type*, as we discussed in section 2.4.10, "User-Defined Types," in the subsection called "Distinct Types." As you learned in that section, distinct types give application developers the ability to use strong typing to protect them against accidental mixing of data types in contexts where it wouldn't make sense.

But it's worth considering the relationship between SQL:1999's distinct types and the domain capability that first appeared in SQL-92. It would be easy to conclude that they serve similar functions, but is that really accurate?

When we discussed domains in section 4.3.2, we told you that you could define default values and constraints on your domains, and that those characteristics were applied to all data defined on those domains. What we did not mention was that you can write SQL expressions—in your WHERE clauses, for example—that mix values defined on any domain (well, as long as their underlying data types are compatible) without SQL having any complaints about it.

By contrast, SQL:1999's distinct types gives you better protection against inappropriate mixing of data types in expressions, but they do not permit you to define constraints or default values. Consequently, when you define a column to have a data type that is some distinct type, you have to specify the column's default value and any constraints in the column definition; the column cannot

---

2   For details of Unicode, refer to The Unicode Consortium, *The Unicode Standard, Version 3.0,* 2000.

inherit these characteristics from the distinct type definition, because the distinct type definition cannot have them.

Therefore, we conclude that SQL's domains and SQL:1999's new distinct types have some conceptual notions in common, but the details are significantly different. Could distinct types be enhanced—for example, by allowing you to specify default values and constraints on them—in such a way that would permit them to completely replace domains? Sure, but we question whether that will ever happen. The reason is a bit subtle, but it comes down to this: distinct types in SQL:1999 can be used to define many sites (see section 2.4.13, "Sites") for which neither a default value nor a constraint is applicable. This alone may make it impossible to ever reach agreement in the SQL standards groups to enhance distinct types with those characteristics.

4.3.5 Temporary Tables

As we discussed earlier in this chapter, there may be cases where you only want a table to exist during a specific period of time. One way to accomplish this is to CREATE a table and subsequently DROP it. Alternatively, SQL:1999 permits tables to be created on a temporary basis. Assume that you wish to create a table into which you can group and organize video and music sales information for end-of-month processing, but that the table's data is meaningless after reports are printed and mailed—that is, the data needn't be preserved. You might issue the DDL statement shown in Example 4-5.

Example 4-5 *Creating a Local Temporary Table*

```
CREATE LOCAL TEMPORARY TABLE sales_summary_info (
  column_definition_1,
  column_definition_2, ... ) ;
```

The expanded syntax of the CREATE TABLE statement permits the creation of temporary tables (as designated by the word TEMPORARY) whose data are either LOCAL (as in the previous case) or GLOBAL in scope.

Additionally, the syntax permits you to specify whether you want the contents of these temporary tables to be preserved for the duration of your entire session or to be deleted at the end of every transaction during your session. Note that the contents of a temporary table can never be preserved between sessions except by copying them into a persistent base table.

The definition of a created local temporary table looks like that shown in Example 4-6.

Example 4-6 *Another Local Temporary Table Definition*

```
CREATE LOCAL TEMPORARY TABLE dvds_on_special (
  title CHARACTER(30),
  {{{the rest of the columns you want to define}}}
)
```

When this definition is executed, the metadata for the temporary table is put into your schema, but no space is allocated to hold data.

When you execute the first SQL statement in your session that references this table (for example, SELECT title FROM dvds_on_special or, more useful, INSERT INTO dvds_on_special...), the table automatically comes into being. That is, the database system allocates space to hold the table's data *for your session*. If some other user (in another session, of course) executes the same statement, the DBMS allocates *more* space to hold the table's data for *that* user's session. When you have finished executing all of your SQL statements and have completed your session, the DBMS deallocates all of the space for the table (possibly deleting any data still in the table).

Now, recall that a *local* temporary table cannot be shared between different modules (or compilation units) in your session. Therefore, if you are running two compiled pieces of embedded SQL, they will each get their own allocated space for the local temporary table, and they cannot share the data in that table.

If your application is written using modular programming techniques and you want to share temporary table data between various modules, you will have to create a *global* temporary table, as shown in Example 4-7.

Example 4-7 *Creating a Global Temporary Table*

```
CREATE GLOBAL TEMPORARY TABLE dvds_on_special (
  title CHARACTER(30),
  {{{other columns}}}
)
```

When that definition is executed, the metadata for the temporary table is put into your schema, but no space is allocated to hold data. In this respect, the global temporary table is just like the local temporary table.

The difference is that multiple modules (or compilation units of embedded SQL) can share the data in a global temporary table; however, other sessions simultaneously using a temporary table with the identical name actually get their own, personalized copies of it. This permits applications to share definitions (metadata) for tables without the worry of interfering with data contributed by fellow users.

In both cases, you can specify ON COMMIT DELETE ROWS or ON COMMIT PRESERVE ROWS. If you specify ON COMMIT DELETE ROWS in a temporary table definition, the contents of the table will be deleted every time you commit your transaction. (You don't have to worry about this when you abort your transaction with a ROLLBACK statement [see Chapter 15, "Transaction Management"] because any data you put into the table will be removed automatically as the effects of all statements in the transaction are undone.) If you specify ON COMMIT PRESERVE ROWS, the data will not be deleted at the end of the transaction; this permits you to commit your work without having to recreate the contents of the temporary tables. Of course, the data will be deleted at the end of your session in any case.

4.3.6 Modification of Table Structures: The ALTER and DROP Statements

Tables can be removed from your database via the DROP TABLE statement. For example,

```
DROP TABLE movies_stars ;
```

will remove from your database all data within the movie_stars table, as well as the structure itself. Note that the actions of this statement are *not* the same as

```
DELETE FROM movies_stars ;
```

The DELETE statement removes all data but leaves the table structure and associated metadata intact. The DROP statement likewise removes all data, but also removes the table structure and associated metadata; it's as if the table never existed (see Figure 4-3).

A caution with regard to the above syntax: The SQL:1999 standard requires that either RESTRICT or CASCADE be used with a DROP TABLE statement, but many implementations do *not* have that restriction (i.e., neither RESTRICT nor CASCADE *must* be used). Later, we'll show how RESTRICT and CASCADE are used; we elected to use the simplest syntax allowed by some implementations to introduce the concept of dropping a table.

The structure of a table may be modified through the ALTER TABLE statement. Within the context of this statement, columns may be added, modified, or removed. For example, assume that the e-tailer in our example had its roots as a walk-in video store that existed back in the early 1980s, and which did most of its business through rentals rather than from sales. The application that they use

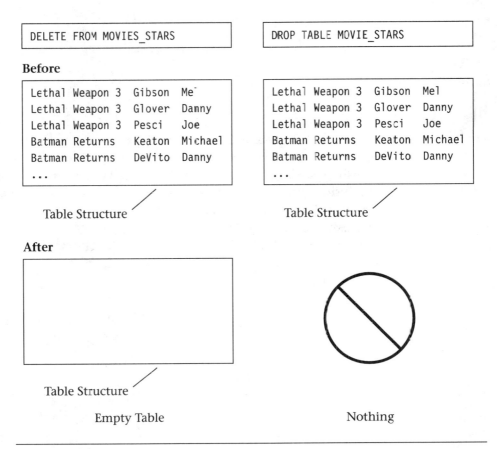

Figure 4-3   DROP versus DELETE Statements

has evolved over the years, and at one time they had Beta format tapes in the database. By the late 1980s, Beta sales were abysmal so the store decided to drop that format from their inventory. To remove the columns related to Beta tapes from your movie_titles table, the statements shown in Example 4-8 would have been used.

Example 4-8 *Removing Columns Related to Beta Tapes*

```
ALTER TABLE movie_titles
  DROP COLUMN beta_owned ;

ALTER TABLE movie_titles
  DROP COLUMN beta_in_stock ;
```

```
ALTER TABLE movie_titles
  DROP COLUMN total_beta_units_rented ;
|
|
|
```

Note that in the above course of actions, the structures for the specified columns as well as the data contained within those columns are removed from the database. Let's say that they wanted to preserve the data that existed—specifically, historical Beta format revenue data, for both sales and rentals—you might perform actions such those in Example 4-9. (Advance warning: There is a caveat, which we discuss immediately after the example.)

As with DROP TABLE, the standard requires DROP COLUMN to have either RESTRICT or CASCADE (explained shortly), but many implementations don't have that requirement.

Example 4-9 *Mixing DML and DDL in a Transaction*

```
UPDATE movie_titles
  SET total_vhs_rental_revenue =
        total_vhs_rental_revenue +
        total_beta_rental_revenue,
      total_vhs_sales_revenue =
        total_vhs_sales_revenue +
        total_beta_sales_revenue ;

ALTER TABLE movie_titles
  DROP COLUMN beta_rental_revenue ;

ALTER TABLE movie_titles
  DROP COLUMN beta_sales_revenue ;
```

However—and this is *very* important—SQL:1999 does not *require* that an implementation permit both data manipulation statements and data definition statements to be executed in the same transaction. If your implementation permits this, you can probably execute the preceding sequence of statements; if not, the first ALTER TABLE statement in this sequence will get an error. Even if your implementation does support the mixing of DML and DDL statements in a transaction, SQL:1999 doesn't specify the semantics of that mixture; your implementor is required to tell you (in the product documentation, for example) what the behavior is. Therefore, something as intuitively obvious as our sample sequence of statements may not be possible within given implementations. If that's the case, you need to divide the data manipulation and data definition statements among multiple transactions. (Transaction management syntax, including invocation and termination, is discussed in Chapter 15, "Transaction Management.")

Columns can be added to tables; this is also accomplished through the ALTER TABLE statement (Example 4-10). Table 4-3 summarizes this and the other ALTER and DROP statements we've discussed in this section.

Example 4-10 *Adding a Column to a Table*

```
ALTER TABLE movie_titles
ADD COLUMN directed_by VARCHAR (20) ;
```

Assume that as the example business evolves from an in-store chain to an e-tailer, several things happen: DVDs are added to the media types handled, movie rentals are eliminated (i.e., only sales are handled over the Internet, since rentals don't make as much sense in this e-tailing environment), and Beta format tapes are also eliminated (and thus the need for distinguishing between different tape formats in the database). The database table structures can be modified to take these new business conditions into consideration. For simplicity's sake, let's focus on only a few columns in Example 4-11.

Example 4-11 *Statements That Merge Data*

```
ALTER TABLE movie_titles
  ADD COLUMN dvds_in_stock INTEGER;

ALTER TABLE movie_titles
  ADD COLUMN tapes_in_stock INTEGER ;

UPDATE movie_titles
  SET tapes_in_stock = vhs_in_stock + beta_in_stock;

ALTER TABLE movie_titles
  DROP COLUMN vhs_in_stock;

ALTER TABLE movie_titles
  DROP COLUMN beta_in_stock;
```

Of course, the same caveat mentioned earlier about mixing DML and DDL in a transaction applies.

As you see in Table 4-3, SQL:1999 allows you to add columns to your existing tables, to remove columns from those existing tables, and to alter the definitions of existing columns in your tables. (You can alter the definition of a column by changing its default value or by removing its explicit default value entirely.) You can also add new constraints to existing tables—subject to those constraints being satisfied by the data stored in the table at the time they are added—and drop existing constraints from your tables.

Table 4-3 *Altering the Definition of Existing SQL:1999 Tables*

Desired Action	Statement
Add a new column to a table	```ALTER TABLE table_name ADD [COLUMN] column-definition```
Modify a column within a table	```ALTER TABLE table_name ALTER [COLUMN] column_name SET default-value or DROP DEFAULT```
Remove a column from a table	```ALTER TABLE table_name DROP COLUMN column_name behavior```
Add a constraint on a table	```ALTER TABLE table_name ADD constraint-definition```
Remove a constraint from a table	```ALTER TABLE table_name DROP CONSTRAINT constraint_name behavior```

4.3.7 Schemas

As we mentioned earlier in this chapter, a schema consists of the collection of objects associated with a particular schema name that is known to the system at a particular instant in time. Schemas are created using the CREATE SCHEMA statement, followed by the creation of objects—primarily tables, domains, and views—within that schema.

```
CREATE SCHEMA movie_information ...

CREATE TABLE movie_titles ...

CREATE TABLE movies_stars ...
```

In Chapter 14, "Privileges, Users, and Security," we'll discuss SQL:1999 security and permission issues. When a schema is created, an AUTHORIZATION clause can be specified to identify the owner of the schema and of the objects in the schema. Among other things, this clause specifies who can determine access privileges for objects in the schema.

Schemas can be removed via the DROP SCHEMA statement. The standard requires issuers to state whether the removal of the schema CASCADEs, or ripples, to contents of the schema. Alternatively, the RESTRICT clause specifies, "If there are still any schema contents remaining, don't execute the DROP command." The DROP SCHEMA statement,

```
DROP SCHEMA movie_information CASCADE ;
```

will remove the schema, all associated tables and columns, as well as the data contained in those tables. If objects in *other* schemas reference an object in the schema being dropped, they will automatically be resolved by dropping those referencing objects or updating them to eliminate the reference. Alternatively,

```
DROP SCHEMA movie_information RESTRICT ;
```

will be successfully executed *only* if all contained tables (and other objects) were dropped prior to the execution of the statement.

4.3.8 Views

An SQL:1999 view can be considered a virtual table—that is, a table that doesn't physically exist, but rather is formed by a query expression against one or more tables. In this chapter, we discuss views derived from single tables. In Chapter 9, "Advanced SQL Query Expressions," we'll introduce multiple-table views.

Assume that you would like to perform a number of operations against your table movie_titles, but including only titles that are on sale. You can always issue a number of SELECT, UPDATE, INSERT, and DELETE statements against the movie_titles table, always including

```
...
FROM movie_titles
WHERE
  ( current_dvd_sale_price < regular_dvd_sale_price )
 OR
  ( current_tape_sale_price < regular_tape_sale_price ) ;
```

along with other parts of query expressions.

An easier way—one that requires far less typing overall—is to create a view against which your operations can be run (see Example 4-12).

Example 4-12 *Defining a View That Encapsulates Movies on Sale*

```
CREATE VIEW movies_on_sale AS
 SELECT * FROM movie_titles
 WHERE
   ( current_dvd_sale_price < regular_dvd_sale_price )
 OR
   ( current_tape_sale_price < regular_tape_sale_price ) ;
```

Following creation of the preceding view, you can then issue your data manipulation statements against `movies_on_sale` and be guaranteed that only the movies that meet the on-sale constraint are included. To see which DVD-format titles that are on sale have less than 100 units in inventory, you would issue the `SELECT *` statement shown in Example 4-13. (Don't forget our cautionary remark about `SELECT *`: it's just as important in view definitions.)

Example 4-13 *Querying That View*

```
SELECT *
FROM movies_on_sale
WHERE dvds_in_stock < 100 ;
```

Views can also include a subset of all the columns of a particular table. Assume that you wish to create a view that contains only the information about DVDs; no videotape-format titles would be included. You might use the statement shown in Example 4-14.

Example 4-14 *Creating Another View*

```
CREATE VIEW dvds_only (
   title, year_released, our_dvd_cost,
   regular_dvd_sale_price, current_dvd_sale_price,
   part_of_series, movie_type,
   dvds_owned, dvds_in_stock,
   total_dvd_units_sold, total_dvd_sales_revenue )
 AS SELECT
   title, year_released, our_dvd_cost,
   regular_dvd_sale_price, current_dvd_sale_price,
```

```
    part_of_series, movie_type,
    dvds_owned, dvds_in_stock,
    total_dvd_units_sold, total_dvd_sales_revenue
FROM movie_titles ;
```

Here's a recommended shortcut for the preceding view definition: you can exclude the column names from the CREATE VIEW part of the statement and automatically create your view with the columns and names specified after the SELECT portion of the statement. You would write the following instead (see Example 4-15):

Example 4-15 *Simpler View Definition*

```
CREATE VIEW dvds_only AS
 select title, year_released, our_dvd_cost,
   regular_dvd_sale_price, current_dvd_sale_price,
   part_of_series, movie_type,
   dvds_owned, dvds_in_stock,
   total_dvd_units_sold, total_dvd_sales_revenue
 FROM movie_titles ;
```

You can then issue SELECT * FROM dvds_only and receive a complete list of only the specified columns. You could, for example, issue the statement shown in Example 4-16:

Example 4-16 *Retrieving All Columns from the View*

```
SELECT *
FROM dvds_only
WHERE total_dvd_units_sold > 50000 ;
```

and receive a list of movies, with information contained in the other columns, that have sold in excess of 50,000 DVD units.

Why would you want to specify column names in the first part of your view definition? One reason is to create virtual columns whose values are derivations of the values of other columns. For example, you might want to create a view units_sold as shown in Example 4-17.

Example 4-17 *Creating a View with a Computed Column*

```
CREATE VIEW units_sold (
  title,
```

```
      total_dvd_units_sold,
      total_tape_units_sold,
      total_units_sold
   AS SELECT title,
        total_dvd_units_sold,
        total_tape_units_sold,
        total_dvd_units_sold + total_tape_units_sold
     FROM movie_titles   );
```

In Example 4-17, the column `total_units_sold` doesn't really exist. If you issue a `SELECT * FROM units_sold`, the tape and DVD sales unit values for each title will be added together and appear as a column along with the real columns' values.

Views that are updatable result in `UPDATE`, `INSERT`, and `DELETE` operations being applied against the underlying base table or tables (see Example 4-18).

Example 4-18 *Updating Rows Using a View*

```
UPDATE movies_on_sale
SET current_tape_sale_price = 10.99
WHERE title = 'The Story of Us' ;
```

This will update the current sales price for this movie both in the view and in the `movie_titles` base table. Therefore, queries issued against `movie_titles` as well as `movies_on_sale` will reflect the correct sales price for the movie *The Story of Us*.

Views cannot be ALTERed. A view definition really consists of its name, the names of its columns, and the query expression used to derive its rows; none of these is an obvious candidate to modify, so SQL:1999 prohibits it. In a future version, perhaps this capability will be allowed.

View definitions can, however, be dropped, as in

```
DROP VIEW movies_on_sale ;
```

Dropping a view doesn't make any changes to any data in your database. The only effect it has is to remove from the schema the metadata describing the view. Obviously, you won't be able to use that view any more, but the data in the underlying base table remains unchanged.

Views are also widely used to assist with security and permission/accessibility issues. We will discuss these uses further in Chapter 14, "Privileges, Users, and Security."

4.4 | WITH CHECK OPTION

If a view is updatable, then you can update rows through the view, delete rows seen through the view, and insert new rows through the view. Of course, these operations "translate" into the corresponding operations on the table on which the view is based. In SQL-92, only those views that were defined in a very limited way on a single underlying table were updatable, but that is still fairly powerful. In SQL:1999, the range of views that are updatable has been extended considerably (which we'll discuss in some detail in section 9.3, "Functional Dependencies: Rules for Updatability.'

However, there is a difficult question to be answered about such changes, with or without the SQL:1999 extensions: What happens when the change (update or insert) causes the existence of a row that would not have appeared in the view in the first place? This question is addressed by the optional syntax WITH CHECK OPTION that can be added to a view definition. If you define the view shown in Example 4-19,

Example 4-19 *Creating a View WITH CHECK OPTION*

```
CREATE VIEW cheap_movies AS
 SELECT title, current_tape_sale_price
 FROM movie_titles
 WHERE current_tape_sale_price < 10.00
WITH CHECK OPTION ;
```

then you are instructing the database system to reject a statement such as

```
UPDATE cheap_movies
 SET current_tape_sale_price = 15.00
WHERE title = 'The Wedding Singer' ;
```

In this case, the database system would raise a special exception for a WITH CHECK OPTION violation because the row that resulted from the UPDATE operation violated the WHERE clause of the view. If you omitted the WITH CHECK OPTION from the view definition, then the UPDATE statement would quietly succeed.

The situation is complicated even more when you consider views defined on top of other views, because any views in the hierarchy might have the WITH CHECK OPTION syntax. To resolve this issue, SQL:1999 allows you to use the keywords CASCADED or LOCAL in the WITH CHECK OPTION clause. WITH LOCAL CHECK OPTION means that only the WHERE clause of the view in which it appears is checked when an

INSERT or UPDATE statement is executed. WITH CASCADED CHECK OPTION means that the WHERE clause of the view in which it appears as well as *all* views on which that view is based are checked (regardless of the appearance or absence of other WITH LOCAL CHECK OPTION clauses in those views' definitions). CASCADED is the default when neither keyword is used.

4.5 | Chapter Summary

In this chapter we discussed a number of SQL:1999 objects, as well as their creation, modification where applicable, and deletion. From the basic concept of tables and columns to the use of views and domains, SQL:1999 database environments can be tailored to your individual application and system needs.

So far, we have concentrated on simple object creation and manipulation. Many simple applications can be built around the statements we have discussed to this point. In the upcoming chapters, we'll discuss further query expression characteristics, as well as the use of multiple tables within query expressions.

Chapter

5

Values, Basic Functions, and Expressions

5.1 Introduction

Thus far, we have taken a somewhat cavalier approach to describing SQL:1999 values and related concepts such as value functions and value expressions. That is, our examples have presumed the placement of some type of values into the database and the corresponding retrieval of those values from appropriate tables, as well as the use of values in our statements. Now, we discuss these concepts more formally and explain how they apply to SQL:1999.

We discuss basic SQL functions and expressions, deferring discussion of some of the more advanced topics (such as CASE, NULLIF, COALESCE, and CAST) until Chapter 6, "Advanced Value Expressions: CASE, CAST, and Row Value Expressions." Many of the functions and expressions that we discuss—such as string concatenation, substring extraction, date-related functions, and others—will look conceptually familiar to users of commercial DBMS packages. In this chapter, you learn how these facilities are supported in SQL:1999.

5.2 Types of SQL Values

Intuitively, we all know what a value is. However, in the context of SQL, the word has a fairly precise meaning. The SQL meaning is, in fact, consistent with the meaning that we infer, but let's have a look at it anyway. There are several types of values in SQL, and each has important characteristics that we should understand.

One type of value in SQL is the value stored as some row of a table. That value is the value of the row (called a *row value,* cleverly enough), and it usually has more than one component (one for each column of the table). Each of the components is also a value—often a scalar, or atomic, value. SQL:1999 allows nonscalar values to be stored in its columns, too: ROW, ARRAY, and structured user-defined types can be used as the data types of columns. Therefore, every row of a table has one value for each column of the table. If the column's data type is a nonatomic type, then the value stored there may be decomposable, but it's still considered a single value for purposes of this discussion. Of course, some of these values may be null, but this is merely a special case of value.

A literal value is another type of SQL value. A literal represents a value that you can "see" just by looking at it. Still another type of SQL value is the information that is passed between the SQL statement and the 3GL program that invokes the statement. These values are passed in *parameters* and *host variables.* We learn more about these two types of SQL values later in this chapter.

Finally, SQL has a type of value that is computed by the DBMS, either as an expression of some sort that is based on the other types of values or as a function that operates on other types of values, producing a new value.

5.3 | Literals

In Chapter 2, "Introduction to SQL:1999," we discussed the many data types supported by SQL:1999. Each corresponding data type can have literals associated with it. The formal definition of a literal is a non-null value, but for our purposes a literal may be viewed as a constant: a specific unchangeable value that satisfies the constraints of its data type. Literals can be further decomposed into several categories, which in turn are further decomposed, as illustrated in Figure 5-1.

In Table 5-1, we take a look at some examples of literals for the various SQL data types. Note that the literals shown in this table demonstrate valid literals that, if assigned to some item of the specified data type, will be stored there without loss of data. However, SQL does not actually categorize literal numbers as (for example) INTEGER or NUMERIC; instead, it categorizes them as *exact numeric,* of which both INTEGER and NUMERIC are example data types.

Table 5-1 *Literals for SQL Data Types*

SQL:1999 Data Type	*Literal Example(s)*
CHARACTER	'Lethal Weapon 4'
CHARACTER VARYING	'American Beauty'
CHARACTER LARGE OBJECT	'The last film by director Stanley Kubrick, "Eyes Wide Shut", has been the subject of tremendous controversy, which has not eased at all following the release of the DVD for the film. The DVD release in the United States was not the "unrated" version that most observers had expected, but was the bowdlerized version that had been released to theaters in the USA; by contrast, the rest of the Western world got to see the film, in the theaters and on DVD, that Kubrick actually shot.'[1]
NATIONAL CHARACTER	N'乱'[2]
NATIONAL CHARACTER VARYING	N'タンポポ'[3]
NATIONAL CHARACTER LARGE OBJECT	N'風 の 谷 の ナウシカ'[4]
INTEGER	258734
SMALLINT	98
NUMERIC	2.99 3
DECIMAL	1.99 5
FLOAT	1.56E-4 200E10
REAL	1.56E-4
DOUBLE PRECISION	3.1415929265432E00
BIT	B'01111110' X'7E'

(Continued)

Table 5-1 *Continued*

SQL:1999 Data Type	Literal Example(s)
BIT VARYING	B'01111110011111' X'1F3A2'
BINARY LARGE OBJECT	X'001F2E3D4C5B6A798897A6B5C4D3E2'[5]
DATE	DATE '1929-10-29'
TIME	TIME '09:00:05.01'
TIMESTAMP	TIMESTAMP '1987-10-19 16:00:00.00'
TIME WITH TIME ZONE	TIME '10:45-07:00'
TIMESTAMP WITH TIME ZONE	TIMESTAMP '1933-04-05 03:00:00+01:00'
INTERVAL	INTERVAL '10:30' MINUTE TO SECOND

1. This rather long literal is shown here on multiple lines, due entirely to the limitations of printing a book; in order for this to be a valid character string literal, however, it would probably appear in your SQL programs as a single string uninterrupted by newlines.

2. This is the film title *Ran* in Japanese (Kanji character set).

3. This is the film title *Tampopo* in the Japanese Katakana character set.

4. This is the film title *Nausicca of the Valley of the Wind* containing both Kanji and Katakana characters in a Japanese character set.

5. The number of hexadecimal digits in a BINARY LARGE OBJECT literal must always be an even number; by contrast, the number of hexadecimal digits in a BIT or BIT VARYING literal expressed in hexadecimal form depends on the length of the BIT or BIT VARYING data that is required and may be either an even number or an odd number.

Note: The "data types" in the left column of the preceding table are only the names of the data type, exclusive of any lengths, precisions, or scales. Take a moment to derive the complete data type for some of the literals. It is also possible, as we shall see in Chapter 6, to write a literal for an entire row or a table.

Literals, like all values in SQL, can only be used in specific places in the language. Generally, you can use an SQL literal anywhere that you can supply a value to the database system. You can also use literals in value expressions. Because literals have a data type, you can only use them in places where data of that type are permitted.

In Table 5-1, we showed you some sample literals for each SQL data type. However, what the DBMS must know is what data type a given literal is. Now, let's look at the *exact* data type of several literals in Table 5-2.

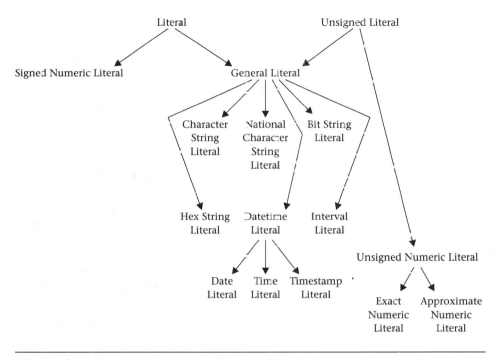

Figure 5-1   SQL Literals

Table 5-2 *Examples of Literals*

Literal	*SQL:1999 Data Type*
'This is a literal'	CHARACTER(17)
N'Σπφ'	NATICNAL CHARACTER(3)
135	Exact numeric data type (INTEGER or SMALLINT). The precise data type is implementation-defined, but SMALLINT is a reasonable choice.
64591.645	Exact numeric data type (DECIMAL or NUMERIC). The precise data type is implementation-defined, but DECIMAL (8,3) might be chosen.
12E-5	Approximate numeric data type (REAL, FLOAT, or DOUBLE PRECISION). The exact data type is implementation-defined, but REAL is possible.

(Continued)

Table 5-2 *Continued*

Literal	SQL:1999 Data Type
B'10101'	BIT(5)
X'1F30'	BIT(16) or BLOB(2)
DATE '12-10-1980'	DATE
TIME '14:35:10.55'	TIME(2)*
TIME '12:20:00.000+05:50'	TIME(3) WITH TIME ZONE
TIMESTAMP '12-10-1980 08:00:00'	TIMESTAMP(0)

* The parenthesized value associated with TIME and TIMESTAMP declarations indicates the number of digits of fractional seconds precision of the type.

You will notice immediately that SQL uses the apostrophe (') to enclose character string literals (as well as some other types of literals). However, the apostrophe is a character that you might wish to put into a character string literal. SQL allows you to do this by using two consecutive apostrophes in the literal to represent one apostrophe:

```
'John''s house'
```

The two consecutive apostrophes cannot be separated by any white space, comments, or a newline.

Unlike the C programming language, SQL does not provide any sort of escape character for character string literals that might give, for example, the ability to encode arbitrary values as though they were characters. (This has been raised as an issue, however, and is something that might be addressed in a future version of the standard.)

Occasionally, you will find that your application requires you to provide a very lengthy literal, perhaps longer than the width of your terminal (or, heaven help you, your punch cards). SQL:1999 provides for this problem by permitting character string literals and bit string literals to cross line boundaries. The syntax is really pretty simple. For example, you could write

```
'This is a very long character string literal that will not fit '
'on a single line, so we can continue it across multiple lines if '
'that''s the best way to represent our data.'
```

As we said earlier, SQL is generally a free-format language without any reliance on line boundaries. However, there are two instances in SQL where line boundaries make a difference, as we shall see later in Chapter 12, "Accessing SQL from the Real World," in our discussion of language embeddings. One of these instances stems from the fact that all implementations of any computer language, including SQL, have physical limits on the number of source characters that can be coded between line boundaries (represented in SQL by the concept *newline*). To get around this limitation, SQL:1999 gives you the ability to write literals that cross line boundaries. Actually, you can put any number of *separators* (white space, newline indicators, and SQL comments[1]) between the parts of a literal; the only requirement is that at least one newline be included between each part. Therefore, you can write literals like this:

```
B'10101011100000011010100'  -- This example illustrates
'11001110001010101111100'    -- multiple separators, including
'11'                         -- comments, white space, and newlines
```

Of course, the actual value of that literal is

```
B'1010101110000011010100110011100010101110011'
```

The separators are completely ignored, as long as at least one newline is included. The following example would *not* be valid, since no newline is included.

```
B'10101' '1011101'
```

Sometimes, you may need to specify a character string literal with no characters in it (not even a blank). SQL:1999 permits this: you just use two consecutive apostrophes ('') and the character string literal's data type is CHARACTER, but with length 0 (which is not a permitted data type for a column definition). Please notice, however, that a character string with length 0 is not the same as a character string with the null value; in the former case, the value of the string is known (it has no characters), while in the latter case, the value is not known. (The concepts are sometimes confused by programmers more familiar with programming languages like C that use the phrase "null string" to mean a string of length 0.)

5.4 | Parameters

When you write SQL statements to accomplish the purposes of your application, you can occasionally code the entire context of the statement as a simple

---

[1] An SQL comment may start with two consecutive hyphens (--) and terminate with the end of a line, or may be bracketed between /* and */, as in C and several other programming languages.

character string. For example, you might know that your application will give all employees a 10% raise after your company completes its initial public offering (IPO) and the stock goes public, an event that will occur only once. In that case, you can write

```
UPDATE employees
  SET salary = salary * 1.1
```

In most cases, however, you have other criteria for your SQL statements, and those criteria will change from execution to execution. For example, you might give your back-office employees a 10% raise, but your employees who staff the company's call center and Internet-based customer support site a 20% raise. Of course, you could write two statements:

```
UPDATE employees
  SET salary = salary * 1.1
WHERE dept = 'Administrative'

UPDATE employees
  SET salary = salary * 1.2
WHERE dept = 'Customer Support'
```

But that doesn't really solve the problem; it merely puts it off. Suppose those values are correct this year, but next year the values are different, you add new departments, or you get rid of one department. You would have to rewrite your application if you used this technique, and that's not a good thing to have to do.

Instead, SQL permits you to write your SQL statement so that it accepts values to be passed to the statement from the application. This technique requires a special type of SQL value called a *parameter* or *host variable*. If you write your application using SQL module language, then *parameter* is the appropriate word; if you use embedded SQL, then *host variable* is the right phrase. (See Chapter 12, "Accessing SQL from the Real World," for more information on module language and embedded SQL in the discussion on language bindings.) In SQL:1999, both parameters and host variables (see section 5.4.2) are signaled by a colon (:). For example, the following statement uses two parameters. (We will use this term because it's more generic. In almost every situation, you can substitute the phrase "host variable" and still be correct. When there's a need to distinguish, we'll make it clear.)

```
UPDATE employees
SET salary = salary * :raise
WHERE dept = :department ;
```

The use of the colon preceding an identifier tells SQL that the identifier is the name of a host parameter or host variable, and not the name of a column in a table being accessed by the statement. This allows you to write your programs using variable names that are meaningful to your application without having to worry about whether you might accidentally pick a variable name that is the same as some column name.

By the way, the use of lowercase letters for the parameter names has no significance; we use that convention for illustration purposes only. SQL's parameter names, like other identifiers, are not affected by the case in which they are written. (Host variable names, on the other hand, are governed by the rules of the language in which the SQL statements are embedded.)

When our host program invokes that SQL statement, it has to supply two values: a numeric value and a character string. If you provide an INTEGER for the numeric value, you might not get the result you expect. You can't give a 10% raise by specifying the value 10, because that will multiply salaries by 10! Instead, you might use a DECIMAL or NUMERIC parameter to pass the more reasonable value of 1.1. (Prior to SQL-92, SQL didn't require the colon before a module language parameter, but the colon before an embedded SQL host variable has always been required.)

5.4.1 Types of Parameters

SQL distinguishes three categories of parameters: *status parameters, data parameters,* and *indicator parameters.* The distinction between data parameters and indicator parameters is based on use, as we shall see in a moment. But let's see what we mean by these three categories first

A status parameter is used to return (to the application) status information about the execution of an SQL statement. While SQL-92 defined two status parameters, SQLCODE and SQLSTATE, SQL:1999 only supports one: SQLSTATE. Earlier versions of SQL defined only the SQLCODE status parameter. Chapter 20, "Diagnostics and Error Management," contains more information about these parameters. For now, we will simply note that SQLSTATE is a character string with 5 characters. (You should plan to use SQLSTATE most of the time; SQLCODE is still supported by most implementations for compatibility with existing applications, but it is no longer part of the SQL standard, meaning that it might not be supported in future versions of some products.)

A data parameter is used to pass data from an application to the DBMS or from the DBMS to an application. Data parameters can be any data type, but your choice of application programming language will make restrictions on the data types that you can use in any given application. When you retrieve data from your database, you will use a data parameter to tell the DBMS where to put the data, as follows:

```
SELECT distributor INTO :dist
FROM movie_titles
WHERE title = 'Notting Hill' ;
```

As we saw in the previous example, you also use a data parameter to supply information to your SQL statements. This can also be data that will be put into the database. For example,

```
INSERT INTO movies_stars
    VALUES ('Hamlet', 1990, 'Gibson', 'Mel', '') ;
```

will do just fine when you know the information in advance, but the general case would be

```
INSERT INTO movies_stars
    VALUES (:title, :year, :last_name, :first_name, :middle_name) ;
```

An indicator parameter (whose data type must be exact numeric with scale 0—most users choose SMALLINT or INTEGER) has two purposes. The first (indeed, the primary) purpose is to allow the DBMS and the host program to exchange information about whether the data parameter is meaningful or whether the data exchanged is null. If you specified the use of an indicator parameter to accompany a data parameter and the data returned from the DBMS to the host program in that data parameter is not null (that is, it's a real value), then the DBMS will set the indicator parameter to 0. If the data that the DBMS would like to pass to the host program is null, then the DBMS will set the indicator parameter to –1. The value of the data parameter is undefined, and the host program should not use it. An implementation may choose to leave the prior value there, it may set its value to zero, or store something there that is entirely unpredictable.

Yes, that seems a little complicated. It is, but it's caused by the fact that most conventional programming languages (e.g., 3GLs, or third-generation languages) don't support the concept of nulls. The only way that the DBMS can indicate the "nullness" of a data item is to pass the flag back to the host program separately. By the way, if you try to retrieve data that is null and you don't specify an indicator parameter, the DBMS will give you an error; therefore, unless you're sure you won't encounter any null values, it's a good idea to use indicator parameters.

If the host program wishes to *send* a null value to the database, it sets the indicator parameter to some negative value (although we strongly recommend the use of –1 for compatibility with possible future enhancements to SQL). If the DBMS sees the negative value in an indicator parameter, it won't even look at the associated data parameter; if the indicator parameter is 0, the DBMS will retrieve the value stored in the data parameter.

The secondary purpose of indicator parameters is to let you know whether the DBMS had to truncate (chop off) characters in a character string when you retrieved it. Suppose you are retrieving a column from the database that is defined as

```
name CHARACTER(50)
```

but you had decided to allocate only 30 characters in your host program (okay, maybe that wasn't too smart, but you probably had a really good reason at the time). If you happen to retrieve a row where the value in the NAME column is longer than 30 characters, SQL will put the first 30 characters of the data into your host program buffer and will set the indicator parameter—assuming you specified one, that is—to 50, telling you how much room you should have allowed. This use of the indicator parameter applies only to retrieval of data from the DBMS and not to sending data to the DBMS. By the way, if you didn't specify an indicator parameter, you would get a warning to let you know about the truncation. Syntax 5-1 demonstrates the format of the indicator parameter.

Syntax 5-1 *Syntax for Host Parameters with Indicator Parameters*

```
: parameter-name [ INDICATOR ] : indicator-name
```

You will have noticed by now that we keep using the word *associated*. We do this because indicator parameters are not distinguishable by the way in which they're declared. You can determine that a parameter is an indicator parameter only by the way in which it's used. In particular, you would write something like

```
:dist INDICATOR :dist_ind
```

to specify that the data parameter :DIST has an associated indicator parameter named :DIST_IND. The keyword INDICATOR is optional, too, so you could have written

```
:dist :dist_ind
```

However, we prefer to always use the keyword INDICATOR to avoid confusion about whether or not we forgot a comma. Let's see what it looks like in a statement.

```
SELECT distributor
INTO :dist :dist_ind
FROM movie_titles
WHERE title = 'Notting Hill' ;
```

Similarly, you might write

```
INSERT INTO movie_stars
VALUES (:title, :year, :last_name, :first_name INDICATOR :first_ind,
        :middle_name INDICATOR :middle_ind) ;
```

in the (likely) case that not all movie stars have two names (Cher, Sting, and Madonna, to name a few) nor use their middle names professionally (as do, e.g., James Earl Jones or Tommy Lee Jones).

Note: To be more precise, you could use (1) the null value if some middle or first name is not known, and (2) a zero-length string when you know that there is no first and/or middle name at all. (This is a situation where you might find it useful to distinguish a null-valued string from a zero-length string.)

5.4.2 Relationship to Host Variables

Several times so far (see section 5.4, for example), we've alluded to the notion of a *module* or an *SQL-client module*. As you'll see in Chapter 12, "Accessing SQL from the Real World," most SQL implementations allow you to write application programs, using a conventional programming language like C or COBOL, that are fairly ordinary except that they also contain SQL statements embedded in them (this is called *embedded SQL*). However, the SQL standard takes a purist approach to defining the language. It defines SQL statements written in pure-SQL procedures that an application program can invoke through the use of a "call statement," and those procedures (called *externally-invoked procedures*) are collected into pure-SQL modules (called *SQL-client modules*).

In section 5.4, we told you about the use of the colon to let SQL easily distinguish your host parameter names (in module language) and host variable names (in embedded SQL) from column names. The reason that the SQL standard uses the same convention for both host parameter names and host variable names is simple: any given SQL statement (indeed, any SQL program) can only have one or the other—not both. Therefore, you don't need a way to avoid giving the same name to a host variable and a host parameter. In fact, because of the way that embedded SQL[2] is defined (as you'll see in Chapter 12, "Accessing SQL from the Real World"), an embedded SQL statement that has a reference to a host variable is converted into a module language SQL statement in an externally-invoked procedure with a host parameter that corresponds to the host variable. That is, there is a one-to-one correspondence between host variable names that you use in embedded SQL statements and host parameter names that you would use in a module language SQL statement.

5.5 | Special Values

SQL:1999 supports a number of special values that can be important to your applications. The value specified by SESSION_USER is equal to the value of the user authorization identifier (authID, for short) of the current SQL-session (sessions were briefly mentioned in Chapter 2, "Introduction to SQL:1999," and are discussed in Chapter 16, "Connections and Remote Database Access"). In this way, your programs can access SESSION_USER to determine the authID of the user executing SQL statements.

SQL:1999 allows SQL statements to execute under the authorization identifier of the session or under a user-specified authorization identifier associated with the module containing the SQL statements, usually called the *definer*. (See Chapter 12, "Accessing SQL from the Real World," for more information on this topic.) If your module doesn't specify an authorization identifier, then the session authorization identifier is used, usually called the *invoker*. In any case, the authorization identifier associated with the module is specified by CURRENT_USER. If the module has no authID, then CURRENT_USER and SESSION_USER are the same.

For example, suppose you have logged into your computer system using the login ID of 'JOE_USER', but you identified yourself to your SQL database as 'PAYROLL_CLERK'. In this case, the value returned by SESSION_USER will be 'PAYROLL_CLERK'. If you're executing an SQL statement in a module that does not have an explicit module authorization identifier and that statement uses the special value CURRENT_USER, then it will also return the value 'PAYROLL_CLERK'.

---

2 Except for embedding in the programming language Java, for which a different approach is used. You can read about embedding in Java in another book, by Jim Melton and Andrew Eisenberg, *Understanding SQL and Java Together: A Guide to SQLJ, JDBC, and Related Technologies* (San Francisco: Morgan Kaufmann Publishers, 2000).

Similarly, SYSTEM_USER is another special value that contains an implementation-defined string. This string identifies the operating system user who has executed an SQL:1999 module. In our example in the previous paragraph, SYSTEM_USER would return 'JOE_USER'. Note, though, that not all operating systems provide a meaningful value for SYSTEM_USER.

SESSION_USER, CURRENT_USER, and SYSTEM_USER have a character string data type. An individual SQL:1999 implementation can specify the length of the strings and whether fixed- or variable-length character strings are used. For compatibility with applications written to use earlier versions of SQL, you can simply code USER when you mean CURRENT_USER.

Note that all of these values have been folded to uppercase. Remember the discussion about identifiers in Chapter 2, "Introduction to SQL:1999"? Because these identifiers are regular identifiers (as opposed to delimited identifiers), the database system will fold them to uppercase for all operations. If you prefer to use delimited identifiers, then you might have identified yourself to the SQL database as "Payroll_clerk" and SESSION_USER will return the value 'Payroll_clerk' to you.

One important use of these special values is recording the identity of a user (for example, in a table designed to capture information about who is executing certain applications). An application might invoke the following SQL statement:

```
INSERT INTO log (information)
    VALUES ('User ' || SYSTEM_USER
            || ', using authID ' || SESSION_USER
            || ' executed at ' || CURRENT_TIMESTAMP) ;
```

(The two vertical bars, ||, mean "concatenate," as we shall see shortly.)

5.6 | Column References and Field References

SQL:1999 gives you the ability to reference SQL data stored in columns, as well as data provided by literals and data supplied in a host variable or a host parameter. In SQL-92, that data stored in columns was always atomic data—meaning data that cannot be decomposed into smaller chunks (except through operations like extracting a substring of a character string). As you saw in section 2.4.8, "Collection (or Array) Types," and section 2.4.9, "Anonymous Row Types," SQL:1999 adds new "nonatomic" data types like row types. Naturally, it also provides a way to reference components of the data stored in a column.

5.6.1 Column References

In SQL, you can reference a column in many of the same places you can use any other value. Obviously, there are situations where it's not meaningful to reference a column, the restriction being that you must have created a context for the column reference.

A column reference can be as little as the name of a column, but the full form is a qualifier, a period, and a column name. For example:

```
movie_titles.title
```

The table name (movie_titles, in this case) gives us the required context. That qualifier has to identify a table that is being *processed* by the SQL statement. Consider the following (erroneous) example:

```
SELECT movie_titles.title
FROM music_supply_cost
WHERE music_supply_cost.supplier =
      'Random Distributors'
```

In this case, even though movie_titles is a valid table name (that is, it is the name of a table that we know about), it has no meaning in this SQL statement. This statement deals only with the table named music_supply_cost, so we can reference only columns that are in that table. The statement

```
SELECT music_supply_cost.music_title
FROM music_supply_cost
WHERE supplier = 'Random Distributors'
```

is valid. It is equivalent to

```
SELECT music_title
FROM music_supply_cost
WHERE supplier = 'Random Distributors'
```

because the column has an *implicit* qualifier equal to the name of the (only) table.

The rule is that the column reference has to be in the *scope* of a table reference. One way of accomplishing this is to qualify a column name with the name of the table that contains the column. Another way is to use a *correlation name* to qualify the column name, about which more shortly. There will be situations where there are two (or more) tables involved (see Chapter 8, "Working with Multiple Tables: The Relational Operators"). When you find yourself in this situation, there are two possibilities:

- the name of each column that you reference is unique over all of the tables that you're using; or
- the names of one or more columns that you reference exist in two or more of the tables that you're using.

In the first case, you can simply use the column name when you want to reference the column. In the second case, you must qualify the column name to tell the database system *which* column you mean. For example, suppose you have a column called NAME in two tables (EMPLOYEE and CUSTOMER, perhaps). If you wanted to retrieve the name of an employee who sold some goods to a particular customer, you would have to specify EMPLOYEE.NAME in your select list and CUSTOMER.NAME in your WHERE clause.

Sometimes, it is inconvenient to use the actual name of the table to qualify a column name, perhaps because the table name is rather long or difficult to type. In that case, SQL allows you to define a correlation name for the table that you can use as a qualifier. (Note: There are other reasons why you might—or must—use a correlation name. You'll read about this in Chapter 8, "Working with Multiple Tables: The Relational Operators.") For example, you might code a query as

```
SELECT msc.music_title
FROM music_supply_cost AS msc
WHERE supplier = 'Random Distributors'
```

In this example, MSC is a correlation name for the table MUSIC_SUPPLY_COST. The keyword AS is optional and may be omitted, although we always prefer to include it for clarity. (If you like, you can think of correlation names as a sort of *alias* for tables, but the SQL:1999 standard doesn't use that term.)

Correlation names are actually a lot more interesting than they would seem from the preceding discussion. Let's take a slightly longer look at them to better understand their usefulness and the rules associated with them.

First, it's important to remember that a correlation name always hides the name of the table. Therefore, if you write

```
SELECT *
FROM movie_titles AS mt
WHERE movie_titles.our_tape_cost > 10.95
```

you will get an error. In the context of this SELECT statement, the table name movie_titles simply doesn't exist once the correlation name has been defined. Instead, you'll have to write

```
SELECT *
FROM movie_titles AS mt
WHERE mt.our_tape_cost > 10.95
```

Second, although you can often use the table name as a sort of implicit correlation name (as though you specified movie_titles AS movie_titles), they're *not* really the same thing. The following statement is *valid* SQL:

```
SELECT *
FROM catalog1.myschema.movie_titles
WHERE catalog1.myschema.movie_titles.our_tape_cost > 10.95
```

but this next one is *invalid* and will give you an error:

```
SELECT *
FROM catalog1.myschema.movie_titles AS mt
WHERE catalog1.myschema.mt.our_tape_cost > 10.95
```

Why? Simply because the correlation name acts as a replacement for the *entire* qualified table name, not just the identifier alone! Therefore, don't think of FROM movie_titles as a shorthand for FROM movie_titles AS movie_titles—they're different in that very important way.

We just told you that you could use a column reference only in the scope of a table reference. Let's try to define this scope a little more carefully.

If the column reference contains an explicit qualifier, then the column reference must be in the scope of a table name or a correlation name that is the same as that qualifier. In other words, you can't qualify a column name with a table name or correlation name that doesn't exist in the same scope as the column reference. Furthermore, there can be only one such table name or correlation name; otherwise, the reference is ambiguous. Actually, scopes can be nested, and in the innermost such scope, there can only be one such name. Naturally, the table identified by the qualifier must actually contain a column with the name you use in the column reference. Therefore,

```
SELECT msc.music_title
FROM movie_titles AS msc
```

isn't valid, even though MSC is a valid correlation name. Why? Because, the table associated with MSC doesn't have a column named music_title.

If the column reference doesn't have an explicit qualifier, then it has an *implicit* qualifier. The database system decides what that qualifier is. In this case, the column reference has to appear in the scope of one or more table names or correlation names that identify a table containing a column with the name you gave in the column reference. If there's exactly one such table name or correlation name, then that name is the implicit qualifier for the table reference. If it turns out that there are two or more such table names or correlation names in the innermost scope, then you'll get an error, *unless* they both (all) identify tables that are part of a joined table (discussed in Chapter 8, "Working with Multiple Tables: The Relational Operators"); in this case, the column name must identify a column in every one of those tables and the column reference identifies any and all of the columns at the same time! If this occurs, the column is actually coalesced from the two source columns and doesn't belong (strictly speaking) to either source table; in other words, you reference such columns solely by their column name without qualifying them with the table name or correlation name.

And, it's almost too obvious to say, but the data type of a column reference is the same as the data type of the column that it references (bet you were surprised by that!).

5.6.2 Field References

As we said in the introduction to section 5.6, SQL:1999 allows you to reference components of decomposable (that is, nonatomic) data stored in columns of your databases. One of the decomposable data types that can be the data type of a column is the anonymous row type introduced in section 2.4.9, "Anonymous Row Types." As you read there, a row type is made up of one or more fields, each having a name and a data type. To reference the value stored in some field of a column whose data type is some row type, you (perhaps obviously) use a field reference.

An SQL:1999 field reference is actually nothing more than the name of some data item whose data type is a row type, followed by a period, followed by the name of a field of that row type. Syntax 5-2 shows the syntax of field references.

Syntax 5-2 *Syntax of Field Reference*

```
source . field_name
```

The source in Syntax 5-2 must be the name of some column (or, for that matter, some SQL parameter—which we will discuss in Chapter 17, "Routines and

Routine Invocation (Procedures and Functions)"—or some SQL variable; SQL variables are discussed in a different book,[3] but row types are not addressed in that book, since they are new to SQL:1999) whose data type is a row type having a field of the specified name. There's nothing tricky about this at all; it's precisely what you'd expect it to be.

Partly because of the requirement to use the period (.) as a separator wherever possible, SQL:1999 had to adopt an unusual restriction regarding the syntax of field references. To explain the underlying problem, let's consider the two tables shown in Example 5-1. For illustrative purposes, assume that the default schema is named S1.

Example 5-1 *Illustrating Row References*

```
CREATE TABLE t1 ( c1 INTEGER );
CREATE TABLE s1 ( t1 ROW ( c1 INTEGER ) );
```

We point out that the second table has a column with the same name as the first table and that column has a row with a field that has the same name as the column of the first table. Next, we attempt to execute the code shown in Example 5-2.

Example 5-2 *Using Row References*

```
SELECT s1.t1.c1
FROM s1, s1.t1
```

Does that code retrieve the value of field C1 from column T1 of table S1, or does it retrieve the value of column C1 from table T1 (both tables in schema S1)?

SQL:1999 resolved this dilemma by observing that compatibility with SQL-92 and earlier versions of the standard requires that the statement be interpreted to mean a retrieval of column C1 from table T1 in schema S1. In order to allow the other semantic, SQL:1999 requires that a *correlation name* be used to qualify column names whenever your code is "reaching inside" a column—for example, to retrieve the value of a field. You can read more about correlation names in Chapter 8, "Working with Multiple Tables: The Relational Operators," and more about this restriction on qualifying names in section 9.2.1, "Qualified Asterisk."

The one additional issue that you might not have considered is this: What is the value of a field reference R.F if the row data item (e.g., a column) identified by R happens to be null? Easy. The field reference's value is also null! Again, it's just what you'd expect it to be.

---

3 Jim Melton, *Understanding SQL's Stored Procedures: A Complete Guide to SQL/PSM* (San Francisco, CA: Morgan Kaufmann Publishers, 1998).

5.7 | Some Terminology

SQL:1999 uses a few special terms to distinguish among various classifications of values.

- *Value specification:* This is a value specified by itself without any operators (not an expression). It can be a literal, a parameter, or host variable (including an indicator), a dynamic parameter, or one of the special values, such as CURRENT_USER, SESSION_USER, or SYSTEM_USER. In a domain definition, the special value VALUE is included (meaning the value of the column in the row).

- *Unsigned value specification:* This is the same as a value specification except that a literal, if applicable, is specifically noted as being unsigned (and, by implication, never negative).

- *Simple value specification:* This is a more limited set of values; it can only be a parameter or host variable (without an indicator) or a literal.

- *Target specification:* This isn't really a value but is a way to specify the place (target) to put output from an SQL statement; it is either a parameter or host variable (with indicators allowed).

- *Simple target specification:* This simplest form is only a parameter or host variable without an indicator.

- *Host parameter specification:* This form contains a host parameter name, followed by optional indicator parameters.

5.8 | Set Functions

Since SQL:1999 supports management of database data as a set (or, more accurately, as a multiset), a number of special set-oriented functions are provided. Set functions can best be viewed as a collection of functions that process the data in a table and perform behind-the-scenes calculations that you would otherwise have to do yourself in your programs. Set functions include facilities to count the number of rows in a table, return the maximum and minimum values within specific columns, and calculate averages and sums (many people call these *aggregate functions*).

As that term implies, these functions perform operations that aggregate data from *groups of one or more rows*. We'll discuss SQL's grouping operations extensively in Chapter 9, "Advanced SQL Query Expressions." For now, we'll just note that application of these functions always requires that the table to which they are applied be grouped in some way; SQL will treat the entire table as a single group if you don't specify a different grouping in your queries.

5.8.1 COUNT

The COUNT(*) set function returns the number of rows in the specified table. For example, let's go back to our MOVIE_TITLES table. The complete syntax of COUNT is shown in Syntax 5-3.

Syntax 5-3 *Syntax of COUNT function*

- COUNT ([DISTINCT] column name)
- COUNT ([ALL] column name)
- COUNT (*)

Assume that we jump into our time-traveling Delorean (from *Back to the Future*) and go back to the early days of video rental stores where we have only a few movies in stock, and therefore small database tables (see Table 5-3).

Table 5-3 *MOVIES Table for a Small Store*

TITLE	OUR_COST	REGULAR_ RENTAL_PRICE	CURRENT_ RENTAL_PRICE
The Way We Were	14.95	1.99	1.99
Prince of Tides	55.95	3.99	3.99
Yentl	24.95	1.99	1.99
48 Hours	29.95	2.99	1.99
A Star Is Born	24.95	1.99	1.99
Another 48 Hours	29.95	2.99	1.99
Beverly Hills Cop	29.95	2.99	1.99
Beverly Hills Cop II	29.95	2.99	1.99
Pretty Woman	55.95	3.99	3.99
Silverado	24.95	1.99	1.99
Moonstruck	35.95	2.99	2.99
Raising Arizona	24.95	1.99	1.99
The Outlaw Josey Wales	24.95	1.99	1.99
Duck Soup	14.95	1.99	1.99

(Continued)

Table 5-3 *Continued*

TITLE	OUR_COST	REGULAR_ RENTAL_PRICE	CURRENT_ RENTAL_PRICE
A Night at the Opera	14.95	1.99	1.99
About Last Night	14.95	1.99	1.99
Animal House	14.95	1.99	1.99
Ten	14.95	1.99	1.99

The statement

```
SELECT COUNT (*)
FROM movie_titles ;
```

will yield the result of 18, indicating that 18 rows are in the table. Of course, in real life post-2000, our example Internet retailer's database tables would contain many, many more rows than that and would therefore yield a larger number as a result.

Let's go back to our MOVIES_STARS table (see Table 5-4 for a subset sample we'll use for this example).

Table 5-4 *MOVIES_STARS Redux*

MOVIE_TITLE	ACTOR_ LAST_NAME	ACTOR_ FIRST_NAME	ACTOR_ MIDDLE_NAME
The Way We Were	Redford	Robert	
The Way We Were	Streisand	Barbra	
Prince of Tides	Nolte	Nick	
Prince of Tides	Streisand	Barbra	
Yentl	Streisand	Barbra	
48 Hours	Nolte	Nick	
48 Hours	Murphy	Eddie	
A Star Is Born	Kristofferson	Kris	
A Star Is Born	Streisand	Barbra	
Another 48 Hours	Murphy	Eddie	
Another 48 Hours	Nolte	Nick	
Beverly Hills Cop	Murphy	Eddie	
Beverly Hills Cop	Reinhold	Judge	
Beverly Hills Cop II	Murphy	Eddie	
Beverly Hills Cop II	Reinhold	Judge	

(Continued)

Table 5-4 *Continued*

MOVIE_TITLE	ACTOR_ LAST_NAME	ACTOR_ FIRST_NAME	ACTOR_ MIDDLE_NAME
Beverly Hills Cop III	Murphy	Eddie	
Beverly Hills Cop III	Reinhold	Judge	
Pretty Woman	Roberts	Julia	
Pretty Woman	Gere	Richard	
Runaway Bride	Roberts	Julia	
Runaway Bride	Gere	Richard	
Silverado	Costner	Kevin	
Silverado	Kline	Kevin	
Silverado	Glover	Danny	
Silverado	Dennehy	Brian	
Moonstruck	Cher		
Moonstruck	Cage	Nicholas	
Raising Arizona	Cage	Nicholas	
Raising Arizona	Hunter	Holly	
The Outlaw Josey Wales	Eastwood	Clint	
The Outlaw Josey Wales	Locke	Sondra	
Duck Soup	Marx Brothers		
A Night at the Opera	Marx Brothers		
About Last Night	Belushi	James	
About Last Night	Lowe	Rob	
About Last Night	Moore	Demi	
Animal House	Belushi	John	
Animal House	Matheson	Tim	
Ten	Derek	Bo	
Ten	Moore	Dudley	

The COUNT(*) set function will yield a result of 40. Just as we discussed in Chapter 3, "Basic Table Creation and Data Manipulation," there may be times when you wish to eliminate duplicate rows from your specific query. The DISTINCT set quantifier can be used to specify a column from which duplicates will be eliminated from consideration. The statement

```
SELECT COUNT (DISTINCT movie_title)
FROM movies_stars ;
```

will result in an answer of 20.

You can also make additional restrictions on the table that you are counting. That is, you don't have to retrieve the count of rows in a physical base table, but from a virtual table that is generated by the statement that contains the COUNT expression. For example, you could say

```
SELECT COUNT(*)
FROM movies_stars
WHERE actor_last_name = 'Moore'
```

which would return the value of the number of movies starring Dudley Moore, Demi Moore, Mary Tyler Moore, and others with the same last name. Be aware, though, that if there were a movie starring more than one actor with the last name of Moore, that title would be counted twice, three times, or some other multiple, depending on exactly how many credited actors named Moore were in the film. To filter out the duplicates, you could say

```
SELECT COUNT(DISTINCT movie_title)
FROM movies_stars
WHERE actor_last_name = 'Moore'
```

5.8.2 MAX

The MAX function is used to return the maximum value within a specified column. Assume that you wish to learn the most expensive DVD sale price that you have in stock (see Table 5-5).

Table 5-5 *Movies in Stock*

TITLE	REGULAR_ TAPE_ SALE_PRICE	CURRENT_ TAPE_ SALE_PRICE	REGULAR_ DVD_ SALE_PRICE	CURRENT_ DVD_ SALE_PRICE
The Sixth Sense	19.95	19.95	29.95	29.95
Three Kings	15.95	15.95	25.95	22.95
The Thomas Crown Affair	14.95	11.95	24.95	22.95
The 13th Warrior	19.95	19.95	29.95	29.95
The Matrix	18.95	18.95	28.95	28.95
Runaway Bride	19.95	17.95	29.95	27.95
Austin Powers	18.95	17.95	28.95	27.95
Austin Powers: The Spy Who Shagged Me	18.95	18.95	28.95	28.95

(Continued)

Table 5-5 *Continued*

TITLE	REGULAR_ TAPE_ SALE_PRICE	CURRENT_ TAPE_ SALE_PRICE	REGULAR_ DVD_ SALE_PRICE	CURRENT_ DVD_ SALE_PRICE
Notting Hill	16.95	16.95	26.95	26.95
Big Daddy	19.95	15.95	29.95	29.95
The Waterboy	19.95	15.95	29.95	29.95
|				
|				
|				
Bowfinger	19.95	19.95	29.95	29.95
Man on the Moon	19.95	19.95	29.95	25.95

The statement

```
SELECT MAX(current_dvd_sale_price)
FROM movie_titles ;
```

will yield an answer of 29.95. Behind the scenes, only one of the rows that meet the MAX (CURRENT_DVD_SALE_PRICE) restriction (five do so in our example, but it doesn't matter how many) will be retained; it doesn't matter which one, since the value is the same in all such rows.

Now, let's see why it's important to understand the behavior of SQL. Suppose you wanted, for some reason, to expand the preceding query to get the titles of all movies priced at the maximum and to get that maximum price. If you quickly sounded out the query, you'd probably say

select the title and the maximum current DVD sale price, from the movie titles table

and you might be tempted to write

```
SELECT title, MAX (current_dvd_sale_price)
FROM movie_titles ;
```

but that is *not* valid SQL syntax. SQL has a rule that says if any column of the select list is (or uses) a set function, then all of them have to be (or use) set functions. (As we'll see in Chapter 9, "Advanced SQL Query Expressions," there are a small number of exceptions, but this isn't one of them.)

You could write

```
SELECT title, ( SELECT MAX ( current_dvd_sale_price )
                FROM movie_titles )
FROM movie_titles
```

to satisfy this rule, but that would give you the names of *all* movies (Result 5-1), no matter what their price (along with the price of the most expensive movie).

Result 5-1 *The Names of All Movies with the Maximum Movie Price*

The Sixth Sense	29.95
Three Kings	29.95
The Thomas Crown Affair	29.95
The 13th Warrior	29.95
The Matrix	29.95
Runaway Bride	29.95

Instead, you need to use a *subquery* in your WHERE clause as we do just below. We cover subqueries briefly in Chapter 7, "Predicates," and discuss them further in Chapter 9, section 9.10, "Subqueries." For now, look at subqueries as a query that yields some type of intermediate result within another query.

For example, let's take our request again, and do a better job of sounding it out. In fact, let's do that in two parts:

- *Part 1:* What is the maximum current DVD sales price within the MOVIE_ TITLES table?

- *Part 2:* What movies sell at that price (from Part 1)?

The SQL manner of doing this is

```
SELECT title, current_dvd_sale_price
FROM movie_titles
WHERE current_dvd_sale_price =
      ( SELECT MAX ( current_dvd_sale_price )
        FROM movie_titles )
```

Our Part 1 query is this subquery: SELECT MAX (CURRENT_DVD_SALES_PRICE)....
The subquery will yield the result of 29.95, which then becomes the comparison
value for the main query: SELECT TITLE,... WHERE CURRENT_DVD_SALE_PRICE =
29.95. This then will yield the correct result shown in Result 5-2.

Result 5-2 *The Names of All Movies Priced at the Maximum*

The Sixth Sense	29.95
The13th Warrior	29.95
Big Daddy	29.95
The Waterboy	29.95
Bowfinger	29.95

Note that the MAX function is not restricted to numeric data types (INTEGER,
REAL, and the like). CHARACTER, DATE, and other data types can have the MAX
function used for columns of that type. The statement

```
SELECT MAX (actor_last_name)
FROM movie_titles ;
```

would probably give an answer of 'ZZ Top' (from the movie *Back to the Future 3*).

5.8.3 MIN

Assume you have that portion of the MOVIE_TITLES table shown in Table 5-6.

Table 5-6 *A Portion of the MOVIE_TITLES Table*

TITLE	TOTAL_TAPE_ UNITS_SOLD	TOTAL_DVD_ UNITS_SOLD
The Sixth Sense	321	89
Three Kings	875	132
The Thomas Crown Affair	562	76
The 13th Warrior	1234	234
The Matrix	987	143
Runaway Bride	987	145
Austin Powers	453	78
		(Continued)

Table 5-6 *Continued*

TITLE	*TOTAL_TAPE_ UNITS_SOLD*	*TOTAL_DVD_ UNITS_SOLD*
Austin Powers: The Spy Who Shagged Me	542	98
Notting Hill	1702	265
Big Daddy	432	87
The Waterboy	131	92
Beverly Hills Cop I	765	134
Beverly Hills Cop II	234	45
Beverly Hills Cop III	132	32
Doctor Doolittle	452	29
Coming to America	214	89
Animal Farm	2450	346
The Way We Were	890	123

The MIN function can be used in a manner similar to that of MAX, except in finding the smallest value in a given column. The statement

```
SELECT MIN (total_tape_units_sold)
FROM movie_titles ;
```

will yield a result of 131 (assuming for this example that the above rows constitute the entire table).

The MAX and MIN functions can be combined in a single statement, if desired. The statement

```
SELECT MAX ( total_dvd_units_sold ),
       MIN ( total_dvd_units_sold )
FROM movie_titles ;
```

provides a result of 346 and 29. As with the MAX function, MIN is not restricted to numeric data types.

5.8.4 SUM

The SUM set function allows you to sum the values in a specified column. Only numeric data types and INTERVALs are acceptable as input, so both integer-based data types (INTEGER and SMALLINT) and other numeric data types (REAL, DECIMAL, FLOAT, and the like) can be used. An additional constraint is that the result of the

SUM function must be within the range of the source data type. More exactly, the result type is exact numeric if the source is exact numeric, with the same scale and implementation-defined precision. Otherwise, the result type is approximate numeric or INTERVAL (as indicated by the source type) of at least the same precision as the source. Implementations vary about whether they automatically promote to a larger exact numeric type in order to avoid overflow problems. The user is safest, especially for portability, to assume the worst. The consequence is that the user ought to explicitly cast exact numerics to a size large enough to handle any overflows caused by accumulating a result larger than otherwise permitted.

If, for example, you were SUMming a column of type SMALLINT and your particular SQL:1999 implementation designates 2047 as the largest number acceptable for SMALLINT data, then the SUM of each row's value must be less than or equal to 2047 even though each row's value is already within range.

Given Table 5-6, the statement

```
SELECT SUM(total_dvd_units_sold)
FROM movie_titles ;
```

will yield the result of 2237.

Incidentally, SQL:1999 prohibits taking a sum of a column whose data type is a collection type, a row type, a user-defined type, a reference type, or a large object type—because they're not numeric types. Obviously, character, bit, and datetime types are also prohibited for the same reason.

5.8.5 AVG

The AVG set function returns the average of the values in the specified column, computed as the sum of all the values in the specified column divided by the number of rows. As with the SUM function, only numeric data types and INTERVALs are permitted. The statement

```
SELECT AVG (total_tape_units_sold)
FROM movie_titles ;
```

will yield the answer that the average number of units sold for all movies is 742.3888.

SQL:1999 also prohibits taking an average of a column whose data type is a collection type, a row type, a user-defined type, a reference type, a large object type, a character type, or a datetime type.

5.8.6 The Rest of the Set Functions: EVERY, ANY, and SOME

We've now looked at most of the SQL:1999 set functions. Together, the complete syntax for these set functions can be written in BNF as shown in Syntax 5-4.

Syntax 5-4 *Syntax of Set Functions*

```
<set function specification> ::=
      COUNT <left paren> <asterisk> <right paren>
    | <general set function>
    | <grouping operation>

<general set function> ::=
    <set function type>
        <left paren> [ <set quantifier> ] <value expression> <right paren>

<set function type> ::=
    <computational operation>

<computational operation> ::=
      AVG | MAX | MIN | SUM
    | EVERY | ANY | SOME
    | COUNT

<grouping operation> ::=
    GROUPING <left paren> <column reference> <right paren>

<set quantifier> ::=
      DISTINCT
    | ALL
```

Let's break that BNF down a bit to make it less intimidating.

We first see that one alternative for a valid set function is simply COUNT(*), which we demonstrated for you in section 5.8.1.

The next alternative is the *general set function,* which is initiated by a keyword indicating which sort of computation is being requested (you've seen most of these in sections 5.8.1 through 5.8.5), followed by a value expression—optionally preceded by either DISTINCT or ALL—enclosed in parentheses.

The keywords that you haven't seen yet are EVERY, ANY, and SOME. If you specify one of these keywords in a set function, then the data type of the parenthesized value expression must be a Boolean type. The value computed by EVERY will be

True if and only if the value of the expression in every row is True. The value computed by either ANY or SOME (they are synonyms here) will be True if the value of the expression in at least one row is True.

Finally, let's look at the final alternative, the *grouping operation*. You can specify this alternative only if the query in which it's specified is a grouped query, which we will consider in Chapter 9, "Advanced SQL Query Expressions," at which time we'll come back to the grouping operation alternative for set functions.

We now look at some other useful functions of SQL:1999, starting with value functions.

5.9 | Value Functions

Those readers familiar with commercial database management software, particularly those packages used on personal computers, are accustomed to a wide variety of functions used for string manipulation, date-related tasks, and other such facilities. SQL:1999 contains four types of value functions, designed to help you perform these necessary chores within your programs. These four categories are

- numeric value functions
- string value functions
- datetime value functions
- interval value functions

5.9.1 Numeric Value Functions

Numeric value functions always return a numeric value, though they may operate on other types of data. The numeric value functions are

- POSITION
- CHARACTER_LENGTH
- OCTET_LENGTH
- BIT_LENGTH
- EXTRACT

- CARDINALITY
- ABS
- MOD

The complete syntax for SQL:1999's numeric value functions is shown in Syntax 5-5.

Syntax 5-5 *Syntax of Numeric Value Functions*

- POSITION (string-value IN string-value)
- EXTRACT (datetime-field FROM datetime-value)
- EXTRACT (datetime-field FROM interval-value)
- EXTRACT (timezone-field FROM datetime-value)
- CHAR_LENGTH (character-string)
- CHARACTER_LENGTH (character-string)
- OCTET_LENGTH (string-value)
- BIT_LENGTH (string-value)
- CARDINALITY (collection-value)
- ABS (numeric-value)
- MOD (numeric-dividend , numeric-divisor)

Let's take a look at each of those variations.

POSITION searches for the presence of a particular string in another string. If the search string is located, the POSITION function returns a numeric value that indicates the position in the source string where the search string was found (the string's first character is at position 1). If the search string is not found in the source string, the function returns a 0 value.

Some examples of POSITION are as follows:

```
POSITION ('4' IN '48 Hours')           -- returns a value of 1
POSITION ('48' IN '48 Hours')          -- returns a value of 1
POSITION ('48' IN 'Another 48 Hours')  -- returns a value of 9
POSITION ('Entertaining' IN 'The Waterboy')  -- returns a value of 0,
                                       -- indicating that the search
                                       -- string wasn't found
POSITION ('' IN 'The Way We Were')     -- returns a value of 1;
                                       -- a search string with a
```

```
                                        -- length of 0
                                        -- always returns a value of 1
POSITION (B'101' IN B'0001010010010') -- returns a value of 4
```

CHARACTER_LENGTH, or its synonym CHAR_LENGTH, returns the length in characters of a character string. Some examples follow:

```
CHARACTER_LENGTH ('Duck Soup')    -- returns a value of 9
CHAR_LENGTH ('True Lies')         -- returns a value of 9
```

Two numeric value functions can be used for system programming tasks that you might need to do. OCTET_LENGTH returns the length in octets of a character or string, while BIT_LENGTH returns the length in bits.

If you use BIT_LENGTH on a character string, it returns the value of OCTET_LENGTH times 8. If you use CHARACTER_LENGTH on a bit string, the value returned is the same as the value returned by OCTET_LENGTH applied to the same bit string.

Example 5-3 *Examples of Length Functions*

```
OCTET_LENGTH ('Annie Hall')    -- returns a value of 10, assuming one
                               -- octet per character; for multi-octet
                               -- implementations, the returned value
                               -- would be different
OCTET_LENGTH (B'1011100001')   -- returns a value of 2, because 10 bits
                               -- require at least 2 octets for
                               -- representation ("octet" = 8 bits)
BIT_LENGTH (B'0111110')        -- returns a value of 8
```

Another SQL:1999 numeric value function is the EXTRACT function, which isolates a single field of a datetime or an interval (see Chapter 4, "Basic Data Definition Language (DDL)") and converts it to a number.

Example 5-4 *EXTRACT Function Example*

```
EXTRACT (YEAR FROM DATE '1992-06-01') -- returns a numeric value of 1992
```

CARDINALITY is used to find out how many elements there are in an array value. So far, we haven't used arrays to represent data in our video store's database, but the following example illustrates the possibility. Suppose that, in our MOVIE_TITLES table, instead of having four columns named REGULAR_

TAPE_SALE_PRICE, CURRENT_TAPE_SALE_PRICE, REGULAR_DVD_SALE_PRICE, and CURRENT_DVD_SALE_PRICE, we had a single column named SALE_PRICES and wanted to hold four values at once in that column. We could define that column as shown in Example 5-5.

Example 5-5 *Column Definition with an Array*

```
sale_prices                     DECIMAL( 5,2 ) ARRAY[4],
```

Having done that, we can then decide that the regular sales price for a VHS tape will always appear in the first element of the array, SALES_PRICES[1]. Similarly, the current sales price for a VHS tape will be found in the second element, the regular sales price for a DVD in the third element, and the current DVD price in the fourth. In this environment, the expression

```
CARDINALITY ( sales_prices )
```

will always return the value 4. However, as you'll recall from the discussion in section 2.4.8, "Collection (or Array) Types," SQL:1999's arrays are variable in length so that you might sometimes have only one or two values stored in an array whose maximum cardinality is 4, and other times have four values stored in there. (That wouldn't make sense, of course, for the rather contrived example we just used, but it's a possible use of SQL:1999's array type.)

ABS is used to compute the absolute value of an expression. You'll undoubtedly recall from your middle school math classes that the absolute value of a positive number or of zero is just that same number, while the absolute value of a negative number is the same number given a positive sign. In other words,

```
ABS ( expression )
```

returns a value that is just the *magnitude* of the value of the expression.

MOD is a little—but only a little—bit more complex. SQL requires that data types of the two operands of the MOD function have scale 0 (that is, they can only be integer values). The value returned by MOD is the remainder that results when you divide the value of the first operand by the value of the second. The returned value always has the same sign (positive or negative) as the first operand, and its absolute value is less than the absolute value of the second operand. To see how this function operates, let's consider the expression

```
MOD ( 25 , 3 )
```

We know that the result will be positive because the first operand is positive (25). We also know that its value will be less than 3 (the value of the second operand). The result of 25 divided by 3 is 8, with a remainder of 1. Therefore, the returned value is 1.

Let's make it a little more complicated. If we compute

```
MOD ( 37 , -8 )
```

the returned value is 5—which has the same sign as 37 and has an absolute value less than the absolute value of –8.

5.9.2 String Value Functions

String value functions are perhaps the most familiar SQL:1999 functions to longtime DEMS users. The complete syntax of SQL:1999's string value expression is shown in Syntax 5-6. Let's look at each individually.

Syntax 5-6 *Syntax of String Value Functions*

- SUBSTRING (string-value FROM start [FOR length])
- SUBSTRING (string-value SIMILAR string-value ESCAPE character-value)
- UPPER (char-string-value)
- LOWER (char-string-value)
- TRIM ([BOTH | LEADING TRAILING] character FROM char-string-value)
- TRANSLATE (char-string-value USING translation)
- CONVERT (char-string-value USING conversion)
- OVERLAY (string-value PLACING string-value FROM start [FOR length])

SUBSTRING

The SUBSTRING function is used to extract a substring—either bit or character, depending on the type of the source string (bit string or character string, respectively). There are two variants of SUBSTRING in SQL:1999. One, which first appeared in SQL-92, is just an ordinary substring, as shown in Example 5-6.

Example 5-6 *SUBSTRING Example*

```
SUBSTRING ('Another 48 Hours' FROM 1 FOR 9)
```

returns Another 4.

As this example shows, the SUBSTRING value function takes three operands. The first is the string from which a substring is to be taken, the second is the starting point for the substring, and the last (which is optional and has a default value of "the rest of the string") specifies the length of the substring to be taken.

SUBSTRING has a couple of interesting behaviors that make it a little easier to use. If the start position is after the string (for example, SUBSTRING('abc' FROM 10)), then the result of the substring is an empty string (''). If the start is before the string and the length is enough to take the substring into the string (for example, SUBSTRING('abc' FROM -2 FOR 4)), then the SUBSTRING acts as if the source string has a bunch of "noncharacters" preceding it. The result of the last example would be 'a'. If any of the three operands is null, then the result is also null.

The operands can be literals, as in our examples so far, but they can also be any sort of value expression (as long as the first one is a character string and the other two are exact numerics, that is).

Example 5-7 *More SUBSTRING Examples*

```
SUBSTRING ('abcdef' FROM -8 FOR 2)
```

has the value ''.

```
SUBSTRING ('abcdef' FROM -2 FOR 6)
```

has the value 'abc'.

```
SUBSTRING ('abcdef' FROM 0 FOR 4)
```

has the value 'abc'.

```
SUBSTRING ('abcdef' FROM 3 FOR -2)
```

returns an error, because the end of the substring preceded the beginning.

```
SUBSTRING ('abcdef' FROM 7 FOR 3)
```

has the value ''.

```
SUBSTRING ('abcdef' FROM 3)
```

has the value 'cdef'.

```
SUBSTRING (B'101101' FROM 3 FOR 2)
```

has the value B'11'.

These examples all use a character string literal as the source of the substring, but you can use any meaningful character value, including expressions, columns, parameters, and so forth. You can also take substrings of CHARACTER LARGE strings, BINARY LARGE OBJECT strings, and even BIT strings.

The second sort of SUBSTRING is the regular expression substring function. This is rather more complicated than the first variation. The purpose of this function is to locate and return a substring from within another expression using *regular expressions* to locate the desired substring (instead of identifying the desired substring by its starting position and length). We'll discuss regular expressions in the context of the SIMILAR predicate in section 7.7.2, "SIMILAR Predicate," but for now we'll just say that a regular expression is one that specifies the rules (sometimes complex rules) for matching one character string to another.

In a regular expression substring function, the second string value *must* have three distinct sections, separated by a specific notation. That "specific notation" is required to be the character given in the third operand (the character value following ESCAPE) immediately followed by a double-quote ("). The three distinct sections of that second string value must each be a valid regular expression (see the discussion in section 7.7.2, "SIMILAR Predicate").

The regular expression substring function then analyzes the character string value of the first operand, attempting to partition it into three sections. The first section is matched by the regular expression comprising the first section of the second operand; the second section is matched by the regular expression comprising the second section of the second operand; and the last section is matched by the regular expression comprising the third section of the second operand. The value returned by this function is the middle portion of the first operand.

Let's look at a very simple example that will help explain this function:

```
SUBSTRING ( 'The Thomas Crown Affair'
            SIMILAR 'The \"[:ALPHA:]+\" Crown Affair'
            ESCAPE '\' )
```

In this example, the operand following the keyword SIMILAR is a character string literal whose contents include a regular expression in the form of another character string literal (which matches exactly that sequence of characters), the separator indicated by the backslash and double-quote (\"), a second regular expression whose meaning is "one or more alphabetic characters," the separator again, and a third regular expression in the form of a different character string literal.

The value returned by this expression is simply

```
Thomas
```

UPPER and LOWER

The UPPER and LOWER value functions convert (or fold) a particular string to all upper- or lowercase characters, respectively.

Example 5-8 *Examples of UPPER and LOWER*

```
UPPER ('Batman')        -- returns 'BATMAN'
LOWER ('SUPERMAN')      -- returns 'superman'
```

A couple of quick notes regarding UPPER and LOWER: if you use either of these functions on an accented character (example: the German ö), the case conversion would be applied (UPPER ('ö') would become an 'Ö'). Other character sets with no concept of upper and lower case—Hebrew or Japanese Katakana, for example—would not be affected by usage of these functions.

TRIM

The TRIM function allows you to strip leading blanks, trailing blanks, or both from a character string. In fact, SQL allows you to strip off any character, such as leading and trailing zeros, asterisks, or whatever you (don't) want. For example:

```
TRIM (LEADING ' ' FROM ' TEST ')    has the value    'TEST '
TRIM (TRAILING ' ' FROM ' TEST ')   has the value    ' TEST'
TRIM (BOTH ' ' FROM ' TEST ')       has the value    'TEST'
TRIM (BOTH 'T' FROM 'TEST')         has the value    'ES'
```

If you write TRIM (LEADING FROM ' TEST '), this is the equivalent to the first example, where you specified a blank character; that is, blanks are the default to the TRIM function. If you specify none of LEADING, TRAILING, or BOTH in your statement, BOTH is the default.

TRANSLATE and CONVERT

Several other string functions belong to the area of internationalization, a subject we discuss in Chapter 21, "Internationalization Aspects of SQL:1999." We'll briefly introduce them for the sake of continuity with the other string functions, but don't get too stressed about them at this point. The TRANSLATE function translates a source string from its character set to the same or a different character set, using the rules specified in a particular translation.

The CONVERT function converts a source string from its form-of-use to another form-of-use, using rules specified in a conversion.

OVERLAY

SQL:1999's OVERLAY string function allows you to replace a portion of a string (character or binary) with new data. You can think of the OVERLAY function as a function that locates a substring in another string (in the same sense that SUBSTRING does, using a start position and a length) and then replaces that string with the value specified in the second operand of the function. For example, the result of

```
OVERLAY ( 'Any Given Sunday' PLACING 'Never On' FROM 1 FOR 9 )
```

is

```
Never On Sunday
```

Note that the length of the replacement text can be different from the length of the text being replaced. You can use the OVERLAY function for character string data and for large object string data.

5.9.3 Datetime Value Functions

Three "current" functions are used in SQL:1999 to get the current date, time, or timestamp. CURRENT_DATE is fairly straightforward and takes no arguments. CURRENT_TIME, LOCALTIME, CURRENT_TIMESTAMP, and LOCALTIMESTAMP each have one argument—precision—that specifies the fractional seconds precision to be returned with the time. CURRENT_TIME and LOCALTIME return a time, while CURRENT_TIMESTAMP and LOCALTIMESTAMP return a timestamp (date + time, as we mentioned in Chapter 4, "Basic Data Definition Language (DDL)"). The complete format for SQL:1999's datetime value function is given in Syntax 5-7.

Syntax 5-7 *Syntax of Datetime Value Functions*

```
CURRENT_DATE
CURRENT_TIME [ ( precision ) ]
LOCALTIME [ ( precision ) ]
CURRENT_TIMESTAMP [ ( precision ) ]
LOCALTIMESTAMP [ ( precision ) ]
```

Three of these (CURRENT_DATE, CURRENT_TIME, and CURRENT_TIMESTAMP) were defined in SQL-92, while the other two (LOCALTIME and LOCALTIMESTAMP) are new to SQL:1999.

The operation of these functions is shown in Example 5-9.

Example 5-9 *Datetime Value Function Examples*

```
CURRENT_DATE            -- returns whatever the current date is, such
                        -- as 1992-06-01; note that the returned value
                        -- is of type DATE, and not a string value
CURRENT_TIME (2)        -- returns the current time to 2 decimal places
                        -- of precision, such as 12:00:05.54-06:00
CURRENT_TIMESTAMP (1)   -- returns a timestamp, such as
                        -- 1980-05-17:09:00:05.2+02:00
LOCALTIME (2)           -- returns the current time to 2 decimal places
                        -- of precision, such as 12:00:05.54
LOCALTIMESTAMP (1)      -- returns a timestamp, such as
                        -- 1980-05-17:09:00:05.2
```

Note that the value returned by CURRENT_TIME or CURRENT_TIMESTAMP is correct for the time zone of your session and includes the time-zone displacement for that time zone. The two new datetime value functions—LOCALTIME and LOCALTIMESTAMP—are respectively analogous to CURRENT_TIME and CURRENT_TIMESTAMP, except that the values returned are "time-zone-less."

5.9.4 Interval Value Functions

SQL:1999 introduces an interval value function that SQL-92 didn't provide. This function is the ABS function and is completely analogous to the ABS numeric value function. It takes a single operand, whose data type must be an interval type, and returns an interval of the identical precision that is guaranteed not to be a negative interval. For example, the value of

```
ABS ( TIME '12:00:00' — TIME '13:00:00' )
```

is the interval that can be expressed by the interval literal

```
INTERVAL +'1:00:00' HOUR TO SECOND
```

5.10 | Value Expressions

There are 10 categories of SQL:1999 value expressions:

1. Numeric value expressions
2. String value expressions
3. Datetime value expressions
4. Interval value expressions
5. Boolean value expressions
6. Array value expressions
7. Row value expressions
8. User-defined type value expressions
9. Reference value expressions
10. Conditional value expressions

We'll discuss the first six types, deferring discussion of row value expressions and of CASE, NULLIF, and COALESCE (the conditional value expressions) until Chapter 6, "Advanced Value Expressions: CASE, CAST, and Row Value Expressions." (Well, we very briefly discuss row value expressions in section 5.10.7 by way of introduction to the subject.) User-defined type value expressions and reference value expressions are mentioned here for completeness only; they are discussed only in Volume 2 of this book.

5.10.1 Numeric Value Expressions

Numeric value expressions allow computation of numeric values using addition, subtraction, multiplication, and division. Any numeric type can participate in such expressions, and they can be mixed. SQL defines rules for the data type of the result of an arithmetic expression based on the data types of the operands. In general, if any approximate numeric type participates in a numeric value expression, the result will have some approximate numeric type. If both operands are exact numeric, the result is also exact numeric; if the operation is division, the result will have implementation-defined precision. The specifics of the result will be defined by your implementation; the standard doesn't define it because of the widely differing platforms on which SQL systems are implemented.

Let's take a look at the complete syntax of the numeric value expression, as shown in Syntax 5-8.

Syntax 5-8 *Syntax of Numeric Value Expressions*

```
<numeric value expression> ::=
    <term>
  | <numeric value expression> <plus sign> <term>
  | <numeric value expression> <minus sign> <term>

<term> ::=
    <factor>
  | <term> <asterisk> <factor>
  | <term> <solidus> <factor>

<factor> ::=
    [ <sign> ] <numeric primary>

<numeric primary> ::=
    <value expression primary>
  | <numeric value function>
```

(Note: In the above BNF, a "solidus" is a forward slash: /.)

As you can see from the BNF, numeric value expressions allow leading ("monadic") signs that have higher priority than multiplication and division, which in turn have higher precedence than addition and subtraction; in other words, the normal rules of arithmetic apply to SQL's numeric value expressions.

Some examples of valid numeric value expressions are

- -3
- 5 + 1
- 8/3-15
- 16* (5-4)

All of the preceding examples show the use of numeric literals in numeric value expressions, but you can use column names, parameters and host variables, and subqueries (see Chapter 9, "Advanced SQL Query Expressions"), like the following:

- +estimate
- sal * 1.15
- :velocity / 2.0E3
- 18 + (cost - (price / 6.5 + 2 * :adjust))

5.10.2 String Value Expressions

Concatenation is the only operator allowed in string value expressions in the SQL:1999 standard, but it is possible that implementations might provide other operators as an extension. Concatenation is denoted by two vertical bars (||). Two or more input values are concatenated together to form a new string value.

Example 5-10 *Examples of Concatenation*

```
'Star ' || 'Wars'          -- results in 'Star Wars'
'Notting' || ' ' || 'Hill'  -- results in 'Notting Hill'
cust_name || ' ' || cust_address
                            -- results in a single string with a
                            -- customer name and address
B'101011' || B'0001'        -- results in B'1010110001'
```

String value expressions apply to character strings, bit strings, and binary strings, but you cannot mix those three types in a single expression.

5.10.3 Datetime Value Expressions

Datetime value expressions allow you to combine datetime and interval values in your SQL statements. The syntax is shown in Syntax 5-9.

Syntax 5-9 *Syntax of Datetime Value Expressions*

```
<datetime value expression> ::=
      <datetime term>
    | <interval value expression> <plus sign> <datetime term>
```

```
            | <datetime value expression> <plus sign> <interval term>
            | <datetime value expression> <minus sign> <interval term>

       <datetime term> ::=
           <datetime factor>

       <datetime factor> ::=
           <datetime primary> [ <time zone> ]

       <datetime primary> ::=
               <value expression primary>
            | <datetime value function>

       <time zone> ::=
           AT <time zone specifier>

       <time zone specifier> ::=
               LOCAL
            | TIME ZONE <interval primary>
```

Datetime value expressions operate on date-oriented data types, including DATE, TIME, TIMESTAMP, and INTERVAL. (We will use the word *datetime* to express dates and times in general when we don't need to distinguish between the two.)

The result of a datetime value expression is always another datetime. Actually, that's part of the definition of the term *datetime value expression:* some expressions that might seem to be datetime value expressions, such as subtracting one datetime from another, actually produce intervals or other data types and are not classified as datetime value expressions in SQL:1999. For example, if you subtract an interval from a datetime, or add an interval to a datetime, the result is another datetime. The expression

```
CURRENT_DATE + INTERVAL '1' DAY
```

has the same value that CURRENT_DATE would give you tomorrow. (Recall that addition is commutative; therefore, you can add a datetime to an interval or an interval to a datetime and get the same result—although the same isn't true for subtraction.)

SQL optionally manages time zone information along with datetimes, if you use the data types TIME WITH TIME ZONE or TIMESTAMP WITH TIME ZONE. Times are handled by the database system in UTC (universal coordinated time), which we all used to call GMT (Greenwich mean time). Time zones are really nothing more than offsets from UTC. (We addressed this in Chapter 2, "Introduction to SQL:1999," so we won't repeat it here.)

You can tell SQL that a datetime is expressed as a local time (in the time zone associated with your SQL session), or you can give it an explicit time zone. For example, a valid datetime value expression is

```
TIME '10:45:00' AT LOCAL
```

This tells the database system that we want it to represent (or store, perhaps) the time of 10:45 A.M. in our local time zone. On the other hand, we could have said

```
TIME '10:45:00' AT TIME ZONE INTERVAL '+09:00' HOUR TO MINUTE
```

and it would tell the database system that we want to represent the time in Tokyo. The expression that follows the words TIME ZONE represents an interval (with only hours and minutes fields, of course); it can be a literal, a host variable or parameter, a database column, or any other value. Its value has to be between +13:00 and −12:59, though.

5.10.4 Interval Value Expressions

If you subtract one datetime from another, you will get an interval as the result. Example 5-11 illustrates this capability in a casual manner.

Example 5-11 *Example of Interval Value Expression*

```
CURRENT_DATE - date_released -- results in the time a
                             -- movie or CD has been available
```

The correct syntax for this expression is a little different from the example. You must express that concept as follows:

```
(CURRENT_DATE - date_released) YEAR TO MONTH
```

The reason that the previous expression is required arises from the fact that the subtraction of two datetimes *could* (theoretically) result in an invalid interval (that is, an interval that is neither a year-month interval nor a day-time interval).

However, SQL requires you to specify what sort of interval you wish to get from the subtraction. We chose a year-month interval for this example, but you could also choose a day-time interval if that serves your needs better. With that specification, SQL is able to produce a valid interval of the correct precision.

In addition, you can add two intervals together or subtract two intervals to get another interval.

```
INTERVAL '6' DAY - INTERVAL '1' DAY -- results in an interval of 5 days
INTERVAL '6' DAY + INTERVAL '1' DAY -- results in an interval of 7 days
```

You cannot mix year-month and day-time intervals in a single interval value expression because the result would not meet the condition of being either a year-month interval or a day-time interval. However, it is valid in SQL to write some expressions that *appear* to violate this restriction:

```
DATE '1999-12-01' + INTERVAL '01' MONTH + INTERVAL '01' DAY
```

In that expression, we've added one month and one day to a specific date, which certainly appears to mix two different types of interval (year-month and day-time) into a single expression. If we used parentheses to group the expression like this:

```
DATE '1999-12-01' + ( INTERVAL '01' MONTH + INTERVAL '01' DAY )
```

then it would, indeed, be an invalid expression. However, SQL groups the expression like this:

```
( DATE '1999-12-01' + INTERVAL '01' MONTH ) + INTERVAL '01' DAY
```

making the result acceptable, since the intermediate result of adding the DATE to the year-month interval is just another DATE to which the day-time interval can be added.

You can also multiply or divide an interval by a numeric constant to get another interval.

```
INTERVAL '2' DAY * 3    -- results in an interval of 6 days
3 * INTERVAL '2' DAY    -- results in an interval of 6 days
INTERVAL '6' DAY / 2    -- results in an interval of 3 days
```

And, of course, intervals can be negative or positive, so you can also write things like

```
INTERVAL -'6' DAY        -- results in an interval of -6 days
```

which is equivalent to

```
- INTERVAL '6' DAY
```

However, the preferred syntax is to put the minus sign inside the apostrophes, like this:

```
INTERVAL '-6' DAY        -- results in an interval of -6 days
```

As always, although we have used literals in our examples, you can use any appropriate value expression throughout.

5.10.5 Boolean Value Expression

As you read in section 2.4.7, "Booleans," a Boolean value is one that expresses only the concepts of True, False, and Unknown (the last concept arising from SQL's three-valued logic and null values, about which you learned in section 2.5, "Logic and Null Values").

As with (most) other SQL data types, SQL:1999 has the ability to combine Boolean values through value expressions. However, the operators that SQL provides for use in Boolean value expressions are not the special-character sorts of operators that SQL provides for numeric, string, and datetime expressions, or that some other programming languages—C comes immediately to mind—for their Boolean expressions. Instead of operators like +, -, *, or ||, or even &, |, and ^, SQL:1999's Boolean operators are expressed using the keywords AND, OR, NOT, and IS. The syntax for SQL:1999's Boolean value expressions is shown in Syntax 5-10. If you compare this with SQL-92's syntax for search conditions (included for your convenience in Syntax 7-9, "SQL-92 Syntax of Search Conditions"), you'll immediately observe the similarities. The reasons are obvious: search conditions combine the results of predicates, and the results of predicates are truth values—that is, Boolean values. You can also see in Syntax 7-10, "SQL:1999 Syntax of Search Conditions," that SQL:1999 has defined a search condition to be nothing more than a Boolean value expression.

Syntax 5-10 *Boolean Value Expression Syntax*

```
<boolean value expression> ::=
    <boolean term>
  | <boolean value expression> OR <boolean term>

<boolean term> ::=
    <boolean factor>
  | <boolean term> AND <boolean factor>

<boolean factor> ::=
    [ NOT ] <boolean test>

<boolean test> ::=
    <boolean primary> [ IS [ NOT ] <truth value> ]

<truth value> ::=
    TRUE
  | FALSE
  | UNKNOWN

<boolean primary> ::=
    <predicate>
  | <parenthesized boolean value expression>
  | <nonparenthesized value expression primary>

<parenthesized boolean value expression> ::=
    <left paren> <boolean value expression> <right paren>
```

Because Boolean value expressions and search conditions have so much in common (they are, after all, the same thing), we won't go into the details of Boolean logic in SQL at this point, but we'll defer that discussion to the place where it's the most relevant—section 7.14, "Search Conditions."

5.10.6 Array Value Expressions

Section 2.4.8, "Collection (or Array) Types," introduced you to SQL:1999's array type. In that section, you learned that SQL's arrays are a little different from the arrays provided by some of the more traditional programming languages such as C, COBOL, or Pascal. (Different languages specify different index values—0,

1, or even user-specified—for the first element of an array. SQL:1999 specifies that the first element of an array is element number 1.) In particular, we told you that SQL's ARRAY type is rather analogous to SQL's CHARACTER VARYING data type in that a specific ARRAY type can hold any number of elements, from no elements up to the maximum number declared for it. We call that maximum number of elements declared for some site to be the maximum cardinality of the ARRAY type and the number of elements in the array at any instant to be its actual cardinality.

One consequence of this aspect of arrays in SQL is that you can combine two arrays into a new array in much the same way that you can combine two character strings: through the use of the concatenation operator, as seen in Example 5-12.

Example 5-12 *Array Concatenation*

```
SELECT CARDINALITY(column1 || column2)
FROM some_table
WHERE column1[1] = 10
```

In Example 5-12, we used the CARDINALITY function that you saw in section 5.9.1 to learn the combined cardinalities of the arrays stored in two columns of rows where the first element of the array in one of those columns has the value 10. The concatenation operator (||) was used to combine the two arrays into one. If column1 had been declared to have a maximum cardinality of 20 and column2 had been declared to have a maximum cardinality of 50, then the greatest value that would ever be returned from the CARDINALITY function would be 70; however, it could return any value from 0 through 70, depending on the actual number of elements stored in the arrays for specific rows in the table. (Actually, the value returned in this case will be between 1 and 70, since our WHERE clause requires that the ARRAY in COLUMN1 have at least one element, COLUMN1[1].)

The only other type of array value expression is one that represents an array as a sort of pseudo-literal value, called an *array value constructor*, which you can see in Example 5-13.

Example 5-13 *Array Value Constructor*

```
ARRAY [10, 12, -5, 2000]
```

The array value constructor shown in Example 5-13 would generate an array having four elements and whose element type is some numeric type (in fact, SQL:1999's rules make it an exact numeric type, with implementation-defined precision and scale 0). The array thus constructed can be readily assigned to any site whose type is a numeric array with maximum cardinality of at least 4. Depending on the type of operation causing the assignment (e.g., retrieval from a column of a table, updating a row of a table), the operation might result in the raising of a warning condition or even an exception condition, quite analogous to assignment of varying length character strings.

A special case of the array value constructor is ARRAY[], which creates an array whose cardinality is 0—it has no elements in it. Of course, because no elements were specified, the element type of this array is not known; however, this array can be assigned to any site whose type is some array type, regardless of the element type of the site.

5.10.7 Row Value Expressions

As you are aware by now, one of the most basic of SQL's data constructs is the row. In SQL-92, there was no way to declare a column (or a variable or a parameter) to have a data type that was a row type, but SQL:1999 has added this capability (called *anonymous row types,* as we discussed in section 2.4.9, "Anonymous Row Types").

Although SQL:1999 provides a syntactic element that it calls <row value expression>, the truth is that you cannot combine two (or more) row values together in any operators.

Therefore, the only valid <row value expression>s in SQL:1999 are the names of data elements whose data types are row types (such as column names) and the "row value constructor" that SQL:1999 provides:

```
[ ROW ] ( field-value , field-value , ... )
```

The number and data types of the field values are determined by the context in which the row value constructor appears; for example, they would have to match the number and data types of the fields of the row type of the site to which they are being assigned.

5.11 | Chapter Summary

In this chapter we've covered SQL:1999's basic functions and expressions. You should be aware, however, that there are some functions and expressions with which you may be familiar that aren't supported by SQL:1999. For example, some string operations, such as "stuffing" a substring into another string at a particular starting point, aren't included among the formal SQL:1999 functions. Some SQL:1999 implementations may include extensions to support these operations; product reference manuals often provide details and, if supported, applicable syntax. SQL:1999 does, however, support a far richer set of functions than do previous versions, bringing SQL standard capabilities more in line with those many readers are accustomed to in personal computer and other database environments.

The subjects discussed in this chapter will help you round out the basic operations discussed in Chapter 3, "Basic Table Creation and Data Manipulation," especially in terms of expanding your repertoire of manipulation tasks with respect to obtaining summary information using set functions. In Chapter 6, "Advanced Value Expressions: CASE, CAST, and Row Value Expressions," we'll discuss how to perform explicit data conversions using the CAST specification, as well as conditional value expressions using CASE, NULLIF, and COALESCE.

Advanced Value Expressions: CASE, CAST, and Row Value Expressions

6.1 | Introduction

In Chapter 5, "Values, Basic Functions, and Expressions," we covered the basic set functions, value functions, and value expressions incorporated into SQL. To write complex applications, however, you will often need more power than is available through these basic facilities. Data sublanguages have often been criticized for their lack of rich programming constructs, forcing users and developers to rely on the facilities of host languages or external environments. SQL:1999 introduces some of these facilities to the SQL world, including

- a conditional expression (CASE)
- a data conversion expression (CAST)
- a way to deal with an entire row of data at one time (row value constructor)

6.2 | The CASE Expression

There are many application situations where you might find it necessary to change the representation of some of your data. Applications developers often strive to find a balance among storage requirements (limiting the amount of storage needed), understandability, and other factors. For example, you might code Marital Status as 1, 2, 3, 4, meaning single, married, divorced, or widowed. It is often more efficient to store the short code than the long one, but human readers of reports will prefer the longer words. Furthermore, short numeric codes tend to be independent of local language requirements, while human readers of reports usually prefer the reports to use words and phrases from their own languages. This conversion shouldn't require host program intervention but should be manageable in the DBMS.

Additionally, applications sometimes need to generate null values based on information derived from the database and should be able to do so without involving the host programs. Conversely, you may wish to convert a null into some more concrete value, like a zero (0).

The SQL:1999 solution to these problems is a CASE expression. This is similar in concept to the CASE statement of some programming languages but is a conditional *expression,* not an executable statement. Therefore, it can be used everywhere that a value expression can be used.

6.2.1 CASE and Search Conditions

The syntax of CASE is shown in Syntax 6-1.

Syntax 6-1 *CASE Statement*

```
CASE
   WHEN search-condition₁ THEN result₁
   WHEN search-condition₂ THEN result₂
   ...
   WHEN search-conditionₙ THEN resultₙ
   ELSE resultₓ
END
```

If search-condition$_1$ is true, then the value of the CASE is result$_1$. If not, then search-condition$_2$ is tested; if it is true, then the value is result$_2$. If none of the search-condition$_i$ is true, then the value of the CASE is result$_x$. All of the result$_i$ must have *comparable* data types. The data type of the CASE is the data type determined by the union data type rules (discussed in section 9.7, "Result Data Types of Columns of UNION, EXCEPT, and INTERSECT").

The ELSE result$_x$ is optional. If it's not specified, then ELSE NULL is implicit. At least one of the result$_i$ has to be something besides the keyword NULL.

As an example, say that we need to make some type of calculation based on the NUMBER_OF_PROBLEMS column in a CUSTOMERS table to maintain a moving average of our customer support effectiveness. Let's say we assign some type of weighting that will be used for problem resolution priorities. We can use the CASE expression with predicates, as shown in Example 6-1.

Example 6-1 *Simple CASE Statement*

```
SELECT cust_name,
       CASE
         WHEN number_of_problems = 0
           THEN 100
         WHEN number_of_problems > 0
          AND number_of_problems < 4
           THEN number_of_problems * 500
         WHEN number_of_problems >= 4
          AND number_of_problems <= 9
           THEN number_of_problems * 400
          ELSE (number_of_problems * 300) + 250
       END,
       cust_address
FROM customers
```

Let's take a look at another example using CASE (Example 6-2).

Example 6-2 *Using CASE with an SQL UPDATE Statement*

```
UPDATE employees
  SET salary = CASE
                 WHEN dept = 'Video'
                   THEN salary * 1.1
                 WHEN dept = 'Music'
                   THEN salary * 1.2
                 ELSE 0
               END
```

Still another example—which can help avoid getting certain types of errors with which most programmers are familiar—is illustrated in Example 6-3.

Example 6-3 *Using CASE to Avoid Unwanted Exception*

```
...
CASE
  WHEN n <> 0 THEN x/n
  ELSE 0
END
```

6.2.2 CASE and Values

You can use a shorthand version of the CASE statement for value comparisons. If $value_t = value_1$, then the value of the CASE is $result_1$. If not, then if $value_t = value_2$, then the result is $result_2$. If none of $value_1 \ldots value_n$ are equal to the desired $value_t$, then the value of the CASE is $result_x$. All of the $result_i$ can be a value expression, and at least one of them must be an expression and not the keyword NULL. All of the $value_i$ must be comparable, and all of the results must have comparable data types. The data type of the CASE is the data type determined by the union data type rules.

The syntax for this shorthand version of CASE is shown in Syntax 6-2.

Syntax 6-2 *Shorthand CASE Syntax*

```
CASE value_t
  WHEN value_1 THEN result_1
  WHEN value_2 THEN result_2
  ...
  WHEN value_n THEN result_n
  ELSE result_x
END
```

In fact, this is really just a shorthand for the equivalent CASE expression:

```
CASE
  WHEN value_t = value_1 THEN result_1
  WHEN value_t = value_2 THEN result_2
  ...
  WHEN value_t = value_n THEN result_n
  ELSE result_x
END
```

The ELSE $result_x$ is again optional. If it's not specified, then ELSE NULL is implicit. At least one of the $result_i$ has to be something besides the keyword NULL. The longer, more explicit form of the CASE statement and the shorter version can be transformed to one another in many cases. However, it is easy to find examples of the longer version that cannot be transformed into the shorter version (examples in which the search-condition$_i$ are not all of the form value$_t$ = value$_i$).

Assume that in our movie_titles table we decided to encode the column movie_type with an integer rather than the CHARACTER(10) needed to spell out Horror, Comedy, Romance, and our other movie types. We can still return a text string to applications through the use of the CASE expression, as shown in Example 6-4.

Example 6-4 *Using CASE with Encoded Values*

```
SELECT title,
       CASE movie_type
          WHEN 1 THEN 'Horror'
          WHEN 2 THEN 'Comedy'
          WHEN 3 THEN 'Romance'
          WHEN 4 THEN 'Western'
          WHEN.....
          ELSE NULL
       END,
       our_cost
FROM movie_titles ;
```

6.2.3 NULLIF

SQL provides null values and defines the behavior of the various arithmetic and other operators when applied to null values. Sometimes, however, people choose to represent missing or unknown or inapplicable information in other ways, either for historical reasons or general preference. For example, missing OUR_COST values might be represented by a value of –1. And, it is sometimes useful to convert such missing information flags to null values, in order to get the null behavior defined by SQL. This can be done with a CASE expression, as follows:

```
...WHERE tape_sales_revenue / CASE
                                 WHEN our_tape_cost = -1
                                    THEN NULL
                                 ELSE our_tape_cost
                              END > 52
```

Such a CASE expression is expected to be relatively common, so a special syntax shorthand is provided for it. In the WHERE clause,

```
...WHERE tape_sales_revenue / NULLIF(our_tape_cost, -1) > 52
```

the expression NULLIF(our_cost, -1), is simply a shorthand for

```
CASE WHEN our_tape_cost=-1 THEN NULL ELSE our_tape_cost END
```

6.2.4 COALESCE

The final form of the CASE expression is the COALESCE expression, whose syntax is given in Syntax 6-3:

Syntax 6-3 *COALESCE Syntax*

```
COALESCE (value₁, value₂, . . . valueₙ)
```

If $value_1$ is not null, then the value of the COALESCE is $value_1$. If $value_1$ is null, then $value_2$ is checked. This continues until either a non-null value $value_i$ is found—in which case, the value of the COALESCE is $value_i$—or every value, including $value_n$, is found to be null, in which case the value of the COALESCE is NULL. The data types of all the $value_1 \ldots value_n$ must be *comparable*; the data type of the COALESCE is the data type determined by the same union data type rules applicable to the NULLIF expression.

COALESCE is also just a shorthand (as is NULLIF) for a variation of CASE that is used quite often. Therefore,

```
COALESCE (value₁, value₂, value₃)
```

is equivalent to

```
CASE
    WHEN value₁ IS NOT NULL
        THEN value₁
    WHEN value₂ IS NOT NULL
        THEN value₂
    ELSE value₃
END
```

For example:

```
COALESCE (salary, commission, subsistence)
```

In the context of a query expression, you might issue the SQL statement shown in Example 6-5:

Example 6-5 *Using COALESCE*

```
SELECT name, job_title, COALESCE (salary, commission, subsistence)
FROM job_assignments
```

This expression would first attempt to return a person's salary. In the absence of a regular salary (that is, the stored value is null), a commission is sought. Subsequently, in the absence of a commission, a subsistence (allowance) is checked. If none of the columns has a non-null value, then null is returned.

Actually, there are other, more important uses for COALESCE, which we will discuss in Chapter 8, "Working with Multiple Tables: The Relational Operators," in the context of the OUTER JOIN.

Syntax 6-4 summarizes the syntax of the CASE expression.

Syntax 6-4 *The Syntax of CASE Expressions*

- NULLIF (value-expression , value-expression)
- COALESCE (value-expression , value-expression , ...)
- CASE test-expression
    WHEN compare-expression THEN { result-expression | NULL }
    ...
  [ELSE { result-expression | NULL }]
- CASE
    WHEN search-condition THEN { result-expression | NULL }
    ...
  [ELSE { result-expression | NULL }]

6.3 | The CAST Expression

SQL has always been considered a *strongly typed* language. This means that you cannot have expressions that contain mixes of arbitrary data types. Some languages, such as PL/I, allow almost completely arbitrary mixing of data types in expressions; for example, you can add an integer and a character string together (as long as the character string "looks like" an integer), or you can concatenate an integer and a character string. Other languages, such as Pascal, don't allow mixing of *any* sort; you cannot even add a short integer with a long integer in a language as strongly typed as Pascal.

SQL falls somewhere in between these extremes but is closer to Pascal than to PL/I. In SQL-86 and SQL-89, you could compare or add an INTEGER with a SMALLINT, but not with a CHARACTER. In SQL:1999, as in SQL-92, you can mix exact numerics and characters in a single expression by CASTing to appropriate data types.

There are many times when your application knows that the contents of a character string are limited to digits that can be readily interpreted as an integer. You would like to be able to add the integer value corresponding to that character string to an actual INTEGER, but SQL-86 and SQL-89 wouldn't let you. Well, SQL:1999 doesn't let you do it indiscriminately—that is, without expressing it precisely. However, if you express it appropriately, you can do it in SQL:1999 and needn't escape to your host program to perform the necessary type mixing and conversion functions.

The appropriate way to express this is to explicitly do a data conversion using the CAST expression. CAST allows you to convert data of one type to a different type, subject to a few restrictions:

1. You can convert any exact or approximate numeric value to any other numeric data type. If the value being converted doesn't fit in the new data type (if you attempt to convert a very large INTEGER to a SMALLINT, for example), then you get an error. If you try to convert a value with a fractional component to a type with less fractional precision, then the system will round or truncate (the choice of which is implementation-defined) for you.

2. You can convert any exact or approximate numeric value to any character string type.

3. You can convert any exact numeric value to a single-component interval, such as INTERVAL MINUTE or INTERVAL YEAR.

4. You can convert any character string to any other data type, with a few restrictions. First, if you are converting to another character string type, then they must have the same character set (see Chapter 21, "Internationalization Aspects of SQL:1999"). Second, the contents of the character string must make sense for the target data type; for example, if the new type is DATE, then the character string must contain four digits, a hyphen,

two digits, another hyphen, and two more digits. In fact, the character string must exactly mimic a valid literal of the data type to which you are CASTing. When converting character strings to numeric, datetime, or interval types, leading and trailing spaces are ignored. When converting a character string to a bit string, the bit representation of the characters (in the encoding used by the character string's coded character set) are placed into the bit string.

5. You can convert a DATE to a character string or to a TIMESTAMP (filling in the TIME part of the TIMESTAMP with 00:00:00). You can convert a TIME to a character string, a TIME with different fractional seconds precision, or a TIMESTAMP (filling in the DATE part of the TIMESTAMP with values for "today"). You can convert a TIMESTAMP to a character string, a DATE, a TIME, or another TIMESTAMP with different fractional seconds precision.

6. You can convert a year-month INTERVAL to a character string, to an exact numeric, or to another year-month INTERVAL with different leading field precision. You can convert a day-time INTERVAL to a character string, to an exact numeric, or to another day-time INTERVAL with different leading field precision.

7. You can convert a bit string to a character string, or to a bit string (which, of course, has no real effect). When converting a bit string to a character string, the bits are placed into the character string as though they were the bits of characters.

8. You can convert a binary string to another binary string or to a character string. Since binary strings are inherently variable in length, this doesn't add much value, except that you might get a warning condition raised if you attempt to convert a binary string to another binary string whose maximum length is shorter than the value you're trying to convert.

9. You can convert a Boolean to a character string (or to another Boolean, but that doesn't really change things, does it?). If you do, then the Boolean value True is converted to the character string 'TRUE' and False is converted to 'FALSE'.

The entire syntax for CAST is summarized in Syntax 6-5.

Syntax 6-5 *The Syntax of CAST Expressions*

```
CAST ( { value-expression | NULL } AS { data-type | domain } )
```

One use for CAST is to make (one or both of) two tables that are not quite the same structure look enough alike for them to be combined in, for example, a

UNION operation. For example, if you have one table of EMPLOYEES that has HIRE_ DATE defined as a DATE and a second table of INTERVIEWEES that has INTERVIEW_DATE defined as a CHARACTER, you could CAST one of these two columns to be the same data type as the other. This would make the columns into the same data type and would contribute to making it possible to union the two tables, an operation that requires very similar column properties (see Chapter 8, "Working with Multiple Tables: The Relational Operators").

Another use is to make it possible to compare rows drawn from two tables. In the previous example, if you wanted to JOIN the tables (also discussed in Chapter 8, "Working with Multiple Tables: The Relational Operators") based on certain column values in two tables being equal to one another, you could have a WHERE clause as shown in Example 6-6.

Example 6-6 *Using CAST in a WHERE clause*

```
WHERE employees.hire_date =
        CAST (interviewees.interview_date AS DATE)
```

For making two tables union-compatible with each other, the ability to CAST (NULL AS datatype) is invaluable. It allows you to "fill" in a column that has no correspondence in one table with a column of the proper data type containing null values.

A very important use for CAST is to allow you to access database data that your host language can't handle (for example, DATE data from any host language). By using CAST, you can retrieve and store such data easily. (For the datetime types, you would CAST to and from CHARACTER, for example.)

6.4 Row Value Constructors

In SQL-86 and SQL-89, virtually all data operations were on single values or single columns. For example, if you needed to compare all columns of a row in one table with all columns in a row of another table, you would have to write a fairly complicated expression.

Beginning in SQL-92 and continuing in SQL:1999, however, you can do it (for some predicates, but not all of them) very simply. For example, you might write

```
WHERE (C1, C2, C3) = (CA, CB, CC)
```

whereas, in SQL-89, you would need to have written

```
WHERE C1 = CA AND C2 = CB AND C3 = CC
```

A row value constructor is basically a parenthesized list of values. It can be used in many places where a value is permitted (but, unfortunately, not in every place) as long as the number of those values is appropriate for the context in which the constructor is used. (The number of values in a row value constructor is called its *degree*; this concept is discussed in section 6.5.) The syntax for a row value is given in Syntax 6-6, with six distinct alternatives from which you can choose, depending on the circumstances.

Syntax 6-6 *Syntax of Row Value Constructors*

- value-expression
- NULL
- DEFAULT
- ARRAY[]
- row-subquery
- (row-value-constructor , row-value-constructor , ...)
- ROW (row-value-constructor , row-value-constructor , ...)

If the row value constructor is used as the insert-values of an INSERT statement, then any value can be NULL, DEFAULT, or ARRAY[]. NULL obviously makes the inserted value for the corresponding column in the table null, while DEFAULT makes the inserted value the default value for the column. ARRAY[] is valid only if the destination is an array and it causes an empty array (one with no elements) to be inserted.

The values (other than NULL, DEFAULT, and ARRAY[]) can be simple values or value expressions. In cases where the row value constructor can be only a single value (degree equal to 1), the parentheses may be left off.

A row value constructor can be thought of as a literal for an entire row. Although this is probably carrying the analogy too far, the individual values don't have to be literals, but can be parameters, host variables, or even subqueries. A row value constructor can itself be a *subquery* (a concept introduced in Chapter 7, "Predicates," and explored in detail in Chapter 9, section 9.10, "Subqueries"). In this case, if the cardinality of the subquery (that is, the number of rows returned by the subquery) is 0, then the row value constructor is a row of null values; if it's 1, then the row value constructor is the row returned by the subquery; if it's greater than 1, then you get an error.

Let's look at another example, one somewhat more complicated. If you were to write

```
WHERE ( c1, c2, c3 ) < ( ca, cb, cc)
```

you would get exactly the same effect as

```
WHERE ( c1 < ca ) OR
      ( c1 = ca AND c2 < cb ) OR
      ( c1 = ca AND c2 = cb AND c3 < cc )
```

The less-than operation is evaluated left to right on the row values and stops whenever it finds a pair that satisfies the comparison. Note that this is the same result that ORDER BY (see Chapter 13, "Cursors") would give if the two expressions were rows in a table.

6.5 | Table Value Constructors

A table value constructor is nothing more than a way for you to write a "table literal" in your SQL code. As with the row value constructor, the contents do not have to be literals—they can also be value expressions, depending on the context—but it's convenient to think of this as a table literal, even if it is not strictly accurate.

The syntax for SQL:1999's table value constructor is shown in Syntax 6-7.

Syntax 6-7 *Table Value Constructor Syntax*

```
VALUES row-value-expression , row-value-expression , ...
```

You can have as few as one row-value-expression or as many as your implementation allows (usually limited by the permitted length of an SQL statement). The value of a table value constructor is not permitted to be null, meaning that the value of none of the row-value-expressions it contains can be null (but, of course, that does not prohibit the value of one element of a given row-value-expression from being null). That is mostly likely to occur if the row-value-expression is a subquery that returns no rows. Furthermore, the degree (that is, the number of columns) of all of the row-value-expressions in a table value constructor must be the same. In addition, the data types of corresponding columns in those row-value-expressions must be compatible, using SQL's rules for UNION compatibility (and the data type of the corresponding column of the table value constructor is determined by those same UNION compatibility rules).

6.6 | Array Value Constructors

The array value constructor is analogous to the table value constructor in several ways. First, it can be conveniently thought of as an array literal, although its elements are not strictly limited to literals. Second, there are restrictions on the relationships among the components. The syntax of the array value constructor is shown in Syntax 6-8.

Syntax 6-8 *Array Value Constructor Syntax*

```
ARRAY [ array-element , array-element , ... ]
```

The data type of the array that results is determined by the data types of the various array-elements. The data types of each array-element is considered, and SQL's rules for UNION compatibility are applied to determine the data type of the array as a whole. The values actually used in the array that is constructed are cast from their apparent data type to the data type determined for the array. See Example 6-7 to understand how this works.

Example 6-7 *Array Value Constructor Example*

```
ARRAY [ 10 , 13.5 , 5.3E2 ]
```

In the array constructed in Example 6-7, there are three elements. The first element looks an awful lot like an integer; and we know it's a number, in any case. The second element, also a number, isn't an integer but is apparently exact numeric. The third is also a number but has the characteristics of an approximate numeric value. According to SQL's rules for UNION compatibility, the result data type is approximate numeric with implementation-defined precision. In this case, let's assume that the implementation chooses REAL as the result data type. Therefore, the array we just constructed can be specified to have the data type

```
REAL ARRAY[3]
```

6.7 | Chapter Summary

In this chapter, we discussed how to use SQL's more advanced value expressions. The CASE expression allows you to return values that are computed from database values (or, for that matter, to store values that are computed from input values). The CAST expression allows you to perform explicit data conversions in your SQL application. The row value constructor allows you to manipulate rows of data at one time instead of one value at a time.

Beginning in SQL-92, and continuing with SQL:1999, the advanced value expressions were among the most significant enhancements as compared with previous versions of the standard. For example, the CAST data conversions are far easier to use than the old way that required host program intervention. Similarly, the CASE expression brings host language programming constructs (somewhat) into the data sublanguage world, permitting multiple-choice operations within the context of your SQL statements. Finally, row value constructors provide an alternative, easier-to-use method of multiple column value comparisons and other operations than previous SQL syntax permitted.

In this chapter and in Chapter 5, "Values, Basic Functions, and Expressions," we've taken our first steps beyond basic SQL syntax. You already knew, for example, how to create simple tables (introduced in Chapter 3, "Basic Table Creation and Data Manipulation") as well as other data objects such as schemas, views, domains, and the like (discussed in Chapter 4, "Basic Data Definition Language (DDL)"). The basic data manipulation statements discussed in Chapter 3, "Basic Table Creation and Data Manipulation," have been enhanced with simple value expressions and value specifications, special values, and now *advanced* value expressions.

In Chapter 7, "Predicates," we turn our attention to the subject of *predicates*, features that allow you to perform wildcard pattern matching, range of value and list of value searching, and other functions that will further add to your SQL repertoire.

Chapter 7

Predicates

7.1 | Introduction

In Chapter 3, "Basic Table Creation and Data Manipulation," we discussed basic SQL:1999 data manipulation statements. We illustrated that the power of SQL:1999 is unleashed when you can specify criteria for your data retrieval and modification operations. For example, SELECT * FROM MOVIE_TITLES is a valid data retrieval statement, but the SELECT statement becomes far more useful when you specify search parameters through the use of facilities such as the WHERE clause.

Even though we didn't explicitly state it in Chapter 3, "Basic Table Creation and Data Manipulation," we looked at some basic predicates in that chapter. More specifically, we illustrated how simple comparison predicates, using familiar symbols such as =, <, and >, can be used to restrict your data manipulation statements to operations on certain data.

In this chapter, we take a more extensive look at the different types of SQL:1999 predicates, including other comparison predicates. We discuss IN, LIKE, NULL, EXISTS, and others. We also introduce the concept of a subquery in the context of certain predicates. As we've discussed with regard to the contents of previous chapters, much of this chapter also applies to user-defined types, but discussion of that topic is deferred until Volume 2.

7.2 | What Is a Predicate?

A predicate is really an expression that asserts a fact about values. The expression can be True, meaning that the fact is correct; it can be False, meaning that the fact is incorrect; or it can (often) be Unknown, meaning that the DBMS is unable to determine whether the fact is correct or incorrect. (Unknown can occur if some of the values are null, for example.)

7.3 | Subqueries

In order to understand how some of the SQL:1999 predicates function, we need to briefly explain the concept of a subquery. We introduced an example of a subquery in Chapter 5, "Values, Basic Functions, and Expressions," and we discuss them in more detail in Chapter 9, "Advanced SQL Query Expressions."

A subquery is a query expression that appears in the body of another expression, such as a SELECT statement, an UPDATE statement, or a DELETE statement. The statement shown in Example 7-1 uses a subquery to locate movies whose titles are found in a selection of movies in which Mel Gibson stars.

Example 7-1 *Using a Subquery*

```
SELECT title, dvds_in_stock
FROM movie_titles
WHERE title IN
      ( SELECT movie_title
        FROM movies_stars
        WHERE
            actor_last_name = 'Gibson'
          AND
            actor_first_name = 'Mel' )   ;
```

Subqueries are one method by which information from multiple tables can be related to one another. In the above example, the subquery—the SELECT of movie titles in which Mel Gibson stars—is evaluated, and a list of movie titles is produced, internal to the system. Then, the main query—matching the TITLE column from MOVIE_TITLES with the produced list of Mel Gibson films—produces the list of titles from the number of DVD titles we have in stock. (Incidentally, there is at least one more way to handle this request, by joining the two tables and filtering the result with a WHERE clause. We leave that solution as an exercise for the reader after Chapter 8 has been read. We will discuss the various types of JOIN operations in the next chapter.)

Note the use of the keyword IN, which we discuss later in this chapter as one of our predicates. The IN predicate is used to perform subquery searching and matching, as we shall see.

Again, we'll discuss subqueries in more detail in Chapter 9, "Advanced SQL Query Expressions," specifically in the context of multiple nestings. For the purposes of this chapter, we discuss several predicates—IN, EXISTS, UNIQUE, and MATCH—that utilize subqueries in their operations. We point out that most predicates can be True, False, or Unknown, but a few (e.g., NULL) can only be True or False.

7.4 | Comparison Predicate

Among the most commonly used predicates are those that perform comparisons. First, we'll discuss the basic ones with which you're no doubt already familiar from your own programming background, and then discuss SQL comparison predicates not commonly found in other languages.

Before we start examining specific predicates, we think that a word about comparisons involving null values is in order. In SQL, two values can either be equal or not equal, unless one or both of them are the null value. If either or both are the null value, then we cannot say whether or not they are equal or unequal; the result of the comparison is *unknown*. Some predicates (for example, see section 7.5) account for null values directly, but most of them involve comparisons that cannot be decided True or False when null values are involved.

7.4.1 The Big Six Comparison Types

The comparison predicate uses the so-called Big Six comparison types (see Table 7-1), which are common to most programming languages.

Table 7-1 *Big Six Comparison Types*

Comparison	SQL:1999 Symbol
1. equal	=
2. not equal	<>
3. less than	<
4. greater than	>
5. less than or equal	<=
6. greater than or equal	>=

The usage of these comparison predicates is fairly self-explanatory for those familiar with programming or even basic mathematics. However, let's briefly look at some, using Table 7-2 in our examples.

Table 7-2 *MOVIE_TITLES*

TITLE	OUR_ TAPE_ COST	OUR_ DVD_ COST	REGULAR_ TAPE_ SALE_PRICE	CURRENT_ TAPE_ SALE_PRICE	REGULAR_ DVD_ SALE_PRICE	CURRENT_ DVD_ SALE_PRICE
The Sixth Sense	9.95	18.95	19.95	19.95	29.95	29.95
Three Kings	9.95	17.95	15.95	15.95	25.95	22.95
The Thomas Crown Affair	9.95	18.95	14.95	11.95	24.95	22.95
The 13th Warrior	8.95	18.95	19.95	19.95	29.95	29.95
The Matrix	9.95	17.95	18.95	18.95	28.95	28.95
Runaway Bride	8.95	18.95	19.95	17.95	29.95	27.95
Austin Powers	8.95	17.95	18.95	17.95	28.95	27.95
Austin Powers: The Spy Who Shagged Me	9.95	17.95	18.95	18.95	28.95	28.95
Notting Hill	8.95	17.95	16.95	16.95	26.95	26.95
Big Daddy	9.95	18.95	19.95	15.95	29.95	29.95
The Waterboy	9.95	18.95	19.95	15.95	29.95	29.95
|						
|						
|						
Bowfinger	9.95	18.95	19.95	19.95	29.95	29.95
Man on the Moon	9.95	18.95	19.95	19.95	29.95	25.95

Example 7-2 *Finding Expensive Videotapes*

```
SELECT title, current_tape_sale_price
  FROM movie_titles
  WHERE current_tape_sale_price >= 19.95 ;
```

Result 7-1 *Expensive Videotapes*

TITLE	CURRENT_TAPE_SALE_PRICE
The Sixth Sense	19.95
The 13th Warrior	19.95
Bowfinger	19.95
Man on the Moon	19.95

Comparisons don't have to be against numeric data types; character, date, and other types can be used as well. Note that the specific collating sequence will determine whether, say, a *4* is greater than or less than a *Q* in terms of value. The following query will return all rows where the TITLE *begins* with a character greater than a capital *Q*: the letters *R* through *Z* and anything else of a greater value in that collating sequence, as shown in Example 7-3 and Result 7-2.

Example 7-3 *Comparison with a Character Date Type*

```
SELECT title
FROM movie_titles
WHERE SUBSTRING(title FROM 1 FOR 1) > 'Q' ;
```

Result 7-2 *Movies Whose Titles Fall Late in the Alphabet*

TITLE
The Way We Were
Yentl
Silverado
Raising Arizona
The Outlaw Josey Wales
Ten

In our next example (Example 7-4), the entire table (Table 7-2) will be returned, since all titles have a DVD sales price greater than or equal to our cost for that DVD (or at least we hope so!).

Example 7-4 *A Comparison Returning the Entire Table in the Result*

```
SELECT *
FROM movie_titles
WHERE regular_dvd_sale_price >= our_dvd_cost ;
```

The query shown in Example 7-5 will give us a list (Result 7-3) of DVDs that aren't currently priced at $29.95, our current top price.

Example 7-5 *Finding DVDs Not Priced at Our Current Top Price*

```
SELECT title, current_dvd_sale_price
FROM movie_titles
WHERE current_dvd_sale_price <> 29.95 ;
```

Result 7-3 *DVDs Not Priced at 29.95*

TITLE	CURRENT_DVD_SALE_PRICE
Three Kings	22.95
The Thomas Crown Affair	22.95
The Matrix	28.95
Runaway Bride	27.95
Austin Powers	27.95
Austin Powers: The Spy Who Shagged Me	28.95
Notting Hill	26.95

7.4.2 BETWEEN

A special variant of the comparison predicate is the BETWEEN predicate, which has the form

```
value1 BETWEEN value2 AND value3
```

This is equivalent to

```
value1 >= value2 AND value1 <= value3
```

Example 7-6 illustrates an example using BETWEEN to find videotapes within a specific price range, resulting in the table shown in Result 7-4.

Example 7-6 *Using BETWEEN*

```
SELECT title, current_tape_sale_price
FROM movie_titles
WHERE current_tape_sale_price BETWEEN 15.95 and 17.95 ;
```

Result 7-4 *Result of Using BETWEEN*

TITLE	CURRENT_TAPE_SALE_PRICE
Three Kings	15.95
Runaway Bride	17.95
Austin Powers	17.95
Notting Hill	16.95
Big Daddy	15.95
The Waterboy	15.95

You should take note of the details of the equivalent expression of this predicate. The order of the operands has some unexpected implications that can catch you off guard if you don't pay close attention:

```
10 BETWEEN 5 AND 15
```

is True, but

```
10 BETWEEN 15 AND 5
```

is False! That's because the equivalent way of expressing BETWEEN (using AND) has a specific order to it. This obviously doesn't matter much when you're using literals, as our example does, but it might matter a lot if you provide value2 and value3 by using host variables, parameters, or even subqueries.

7.4.3 NOT BETWEEN

Still another variant of the comparison predicate is the use of NOT BETWEEN, as in

```
value1 NOT BETWEEN value2 AND value3
```

This predicate is equivalent to

```
NOT (value1 BETWEEN value2 AND value3)
```

or, in other words, value1 is outside the range between value2 and value3. (The same one-way characteristic applies to NOT BETWEEN, too.)

The statement in Example 7-7 will result in the table shown in Result 7-5.

Example 7-7 *Using NOT BETWEEN*

```
SELECT title, current_tape_sale_price
FROM movie_titles
WHERE current_tape_sale_price NOT BETWEEN
      15.95 and 17.95 ;
```

Result 7-5 *Movies Outside of a Specific Price Range*

TITLE	CURRENT_TAPE_ SALE_PRICE
The Sixth Sense	19.95
The Thomas Crown Affair	11.95
The 13th Warrior	19.95
The Matrix	18.95
Austin Powers: The Spy Who Shagged Me	18.95
|	
|	
|	
Bowfinger	19.95
Man on the Moon	19.95

BETWEEN is also used with the various character, bit, and datetime data types as well.

IS NULL Predicate

The NULL predicate is used to determine if the value of some expression is the null value. The syntax is as follows:

```
value-expression IS NULL
```

Using the rows shown in Table 7-3, the query shown in Example 7-8 will give the result set shown in Result 7-6. For purposes of this example, assume that any empty value in ACTOR_FIRST_NAME is a null value, not one or more blanks or a zero-length string.

Example 7-8 *Looking for Movies Whose Stars Have No First Name*

```
SELECT movie_title, actor_last_name, actor_first_name
FROM movies_stars
WHERE actor_first_name IS NULL ;
```

Table 7-3 *A Portion of the MOVIES_STARS Table*

MOVIE_TITLE	ACTOR_LAST_NAME	ACTOR_FIRST_NAME
Silverado	Costner	Kevin
Silverado	Kline	Kevin
Silverado	Glover	Danny
Silverado	Dennehy	Brian
Moonstruck	Cher	
Moonstruck	Cage	Nicholas
Raising Arizona	Cage	Nicholas
Raising Arizona	Hunter	Holly
The Outlaw Josey Wales	Eastwood	Clint
The Outlaw Josey Wales	Locke	Sondra
Duck Soup	Marx Brothers	
A Night at the Opera	Marx Brothers	
A League of Their Own	Davis	Geena
A League of Their Own	Madonna	
G.I. Jane	Moore	Demi
Animal House	Belushi	John

Result 7-6 *Movies with Actors Having No First Name*

MOVIE_TITLE	ACTOR_LAST_NAME	ACTOR_FIRST_NAME
Moonstruck	Cher	
Duck Soup	Marx Brothers	
A Night at the Opera	Marx Brothers	
A League of Their Own	Madonna	

You won't be surprised to learn that you can combine the NOT operator with the NULL predicate. The format is

```
value IS NOT NULL
```

and the predicate is True if and only if the provided value is not null. If the value is null, then the predicate is False.

One place where the IS NULL predicate might not behave exactly as you expect it to is when it operates on a row with more than one column:

```
WHERE (actor_last_name, actor_first_name) IS NULL
```

will be True only if *both* values are null. However, with

```
WHERE (actor_last_name, actor_first_name) IS NOT NULL
```

also will be True only if *both* values are not null!

There are two more possible variations:

```
WHERE NOT (actor_last_name, actor_first_name) IS NULL
```

will be True if both are null, and otherwise False. Similarly,

```
WHERE NOT (actor_last_name, actor_first_name) IS NOT NULL
```

is True if either or both is null and False only if neither is null.

Confused? This is why you were taught in elementary school not to use double negatives! Table 7-4 captures and makes some sense out of the preceding examples.

Table 7-4 *Null Predicate Semantics*

Expression	R IS NULL	R IS NOT NULL	NOT R IS NULL	NOT R IS NOT NULL
Degree 1: null	True	False	False	True
Degree 1: not null	False	True	True	False
Degree >1: all null	True	False	False	True
Degree >1: some null	False	False	True	True
Degree >1: none null	False	True	True	False

<h2>7.6 | IN Predicate</h2>

We introduced you to the IN predicate earlier, while introducing subqueries. The format of the IN predicate is either of the two alternatives shown in Syntax 7-1.

Syntax 7-1 *Two Alternatives for IN Predicate Syntax*

- $value_t$ IN ($value_1$, $value_2$, ...)
- $value_t$ IN subquery

The first form of the IN predicate permits the usage of a list of values in place of a subquery. Assume that we want to examine our current rental prices for selected movie costs (that is, our costs), the goal being searching for inconsistencies. We could issue the following statement:

```
SELECT title, current_dvd_sale_price
FROM movie_titles
WHERE current_dvd_sale_price IN
    (24.95, 25.95, 28.95 ) ;
```

All movies that have a current DVD sale price of $24.95, $25.95, or $28.95 will evaluate True to the IN predicate, and in turn produce a list of titles and accompanying current DVD sale prices for those movies.

In the second form, the subquery is evaluated to produce an intermediate result, against which further processing can be performed. We've already looked at a brief example of a subquery within a SELECT statement. As we mentioned earlier, subqueries can also be contained within statements that modify data, such as UPDATE statements. For example, to promote our *Animal House* storewide

promotion, we decide to put all movies in which John Belushi starred on sale
with a 10% discount (videotape only, not DVD). Note that as a result of our
mostly normalized database design (discussed briefly in section 1.2.3, subsection
entitled "Normal Forms"), the various columns required to do this are contained
in two different tables: `regular_tape_sale_price` and `current_tape_sale_price`
are contained within `movie_titles`, while `actor_last_name` and `actor_first_name`
reside in `movies_stars`. By using a subquery, accompanied by the IN predicate, we
can accomplish our goal, as shown in Example 7-9.

Example 7-9 *Using IN as Part of a Subquery*

```
UPDATE movie_titles
  SET current_tape_sale_price =
      ( regular_tape_sale_price * .9 )
WHERE title IN
      ( SELECT movie_title
        FROM movies_stars
        WHERE actor_last_name = 'Belushi'
          AND actor_first_name = 'John' )   ;
```

   Once the subquery produces its list of selected movie titles, that list is processed against the `movie_titles` table and the appropriate rental prices are
discounted for *Animal House, Blues Brothers, Neighbors,* and others in which John
Belushi appeared.

   As you must surely expect by now, the IN predicate has a negative companion, NOT IN. The format of this is exactly the same as the IN predicate, but you
substitute NOT IN for IN. And, as you guessed, NOT IN is True only if the provided
value is not found in the values returned by the subquery or in the parenthesized
list of values.

7.7 LIKE and SIMILAR Predicates

The predicates we've examined so far can deal with data of almost any type:
numeric, character string, datetime, and so forth. However, when the data with
which you're dealing is character data, you'll often want your queries to find
rows based on matches that are based on only part of the values in character
strings stored in one or more columns.

   Virtually all client applications—including operating system command line
interfaces, email clients, and Web browsers—and most server environments pro-

vide facilities for identifying data through partial matches of data, filenames, and so forth. SQL is no different in this respect. In fact, SQL:1999 provides two predicates to help you write powerful queries. SQL's LIKE predicate uses simple wildcard matching, while SQL:1999's new SIMILAR predicate gives you even more powerful facilities.

7.7.1 LIKE Predicate

Users of any commercial database product are familiar with wildcards or special characters used to perform partial matches. SQL has long provided the LIKE predicate, together with the % and _ special characters, to do basic pattern matching against character string data. The LIKE predicate can also be used with binary string data: BINARY LARGE OBJECTs, or BLOBs (but we must emphasize that this is not the same as the BIT and BIT VARYING types, which cannot participate in the LIKE predicate). The LIKE predicate can be used anywhere a predicate can appear.

The syntax of the LIKE predicate is straightforward, as shown in Syntax 7-2.

Syntax 7-2 *Syntax of the LIKE Predicate*

```
source_value [ NOT ] LIKE pattern_value [ ESCAPE escape_value ]
```

As with other predicates that support the optional keyword NOT, you'll find that NOT LIKE merely inverts the sense of LIKE. In other words, if "x LIKE y" is True, then "x NOT LIKE y" is False. In the LIKE predicate's syntax, the source_value can be any expression whose data type is either a character string type or a binary string type, such as a database column, a host variable, a character string literal, or even a concatenation of other values (of the appropriate type, of course). The pattern_value has the same flexibility but will probably be a literal in most of your applications. The escape_value, which you'll note is optional, also has that flexibility, but it is limited to values with a length of exactly one character or one octet, depending on the types of the other values. Perhaps obviously, if one of those values is a character string value, then they all must be; similarly, if one of them is a binary string value, they all must be. We're first going to consider the use of the LIKE predicate with character string values. Once we've covered this usage, we'll show you the slight changes needed to use it with binary string values.

The pattern_value can use one or both of two possible wildcard characters. The percent sign (%) is used to stand for zero or more arbitrary characters (not any specific characters) in the source_value, while the underscore (_) stands for exactly one arbitrary character (again, not any specific character) in the source_value. Every other character in the pattern_value stands only for itself (although the use of an escape_value changes this rule slightly, as you'll see below). More than one of either special character may be used, depending on the specific search criteria you have in mind (see Table 7-5). If you have a need to match exactly two arbitrary characters, you'd use two consecutive underscores. Since a single percent sign matches zero or more characters, there's never a need to use two or more consecutive percent signs, because the result would be exactly the same as a single percent sign.

Table 7-5 *LIKE Predicate Wildcard Usage*

Pattern	Explanation	Would Match
'ABC%'	Match any character string value beginning with 'ABC'	'ABCDEF' 'ABC'
'%ABC'	Match any character string value ending with 'ABC'	'XYZABC' 'ABC'
'%%ABC'	Match any character string value ending with 'ABC'	'XYZABC' 'ABC'
'%ABC%'	Match any character string value that contains 'ABC' anywhere in the string	'ABC' 'ABCDEF' 'XYZABC' 'XYZABCDEF'
'ABC_'	Match any character string value that begins with 'ABC' and is followed by a single character	'ABCD'
'ABC__'	Match any character string value that begins with 'ABC' and is followed by exactly two characters	'ABCDE'
'_ABC'	Match any character string value that is four characters in length and ends with 'ABC'	'XABC'
'__ABC'	Match any character string value that is five characters in length and ends with 'ABC'	
'_ABC%'	Match any character string value that begins with any character, has 'ABC' as the second, third, and fourth characters, respectively, and ends with any number of other characters	'XABCDEFG' 'XABC'

There might be occasions where you want to match a percent sign (%) or an underscore (_) in your source_value (see Table 7-6). To do this, you can use the keyword ESCAPE to designate another character as the *escape* character in your pattern_value, which in turn designates a *real* percent sign or underscore immediately following the escape character. Your escape character must be one that is not used explicitly elsewhere in your pattern_value.

Table 7-6 *Using the LIKE Predicate to Match the Special Characters*

Desired Match Value	SQL:1999 Predicate	Would Match
'10%'	LIKE '%10$%'	'10%'
	ESCAPE '$'	'810%'
		'A 10%'
	LIKE '%10*%%'	'10%'
	ESCAPE '*'	'10% DISCOUNT'
		'A 10% DISCOUNT'

By the way, the LIKE predicate can't deal with row values, so you can only test one character string at a time.

Before we leave our discussion of the LIKE predicate, let's look at some examples from our movie_titles table. Note that some of the retrieved titles don't appear in the abbreviated master table (Table 7-2) found earlier in this chapter but are included in the results to illustrate the respective query. First, consider Example 7-10, whose result is shown in Result 7-7.

Example 7-10 *Using LIKE 'Bev%'*

```
SELECT title
FROM movie_titles
WHERE title LIKE 'Bev%' ;
```

Result 7-7 *Result of LIKE 'Bev%'*

TITLE
Beverly Hills Cop
Beverly Hills Cop II

Next, consider Example 7-11 and its result, in Result 7-8.

Example 7-11 *Using LIKE '%Bev%'*

```
SELECT title
FROM movie_titles
WHERE title LIKE '%Bev%' ;
```

Result 7-8 *Result of LIKE '%Bev%'*

TITLE

Beverly Hills Cop
Beverly Hills Cop II
Down and Out in Beverly Hills
Slums of Beverly Hills
Troop Beverly Hills

Now, let's see Example 7-12 and the corresponding Result 7-9.

Example 7-12 *Using LIKE '%#%%' ESCAPE '#'*

```
SELECT title
FROM movie_titles
WHERE title LIKE '%#%%' ESCAPE '#' ;
```

Result 7-9 *Result of LIKE '%#%%' ESCAPE '#'*

TITLE

The Ten % Solution

Finally, let's look at Example 7-13 and Result 7-10.

Example 7-13 *Using LIKE '_*_*_*%' ESCAPE '#'*

```
SELECT title
FROM movie_titles
WHERE title LIKE '_*_*_*%' ESCAPE '#' ;
```

Result 7-10 *Result of LIKE '_*_*_*%' ESCAPE '#'*

TITLE

M*A*S*H
F*I*S*T

In the preceding LIKE predicate, the first underscore in the string designates a single character "wildcard" match; the next character (*) signifies that an asterisk is specifically desired; this is repeated two more times, and then the % is used to match multiple characters (or none at all). In this case, the ESCAPE serves no function (but does no harm).

Unlike comparison predicates (= and <> in particular), blanks are significant in the LIKE predicate. Therefore, although

```
'Rocky' = 'Rocky   '
```

is usually True, and

```
'Rocky' LIKE 'Rocky'
```

is True, you'll find that

```
'Rocky' LIKE 'Rocky   '
```

is always False!

You can use TRIM to trim trailing blanks from the pattern to ensure that a string with trailing blanks can match the pattern when you're using LIKE.

Now that we've gained some familiarity with the LIKE predicate and its use with character string values, let's explore its use with binary string values. In fact, the changes are pretty obvious. Mostly, you have to use binary string literals instead of character string literals, as seen in Example 7-14.

Example 7-14 *LIKE Predicate Using Binary String Literals*

```
X'01234ABCD5' LIKE column_value
```

Let's consider the implications of that information for a moment. Suppose we'd like to write a LIKE predicate that can match the value stored in a column with a few specific octets whose values we can express in hexadecimal, and we want to use our wildcards while performing that match. Binary string literals can only contain hexadecimal digits, not characters such as percent and underscore. How, then, can we construct a pattern_value for this purpose?

Obviously, we can't write something like that in Example 7-15, because the hexadecimal literal is only permitted to contain hexadecimal digits, and neither the underscore nor the percent sign meet that requirement.

Example 7-15 *Incorrect Attempt to Use Wildcards in LIKE Predicate*

```
my_column LIKE X'0123_AB%'
```

You might think that you could get around this problem by writing an expression that uses concatenation, as we attempt in Example 7-16.

Example 7-16 *Another Incorrect Attempt to Use Wildcards in LIKE Predicate*

```
my_column LIKE X'0123' || '_' || X'AB' || '%'
```

That's a clever effort, but it's doomed immediately, because the concatenation operator requires that its operands both be character strings or both be binary strings; mix-and-match of data types isn't supported.

The answer lies in SQL:1999's requirement that a one-octet representation of the two wildcard characters exist (in the special character set used to describe SQL statements, SQL_CHARACTER). The bad news is that you have to know, or be able to discover, what that one-octet representation is! For the purposes of discussing this feature, we're going to assume that the SQL_CHARACTER character set is really ASCII or some proper subset of ASCII; that means that the hexadecimal representation of a percent sign is X'25', and the hexadecimal representation of an underscore is X'5F'. Unfortunately, SQL:1999 fails to provide you with a foolproof, automatic way to represent the wildcard characters for use in situations like this. You simply have to figure out what the hexadecimal values are and then use them as we illustrate (correctly, this time) in Example 7-17.

Example 7-17 *Correct Use of Wildcards in LIKE Predicate with Binary String Values*

```
my_column LIKE X'0123' || '5F' || X'AB' || X'25'
my_column LIKE X'01235FAB25'
```

Example 7-17 has two variations of the same example; the concatenation operator effectively constructs the second example from the first. Either variation can be described as matching values in the column named my_column that start with two octets whose hexadecimal values are X'0123' followed by any octet at all, followed by one octet whose hexadecimal value is X'AB', followed by zero or more additional octets.

As you'd expect, that means that you cannot match octets whose values are X'25' or X'5F' without using the escape octet capability to flag them, as illustrated in Example 7-18.

Example 7-18 *Wildcards in LIKE Predicate with ESCAPE Octet*

```
my_column LIKE X'0123FF5F5FAB25' ESCAPE X'FF'
```

This example matches values in my_column that start with three octets whose hexadecimal values are X'01235F' followed by any octet at all, followed by one octet whose hexadecimal value is X'AB' followed by zero or more additional octets. The sequence of octets whose value is X'FF5F' will match a single octet whose value is X'5F', while the following octet (also X'5F') just represents the wildcard underscore, matching any single octet.

7.7.2 SIMILAR Predicate

Sometimes, simple pattern matching using the wildcards % and _ just doesn't give you the power you need in your queries. Instead, you may find that you need to match character strings based on more complex criteria.

SQL:1999 features the SIMILAR predicate to give you the full power of UNIX's regular expressions. If you've never used some variation of the UNIX operating system, or any other operating system that supports that type of capability, you may not already be familiar with this extremely useful facility. If you are familiar with UNIX's regular expressions, then you'll quickly become comfortable with the SIMILAR predicate; but don't skip this section, because there are some minor differences between the syntax of UNIX regular expressions and SQL:1999's.

By contrast with the LIKE predicate, the SIMILAR predicate applies only to character strings—that is, not to binary strings. However, in common with the LIKE predicate, the SIMILAR predicate has either two or three parameters and can be negated, as you'll see in Example 7-19.

Example 7-19 *Syntax of the SIMILAR Predicate*

```
source_value [ NOT ] SIMILAR TO pattern_value [ ESCAPE escape_value ]
```

As with the LIKE predicate, specification of NOT SIMILAR TO merely inverts the sense of SIMILAR TO. In other words, if "x SIMILAR TO y" is True, then "x NOT SIMILAR TO y" is False. In the SIMILAR predicate's syntax, the source_value can be any expression whose data type is a character string type, such as a database column, a host variable, a character string literal, or even a concatenation of other values (of character string type, of course). The pattern_value has the same flexibility but will most often be a literal in most of your applications. The escape_value, which is optional, has the same flexibility but is limited to values with a length of exactly one character. In this chapter, as in much of the book, we'll mostly use literals for our examples, but we'll show at least one example using a host variable, just to show you the unfortunate (and, in our opinion, unattractive) syntax that has to be used.

In the LIKE predicate, the pattern_value has a very simple structure in which only the percent sign and underscore (and the escape character or octet) had special meanings. The SIMILAR predicate, in order to provide its greater power, has a substantially more complex set of rules and structures in its pattern_value, as we show you in Syntax 7-3 (this time, the BNF is more formal than many of the syntax structures we've shown; that's largely because of its complexity and use of some very formal terminology). This set of rules and structures is instantiated by a special type of character expression called a *regular expression*. Regular expressions allow you to match strings that have a particular content and structure. A regular expression describes a set of strings: the strings that are matched by the regular expression. That's right, a regular expression gives you the ability to find things in your database using pattern matching.

Syntax 7-3 *Syntax of SIMILAR Predicate's Regular Expressions*

```
<regular expression> ::=
    <regular term>
  | <regular expression> <vertical bar> <regular term>

<regular term> ::=
    <regular factor>
  | <regular term> <regular factor>

<regular factor> ::=
    <regular primary>
  | <regular primary> <asterisk>
  | <regular primary> <plus sign>

<regular primary> ::=
    <character specifier>
  | <percent>
  | <regular character set>
  | <left paren> <regular expression> <right paren>

<character specifier> ::=
    <non-escaped character>
  | <escaped character>

<regular character set> ::=
    <underscore>
  | <left bracket> <character enumeration>... <right bracket>
  | <left bracket> <circumflex> <character enumeration>... <right bracket>
  | <left bracket> <colon> <regular charset id> <colon> <right bracket>
```

```
<character enumeration> ::=
    <character specifier>
  | <character specifier> <minus sign> <character specifier>

<regular charset id> ::=
    ALPHA
  | UPPER
  | LOWER
  | DIGIT
  | ALNUM
```

Now, don't get too intimidated by that lengthy sequence of BNF; we'll make it clear in the next few paragraphs. The first thing we want to point out is that SQL:1999 has chosen to use the terminology of traditional math, words such as *expression, term,* and *factor*. The use of those words implies the precedence of the operators: the vertical bar operator has lowest priority, and adjacency (or implicit concatenation) is the "operator" with the second lowest priority.

In general, you specify a regular expression by creating a character string that contains the characters you want to match explicitly, interspersed with wildcard characters like those used in the LIKE predicate, operators such as alternation, and quantifiers that modify the meanings of various components of the regular expression (by specifying things such as how often those components are to be applied in performing the match). In Syntax 7-3, the wildcard characters are represented by the <percent> and <underscore> nonterminal symbols, and they have precisely the same meanings as the percent sign and underscore have in the LIKE predicate.

The simplest regular expression is one that matches exactly a particular string value. For example, the regular expression

```
Conspiracy Theory
```

matches the character string value

```
Conspiracy Theory
```

and no other value. You can see this in the context of a SIMILAR predicate in Example 7-20, which (trivially) evaluates to True.

Example 7-20 *Trivial Use of SIMILAR Predicate*

```
'Conspiracy Theory' SIMILAR TO 'Conspiracy Theory'
```

In fact, we could have constructed the regular expression (that is, the `pattern_value`) by using implicit concatenation (as opposed to explicit concatenation, using two vertical bars, ||, that you must use in character value expressions) of two regular expressions, like that in Example 7-21.

Example 7-21 *Using Implicit Concatenation*

```
'Conspiracy Theory' SIMILAR TO '(Conspiracy )(Theory)'
```

You should note several points here. First, the second operand is itself a character string literal. Second, we enclosed each of the two character string values within the overall regular expression in parentheses; that's the convention you must use to enclose a regular expression when you need to delimit it from another regular expression. Third, the use of implicit concatenation means that the two examples (Example 7-20 and Example 7-21) are identical in behavior. And, of course, each of the nested character strings is itself a regular expression (any sequence of characters that doesn't span any of the SIMILAR predicate's "special characters" is itself a valid regular expression that matches itself).

While both examples are simple and easy to understand, they're not very useful, because replacing the SIMILAR TO keywords with an equals sign in Example 7-20 would give the same result, as would using the equal sign and explicit concatenation (||) in Example 7-21. For a regular expression to be more interesting, we're going to have to use some of those operators, wildcards, and modifiers. For example, if we want to match either of two strings, we could write a SIMILAR predicate such as the one in Example 7-22.

Example 7-22 *Slightly More Interesting Regular Expression*

```
movie_title SIMILAR TO '(Conspiracy Theory)|(Enemy of the State)'
```

In this case, the predicate is satisfied whenever `movie_title` contains the name of either one of those two paranoid thrillers. Example 7-22 uses the <vertical bar> operator that appeared in the BNF production for <regular expression> (see Syntax 7-3), which shows you how the <vertical bar> is used. It specifies that the source string has to match either the regular expression on the left of the vertical bar *or* the regular expression contained in the regular term on its right.

That's still not very interesting, since we could have simply used the IN predicate just as conveniently. Obviously, we've got to start using more complex regular expressions that match strings whose entire contents we don't know in advance, using quantifiers, operators, and wildcards.

Suppose we'd like to retrieve rows from our database that correspond to one of the movies *Scream, Scream 2,* or *Scream 3.* Consider Example 7-23.

Example 7-23 *Regular Expression Using Regular Character Set and Quantifier*

```
movie_title SIMILAR TO '(Scream)|(Scream [23]*)'
```

In this example, we've used two new facilities. The first is the square brackets that surround the digits 2 and 3; this convention (an alternative of <regular character set> in Syntax 7-3) has nothing to do with optionality, even though we use square brackets in BNF for that purpose. Instead, it means "use exactly one of the characters within these brackets as part of the regular expression"; therefore, the regular expression formed along with the character string literal 'Scream ' and the following [23] would be either 'Scream 2' or 'Scream 3'.

The asterisk (which you can see in an alternative to <regular factor> in Syntax 7-3) is used to indicate that "the immediately preceding regular expression component can appear zero or more times." This means that movie_title values that satisfy the SIMILAR predicate in Example 7-23 include *Scream* (matched by the part of the regular expression to the left of the vertical bar), "*Scream* " (that trailing space doesn't really stand out visually, so we enclosed this title in quotation marks), *Scream 2*, and *Scream 3*. Unfortunately, the predicate would be equally satisfied by *Scream 23*, *Scream 32*, and even *Scream 323223332*, none of which (we very sincerely hope) are even in preproduction!

SQL:1999's regular expressions have a second quantifier that behaves very much like the asterisk. The plus sign (+) is used to indicate that "the immediately preceding regular expression component must appear one or more times." If Example 7-23 had used + where the * appeared, then all of those titles would still have been valid, except for "*Scream* " (the version with the trailing space) itself—the one that would be matched with 0 instances of "2" or "3".

Unfortunately, SQL:1999's regular expressions don't support an operator or quantifier to specify "the immediately preceding regular expression component can appear zero or one time" (some systems' regular expressions use a question mark for that purpose). That's a significant disadvantage, because it forces us to use a more cumbersome solution, such as that in Example 7-24.

Example 7-24 *Corrected Regular Expression Example Using Regular Character Set*

```
movie_title SIMILAR TO '(Scream)|(Scream [23])'
```

That solution isn't too bad, but it's awkward to have to repeat the common part of the movies' names in an alternative for the original film and in the alternative for the sequels. We anticipate that a future generation of the SQL standard will include a "zero or one time" quantifier to make this type of query simpler to write.

Since Hollywood seems convinced that sequels are easier to produce than genuinely new ideas, perhaps our store ought to assume that the *Scream* franchise will last for nine films in all. We can accommodate that possibility by using a regular character set identifier as shown in Example 7-25.

Example 7-25 *Regular Expression Using Regular Character Set Identifier*

```
movie_title SIMILAR TO '(Scream)|(Scream [:DIGIT:])'
```

The convention [:DIGIT:] specifies that the final component of the regular expression is any single character that belongs to the regular character set known as DIGIT—which you will quickly realize is the set of digits 0 through 9. This construct allows us to retrieve movies through *Scream 9*, should that film (oh, horrors!) eventually be produced. The other regular character set identifiers supported in SQL:1999 are ALPHA (any alphabetic character), UPPER (any uppercase alphabetic character), LOWER (any lowercase alphabetic character), and ALNUM (any character that is either an alphabetic character or a digit—the name should make you think "alphanumeric").

Unfortunately, using [:DIGIT:] will find the movie *Scream 1,* which simply doesn't exist, and *Scream 0,* which we doubt will ever be made. Now, that's not a problem at our movie store, since we won't have any rows in our MOVIES table that specify those names, but it's still an inelegant use of the regular expression. A better solution can be seen in Example 7-26.

Example 7-26 *Regular Expression Using Character Range*

```
movie_title SIMILAR TO '(Scream)|(Scream [2-9])'
```

The regular expression [2-9] means "use any one digit in the range between 2 and 9, inclusive." And that, finally, solves our problem accurately and (reasonably) elegantly.

A regular character set specified using the range notation, such as that in Example 7-26, allows you to specify the first and last characters of a range of characters. But you have to know the coded character set (not the "regular character set," which is a term used only in regular expressions!) involved in order to know what that range means. Most modern coded character sets group all their digits together, and many of them group all their lowercase alphabetic characters together and their uppercase alphabetic characters together. But there are some pretty important exceptions, the most notable of which are Unicode and EBCDIC. We're not going to go into coded character set issues until Chapter 21, "Internationalization Aspects of SQL:1999," but we want you to be conscious of the possible implications of character ranges when the coded character set of the data being interrogated is something more complex than ASCII or Latin 1. This aspect of regular expressions might seem intuitive when the range is something like [a-j] or [M-Z], but it can be frustrating to figure out exactly what characters are supported by [;-+] in an arbitrary coded character set.

Before we leave the subject of quantifiers (* and +) completely, we want to be sure that you understand an important attribute they share: they always apply to the smallest expression that precedes them. Consider the two regular expressions in Example 7-27.

Example 7-27 *Quantifiers and Preceding Expressions*

```
(I )(Still )*(Know What You Did Last Summer)
(I )(Still )+(Know What You Did Last Summer)
```

The first of those regular expressions—the one with the asterisk quantifier—would allow us to match the movie *I Know What You Did Last Summer,* but the second one—using the plus sign—would not, because the preceding expression, ('Still '), is required to appear at least once. Of course, the nonexistent movie *I Still Still Still Know What You Did Last Summer* would be supported by both expressions, but that's a different problem. Neither expression would support the (also nonexistent) movie *I I I I Know What You Did Last Summer,* or even *I Still I Still I Still I Still Know What You Did Last Summer,* because the qualifiers apply to the smallest preceding expression.

You'll sometimes encounter a need to match character strings that *do not* have some characteristic. For example, you might want to locate all movies in which the characters "L" and "A" appear without a period between them. A movie like *L.A. Story* wouldn't be found by the predicate in Example 7-28, but a movie with Louisiana's postal abbreviation would. (For those readers from outside the USA who may not be familiar with the official U.S. Postal Service abbreviations for states, LA is the postal code used for the state of Louisiana.)

Example 7-28 *SIMILAR Predicate Matching "LA" and not "L.A."*

```
movie_title SIMILAR TO '%L[^.]*A%'
```

Notice that we've used the percent sign wildcard character to match zero or more arbitrary characters, and we've also indicated that the regular expression allows any characters other than a period between an "L" and an "A". The caret (^) is used in SQL:1999 regular expressions to change the meaning of the regular character set in which it occurs so that all characters in the character set are excluded, rather than included. That rule applies only if the caret appears as the first character of the regular character set (i.e., within square brackets). If it appears anywhere else within those square brackets, it's just another character that's part of the regular character set.

By now, you've probably begun to wonder how on earth you'd match character strings that included any of our special characters, like the square brackets, parentheses, caret, percent sign, underscore, asterisk, or plus sign. Suppose we believe that we've got an error in our database so that the movie *The 7% Solution* is stored correctly, but a careless data entry episode may have also stored rows for *The 6% Solution* and *The 8% Solution*. We need to check for the existence of such an error, and we'd like to do so as simply as possible. Example 7-29 shows one way to accomplish this.

Example 7-29 *Using Escape Characters in Regular Expressions*

```
movie_title SIMILAR TO 'The [678]\% Solution' ESCAPE '\'
```

We didn't really think you'd be surprised by that! The SIMILAR predicate provides us with an ESCAPE clause that works precisely like the corresponding clause of the LIKE predicate. If your predicate requires the use of a regular expression that includes any of the special characters in a text string, you must precede them with an escape character that is specified in the ESCAPE clause.

Before we finish discussing the SIMILAR predicate, we'll fulfill the promise we made when we started: to show you an example in which a host variable is used to pass information into the predicate. Most likely, using a host variable to pass an entire regular expression won't surprise you; it would look like this:

```
movie_title SIMILAR TO :regexp
```

It's somewhat more interesting if we pass only *part* of a regular expression. Suppose that, in Example 7-29, we had wanted to pass the possible digits to be used in the search. We could do something like that shown in Example 7-30.

Example 7-30 *Using a Host Variable to Provide Part of a Regular Expression*

```
movie_title SIMILAR TO 'The ' || :regexp || '\% Solution' ESCAPE '\'
```

That's a little bit clumsy but, all in all, it's certainly usable.

In spite of the extra expressive power that the SIMILAR predicate gives you when compared with the LIKE predicate, it's not as useful as it could be. Several other implementations of regular expressions are commonly used, including some UNIX utilities and even some aspects of XML. Those implementations have a few features that SQL:1999 does not, although we have great hopes that some future version of the SQL standard will provide them.

The following list is probably not comprehensive, but it does include the most obvious omissions from SQL:1999's regular expression facilities:

- White space: It is often important to explicitly match arbitrary "white space"—that is, nonprinting characters, such as spaces, tabs, newlines, and so forth. SQL:1999 allows matching of an arbitrary number of space characters but doesn't address other white space issues. The convention "[:WHITESPACE:]" or something similar might be provided in the future.

- Optional single instance: Several implementations of regular expressions use the question mark (?) to mean "match exactly zero or one instance of the preceding regular expression." SQL:1999 has no obvious way to express this concept.

- Range of characters with exclusions: SQL:1999 provides no easy way to represent the notion "match all characters in this range, except for this list of exceptions," such as matching all digits other than 5. Other regular expression implementations often provide this facility. One possibility would be a notation like "[0-9^5]" or "[:DIGIT:^5]".

- Specific number of characters: SQL:1999 doesn't have convenient syntax to express the notion "exactly 3 digits," which would be very convenient for expressing fixed-format values like North American telephone numbers. A future version of the SQL standard could support a notation like "[:DIGIT:]{3}" to mean "exactly three digits" or "[AEIOU]{2,5}" to mean "at least two and no more than five vowels."

7.8 | EXISTS and UNIQUE Predicates

The EXISTS predicate is somewhat similar in function to the IN predicate. It is True if and only if the cardinality of the subquery is greater than 0 and is False otherwise. The format of the EXISTS predicate is given in Syntax 7-4.

Syntax 7-4 *Syntax of EXISTS Predicate*

```
EXISTS subquery
```

The statement in Example 7-31 produces an in-stock list of Mel Gibson videotapes using the EXISTS predicate rather than using IN, as we did when putting the John Belushi videotapes on sale (see Example 7-9).

Example 7-31 *Using EXISTS*

```
SELECT title, tapes_in_stock
FROM movie_titles m
WHERE EXISTS
   ( SELECT *
     FROM movies_stars
     WHERE
        movie_title = m.title
      AND
        actor_last_name = 'Gibson'
      AND
        actor_first_name = 'Mel' )   ;
```

Note that this predicate tests to see whether the subquery is empty or not, not whether some value appears in the values returned by the subquery. However, the analog with the IN predicate is real. (Example 7-31 shows a *correlated subquery,* a topic we'll discuss in section 9.10, "Subqueries").

The EXISTS predicate has been criticized because it is True only when there is *definitely* at least one row that meets the criteria of the subquery. If you apply the meaning "maybe" to a predicate that is neither False nor True, but is Unknown, then you might get unexpected results. For example, in the example above, you may have rows for some actor whose last name is Gibson, but whose first name is null for some reason. Those rows will not meet the criteria for the subquery and will therefore not satisfy the EXISTS criteria, either. However, it may be that those rows *should* satisfy the criteria because you know that you're going to put Mel's first name into those rows later on. All we can offer you here is this: be very careful that you know the semantics of your data and that you write the intended query; and, if you think that you might have the problem we've suggested, consider coding your query a little differently. For example, you might use this in the last line of Example 7-31:

```
( actor_first_name = 'Mel' OR actor_first_name IS NULL )
```

The UNIQUE predicate is used to determine if duplicate rows exist in a virtual table (one returned from a subquery). The format is

```
UNIQUE subquery
```

If any two rows in the subquery are equal to one another, the UNIQUE predicate evaluates to False.

Suppose we've decided that it's confusing to stock movies and CDs with the same title (there go all the soundtrack sales!). We could check to see if we've violated this rule by using a UNIQUE predicate:

```
UNIQUE ( SELECT name
              FROM ( SELECT title AS name
                     FROM movie_titles )
              UNION
              ( SELECT title as name
                FROM music_titles ) )
```

7.9 OVERLAPS Predicate

The OVERLAPS predicate has a very specific purpose: to determine whether two periods of time overlap with one another. Suppose your database includes a schedule of meetings at your company and you'd like to ensure that any new meetings that you want to schedule don't conflict with any other meetings already scheduled. You might express your meeting as starting at 1:00 P.M. on the first of June, 1995, and lasting for two hours, while somebody else listed their meeting as starting at 12:30 P.M. on the same day and lasting until 1:30 P.M. Do those meetings overlap? Yes, we can see that they do. The challenge is to allow SQL to make the determination.

The format of the OVERLAPS predicate can be seen in Syntax 7-5.

Syntax 7-5 *Syntax of OVERLAPS Predicate*

```
event-information OVERLAPS event-information
```

Either event-information can be of the form

```
( start-time, duration )
```

or

```
( start-time, end-time )
```

but they don't have to have the same form. If the first form (using duration) is specified, then that form is effectively converted to the second form by adding the duration value to the start-time value to calculate the effective end-time value.

Both start-time and end-time have to be the same variety of datetime (that is, either DATE, TIME, or TIMESTAMP). If the first form is used, then the duration has to be an interval that can be added to the datetime form used by start-time. Those rules were discussed in Chapter 2, "Introduction to SQL:1999."

If the starting time of either event or the ending time of either event (remember that the ending time can be computed as the starting time plus the duration) lies between the starting and ending times of the other event, then the events overlap.[1] Sometimes, even when the starting time or the ending time is null, we can tell that there is an overlap, but other times it's not clear.

For example:

```
( TIME '10:45:00', INTERVAL '1' HOUR )
OVERLAPS
( TIME '10:00:00', TIME '10:30:00')
```

is False. But

```
( TIME '10:45:00', INTERVAL '1' HOUR )
OVERLAPS
( TIME '10:00:00', TIME '11:30:00')
```

is True. And

```
( TIME '10:45:00', INTERVAL '1' HOUR )
OVERLAPS
( TIME '11:00:00', NULL)
```

is True, because the length of the interval is unimportant since 11:00 is always going to be during the period 10:45 to 11:45. Incidentally, the intervals can also be negative, so that the start-time is really the end of the event. SQL even allows you to reverse the start and end times. That makes the OVERLAPS predicate symmetrical, unlike the BETWEEN predicate.

---

1   The statement is generally True, but there are boundary conditions that need to be explained. If the second interval is a point in time (an instant with duration 0), then it overlaps the first interval even if it is exactly equal to the starting time of the first interval—but not if it is exactly equal to the ending time of that first interval. If the second interval is longer than a single point in time, then it does not overlap the first interval if its ending time is equal to the first interval's starting time or if its starting time is equal to the first interval's ending time. These rules seem somewhat arbitrary, but the designers of the SQL standard believe that they satisfy most users' expectations of datetime and interval behaviors.

If two intervals touch without overlapping, then the OVERLAPS predicate will report False.

```
( TIME '10:00:00' , TIME '11:00 00' )
OVERLAPS
( TIME '11:00:00' , TIME '12:00 00' )
```

is False: the two intervals don't overlap.

Note also that the start-time does not have to be before the end-time, nor does the duration need to be positive. (Time travel, anyone?) If the start-time is after the end-time, then the pair of values is effectively swapped.

7.10 SOME, ANY, and ALL

SQL also provides a type of predicate called a *quantified comparison predicate*. This sort of predicate allows the application of an existential quantifier or a universal quantifier to a comparison operator. The *existential quantifier* asks, Is there *any* value at all in the stuff we're searching that meets our requirements? By contrast, a *universal quantifier* asks, Does *every* value in the stuff we're looking at meet the requirements? Let's look at some examples to clarify this admittedly murky subject. Consider the question, "Are there any movies whose titles are the same as the last name of a movie star in that movie?" There are a couple of ways that we could ask the question, but let's start by using the IN predicate that we learned in this chapter:

```
SELECT COUNT(*)
FROM movie_titles AS m
WHERE title
   IN ( SELECT movie_title
        FROM movies_stars AS s
        WHERE s.movie_title = m.title
          AND s.actor_last_name = s.title )
```

However, that returns to *us* (or to our application) the number of such movies, and we have to use that number to make a decision: zero or nonzero. If we want to actually use that information as part of another query, then we could use something really awkward like this (let's just look at segments of the code, following WHERE):

```
SELECT....
WHERE ( SELECT COUNT(*)
           FROM movie_titles AS m
           WHERE title
              IN ( SELECT movie_title
                      FROM movies_stars AS s
                      WHERE s.movie_title = m.title
                        AND s.actor_last_name = m.title ) ) > 0
```

but that's unnatural and probably not very efficient in most DBMS implementations. It is also possible simply to use the IN predicate directly, which is certainly more natural:

```
SELECT....
WHERE title
   IN ( SELECT movie_title
           FROM movies_stars AS s
           WHERE s.movie_title = m.title
             AND s.actor_last_name = m.title )
```

This is better, but not always what we want to ask, as we shall shortly see. Instead, SQL allows us to use something like

```
SELECT...
WHERE title
   = SOME ( SELECT movie_title
               FROM movies_stars
               WHERE s.movie_title = m.title
                 AND s.actor_last_name = m.title )
```

Now, this WHERE clause will return all rows whose title appears anywhere in the titles returned from the subquery. That's exactly what the IN variant just preceding does. In fact, the SQL standard actually defines the IN predicate to be equivalent to a quantified comparison predicate, using equality for the operator and SOME to signal the existential quantifier. However, there are variations available using the quantified comparison predicate that the IN predicate can't hope to match.

For example, if we needed to use a greater-than relationship instead of equality, we can use the quantified comparison predicate, but couldn't use the IN predicate. Furthermore, if we wanted to find out if *every* row in the subquery—

instead of at least one row—met the criteria, then a quantified comparison predicate is required and the IN predicate doesn't help at all.

We might want to know whether some actor happens to star in *every* movie whose title is the same as his last name. That query might look like

```
...
WHERE a.actor_last_name
    = ALL ( SELECT title
            FROM movie_titles m. movies_stars s
            WHERE s.movie_title = m.title
              AND s.actor_last_name = m.title
              AND a.actor_last_name = s.actor_last_name )
```

Interestingly, this condition is satisfied by an actor who stars in no movies whose titles are the same as his last name. After all, he stars in all zero of those movies!

The format of the quantified comparison predicate is shown in Syntax 7-6.

Syntax 7-6 *Syntax of Quantified Comparison Predicate*

```
value comparison-operator quantifier subquery
```

The comparison-operator refers to the Big Six comparison operators that we discussed in section 7.4.1, under comparison predicates. The symbol quantifier refers to the keyword ALL, for the universal quantifier, or one of the keywords SOME or ANY, for the existential quantifier (SOME and ANY produce the same result, but sometimes one is more semantically intuitive than the other). And, of course, value and subquery are the value and the subquery against which that value is to be checked.

As you might expect, if the supplied value is null, then the result cannot be evaluated and the result of the predicate is unknown. If the subquery returns no rows, then the result of the predicate is False, since there are no rows for which the implied comparison can be True!

There isn't a negative version of this subquery—at least, there's not one that uses the NOT keyword. If you want to ask

```
value = NOT SOME subquery -- Not valid SQL!
```

which is not valid SQL, then you simply rephrase it to read

```
value <> SOME subquery
```

or

```
NOT ( value = SOME subquery )
```

If the value is really a row value, then the degree of the table produced by the subquery must match the degree of the row value; otherwise, the subquery must be of degree 1.

7.11 | MATCH Predicate

SQL:1999 provides a MATCH predicate that corresponds to the referential integrity restrictions that you can place on your tables (discussed in Chapter 10, "Constraints, Assertions, and Referential Integrity"). To give you a brief introduction to referential integrity for purposes of this discussion, we'll mention that a table may have a FOREIGN KEY through which its rows correspond (by values in one or more columns) to rows in some other table. FOREIGN KEYs usually (but don't have to) relate to a PRIMARY KEY in the other table.

By using this query, you can test rows before attempting to insert them into a table to ensure that they won't violate a referential integrity constraint. This advance check might help you avoid getting certain errors and might therefore make your application logic simpler.

The syntax for the MATCH predicate is shown in Syntax 7-7.

Syntax 7-7 *Syntax of MATCH Predicate*

```
row-value MATCH [ UNIQUE ] [ criterion ] subquery
```

In this predicate, row-value is the value of the candidate row that you are considering inserting into your table; like any row value, it contains one or more column values. UNIQUE is used to simulate a PRIMARY KEY constraint on the target table. The subquery is normally one that selects (one or more specified columns of) every row from the target table (but, because the predicate is available for more general use, you're not restricted to that convention). The criterion is either nothing at all or one of the keywords SIMPLE, PARTIAL, or FULL. Naturally, the number of columns in the row-value has to match the number of columns in the select-list of the subquery, and the data types of corresponding columns have to be compatible. We note that for row-values and subquerys whose degrees are 1, the three cases are equivalent; the distinction only arises for degrees greater than 1.

If you provide no criterion or if you specify SIMPLE (which is equivalent to not specifying anything at all), then the predicate is True if and only if

- any value in row-value is null; or
- no value in row-value is null and there is at least one row (exactly one row if UNIQUE is specified) of the subquery for which every value is equal to the corresponding value in row-value.

Otherwise, the predicate is False. (Just to be clear, every value in row-value must be equal to the corresponding value in a *single* row of the subquery; it doesn't count if the first column value in row-value is equal to the first column value in one row of subquery and the second column value in row-value is equal to the second column value in a different row of subquery!)

If you specify FULL, then the predicate is True if and only if

- every value in row-value is null; or
- no value in row-value is null and there exists at least one row (exactly one row if UNIQUE is specified) of the subquery for which every value is equal to the corresponding value in row-value.

Otherwise (including the case where *any* value in row-value is null), the predicate is False.

If you specify PARTIAL, then the predicate is True if and only if

- every value in row-value is null; or
- there exists at least one row (exactly one row if UNIQUE is specified) of the subquery such that every non-null value in row-value is equal to the corresponding value of the row of the subquery.

Otherwise, the predicate is False.

How would this work for you? In our sample database, we have a rule that requires every row in the MOVIES_STARS table to have a corresponding row in the MOVIE_TITLES table (identified by the TITLE columns in the tables having the same value). We use both the TITLE and the YEAR_PRODUCED columns for the PRIMARY KEY of the MOVIE_TITLES table and for the FOREIGN KEY of the MOVIES_STARS table (MOVIE_TITLE and YEAR_PRODUCED are the column names in the latter table).

Now, we could define the rule to say that if either FOREIGN KEY field is null in MOVIES_STARS, then the row is all right, because we're not going to be compulsive about matching up rows when we have only partial information. That means that we could store a row in the MOVIES_STARS table that claimed that Mel Gibson starred in *The Year of Living Foolishly* simply by leaving the YEAR_PRODUCED field null—that is, the movie title doesn't even have to correspond to a real movie. Okay, that's probably not a reasonable thing to do in *this* application, but it could be done. This corresponds to the option of not specifying a criterion.

Alternatively, we could allow storage of Mel's row only if the values for the FOREIGN KEY were all filled in correctly, or if they were all null. This obviously corresponds to our FULL option.

Finally, we could allow insertion of rows for Mr. Gibson as long as any values that were filled in actually corresponded to meaningful movies or actual years of production of *some* movie. It still might not be a movie that has Mel in it, but that's a problem of external accuracy (valid data) and not, strictly speaking, one of database integrity.

Those three situations would correspond to

```
 . . .
WHERE ( 'The Year of Living Foolishly', NULL )
     MATCH SIMPLE ( SELECT title, year_released
                          FROM movie_titles )
```

and

```
 . . .
WHERE ( 'The Year of Living Foolishly', NULL )
     MATCH FULL ( SELECT title, year_released
                        FROM movie_titles )
```

and

```
 . . .
WHERE ( 'The Year of Living Foolishly', NULL )
     MATCH PARTIAL ( SELECT title, year_released
                           FROM movie_titles )
```

respectively. In this case, the second (MATCH FULL) example would always be False because of the NULL.

7.12 | DISTINCT Predicate

In section 7.8, "EXISTS and UNIQUE Predicates," we showed you the UNIQUE predicate that you can use in your applications to see if a virtual table contains two or more rows that are equal to one another. As you can infer from our use of the word "equal," the UNIQUE predicate uses an equality test to make this determination. But, as you learned in section 2.5, "Logic and Null Values," if you compare two null values, the answer is never "yes, they're equal," but always "whether or not they're equal is unknown." Similarly, in section 7.4.1, "The Big Six Comparison Types," we showed you how you could compare two values or row values to see whether or not they are equal to one another (or unequal, or one less than the other, and so forth).

There are times when your applications need to compare two rows to determine whether every non-null column in each of the rows is equal and every null-valued column in one of the otherwise equal rows is matched with a column whose value is also null. In SQL:1999, we refer to this situation using the term *not distinct.*

In SQL:1999, two values can either be equal or not equal, unless one or both of them are the null value. If they are both the null value, then they are not distinct, even though we cannot say whether or not they are equal or unequal. If one value is null and another is not null, then the two values are distinct, even though we still cannot say whether or not they are equal or unequal. Syntax 7-8 shows the syntax of the DISTINCT predicate.

Syntax 7-8 *Syntax of DISTINCT Predicate*

```
row-value-1 IS DISTINCT FROM row-value-2
```

You will immediately note that there is no subquery involved in the DISTINCT predicate, so you cannot use it in the same manner as you would use the UNIQUE predicate; instead, you'd use it more like you would an equality comparison predicate, in which you compare two specific row values. To understand this, consider the three uses of the DISTINCT predicate in Example 7-32:

Example 7-32 *Three DISTINCT Predicate Examples*

```
(10, 20, 30) IS DISTINCT FROM (10, 20, 30)
(10, 20, NULL) IS DISTINCT FROM (10, 20, 30)
(10, 20, NULL) IS DISTINCT FROM (10, 20, NULL)
```

The first line, comparing two row values each of which have three non-null values, would result in False, since all of the corresponding values are equal to one another (which, of course, requires that none of them are null). In this case, False is what we want to get, since the two row values are obviously not distinct from each other—two equal values are not distinct. We would have achieved precisely the same answer if we were to replace IS DISTINCT FROM with <> (not equal).

The second line, which compares two row values for which the first two columns contain non-null values and the third has a null value in one row value only, will result in True. This is also precisely what we expect, since a null value is distinct from the number 30, even though the corresponding values of the first two columns of the two row values are equal and thus not distinct. Now, however, we would not get the same answer if we were to replace IS DISTINCT FROM with <> (not equal), because comparison with a null value results in *Unknown*.

The third line really illustrates the value added by the DISTINCT predicate. In this example, the corresponding values of the first two columns of the two row values remain equal to one another, but the third column in each row value has the null value. In this case, the use of any equality-type predicate (such as <>) would result in Unknown. But the IS DISTINCT FROM predicate would return False, which is appropriate, since two null values are not distinct from one another according to SQL:1999's rules.

In our opinion, the DISTINCT predicate has a minor omission that makes it slightly inconvenient to use. That omission is the lack of the ability to negate the predicate: that is, SQL:1999 does not support the syntax IS NOT DISTINCT FROM. Instead, you have to use a construction like this:

```
NOT (10, 20, 30) IS DISTINCT FROM (10, 20, 30)
```

That is, you have to put the keyword NOT in front of the whole predicate, which makes it sound a bit awkward from most readers' viewpoints.

The DISTINCT predicate requires a special rule when the data type of one (or more) of the row values' columns is an array type. In particular, two values whose types are array types are distinct from each other if either of the following three characteristics are met:

- One array is null and the other is non-null.
- The number of elements in the array values differs.
- For corresponding array elements in the two array values, the values of the array elements are distinct.

Incidentally, if the number of elements in each array value is zero, then the arrays are not distinct from each other.

<h2>7.13 | Type Predicate</h2>

In the interests of completeness, we're going to mention the type predicate here. However, because this predicate is only used in the context of SQL:1999's object facilities, it is dealt with in detail in Volume 2 of this book, and so we will only briefly discuss it here.

The type predicate is provided in SQL:1999 so that SQL code can determine whether or not the data type of some value is one of a specified list of user-defined types. The predicate can return Unknown if the provided value is the null value, True if the value's type is one of the types specified in the list, or False if the value's type is not among those specified in the list.

<h2>7.14 | Search Conditions</h2>

SQL uses the term search-condition to indicate any combination of predicates that are used together to make a combined test. The SQL-92 syntax for a search condition is given in Syntax 7-9.

Syntax 7-9 *SQL-92 Syntax of Search Conditions*

```
<search condition> ::=
    <boolean term>
  | <search condition> OR <boolean term>

<boolean term> ::=
    <boolean factor>
  | <boolean term> AND <boolean factor>

<boolean factor> ::=
    [ NOT ] <boolean test>

<boolean test> ::=
    <boolean primary> [ IS [ NOT ] <truth value> ]
```

```
<truth value> ::=
      TRUE
    | FALSE
    | UNKNOWN


<boolean primary> ::=
      <predicate>
    | <left paren> <search condition> <right paren>
```

In SQL:1999, because of the introduction of the Boolean data type, the syntax of search conditions has been significantly simplified, as shown in Syntax 7-10.

Syntax 7-10 *SQL:1999 Syntax of Search Conditions*

```
<search condition> ::=
    <boolean value expression>
```

In reality, of course, the syntax hasn't been simplified at all; it's just hidden in the syntax of Boolean value expressions, which we covered in section 5.10.5, "Boolean Value Expression." In spite of that fact, we're going to cover search conditions here. While it may be a bit redundant, it's appropriate, since the most important semantics of combining predicates is encountered in the context of search conditions and not in the context of Boolean values themselves.

In some of our examples, we've used two predicates hooked together with the keyword AND to ensure that *both* predicates are True in order for a row to meet our criteria. Similarly, we've sometimes used OR to permit a row to meet the criteria if *either* predicate is True. And, as we mentioned above, SQL allows you to precede any predicate with NOT to invert the meaning of the predicate. The combination of predicates with AND, OR, and NOT comprises a search-condition.

Because SQL supports null values and predicates whose results are Unknown, we say that the language uses three-valued logic (True, False, and Unknown; we discussed these in Chapter 2, "Introduction to SQL:1999"). You will recall that Boolean logic tells us that the result of an AND is True if and only if *both* of the operands are True. Therefore, True AND True is True, but True AND False is False. How about True AND Unknown, though? If the Unknown were replaced by True, then the predicate would be True, but if it were replaced by False, then the predicate would be False. To resolve the dilemma, we say that True AND Unknown is Unknown. Similar rules apply for OR: True OR True is true, as is True OR False, but False OR False is always False. How about False OR Unknown? In this case, if the

Unknown were replaced by False, then the result would be False, but a replacement with True would make the result True. As a result, we make the result of False OR Unknown also Unknown. (By the way, the AND and OR operations are *commutative*, which means that the operands can be in either order with the same result.) Finally, NOT True is False, NOT False is True, and NOT Unknown is (although it sounds funny to say it) still Unknown. We've summarized the rules of three-valued logic for you in Tables 7-7 through 7-10. (We note that Table 7-7 and Table 7-8 are essentially duplicates of Table 2-3, "Truth Table for AND," and Table 2-4, "Truth Table for OR," respectively, repeated here for your convenience.)

Table 7-7 *Truth Table for the AND Boolean Operator*

AND	True	False	Unknown
True	True	False	Unknown
False	False	False	False
Unknown	Unknown	False	Unknown

Table 7-8 *Truth Table for the OR Boolean Operator*

OR	True	False	Unknown
True	True	True	True
False	True	False	Unknown
Unknown	True	Unknown	Unknown

Table 7-9 *Truth Table for the NOT Boolean Operator*

NOT	
True	False
False	True
Unknown	Unknown

Table 7-10 *Truth Table for the IS Boolean Operator*

IS	True	False	Unknown
True	True	False	False
False	False	True	False
Unknown	False	False	True

Sometimes, predicates combined into search conditions sound funny when you read them aloud. It might sound better if you could say, "this test is False" or "this one is True." To support this occasional need, SQL:1999 search conditions allow you to use the keywords TRUE, FALSE, and UNKNOWN to expand the evaluation of predicates. These Boolean search conditions are an alternative means to express the basic search conditions we've been exploring so far. For example, an alternative manner to express the query "list all movies that don't have a current DVD sales price of $29.95" would be

```
SELECT title
FROM movie_titles
WHERE current_dvd_sales_price = 29.95 IS FALSE ;
```

Now, this one doesn't sound better than (in our opinion, it doesn't even sound as good as) the same query without the IS FALSE. However, others might think it does.

Similarly, a list of all movies starring Eddie Murphy can be found using

```
SELECT movie_title
FROM movies_stars
WHERE ( actor_last_name = 'Murphy'
    AND actor_first_name = 'Eddie' ) IS TRUE ;
```

A guideline: The more complex a search condition is, the more likely you will want to at least consider using the IS TRUE, IS FALSE, or IS UNKNOWN variations. For instance, if you wanted to retrieve all movies where the actors' first names, last names, or both are null, you could write the following:

```
SELECT movie_title
FROM movies_stars
WHERE ( actor_last_name = 'X'
    AND actor_first_name = 'X' ) IS UNKNOWN
```

Note that we don't have to ask for a real name, just any non-null value. Yes, there are other ways to ask the same query, but this one might sound better to some application programmers.

What exactly does IS UNKNOWN mean? First, IS UNKNOWN is not the same as IS NULL. Remember that "nullness" is a characteristic of an SQL data item. "Unknown-ness," in contrast, is a characteristic of a predicate or other Boolean value. The differences between the two concepts and the corresponding syntactical expressions may appear to be subtle, but they must be used correctly in order to develop SQL applications.

7.15 | Chapter Summary

Predicates, as we have seen, are a valuable mechanism to assist your database searches. Rather than having to manually sift through voluminous amounts of data, you'll find that comparison operators, LIKE, subqueries, IN, and so forth can help you expand or limit your searches to the most appropriate degree of precision. In Chapter 8, "Working with Multiple Tables: The Relational Operators," we'll discuss the relational operators and how they are represented and used in SQL:1999. Together with the material we've discussed so far, particularly predicates, you can start to build real-world systems to handle your information processing requirements.

Chapter
8

Working with Multiple Tables: The Relational Operators

8.1 ## Introduction

So far, except for a brief discussion of subqueries, we have discussed SQL:1999 statements that deal with single tables. Since one of the primary purposes of relational databases is to relate information among tables in a database, we now examine the major SQL:1999 facilities that help you do this. In this chapter, we discuss the many different types of join operations. We also discuss the UNION, INTERSECT, and EXCEPT operators and how they are used for multiple table management. In addition, we explore a number of relational operators and learn how they behave in a fairly informal way. In Chapter 9, "Advanced SQL Query Expressions," we'll cover the material in a more substantial manner.

8.2 Join Operations: An Overview

In Chapter 7, "Predicates," we briefly examined how SQL:1999 subqueries can be used to relate one table to another to retrieve cross-referenced data. Information may be *joined* among tables even without using subqueries. The earliest versions of SQL (SQL-85 and SQL-89) supported the relational join operation through the basic SELECT...FROM...WHERE statement. SQL:1999 builds on syntax added in SQL-92, greatly expanding the toolbox of operators you can use to join information across tables.

To assist with our examples in this chapter, let's introduce several new tables into our sample database. Since, as we've mentioned in earlier chapters, our example e-tailer handles both video and audio media products, we will now create several tables relating to the music side of our business. These table definitions, shown below, contain information for (in the order shown) (1) the music titles, artists, and pricing information (regular and current prices for both CD and cassettes); (2) music distributors from whom we purchase CDs and cassettes; (3) current and historical inventory data for each music title; and (4) an "intersection" table that contains current CD and cassette costs for each title available from each distributor.

```
CREATE TABLE music_titles (
    music_id                    CHAR (12) NOT NULL,
    title                       CHAR (30) NOT NULL,
    artist                      CHAR (40),
    artist_more                 CHAR (50),
    record_label                CHAR (20),
    type                        CHAR (10),
    greatest_hits_collection    BOOLEAN,
    category                    CHAR (10),
    date_released               DATE,
    cd_list_price               DECIMAL (9,2),
    cd_current_price            DECIMAL (9,2),
    cassette_list_price         DECIMAL (9,2),
    cassette_current_price      DECIMAL (9,2) ) ;

CREATE TABLE music_distributors (
    distributor_id              CHAR (15) NOT NULL,
    distributor_name            CHAR (25) NOT NULL,
    distributor_address         CHAR (40),
    distributor_city            CHAR (30),
    distributor_state           CHAR (2),
    distributor_zip_code_full   CHAR (10),
    distributor_phone_1         CHAR (10),
    distributor_phone_2         CHAR (10),
    distributor_fax_number_1    CHAR (10),
    distributor_fax_number_2    CHAR (10),
    distributor_web_site_addr   CHAR (40) ) ;
```

```
CREATE TABLE music_inventory (
    music_id                       CHAR (12) NOT NULL,
    number_cd_now_in_stock         INTEGER,
    number_cassette_now_in_stock   INTEGER,
    total_cd_sold                  INTEGER,
    total_cassette_sold            INTEGER,
    total_cd_returned              INTEGER,
    total_cassette_returned        INTEGER) ;

CREATE TABLE current_distributor_costs (
    music_id                       CHAR (12) NOT NULL,
    distributor_id                 CHAR (15) NOT NULL,
    our_cd_cost                    DECIMAL (9,2),
    our_cassette_cost              DECIMAL (9,2) ) ;
```

Note that in the music_titles table, the column artist_more is used primarily for an artist's first name if the artist is a person and not a group (excepting, as in our video movie examples earlier, people like Cher and Sting). Alternatively, it might be used to distinguish between two artists of the same name, such as long ago, when the original Jefferson Airplane became the Jefferson Starship but then there was a new Jefferson Airplane with some, but not all, of the original members of the band. Or, perhaps, you could put the "unpronounceable symbol" (unfortunately, we don't believe the symbol is a part even of the Unicode character set) for "The Artist Formerly Known as Prince" in the artist column, while in the artist_more column you might somehow note the relationship between that symbol and Prince. (Actually, we've taken to simply calling him "TAFKAP" to avoid that strange symbol!) Anyway, some sort of additional clarifying information as to which artist it is could go into this column. Tables 8-1 through 8-4 show portions of the contents of these respective SQL tables.

8.3 | Types of Join Operations

In this chapter, we discuss several different types of join operations. These include

- classic, comma-separated joins
- cross joins
- natural joins

- condition joins
- column name joins
- inner joins
- outer joins (left, right, or full)

Table 8-1 *Portion of Populated Table MUSIC_TITLES*

MUSIC_ID	TITLE	ARTIST ...	ARTIST_ MORE	GREATEST_ HITS_ COLLECTION	CATEGORY
SD328	Two Against Nature	Steely Dan		FALSE	Rock
TE765	Blue	Third Eye Blind		FALSE	Rock
DC95	Fly	Dixie Chicks		FALSE	Country
ST972	Supernatural	Santana		FALSE	Rock
ST3312	Latest Greatest Straitest Hits	Straight	George	TRUE	Country
CG097	The Red Violin	Corigliano	John	FALSE	Soundtrack
AC9982	Stiff Upper Lip	AC/DC		FALSE	Rock
TW3211	Come on Over	Twain	Shania	FALSE	Country
EG22334	Eagles' Greatest Hits	The Eagles		TRUE	Rock
MA5552	Magnolia: Music from the Motion Picture	Mann	Aimee	FALSE	Soundtrack
MG4411	A Place in the Sun	McGraw	Tim	FALSE	Country
KR9965	When I Look in Your Eyes	Krall	Diana	FALSE	Jazz
HA4313	Camelot	Harris	Richard	FALSE	Soundtrack
GS8756	Herding Cats	Gaelic Storm		FALSE	International

Table 8-2 *Portion of Populated Table MUSIC_DISTRIBUTORS*

DISTRIBUTOR_ID	DISTRIBUTOR_NAME	DISTRIBUTOR_ PHONE_1	DISTRIBUTOR_ PHONE_2	DISTRIBUTOR_ FAX_1
US776432	Music All the Time	4125559987		4125559999
US998553	CD Wholesalers, Inc.	2135553219	2135553220	2135553221
US445678	Yesterday's Music Found	6025553489		6025557812

Table 8-3 *Portion of Populated Table MUSIC_INVENTORY*

MUSIC_ID	NUMBER_ CD_NOW_ IN_STOCK	NUMBER_ CASSETTE_ NOW_IN_STOCK	TOTAL_ CD_SOLD	TOTAL_ CASSETTE_ SOLD	TOTAL_CD_ RETURNED	TOTAL_ CASSETTE_ RETURNED
SD328	62	34	986	192	3	15
TE765	56	53	876	221	3	3
DC95	77	21	890	431	4	4
ST972	124	52	1232	334	1	7
ST3312	86	28	553	112	3	12
CG097	3	26	879	31	8	4
AC9982	110	31	1119	346	9	11
TW3211	99	36	975	112	18	7
EG22334	76	22	4312	967	0	2
MA5552	35	29	312	98	2	4
MG4411	87	11	443	231	31	14
KR9965	111	17	997	222	2	2
HA4313	97	15	1000	312	8	13
GS8756	100	85	1566	234	0	0

Table 8-4 *Portion of Populated Table CURRENT_DISTRIBUTOR_COSTS*

MUSIC_ID	DISTRIBUTOR_ID	OUR_CD_COST	OUR_CASSETTE_COST
SD328	US776432	10.95	6.95
SD328	US998553	10.95	6.95
SD328	US445678	10.95	6.95
TE765	US776432	11.95	7.45
TE765	US998553	10.95	6.95
DC95	US776432	10.95	6.95
DC95	US998553	11.95	7.45
DC95	US445678	11.95	7.25
ST972	US998553	10.95	6.95
ST972	US445678	10.95	6.95
ST3312	US776432	11.95	7.95
ST3312	US998553	11.95	7.45
ST3312	US445678	10.95	6.95

(Continued)

Table 8-4 *Continued*

MUSIC_ID	DISTRIBUTOR_ID	OUR_CD_COST	OUR_CASSETTE_COST
CG097	US776432	11.95	7.95
CG097	US998553	10.95	6.95
CG097	US445678	10.95	6.95
AC9982	US776432	11.95	7.45
AC9982	US998553	10.95	6.95
AC9982	US445678	10.95	6.95
TW3211	US776432	10.95	6.95
TW3211	US998553	11.95	7.45
TW3211	US445678	10.95	6.95
EG22334	US776432	10.95	6.95
EG22334	US998553	11.95	7.45
EG22334	US445678	10.95	6.95
MA5552	US776432	11.95	7.95
MA5552	US998553	10.95	6.95
MA5552	US445678	10.95	6.95
MG4411	US776432	10.95	6.95
MG4411	US998553	10.95	6.95
MG4411	US445678	11.95	7.45
KR9965	US776432	11.95	7.95
KR9965	US998553	10.95	6.95
KR9965	US445678	10.95	6.95
HA4313	US776432	10.95	6.95
HA4313	US998553	11.95	7.25
HA4313	US445678	10.95	6.95
GS8756	US445678	12.95	8.95

There is also another type of join operation, the union join, which we discuss following our coverage of union operations in general. The complete syntax for all the ways of joining tables is illustrated in Syntax 8-1.

Syntax 8-1 *Syntax of Joined Table Operation*

```
<joined table> ::=
      <cross join>
```

```
    | <qualified join>
    | <natural join>
    | <union join>

<cross join> ::=
    <table reference> CROSS JOIN <table primary>

<qualified join> ::=
    <table reference> [ <join type> ] JOIN <table reference>
        <join specification>

<natural join> ::=
    <table reference> NATURAL [ <join type> ] JOIN <table primary>

<union join> ::=
    <table reference> UNION JOIN <table primary>

<join specification> ::=
        <join condition>
    | <named columns join>

<join condition> ::= ON <search condition>

<named columns join> ::=
    USING <left paren> <join column list> <right paren>

<join type> ::=
        INNER
    | <outer join type> [ OUTER ]

<outer join type> ::=
        LEFT
    | RIGHT
    | FULL

<join column list> ::= <column name list>
```

That much BNF can be rather intimidating, but it's really not as complicated as it may appear at first glance. We'll go over each piece as needed, and we'll do so methodically. Let's now take a look at each of these join operations, in turn.

8.3.1 Classic, Comma-Separated Joins

So far, the SELECT statements we have examined have always included a single table name following the keyword FROM, as in

```
SELECT column-list
FROM  single-table-name
```

You can, however, specify multiple table names after the FROM, which causes SQL to perform a relational join operation, as in

```
SELECT table1.*, table2.*
FROM table1, table2  ;
```

(In spite of our using it in a few examples here and there, we strongly recommend that you code * in a select list—meaning "all columns of the table"—only when you're using interactive SQL, but never in an application program.)
The above SQL statement causes a virtual table to be produced that includes the Cartesian product (i.e., the cross-product) of the source tables, as illustrated in Result 8-1 when the music_titles and current_distributor_costs tables are joined together in this manner. The resulting table is basically meaningless, since the cross-product of the join causes each row from the first table to be matched with each possible row from the second table.

Result 8-1 *Sample "Old-Style" Join with Cartesian Product Result*

MUSIC_ ID	TITLE	ARTIST...	MUSIC_ ID	DISTRIBUTOR_ ID	OUR_ CD_COST	OUR_CASSETTE_ COST
SD328	Two Against Nature	Steely Dan	SD328	US776432	10.95	6.95
SD328	Two Against Nature	Steely Dan	SD328	US998553	10.95	6.95
SD328	Two Against Nature	Steely Dan	SD328	US445678	10.95	6.95
SD328	Two Against Nature	Steely Dan	TE765	US776432	11.95	7.45
SD328	Two Against Nature	Steely Dan	TE765	US998553	10.95	6.95
SD328	Two Against Nature	Steely Dan	DC95	US776432	10.95	6.95
SD328	Two Against Nature	Steely Dan	DC95	US998553	11.95	7.45
SD328	Two Against Nature	Steely Dan	DC95	US445678	11.95	7.25
SD328	Two Against Nature	Steely Dan	ST972	US998553	10.95	6.95
SD328	Two Against Nature	Steely Dan	ST972	US445678	10.95	6.95
SD328	Two Against Nature	Steely Dan	ST3312	US776432	11.95	7.95

A more meaningful result can be obtained by using the WHERE clause in the SELECT statement to create an *equi-join*, the structure of which is shown in Example 8-1.

Example 8-1 *Equi-Join Structure*

```
SELECT table1.*, table2.*
FROM table1, table2
WHERE table1.colname = table2.colname ;
```

For example, the SQL statement shown in Example 8-2 yields the result table shown in Result 8-2.

Example 8-2 *Sample Equi-Join Statement*

```
SELECT music_titles.*, current_distributor_costs.*
       FROM music_titles, current_distributor_costs
       WHERE music_titles.music_id = current_distributor_costs.music_id ;
```

Result 8-2 *More Meaningful Joined Table*

MUSIC_ID	TITLE	ARTIST...	MUSIC_ID	DISTRIBUTOR_ID	OUR_CD_COST	OUR_CASSETTE_COST
SD328	Two Against Nature	Steely Dan	SD328	US776432	10.95	6.95
SD328	Two Against Nature	Steely Dan	SD328	US998553	10.95	6.95
SD328	Two Against Nature	Steely Dan	SD328	US445678	10.95	6.95
TE765	Blue	Third Eye Blind	TE765	US776432	11.95	7.45
TE765	Blue	Third Eye Blind	TE765	US998553	10.95	6.95
DC95	Fly	Dixie Chicks	DC95	US776432	10.95	6.95
DC95	Fly	Dixie Chicks	DC95	US998553	11.95	7.45
DC95	Fly	Dixie Chicks	DC95	US445678	11.95	7.25

Note that the music_id column appears twice in the result table, since we specified all columns (via the *) in each table to be included in the newly created table. We can further refine our join to produce Result 8-3, as shown in Example 8-3 where we only want to see the ID numbers of distributors from whom we can order our CDs (not worrying about cassettes), and their respective prices.

Example 8-3 *Refining the Column Selection Criteria in a Join Operation*

```
SELECT music_titles.*,
       current_distributor_costs.distributor_id,
       current_distributor_costs.our_cd_cost
  FROM music_titles, current_distributor_costs
 WHERE music_titles.music_id
     = current_distributor_costs.music_id ;
```

Result 8-3 *Refined Equi-Join*

MUSIC_ID	TITLE	ARTIST...	DISTRIBUTOR_ID	OUR_CD_COST
SD328	Two Against Nature	Steely Dan	US776432	10.95
SD328	Two Against Nature	Steely Dan	US998553	10.95
SD328	Two Against Nature	Steely Dan	US445678	10.95
TE765	Blue	Third Eye Blind	US776432	11.95
TE765	Blue	Third Eye Blind	US998553	10.95
DC95	Fly	Dixie Chicks	US776432	10.95
DC95	Fly	Dixie Chicks	US998553	11.95
DC95	Fly	Dixie Chicks	US445678	11.95

Note that by eliminating the duplicate column from the resulting table (along with columns containing information that we don't need at the moment), we not only make the result a bit more intuitive, but we are actually improving performance by reducing the amount of data to be transferred.

The simplest way to view this form of SQL:1999 join processing is that the first example—the Cartesian product table—is always internally created (logically, anyway; optimizers will certainly take shortcuts), after which any WHERE conditions, such as those that specify an equi-join, are subsequently processed against the complete virtual table in much the same way as WHERE conditions are processed against any individual table. That is, in our simple example above, the 52-row table (13 rows from music_titles times 4 rows from current_distributor_costs) is created, and the equality condition of

```
music_titles.music_id = current_distributor_costs.music_id
```

is checked against each of the 17 rows; only those that pass the test will become part of the final result; the rest are "filtered out." Failure to understand this concept is common among those new to SQL and can lead to endless confusion related to how a query can produce more result rows than appear in any of the individual tables involved in the query.

You may have noticed that the table names we selected for the examples in this chapter, particularly Table 8-4, can be somewhat cumbersome to use in an SQL statement, particularly when we are selecting individual columns (as in Example 8-3) rather than using * to return all columns from all tables. *Correlation names* can be used in place of full table names. For example, suppose that we want to produce a list of all entertainers for whom we have both movies and music in stock as part of a special "William Shatner Singing and Acting" promotion (referring to Mr. Shatner's "interpretations" of such rock classics as "Freebird" and "Two Tickets to Paradise" on his commercials for *priceline.com*). The statement shown in Example 8-4 shows how this may be done, referring back to our movies_stars table that we introduced in Chapter 2, "Introduction to SQL:1999," and the music_titles table introduced in this chapter.

Example 8-4 *Using Correlation Names in an SQL Statement*

```
SELECT m.actor_last_name, m.actor_first_name
FROM movies_stars AS m, music_titles AS t
WHERE m.actor_last_name = t.artist
  AND m.actor_first_name = t.artist_more ;
```

Recall that we now must use M and T as correlation names (aliases) for movies_stars and music_titles, respectively. The statement in Example 8-4 creates a virtual table that initially matches each row from movies_stars with each row from music_titles. Following the initial table creation, the last and first names of the actors are compared with those of the music artists. Matches are reflected in the final result table, Result 8-4.

Result 8-4 *Result of Using Correlation Names*

ACTOR_LAST_NAME	ACTOR_FIRST_NAME
Streisand	Barbra
Streisand	Barbra
Streisand	Barbra
Harris	Richard
Harris	Richard

(Continued)

Result 8-4 *Continued*

ACTOR_LAST_NAME	ACTOR_FIRST_NAME
Sinatra	Frank
Sinatra	Frank
Sinatra	Frank
Sinatra	Frank
Sinatra	Frank

Note that duplicate data occurs as a result of multiple matches for Barbra Streisand, Richard Harris, Frank Sinatra, and others due to multiple entries in each of our two source tables. Use of DISTINCT (Example 8-5) will eliminate duplicate data results to give us Result 8-5.

Example 8-5 *Using DISTINCT to Eliminate Duplicates in a Join Operation*

```
SELECT DISTINCT m.actor_last_name, m.actor_first_name
FROM movies_stars m, music_titles t
WHERE m.actor_last_name = t.artist
  AND m.actor_first_name = t.artist_more ;
```

Result 8-5 *SELECT DISTINCT in Joined Table*

ACTOR_LAST_NAME	ACTOR_FIRST_NAME
Streisand	Barbra
Harris	Richard
Sinatra	Frank

Going back to Example 8-3, a deficiency in being able to use the result of the join operation effectively is that only the distributor's ID number shows up, since only the ID number is stored in the current_distributor_costs table. It would be useful to have the distributor's name and contact information available as part of the result. Join operations can include columns from more than two tables, as shown in Example 8-6, resulting in the table shown in Result 8-6.

Example 8-6 *A Join Operation Using Columns from Three Tables*

```
SELECT t.*, c.distributor_id, d.distributor_name,
       d.distributor_phone_1, d.distributor_fax_1,
       c.our_cd_cost
FROM music_titles t, current_distributor_costs c,
     music_distributors d
WHERE t.music_id = c.music_id
  AND c.distributor_id = d.distributor_id ;
```

Result 8-6 *Result of a Three-Way Join*

MUSIC_ ID	TITLE	ARTIST ...	DISTRIBUTOR_ ID	DISTRIBUTOR_NAME	DISTRIBUTOR_ PHONE_1	DISTRIBUTOR_ FAX_1	OUR_CD_ COST
SD328	Two Against Nature	Steely Dan	US776432	Music All the Time	4125559987	4125559999	10.95
SD328	Two Against Nature	Steely Dan	US998553	CD Wholesalers, Inc.	2135553219	2135553221	10.95
SD328	Two Against Nature	Steely Dan	US445678	Yesterday's Music Found	6025553489	6025557812	10.95
TE765	Blue	Third Eye Blind	US776432	Music All the Time	4125559987	4125559999	11.95
TE765	Blue	Third Eye Blind	US998553	CD Wholesalers, Inc.	2135553219	2135553221	10.95
DC95	Fly	Dixie Chicks	US776432	Music All the Time	4125559987	4125559999	10.95
DC95	Fly	Dixie Chicks	US998553	CD Wholesalers, Inc.	2135553219	2135553221	11.95
DC95	Fly	Dixie Chicks	US445678	Yesterday's Music Found	6025553489	6025557812	11.95

Before we begin addressing the new syntax that SQL-92 and SQL:1999 provide for join operations, we want to briefly go over the concept of joining a table to itself (often called a *self-join* operation). There are many cases where the information that you need to derive can be acquired from a single table, but only when matching some information in that table with other information in the same table.

For example, suppose we wanted to publicize our fascination with artists who release eponymous albums (that is, albums having the same name as the artist). We might write a query like the one shown in Example 8-7.

Example 8-7 *Self-Joins*

```
SELECT a.artist
FROM   music_titles AS t, music_titles AS a
WHERE  t.title = a.artist
```

That query (effectively) produces a cross-product of the `music_titles` table with itself, then eliminates all rows for which the `title` column is not equal to the `artist` column, leaving only rows identifying music whose title is the same as the artist's name. A sample of the output is seen in Result 8-7.

Result 8-7 *Eponymous Music*

ARTIST

'N Sync
Backstreet Boys
Foo Fighters
James Taylor
The Beatles
The Eagles
The Velvet Underground
|

|

Queries like this are used for many purposes, including, for example, to retrieve information about employees and their managers, for which your application would include a query that joined the `employees` table with itself, matching the `manager` column with the `employee_id` column. While our example doesn't include personnel tables, the following example is readily understood:

```
SELECT  e.name, m.name
FROM    employees AS e, employees AS t
WHERE   e.employee_manager = m employee_id
```

8.3.2 The CROSS JOIN

The `CROSS JOIN` produces the same cross-product (see Result 8-1) that we saw above when no conditions were expressed via a `WHERE` clause. The syntax is shown in Example 8-8.

Example 8-8 *CROSS JOIN Syntax*

```
SELECT *
FROM table1 CROSS JOIN table2 ;
```

Therefore, it is equivalent to the basic old-style comma-separated join without a `WHERE` clause.

8.3.3 The NATURAL JOIN

A natural join (more properly known as a natural equi-join, because it selects rows from the two tables that have equal values in the relevant columns) is based on all columns in the two tables that share the same name. Example 8-9 shows the syntax for the natural join.

Example 8-9 *NATURAL JOIN Syntax*

```
SELECT *
FROM t1 NATURAL JOIN t2  ;
```

Note that when we matched up actors and musicians in Example 8-4, we didn't perform a natural join because the column names we used for comparison purposes had different names (actor_last_name and actor_first_name compared against artist and artist_more). However, suppose we want to join data from our music_titles and music_inventory tables. We can use a natural join because both tables have a column with the name music_id as shown in Example 8-10, with the result shown in Result 8-8. You could, of course, use correlation names or specify only selected columns to be part of the result table (or both), as shown in the earlier examples in the chapter, but for illustrative purposes we'll use SELECT * as part of the example.

Example 8-10 *NATURAL JOIN for Two Tables*

```
SELECT *
FROM music_titles NATURAL JOIN music_inventory  ;
```

Result 8-8 *Result of a NATURAL JOIN*

MUSIC_ ID	TITLE	ARTIST	...	NUMBER_ CD_NOW_ IN_STOCK	NUMBER_ CASSETTE_ NOW_IN_ STOCK	TOTAL_ CD_SOLD	...
SD328	Two Against Nature	Steely Dan		62	34	986	
TE765	Blue	Third Eye Blind		56	53	876	
DC95	Fly	Dixie Chicks		77	21	890	
ST972	Supernatural	Santana		124	52	1232	
ST3312	Latest Greatest Straitest Hits	Strait		86	28	553	
CG097	The Red Violin	Corigliano		3	26	879	
AC9982	Stiff Upper Lip	AC/DC		110	31	1119	

NATURAL can also be used to qualify some of the other join types we investigate in the coming sections: inner, outer, and union, as we'll show later.

It's also important to note that every row in either table that does not have a "companion" row in the other table—that is, there is no row with an identical value in the same column on which the natural join is taking place—is eliminated from the result table. The following simple example (Table 8-5 and Result 8-9) illustrates this, where the second row in each table is dropped from the final result because (1) there isn't a value of "20" in column c1 in table t2, nor (2) is there a value of "15" in column c1 in table t1.

Table 8-5 *Two Tables for NATURAL JOIN Example*

T1		T2	
C1	C2	C1	C4
10	15	10	BB
20	25	15	DD

Result 8-9 *Result of NATURAL JOIN of Two Tables*

Joined Table		
C1	C2	C4
10	15	BB

You've got to be careful with NATURAL JOIN operations, though. In many application development environments, there is little control over the identifiers that are assigned to tables and columns, and one ends up with the situation where a single identifier is used for multiple purposes. For example, NAME may be used for employees, suppliers, customers, departments, and even parts. Obviously, if you do a NATURAL JOIN of a table containing supplier information with a table containing information about parts that you stock, and both tables have a column whose identifier is NAME, you're going to get some surprising results! (In fact, the most likely result you'll get is an empty result; it seems likely that very few parts have the same name as a company that supplies parts.) In other words, use a NATURAL JOIN only when you are certain that the columns having the same identifier in each table also have the same semantics.

Also, be aware that there is a risk of having the meaning of a NATURAL JOIN change when you are changing the columns (e.g., adding or removing columns) of one or more of the tables involved in the join.

8.3.4 Condition JOIN

Any columns may be used to match rows from one table against those from another table. Example 8-11 illustrates the syntax of the condition join. Note the use of the keyword ON, as opposed to WHERE; this permits you to also use a WHERE clause to further filter the results of the JOIN operation.

Example 8-11 *Structure of Condition JOIN*

```
SELECT *
FROM t1 JOIN t2
  ON t1.c1 = t2.c3  ;
```

The query related to our William Shatner Singing and Acting Promotion (Example 8-4) could also be written as shown in Example 8-12.

Example 8-12 *Condition JOIN Example*

```
SELECT m.actor_last_name, m.actor_first_name
FROM movies_stars AS m
JOIN music_titles AS t
  ON   ( m.actor_last_name = t.artist )
    AND ( m.actor_first_name = t.artist_more ) ;
```

This sort of JOIN has an interesting—perhaps even surprising—side effect on the *scope* of qualifiers (correlation names and exposed table names) that is worth spending a few moments discussing. Let's consider an example of a three-way join (we could use inner or outer joins, the latter covered in section 8.3.8):

```
SELECT select-list
FROM music_titles AS t
JOIN music_inventory AS i
  ON join-condition-1
JOIN some_other_table AS x
  ON join-condition-2
WHERE search-condition
```

Because JOINs are (effectively) performed from left to right (that is, using mathematical terminology, they are left associative), the first JOIN to be performed is

```
music_titles AS t JOIN music_inventory AS i
```

That JOIN has an ON clause with a search condition, represented here as join-condition-1. The search condition in join-condition-1 can reference columns in music_titles and in music_inventory but *cannot* reference any columns in some_other_table. That's because the *scope* of join-condition-1 is only that first JOIN.

The second JOIN is, of course,

```
( result-of-first-JOIN ) JOIN some_other_table AS x
```

which also has an ON clause with a second search condition (join-condition-2). That search condition can reference columns in some_other_table and can also reference columns in the result of the first JOIN. Because the first JOIN doesn't obscure its source tables, the second search-condition *can* reference columns in music_titles and music_inventory as well as some_other_table!

We should point out that, in many cases, especially when the joins are inner joins and you don't use an ON condition, the order in which the joins are performed is irrelevant.

You will want to use your knowledge of this scoping characteristic to help you decide how to code your ON clauses; sometimes you'll put a particular predicate in one ON clause and sometimes in another. Of course, the search-condition in the WHERE clause and the select-list can both reference columns from all three tables.

8.3.5 Column Name JOIN

Natural JOINs use all columns with the same names to manage the matching process. If we only want to use some of those columns (perhaps because we know that some columns in the two tables that share a column name do not share semantics), we can explicitly specify those column names, as shown in Example 8-13.

Example 8-13 *The Column Name JOIN*

```
SELECT *
FROM t1 JOIN t2
USING (c1, c2)  ;
```

In our relatively simple examples in this chapter, we don't have any tables with a *compound key*; that is, in the examples of this chapter, the values that uniquely identify each row in a table are taken from exactly one column. In a real-world example, however, we would likely have tables in our database that not only have some type of unique identifying number (such as music_title), but also additional columns that appear in more than one table in the database, such as month_year in a set of tables that capture monthly sales statistics. So should you wish to disregard one or more of these other columns, you can use USING to do so.

There is a surprise waiting for you when you use JOIN with a USING clause: the columns referenced in the USING clause have no qualifier. Let's see an example to illustrate this.

```
SELECT select-list
FROM music_titles
JOIN current_distributor_costs
USING (music_id)
WHERE search-condition
```

In this example, the select-list might contain references to music_titles.cd_list_price and to current_distributor_costs.our_cd_cost; so can the search-condition in the WHERE clause. However, *neither* one of them can reference music_titles.music_id or current_distributor_costs.music_id! Instead, if they reference the column on which the JOIN is performed at all, it can only be with the simple identifier music_id. That is, the JOIN...USING syntax "projects out" both tables' column named MUSIC_ID and replaces them both with a single column with that name; since that replacement column is not "the" column from either table, it has no qualifier. To emphasize this point, let us speculate that one of the columns identified in a USING clause is defined as CHARACTER(10), but the corresponding column from the other joined table is defined as CHARACTER VARYING(8). SQL's rules for determining the data type of the result column would choose a data type of CHARACTER VARYING(10), which is not the data type of either of the source columns. That is, the replacement column is *neither* the column from the first table, nor the column from the second table, but a new column created by SQL to capture information from both columns.

Therefore,

```
SELECT music_titles.cd_list_price, music_id
FROM music_titles
JOIN current_distributor_costs
USING (music_id)
WHERE music_id = "SD328" ;
```

is valid, but

```
SELECT music_titles.cd_list_price, music_titles.music_id
FROM music_titles
```

```
JOIN current_distributor_costs
USING (music_id)
WHERE music_titles.music_id = "SD328" ;
```

is invalid.

The same restriction exists in the NATURAL JOIN:

```
SELECT music_id, t.title, t.cd_list_price, c.our_cd_cost
FROM music_titles AS t
NATURAL JOIN
    current_distributor_costs AS c ;
```

is valid, since music_id is the column that SQL provides to coalesce the values taken from t.music_id and c.music_id, but substituting t.music_id or c.music_id would be invalid, since neither of those two columns are part of the result of the JOIN...USING or of the NATURAL JOIN. If your application absolutely, positively has to have access to the value of the source columns, then you must code your joins without the USING clause (and, for the same reason, avoid the NATURAL JOIN).

8.3.6 Joins So Far

So far, we've discussed several styles of joins. The old-style JOIN (comma-separated list of table names) and the CROSS JOIN are essentially the same. The NATURAL JOIN uses all columns with the same name in the two source tables for an implicit equi-join (a JOIN in which the values in those columns are equal), while the column name JOIN allows you to specify a USING clause so that you can further restrict the columns used to a subset of those columns having the same name.

By contrast, the *condition* JOIN lets you specify an arbitrary search condition to determine how the rows of the two tables will be joined. Sometimes, the ON clause is redundant with the WHERE clause; however, we like to use the ON clause to specify conditions specifically related to the JOIN and use the WHERE clause for additional filtering of the result of the JOIN.

ON and WHERE are not interchangeable, though; our discussion of OUTER JOINs will make that clear shortly.

8.3.7 The INNER JOIN

The types of JOIN operations we've discussed thus far are known in the relational model and in SQL:1999 terminology as *inner joins*. For the sake of clarity, you can explicitly specify that a particular statement represents an INNER JOIN, as shown in Example 8-14.

Example 8-14 *INNER JOIN Syntax*

```
SELECT *
FROM t1 INNER JOIN t2
USING (c1, c2)  ;
```

The use of INNER has no additional effects, but it does help your statement to be completely self-documenting.

8.3.8 The OUTER JOIN

As opposed to the INNER JOIN, the OUTER JOIN operation preserves *unmatched* rows from one or both tables, depending on the keyword used: LEFT, RIGHT, or FULL. That is, an INNER JOIN disregards any rows where the specific search condition isn't met, while an OUTER JOIN maintains some or all of the unmatched data. Let's look at some examples.

LEFT OUTER JOIN

The LEFT OUTER JOIN preserves unmatched rows from the *left table,* the one that precedes the keyword JOIN. Let's look at our condition JOIN example earlier from Example 8-11, where we use values in differently named columns as our matching criteria. In Example 8-15, you see the new text of the query, using a LEFT OUTER JOIN.

Example 8-15 *LEFT OUTER JOIN*

```
SELECT *
FROM t1 LEFT OUTER JOIN t2
  ON t1.c1 = t2.c3  ;
```

Table 8-6 *Two Tables for LEFT OUTER JOIN*

C1	C2	C3	C4
10	15	10	BB
20	25	15	DD

Result 8-10   *Result of Ordinary Inner Condition Join*

Joined Table

C1	C2	C3	C4
10	15	10	BB

Result 8-11   *Result of LEFT OUTER JOIN*

Joined Table

C1	C2	C3	C4
10	15	10	BB
20	25	null	null

Example 8-15 operates on the two tables illustrated in Table 8-6; if we had written an ordinary condition join (that is, an inner join with either an ON clause or an equivalent WHERE clause), then we would have gotten the results shown in Result 8-10. However, the LEFT OUTER JOIN produces a result with additional data as seen in Result 8-11. By definition, each row in the first table in a LEFT OUTER JOIN must be included in the result table—whether or not there is a row in the second table that matches, based on the criteria given in the ON clause. The first row, where C1 = 10, had a match found in the right table (T2), and the join operation is completed to produce a new row. The second row, however, has no corresponding row in T2 where C3 = 20. Therefore, the values from T1 (C1 = 10, C2 = 25) are added to a new row in the resulting virtual table, accompanied by *null* values for columns C3 and C4 of that new row.

Because the row representing the unmatched row from the first (left) table has nulls in the columns that correspond to the second (right) table, most SQL practitioners refer to such rows as *null-extended* rows. We think that term is appropriate and clearly evocative of the behavior of the OUTER JOIN operation.

Of course, inclusion of rows by an OUTER JOIN operation doesn't mean that those very same rows might not then be excluded by the query's WHERE clause. If we were silly enough, we could write something like this:

```
SELECT *
FROM t1 LEFT OUTER JOIN t2
ON t1.c1 = t2.c3
WHERE t2.c3 IS NOT NULL AND t2.c4 IS NOT NULL
```

That would defeat the purpose of doing the LEFT OUTER JOIN, since the WHERE clause would carefully delete the very rows that the LEFT OUTER JOIN would have retained.

RIGHT OUTER JOIN

The RIGHT OUTER JOIN operates similarly to a LEFT OUTER JOIN, except the *right*, or second-named, table has its rows preserved.

Example 8-16 *RIGHT OUTER JOIN*

```
SELECT *
FROM t1 RIGHT OUTER JOIN t2
ON t1.c1 = t2.c3  ;
```

Table 8-7 *Two Tables for RIGHT OUTER JOIN*

C1	C2		C3	C4
\multicolumn{2}{c}{T1}		\multicolumn{2}{c}{T2}	
10	15		10	BB
20	25		15	DD

Result 8-12 *Result of RIGHT OUTER JOIN*

C1	C2	C3	C4
\multicolumn{4}{c}{Joined Table}			
10	15	10	BB
null	null	15	DD

FULL OUTER JOIN

The FULL OUTER JOIN acts as a combination of LEFT and RIGHT OUTER JOINs.

Example 8-17 *FULL OUTER JOIN*

```
SELECT *
FROM t1 FULL OUTER JOIN t2
ON t1.c1 = t2.c3  ;
```

Table 8-8 *Two Tables for FULL OUTER JOIN*

C1	C2		C3	C2
\multicolumn{2}{c}{T1}		\multicolumn{2}{c}{T2}	
10	15		10	BB
20	25		15	DD

Result 8-13 *Result of FULL OUTER JOIN*

Joined Table

C1		C3	
10	15	10	BB
20	25	*null*	*null*
null	*null*	15	DD

In Chapter 6, "Advanced Value Expressions: CASE, CAST, and Row Value Expressions," we promised that we'd show you a more interesting use of COALESCE—well, here it is. We're going to show a four-way OUTER JOIN (without a net, no less) to illustrate that your joins won't always be simple two-way A JOIN B operations; among other things, we'll try to show you that OUTER JOINs are not commutative (even though INNER JOINs are), and we'll show how COALESCE is really helpful.

Suppose we have tables q1, q2, q3, and q4 to hold quarterly video and music sales results; each table has an id and a total column (id is the account number and total is the sales total for that account for the appropriate quarter). Any account can have one record for the quarter, or no entry at all. To select sales by quarter, you'd write the following:

```
SELECT *
FROM q1
FULL OUTER JOIN
      q2
   ON (on-clause-1-2)
FULL OUTER JOIN
      q3
   ON (on-clause-12-3)
FULL OUTER JOIN
      q4
   ON (on-clause-123-4)
```

which would give you a table containing one row for each account that had some sales activity during any one (or more) of the four quarters. Without a COALESCE, this table will end up with four different copies of the id column, so a careful programmer would eliminate such redundant data by *coalescing* the four copies into one result column.

Now, on-clause-1-2 is obviously Q1.ID = Q2.ID. We might initially write on-clause-12-3 as Q1.ID = Q3.ID. But, then we would only match q3 rows with the q1-q2 result rows that have non-null values for q1.id; otherwise, we would miss q1-q2 result rows that are null for q1.id but have a value for q2.id. Thus, on-clause-12-3 must be one of the following:

```
ON ( q1.id = q3.id   OR   q2.id = q3.id )
```

```
ON ( COALESCE ( q1.id , q2.id ) = q3.id )
```

Then we need a similar analysis for on-clause-123-4. We might initially write it as ON(q1.id=q4.id), but then we would match only q1-q2-q3 result rows with values for q1.id So, our on-clause-123-4 must be one of the following:

```
ON ( q1.id = q4.id OR q2.id = q4.id OR q3.id = q4.id )
```

```
ON ( COALESCE(q1.id, q2.id, q3.id) = q4.id )
```

(Caution: In this instance, the two variants of the ON clause have the same effect, but don't be misled into believing that a COALESCE like this one is syntactically equivalent or always semantically equivalent to the series of comparisons connected by OR.)

The previous example demonstrates how COALESCE can really make multi-way OUTER JOINs possible (although you might easily conclude that nothing can make them pretty).

Now, let's quickly explore commutativity (or the lack thereof) of OUTER JOINs. If you did a three-way inner join, like

```
SELECT * FROM t1, t2, t3
```

the result would be exactly the same (except for the order of the columns) as

```
SELECT * FROM t2, t3, t1
```

This is called *commutative* behavior, meaning that you can interchange the positions of the various table names in the list of table names without changing the result of the operations. However, OUTER JOINs are less friendly in this way. Specifically,

```
SELECT *
FROM t1
LEFT OUTER JOIN t2
LEFT OUTER JOIN t3
```

will give you very different results than

```
SELECT *
FROM t2
LEFT OUTER JOIN t3
LEFT OUTER JOIN t1
```

We'll let you work out the differences yourself—an exercise for the reader. (Hint: Using what you've learned in this section, derive the result of the first LEFT OUTER JOIN in each case, then use that result in the derivation of the result of the second LEFT OUTER JOIN.) The message is that you need to be *very* careful how you write your outer joins or you'll get some really unexpected results.

Product Caveats

Unfortunately, the SQL vendors have been slow in implementing the style of OUTER JOIN operators that the SQL standard has provided since 1992. Most major vendors had already implemented outer joins using a proprietary syntax that unfortunately did not lend itself well to generalization when combined in queries with other outer joins (or, indeed, any other relational operators).

For example, Sybase, Inc. Adaptive Server Anywhere version 12 provides both standard OUTER JOIN syntax and the earlier proprietary Transact-SQL syntax illustrated in Example 8-18.

Example 8-18 *Sybase Proprietary Syntax for Left Outer Join*

```
SELECT column-list
FROM   table1, table2
WHERE  table1.column1 *= table2.column2
```

The use of the *= syntax is intended to signal that unmatched rows from the table on the same side of the equal sign as the asterisk (the left side, in this case) are to be retained in the result. Similarly, you could use =* for a right outer join. Transact-SQL did not provide any syntax, such as *=*, for full outer joins.

Oracle Corp. defined analogous capabilities, but used a different syntactic convention. Instead of specifying the outer join through a modification of the comparison operator in the WHERE clause, Oracle's syntax used the notation illustrated in Example 8-19.

Example 8-19 *Oracle Proprietary Syntax for Right Outer Join*

```
SELECT column-list
FROM   table1, table2
WHERE  table1.column1 = table2.column2(+)
```

In Oracle's syntax, the use of (+) identifies the column in the table for which unmatched rows are to be maintained. If the (+) notation were applied to the column identifier on the left side of the equal sign, then a left outer join would be performed instead. Oracle's syntax does not permit the (+) notation to be used on both sides of the equal sign; therefore, no full outer join is possible.

With all vendors' proprietary extensions, we have to give you an additional caution: because those extensions are somewhat ad hoc in nature, you'll find that they are associated with numerous restrictions that aren't applicable to the standard's OUTER JOIN facilities. Be sure you understand those restrictions before you use the proprietary language.

Many other SQL vendors have provided analogous proprietary ways of specifying outer joins, but all of those vendors are—as far as we are able to tell, at least—actively moving toward providing SQL standard syntax for outer joins. Some of them (e.g., Sybase) have already released products with standard outer join syntax, while others are expected to do so shortly, perhaps before you have read these words. IBM's DB2 is a notable exception, because it implemented the SQL standard syntax for outer joins from the beginning without going through that first awkward step of providing proprietary language.

8.4 | The UNION Operator

Before we discuss our next—and final—type of JOIN operator, we need to examine the UNION operator and how it works. UNION is used to combine two tables whose respective column data types are *union compatible* (that is, comparable; you can learn more about these rules in section 9.7, "Result Data Types of Columns of UNION, EXCEPT, and INTERSECT"). We note that the *names* of the columns of the source tables are not relevant in determining whether the source tables are union compatible. The data type of each column of the result is determined from the data types of the columns in the source tables; see the rules for union data types in section 9.7). With SQL-86 and SQL-89, UNION was limited to cursor operations (we discuss cursors in Chapter 13, "Cursors"). SQL:1999 permits UNION operations to be performed within query expressions, as did SQL-92.

Assume that in addition to our `music_titles` table (Table 8-1), we also have a table with the identical structure (same column names and definitions, etc.) called `discontinued_music_titles` that contains CDs and cassettes that are no longer being produced by their respective labels. Given that the column names, data types, and other properties of these two tables are identical, we can create a consolidated list of all music titles, both those available now as well as those that are discontinued, through the statement shown in Example 8-20:

Example 8-20 *UNION Example*

```
SELECT *
FROM music_titles
UNION
SELECT *
FROM discontinued_music_titles ;
```

The preceding statement will produce a resulting virtual table with all rows from the first table *plus* all rows from the second table (again, be careful about the use of SELECT * as compared with specifying all columns; care should be taken as to which form you use in various circumstances). Naturally, the resulting virtual table has the same "shape" (that is, the same number of columns, in the same order, and with the same data types) as the two source tables.

Several items must be noted. First, the virtual tables are a very important consideration in UNION operations. Therefore, the following statement is *incorrect:*

```
SELECT title, greatest_hits_collection
FROM music_titles
UNION DISTINCT
SELECT record_label, date_released
FROM discontinued_music_titles ;
```

Even though the source tables are union compatible in their entirety, the different column projections within each query expression above make the statement syntactically invalid (because the *virtual tables* that are being UNIONed don't have union-compatible columns—specifically, SQL doesn't permit a DATE column to be unioned with a BOOLEAN column).

If you don't specify the optional keyword DISTINCT, then UNION will eliminate duplicate rows anyway. (SQL:1999 provides the optional keyword DISTINCT to allow you to write fully self-documenting queries.) If MUSIC_TITLES was somehow to have a row entry that was identical to one found in DISCONTINUED_

ALBUMS, only one copy of that row will find its way into the resulting virtual table.

The relational model of data (see section 1.2.3, "The Relational Model") depends on—requires, in fact—that no relation (which SQL calls *table*) contain two or more rows that are equal to one another. Every row must be unique in the relation. SQL, as we've seen, does not require that limitation, but it allows you to specify the restriction on your own tables. You can define tables with a PRIMARY KEY (see Chapter 4, "Basic Data Definition Language (DLL)") to ensure that your stored data does not contain duplicate rows. You can also ensure that the virtual tables that are the results of your queries do not contain duplicate rows by using the keyword DISTINCT in the select lists of those queries.

To enforce the relational model's semantics that depend on never having duplicate rows throughout the partial results that are computed during query evaluation, you can also use DISTINCT on operators such as UNION, EXCEPT, and INTERSECT.

You can, if desired, preserve duplicate rows in the virtual table through the use of ALL in place of DISTINCT. Suppose we have a table for inventory available through our Web site, plus another table containing inventory from a retail store that we still operated in the pre-Internet days when we started out in the music business. The result might not be meaningful without identification by store or site, but we could produce a comprehensive inventory list with each row preserved as follows:

```
SELECT title, artist, ...
FROM music_titles
UNION ALL
SELECT title, artist, ...
FROM music_titles_mall_store ;
```

The use of CORRESPONDING will sometimes make it possible to form the UNION, intersection (INTERSECT), or difference (EXCEPT) of two tables that have common columns but that aren't actually union compatible. CORRESPONDING without a column list will form virtual tables that have only the common columns (columns with the same name) from the two source tables and then UNION (or INTERSECT or EXCEPT) them. Specifying a column list further restricts the columns in the source virtual tables (and the result) to the common columns in the list. (Perhaps obviously, the column list can contain only names of columns that are common columns in the two source tables.)

In our example above, it would be unlikely that each album's inventory data at each store would be identical, but we use ALL to be sure that each row is preserved. Suppose we just want to produce a comprehensive list of titles and artists that we have on the Web site along with those in the mall store. (While our Internet e-tail site has a far greater inventory of currently available music, our store also contains discontinued titles that we don't carry on our Web site because of low volume and unpredictable availability.) We could use

```
SELECT * FROM music_titles
UNION CORRESPONDING BY (title, artist, artist_more)
SELECT * FROM music_titles_mall_store  ;
```

This example selects the three *interesting* columns (for the purposes of this example, that is) from each store's table and produces a result that has all the rows from both stores. Even though we used SELECT *, the additional use of CORRESPONDING (...) reduced the columns from each store—and in the result—to just the three in the column list.

Now, something about this SELECT...UNION CORRESPONDING statement and the result must be understood. We asked for a SELECT * for each source table, which, as we discussed in Chapter 3, "Basic Table Creation and Data Manipulation," translates to a column select list of all of the columns in the table(s): title, artist, artist_more, record_label, type, and so on. Our result, however, only has three columns: the same three we specified after the UNION CORRESPONDING. What happened? The following logical sequence of actions takes place as the statement is processed and executed.

1. The asterisks (*) are translated into the complete column list as part of the SELECTs.

2. Those new column lists from step 1 above are then *further reduced* by the CORRESPONDING specification; in effect, the columns whose names do not appear in the CORRESPONDING list (whether explicit or implicit) are thrown away, as if they were never specified at all.

3. The UNION CORRESPONDING processing will eliminate duplicates (because DISTINCT is the default if ALL is not specified) and produce the query result, with only three columns.

Therefore, even though you may specify SELECT * ..., your result will only contain the specific columns you specify as part of UNION CORRESPONDING, regardless of whether your source tables have 10 or 1000 columns. If you do not specify an explicit CORRESPONDING column list, then all columns with the same name in both tables form an implicit list.

The syntax of CORRESPONDING is shown in Syntax 8-2.

Syntax 8-2 *Syntax of CORRESPONDING*

```
<corresponding spec> ::=
  CORRESPONDING [ BY <left paren> <corresponding column list> <right paren> ]

<corresponding column list> ::= <column name list>
```

8.4.1 Alternative Syntax

It is inconvenient, as well as nonintuitive, to keep repeating the SELECT * FROM...
phrase in UNION queries, but the potential syntax ambiguities make it *impossible*
to specify something like

```
SELECT *
FROM t1 UNION t2  ;
```

There is, however, a parentheses-assisted shortcut that can be used:

```
SELECT *
FROM ( TABLE t1 UNION TABLE t2 ) AS tbl_union;
```

SQL-92 defined (and SQL:1999 retained) the shorthand notation TABLE table-
name to be equivalent to SELECT * FROM table-name. Therefore, the preceding
shortcut is equivalent to specifying the following:

```
SELECT *
FROM (( SELECT *
        FROM t1 )
  UNION
      ( SELECT *
        FROM t2 )
      ) AS tbl_union
```

(SQL syntax requires that a correlation name be specified after a subquery that
appears in the FROM clause, as we've done here.)

8.5 | UNION JOIN

Earlier, we mentioned that there was a final type of join operation, one we would discuss after introducing UNION. The SQL:1999 UNION JOIN works in a manner similar to that of the FULL OUTER JOIN, with one major difference. Recall that with the FULL OUTER JOIN, column matches may be specified that result in a single consolidated row. The UNION JOIN has no provisions for column matching, but rather

- creates a new virtual table with the union of all columns from the source tables, and
- creates a row in the new table with the values from the respective columns from each source table, with null values assigned to columns within each row from the other table.

For example, let's look at our FULL OUTER JOIN example from earlier:

Table 8-9 *Two Tables for FULL OUTER JOIN (Again)*

	T1			T2	
C1	C2		C3	C2	
10	15		10	BB	
20	25		15	DD	

The UNION JOIN results are shown in Result 8-14.

Result 8-14 *Result of UNION JOIN*

Joined Table

C1			C3	
10	15	null	null	
20	25	null	null	
null	null	10	BB	
null	null	15	DD	

Unlike the FULL OUTER JOIN, *no attempt* is made to match rows by column name or in any other manner.

It is also interesting to note these equivalencies:

```
a CROSS JOIN b
```

is equivalent to any and all of the following:

```
a INNER JOIN b ON 2=2
a LEFT CUTER JOIN b ON 2=2
a RIGHT OUTER JOIN b ON 2=2
a FULL CUTER JOIN b ON 2=2
```

(where $2 = 2$ is any predicate that is *always* True). Similarly,

```
a UNION JOIN b
```

is equivalent to

```
a FULL OUTER JOIN b ON 2=3
```

(where $2 = 3$ could be any predicate that is *always* False).

There's actually a relationship between various sorts of the join operations we've discussed:

- FULL OUTER JOIN contains both LEFT OUTER JOIN and RIGHT OUTER JOIN.
- Both LEFT OUTER JOIN and RIGHT CUTER JOIN contain INNER JOIN.
- CROSS JOIN contains INNER JOIN.
- LEFT OUTER JOIN INTERSECT RIGHT OUTER JOIN is very similar to INNER JOIN (although the presence of null values in the columns of one or both of the tables being joined affects the results of the INNER JOIN differently than the INTERSECTion of the two OUTER JOINs due to the sequence in which comparisons are made).

As you can see, SQL:1999 could have provided fewer ways to express these concepts, but the existence of the various options often makes it easier and more direct to write many queries—once you've learned how to use the various alternatives, at least.

UNION JOIN has not been implemented in any SQL product of which we're aware, and the next version of the SQL standard might actually omit this feature (SQL:1999 deprecated the feature, thus allowing its deletion in a future version).

8.6   The INTERSECT and EXCEPT Operators

When working with two tables, there may be occasions when you would like to easily determine which rows exist in both of those tables or, alternatively, which rows exist in one table but not in another. The SQL:1999 INTERSECT and EXCEPT set operators are used in these cases.

INTERSECT returns all rows that exist in the intersection of two tables—that is, in both tables.

```
SELECT *
FROM music_titles
INTERSECT
SELECT *
FROM discontinued_albums ;
```

The preceding query will return, for example, all discontinued albums that have been re-released.

DISTINCT, ALL, and CORRESPONDING function with INTERSECT in much the same manner as with UNION. To perform the preceding query, but eliminate from "sameness" consideration all information about numbers in stock, pricing, and the like, you can write

```
SELECT *
FROM music_titles
INTERSECT CORRESPONDING BY
    ( title, artist, artist_more, distributor, record_label )
SELECT *
FROM discontinued_albums ;
```

EXCEPT is used to return all rows that are in the first table *except* those that also appear in the second table. To obtain a list of all albums in current release that have never been discontinued, you could issue

```
SELECT *
FROM music_titles
EXCEPT CORRESPONDING BY
    ( title, artist, artist_more, distributor, record_label )
SELECT *
FROM discontinued_albums ;
```

If the two tables that you're combining (whether with UNION, EXCEPT, or INTERSECT) do not contain any duplicate rows, nor do any of either table's rows duplicate any of the other table's rows, then it's irrelevant whether or not you specify DISTINCT when using any of these three operators.

On the other hand, if you're not sure of the possibility of duplicates being present (whether in just one of the two tables or in the two tables taken together), then you need to understand the implications of using ALL versus DISTINCT. To make this as simple as possible, we'll use the two tables illustrated in Table 8-10 and Table 8-11. We've sorted the rows in each table to make it easier for us to see how many duplicate rows there are in each of the tables.

Table 8-10 *One Sample Table*

TABLE_1

COLUMN_1	COLUMN_2
10	AAA
10	AAA
10	AAA
20	BBB
30	CCC
40	DDD

Table 8-11 *Another Sample Table*

TABLE_2

COLUMN_1	COLUMN_2
10	AAA
10	AAA
40	DDD
50	EEE
60	FFF

Given those two tables, let's see what the results of each combination of UNION, EXCEPT, and INTERSECT with DISTINCT and ALL will give. The results can be seen in Results 8-15 through 8-20. We've sorted the values in the columns to make it easy for you to see the effects.

Result 8-15 *TABLE_1 UNION ALL TABLE_2*

Result

COLUMN_1	COLUMN_2
10	AAA
10	AAA
10	AAA
10	AAA
10	AAA
20	BBB
30	CCC
40	DDD
40	DDD
50	EEE
60	FFF

It's readily apparent that the UNION ALL operation retained every row from both tables.

Result 8-16 *TABLE_1 UNION DISTINCT TABLE_2*

Result

COLUMN_1	COLUMN_2
10	AAA
20	BBB
30	CCC
40	DDD
50	EEE
60	FFF

There are no duplicates in the result, which we would expect from specifying UNION DISTINCT, but one copy of each row from each table has been retained in the result.

Result 8-17 *TABLE_1 EXCEPT ALL TABLE_2*

Result

COLUMN_1	COLUMN_2
10	AAA
20	BBB
30	CCC

TABLE_1 contains three rows (or, if you prefer, three copies of the row) in which the value of COLUMN_1 is 10. TABLE_2 contains two such rows (or copies), so the result contained (3 – 2), or 1, such rows. Since TABLE_1 and TABLE_2 each contain one copy of a row in which COLUMN_1 has the value 40, there is no such row in the result. TABLE_1 contains two rows (COLUMN_1 = 20 and COLUMN_1 = 30) with no corresponding row in TABLE_2, so those rows are retained in the result. Finally, TABLE_2 contains two rows (COLUMN_1 = 50 and COLUMN_1 = 60) with no corresponding rows in TABLE_1; however, because the operation returns all rows in the first table *except* equal rows in the second table, these TABLE_2-only rows do not affect the result.

Result 8-18 *TABLE_1 EXCEPT DISTINCT TABLE_2*

Result

COLUMN_1	COLUMN_2
20	BBB
30	CCC

EXCEPT DISTINCT operates similarly to EXCEPT ALL, but it eliminates all duplicates before it inserts into the result the (now unique) rows from the first table and then removes from the result the (also unique) rows from the second table. Therefore, the rows with COLUMN_1 = 10 are removed entirely.

Result 8-19 *TABLE_1 INTERSECT ALL TABLE_2*

Result

COLUMN_1	COLUMN_2
10	AAA
10	AAA
40	DDD

The INTERSECT ALL operation returns all rows from the first table that are also found in the second table. Since TABLE_1 contains three rows whose COLUMN_1 value is 10, but TABLE_2 contains only two such rows, the result has only two such rows. Both tables contain one row in which COLUMN_1 = 40, so the result has one such row. The remaining rows appear only in one of the two tables (not in both) and thus are not represented at all in the result.

Result 8-20 *TABLE_1 INTERSECT DISTINCT TABLE_2*

Result

COLUMN_1	COLUMN_2
10	AAA
40	DDD

Finally, INTERSECT DISTINCT behaves similarly to INTERSECT ALL, except that duplicates are eliminated before the intersection is computed. Therefore, the result contains only one copy of rows for which at least one copy appears in both tables.

8.7 | Another Example

Let's look at one more example from our video and music store database that uses one of the operators we've discussed in this chapter; we'll also see some more examples in Appendix B, "A Complete SQL:1999 Example."

Suppose we want to produce a comprehensive list of all videos we have in stock, along with the soundtrack album information, if indeed there is a soundtrack for that movie. That is, we want all of our movies to be included and some of our CDs or tapes. We can use the LEFT OUTER JOIN, which you'll recall preserves all rows from the *left* table regardless of whether there is a match with a row in the *right* table. Assume that we have no non-soundtrack albums that have the same title as that of a movie, and that the year a movie was released is the same as the year the soundtrack was released.

```
SELECT movie_titles.title, movie_titles.year_released,
       music_titles.record_label,...{rest of select list}
FROM movie_titles
```

```
LEFT OUTER JOIN
    music_titles
 ON movie_titles.title = music_titles.title
AND movie_titles.year_released = music_titles.date_released
```

Table 8-12 *Relevant Columns of MOVIE_TITLES*

TITLE	YEAR_RELEASED
Erin Brockovich	2000
Dirty Dancing	1987
The Rose	1979
Titanic	1997
The Blair Witch Project	1999
U-571	2000

Table 8-13 *Relevant Columns of MUSIC_TITLES*

TITLE	YEAR_RELEASED	RECORD_LABEL
Erin Brockovich	2000	Sony Classics
Dirty Dancing	1987	BMG/RCA
The Rose	1979	WEA/Atlantic
Titanic	1997	Sony Classics

Table 8-14 *Result Table*

TITLE	YEAR_RELEASED	RECORD_LABEL
Erin Brockovich	2000	Sony Classics
Dirty Dancing	1987	BMG/RCA
The Rose	1979	WEA/Atlantic
Titanic	1997	Sony Classics
The Blair Witch Project	1999	*null*
U-571	2000	*null*

Syntax 8-3 *Complete Syntax of Joined Table*

- `<cross join> ::=`
    `<table reference> CROSS JOIN <table primary>`

- `<qualified join> ::=`
    `<table reference> [ <join type> ] JOIN`
    `<table reference> <join specification>`

  `<join type> ::=`
     `INNER`
   `| <outer join type> [ OUTER ]`

  `<outer join type> ::=`
     `LEFT`
   `| RIGHT`
   `| FULL`

  `<join specification> ::=`
     `<join condition>`
   `| <named columns join>`

  `<join condition> ::= ON <search condition>`

  `<named columns join> ::=`
     `USING <left paren> <join column list> <right paren>`

  `<join column list> ::= <column name list>`

- `<natural join> ::=`
    `<table reference> NATURAL [ <join type> ] JOIN`
    `<table primary>`

- `<union join> ::=`
    `<table reference> UNION JOIN <table primary>`

8.8 | Chapter Summary

As we've seen in this chapter, there are many ways in which tables can be combined with one another to provide consolidated information through a combination of old SQL syntax and newer, join-specific syntax. Depending on the needs of your applications, you now have access to a robust set of operators, from which you can likely choose exactly the statement that meets your specific needs of the moment. You can

- find all rows that appear in one table but not another
- find all rows that appear in more than one table
- explicitly eliminate certain columns from consideration when performing JOIN and UNION operations

and many of the other types of functions we discussed.

In the next couple of chapters, we'll look at some more advanced DML (data manipulation language) operations and, in the spirit of working with multiple tables, the means through which integrity of data may be maintained among those tables.

Chapter

9

Advanced SQL Query Expressions

Introduction

To this point, we've discussed the basic SQL statements that you will use to write your applications, and we've talked about the kinds of values and basic relational operators that you can use in those statements. Now, it's time to delve a bit deeper and clarify the more complex query expression facilities of SQL.

In this chapter, we dissect SQL's query expression and study each of its components; then we see how they build on one another. After that, we look more closely at the relational operators to understand their precise syntax and semantics. We also tackle the concept of grouped tables that causes so much confusion; during that discussion, we'll have to reexamine the set functions to see how their behavior is affected by grouping operations. Many of the statements we've discussed in the preceding chapters are revisited, this time from a more formal orientation.

We also introduce the *table value* concept and show where it can help you write your applications. We also take a very close look at subqueries and discuss their uses and restrictions, a subject we briefly introduced earlier. Initially, we diverge from our music and video examples to concentrate on more abstract examples that may be easier to follow as we explore statement internals.

We have included some very advanced material at the end of this chapter, including SQL:1999's CUBE and ROLLUP analytical operations, as well as its new ability to perform recursive queries.

This chapter tells you the inside story about the most important elements of SQL: the query expression and the query specification. The two phrases sound awfully similar, don't they? Well, there's an easy way to remember the difference: use an analogy with value specifications and value expressions (we discussed them in Chapter 5, "Values, Basic Functions, and Expressions"). You may recall that a value specification is a simple value, such as a literal. The value may be provided by a host variable or a parameter, or the value given by a special value function such as CURRENT_TIME. A value expression is a way to combine value specifications with appropriate operators to produce a new value; the simplest value expression is just a value specification.

Using this analogy, we can see that a query specification is a way to produce a virtual table in SQL that can be used in a query expression to combine with other query specifications to produce a new virtual table. And the simplest form of query expression should be just a query specification. Actually, that's not quite right. There are three "simplest forms" of query expression, and we cover them all in this chapter. (If you want to keep track of these three forms, they are the <query specification> that is covered in section 9.2, the <explicit table> discussed briefly at the end of section 9.4, and the <table value constructor> that we address in section 9.9.)

We recognize that the material in this chapter, especially that toward the end of the chapter, is quite complex and may be difficult to get through, especially if you're not thoroughly familiar with the earlier material in the chapter. We encourage you not to be too dismayed by this complexity, but to feel free to skip ahead to the next chapter after you've gotten through section 9.11. You can always come back to the later sections of this chapter.

9.2 | Query Specifications

The query specification of SQL is what many people call the SELECT statement because it starts off with the keyword SELECT. As we have seen before, the SELECT statement is really a different beast, subtly different, but different in important ways. You will recall (see section 3.5.2, "Inside the SELECT Statement") that the SELECT statement is really a statement that can be executed by itself and that it must return no more than one row; in fact, in the SQL standard, it's called the *single row SELECT statement*. By contrast, a query specification is an expression (a *table-valued expression*) that starts with the keyword SELECT and has other syntactic similarities with the SELECT statement. Many users who understand that a SELECT expression is just part of an SQL statement refer to it as a *query block*. However, a query specification cannot be used by itself (it must be used as part of another SQL statement), and it is allowed to return more than one row. The syntax for a query specification is shown in Syntax 9-1. (As you see, this is obviously more complete than the brief version that we showed you in Syntax 3-1, "Syntax of the SELECT Statement.")

Syntax 9.1 *Syntax of Query Specification*

```
<query specification> ::=
    SELECT [ <set quantifier> ] <select list> <table expression>

<select list> ::=
      <asterisk>
    | <select sublist> [ { <comma> <select sublist> }... ]

<select sublist> ::=
      <derived column>
    | <qualified asterisk>

<qualified asterisk> ::=
      <asterisked identifier chain> <period> <asterisk>
    | <all fields reference>

<asterisked identifier chain> ::=
    <asterisked identifier>
        [ { <period> <asterisked identifier> }... ]

<asterisked identifier> ::= <identifier>

<derived column> ::=
    <value expression> [ <as clause> ]

<as clause> ::= [ A S ] <column name>

<all fields reference> ::=
    <value expression primary> <period> <asterisk>
```

Like lots of BNF, Syntax 9-1 might seem overwhelming, but it's mostly straightforward. Don't worry: we'll cover it all and clarify the confusing bits.

The query specification is the most basic operation that deals with tables in SQL. It is the building block on which other virtual tables are built. A query specification is not used *directly* in many other places in SQL, because it is part of another important building block, the query expression, which we'll discuss shortly.

Like several other SQL components, the query specification creates a virtual table. (We say *virtual* table because the table is not normally materialized. Instead, the rows of the table are produced, even computed, as they are required.) Like any other tables, these virtual tables have columns and rows. The columns of these tables have data types, names (but see below for more information about names of the columns), and all the other attributes of columns. The table has a degree (number of columns) and cardinality (number of rows).

Let's take a very close look at the query specification. Because it's so important to an understanding of SQL, we're going to take it slowly and work through all of the details. The basic form of a query specification is given in Syntax 9-2.

Syntax 9-2 *Syntax of Query Specification, Alternative 1*

```
SELECT select-list table-expression
```

There is another form that you can use, too, shown in Syntax 9-3,

Syntax 9-3 *Syntax of Query Specification, Alternative 2*

```
SELECT quantifier select-list table-expression
```

where quantifier is either DISTINCT or ALL. If you don't specify a quantifier, then ALL is the default and means "don't eliminate any duplicates from the resulting table." DISTINCT, on the other hand, means "if the table that results from the query specification has any duplicate rows, eliminate all redundant duplicates— all of them except one."

The essence of the basic form of query specification seen in Syntax 9-2 and Syntax 9-3 is this: remove all unspecified columns from the virtual table produced by the table expression and, if DISTINCT is specified, delete all redundant duplicate rows from the table comprising the remaining columns. Even though the select list comes earlier in the query specification syntax than the table-expression, the table-expression is (effectively) performed before the operations implied by the select list.

The select list comes in two forms. You can either use just an asterisk (represented in Syntax 9-1 as <asterisk>):

```
*
```

meaning "all columns that are part of the table corresponding to the table-expression," or you can use

```
select-sublist [ , select-sublist ]...
```

In this case, a select sublist is either a derived column or a qualified asterisk, which is *normally* (in section 9.2.1, we'll examine the implications of saying "normally") a qualifier followed by a period and an asterisk:

```
qualifier . *
```

Remember from Chapter 5, "Values, Basic Functions, and Expressions," that a qualifier is either a table name or a correlation name that identifies a table in a particular scope.

A derived column is a value expression (which may be as simple as a column name, possibly with a qualifier), optionally followed by the keyword AS and a derived column name:

```
value-expression [ A S derived-column-name ]
```

The derived column name gives the derived column a name. Now, if your value expression is

```
movie_titles.title
```

then the column already has a name: TITLE. However, if your value expression was

```
movie_titles.current_dvd_sale_price/2
```

the column doesn't have a name. In many situations, you must know the names of all of your columns (actually, some of the rules of SQL simply don't work correctly if columns don't have names). As a result, the SQL standard says that an implementation must *assign* a name to any columns that do not have names (however, it may not be easy to learn what those names are, especially if your implementation makes the decision differently for every program you compile or run). If you anticipate using such columns, we strongly recommend that you use the AS clause to give those columns names that are meaningful to you:

```
movie_titles.current_dvd_price/2 AS special_discounted_price
```

Let's look at some examples of query specifications with what we know now (we haven't looked at the table expression yet, so we'll leave that placeholder there).

```
SELECT DISTINCT current_dvd_sale_price table-expression
```

This example will return a set (not a multiset, because we used DISTINCT) of the `current_dvd_sale_prices` in our `table expression`. This will allow us, for example, to determine the unique, different prices of all our movies. Let's see another one.

```
SELECT movie_titles.*, music_titles.* table-expression
```

This example will select *all* columns from the `movie_titles` table and all columns from the `music_titles` table as they appear in the `table expression`.

```
SELECT * table-expression
```

This last example will select all columns from the `table expression`. When you use the standalone asterisk, or the `select sublist` of `qualifier.*`, you are telling the DBMS that you want all the columns from the `table expression` (or all columns that are available with the specified qualifier). However, because you can add columns to or drop columns from base tables (see Chapter 4, "Basic Data Definition Language (DDL)"), the *meaning* of "all columns" might change. Because of this, your programs might quit working or start working incorrectly—without warning, just because some other application developer modified the definition of a table. *We strongly recommend that you avoid the use of the asterisk as a* `select list` *or as a* `select sublist`. In interactive SQL, the asterisk is extremely useful (it beats the heck out of repeatedly entering a long list of column names), but it can cause very surprising results in embedded SQL programs or in module language.

9.2.1 Qualified Asterisk

Earlier in this chapter, we told you that a `qualified asterisk` was *normally* a qualifier followed by a period and an asterisk. That was the only possibility in SQL-92, but SQL:1999's support for anonymous row types and structured user-defined types adds complexity that shows up right here.

In Syntax 9-1, you saw that a `qualified asterisk` is defined like this:

```
<qualified asterisk> ::=
     <asterisked identifier chain> <period> <asterisk>
   | <all fields reference>
```

That's obviously got more to it than simply an identifier, a period, and an asterisk. But it's fairly easy to understand, once you know *why* it's defined this way. Let's first look at the alternative containing the asterisked identifier chain.

By way of explanation, we first need to remind you that anonymous row types have one or more fields, each of which has a name and a data type; similarly, structured user-defined types (about which you can learn more in Volume 2 of this book) have one or more attributes, each of which has a name and a data type. SQL:1999 chose (by popular demand, we hasten to add) the familiar convention of using a period as the delimiter appearing between the name of a site whose data type is some anonymous row type or some structured user-defined type and the name of a field or attribute of that type.

However, in using a period as that delimiter, potential syntax ambiguities were introduced. Consider the two tables shown in Example 9-1.

Example 9-1 *Tables Illustrating Potential Syntax Ambiguity*

```
CREATE TABLE T1 (
    C1        INTEGER,
    C2        ROW (
                    F1        INTEGER,
                    F2        CHARACTER(10)  )
    C3        REAL )  ;

CREATE TABLE C2 (
    F1        INTEGER,
    F2        DATE )  ;
```

In particular, you should observe that one table (T1) has a column named C2 whose type is an anonymous row type, one of whose fields is named F1, while the other table is named C2 and has a column named F1. In this situation, the query shown in Example 9-2 is potentially ambiguous.

Example 9-2 *Potentially Ambiguous Query*

```
SELECT C2.F1
FROM    T1, C2
```

The reason that the query in Example 9-2 is ambiguous is easy to observe: We cannot immediately determine whether "C2.F1" means "the column named F1 from the table named C2" or "the field named F1 in the column named C2 in the table named T1." Both interpretations are equally valid unless we have additional rules (new to SQL:1999, of course) to tell us which interpretation is the right one.

(SQL:1999's rules, which require that you use a correlation name when you want to use a column name as a qualifier, gives the interpretation that C2.F1 is column F1 of table C2.) Similarly (and here we finally get to the issue dealing with qualified asterisk), the query in Example 9-3 is ambiguous, for the same reason.

Example 9-3 *Another Potentially Ambiguous Query*

```
SELECT C2.*
FROM   T1, C2
```

That query's use of "C2.*" could mean "all columns from table C2," or it could mean "all fields in column C2 from table T1"; again, either interpretation is valid without some rule to help us (and SQL implementations) to determine which is intended. Of course, both interpretations are useful, so we wouldn't want SQL to *arbitrarily* choose one and disallow the other. If there's a genuine and unresolvable ambiguity, then the programmer should be informed and required to clarify the code. On the other hand, if there's not a true ambiguity, but a way to determine a "most correct" interpretation, then SQL does the programmer a service by choosing that interpretation.

Of course, we could have chosen to write "T1.C2.*" to disambiguate—if that's what we meant! And SQL:1999 could have been written to require us to write that out if we intend that interpretation and to choose the alternate interpretation if we didn't write it out completely. That may have proved consistent, but it would cause application developers to use awkward and inconvenient coding rules in unnecessary situations. Worse, that chain of identifier-followed-by-period can be several identifiers in length (consider a table with a column whose data type is an anonymous row type, one of whose fields is another anonymous row type, one of whose fields is yet another anonymous row type, and so forth). As a final complication, don't overlook the fact that you can always precede a table name with the name of its schema (followed by a period, of course) and precede that with the name of the catalog containing the schema (again, followed by a period). SQL:1999's designers chose instead to use heuristic rules to determine the programmer's intent most of the time. In Example 9-3, SQL:1999's rules resolve C2.* to mean "all columns from table C2."

SQL:1999's rules for making this determination are (to put it charitably) dense and complex. We don't pretend that we can make them seem trivially simple, but we will give you the essence of the solution, which reduces to the following points:

- Find all possible meanings of the first identifier, all possible meanings of the first two identifiers, and all possible meanings of the first three identifiers. The acceptable possible meanings are the following:

- an SQL variable name (only if SQL/PSM is involved)
- an SQL parameter name
- correlation-name . column-name, where the type of the column is a row type or a structured type
- an exposed table name that is equivalent to the entire chain of identifiers

- If only one of the possible interpretations is found, then we know how to interpret the expression.

- If more than one of these possible interpretations are found, then the one in which the first identifier was declared "closest" to the use of the identifier is chosen as the correct interpretation. (SQL:1999 expresses this using the phrase "with the *innermost scope.*")

- If more than one of the interpretations have the same innermost scope, then there really is an ambiguity.

In fact, SQL:1999's rules prohibit an interpretation of Example 9-3 to mean "all fields in column C2 from table T1" by requiring that all references to a field (or, in this case, to all fields, using the asterisk) of the row type of a column be qualified by a correlation name that qualifies the name of the column whose row type contains the field. Therefore, if we intended to retrieve "all fields in column C2 from table T1," we would have to write

```
SELECT T.C2.*
FROM   T1 AS T, C2
```

That is arguably awkward (particularly since it requires defining a correlation name), but it is also precise and unambiguous.

Since the ambiguity is removed by that requirement, the query in Example 9-3 must be interpreted to mean "all columns from table C2."

The second alternative for qualified asterisk is all fields reference, which is defined as follows:

```
<all fields reference> ::=
    <value expression primary> <period> <asterisk>
```

In this case, the use of a <value expression primary> allows application writers to enclose their qualifiers (including a chain of identifiers) in parentheses to disambiguate things themselves, thus avoiding a syntax error when there are (or might be) multiple interpretations of an identifier or identifier chain that all have equal validity. Therefore, if Example 9-3 had been written as shown in Example 9-4, the ambiguity would have been eliminated. How? By SQL:1999's rule requiring that the expression "(C2)" be interpreted as the name of a site (we defined *site* in section 2.4.13, "Sites") whose data type is some anonymous row type, and there's only one possibility: the column named C2 in table T1.

Example 9-4 *Resolving the Ambiguity*

```
SELECT (C2).*
FROM   T1, C2
```

9.2.2 Table Expressions

Okay, now it's finally time to see what a table expression is. You probably won't be surprised to learn that it is an expression involving tables and that it produces a virtual table. A table expression is shown in Syntax 9-4:

Syntax 9-4 *Syntax of Table Expression*

```
from-clause
[ where-clause ]
[ group-by-clause ]
[ having-clause ]
```

The from-clause is always required. As you see from the syntax, the other clauses are all optional. If you specify them, they must be in the given order, but you can skip any or all of them.

Think of these clauses as operators that take input and produce output. Each clause in a table expression produces a virtual table. In fact, the input to the from-clause is one or more tables (base tables or views). The input to the where-clause is the virtual table produced by the from-clause. The input to the group-by-clause is the virtual table produced by the where-clause; if there is no where-clause, then it is the virtual table produced by the from-clause. Finally, the input to the having-clause is the virtual table produced by the group-by-clause, where-clause, or from-clause.

The format of the from-clause is given in Syntax 9-5.

Syntax 9-5 *FROM Clause Syntax*

```
FROM table-reference [ , table-reference ]...
```

table references were partially covered in Chapter 8, "Working with Multiple Tables: The Relational Operators." Briefly, a table reference is usually either a table name or a joined table. (Actually, there are other alternatives as well, but they're not relevant for this discussion; see section 9.11 for those other alternatives.) Therefore, a from-clause might look like this:

```
FROM t1, t2
```

or, more likely, in our example application:

```
FROM movie_titles, distributors
```

If there is only one table reference in the from-clause, the resulting virtual table has exactly the same number of columns (with the same names, data types, and other attributes) as the table identified by the table reference. If there are two or more table references, then the columns of the resulting virtual table are the same as the columns of each of the input tables in the order that those tables are listed in the from-clause. Therefore, if the table MOVIE_TITLES has columns TITLE, OUR_DVD_COST, and CURRENT_DVD_SALE_PRICE; and DISTRIBUTORS has columns DIST_NAME, and DIST_PHONE; then the resulting virtual table of our example would have columns TITLE, OUR_DVD_COST, CURRENT_DVD_PRICE, DIST_NAME, and DIST_PHONE. Finally, the resulting virtual table's *degree* is the *sum* of the degrees of each participating input table.

If there is only one table reference in the from-clause, the resulting virtual table has exactly the same number of rows as the table identified by the table reference, and the rows are identical to the rows of that table (except, of course, for the order of rows, since order is irrelevant in tables). If there is more than one table reference, the rows of the resulting virtual table are determined by joining each row of each input table with each row of each other input table. So, the first row retrieved from MOVIE_TITLES would be combined with the first row retrieved from DISTRIBUTORS; next, the first row retrieved from MOVIE_TITLES would be combined with the second row retrieved from DISTRIBUTORS; and so forth until the first row retrieved from MOVIE_TITLES is combined with the last row retrieved from DISTRIBUTORS. Then the second row retrieved from MOVIE_TITLES is combined with the first row retrieved from DISTRIBUTORS. You can probably guess the rest. This is the *Cartesian product* of the input tables. The resulting virtual table's *cardinality* is therefore the *product* of the cardinalities of each participating input table.

Let's make this a bit more precise by looking at Table 9-1 and Table 9-2, MOVIE_TITLES and DISTRIBUTORS. The resulting virtual table of

```
FROM movie_titles, distributors
```

is shown in Result 9-1.

Table 9-1 *MOVIE_TITLES*

TITLE	OUR_DVD_ COST	CURRENT_DVD_ SALE_PRICE
Unforgiven	21.95	24.95
Batman Returns	22.95	25.95
Lethal Weapon 3	21.95	24.95
Young Frankenstein	18.95	22.95

Table 9-2 *DISTRIBUTORS*

DIST_NAME	DIST_PHONE
Cheaper Distributors	555-9999
Eastern Movies, Inc.	555-8888
Western Films, Inc.	555-4444

Result 9-1 *Result of Unrestricted Join*

TITLE	OUR_DVD_ COST	CURRENT_DVD_ SALE_PRICE	DIST_NAME	DIST_PHONE
Unforgiven	21.95	24.95	Cheaper Distributors	555-9999
Unforgiven	21.95	24.95	Eastern Movies, Inc.	555-8888
Unforgiven	21.95	24.95	Western Films, Inc.	555-4444
Batman Returns	22.95	25.95	Cheaper Distributors	555-9999
Batman Returns	22.95	25.95	Eastern Movies, Inc.	555-8888
Batman Returns	22.95	25.95	Western Films, Inc.	555-4444
Lethal Weapon 3	21.95	24.95	Cheaper Distributors	555-9999
Lethal Weapon 3	21.95	24.95	Eastern Movies, Inc.	555-8888
Lethal Weapon 3	21.95	24.95	Western Films, Inc.	555-4444
Young Frankenstein	18.95	22.95	Cheaper Distributors	555-9999
Young Frankenstein	18.95	22.95	Eastern Movies, Inc.	555-8888
Young Frankenstein	18.95	22.95	Western Films, Inc.	555-4444

A close examination of Result 9-1 will reveal that the result of the unrestricted join is nothing more than the Cartesian product of the two tables that were joined together.

The degrees of the input tables were 3 and 2, respectively, so the degree of the resulting table is 3 + 2, or 5. The cardinalities of the input tables were 4 and 3, respectively, so the cardinality of the resulting virtual table is 4 * 3, or 12. Also, note that the names of the columns of the resulting virtual table are taken from the input tables. If the two tables have columns named with the same identifier, then the resulting virtual table will have two columns with the same name! Of course, that's not valid for a base table or a view, but it's possible (and valid) for a FROM clause.

The from-clause creates a virtual table that may (if there is more than one input table) have a different shape than its input table has. (The word *shape* is occasionally used to express the degree of a table, along with the names, data types, and other attributes of its columns.) By contrast, the where-clause produces an output table with exactly the same shape as its input table.

The format of the where-clause is shown in Syntax 9-6:

Syntax 9-6 *Syntax of WHERE Clause*

```
WHERE search-condition
```

(Note: search condition was defined in Chapter 7, "Predicates.") Think of the where-clause as a sort of filter that examines each row in the input table and decides whether to pass it on or toss it out. It passes on every row that satisfies the search condition (that is, for which the search condition is True) and throws out all rows for which the search condition is either False or Unknown. For example, if we apply the following where-clause,

```
WHERE movie_titles.title <> 'Young Frankenstein'
   AND ( distributors.dist_name NOT LIKE 'Eastern%' )
```

to our example above, the resulting virtual table would be as shown in Result 9-2.

Result 9-2 *Result of Join Restricted by WHERE Clause*

TITLE	OUR_DVD_ COST	CURRENT_DVD_ SALE_PRICE	DIST_NAME	DIST_PHONE
Unforgiven	21.95	24.95	Cheaper Distributors	555-9999
Unforgiven	21.95	24.95	Western Films, Inc.	555-4444
Batman Returns	22.95	25.95	Cheaper Distributors	555-9999
Batman Returns	22.95	25.95	Western Films, Inc.	555-4444
Lethal Weapon 3	21.95	24.95	Cheaper Distributors	555-9999
Lethal Weapon 3	21.95	24.95	Western Films, Inc.	555-4444

Note that the shape of the table hasn't changed, but there are fewer rows in the result because all rows that didn't satisfy the `search condition` have been eliminated.

9.2.3 GROUP BY and HAVING

The `GROUP BY` and `HAVING` clauses are part of `table expression` and thus might seem to have logically been included in the previous section. However, they are used a bit less often than the `FROM` and `WHERE` clauses, so it seemed appropriate to highlight them by giving them their own section in this chapter.

Even though a great many queries against databases are of the simple form "retrieve these specific columns from all rows that satisfy this condition," there are many applications that have to do more analysis on the data. For example, you may need to find the total value of all CDs currently in stock, or perhaps the total number of DVDs starring Leonardo DiCaprio that are available for rent. SQL allows you to use several "statistical functions" (such as `COUNT`, `SUM`, `AVG`, `MIN`, and `MAX`) to perform such analysis. To find the total value of CDs currently in stock, you might use the `SUM` function applied to rows identifying CDs that are in stock.

However, analyzing your data using such functions often requires that you *partition* the data into groups based on some criteria applicable to your needs. If your application needs access to the value of all CDs currently in stock, broken down by music category, you must have a way to inform the database system of how you want the CDs partitioned. SQL provides syntax to accomplish this in the form of the `group-by-clause`. The effect of this clause is to *group* together all rows of the virtual table supplied by the table expression so far, so that all rows in which certain columns (called *grouping columns*) have equal values are grouped together.

The format of the `group-by-clause`, as it was defined in SQL-92, is given in Syntax 9-7:

Syntax 9-7 *Syntax of GROUP BY Clause*

```
GROUP BY grouping-column [ , grouping-column ]...
```

where `grouping column` is a `column reference` optionally followed by a `collate-clause`. (Actually, the `collate-clause` can appear only if the `column reference` identifies a column whose data type is character string.) The `collate-clause` identifies the collation used for comparing the columns (see Chapter 21, "Internationalization Aspects of SQL:1999'). In SQL:1999, several new features have been added to the group-by-clause. These new alternatives provide OLAP (online analytical processing) capabilities and are addressed in section 9.11, after we've covered the fundamentals.

The result of a group-by-clause is a virtual table, as we've already said, and that result is called a *grouped table*. The input table is partitioned into one or more groups; the number of groups is the minimum such that, for each grouping column, no two rows of any group have different values for that grouping column. (For this purpose, all null values are considered to have the same value.) That is, for any group in the resulting grouped table, every row in the group has the same value for the grouping column. Furthermore, no other group has the same value for the complete set of grouping columns. Otherwise, the group-by-clause produces an output table that is identical to the input table. The code in Example 9-5 and in Table 9-3 show what a group-by-clause might look like. (For ease of understanding this example, assume that the table MOVIE_TITLES contains *only* the six rows shown in Table 9-3.)

Example 9-5 *GROUP BY Example*

```
SELECT movie_type, AVG (current_dvd_sale_price) AS avg_dvd_sale_price
FROM movie_titles
GROUP BY movie_type
```

Table 9-3 *MOVIE_TITLES*

TITLE	MOVIE_TYPE	CURRENT_DVD_SALE_PRICE
Lethal Weapon 3	Action	24.95
Unforgiven	Western	24.95
The Outlaw Josey Wales	Western	22.95
Kelly's Heroes	War	25.95
Shaft	Action	23.95
Shaft's Big Score	Action	25.95

The grouped table that is produced by the GROUP BY clause is shown in Result 9-3, and the query's resulting table would look like Result 9-4.

Result 9-3   *Grouped Table Resulting from the GROUP BY*

TITLE	MOVIE_TYPE	CURRENT_DVD_SALE_PRICE
Lethal Weapon 3	Action	24.95
Shaft	Action	23.95
Shaft's Big Score	Action	25.95
Kelly's Heroes	War	25.95
Unforgiven	Western	24.95
The Outlaw Josey Wales	Western	22.95

Note that all we've done is collect together all rows that have the same value for the MOVIE_TYPE column. Each of those collections of rows is a *group* in the *grouped table*. (We've highlighted the boundaries between each group for clarity.)

Of course, the grouped table that you see in Result 9-3 isn't the end of the story, because the select list takes as its input that grouped table, reduces the number of columns to just two, and collapses each group into a single row by applying the AVG function to the group.

Result 9-4   *Result of Query with GROUP BY*

MOVIE_TYPE	AVG_DVD_SALE_PRICE
Action	24.95
Western	23.95
War	25.95

Note that the intermediate virtual table (the grouped table) has the same number of columns and (presumably, although we haven't shown this explicitly) the same data types and other attributes as the source table. MOVIE_TYPE is the grouping column for this group-by-clause.

If the column (or columns) on which we're grouping contains null values in some rows, then SQL collects together all of the rows with null values in the grouping columns into a single group. (Even though one null value isn't *equal* to another null value, as we discussed in section 7.4, "Comparison Predicate," they are considered *not distinct* from one another for the purposes of grouping.)

Now, the having-clause is the source of some confusion among those just getting comfortable with SQL. This clause gives you another filter, one that filters groups, not individual rows. Its purpose is to remove from your query results all *groups* that don't satisfy the specified criteria, such as groups of CDs for which the total value is less than $100. The filtering operation is applied to the grouped table resulting from the preceding clause. If there is a group-by-clause, the grouped table resulting from it is the input to the having-clause. On the other hand, if there is no group-by-clause, the entire table resulting from the where-clause (or from-clause if there is no where-clause) is treated as a grouped table with exactly one group. In this case, there is no grouping-column. The format of the having-clause is shown in Syntax 9-8:

Syntax 9-8 *Syntax of HAVING Clause*

```
HAVING search-condition
```

The search condition is applied to each *group* of the grouped table, although not really to the *rows* of the groups. That's because the only columns of the input table that the having-clause can reference are the grouping columns (and columns that are functionally dependent on grouping columns; see section 9.3 for information about functional dependencies), unless the columns are used in a set function. Therefore, the following is a valid having-clause for our example:

```
HAVING movie_type = 'Western'
    OR movie_type = 'War'
```

The result of applying this having-clause to our example is shown in Result 9-5.

Result 9-5 *Result of Query with HAVING Clause*

MOVIE_TYPE	AVG_DVD_ SALE_PRICE
Western	23.95
War	25.95

This, by contrast, is *not* a valid having-clause:

```
HAVING our_dvd_cost = 21.95
```

because our_dvd_cost is not a grouping column. However, we could have written

```
HAVING AVG(current_dvd_sale_price) < 25.0
```

That would, of course, have returned the rows seen in Result 9-6. (You might wonder why we didn't use the column name AVG_DVD_SALE_PRICE in the

HAVING clause. The reason is that the name isn't defined at this point; it's defined to be part of the *result* of the query, but not part of the input to any of the query's clauses. We find this limitation frustrating, but it's logical in the context of SQL's architecture.)

Result 9-6 *Another Result of Query with HAVING Clause*

MOVIE_TYPE	AVG_DVD_ SALE_PRICE
Action	24.95
Western	23.95

On the other hand, you might be interested only in movies whose DVD cost is greater than $22.00 and only want to compute the average current sale price of those. You can use SQL:1999's *nested table* facility for that.

```
SELECT movie_type, AVG (current_dvd_sale_price)
FROM ( SELECT *
       FROM movie_titles
       WHERE current_dvd_cost > 22.00 )
GROUP BY movie_type
```

Even though you may often hear it said that a subquery is "just a query expression in parentheses," the nested SELECT * FROM... isn't actually a subquery (see section 9.10) by SQL's definition of the term, but is instead a *nested table expression*. (Having said that, we must admit that the distinction has no major significance, and you won't cause yourself any difficulties if you fail to distinguish the two.) Therefore, the GROUP BY (and the select list) only operates on a virtual table (unnamed, by the way) of movies whose current_ dvd_cost is more than $22.00.

By the way, we used a nested table expression in that previous query just to illustrate the facility. Most SQL database systems will do a better job of optimizing that query if you don't use the nested table expression, which certainly isn't required in this example. Instead, you'd probably be better off writing the query like this:

```
SELECT movie_type, AVG (current_dvd_sale_price)
FROM movie_titles
WHERE current_dvd_cost > 22.00
GROUP BY movie_type
```

The search condition of a having-clause can also contain subqueries, which we'll cover later in this chapter. It's worth mentioning here, however, that such subqueries are evaluated once for each *group* in the input grouped table, and the values of such subqueries are used in the application of the search condition to the group.

Like the where-clause and group-by-clause, the having-clause produces a resulting table with the same shape as its input table.

Okay, let's see what an entire table expression looks like at one shot:

```
FROM t1, t2              -- FROM Clause
WHERE t1.c11 <> 'W'      -- WHERE Clause
  AND ( t2.c21 = 'R'
     OR t2.c21 = 'T' )
GROUP BY t1.c13          -- GROUP BY Clause
HAVING t1.c13 = 'XYZ'    -- HAVING Clause
```

9.2.4 Updatable Query Specifications

Query specifications are not only applicable when retrieving information, but also when you need to update data. According to SQL-92, a query specification is *updatable* if and only if

- You don't use DISTINCT as a quantifier.

- The value expressions in the select list are all column references, and none of them appears more than once.

- The from-clause has only one table reference, and it identifies either a base table or an updatable derived table.

- The base table ultimately identified by the table reference isn't referenced (directly or indirectly) in any FROM clause of a subquery in the where-clause (other than as a qualifier to identify a column of the table, of course).

- You don't use a group-by-clause or a having-clause.

If you violate any of these, then the query specification is read-only. If you use it in a view definition or a cursor specification, you cannot execute UPDATE, DELETE, or INSERT (for a view) on it.

In SQL:1999, the situation has become a little bit more complicated, largely because of new features in this generation of the standard. SQL:1999 defines several terms that correspond to SQL-92's "updatable"; these terms include *poten-*

tially updatable, updatable, simply updatable, and *insertable-into.* We'll explain each of these one at a time. But, first, we want to point out the new (to SQL:1999) distinction between the ability to update rows in a table (the various sorts of *updatable*) and the ability to insert rows into a table (*insertable-into*).

A query specification is *potentially updatable* (under SQL:1999's rules) if and only if

- You don't use DISTINCT as a quantifier.
- None of the derived columns in the select list that are column references appear more than once.
- You don't use a group-by-clause or a having-clause.

If a query expression is potentially updatable and its from-clause contains exactly one table reference, then each column of the query expression that corresponds to a single column of the table identified by the table reference is updatable. If a query expression is potentially updatable, but its from-clause contains two or more table references, then a column of the query expression is updatable only if

- it is derived from a column of exactly one table identified by one of those table references, and
- that table is used in the query expression in such a way that its primary key or other candidate key relationships are preserved.

In other words, a column of a potentially updatable query expression is updatable only when that column can be unambiguously traced back to a single column in a single table participating in the query expression *and* each row of that column can be unambiguously traced back to a single row in that participating table.

Therefore, a query expression is *updatable* if it is potentially updatable and at least one of its columns is updatable. A query expression is *simply updatable* if it is updatable, its from-clause contains exactly one table reference, and every column of the query expression is updatable.

Finally, a query expression is *insertable-into* if it is updatable, if every one of the tables on which it depends (the tables referenced by table references in the from-clause) are also insertable-into, and if the query expression does not include a UNION, INTERSECT, or EXCEPT set operator. As you'd expect, all base tables are insertable-into (given the appropriate INSERT privilege, of course).

9.3 | Functional Dependencies: Rules for Updatability

The discussion in section 9.2.4 concerns the rules for determining whether or not a query specification is updatable (and insertable-into). In fact, SQL:1999 has rather lengthy (and dense) rules for determining the updatability of many of the language's components. These rules were developed in pursuit of increasing the sorts of views (and other virtual tables) that can be updated, inserted into, or deleted from by SQL statements. In this section, we'll summarize many of those rules, but we'll still address the updatability issue in certain individual sections where it makes sense to do so.

Before we delve into this subject, it's only fair to warn you that much of this section reads like it was pulled from a math textbook. In some sense, it has been—not literally, of course, but it does involve relational theory. We've included it for completeness, but we don't pretend that it's easy to get through, nor do we want to trivialize it by cutting its discussion too short. Unless you're concerned with data modeling issues, you would not be shortchanging yourself by merely skimming this material, at least on first reading.

The title of this section, "Functional Dependencies: Rules for Updatability," refers to an aspect of the relational model in which one determines whether or not specific columns of data are dependent, in a very specific way, on other columns of data. Consider the data in Table 9-1, which we repeat here in Table 9-4 for convenient reference:

Table 9-4 MOVIE_TITLES

TITLE	OUR_DVD_COST	CURRENT_DVD_SALE_PRICE
Unforgiven	21.95	24.95
Batman Returns	22.95	25.95
Lethal Weapon 3	21.95	24.95
Young Frankenstein	18.95	22.95

Observe that the data in the OUR_DVD_COST and CURRENT_DVD_SALE_PRICE columns do *not* have a one-to-one relationship with the data in the TITLE column; for example, there are duplicate values (24.95) in the CURRENT_DVD_SALE_PRICE column. While you might reasonably argue that you cannot determine the meaning of the value 24.95 without knowing the value in the TITLE column, too, that relationship is not one of functional dependency.

Instead, imagine that Table 9-4 contained an additional column, named FRENCH_TITLE, and imagine that the world is so well ordered that every English TITLE had exactly one FRENCH_TITLE translation. See Table 9-5, in which we've used naive translations of our English titles (we do not pretend that the movies in question were released in France or Canada with the FRENCH_TITLEs we've given, or even that all movie titles are automatically translated into French when released in French-speaking countries, as illustrated by our representation of "Unforgiven").

Table 9-5 *Enhanced MOVIE_TITLES*

TITLE	FRENCH_TITLE	OUR_DVD_ COST	CURRENT_DVD_ SALE_PRICE
Unforgiven	Unforgiven	21.95	24.95
Batman Returns	Batman Retourne	22.95	25.95
Lethal Weapon 3	Mortelle Arme 3	21.95	24.95
Young Frankenstein	Jeune Frankenstein	22.95	22.95

In this example table, we say that the FRENCH_TITLE column is *functionally dependent* on the TITLE column—that is, the data in the FRENCH_TITLE column of a given row of the table corresponds to the data in the TITLE column of that same row and of no other row. (It is also true that the TITLE column is functionally dependent on the FRENCH_TITLE column. The functional dependency means that a change in the value of one column implies a change in the value of the column or columns that are functionally dependent on it. By no means is it always true that functional dependencies are bidirectional in this way, but it happens to be true here.)

In the relational model, the primary use of functional dependencies (which, by the way, you have to determine by knowing and examining your data, not by inspecting table definitions or column definitions in the absence of data) is to normalize your data and your table definitions. We briefly addressed this in Section 1.2.3, in the subsection called "Normal Forms," which you should review if you're uncertain about the meaning of the term or about the concept.

However, a good understanding of the functional dependencies in your data, and those that arise from your queries and their use of tables and columns, can identify very useful and interesting relationships between the virtual tables produced by queries and the underlying base tables on which those queries depend. Those relationships can often be used to determine whether or not the virtual table produced by a query is updatable—and, if it is updatable, how to update rows in the underlying base tables to produce the effect of the update as it might be seen in the query.

We're not even going to attempt to spell out all of SQL:1999's rules related to functional dependencies. A summary alone would take more space in this book than it would be worth to you when you're writing your applications, unless you happen to be responsible for designing your enterprise's data model. (You might well ask why SQL's designers felt that it was appropriate to put into the standard rules so complex that even a summary would be unwieldy. The simplest answer is "for completeness." Although summarizing the rules might take several pages in this book, they are generally derivable from a good understanding of the principles of functional dependencies and of the various SQL objects to which those principles are applied.)

One reason we have chosen not to attempt to detail the rules here is that we expect implementations to find even more ways of making views and other virtual tables updatable, using functional dependencies and other relationships among data; therefore, you have to understand your implementation's rules about updatable virtual tables—or let your implementation inform you about the updatability of a specific query. However, we will give a very high-level overview of the subject to help you understand your implementation's rules when you encounter them. We believe that most implementations that provide good support for updatable query expressions will document their restrictions and permissions fairly well to help guide their users.

In Table 9-5, you saw that FRENCH_TITLE is functionally dependent on TITLE. We could also say that TITLE *determines* FRENCH_TITLE, because "functionally dependent" and "determines" are the two sides of this particular coin. Many sources, including SQL:1999, represent this relationship by this notation:

MOVIE_TITLES: TITLE $\mapsto$ FRENCH_TITLE

That funny symbol $\mapsto$ is pronounced "determines," or "is a determinant of," when reading from left to right: "In MOVIE_TITLES, TITLE determines FRENCH_TITLE," or perhaps "TITLE is a determinant of FRENCH_TITLE in MOVIE_TITLES." If you prefer reading right to left, it's pronounced "is functionally dependent on": "In MOVIE_TITLES, FRENCH_TITLE is functionally dependent on TITLE." (If you wanted to pronounce the right-to-left version "is determined by," you wouldn't be incorrect, but you wouldn't be as readily understood as you would be using "is functionally dependent on.") If the table context is clear, then you can leave off its name and the colon:

TITLE $\mapsto$ FRENCH_TITLE

Of course, since this particular example involves two columns that happen to be functionally dependent on each other, it is also correct to write

FRENCH_TITLE $\mapsto$ TITLE

That's not always true, as we mentioned earlier.

Since we're not concerned here with normalizing your table definitions, you might conclude that functional dependencies like the one demonstrated in Table 9-5 are not considered further in this chapter. That's not quite accurate: we're going to address functional dependencies created by various components of SQL:1999, and there are 11 such components, including base tables, for which the standard specifies the functional dependency rules. Before we start describing those, however, there are some definitions we need to get in place.

- If S is a set of columns in some table T and SS is a subset of S (that is, another set of columns in T, but limited just to those columns in S), then we define both "T: S $\mapsto$ S" and "T: S $\mapsto$ SS" to be *axiomatic functional dependencies*. These are "axiomatic" because the relational model provides axioms stating that any column is functionally dependent on itself, any set of columns is functionally dependent on itself, and any set of columns is functionally dependent on any other set of columns of which it is a subset. There are no other axiomatic functional dependencies; all other functional dependencies are *nonaxiomatic functional dependencies*. These two definitions give us a starting point from which we can determine other functional dependencies.

- All axiomatic functional dependencies are also *known functional dependencies*. SQL:1999's rules define how other known functional dependencies are determined, and SQL implementations are free to augment those rules by finding other known functional dependencies not specified by SQL:1999. We anticipate that future versions of the SQL standard may also enhance these rules.

- If some column (let's call it C1) in a virtual table is specified by a column reference identifying some other column, C2, in a table (base table or otherwise), T, from which the virtual table is derived, then we say that C1 is a *counterpart* of C2. More precisely, we say that C1 is a counterpart of C2 *under qualifying table* T.

- The notion of counterparts extends to sets of columns. If a set of columns S1 in a virtual table is specified by a set of column references that identify, in a one-to-one mapping, another set of columns S2 in an underlying table

T, and each column in S1 is a counterpart of its corresponding column in S2, then S1 is a counterpart of S2 under qualifying table T.

- If every column of a unique constraint is a non-null column, then the set of those columns is called a BUC-set (the acronym BUC implies "base table unique constraint"). A set of columns that is a counterpart to a BUC-set is also a BUC-set, so this property propagates through various expressions that produce virtual tables. If S1 and S2 are both sets of columns, S1 is a subset of S2, $S1 \mapsto S2$, and S2 is a BUC-set, then S1 is also a BUC-set. A BUC-set for a table can be empty (that is, have no columns), which implies that the table can have at most one row;[1] by contrast, a table might have no BUC-set at all which isn't the same thing as an empty BUC-set.

- The set of columns that make up a PRIMARY KEY are called a BPK-set (BPK implies "base table primary key"). Every BPK-set is necessarily a BUC-set, because a PRIMARY KEY is a unique constraint comprising only non-null columns. Like the BUC-set property, the BPK-set property propagates through expressions producing virtual tables using counterparts. If S1 and S2 are both sets of columns, S1 is a subset of S2, $S1 \mapsto S2$, and S2 is a BPK-set, then S1 is also a BPK-set. And, like BUC-sets, BPK-sets can be empty.

With those definitions available for our use, let's look at some (but only some) of the 11 components for which SQL:1999 provides functional dependency rules.

- *Base tables:* The set of columns in a base table's PRIMARY KEY (if any) make up a BPK-set. If a base table has a non-deferrable unique constraint, then the set of non-nullable columns identified in that unique constraint make up a BUC-set. If UCL is a set of columns in a base table such that UCL is a BUC-set, and CT is the set of all columns of that base table, then $UCL \mapsto CT$ is a *known functional dependency* in that base table.

- *Table value constructors:* Since you cannot specify constraints for table value constructors, there are no BUC-sets or BPK-sets for them defined by SQL:1999. Other than axiomatic functional dependencies, there are no known functional dependencies defined for them by SQL:1999, although implementations might examine the data in them to determine known functional dependencies.

- *Joined tables:* Because of the inherent nature of joining tables, you'll immediately realize that every column in the virtual table that results from a

---

1   The implication that a table can have at most one row when that table is constrained by a unique constraint defined on no columns at all is an admittedly obscure artifact of set theory.

joined table has a counterpart in one or both of the source tables ("both" only if the joined table is a natural join or a named-columns join). If S is some set of columns in the result table and CT is the set of all columns in the result table, then S is a BPK-set if it has a counterpart in either or both of the input tables that is a BPK-set, all columns of S are not nullable, and S $\mapsto$ CT is a known functional dependency. Analogously, S is a BUC-set if it has a counterpart in either or both of the input tables that is a BUC-set, all columns of S are not nullable, and S $\mapsto$ CT is a known functional dependency.

There are several rules that participate in determining the known functional dependencies of joined tables, but, in the interests of brevity, we're only going to state one of them (which, believe it or not, is the simplest of the several rules). This rule has multiple steps and depends on a number of SQL features with which you might not be familiar, but we'll explain them sufficiently for you to work through the rule.

If the joined table is either a named-columns join or a natural join, then there are one or more columns in the first source table that correspond to a column with the same name from the second source table. Let's define SLCC to be a select list of the following expressions, one per such common column:

```
COALESCE (t1.colname, t2.colname) AS colname
```

The COALESCE expression was discussed in section 6.2.4, "COALESCE"; feel free to quickly review it if you need to do so.

Let's also define the symbol JT to be the keywords that specify the type of join (if any) and TN1 and TN2 to be either the table names or (if specified) the correlation names of the two source tables, respectively. Furthermore, we can define the symbol SC to be the search condition specified with the joined table operation. Then, we can define the symbol IR to be the result of the query expression:

```
SELECT SLCC, TN1.*, TN2.*
FROM TN1 JT JOIN TN2
ON SC
```

The following are recognized as additional known functional dependencies of IR:

- If INNER or LEFT is specified, then COALESCE(TN1.Ci, TN2.Ci) $\mapsto$ TN1.Ci, for all i between 1 (one) and the number of columns in IR.
- If INNER or RIGHT is specified, then COALESCE(TN1.Ci, TN2.Ci) $\mapsto$ TN2.Ci, for all i between 1 (one) and the number of columns in IR.

Now, let's define SL to be a select list. If every column of the first and second source tables are common columns, then SL is the same as SLCC. If no columns of either source table are common columns, then SL is just a select list containing the names of the columns of the first source table ₉ followed by the names of the columns of the second source table. If the first source table has only common columns, but the second table has columns in addition to the common columns, then SL is a select list made up of SLCC followed by the names of the additional columns in the second source table. Similarly, if the second source table has only common columns, but the first table has columns in addition to the common columns, then SL is a select list made up of SLCC followed by the names of the additional columns in the first source table. Finally, if there are common columns and both source tables have additional columns, then SL is SLCC followed by the names of the additional columns from the first source table followed by the names of the additional columns from the second source table. (Whew!)

Finally, we can say that one group of known functional dependencies of the virtual table that results from the join are the known functional dependencies of

```
SELECT SL FROM IR
```

(We say "one result" because, as we stated in the second paragraph of this bullet, there are several rules that are contributors to known functional dependencies of joined tables.)

Complex? Yes! Necessary? Probably. Helpful to vendors and, ultimately, to users? Very much so.

- *Table reference:* There are several types of table reference; for example, a table name or a query name (see section 9.4.4 for information about query names) are table references. The columns of the virtual table resulting from a table reference are naturally counterparts of the columns of the table identified by the table reference; therefore, the BUC-sets and BPK-sets of the result table are counterparts of the BUC-sets and BPK-sets of the source table, and the known functional dependencies of the result table are derived by substituting the column names of the result table for the column names of the source table in the known functional dependencies of the source table. The other types of table reference have analogous rules for determining the BUC-sets, BPK-sets, and known functional dependencies.

- *FROM clause:* In section 9.2.2, we told you that a FROM clause produces a virtual table that is used in subsequent clauses of a table expression. Naturally, that virtual table may have BUC-sets, BPK-sets, and known functional dependencies. If the FROM clause contains only a single table reference, then the BUC-sets and BPK-sets of the FROM clause are counterparts to those of the table associated with that table reference. If the FROM clause contains more than one table reference, then it has no BUC-sets or BPK-sets identified by SQL:1999. The known functional dependencies of the result table of the FROM clause are the functional dependencies of every source table of the FROM clause.

There are five other components of SQL:1999 for which functional dependency rules are contained in the standard. None of them have rules as complex as those for joined tables, but none of them have rules as simple as those for base tables; their complexities all fall somewhere in between those two extremes. Instead of continuing the tedious exercise of detailing them, the next five bullets merely identify unusually interesting aspects of the rules.

- *WHERE clause:* Because WHERE clauses contain search conditions that might use the AND operator to combine multiple predicates, SQL:1999 provides some rules to derive information about known functional dependencies (as well as about BUC-sets and BPK-sets) using knowledge about the behavior of the Boolean operator AND, as well as the equality comparison operator =.

- *GROUP BY clause:* Determining the BUC-sets, BPK-sets, and known functional dependencies of the virtual table resulting from a GROUP BY clause requires effectively generating in that result table a new column whose values somehow identify the rows in the source table that have been grouped together for each row of the result table.

- *HAVING clause:* The BUC-sets, BPK-sets, and known functional dependencies of the virtual table resulting from a HAVING clause are those of its input table (that is, the table coming from the GROUP BY clause, if any, the WHERE clause, if any, or the FROM clause), after applying the rules related to the search condition of the HAVING clause in the same way that such rules were applied for the WHERE clause.

- *Query specification:* The use of value expressions other than column references in the select list influences the computation of BUC-sets, BPK-sets, and known functional dependencies.

- *Query expression:* The BUC-sets, BPK-sets, and known functional dependencies are influenced by the relational operators (UNION, INTERSECT, and EXCEPT). In addition, the BPK-sets, BUC-sets, and known functional dependencies of a recursive query (see section 9.13) are entirely implementation-defined.

We realize that the material in this section is complex and abstract in the extreme. We have included it in spite of the complexity to serve readers who need to understand SQL:1999's enhancements in updatability and who are sufficiently involved with data modeling to have or pursue the background in relational theory. However, in practical terms, we have rarely found ourselves using knowledge of all of these functional dependency relationships when writing our applications.

9.4 | Query Expressions

You've already had an introduction to query expressions in Chapter 4, "Basic Data Definition Language (DDL)" (and other places). In fact, we used the concept a lot in Chapter 8, "Working with Multiple Tables: The Relational Operators," without really calling it by name. However, in this chapter, we are going to examine thoroughly this important element of the SQL language.

In its simplest form, a query expression is merely a query specification. There are two other "simplest forms" of query expressions that we also cover later in this chapter (TABLE table-name and VALUES row-value), but just now, we're going to explore the more complex forms of the query expression. First, let's review what we learned in Chapter 8, "Working with Multiple Tables: The Relational Operators."

There are many different forms of a query expression; that is, the format is very flexible and you can write a wide variety of query expressions. A query expression can be either a joined table (more on that later, too) or a non-join query expression, which is either a non-join query term or a query expression and a query term separated by some operators. The operators are UNION or EXCEPT, and they can optionally be followed by ALL and/or a corresponding specification.

As you recall, UNION specifies that the table indicated by the query expression and the table indicated by the query term are to be combined with a union operation. If ALL is specified, then redundant duplicate rows are retained; otherwise, they are eliminated. EXCEPT specifies that the resulting virtual table is to contain all rows from the table indicated by the query expression *except* those that also appear in the table indicated by the query term. Again, if ALL is specified, then the number of copies of any specific row value in the result is equal to the number of such copies in the table indicated by the query expression, less the number in the table indicated by the query term.

A query term is either a non-join query term or a joined table, and a non-join query term is either a non-join query primary or a query term and a query primary separated by the operator INTERSECT, optionally followed by ALL and/or a corresponding specification.

If INTERSECT is specified, the resulting virtual table contains rows that appear in both the query term and the query primary. If ALL is specified, then the number of copies of any specific row value in the result is equal to the lesser number of such copies in the table indicated by the query term and the number in the table indicated by the query primary.

The syntax of query expressions gives INTERSECT a higher precedence than UNION and EXCEPT. This means that, in a statement that doesn't use parentheses to resolve precedence relationships, INTERSECT operations will be performed before UNION and EXCEPT operations. For example,

```
t1 UNION t2 INTERSECT t3 EXCEPT t4
```

will (effectively) be performed in this order:

```
t2 INTERSECT t3 (call the result TX)
t1 UNION TX      (call the result TY)
TY EXCEPT t4
```

Note that operators of the same precedence are effectively executed left to right.

A query primary is either a non-join query primary or a joined table. A non-join query primary is either a simple table or a non-join query expression enclosed in parentheses.

And a simple table is either a query specification, a table value, or an explicit table. An explicit table is the keyword TABLE followed by a table name; it is just a shorthand for SELECT * FROM table-name, so you must be careful to use it only when the shape of the table is appropriate. You can see the complete syntax of query expressions in Syntax 9-10.

9.4.1 CORRESPONDING

So far in this chapter, we've left out the definition of a corresponding specification, but now it's time to include it. The format is as shown in Syntax 9-9:

Syntax 9-9 *Format of CORRESPONDING*

```
CORRESPONDING [ BY ( column-name [ , column-name ]... ) ]
```

This shows that you can specify just CORRESPONDING, or you can specify CORRESPONDING BY followed by a parenthesized list of column names. If you leave off the optional BY clause, the DBMS will make up a BY clause for you that includes every column name that appears in both of the tables. If you include the BY clause, every column name that you include must be the name of a column in both of the tables. You first saw this in BNF form, in Syntax 8-2, "Syntax of CORRES- PONDING" (see Chapter 8, "Working with Multiple Tables: The Relational Operators," section 8.4, "The UNION Operator"). In section 8.4, we told you that use of this clause causes the result of the UNION, EXCEPT, or INTERSECT to be limited to just the corresponding columns.

9.4.2 Results of Query Expressions

Like everything else we've discussed in this chapter, the result of a query expres- sion—and of each of its component expressions, terms, and primaries—is a vir- tual table. The rules are fairly simple, too: the tables must have the same number of columns, and the data types of each pair of columns in the two tables that appear in the same relative positions (the first column in each table, the second, and so forth) must be comparable. (The word "comparable" means that values of those types can be legally compared using SQL's rules.) Such pairs of columns are called *corresponding columns*. (This must be distinguished from "the columns named in a corresponding specification" as defined in section 9.4.1.) The names of the corresponding columns need not be identical. If they are, the name of the resulting column is the same name; otherwise, the name of the resulting column is assigned by the DBMS. The data type and other attributes of the result columns are the same as the data types of the input columns, with suitable rules to resolve differences caused by the comparable requirement. For example, if one input column were CHARACTER(5) and the other CHARACTER(10), the output col- umn would be CHARACTER(10). We call such tables *union-compatible tables*.

9.4.3 Examples of Query Expressions

Okay, now that we've presented a rather complicated picture of query expres- sions, let's look at a few examples. The first example,

Example 9-6 *The Simplest Query Expression*

```
SELECT c1 FROM t1
```

is a query expression because it's a query specification. The next example,

Example 9-7 *Surrounding a Query Expression with Parentheses*

```
(SELECT c1 FROM t1)
```

is also a query expression because it's a query expression in parentheses. The third example,

Example 9-8 *A Query Expression with UNION*

```
SELECT * FROM t1
UNION
SELECT * FROM t2
```

is a query expression that is valid only if T1 and T2 have (almost) identical definitions. The last example,

Example 9-9 *A Query Expression with INTERSECT ALL and CORRESPONDING*

```
SELECT c1, c2, c3
FROM t1
INTERSECT ALL CORRESPONDING BY ( c2, c3 )
SELECT c4, c2, c3
FROM t2
```

is also a query expression using several options. (As you learned in section 8.4, "The UNION Operator," the result of that query has only two columns, C2 and C3, because of the effects of using CORRESPONDING.)

9.4.4 WITH Clause

So far, we've discussed only SQL-92-style query expressions. One of the major enhancements made to query expression power in SQL:1999 is the addition of recursive queries, which we discuss in section 9.13. In order to define recursive queries in a reasonable way, the designers chose to provide a clause in query expressions that allows an application developer to assign a sort of alias, called a *query name,* to one or more "inner" query expressions that are used in the definition of the "outer" query expression.

The high-level syntax of a query expression is shown in Syntax 9-10 and doesn't contain many surprises. (This syntax reprises the somewhat more wordy description of query expressions earlier in section 9.4.)

Syntax 9-10 *Syntax of Query Expression*

```
<query expression> ::=
    [ <with clause> ] <query expression body>

<query expression body> ::=
    <non-join query expression>
  | <joined table>

<non-join query expression> ::=
    <non-join query term>
  | <query expression body> UNION [ ALL | DISTINCT ]
    [ <corresponding spec> ] <query term>
  | <query expression body> EXCEPT [ ALL | DISTINCT ]
    [ <corresponding spec> ] <query term>

<query term> ::=
    <non-join query term>
  | <joined table>

<non-join query term> ::=
    <non-join query primary>
  | <query term> INTERSECT [ ALL | DISTINCT ]
    [ <corresponding spec> ] <query primary>

<query primary> ::=
    <non-join query primary>
  | <joined table>

<non-join query primary> ::=
    <simple table>
  | <left paren> <non-join query expression> <right paren>

<simple table> ::=
    <query specification>
  | <table value constructor>
  | <explicit table>

<explicit table> ::= TABLE <table name>
```

```
<corresponding spec> ::=
    CORRESPONDING
      [ BY <left paren> <corresponding column list> <right paren> ]

<corresponding column list> ::= <column name list>
```

In Syntax 9-10, you see that a query expression can optionally begin with a <with clause>, whose definition we omitted from that BNF. The remainder of the BNF should be somewhat familiar to you already, if you started this chapter from its beginning. Now, let's consider the <with clause>, whose syntax is shown in Syntax 9-11.

Syntax 9-11 *Syntax of <with clause>*

```
<with clause> ::= WITH [ RECURSIVE ] <with list>

<with list> ::=
    <with list element> [ { <comma> <with list element> }... ]

<with list element> ::=
    <query name> [ <left paren> <with column list> <right paren> ]
    AS <left paren> <query expression> <right paren>
    [ <search or cycle clause> ]

<with column list> ::= <column name list>
```

We'll defer consideration of RECURSIVE and the associated <search or cycle clause> until section 9.13; at this point, we'll stick to the use of WITH in nonrecursive query expressions.

In SQL, as in most other programming languages, it often happens that expressions end up containing a specific subexpression more than one time. For example, in SQL, you might find it useful to use a subquery (see section 9.10) in two or more predicates in a WHERE clause, as illustrated in Example 9-10. (Assume for purposes of this example that the movie_titles table includes a column current_tape_rental_price.)

Example 9-10 *Using a Subquery Multiple Times in a Query Expression*

```
SELECT title
FROM movie_titles
```

```
WHERE current_tape_rental_price > ( SELECT MAX(our_tape_cost)
                                     FROM movie_titles
                                     WHERE year_released < 1950 ) / 10
  AND current_tape_rental_price < ( SELECT MAX(our_tape_cost)
                                     FROM movie_titles
                                     WHERE year_released < 1950 )
```

This query is intended to find the titles of films whose current rental price in our "old economy" brick-and-mortar store is greater than 1/10 the cost of the most expensive old movie we stock but less than that cost. Note that we had to write that simple, but space-consuming subquery twice. You will not be surprised to find that database implementors have worked very hard to build optimizers that recognize such repeated subexpressions so they can be factored out and executed once instead of multiple times.

Of course, we could create a view containing the query that is contained in the repeated subquery, but that is tedious at best. At a minimum, we'd have to execute a CREATE VIEW statement, which creates persistent metadata, and then perhaps a DROP VIEW to delete that persistent metadata when we're done with our query. That's rather a lot of overhead for this sort of operation. A less cumbersome approach is needed, a way to factor common subexpressions out of a query expression.

The WITH clause in SQL:1999 allows us to rewrite Example 9-10 in a shorter, simpler way, illustrated in Example 9-11.

Example 9-11 *Using WITH Clause to Replace Multiple Subquery Use*

```
WITH max_old_movie (max_cost) AS
     ( SELECT MAX(our_tape_cost)
       FROM movie_titles
       WHERE year_released < 1950 )
SELECT title
FROM movie_titles
WHERE current_tape_rental_price > ( SELECT max_cost
                                    FROM max_old_movies ) / 10
  AND current_tape_rental_price < ( SELECT max_cost
                                    FROM max_old_movies )
```

Superficially, this may not seem to have gained us very much (in fact, it contains almost exactly the same number of keystrokes as Example 9-10). But, recall that the WHERE clause of the subquery can be arbitrarily complex, and that the subquery might also contain a GROUP BY clause and a HAVING clause. The savings from eliminating duplicate coding (and, if the developer fails to actually copy and paste the subquery, the potential for transcription errors) can be very significant. The more complex the expression factored out, the greater the savings in effort, possible errors, and so forth. The optional <with column list> must be used if any of the columns of the subexpression being factored out have duplicate names in that subexpression.

You might well wonder why the subquery that appears twice in the WHERE clause

```
( SELECT max_cost FROM max_old_movies )
```

could not also have been written only once and reused in the second place. Well, it's possible to reduce things only so far; at some point, "repetition happens," to coin a phrase. The best we could have done in this case would have been to replace both instances of the subquery with

```
( TABLE max_old_movies )
```

which is simply syntactic shorthand for

```
( SELECT * FROM max_old_movies )
```

That works in this case because the only column in max_old_movies is max_cost, but it wouldn't have worked if there were other columns in the table.

A strong word of caution: The WITH clause in SQL:1999 does *not* behave like a macro, in which there is merely a syntactic substitution of the expression wherever its name is used, so that the query still might be executed multiple times (if it's not discovered by an optimizer). Instead, the virtual table that results from the query specified in the WITH clause is actually used in each place where it's referenced.

As you can see from Syntax 9-11, you're permitted to factor out more than a single subexpression by coding multiple WITH list elements (separated by commas, as SQL usually provides). The usual rules apply to this situation, including a prohibition against using the same query name for two or more such WITH list elements in any single query expression. Furthermore, the query names you use have to be different from the table names and correlation names used in the containing query expression. Interestingly, you're allowed to reference the query name of one such factored-out subexpression in the definition of another one, as long as the referencing subexpression is defined after the subexpression whose query name is referenced (in other words, only "backward references" are permitted).

9.5 | Joined Table

Now, let's add joined-table to our list. We first covered this material in section 8.3, "Types of Join Operations," but we're going to go into additional detail in this chapter.

9.5.1 Review of Joined Table

You will recall the discussion earlier in this chapter that specified the results of the from-clause; that clause produces a resulting virtual table that was the Cartesian product of its input tables (if there are more than one, at least); the number of columns of the result is the sum of the numbers of columns of the input tables, and the number of rows in the result is the product of the number of rows of the input tables. Well, one alternative of a joined-table is a cross-join:

Syntax 9-12 *Syntax of CROSS JOIN*

```
table-reference CROSS JOIN table-reference
```

The resulting virtual table of FROM T1 CROSS JOIN T2 is exactly the same as FROM T1, T2.

Another alternative of joined-table is a qualified-join, which is

Syntax 9-13 *Syntax of Qualified Join*

```
table-reference [ NATURAL ] [ join-type ] JOIN
table-reference [ join-spec ]
```

The join type is either INNER, UNION, LEFT OUTER, RIGHT OUTER, or FULL OUTER (the keyword OUTER is optional in all three cases, but we recommend that you use it to make your programs more readable) and indicates the type of join that you want. If you don't use join type at all, the result is the same as if you had used INNER.

An INNER JOIN is one where the rows in the result table are the rows from the first table that meet the specified criteria, combined with the corresponding rows from the second table that meet the specified criteria.

An OUTER JOIN, by contrast, is one where the rows in the result table are the rows that would have resulted from an INNER JOIN *and* the rows from the first table (LEFT OUTER JOIN), the second table (RIGHT OUTER JOIN), or both tables (FULL OUTER JOIN) that had no matches in the other table.

A UNION JOIN (sometimes called OUTER UNION in the relational literature) produces only those rows in the first and second tables that had *no* matches in the other table. The behavior of

```
t1 UNION JOIN t2
```

is a bit like that of

```
( t1 FULL OUTER JOIN t2 ) EXCEPT ( t1 INNER JOIN t2 )
```

The join spec gives the criteria for the join. A join spec is either the keyword ON followed by a search condition:

Syntax 9-14 *Syntax of Join Specification, Alternative 1*

```
ON search-condition
```

or the keyword USING followed by a parenthesized list of column names:

Syntax 9-15 *Syntax of Join Specification, Alternative 2*

```
USING ( column-name [ , column-name ]... )
```

If the ON variant is used, the result of the join contains every row of the Cartesian product of the two tables that satisfies the search condition. For example,

```
ON t1.c1 = t2.c2 * 2 AND t1.c3 <> t2.c4
```

The most common case in real applications, though, is commonly known as an *equi-join*. In an equi-join, the criterion is for one or more columns of rows in one table to be equal to one or more columns of rows in the other table:

```
ON t1.c1 = t2.c1 AND t1.c2 = t2.c2
```

Because this practice is so common, SQL:1999 provides the following alternative:

```
USING (c1, c2)
```

This is useful (and valid) only if the columns to be used for the join have the same names in both tables (and have comparable data types), because it is identical to the ON variant just above. In the USING variant, you select the columns that you wish to use to determine the result of the join.

The essential characteristic that defines a join to be an equi-join is that the only comparison operator allowed in the ON clause is an equality operator; if there are multiple comparisons, then they must be connected with AND conjunctions. Thus

```
ON t1.c1 = t2.c2 * 5 AND t1.c3 = t2.c4 + t1.c5
```

is an equi-join. There is no corresponding USING variant for this ON clause, since the column names on the left and right sides of the equality operator are not the same and since one side uses expressions and not simple column names.

If you want to use *every* column with the same name in both tables for the join, you can use the NATURAL variation. A natural join is an equi-join based on the equality of every column with the same name in the two tables. The join

```
t1 NATURAL JOIN t2
```

is equivalent to

```
t1 JOIN t2 USING (Cx, Cy, ...)
```

where Cx, Cy, . . . are the columns with the same name in both tables. That, in turn, is equivalent to

```
t1 JOIN t2 ON t1.Cx = t2.Cx AND t1.Cy = t2.Cy AND...
```

or

```
t1 INNER JOIN t2 ON t1.Cx = t2.Cx AND t1.Cy = t2.Cy AND...
```

Now that we've gone through all of the various types of JOINs in SQL:1999 (both the old-style join and all of the new JOIN types) and the various set operators (UNION, EXCEPT, and INTERSECT) in some detail, we think it would be useful to look at the *formal* definitions of these operators from SQL:1999. We'll do these in list form so you can easily follow the steps and corresponding logic.

We'll start with the JOIN definitions. SQL:1999 approaches the specification of *joined-table* (the way that JOINs are expressed) by decomposing the functions into basic components and then putting them together in ways that produce the desired result. Let's do the same here First we'll see what restrictions there are on the syntax and what the shape of the result is (that is, the number of columns and the names and data types of the columns).

1. Since a JOIN always has two source tables, let's call them T1 and T2. Let's also call the *table references* TR1 and TR2 (to clarify: the tables themselves are T1 and T2; the possibly qualified names of the tables are TR1 and TR2). Since table references always have a correlation name (even if the system assigns one without telling you about it), let's call the correlation names CN1 and CN2.

2. Let's use the symbol CP to mean

   ```
   SELECT * FROM tr1, tr2
   ```

   or, equivalently,

   ```
   SELECT * FROM tr1 CROSS JOIN tr2
   ```

3. If you specify NATURAL JOIN, you cannot specify UNION, ON, or USING.

4. If you specify UNION JOIN, you cannot specify ON or USING.

5. If you don't specify NATURAL or UNION, you must specify either ON or USING.

6. If you specify JOIN without any other join type, then INNER JOIN is implicit.

7. If you specify ON, all of the column references in the search condition have to reference a column of T1 or of T2 (they can also be an "outer reference" to a column in a query expression that contains the joined-table). If any value expression in the search condition is a set function, the joined-table has to be contained in the select list or HAVING clause of some outer query expression *and* the set function must reference a column of that outer query expression.

8. If you specify any JOIN with an ON clause, the shape of the resulting table is the same as the shape of CP.

9. If you specify any JOIN with NATURAL or USING, the shape of the resulting table is determined this way:

   - If you specified NATURAL, let's use the phrase *corresponding join columns* to mean all columns that have the same name in both T1 and T2 (and have no duplicate names in either T1 or T2).

   - If you specified USING, we'll use the phrase *corresponding join columns* to mean all columns whose name appears in the column name list (they must all have the same name in both T1 and T2, and there cannot be other columns in either T1 or T2 whose names are duplicates of these column names).

   - Each pair of corresponding join columns has to be comparable, of course.

- Let's use the term SLCC to mean "a select-list of corresponding join columns," each of which is of the form

  COALESCE (ta.c, tb.c) AS c

  (where c is the name of the corresponding join column), with the COALESCE clauses in the same order as the corresponding join columns appeared in T1 (this was chosen arbitrarily; it could have been T2, but the standards committees chose T1).

- Let's use the term SLT1 to mean "a select-list of column names in T1 that are *not* corresponding join columns, in the order they appear in T1." Let's also use the term SLT2 to mean "a select-list of column names in T2 that are *not* corresponding join columns, in the order they appear in T2."

- The shape of the result is the same as the shape of

  SELECT slcc, slt1, slt2 FROM tr1, tr2

- Therefore, the common columns appear first in the result table, followed by the noncommon columns from T1, and ending with the noncommon columns from T2.

Next, let's see what rows are actually returned in the result.

10. First, let's define the symbol T to mean one of five things:
    - If you specified UNION JOIN, then T is empty (has no rows).
    - If you specified CROSS JOIN, then T has all the rows that CP has.
    - If you specified ON, then T has all the rows of CP that satisfy the search-condition.
    - If you specified NATURAL or USING, and there are some corresponding join columns, then T has all the rows of CP for which the values in the corresponding join columns are equal.
    - If you specified NATURAL or USING, and there were no corresponding join columns, then T has all the rows that CP has.

11. Let's use the symbol P1 to mean "all rows of T1 that appear as a partial row in T" (recall that the rows in T are rows from T1 combined with rows from T2). Similarly, let's use P2 to mean "all rows of T2 that appear as a partial row in T."

12. Let's use the symbol U1 to mean "all rows of T1 that do not appear as a partial row in T" and U2 to mean "all rows of T2 that do not appear as a partial row in T."

13. Now, let's use X1 to be the same rows as U1 except we'll append some null values on the *right* (as many null values as T2 has columns). We'll also use X2 to be the same rows as U2 except we'll append some null values on the *left* (as many null values as T1 has columns).

14. Let's invent two distinct names, N1 and N2, to reference the virtual tables X1 and X2. (Remember, X1 and X2 are sets, or multisets, of rows, not the names of those sets or multisets.) And let's use the name TN to reference the virtual table T.

15. If you specified INNER JOIN or CROSS JOIN, we'll use the symbol S to identify the same rows as T.

16. If you specified LEFT OUTER JOIN, we'll use the symbol S to identify the rows that result from

```
SELECT * FROM tn
UNION ALL
SELECT * FROM n1
```

17. If you specified RIGHT OUTER JOIN, we'll use the symbol S to identify the rows that result from

```
SELECT * FROM tn
UNION ALL
SELECT * FROM n2
```

18. If you specified FULL OUTER JOIN, we'll use the symbol S to identify the rows that result from

```
SELECT * FROM tn
UNION ALL
SELECT * FROM n1
UNION ALL
SELECT * FROM n2
```

19. If you specified UNION JOIN, we'll use the symbol S to identify the rows that result from

```
SELECT * FROM n1
UNION ALL
SELECT * FROM n2
```

20. Now, let's use SN as a name for the virtual table S.

21. If you specified NATURAL or USING, the result of the JOIN is the same rows that would result from

```
SELECT slcc, slt1, slt2 FROM sn
```

22. If you didn't specify NATURAL or USING, the result of the JOIN is the same rows that are in S.

We agree that this seems really confusing when you first read it. However, we encourage you to take the time to read it through carefully. You'll find that it's extremely logical and can help you to understand exactly how the various types of JOIN work.

Now, let's take the same kind of look at the INTERSECT, EXCEPT, and UNION operators that can participate in query expressions. We'll start off with determining the shape of the result.

1. All query expressions use one or more simple tables that may or may not be combined with these set operators. You'll recall from earlier in this chapter that a simple table can be either a query specification, a table value constructor, or TABLE table-name.

   - If the simple table is a query specification, the shape of the simple table is the same as the shape of the query specification.
   - If the simple table is TABLE table-name, the shape of the simple table is the same as the shape of that table.
   - If the simple table is a table value constructor, the shape of the simple table is the same as the shape of the table value constructor except that all the column names are provided by the DBMS (uniquely in the SQL statement).

2. If the query expression doesn't have any UNION, INTERSECT, or EXCEPT operators, then the shape of the query expression is the same as the shape of the simple table. Otherwise, it's more interesting.

3. Let's use the symbol T1 to represent the table on the left of the set operator and TN1 to be its name. Similarly, let's use T2 to represent the table on the right and TN2 to be its name. We'll use the symbol TR to be the result of the operation (not its name, though). Finally, let's use the symbol OP to be the set operator (UNION, etc.).

4. If you do not specify CORRESPONDING, then T1 and T2 must be of the same degree (have the same number of columns). For all respective columns (columns in the same position in the table) in T1 and T2 that happen to have the same name, the respective result column in TR has that name. All other columns of TR have a DBMS-provided name (unique in the SQL statement).

5. If you do specify CORRESPONDING, there has to be at least one column in T1 and in T2 with the same name (and no columns of either T1 or T2 can be duplicates).

   - If you specify a column list with CORRESPONDING, let's use the symbol SL to mean "a select list identical to that column list"; of course, every column in the select list has to be a column in both T1 and T2.

   - If you don't specify a column list, let's define SL to mean "a select list of every column that has the same name in both T1 and T2, in the order they appear in T1."

6. If you specify CORRESPONDING, the expression TN1 OP TN2 is effectively replaced by

   (SELECT sl FROM tn1) OP (SELECT sl FROM tn2)

   This has the effect of eliminating all the columns of T1 and T2 that are not corresponding columns. Because all the respective columns of the two new source tables have the same name, the name of the respective result column in TR has the same name, too.

7. Whether or not you specify CORRESPONDING, the data type of a result column is determined by the data types of the two source columns. (We've already said that the data types of the source columns have to be comparable.) The result column's data type is determined by the union data type rules that we give you in section 9.7.

Okay, now we know the shape of the result table. Let's see how to determine the actual rows of that result.

8. Obviously, if there is no set operator, the result has exactly the same rows as the simple table.

9. If there is a set operator, let's examine the contents of the two source tables. First, we'll define the symbol R as "a copy of any row that is a row of T1, a row of T2, or a row that is in both T1 and T2." We decided to say "a copy" because we're later going to talk about how many copies of R there might be in the result table, and it can get too confusing if we defined R to be a row *in* T1 or T2.

10. Now, tables in SQL are multisets, so R may have one or more copies in T1 or in T2 (or both). Let the symbol M mean "the number of copies of R in T1" and let N be "the number of copies of R in T2." (Of course, both M and N are

greater than or equal to zero since, for example, T1 might not have *any* copies of R if it is a copy of a row that exists only in T2.)

11. If you didn't specify ALL, we have to take care of duplicate elimination.

    - If you specified UNION and either M or N is greater than zero, then the result has exactly one copy of R; otherwise, the result has no copies of R. This means, of course, that R doesn't exist, since it was required to be a copy of a row in either T1 or T2.

    - If you specified EXCEPT and M is greater than zero but N is equal to zero, then the result has exactly one copy of R; otherwise, the result has no copies of R.

    - If you specified INTERSECT and both M and N are greater than zero, the result contains exactly one copy of R; otherwise, the result has no copies of R.

12. If you did specify ALL, we don't eliminate duplicates from the result and the results look like this:

    - If you specified UNION, the number of copies of R in the result is M + N.

    - If you specified EXCEPT, the number of copies of R in the result is M – N, except that it obviously cannot be negative, so the number is zero if N is greater than M.

    - If you specified INTERSECT, the number of copies of R in the result is the smaller of M and N.

Again, we recognize that it can be pretty intimidating to read these rules for the first time. However, if you take the time to really understand them, you'll have a much better grasp of the actions that the DBMS must (effectively) take when processing the set operators. (Our use of the word "effectively" emphasizes that the standard merely describes the effects that the database system must produce. The details of how a given product produces that effect are no business of the standard and are, in fact, among the most important ways in which vendors compete with one another.)

9.6 | Grouped Tables

Earlier in this chapter, we mentioned the notion of a grouped table. In this section, we're going to talk about grouped virtual tables and grouped views.

9.6.1 Grouped Virtual Tables

Put simply, a grouped table is the table that results from the use of a GROUP BY or a HAVING clause. You can think of a grouped table as a "table of tables" or a *table of groups*. Each group has the same value for the grouping column or columns, unless there aren't any grouping columns, in which case there's only one group anyway. Set functions operate on the individual groups in the grouped table, as we illustrated earlier.

In Chapter 5, "Values, Basic Functions, and Expressions," we examined set functions and we learned that the set functions operated on the table that was provided to produce a result. Therefore, if you wrote

```
SELECT SUM(salary)
FROM employees
```

you would get back a single row (with a single column) that contained the total of the salaries for employees. However, the set functions can also be applied in grouped-table situations using explicit GROUP BY clauses. Assume that our EMPLOYEES table looks like Table 9-6.

Table 9-6 *An EMPLOYEES Table*

DEPT_NO	LAST_NAME	FIRST_NAME	SALARY
12	Mitchell	Andrea	20000
15	Walters	Marvin	20000
12	Richards	Martha	30000
15	Young	Gail	40000

Consider the following:

```
SELECT dept_no, SUM(salary), AVG(salary),
       MAX(salary), MIN(salary)
FROM employees
GROUP BY dept_no
```

That query will return as many rows as there are departments that have employees assigned to them; each row will have five columns containing (1) the number of the department, (2) the total of its salaries, (3) the average salary, and (4) the highest and (5) the lowest salary in the group. Our result is shown in Result 9-7.

Result 9-7 *Result of Query*

DEPT_NO	SUM(SALARY)	AVG(SALARY)	MAX(SALARY)	MIN(SALARY)
12	50000	25000	30000	20000
15	60000	30000	40000	20000

You can also use the COUNT functions:

```
SELECT COUNT(*)
FROM employees
GROUP BY dept_no
```

which will return the number of employees *in each group* (in our brief example, two for each group). Contrast this with

```
SELECT COUNT(*)
FROM employees
```

This query will return one row with a value of 4, the total number of employees in the entire EMPLOYEES table. The difference is the absence of the GROUP BY clause, of course. Without that clause, your grouped table has only a single group (the entire table), and the COUNT function counts the entire table instead of the rows in the groups.

When you write a query specification that contains a GROUP BY clause or a HAVING clause, the resulting virtual table is a grouped table (as we said above). In this case, no select list column in the query specification can reference a column of the table expression in the query specification unless that column is a grouping column (or is functionally dependent on a grouping column) or the reference is in the form of a set function invocation that has the column as a parameter.

9.6.2 Grouped Views

Views that are defined using query expressions that define grouped tables are called *grouped views*. Just as a view is merely a virtual table with a name and a persistent definition, a grouped view is merely a grouped virtual table with a name and a persistent definition. There's not really anything special about a grouped view beyond the characteristics of grouped tables. Because some SQL implementations do not yet provide full support for grouped tables, there may be restrictions in the use of grouped views, too. As with all SQL features, especially more advanced features, you must check your product's documentation for any such restrictions.

9.7 | Result Data Types of Columns of UNION, EXCEPT, and INTERSECT

So far in this book, we've mentioned several times the fact that SQL provides rules for determining the data type of a column in a virtual table that results from combining two other tables through the use of UNION, EXCEPT, and INTERSECT. Those rules we've mentioned are often referenced using the phrase *union compatibility* (even though they're applied in several circumstances other than UNION, we'll use that phrase and its companion, *union-compatible,* when we're talking about this attribute of SQL and its data types). During the evolution of SQL, the rules have been extended to cover new data types, but we find them quite predictable and easily understood.

The most basic rule is that all data types in a group of union-compatible data types are mutually comparable—that is, SQL's rules must support comparing values of those types. For example, values of all numeric types can be compared with one another, whether some are INTEGER and others are DOUBLE PRECISION.

The rest of the union compatibility rules are determined by the underlying data types, which we summarize here:

- If any of the source types are character string, then they must all be character string and they must all have the same character repertoire, which is the character repertoire of the result type. (A *character repertoire* is nothing more than the selection of characters in the character set used to express the character string. See Chapter 21, "Internationalization Aspects of SQL:1999," for more information on this subject.) Large object strings dominate over varying-length character strings, which dominate over fixed-length character strings. (When we say "dominate," we mean this: if any of the source types are of the dominating type, then the result is that type. Therefore, for character strings, if at least one of the types is CHARACTER LARGE OBJECT, then the result is CHARACTER LARGE OBJECT; if none are CHARACTER LARGE OBJECT, but at least one is CHARACTER VARYING, then the result will be CHARACTER VARYING. Only if none of the types is CHARACTER LARGE OBJECT or CHARACTER VARYING will the result type be CHARACTER.)

- If any of the source types are bit string, then they must all be bit string. Varying-length bit strings dominate over fixed-length bit strings.

- If any of the source types are binary string (BINARY LARGE OBJECT), then they must all be binary strings.

- If all of the source types are exact numeric, then the result is exact numeric whose precision is defined by the implementation and whose scale is the maximum of the scales of the source types.

- If any of the source types are approximate numeric, then all of the types must be some numeric type and the result is approximate numeric (with implementation-defined precision).

- If any of the source types are a datetime type, then all of the types must be a datetime type with the same fields including the time-zone displacement, and the result is that datetime type whose fractional seconds precision is the largest of the fractional seconds precisions of the source types.

- If any of the source types are a year-month interval type, then they must all be year-month interval types, and the result is a year-month interval type that has all of the fields of the source types. If any of the source types are a day-time interval type, then they must all be day-time interval types, and the result is a day-time interval type that has all of the fields of the source types.

- If any of the source types are Boolean, then they must all be Boolean, as is the result type.

- If any of the source types are a row type, then they must all be a row type with the same number of fields and whose corresponding fields (that is, the ones in the same ordinal positions) must have comparable data types; the result type is a row type with the same number of fields, and these union compatibility rules are applied to the types of the corresponding source fields to determine the types of the result fields. If the names of corresponding source fields are the same, then the result type's fields have the same names; otherwise, the names of the result type's fields are implementation-defined.

- If any of the source types are an array type, then they must all be an array type; the result type is an array type whose maximum cardinality is the largest of the maximum cardinalities of the source types and whose element type is determined by applying these union compatibility rules to the element types of the source array types.

9.8 | Sequence of Evaluation within Query Expression

In this chapter and in Chapter 8, "Working with Multiple Tables: The Relational Operators," we've discussed the sequence in which various relational operations are performed, producing virtual tables that are used by other operations. To summarize those discussions (at a high level, not with all the details), we've prepared Figure 9-1.

Of course, the flow illustrated in Figure 9-1 doesn't represent any specific query, but is intended to show the relationships between various components of the syntax of query expressions. A corresponding, but equally nonspecific, query would look like Example 9-12.

Example 9-12 *Nonspecific, Illustrative Query Expression*

```
SELECT ...
FROM query-term UNION
     SELECT ...
     FROM query-primary
       INTERSECT
         SELECT ...
         FROM T3,
             ( T1 JOIN T2 )
         WHERE search-condition
         GROUP BY grouping-columns
```

Of course, we've used terms like query term and query primary that would really have to be expanded into their component query specifications or query expressions, but the idea should be fairly clear from what we've shown.

In Figure 9-1, we especially wish to note that the application of SELECT is done *after* the joins, GROUP BY, and the like.

Of course, we can't show everything about a query expression in such a figure, because it's more complex than drawings can easily represent (note, for example, that we've left out the WITH clause). But this should give you a better feel—or perhaps, since it's visual, a better image—than we've given you so far.

9.9 | Table Value Constructor

We mentioned earlier in this chapter that there were three "simplest" forms of a query expression. The third of those simplest forms is called a *table value constructor.* Think of it as a table literal, if you must. Although not quite accurate, as we'll

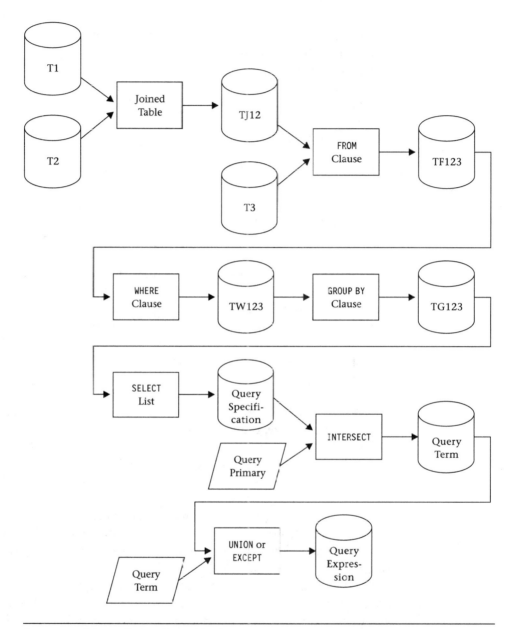

Figure 9-1   Sequence of Query Expression Evaluation

see, it's close enough to give you a fairly decent mental picture of what's intended.

Earlier, in Chapter 6, "Advanced Value Expressions: CASE, CAST, and Row Value Expressions," we discussed the row value constructor as a way of representing an entire tuple, or row, of data at one time. The table value constructor is analogous to that, except that it is used to represent an entire table of data (that is, the cardinality can be greater than 1).

The syntax of the table value constructor is shown in Syntax 9-16. A row value expression is a parenthesized list of value expressions—or the special cases of NULL, DEFAULT, or ARRAY()—separated by commas.

Syntax 9-16 *Syntax of Table Value Constructor*

```
<table value constructor> ::=
    VALUES <row value expression list>

<row value expression list> ::=
    <row value expression> [ { <comma> <row value expression> }... ]
```

The most common place to find a table value constructor is in the INSERT statement, which we've seen already. However, the ability to use a table value constructor in the INSERT statement is hidden in the details. Recall that the format of the INSERT statement uses a query expression.

```
INSERT INTO table-name [ ( column-name [ , column-name ]... ) ]
  query expression
```

Well, one alternative of that query expression is a table value constructor. Using this alternative, the syntax looks like the following:

```
INSERT INTO table-name [ ( column-name [ , column-name ]... ) ]
  VALUES row-value-constructor [ , row-value-constructor ]...
```

Of course, the degree of each row value constructor has to be the same as the number of (explicit or implicit) column names, which means that they all have to have the same degree, too. The rows inserted are represented by the row value constructors (one each).

Similarly, anywhere that you can use a query expression, you can also use a table value constructor of the same degree. Consider the table subquery (more about this below): as we shall see, a subquery (including a table subquery) is really a query expression enclosed in parentheses. That query expression can be a table value constructor, so you can code an IN predicate as follows:

```
IN ( VALUES (5), (10), (15) )
```

To be honest, we don't know why you'd want to do this, since the same effect could be had with

```
IN ( 5, 10, 15 )
```

but there are other cases where it could be more interesting. For example, as we showed you in Chapter 7, "Predicates," the first operand of the IN predicate can be a row value constructor. Thus, you could code something like

```
( title, actor_first_name, actor_last_name ) IN
VALUES ( '10', 'Bo', 'Derek' ),
        ( 'M*A*S*H*', 'Donald', 'Sutherland' ),
        ( 'Unforgiven', 'Clint', 'Eastwood' )
```

which couldn't be coded without the table value constructor.

9.10 | Subqueries

We introduced subqueries in Chapter 5, "Values, Basic Functions, and Expressions"; now let's discuss them further. A subquery is just what it sounds like: a query that is a part of another query. Yet, that's an oversimplification. A subquery is (syntactically the same format as) a query expression in parentheses. Subqueries can return atomic values (degree and cardinality both equal to 1), row values (degree greater than or equal to 1, but cardinality equal to 1), or table values (degree and cardinality both greater than or equal to 1), depending on the situation in which they are used. Actually, in all cases, it's possible for the subquery that you write to have a cardinality of 0 or greater than 1, and the rules of SQL:1999 specify what result you'll get in either case. SQL has been criticized (fairly, in our opinion) for having a single syntactic form for all three sorts of subquery, leaving users to sort out which is really wanted depending on context. If nothing else, this state of affairs leaves the application developer subject to unanticipated errors in some situations. Had SQL been designed to syntactically distinguish (minimally) between scalar or row subqueries and table subqueries, some application development problems might have been avoided.

In general, most situations where you can use a subquery will treat the value of the subquery as the null value if the cardinality is 0. Similarly, when the cardinality is required to be no greater than 1, you'll get an error if the subquery identifies more than one row.

By contrast, when a scalar subquery is required (degree and cardinality = 1), SQL:1999 simply doesn't permit you to specify a subquery that returns more than a single column: any attempt to do so will give you syntax errors. Similarly, for a row subquery or a table subquery, the number of columns returned (the degree of the subquery) must be appropriate for the use of the subquery.

As you've seen in other chapters of this book, and in other sections of this chapter, subqueries can appear in various places throughout a query. They can appear in the select list, but that's not really very common. In fact, programmers who try to use a subquery this way often fall into traps that lead to incorrect results, as the following query (from Chapter 5, "Values, Basic Functions, and Expressions") illustrates:

```
SELECT title, ( SELECT MAX ( current_dvd_sale_price )
                FROM movie_titles )
FROM movie_titles
```

As we saw in Chapter 5, that query returns the name of every movie, with each name accompanied by the price of the most expensive movie in our database—probably not what the application really needs. Much more frequently, you'll use subqueries in a WHERE clause, like this (also found in Chapter 5, "Values, Basic Functions, and Expressions"):

```
SELECT title, current_dvd_sale_price
FROM movie_titles
WHERE current_sale_price =
      ( SELECT MAX ( current_dvd_sale_price )
        FROM movie_titles )
```

or in a predicate that is in a WHERE clause, like one taken from Chapter 7, "Predicates," replicated in Example 9-13.

Example 9-13 *Subquery Used in an IN Predicate*

```
SELECT title, dvds_in_stock
FROM movie_titles
WHERE title IN
      ( SELECT movie_title
        FROM movies_stars
        WHERE actor_last_name = 'Gibson'
          AND
            actor_first_name = 'Mel' ) ;
```

Subqueries like these last two stand on their own—that is, they do not inter-act with the data being accumulated in the rest of the query. In one, we simply wanted to find the most expensive DVD currently being sold, without regard to its title or any other data with which the main query was concerned. In the other, our IN predicate requires the use of a subquery, but we had no need to correlate the outer query and the subquery in any way.

But there are many situations where the information being pursued in a subquery is dependent in some way on data known to the outer query. For instance, let's examine another example taken from Chapter 7, "Predicates," repeated in Example 9-14.

Example 9-14 *Subquery Used in an EXISTS Predicate*

```
SELECT title, tapes_in_stock
FROM movie_titles m
WHERE EXISTS
        ( SELECT *
          FROM movies_stars
          WHERE movie_title = m.title
            AND
                actor_last_name = 'Gibson'
            AND
                actor_first_name = 'Mel' ) ;
```

Like Example 9-13, Example 9-14 uses a subquery as a component of a predicate (an EXISTS predicate, in this case). In that subquery, the first predicate in the WHERE clause uses the column reference m.title. By looking at the FROM clause of the outer query, we see that M is actually a correlation name associated with the movie_titles table being queried in that outer query.

Because the information retrieved by the subquery depends on data being processed in the outer query, we say that the subquery is *correlated* with the outer query. More commonly, we say that this is a *correlated subquery*. Simply put, a correlated subquery is one that uses data from an outer query. Correlated subqueries differ from noncorrelated subqueries in an important aspect that often affects the performance of queries: in general, a correlated subquery cannot be evaluated just once and the result used repeatedly during the evaluation of the outer query; instead, the correlated subquery typically must be evaluated for each row identified by the outer query.

Let's examine Example 9-13 and Example 9-14 again with this new informa-tion in mind. In Example 9-13, the subquery

```
( SELECT movie_title
  FROM movies_stars
  WHERE actor_last_name = 'Gibson'
    AND
       actor_first_name = 'Mel' ) ;
```

can be evaluated just once; of course, the number of rows returned by that subquery may well be more than one, but nothing that we can do in the outer query will change the result of evaluating the subquery. By contrast, the subquery in Example 9-14, repeated here,

```
( SELECT *
  FROM movies_stars
  WHERE movie_title = m.title
    AND
       actor_last_name = 'Gibson'
    AND
       actor_first_name = 'Mel' ) ;
```

cannot be evaluated just once, because the value of m.title will change with every row that is considered by the outer query. As each row is considered by the outer query, the subquery has to be reevaluated with the new value of m.title.

Many (actually, most or even all) such correlated subqueries can be restated in terms of a join operation that has equivalent semantics. The query in Example 9-14 can be replaced with the query in Example 9-15.

Example 9-15 *Rewritten Query without Subquery*

```
SELECT title, tapes_in_stock
FROM movie_titles m, movie_stars ms
WHERE ms.movie_title = m.title
  AND
     ms.actor_last_name = 'Gibson'
  AND
     ms.actor_first_name = 'Mel' ;
```

In fact, the query optimizers of many SQL database products are able to detect situations where subqueries can be avoided by "rewriting" the outer query to use a join operation. These rewrites are effective largely because optimizers are usually better at producing high-performance statement execution for join operations than for repeated subquery evaluation.

In SQL-89, the use of subqueries was severely restricted. They could appear only in a very limited number of places in the language. This was widely viewed as undesirable under the principle of maximum orthogonality (separation of unrelated concepts). Because subqueries are nothing more than a way to produce values, and because there are many places in SQL where values can be used, it was widely believed that SQL should allow the use of subqueries in any place where another kind of value could be used.

SQL-92 went a very long way toward satisfying that requirement, although hardly all the way. While we believe that SQL:1999 represents a substantial improvement in orthogonality over SQL-92, we also recognize that it still doesn't finish that job. We continue to hope that future versions will be yet more thorough.

The format of a subquery (though we just told you what it looks like) is shown in Syntax 9-17.

Syntax 9-17 *Syntax of Subquery*

```
( query-expression )
```

9.11 Table References

In section 9.2.2, we said that a table reference is usually either a table name or a joined table, which we've covered already. We also told you that there are other alternatives and pointed you to this section for a discussion of those alternatives.

The full syntax of table references is shown in Syntax 9-18.

Syntax 9-18 *Syntax of Table Reference*

```
<table reference> ::=
    <table primary>
  | <joined table>

<table primary> ::=
    <table or query name> [ [ AS ] <correlation name>
      [ <left paren> <derived column list> <right paren> ] ]
  | <derived table> [ AS ] <correlation name>
      [ <left paren> <derived column list> <right paren> ]
  | <lateral derived table> [ AS ] <correlation name>
      [ <left paren> <derived column list> <right paren> ]
```

```
    | <collection derived table> [ AS ] <correlation name>
        [ <left paren> <derived column list> <right paren> ]
    | <only spec>
        [ [ AS ] <correlation name>
        [ <left paren> <derived column list> <right paren> ] ]
    | <left paren> <joined table> <right paren>

<only spec> ::=
    ONLY <left paren> <table or query name> <right paren>

<lateral derived table> ::=
    LATERAL <left paren> <query expression> <right paren>

<collection derived table> ::=
    UNNEST <left paren> <collection value expression> <right paren>
    [ WITH ORDINALITY ]

<derived table> ::= <table subquery>

<table or query name> ::=
    <table name>
  | <query name>

<derived column list> ::= <column name list>

<column name list> ::=
    <column name> [ { <comma> <column name> }... ]
```

We're not going to discuss the <only spec> alternative in this volume, as it pertains only to SQL:1999's user-defined types; you will find a discussion of that alternative in Volume 2 of this book. It is included here only for completeness of the syntax.

As you can see from Syntax 9-18, we were not entirely honest—or, at least, we were incomplete—when we said that one alternative of <table reference> is a table name. In fact, that alternative is <table or query name>, implying that you can specify the name of a base table or view or the name of a query defined (in scope, of course) using the WITH clause (discussed in section 9.4.4) to provide another alternative for table references. In the remainder of this section, we're going to concentrate on the two forms of table reference that are truly new in

SQL:1999 (and not related to user-defined types): <collection derived table> and <lateral derived table>.

Astute readers may have already recognized that SQL:1999's ARRAYs make it possible to put collections of rows into a column of a table:

```
...
my_column          ROW ( name CHARACTER(20), birthdate DATE ) ARRAY [50]
...
```

Even though SQL's tables do not have rows in a fixed sequence, while ARRAYs do have their elements in a fixed sequence, the temptation to treat an ARRAY of ROW instances as a sort of degenerate table is obviously present. And the designers of SQL:1999 took advantage of this by providing syntax that allows you to reference and to use such a value in a column as though it were a table, under the right circumstances. That, perhaps obviously, is the purpose of the <collection derived table>: to provide a table derived from the collection formed by an ARRAY. Interestingly enough, ARRAYs of any element type can be used this way; we're not limited to ARRAYs of ROWs.

The syntax for a <collection derived table> requires that you specify a correlation name (after all, you have to have a name with which to qualify the names of columns of the table formed from the ARRAY, and the column name of the ARRAY column won't do for this purpose).

It also permits you to specify the names of the columns of the table formed from the ARRAY. Perhaps surprisingly, that list of column names can contain no more than two names. If you specify WITH ORDINALITY, then you must specify two names (or none); otherwise, you must specify only one name (or none). If you don't specify a column name list at all, the SQL implementation will "invent" the appropriate number of names (one or two) for you.

The result of the <collection derived table> is a virtual table whose name is the correlation name you supply. That virtual table has either two columns or one column, depending respectively on whether or not you specified WITH ORDINALITY. The first (or only) column of each row contains the value of each element of the ARRAY. If you specified WITH ORDINALITY, then the value of the second column in each row is the index (that is, the element number) of the element corresponding to the first column's value in that row. See Figure 9-2 for an illustration of this mechanism.

We've separated the two rows in the musical_groups table to illustrate the fact that the result of the <collection derived table> creates a separate table for each row in the source table. We might use information like this to learn the names of movies in which each of the Beatles have starred:

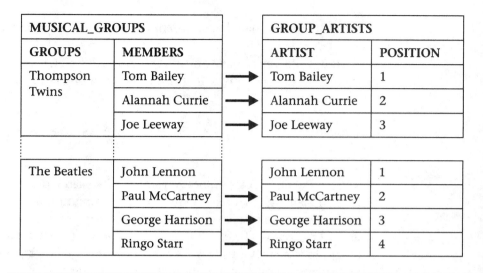

Figure 9-2   Collection Derived Table

Example 9-16 *Finding Movies in which a Beatle Stars*

```
SELECT movie_title
FROM   movies_stars, UNNEST ( SELECT members
                              FROM musical_groups
                              WHERE groups = 'The Beatles' )
                      WITH ORDINALITY
                    AS group_artists ( artist, position )
WHERE  group_artists.artist = movies_stars.actor_first_name ||
                ' ' || movies_stars.actor_last_name
```

Collection derived tables are never updatable in SQL:1999. (Who knows? Perhaps they will be made updatable in some future version of the SQL standard.)

In SQL-92 and earlier versions of the SQL standard, it was forbidden to reference any table appearing in the FROM clause of a query from any other table in the FROM clause. In fact, the table names used in and the correlation names defined in the FROM clause were simply not "visible" in the FROM clause. The scope of their visibility was limited to the other clauses of the table expression: WHERE, GROUP BY, HAVING, and the SELECT list.

SQL:1999 relaxes that restriction, but only to a limited extent: the scope of table names and correlation names in a FROM clause includes lateral derived tables and collection derived tables that appear later in the FROM clause. (Limiting the scope to such derived tables that appear later in the FROM clause eliminates the possibility of cyclic references in which one such derived table references a second one that then references the first.)

In Example 9-16, we joined information from one table (movies_stars) with information retrieved from a collection derived table that unnested an array in a second table (musical_groups). Suppose we'd designed the movies_stars table to include another column—an array of, say, up to 10 character string elements whose values are the names of the children of each star. (That's not very good database design, but we're trying to make a point here!) We could write a different query with a collection derived table that unnests the array containing the star's children's names and use that information to learn the names of movies in which a specific actor stars with his or her oldest child. Such a query would obviously have to correlate the collection derived table with the information being taken from the non-array columns of the movies_stars table; that correlation would necessitate the use of a correlation name given to the movies_stars table in the outer query, as in Example 9-17.

Example 9-17 *Collection Derived Table That References Earlier FROM Clause Table*

```
SELECT  m1.movie_title
FROM    movies_stars m1,
        UNNEST ( SELECT children
                 FROM movies_stars m2
                 WHERE m1.actor_first_name
                     = m2.actor_first_name
                 AND m1.actor_last_name
                     = m2.actor_last_name )
             WITH ORDINALITY
           AS actors_kids ( child, birth_order ),
        movies_stars m3
WHERE   actors_kids.child
    =   m3.actor_first_name || ' ' || m3.actor_last_name
  AND   actors_kids.birth_order = 1
  AND   m1.actor_first_name = :parameter1
  AND   m1.actor_last_name = :parameter2
```

The final alternative for table reference that SQL:1999 provides is the <lateral derived table>. The word "lateral," in this context, means "sideways," and the name is applied here because a <lateral derived table> is one that references a table used earlier in the same FROM clause—to the (left) side of the <lateral derived table> itself. In fact, a collection derived table is a type of lateral derived table, since it is allowed to reference tables used earlier in the same FROM clause as we illustrated in Example 9-17. More general lateral derived tables (that don't unnest array columns into tables) can exist, too. Consider the query in Example 9-18.

Example 9-18 *Lateral Derived Table*

```
SELECT *
FROM Departments D,
    LATERAL ( SELECT *
              FROM Employees E
              WHERE D.DeptNum = E.DeptNum )
```

The query in Example 9-18 would be invalid if it used a conventional <derived table> (without LATERAL), because the correlation name D would not be visible in the <derived table>. That is, the query in Example 9-19 is invalid.

Example 9-19 *Incorrect Attempt to Use Earlier Correlation Names*

```
SELECT *
FROM Departments D,
    ( SELECT *
      FROM Employees E
      WHERE D.DeptNum = E.DeptNum )
```

The reason is that the correlation name D is not in scope in the inner query block. SQL's rules prevent access to that correlation name in the FROM clause except in a lateral derived table (or a collection derived table, which we mentioned above is a type of lateral derived table).

While LATERAL can be used to rewrite primary key/foreign key joins as illustrated in Example 9-18, it is more general than that. The rows of the table or tables declared prior to the lateral derived table in the FROM clause can be viewed as parameters to the <query expression> enclosed by the parentheses of the lateral derived table (as we illustrated in the collection derived table of Example 9-17). Thus a lateral derived table is, in effect, a sort of parameterized in-line view.

9.12 | CUBE and ROLLUP

In section 9.2.3, we told you about the GROUP BY clause in SQL's table expressions, but we didn't cover all of the alternatives; instead, we deferred discussion of some of those alternatives, pointing you to this section. We used the phrase *online analytical processing* (OLAP) to describe the purpose of these (new to SQL:1999) forms of GROUP BY.

In fact, SQL:1999 was initially published only with these two relatively minor OLAP capabilities, but an amendment to the standard, called SQL/OLAP, was published in late 2000. That amendment effectively modified the published SQL:1999 standard by adding major language enhancements to provide significantly more capabilities in that area of technology. The SQL/OLAP amendment is addressed in Volume 2 of this book; in this volume, we cover the basics: the CUBE and ROLLUP operations and their supporting infrastructure.

The ROLLUP operation is often described as a way to do "control breaks" on data, analogous to COBOL's Report Writer features. Simply put, a control break monitors a specific variable (in SQL, this "variable" would be a column) and, whenever the value of that variable changes, causes some aggregating operations to be performed.

In our DVD business, we may wish to analyze sales by movie category and by the year of release. Therefore, we would want to define control breaks on the columns representing those two pieces of information and report total sales volume whenever either of the values changes, thus producing a summary line that aggregates the information for an entire group of movies in one category that were released in a single year with a further summary line that aggregates the information for all movies released in the same year. SQL:1999's ROLLUP operation gives us that capability.

We might also wish to know the aggregate information for all movies of each category regardless of the year in which the movies were released. In order to get all of the information in one query, an extension to ROLLUP, called CUBE, is required. The name CUBE is intended to evoke an image of multidimensional analysis, even though a *cube* is technically three-dimensional; higher dimensions could be said to require a "hypercube" for analysis, but common terminology continues to use *cube,* regardless of the number of dimensions involved.

9.12.1 The Basics

OLAP is a term applied to a large selection of operations that support data analysis (whether done online, whatever that might mean, or not). As you may already realize, data analysis depends on having collections of data to analyze. SQL:1999 focuses on partitioning data into groups as one of the principal mechanisms for providing this capability. In fact, most SQL-based data analysis depends on this kind of partitioning, or grouping, of rows in tables. SQL:1999 was designed to perform the partitioning using the GROUP BY clause, which seems to be quite compatible with the rest of the language.

As we discussed in section 9.2.3, SQL's GROUP BY clause takes as input a virtual table (the one that results from the WHERE clause or, if there is no WHERE clause, the FROM clause). The clause then collects into groups those rows that have equal values in specified columns—called the grouping columns—and produces a new virtual table (the grouped table). In the grouped table, all of the rows belonging to each group (that is, the rows having equal values in the grouping columns) are effectively collected together. The effect is as though a (partial) ordering of the table—a sort on the grouping columns—had been performed. The columns of the grouped table are restricted to include only the grouping columns of the input virtual table and columns created from grouping columns and set functions such as SUM or MAX (sometimes called *aggregate operations*). Once the query's aggregate operations have been applied, the grouped table is further refined into a table that contains one row for each of the identified groups of rows. These rows are sometimes called *aggregate rows,* since they aggregate the values in the rows of the group. The rows of this final refinement of the grouped table contain the value of the grouping columns for each group and the result of the set function computation over the rows of the group.

A ROLLUP grouping extends this notion in an important way, the very raison d'être for the feature: additional rows, called *ordered super-aggregate rows,* are created containing the results of the set functions applied to the ordinary aggregate rows, effectively grouping them into new, higher-order groups. The ordered super-aggregate rows are "ordered" because they are generated along with the groups that they summarize, and they are "super-aggregates" because they further aggregate rows that are already aggregated. We will continue to use the seemingly superfluous adjective "ordered," largely because we will shortly introduce a different sort of super-aggregate row.

In these ordered super-aggregate rows, one or more of the grouping columns is given the null value, the remaining grouping columns have the value of the group from which the row is derived, and the aggregate columns contain the value of the set function for the group of groups summarized by the row. And, yes, we recognize how difficult it is to visualize this without an example, so let's consider the situation in Example 9-20 and Result 9-8, remembering the structure and content of the MOVIE_TITLES table first introduced back in Chapter 3, "Basic Table Creation and Data Manipulation."

Example 9-20 *Ordinary Grouping*

```
SELECT movie_type, year_released, SUM(dvds_owned) AS sum_of_dvds
FROM movie_titles
GROUP BY movie_type, year_released
```

9.12 CUBE and ROLLUP

The query in Example 9-20 retrieves three columns, one of which is computed from a set function. This query gives us a result table with three columns, each of which tells us how many DVDs we own for each movie type in each year for which we have movies of that type. In this example, we've done grouping based on two columns: MOVIE_TYPE and YEAR_RELEASED. As a result, we expect to see summary information for each type of movie during each year of release for movies of that type that we have in our database. Indeed, Result 9-8 shows just such a result.

Result 9-8 *Result of Ordinary Grouping*

MOVIE_TYPE	YEAR_RELEASED	SUM_OF_DVDS
Action	1990	250
Action	1991	374
Action	1992	288
Romance	1990	195
Romance	1991	439
Romance	1992	221
Comecy	1990	347
Comecy	1991	122
Comecy	1992	201

This result (of an ordinary GROUP BY clause) tells us how many DVDs we have for action movies released in 1990, how many DVDs we have for action movies released in 1991, and so forth. What it does not tell us is how many DVDs we have for all action movies. We could have obtained that information with the query in Example 9-21.

Example 9-21 *Alternative Ordinary Grouping*

```
SELECT movie_type, SUM(dvds_owned) AS sum_of_dvds
FROM movie_titles
GROUP BY movie_type
```

However, this alternative approach wouldn't produce the summary by YEAR_RELEASED, as you see illustrated in Result 9-9.

Result 9-9 *Result of Alternative Ordinary Grouping*

MOVIE_TYPE	SUM_OF_DVDS
Action	912
|	
Romance	855
|	
Comedy	670
|	
|	

In other words, we'd have to execute two different queries to get these two pieces of closely related information.

A ROLLUP grouping, by contrast, gives us all of that information in a single result, as you can see in Example 9-22. This example illustrates a ROLLUP across two columns, but the facility is generalized, and any number of columns, determined by your data model and your analysis requirements, can be used. (However, a ROLLUP that specifies only one column is functionally equivalent to a GROUP BY on that same column and is thus not especially interesting.)

Example 9-22 *ROLLUP Grouping*

```
SELECT movie_type, year_released, SUM(dvds_owned) AS sum_of_dvds
FROM movie_titles
GROUP BY ROLLUP ( movie_type, year_released )
```

Result 9-10 *Result of ROLLUP Grouping*

MOVIE_TYPE	YEAR_RELEASED	SUM_OF_DVDS
Action	1990	250
Action	1991	374
Action	1992	288
|		
Action	(null)	912
Romance	1990	195
Romance	1991	439
Romance	1992	221
|		
Romance	(null)	855
	(Continued)	

Result 9-10 *Continued*

MOVIE_TYPE	YEAR_RELEASED	SUM_OF_DVDS
Comedy	1990	347
Comedy	1991	122
Comedy	1992	201
Comedy	(null)	670
(null)	(null)	2437

The rows in which the MOVIE_TYPE column contains a (non-null) value, but the YEAR_RELEASED column contains a null value (represented by "*(null)*") are called *level 1 ordered super-aggregate rows*. The final row in which both of those columns contain a null value is called an *overall total super-aggregate row*.

If you've ever done bookkeeping or accounting, or if you've ever programmed in COBOL, then you've probably encountered the term *control break*. And you'll probably recognize the level 1 ordered super-aggregate rows and the overall total super-aggregate row as rows that contain control break information: information summarizing the rows immediately above them. That's all there is to ROLLUP grouping! It took rather a lot of words and examples to demonstrate it, but it's really quite simple, and very powerful.

Note, if you will, that the summary rows are created based on processing the ROLLUP grouping columns from right to left in the list specified in the GROUP BY clause. If our query had a third ordinary grouping column (perhaps the column indicating whether or not a specific movie is part of a series, PART_OF_SERIES), then we would have seen two levels of ordered super-aggregate rows: level 1 and level 2, one less than the number of grouping columns.

An important question arises here: How does ROLLUP distinguish between a level 1 ordered super-aggregate row for a specific MOVIE_TYPE and an ordinary aggregate row for the same MOVIE_TYPE that summarizes movies of that type whose YEAR_RELEASED data is unknown and therefore contains the null value? The answer lies in a special function added to SQL:1999 for just this purpose:

```
GROUPING ( column-reference )
```

The GROUPING function's return value is an integer. When the grouping column identified by the column reference in a row of the query result has the null value because the row is a super-aggregate row, the GROUPING function returns the value 1. Otherwise (that is, the identified grouping column has a non-null value in a super-aggregate row or a normal aggregate row, or it has the null value in a normal aggregate row), the GROUPING function returns the value 0. We illustrate this use in Example 9-23, whose results are shown in Result 9-11.

Example 9-23 *ROLLUP Grouping with GROUPING Function*

```
SELECT movie_type, year_released, SUM(dvds_owned) AS sum_of_dvds,
       GROUPING (movie_type) AS gm, GROUPING (year_released) AS gy,
FROM movie_titles
GROUP BY ROLLUP ( movie_type, year_released )
```

Result 9-11 *Result of ROLLUP with GROUPING Function*

MOVIE_TYPE	YEAR_RELEASED	SUM_OF_DVDS	GM	GY
Action	1990	250	0	0
Action	1991	374	0	0
Action	1992	288	0	0
Action	(null)	2	0	0
Action	(null)	914	1	0
Romance	1990	195	0	0
Romance	1991	439	0	0
Romance	1992	221	0	0
Romance	(null)	855	1	0
Comedy	1990	347	0	0
Comedy	1991	122	0	0
Comedy	1992	201	0	0
Comedy	(null)	670	1	0
(null)	(null)	2437	1	1

Note, if you will, the two lines for which MOVIE_TYPE specifies Action and YEAR_RELEASED is the null value. The first of those two lines has the value 0 in the GM column, while the second has the value 1 in that column. The second line's 1 means that the null value in YEAR_RELEASED signals that the line is a level 1 ordered super-aggregate row of the result. By contrast, the first line's 0 in the GM column means that the line is an ordinary aggregate (GROUP BY) row reporting that we have 2 Action DVDs for which the YEAR_RELEASED value is not provided in the database.

If you fail to take advantage of the GROUPING function and your data contains null values in the columns over which you're performing ROLLUP operations, then your results are going to be confusing at best. You'll receive results containing rows that have null values in the ROLLUP columns that are not actually super-aggregate rows, in addition to rows that are otherwise indistinguishable that are, in fact, superaggregate rows. *Know your data* and use the GROUPING function whenever you may have null values that will be reported in ROLLUP columns. (As you'll see shortly, the CUBE operation has a lot in common with ROLLUP; therefore, the caution about null values and the use of the GROUPING function applies equally well to that operation.)

What Result 9-10 does not show us (nor does Result 9-11) is summary information by YEAR_RELEASED, regardless of MOVIE_TYPE. Of course, we could have rewritten the query in Example 9-22 like this, reversing the order in which the grouping columns were processed:

```
SELECT movie_type, year_released, SUM(dvds_owned) AS sum_of_dvds
FROM movie_titles
GROUP BY ROLLUP ( year_released, movie_type )
```

But that would give us the opposite problem: summary by YEAR_RELEASED, but no summary by MOVIE_TYPE. Sometimes, we need both kinds of summary simultaneously, and that's where the CUBE comes in.

A CUBE grouping acts a lot like a ROLLUP on steroids: it gives summary rows based on summarizing in every possible dimension, instead of only certain types. In a CUBE grouping, the super-aggregate rows are called *symmetric super-aggregate rows*. The reason for the use of the term *symmetric* is evident when you examine Example 9-24 and Result 9-12. Note that we've illustrated the use of the GROUPING function in this example and its result, even though we (apparently) have no groups with null values in the grouping columns.

Example 9-24 *CUBE Grouping*

```
SELECT movie_type, year_released, SUM(dvds_owned) AS sum_of_dvds
        GROUPING (movie_type) AS gm, GROUPING (year_released) AS gy
FROM movie_titles
GROUP BY CUBE ( movie_type, year_released )
```

Result 9-12 *Result of CUBE Grouping*

MOVIE_TYPE	YEAR_RELEASED	SUM_OF_DVDS	GM	GY
Action	1990	250	0	0
Action	1991	374	0	0
Action	1992	288	0	0
|				
Action	(null)	912	0	1
Romance	1990	195	0	0
Romance	1991	439	0	0
Romance	1992	221	0	0
|				
Romance	(null)	855	0	1
Comedy	1990	347	0	0
Comedy	1991	122	0	0
Comedy	1992	201	0	0
|				
Comedy	(null)	670	0	1
(null)	1990	792	1	0
(null)	1991	935	1	0
(null)	1992	710	1	0
|				
(null)	(null)	2437	1	1

The rows in which the YEAR_RELEASED column is null are the same level 1 ordered super-aggregate rows that we got in our ROLLUP grouping that you saw in Result 9-10. The rows in which the MOVIE_TYPE column is null are called *type 1 symmetric super-aggregate rows*. If we'd had that additional PART_OF_SERIES column in our grouping column list, then the symmetric super-aggregate rows would have been produced in two types. (In fact, the number of types of symmetric super-aggregate rows is always 2^{n-1}, where n is the number of ordinary grouping columns.) And, finally, the row in which both of those columns are null is still an overall total super-aggregate row.

9.12.2 Grouping Operations

You might be surprised to learn that you can combine ordinary grouping operations (without CUBE or ROLLUP) in the same query with either or both of CUBE and

ROLLUP. We've concluded that motivating the need for such combinations isn't worth the space it would take in this book, but we do think you'll appreciate seeing an example of such a query:

```
SELECT title, movie_type, year_released, SUM(dvds_owned) AS sum_of_dvds
FROM movie_titles
GROUP BY title, ROLLUP ( movie_type, year_released )
```

That query produces control breaks by MOVIE_TYPE and YEAR_RELEASED, but does an ordinary grouping by TITLE (that is, without the control break summaries for TITLE).

There are other situations in which you might want different sorts of summary information returned by a single query. Suppose you'd like to see only the figures for the DVDs in our inventory summarized by MOVIE_TYPE and by YEAR_ RELEASED, but without the added detail obtained by having the inventory count broken down by MOVIE_TYPE and YEAR_RELEASED together. You can accomplish this by using SQL:1999's ability to generate multiple *grouping sets* in a single query and "paste" them together as a single result. Accomplishing this requires the use of parentheses in the GROUP BY clause to collect together the grouping instructions for each such grouping set, as we illustrate in Example 9-25.

Example 9-25 *Using Grouping Sets*

```
SELECT movie_type, year_released, SUM(dvds_owned) AS sum_of_dvds
FROM movie_titles
GROUP BY GROUPING SETS
  ( ROLLUP ( movie_type ),
    ROLLUP ( year_released ),
    () )
```

There are several things to note in Example 9-25. First, we used the syntax GROUPING SETS to inform SQL that we're going to ask for the result to be grouped multiple times. Next, we've provided two ROLLUP specifications in a single GROUP BY clause, each of which performs a ROLLUP on a single column. And, finally, we have included an empty pair of parentheses. In SQL:1999's GROUPING SETS, this syntax specifies that a "grand total" is to be included in the result. In Result 9-13, we show the results of this query. Even though in SQL, the order of the rows of a table (even the virtual table resulting from a query execution) is irrelevant, we've carefully given the results of the first ROLLUP specification first, the second ROLLUP specification next, and the grand total last, with a bit of blank space separating each partial result.

Result 9-13 *Result of Grouping Sets Use*

MOVIE_TYPE	YEAR_RELEASED	SUM_OF_DVDS
Action	(null)	912
Romance	(null)	855
Comedy	(null)	670
(null)	1990	792
(null)	1991	935
(null)	1992	710
(null)	(null)	2437

SQL:1999 offers even more expressive power than we've shown you so far. For example, you may sometimes want to perform a ROLLUP or CUBE based on the combination of two columns instead of on each of those two columns. For example, it is fairly common for a director to remake a movie that he or she admires. If the remake uses the same title as the original movie (common, though not universal), then performing a ROLLUP or CUBE using just the TITLE column is not sufficient to uniquely group together rows for the individual movies; using the TITLE column alone would incorrectly group together two movies with the same title. Instead, you might use the combination of the TITLE column and the YEAR_RELEASED column (since it's unlikely to the point of impossibility for a remake to be released in the same year as the original film).

You can accomplish this feat by putting the column's names in parentheses nested within your ROLLUP or CUBE specification:

```
ROLLUP ( movie_type, ( title, year_released ) )
```

Such a specification will avoid control breaks at every change of TITLE but will place a control break when the combination of the two columns together (TITLE and YEAR_RELEASED) changes.

SQL:1999 also allows you to nest CUBEs within ROLLUPs and to nest ROLLUPs within CUBEs. We leave as an exercise for the reader the creation of an example illustrating these possibilities and the results they would generate.

We close this section by showing you the complete SQL:1999 syntax for the GROUP BY clause, including the (rather significant) enhancements associated with the addition of CUBE and ROLLUP. You should especially note the recursive character of this syntax, allowing nesting of the CUBE and ROLLUP clauses (but not the GROUPING SETS clause!) to arbitrary depths. Obviously, specific vendors' implementations of this facility will have some limits; for example, you might be permitted to nest no deeper than four levels deep. (We're not sure we can even visualize the CUBE of a ROLLUP of a CUBE of a ROLLUP, so this limit might well be sufficient for any realistic application!)

Syntax 9-19 *Complete Syntax of GROUP BY Clause*

```
<group by clause> ::=
    GROUP BY <grouping specification>

<grouping specification> ::=
    <grouping column reference>
  | <rollup list>
  | <cube list>
  | <grouping sets specification>
  | <grand total>
  | <concatenated grouping>

<rollup list> ::=
    ROLLUP <left paren> <grouping column reference list> <right paren>

<cube list> ::=
    CUBE <left paren> <grouping column reference list> <right paren>

<grouping sets specification> ::=
    GROUPING SETS <left paren> <grouping set list> <right paren>

<grouping set list> ::=
    <grouping set> [ { <comma> <grouping set> }... ]

<concatenated grouping> ::=
    <grouping set> <comma> <grouping set list>

<grouping set> ::=
    <ordinary grouping set>
  | <rollup list>
  | <cube list>
  | <grand total>
```

```
<ordinary grouping set> ::=
    <grouping column reference>
  | <left paren> <grouping column reference list> <right paren>


<grand total> ::= <left paren> <right paren>


<grouping column reference list> ::=
    <grouping column reference>
      [ { <comma> <grouping column reference> }... ]


<grouping column reference> ::=
    <column reference> [ <collate clause> ]
```

9.13 | Recursive Queries

In section 9.4.4, Syntax 9-11, you saw the overall syntax of SQL:1999's WITH clause, after which we told you that we would defer all discussion of recursion (including the keyword RECURSIVE and the optional <search or cycle clause>) until this point in the chapter.

Recursion in SQL has been a topic of heated debate for many years, and several vendors have produced proprietary ways of providing such functionality for their users. For example, Oracle provides a form of recursion, under the name *hierarchical queries,* that uses a START WITH and CONNECT BY clause. Oracle doesn't use the word *recursion* to describe this feature, but its effects are similar enough to those of true recursion to justify our mentioning it at this point. Other vendors have provided similar proprietary capabilities, but until SQL:1999 this feature was not standardized.

The material in this section is very complex, and some readers may wish to defer its study until they are sufficiently comfortable with the earlier sections of this chapter.

Before we get into the details of SQL:1999's support for recursion, let's take a look at the requirement for having recursion in a relational system and examine some of the underlying concepts.

9.13.1 Parts Is Parts Is Parts, or Who Works for Whom

The classic justification for recursion is often called the *bill-of-materials problem,* probably because the phrase describes an application that is central to a great many manufacturing environments. It could be just as accurately called the *corporate hierarchy problem,* since the solution to the BOM (bill-of-materials) problem handily solves this problem, too Another, less common, name is *computing transitive closure,* which you'll appreciate only if you have a mathematical bent.

Suppose for a moment that, instead of running a video and music operation, we're building jet planes. You won't be surprised to learn that jet planes are typically assembled from a number of complicated subassemblies, or that those subassemblies are usually assembled of several smaller subassemblies. In fact, those smaller subassemblies may well be made of still smaller subassemblies, and so on until we find subassemblies that are made of individual parts. Imagine that we needed to learn the cost of the parts that it takes to build one of these planes (ignoring labor costs). Well, the cost of the plane is the sum of the costs of its subassemblies. The cost of a given subassembly is the sum of the costs of its smaller subassemblies, and so forth until we compute the cost of a subassembly as the cost of its individual parts.

Now, a typical jet plane probably has tens of thousands of individual parts, but those parts aren't filed directly under "jet plane" in our database. Instead, we have to go through the process of finding subassemblies, smaller subassemblies, and so forth until we know how many units of each individual part are required. At that point, we can multiply the quantity of each part by the cost of that part and add the products to find the cost of the plane.

Doing this requires building a hierarchy of components, starting at the *root* of the tree (the jet plane), following *branches* to the subassemblies, smaller branches to the smaller subassemblies, and so on until we get to the *leaves* (the individual parts). See Figure 9-3 for an illustration of this situation. But some individual parts might be used in several subassemblies, possibly at different levels in our tree structure. Therefore, we have to count the number of each individual part as we encounter it in the tree before we can multiply the count by its cost to determine how much cost that part contributes to the cost of the plane.

Naturally, we've greatly simplified the diagram, but you can see that we've broken the plane into three subassemblies. One of those, the wings, is further broken down into three smaller subassemblies, and so forth until we have a coil, a shaft, and an armature. It's possible that one or more of these parts could be required somewhere in the landing gear subassembly or somewhere in the rudder subassembly, complicating the cost implications of those parts. But we think you've got the idea.

Following that hierarchy of parts can be done with some difficulty using several techniques of SQL other than the new RECURSIVE feature, but it's awkward at best and unworkably limited at worst. Using WITH RECURSIVE makes it very easy, as we'll show you in section 9.13.3.

But, first, let's take a look at some of the concepts involved in the definition and use of recursive facilities.

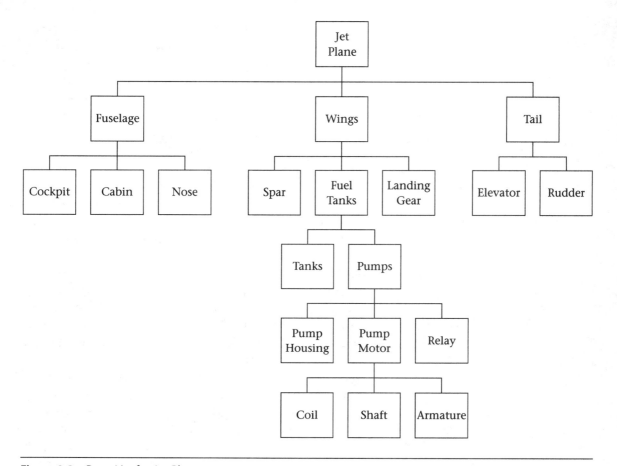

Figure 9-3   Parts List for Jet Plane

9.13.2 Concepts of Recursion

Much of what we discussed in section 9.13.1 applies to the use of hierarchies of data and can be implemented using iterative techniques. However, it is not difficult to find examples for which the data is not structured in a hierarchy or tree and iteration is often insufficient for finding the needed answers to your queries.

For example, one might wish to determine all actors and actresses who have been in a movie with Kevin Bacon—recalling the (never all that popular) party game "Six Degrees of Kevin Bacon." If you have the inclination, feel free to grab a sheet of paper (make it a very large sheet) and start drawing boxes that represent the movies in which Kevin Bacon appears. Write in each box the names of the actors and actresses in the movie represented by the box. Then, for each of those actors and actresses, draw a box for each movie in which they have appeared, listing in the box the names of the actors and actresses in that movie, and connect those boxes with the box from which you started. Then, for each of those boxes . . . well, you get the idea. Clearly, in this process, you're going to encounter (and it won't take too long) some situation where your lines and boxes no longer form a tree, but a more generalized graph. That is, you'll be drawing a line to a box from which there is already a path to the box from which you're drawing the line. In other words, you'll create a "cycle" in the graph.

It's at that point that iterative evaluation no longer works as well. Of course, techniques have been developed to allow some of the more sophisticated iteration designs to handle general graph structures, but they are highly procedural in nature. You may recall from section 1.3.2, "Procedural Versus Nonprocedural Languages," that one of SQL's strengths is its essential nonprocedural nature, allowing the optimizers in products to find better ways of executing queries. An iterative solution to general graph evaluation inhibits just this sort of advantage of SQL, so a nonprocedural solution is preferred: true recursion.

Among other advantages, true recursion allows queries to invoke themselves! While this sounds a little bizarre when we word it that way, it's not bizarre at all in practice. As we get through the details, you'll see examples that illustrate the value of this.

Before we go any further, we'd like to define a number of terms and concepts that participate in SQL:1999's recursion facilities. As part of the definitions we provide, we also inform you of the relationship that the terms and concepts have to SQL:1999. One word of caution, though: Our definitions are strictly related to SQL:1999's recursion and may or may not apply either to other types of recursion or to technologies other than recursion.

- *Breadth-first:* If a tree is traversed in a manner that results in visiting all immediate children of each node before visiting "grandchildren," then the traversal is breadth-first. In Figure 9-3, a breadth-first traversal would result in visiting the node labeled "Jet Plane," followed (in order) by the nodes labeled "Fuselage," "Wings," and "Tail," further followed by "Cockpit," "Cabin," "Nose," "Spar," "Fuel Tanks," "Landing Gear," and so on.

- *Cycle:* In graph theory, a cycle is the result of having a series of connections (arcs) that can be followed to return to a point (node) already visited without traversing any arc twice (once in one direction and once in the reverse direction). In SQL:1999 recursion, the nodes are rows being included in the result of a recursive query, and the arcs are the ways in which processing one row leads to the inclusion of other rows in the result (sometimes resulting from the use of referential integrity).

- *Depth-first:* If a tree is traversed in a manner that results in visiting all descendents of each immediate child of a node before visiting other immediate children of that node, then the traversal is depth-first. In Figure 9-3, a depth-first traversal would result in visiting the node labeled "Jet Plane," followed (in order) by the nodes labeled "Fuselage," "Cockpit," "Cabin," "Nose," "Wings," "Spar," "Fuel Tanks," "Tanks," "Pumps," "Pump Housing," and so on.

- *Direct recursion:* An item uses direct recursion if it invokes itself without invoking an intervening item to do so. In SQL:1999, that "item" corresponds to a recursive query.

- *Linear recursion:* An invocation of a linear recursive item results in at most one direct invocation of that same recursive item. In SQL:1999, every (virtual) table that is defined recursively is referenced in a `<table reference>` at most once in the definition of that table. This means that SQL:1999 places the restriction that the table cannot be referenced both in the FROM clause of the definition's query specification and in a subquery contained in that query specification, nor more than once in the FROM clause of that query specification.

- *Monotonicity:* A monotonic progression is one that never decreases (that is, either always increases or stays the same) or never increases (always decreases or stays the same). In SQL:1999 recursion, the number of rows being accumulated into the result of a recursive query never decreases (see the definition of *negation* below for additional clarification).

- *Mutual recursion:* Two items A and B are related through mutual recursion if A invokes B either with or without invoking an intervening item to do so *and* B invokes A either with or without invoking an intervening item to do so. In SQL:1999, those "items" correspond to recursive queries.

- *Negation:* Removing rows from an accumulated result is negation; in SQL, negation can occur because of set operators like EXCEPT or INTERSECT, because of the use of DISTINCT, because of predicates like NOT EXISTS, and so forth. SQL:1999 does not prohibit the use of negation in recursive queries but avoids the problem of negation causing a violation of monotonicity by requiring that negation be applied only to tables that are completely known (or computed) prior to the application of the negation and not during the process of computing a table, such as during accumulation of the result of a recursion.

- *Nonlinear recursion:* An invocation of a nonlinear recursive item might result in more than one direct invocation of that same recursive item. In SQL:1999, nonlinear recursion is deliberately excluded; while it might be included in a future version of the standard, we consider that somewhat unlikely.

- *Search order:* The choice of breadth-first or depth-first traversal is the search order.

- *Seed:* When performing recursive computations, one usually (but not always) starts off with some initial value, called a seed. In SQL:1999, the seed is a row or (probably small) set of rows that matches some initial condition from which additional rows are located to form the final result.

- *Stratification:* An SQL:1999 query that involves recursion typically contains a "recursive part" and a "nonrecursive part." Stratification is the process by which those two parts are evaluated, or considered, separately. (More complex recursive queries might have several recursive parts and perhaps more than one nonrecursive part, in which case stratification will identify more than two strata.) Negation (see the definition above) can be applied only to the nonrecursive part (or parts) of such a query; this use of stratification is how SQL:1999 avoids the problems associated with violation of monotonicity.

There's one more concept we want to define: *fixpoint semantics*. This concept provides the theoretical underpinnings of SQL:1999's recursion capabilities, yet we find that it is poorly understood (at best) outside of the logic database community. It is often said that the concept isn't "intuitive"—and we agree enthusiastically with that perception! But it's important enough that we feel compelled to provide a definition. One textbook[2] says, "A fixpoint of a function f is a value v such that the function applied to the value returns the same value, that is, $f(v) = v$." That definition is surprisingly simple to grasp and may even be applicable to SQL:1999. But it's probably not obvious how that definition applies to SQL, so let's go a little further.

Another, possibly more helpful, statement comes from the Web site of Universität Tübingen,[3] where we found the notes for a seminar on Constraint Programming taught by Tom Cornell and Frank Moraweitz. The statement that we found helpful reads: "When we reach a fixpoint, that is, when a complete pass through all the relevant pairs fails to make any changes . . . ." Applying this to the notion of collecting rows into a virtual table, we realize that fixpoint semantics in SQL:1999 means that we know that a recursive query is finished when further efforts to identify more rows to insert into the result find no such additional rows.

The technical change proposal[4] that added recursive queries to SQL:1999 goes beyond this to say this: the use of fixpoint properties for capturing the semantics of recursive tables posed a number of questions that have been worked upon by the DB research community:

---

2 Raghu Ramakrishnan, *Database Management Systems* (Boston: WCB/McGraw-Hill, 1998).

3 *http://tcl.sfs.nphil.uni-tuebingen.de*

4 ISO/IEC JTC1/SC21/WG3 DBL:MCI-077 and X3H2-96-075R1. S. Finkelstein, N. Mattos, I. Mumick, and H. Pirahesh, *Expressing Recursive Queries in SQL,* 6 March, 1996.

- Does a fixpoint exist that solves the equation defining the view or named query expression definition?

- Is this solution unique?

- Are there algorithms to determine the desired fixpoint solution?

The proposal goes on to say that it has been shown that fixpoint theory assures that unique solutions really exist as long as the transformation on the right-hand side of a recursive definition is monotonically increasing. That is, adding elements to the input set must not remove or change an element of the result of the transformation.

And, of course, you will not be surprised to learn that SQL:1999's recursive capabilities ensure that unique fixpoint solutions are produced by the naive algorithm by which the standard defines the semantics of recursion. Implementations, of course, are free to use other, probably more highly optimized, algorithms, as long as the final result produced is the same as the naive algorithm specified in the standard.

And with that, we're ready to tell you precisely how SQL:1999 lets you write recursive queries.

9.13.3 WITH RECURSIVE

In Syntax 9-11, we showed you the syntax of the <with clause>, after which we deferred discussion of RECURSIVE and the <search or cycle clause> until this point in the chapter. In Syntax 9-20, we provide the syntax of the <with clause> again, but this time we've added the syntax of the <search or cycle clause>.

Syntax 9-20 *Syntax of <with clause> Redux*

```
<with clause> ::= WITH [ RECURSIVE ] <with list>

<with list> ::=
    <with list element> [ { <comma> <with list element> }... ]

<with list element> ::=
    <query name> [ <left paren> <with column list> <right paren> ]
    AS <left paren> <query expression> <right paren>
    [ <search or cycle clause> ]

<with column list> ::= <column name list>
```

```
<search or cycle clause> ::=
    <search clause>
  | <cycle clause>
  | <search clause> <cycle clause>

<search clause> ::=
    SEARCH <recursive search order> SET <sequence column>

<recursive search order> ::=
    DEPTH FIRST BY <sort specification list>
  | BREADTH FIRST BY <sort specification list>

<sequence column> ::= <column name>

<cycle clause> ::=
    CYCLE <cycle column list>
      SET <cycle mark column> TO <cycle mark value>
      DEFAULT <non-cycle mark value>
      USING <path column>

<cycle column list> ::=
    <cycle column> [ { <comma> <cycle column> }... ]

<cycle column> ::= <column name>

<cycle mark column> ::= <column name>

<path column> ::= <column name>

<cycle mark value> ::= <value expression>

<non-cycle mark value> ::= <value expression>
```

We first want to point out that a <search or cycle clause> can be either a <search clause> or a <cycle clause>, or it can be both clauses—in that order. Before we get into the details of the <search or cycle clause> and the meanings of its variations, we must first show you how to do basic recursion in SQL:1999. To learn what parts it takes to build our airplane from Figure 9-3, we could define a table identifying airplane parts and their relationships like the one in Example 9-26 and then pose a query such as that shown in Example 9-27.

Example 9-26 *The Table Representing Airplane Parts*

```
CREATE TABLE airplane (
    containing_assembly   CHARACTER VARYING(10), -- 0-length string at top
    contained_assembly    CHARACTER VARYING(10), --"This" part number
    quantity_contained    INTEGER,
    is_this_assembly      BOOLEAN,              --False for individual parts
    unit_cost             DECIMAL(6,2) ) ;
```

In Example 9-26, we might expect to find a row in which the containing_ assembly column holds the value Fuselage (or a part number representing the fuselage; see Figure 9-3) and the contained_assemply column holds the value Cockpit (or the corresponding part number). In this row, quantity_contained will probably be 1, since most jet plane fuselages have only a single cockpit. The value of is_this_assembly might contain FALSE, based purely on the data gathered from Figure 9-3, but we suspect that the figure is incomplete and a cockpit is almost certainly going to be an assembly of smaller components (meaning that the column will probably contain TRUE). If is_this_assembly does contain FALSE, the value of unit_cost will contain a number indicating the cost of the part represented by the row.

Example 9-27 *Using Recursion for an Airplane Parts List*

```
WITH RECURSIVE partslist ( part_number, quantity, cost ) AS
    (   SELECT contained_assembly, 1, 0.00
        FROM   airplane
        WHERE  containing_assembly = ''     -- Seed with top-level (the plane)
      UNION ALL
        SELECT airplane.contained_assembly, airplane.quantity_contained,
               airplane.quantity_contained * airplane.unit_cost
        FROM   partslist, airplane
        WHERE  partslist.contained_assembly = airplane.containing_assembly )
SELECT part_number, SUM(quantity), SUM(cost)
FROM   partslist
GROUP BY part_number ;
```

Let's look at that query in a little bit of detail, because it's undoubtedly got some unexpected language in it. The WITH clause defines a named recursive query (the name of this query is partslist) that has three columns (part_number, quantity, and cost). The query itself has two components: a seed (see our definition in section 9.13.2) that finds a row in the database from which we'll start accumulating our result, followed by the recursive part of the query, which accumulates more rows based on their relationship with the rows already included in the query. In this recursive portion of the query, we use a join between the rows accumulated so far and the source table to identify additional rows to be added to the result. That join identifies new rows based on the relationship between the parts represented by those rows and the parts represented by rows already in the result. Since we coded this query using a UNION ALL (as opposed to UNION DISTINCT), no duplicates get eliminated, so monotonicity is maintained and fixpoint semantics are used. Finally, the last three lines of the query comprise a query specification that uses the named query defined in the WITH clause to retrieve, for every part used in constructing the plane, the part number, the quantity of that part used in the entire airplane, and the cost of using the part. If we had wanted the parts to be sorted by part number, we could have created a cursor using this same query and added an ORDER BY clause to the cursor definition (see Chapter 13, "Cursors," for details):

```
ORDER BY part_number
```

We find that a large majority of recursive queries follow a pattern very much like this one: a simple seed that usually selects a single row, to which the recursive part is accumulated using a UNION ALL, as we illustrated in Example 9-27. (The other variant of UNION, UNION DISTINCT, can be used as well, but queries that are intended to accumulate information about a single part number that is used in multiple higher-level assemblies will find that duplicate elimination gives incorrect results.) In fact, SQL:1999 is optimized for queries like this one, since it is only such "simple" recursive queries for which a <search or cycle clause> can be specified. (SQL:1999 permits a <search or cycle clause> only on queries that are linearly recursive, are not mutually recursive, and have only a single UNION operator and no other set operators.)

A <search clause> is, as you can see in Syntax 9-20, simply a way to instruct SQL whether to process your data in depth-first order or in breadth-first order. And, because we defined those terms above, that's almost all we need to say about the <search clause> here—well, almost all . . .

BREADTH FIRST and DEPTH FIRST

In most cases, you don't care about the order in which the rows of your source data are accumulated into the result of your recursive queries, and you can order the result with an ORDER BY clause (if you're using a cursor, at least, or if you're using direct invocation of SQL statements). When your requirements are satisfied with this situation, then you don't need a <search clause>. On some occasions, however, you might have an application-based reason for wanting to query your part (or other) hierarchy with a depth-first or a breadth-first traversal, and that's when a <search clause> is used. Depth-first ordering ensures that each "parent" or "containing" item appears in the result before the items that it contains, as well as before its "siblings" (items with the same parent or container). Breadth-first ordering ensures that items follow their siblings without following the sibling's subordinate items ("children"). Your application requirements will dictate which of these will be used in your queries.

Syntax 9-20 shows that specifying DEPTH or BREADTH is accompanied by a <sort specification list>, which is nothing more than the same list of value expressions that you can use in a cursor definition's ORDER BY clause (as you'll see in Chapter 13, "Cursors"). The value expressions used in the SEARCH clause are restricted to be column references—not more complex value expressions—and the columns referenced must be columns of the query being defined in the WITH clause. The columns that you identify in this clause are the columns whose values in each row are used to identify the next batch of rows to bring into the result. We could enhance Example 9-26 to do a breadth-first search (identifying more complex subassemblies before identifying individual parts) by adding a SEARCH clause as shown in Example 9-28.

Example 9-28 *Performing a Breadth-First Traversal*

```
WITH RECURSIVE partslist ( assembly, part_number, quantity, cost ) AS
   (    SELECT containing_assembly, contained_assembly, 1, 0.00
        FROM    airplane
        WHERE   containing_assembly = ''     -- Seed with top-level (the plane)
      UNION ALL
        SELECT airplane.containing_assembly, airplane.contained_assembly,
               airplane.quantity_contained,
               airplane.quantity_contained * airplane.unit_cost
        FROM    partslist, airplane
        WHERE   partslist.contained_assembly = airplane.containing_assembly )
   SEARCH BREADTH FIRST BY containing_assembly, contained_assembly
     SET order_column
SELECT part_number, quantity, cost
FROM    partslist
ORDER BY order_column ;
```

In order to use the FIRST clause, we had to enhance our recursive query (partslist) by adding yet another column to be retrieved (containing_assembly). However, when we used that query to retrieve our final result, we weren't required to retrieve that column, which we didn't want in any case.

The SET clause that appears at the end of the SEARCH clause identifies a new column name (order_column) that doesn't appear anywhere else. In fact, it's not specified to be part of the recursive query (partslist) at all! This "invented" column is used "under the covers" by SQL to allow us to reorder the recursive result into the desired breadth-first traversal. Behind the scenes, SQL places values into that invented column that can be used later to order the result according to the specified criteria: depth-first, breadth-first, and so on. (But don't conclude from this that you can always use an ORDER BY in a query like this one: as you'll learn in Chapter 13, "Cursors," ORDER BY is valid only when you're defining a cursor.)

A DEPTH FIRST query is written identically, merely substituting the keyword DEPTH where Example 9-28 used BREADTH. While there are valid reasons for BREADTH FIRST queries, we personally find that a majority of applications seem more intuitive when contained parts are listed immediately beneath the parts that contain them. Similarly, it just seems natural for employees reporting to a manager to be listed under that manager in a report. Therefore, we suspect you'll use DEPTH FIRST more often than BREADTH FIRST. But we also suspect that you'll use "no specified order" still more often than either of those two alternatives (if for no other reason than the fact that omitting an ordering specification, in the absence of a requirement for some ordering, may improve the performance of executing the query).

CYCLE Clause

Once in a while, you might run across a problem in which the actual data, not just the data structures, are recursive. In graph theory, we'd say that there are cycles in the data, not just in the table definitions.

For example, some American corporations treat the members of the Board of Directors as though they are the "managers" of the President or of the CEO. In some of those corporations, the employees (perhaps in the form of a trade union) are given a seat on the Board of Directors. It's easy to recognize that the data representing employees in the corporation now has a cycle, because the CEO manages a Vice President, who manages a Senior Manager, who manages a line Manager, who manages a Supervisor, who manages the ordinary worker who just happens to represent the employees on the Board of Directors—and is thus a manager of the CEO! Thus, a cycle exists in the data.

If you're confident that your data does not have any cycles in it, then you need not worry about your recursive queries running forever, like an infinite loop in some programming languages. But, if there is some possibility of a cycle in the data—and this situation is not especially rare—then you must prevent "runaway" queries on such data. SQL:1999 gives you a tool to deal with this problem in the form of a CYCLE clause that you can add to your recursive queries.

In general, we know of no ways to prevent entirely the problem of queries on data with cycles. But SQL's CYCLE clause gives you a way to prevent those queries from running forever. The trick is to "recognize" data that you've already seen once, which isn't terribly complicated a task. When you're accumulating into your result the rows that satisfy the conditions of your query, the CYCLE clause instructs SQL to record a specified value to indicate that those rows have already been identified. Whenever you find a new row to add to your result, SQL checks to see if you've already got that row in the result by determining whether the row has been "marked" with that specified value; if it has been marked, then a cycle is presumed to have been encountered and the query stops looking for more result rows. Of course, this is all complicated a bit by the fact that SQL's operations are supposed to be insensitive to the order in which the implementation chooses rows on which to operate. That means that the solution is slightly more complicated than we've described, but not much.

We've repeated the <cycle clause> syntax from Syntax 9-20 in Syntax 9-21 for easier reference.

Syntax 9-21   *<cycle clause> Syntax*

```
<cycle clause> ::=
    CYCLE <cycle column list>
      SET <cycle mark column> TO <cycle mark value>
      DEFAULT <non-cycle mark value>
      USING <path column>

<cycle column list> ::=
    <cycle column> [ { <comma> <cycle column> }... ]

<cycle column> ::= <column name>

<cycle mark column> ::= <column name>

<path column> ::= <column name>

<cycle mark value> ::= <value expression>

<non-cycle mark value> ::= <value expression>
```

Let's break that BNF down a bit before we show you an example. First, the <cycle column list> is where you provide the names of one or more columns that are used to identify new rows for your result based on rows you already have. For example, in Example 9-26, contained_assembly is the name of the column that "links" between a larger assembly to a smaller assembly or part. In a table describing employees and their supervisors, there would probably be a column named something like subordinate_employee_id to provide this information.

Next, you'll notice the SET clause. That clause generates a new column (one not otherwise specified in your recursive query definition!) in the result and sets the value of that column in almost all rows to <non-cycle mark value>. In rows that have been previously accumulated into your result, the value of that column is set to <cycle mark value>. The data types of those two values are fixed-length character strings with length 1, so you might use '0' and '1' or perhaps 'Y' and 'N' for the two alternatives.

Finally, Syntax 9-21 provides a USING clause, in which yet another new column is generated in the result; this column is how cycles are tracked. The column's data type is an ARRAY type whose cardinality is presumed to be "sufficiently large" to accommodate the number of rows in your result, and whose element type is a row type with one column for each column in your <cycle column list>. The < column> contains an array element for each row that has been accumulated into the result.

To see how all this fits together, look at Example 9-29.

Example 9-29 *Detecting Cycles in Airplane Parts*

```
WITH RECURSIVE partslist ( part_number, quantity, cost ) AS
  (   SELECT contained_assembly, 1, 0.00
      FROM   airplane
      WHERE  containing_assembly = ''    -- Seed with top-level (the plane)
    UNION ALL
      SELECT airplane.contained_assembly, airplane.quantity_contained,
             airplane.quantity_contained * airplane.unit_cost
      FROM   partslist, airplane
      WHERE  partslist.contained_assembly = airplane.containing_assembly )
  CYCLE contained_assembly
    SET cyclemark to 'Y' DEFAULT 'N'
    USING cyclepath
SELECT part_number, SUM(quantity), SUM(cost)
FROM    partslist
GROUP BY part_number ;
```

We've chosen the column names CYCLEMARK and CYCLEPATH for our two newly invented columns. (You get to choose the names for these columns in your queries.) The only restrictions are that you cannot assign a name that is already used as a column name within the scope of this query or a name that is otherwise invalid (such as one spelled the same as a reserved word).

As the query is executed, rows satisfying the query are accumulated into the query's result, but those rows are also "cached" in the invented array column that we've named CYCLEPATH. Whenever a row is accumulated into the result that has not already been accumulated, which is readily detected by the row's absence from every array element in CYCLEPATH, the value of the CYCLEMARK column appended to that row is given the value 'N'. When a row is accumulated into the result that has already been accumulated (that is, the row is found in some array element in CYCLEPATH), the existing row in the result is modified so that its CYCLEMARK column value is changed to 'Y'. This mark indicates that the row starts a cycle.

Recursive Views

In SQL:1999, it is possible to use a recursive query at any place that a query expression can be used. Among the more interesting places in the language where query expressions might be especially useful if they are recursive are in the definition of cursors and in the definition of views.

If you have no need to do depth-first or breadth-first ordering in your recursive queries, then ordinary recursive queries can be used for your applications. Recursion used in cursors (see Chapter 13, "Cursors") is interesting principally because SQL doesn't permit you to specify ordering of result rows anywhere other than in cursors. Therefore, if you want to insist on a BREADTH FIRST or a DEPTH FIRST query, you can do so only as part of a cursor specification.

A recursive view is, of course, one that invokes itself, either using direct recursion or using mutual recursion through some other view. To avoid "accidentally" creating a recursive view (especially one that involves mutual recursion), SQL:1999 requires the use of the keyword RECURSIVE in the view definition itself (in addition to its use in the query expression that defines the view), as seen in Syntax 9-22.

Syntax 9-22 *View Definition with Recursion*

```
CREATE [ RECURSIVE ] VIEW <table name>
    [ <left paren> <view column list> <right paren> ]
  AS <query expression>
  [ WITH [ <levels clause> ] CHECK OPTION ]
```

This syntax differs from "ordinary" view definitions only in the use of the keyword RECURSIVE, which is required if the <query expression> is recursive (which is known by the presence of the same keyword in the <query expression>; SQL:1999 requires that both the <query expression> and the <view definition>

specify RECURSIVE, which is redundant, but nonetheless required by the language). Perhaps surprisingly, specification of a recursive view prohibits the use of the CHECK OPTION clause (see section 4.4, "WITH CHECK OPTION," for more information), undoubtedly because SQL:1999's designers despaired at the task of figuring out how to apply the CHECK OPTION rules to a recursive view. We're very sympathetic with that decision, because the problem is, no doubt, extreme, if not impossible.

And, with that, we've covered all aspects of SQL:1999's recursive query capabilities. We agree that the subject is complex and sometimes difficult to understand. Frankly, we're not sure when standard-conforming implementations will appear on the marketplace, but IBM's DB2 Version 2 implements recursion using syntax and semantics very close to those we've described here. While that may suggest that IBM could implement the standard version more easily than other vendors, nothing's guaranteed until it ships!

9.14 | Chapter Summary

In this chapter, we've taken a more formal approach to, and a much more detailed look at, SQL query expressions. That is, rather than presenting language facets with "to do this, you enter this" or "if you do this, this is what you'll get," we've presented the inside story behind query expressions.

We discussed query specifications and the subtle differences from routine SELECT statements. We looked at table expressions and the GROUP BY and HAVING clauses, including the new OLAP-oriented features. We discussed subqueries in the context of permissible usage within SQL:1999. Finally, we examined the new WITH clause and the expressive power it gives you, especially when its RECURSIVE capabilities are required.

This chapter is not only rather long, it contains some very complicated material that is quite intimidating, especially on a first reading. Most SQL application programmers will rarely, if ever, have to use these advanced SQL capabilities in their work. But, isn't it nice to know that the designers of SQL:1999 provided the ability to solve complex problems when you encounter them? As we suggested in the introduction to this chapter, don't try to absorb everything in one pass, but come back to the more difficult parts later, after you're more comfortable with the language.

In the next chapter, we'll turn our attention away from the data manipulation orientation of the last four chapters. We'll now look at how SQL handles constraints and referential integrity aspects, and how you can use these facilities to enhance the integrity of your databases.

Chapter

10

Constraints, Assertions, and Referential Integrity

10.1 | Introduction

Your organization's databases are only as good as the integrity of the data contained within their tables and records. That is, the reliability and consistency of the data is critical to your applications, decision support and query tools, and other aspects of your information systems environment that utilize your database. Outright errors in the data are an obvious problem, although not the only one. Missing information, lost linkages among data elements, and other problems can result in incorrect reports and can lead the database users to lose confidence in the overall database environment.

The integrity of the data can be ensured by applying *constraints*, or rules, to the structure of the database and its contents. There are two primary methods by which these constraints can be specified, applied, and enforced:

- through the applications programs and software systems that use the database

- through the database management system itself

Traditionally, application programs have been the medium through which such constraints have been applied. Examples include

- Verifying that an input value for a particular data item is within the correct range of values (e.g., a new employee's age must be between 16 and 90, and hourly wage must be greater than the legal minimum wage rate) or is from the correct list of values (e.g., a new movie's type can only be CHILDREN, HORROR, COMEDY, OTHER).

- Verifying that the relationship between two or more values is correct (e.g., comparing the number of copies of a particular CD that we have on hand with the number requested in an incoming order).

The ever-growing use of relational database management systems introduced the concept of *database-enforced constraints* to many information systems users. That is, instead of having to write COBOL, C, or some other type of procedural code to specify and enforce constraints, the data definition language of the database itself provides facilities to perform these functions.

One of the catalysts encouraging the shift from procedural specification and enforcement of constraints to constraint management within the database realm was the explosion of personal computer-based applications in the early and mid-1980s, particularly those using the dBASE product family (particularly dBASE III and III+) or other products such as Clipper or FoxPro based on the Xbase language. These development environments provided a rich set of database-managed constraints for ranges of values, lists of values, and many of the other capabilities we'll discuss in this chapter, and application developers quickly became enamored with the combination of simplicity and power, and the resultant high productivity, of these features. Many of the more powerful relational DBMS products began featuring constraints within their own data definition languages, which of course led to SQL and standardization efforts.

There are a couple of major advantages to database-enforced constraints as compared with those managed through procedural applications code.

- Since the tables in a relational database are used by many different applications, each and every constraint must be specified—and modified, whenever necessary—in each applicable program when the application-enforced model is used. In contrast, database-enforced constraints can usually be designated in a single location (typically in the data definition language) and still apply to all necessary applications.

- Application-enforced constraints are usually more complex to code and manage than are database-enforced constraints. For example, to validate a list-of-values constraint in procedural code, program constructs such as loop control and if-then-else statements are necessary, as illustrated in the following pseudocode:

```
do until all input is correct:
   get movie title
   get movie cost
 . . .
   get movie type
 . . .
   if movie type = 'Children'
      or if movie type = 'Horror'
      or if . . .
   then movie type is correct
   else
         repeat loop
   end if
end do loop
```

A corresponding database-enforced constraint, however, is usually specified through a much less wordy clause in the DDL itself.

The very nature of the relational model—the division of a database's data among logically related tables, together with logical relationships among those tables—introduces an additional consideration with respect to database constraints, namely, that of keeping update anomalies, redundant data, and similar problems to a minimum. This is done through *normalization*. (See section 1.2.3, subsection called "Normal Forms," for a discussion of this concept in the relational model.) Data normalization typically requires several physical SQL tables to constitute some logical application object. For example, a MOVIE is represented by several different SQL tables: MOVIE_TITLES and MOVIES_STARS. In a more comprehensive database environment, perhaps 10 or more SQL tables would be used to describe various aspects of our movies.

Because of this split among multiple tables, it is highly desirable that constraints be used to ensure that the following types of situations do *not* occur. Consider the following scenarios.

Table 10-1 *Rows in MOVIES_STARS Table*

Wall Street	Douglas	Michael
Wall Street	Sheen	Charlie
Wall Street	Sheen	Martin

- Though the rows Table 10-1 exist, there is no row in our "main movie table" (MOVIE_TITLES) for the movie *Wall Street*. Therefore, we have a lost data problem.

- We received prerelease information about a movie called *The Postman, Part II*, and we enter preliminary information in our MOVIE_TITLES and MOVIES_STARS tables. Several months later when the movie is released on videocassette, the title has been changed to *The Last Postman*. We issue an UPDATE MOVIE_TITLES SET... statement to correct the title in one table but forget to do so in the MOVIES_STARS table. Until we remember that we forgot (?!), we have a problem of a lost relationship between these two tables; simple join operations, for example, will not make the association between applicable rows because of the difference in the titles.

In this chapter we look at the facilities provided by SQL:1999 to handle different types of constraint specification and enforcement. First we look at some basic constraints, such as those used to specify whether or not a column can have a NULL value or what values are permissible in a column, and then we turn our attention to those dealing with referential integrity—that is, rules that require values stored in certain columns of the rows of one table also be stored in certain columns of the rows of another table (under certain circumstances, even of the same table).

10.2 | Column Constraints and Table Constraints

Let's expand on our basic table definitions of Chapter 4, "Basic Data Definition Language (DDL)," by adding constraints to the DDL. Let's look at some of the basic constraints you can specify on columns and in tables. Syntax 10-1 shows what these constraints look like in BNF form. Here, we're showing you the high-level syntax of constraints, both table constraints and column constraints. You'll see the syntax for specific types of constraints later: unique constraints in Syntax 10-2, check constraints in Syntax 10-3, and referential constraints in Syntax 10-5.

Syntax 10-1 *Syntax of Constraint Definition*

```
•  <table constraint definition> ::=
      [ <constraint name definition> ]
      <table constraint> [ <constraint characteristics> ]

   <table constraint> ::=
        <unique constraint definition>
      | <referential constraint definition>
      | <check constraint definition
```

- `<column constraint definition> ::=`
    `[ constraint name definition ]`
    `<column constraint> [ <constraint characteristics> ]`

  `<column constraint> ::=`
      `NOT NULL`
    `| <unique constraint definition>`
    `| <referential constraint definition>`
    `| <check constraint definition>`
- `<constraint name definition> ::=`
    `CONSTRAINT <constraint name>`

  `<constraint characteristics> ::=`
      `<constraint check time> [ [ NOT ] DEFERRABLE ]`
    `| [ NOT ] DEFERRABLE [ <constraint check time> ]`

  `<constraint check time> ::=`
      `INITIALLY DEFERRED`
    `| INITIALLY IMMEDIATE`

SQL:1999, like SQL-92, defines its column constraints (constraints that you define as part of a column definition) to be syntactic shorthand for table constraints (constraints that are defined as elements of a table definition). While this might seem unnecessarily complex and even confusing to application developers like yourself, it did simplify the specification of SQL constraints enough to justify doing so. You'll see in Section 10.2.2 why we mentioned this fact.

10.2.1 Constraint Deferral

Before we begin discussing the various types of constraints, let's consider the issue of just when a constraint is checked. In the introduction to this chapter, we saw that constraints are used to enforce valid states of the database. SQL's policy is that constraints are checked, by default, at the end of execution of every SQL statement. Actually, it's more correct to say that SQL requires that no constraint is violated at the time an SQL statement terminates. Saying it this way avoids the implication that the database has to explicitly check constraints that could not have been violated by a specific statement, such as a SELECT statement that makes no changes to the data.

Remember we said that this is SQL's default policy. It's possible that your environment will have some applications that cause certain inconsistencies in your data to span the execution of two or more SQL statements. If the policies of our music and video store included a rule that prohibited stocking more than $1,000,000 of DVDs and a second rule that prohibited returning merchandise before it has been accepted into inventory, we could easily find ourselves unable to return unordered merchandise solely because our inventories are nearing, but less than, that limit. However, if we were able to *temporarily* prevent the database system from checking the constraint that enforces the million-dollar limit, we could accept the merchandise into inventory and then return it to the shipper, all without causing a constraint violation.

SQL:1999, like SQL-92 before it, allows you to declare that your constraints are deferrable. Deferred constraints are not checked at the end of every SQL statement. However, every constraint, even a deferred constraint, is always checked at the end of every transaction.

At the end of Syntax 10-1, there are BNF productions named <constraint characteristics> and <constraint check time>. <constraint characteristics> allow you to specify that a particular constraint either is or is not deferrable. If a constraint is deferrable, then you can also specify whether it is initially deferred— that is, deferred by default when each transaction begins. Deferrable constraints that are not initially deferred can be explicitly deferred by the use of the SET CONSTRAINTS statement. Deferred constraints, whether initially deferred or deferred by the use of SET CONSTRAINTS, can be checked upon demand by using SET CONSTRAINTS to set them to immediate checking.

When a nondeferred constraint is checked and is found to have been violated (that is, the data in the database does not satisfy the constraint), then the effects on the database of the statement causing the constraint to be checked are undone. By undoing the offending statement, the database can be restored to a consistent state. However, if a deferred constraint is checked, either at the end of a transaction or as a result of executing a SET CONSTRAINTS statement, the statement that caused the database to become inconsistent is not necessarily identifiable. As a result, it's not possible to just undo the effects of one statement. Instead, unless your application is somehow able to determine the problem and update the database to become consistent, the entire transaction will have to be undone (see Chapter 15, "Transaction Management"). Because of this difficulty, we recommend that you defer constraint evaluation only in limited circumstances.

10.2.2 NOT NULL

In Chapter 4, "Basic Data Definition Language (DDL)," we briefly mentioned the NOT NULL constraint while discussing basic Data Definition Language syntax.

Since NOT NULL is an example of an SQL:1999 constraint (and, arguably, the simplest to specify and understand), we will quickly repeat our discussion.

NOT NULL indicates that null values are not permissible in any row of that table for the specified column. That is,

```
CREATE TABLE movie_titles (
    title CHARACTER (30) NOT NULL,
    |
    |
)
```

will ensure that no row in the movie_titles table will ever have a null value in the title column. As we previewed in Chapter 4, "Basic Data Definition Language (DDL)," and mention later in this chapter, this restriction can also be specified using the multipurpose CHECK constraint.

In Syntax 10-1, you probably noticed that the alternatives for column constraints and for table constraints were exactly the same, except that NOT NULL is not permitted for table constraints. In the transformation of the column constraint NOT NULL into a table constraint, SQL:1999 converts NOT NULL into a check constraint, described in section 10.2 4.

10.2.3   UNIQUE

In many situations, we want to ensure that a specific column or group of columns designates some type of unique identifier for a table. In Chapter 8, "Working with Multiple Tables: The Relational Operators," we showed an example of a table of music distributors from which we order CDs and tapes. Changing our example from that chapter a little bit, since each distributor has a different unique identifier, we can specify the syntax in Example 10-1.

Example 10-1 *Using the UNIQUE Constraint*

```
CREATE TABLE music_distributors (
    distributor_id CHARACTER (15) UNIQUE,
    |           -- {rest of column definitions}
    |
    |
    ...)
```

Alternatively, we can specify the uniqueness constraint in a slightly different way, as shown in Example 10-2.

Example 10-2 *Alternative Form of UNIQUE Constraint*

```
CREATE TABLE music_distributors (
    distributor_id CHARACTER (15),
    |            -- {rest of column definitions}
    |
    |
    UNIQUE (distributor_id),
    ...)
```

You might be wondering what happened to the NOT NULL constraint if you took a peek back at Chapter 8, "Working with Multiple Tables: The Relational Operators," while reading this example. SQL-89 required you to specify NOT NULL UNIQUE in your constraint definition; you were not permitted to say UNIQUE without also saying NOT NULL. Additionally, the ordering of the two constraints was restrictive; you could not say UNIQUE NOT NULL, but rather had to place the NOT NULL constraint first. SQL-92 relaxed that requirement and allowed UNIQUE to be specified without an accompanying specification of NOT NULL. That is, SQL-92 did not include in the uniqueness check implied by a UNIQUE predicate any rows in which any of the columns participating in the UNIQUE predicate had the null value. The SQL-92 syntax and semantics for the UNIQUE predicate continues into SQL:1999. (That is, UNIQUE alone permits multiple null values in a column.)

Still, specifying UNIQUE without NOT NULL is considered a dangerous practice by leading relational database proponents and is not recommended. (However, see section 10.4 for a different predicate that avoids the problems associated with failing to use NOT NULL along with a UNIQUE predicate.) For syntactical completeness, however, we'll show you what happens if you were to use only the UNIQUE constraint.

(Note that SQL:1999 also defines a UNIQUE column constraint to be exactly the same as a CHECK constraint on the table, as we will see later.)

Let's look at our music_distributors example again. With the above constraint definition, the following table contents would be legal within SQL:1999. That's normally not a good idea, particularly if the column is used to uniquely identify a business entity (like the distributor for the music we sell), but having only a single row with a null value in the unique column makes that possible, if a bit unorthodox.

Table 10-2 *Valid MUSIC_DISTRIBUTORS Table Contents*

DISTRIBUTOR_ID ...

Music All the Time
CD Wholesalers, Inc.
null
Yesterday's Music Found

It's probably worse that the following is also allowed, since it's no longer possible to identify certain rows uniquely at all, since there are multiple rows with the same value (well, the same "nonvalue") in the unique column.

Table 10-3 *Valid, but Even Less Convenient, MUSIC_DISTRIBUTORS Table Contents*

DISTRIBUTOR_ID ...

Music All the Time
null
CD Wholesalers, Inc.
null
Yesterday's Music Found

In SQL:1999 terminology, UNIQUE may be defined as meaning "not equal." In our example, no two music_distributors rows may have distributor_id column values that are equal. (Two rows with null values are considered not equal and are thus not prohibited by UNIQUE.)

The complete syntax for unique constraints can be seen in Syntax 10-2, even though we've described only some of the syntax so far (those alternatives using the keyword UNIQUE); we'll cover primary keys in section 10.4.

Syntax 10-2 *Syntax of UNIQUE Constraints*

```
<unique constraint definition> ::=
    <unique specification>
        <left paren> <unique column list> <right paren>
  | UNIQUE ( VALUE )

<unique specification> ::=
    UNIQUE
  | PRIMARY KEY

<unique column list> ::= <column name list>
```

The alternatives in which a list of column names is specified permit you to force the database system to check that no two rows in the table have the same values in the combination of the specified columns.

The alternative UNIQUE (VALUE) allows you to ensure that a table contains no duplicate rows when all columns of the table are considered; it is merely a shorthand notation for

```
UNIQUE ( column-name-1, column-name-2,..., column-name-n )
```

in which you list every column of the table.

10.2.4 CHECK

One of the most flexible, and therefore useful, constraints within SQL:1999 is the CHECK constraint. This allows you to specify a wide range of rules for your tables, such as range of values, list of values, and others.

The syntax of the CHECK constraint is shown in Syntax 10-3.

Syntax 10-3 *Syntax of CHECK Constraint*

```
CHECK ( search-condition )
```

As we shall see, the search-condition can be any sort of search condition that we've learned to use. However, there is one unusual aspect to them. Let's say that you're defining a CHECK constraint on table movie_titles. In this search condition, you refer to any column of that table (e.g., our_dvd_cost) just by its name; the context is always the current row of that table. By contrast, if you need to access a column in another table, you have to use a subquery.

As with UNIQUE (discussed above), there are several alternate syntax specifications for CHECK. Assume that we want to ensure that our_dvd_cost for all movies is less than $90.00 (Example 10-3).

Example 10-3 *CHECK Clause Example (Column Constraint)*

```
CREATE TABLE movie_titles (
    ...
    our_dvd_cost      DECIMAL (5,2)
      CHECK ( our_dvd_cost < 90.00 ),
    | --{rest of column definitions}
    |
)
```

Alternatively, the constraint could be specified as shown in Example 10-4.

Example 10-4 *Alternative Form of CHECK Clause (Table Constraint)*

```
CREATE TABLE movie_titles (

    ...
    our_dvd_cost      DECIMAL (5,2),
    | --{rest of column definitions}
    |
    CHECK ( our_dvd_cost < 90.00 ) ,
    |
    |
)
```

It is important to note the rule that applies to the search condition of the CHECK constraint. Specifically, the search condition *must not be False* for any row in the table (as opposed to having to be True for every row in the table). This means that the table can be *empty* and the CHECK constraint will be satisfied (that is, no row violates the search condition because there are no rows!). This is rather subtle but is important to understand, especially when analyzing and debugging your applications. That is, the search condition can evaluate to Unknown and the CHECK constraint is satisfied.

Perhaps you also want to be sure that our_dvd_cost is positive. You could specify this with an additional CHECK clause (Example 10-5).

Example 10-5 *Using Two CHECK Constraints Together*

```
...CHECK ( our_dvd_cost < 90 ),
   CHECK ( our_dvd_cost > 0 ) ...
```

(The comma in Example 10-5 would be used only if these two constraints were specified as table constraints; if they're column constraints, then the comma is prohibited.) Or, you could specify the two conditions in a single constraint (Example 10-6).

Example 10-6 *Combining Two CHECK Constraints into One Using AND*

```
...CHECK ( our_dvd_cost < 90 AND our_dvd_cost > 0 )
```

In this case, all of the CHECK clauses in a table are effectively ANDed together. This is true even if the CHECK clauses reference different columns (Example 10-7).

Example 10-7 *Another Example with Two CHECK Constraints and Then Combining Them*

```
...CHECK ( our_dvd_cost < 90 ),
   CHECK ( tapes_owned > 0 )
```

The example in Example 10-7 is equivalent to

```
...CHECK (our_cost < 90 AND tapes_owned > 0)
```

Let's look at some of the typical business rules you are likely to want to specify through your database and how they might be coded using the CHECK constraint. Don't forget that a CHECK constraint uses an ordinary search condition like those that we learned about in Chapter 8, "Working with Multiple Tables: The Relational Operators." There are, however, a couple of limitations. When the CHECK constraint is a column constraint, then it cannot reference any column other than the column with which it is associated; when it is a table constraint, then it can reference only columns that are in the table with which it is associated.

Minimum or Maximum Values

We already saw how a maximum value such as our_dvd_cost < 90 can be specified. Similarly, a minimum value constraint can be designated. To ensure that all of our e-tailer employees earn at least the current minimum wage rate, you might specify the syntax shown in Example 10-8.

Example 10-8 *Employees Table Definition and Minimum Wage CHECK Constraint*

```
CREATE TABLE employees (
    emp_last_name        VARCHAR (30) NOT NULL,
    emp_first_name       VARCHAR (15) NOT NULL,
    emp_address          VARCHAR (30),
    emp_city             VARCHAR (15),
    emp_state            CHAR (2),
    emp_zip              VARCHAR (9),
    emp_phone            CHAR (8),
    emp_start_date       DATE,
    emp_hourly_rate      DECIMAL (7,2)
    |
    |
    |
```

```
       CHECK (emp_hourly_rate >= 5.25),
       |
       |
       |
   )
```

On occasion, you might wish to designate a minimum or maximum value check against some dynamic value rather than a hard-coded one as in the examples above. Assume that some table competition_prices contains information collected about your competitors, and you wish to ensure that none of our DVD format movie titles are sale-priced higher than the maximum price charged by any competitor for any of their DVDs. To accomplish this, you'd use a subquery in the constraint, as shown in Example 10-9.

Example 10-9 *Dynamic Definition of a Maximum Price CHECK Constraint*

```
   CREATE TABLE competition_prices (
       |
       |
       |
       max_dvd_price DECIMAL (5,2),
       |
       |
       | )

   CREATE TABLE movie_titles (
       |
       |
       |
       current_dvd_sale_price DECIMAL (5,2),
       |
       |
       CHECK ( current_dvd_sale_price <=
               ( SELECT MAX ( max_dvd_price )
                 FROM competitior_prices ) )
       |
   )
```

You should be aware that any constraint that references data in more than one table is checked after a change to any one or more of those tables (both competition_prices and movie_titles, in this case). This constraint, therefore, will also cause a failure if an attempt is made to insert a record into `competition_prices` with a `max_dvd_price` that is lower than some `current_dvd_sale_price` in `movie_titles`.

We can also specify constraints for a column's values against other values in the same table. Assume that we want to ensure that no DVD movie has a current sales price that is lower than our lowest cost for *any* DVD movie; this is shown in Example 10-10.

Example 10-10 *CHECK Constraint with Dynamic Checking against Column Values in the Same Table*

```
CREATE TABLE movie_titles (
    |
    |
    |
    our_dvd_cost            DECIMAL (5,2),
    current_dvd_sale_price  DECIMAL (5,2),
    |
    |
    CHECK ( current_dvd_sale_price >=
            ( SELECT MIN ( our_dvd_cost )
              FROM  movie_titles ) )
    |
)
```

Range of Values

It's often desirable to place both minimum and maximum permissible values on one or more columns. Many DBMS products allow you to specify a parameter such as RANGE, in which the boundary values are designated. SQL:1999 allows you to use a combination of CHECK and BETWEEN. Assume that we wish to place "reasonableness" boundaries on our numeric columns within `movie_titles`. We can do so as shown in Example 10-11.

Example 10-11 *CHECK Constraint Used for Range of Values*

```
CREATE TABLE movie_titles (
    title            CHARACTER ( 30 ) NOT NULL,
    year_released    DATE,
    our_tape_cost    DECIMAL ( 5,2 ),
    our_dvd_cost     DECIMAL ( 5,2 ),
```

```
        regular_tape_sale_price        DECIMAL ( 5,2 ),
        current_tape_sale_price        DECIMAL ( 5,2 ),
        regular_dvd_sale_price         DECIMAL ( 5,2 ),
        current_dvd_sale_price         DECIMAL ( 5,2 ),
        part_of_series                 CHARACTER ( 3 ),
        movie_type                     CHARACTER ( 10 ),
        tapes_owned                    INTEGER,
        dvds_owned                     INTEGER,
        tapes_in_stock                 INTEGER,
        dvds_in_stock                  INTEGER,
        total_tape_units_sold          INTEGER,
        total_dvd_units_sold           INTEGER,

    |
    |
    |
CHECK (
  ( our_tape_cost BETWEEN .99 AND 90.00 )
AND
  ( our_dvd_cost BETWEEN .99 AND 90.00 )
AND
  ( regular_tape_sale_price BETWEEN .25 AND 90.00 )
AND
  ( current_tape_sale_price BETWEEN .25 AND 90.00 )
AND
  ( regular_dvd_sale_price BETWEEN .25 AND 90.00 )
AND
  ( current_dvd_sale_price BETWEEN .25 AND 90.00 )
AND
  ( tapes_owned BETWEEN 0 AND 1000 )
AND
  ( dvds_owned BETWEEN 0 AND 1000 )
AND ... )
    |
    |
    |
)
```

Several points are worth noting about the first example. Note the use of AND as part of the above constraint. If applicable, OR may also be used as part of a CHECK constraint, as well as NOT or any Boolean expression (including any predicate).

Additionally, the sign (positive or negative) of a particular column's permissible values can be designated through the CHECK constraint. By specifying that a value is (BETWEEN 0 and {*some value*}) or (BETWEEN ({*some negative value*} and 0), positive and negative values, respectively, can be enforced. An important point to remember is that the ordering of the values within the BETWEEN clause is *very* important. Remember the meaning of BETWEEN: allowable values are (1) greater than or equal to the first value, and (2) less than or equal to the second value (see Chapter 7, "Predicates"). Therefore, the following syntax is *not* very useful:

```
CHECK (some_negative_number BETWEEN 0 AND -10000)
```

In fact, that CHECK constraint can *never* be satisfied (except by an empty table).

List of Values

It's often desirable to specify that a specific list of values, and no others, are permissible values for a given column. For example, we may wish to specify that each and every row in the movie_titles table must have one of a given set of values for the movie_type column. We can do so as shown in Example 10-12.

Example 10-12 *Using a CHECK Constraint for List-of-Values Constraint*

```
CREATE TABLE movie_titles (
    title          CHAR (30) NOT NULL,
    |
    |
    |
    movie_type     CHAR (10),
    |
    |
    |
    CHECK ( movie_type IN
          ( 'Horror', 'Children', 'Comedy', 'Musical',
            'Romance', 'Western', 'Adventure', 'Other' ) ) )
```

Exclusion from Another Table

On occasion, you might wish to make certain that values in some column in a table are different from those of some other table. For example, we may have some table discontinued_music_titles in which we store rows for each music title that has been discontinued. We can ensure that no discontinued title appears in our music_titles table, as shown in Example 10-13.

Example 10-13 *Using CHECK Constraint to Maintain Exclusivity of Contents between Two Tables*

```
CREATE TABLE music_titles (
    music_id                CHAR (12) NOT NULL,
    title                   CHAR (30) NOT NULL,
    artist                  CHAR (40),
    artist_more             CHAR (50),
    |
    |
    |
)

CREATE TABLE discontinued_music_titles (
    music_id                CHAR (12) NOT NULL,
    title                   CHAR (30) NOT NULL,
    artist                  CHAR (40),
    artist_more             CHAR (50),
    |
    |
    |
    CHECK ( music_id <> ANY
            ( SELECT music_id FROM music_titles ) )
    |
    |
    |
)
```

This sort of constraint allows you to effectively form a unique constraint across more than one table. Another way to achieve the same effect is shown in Example 10-14.

Example 10-14 *Alternative Constraint Expression for Exclusivity of Contents*

```
CHECK ( UNIQUE ( SELECT music_id
                 FROM music_titles
                 UNION ALL
                 SELECT music_id
                 FROM discontinued_music_titles ) )
```

10.2.5 Constraint Names

Each of SQL's table constraints and column constraints may, optionally, have a name assigned to it. In reality, all constraints have a name, although not necessarily one assigned by the user. For example, alternative expressions for several of the earlier constraints in this chapter are shown in Example 10-15.

Example 10-15 *Named Constraints*

```
CREATE TABLE movie_titles (
    title               CHARACTER (30)
      CONSTRAINT title_not_null NOT NULL,
    |
    |
    |
    movie_type          CHARACTER(10),
    |
    |
    |
    CONSTRAINT check_movie_type
      CHECK ( movie_type IN
            ( 'Horror', 'Children', 'Comedy', 'Musical',
              'Romance', 'Western', 'Adventure', 'Other' ) )
```

We strongly recommend that constraint names always be used, even though they are optional. Applications can then report more complete information when constraint violations occur, because they can get the name of the violated constraint out of the diagnostics area (see Chapter 20, "Diagnostics and Error Management"), thereby helping with the problem analysis process. Constraint names were new to SQL-92 and have proven to be very useful. If you don't give names to your constraints, the DBMS will assign them for you, but they will probably be less meaningful and less mnemonic than those you have chosen yourself.

Whether you or the DBMS assigns the constraint name, it will be reported with any error caused by violating the constraint, and you can use the name to SET the constraint to DEFERRED or IMMEDIATE (see Chapter 15, "Transaction Management") or to DROP the constraint (see Chapter 4, "Basic Data Definition Language (DDL)").

Note also that constraint names may be assigned as well to the two constraints that don't directly utilize CHECK: NOT NULL and UNIQUE. Additionally, these two constraints could, if desired, be expressed using CHECK, as follows:

```
CONSTRAINT column_not_null
  CHECK (columnname IS NOT NULL)

CONSTRAINT column_unique
  CHECK (UNIQUE (SELECT columnname FROM table) )
```

10.3 | Assertions

As we have seen, SQL has several types of constraints. Of those that we've examined so far, all have been "attached" to tables or, equivalently, to columns in tables. However, SQL:1999 also provides you with a different kind of constraint that isn't attached to a particular table. This constraint, called an *assertion,* is a standalone constraint in a schema and is normally used to specify a restriction that affects more than one table; it was introduced in SQL-92.

A table (or column) constraint is normally used to make a restriction on the data that is stored in the table (or column) to which the constraint is attached. It is possible (given some awkwardness, such as using subqueries) to express restrictions involving multiple tables with regular table CHECK constraints, but this is not really recommended (among other things, performance tends to suffer using this approach, since the database system is less able to determine your real intent). Instead, you should use assertions for that purpose.

Let's suppose that you want to ensure that the total number of movies (DVDs and videocassettes) plus the total number of music items (CDs plus cassettes) in stock at any one time is never greater than some limit imposed by your insurance company or banker, say, 500,000. (This sort of situation illustrates a primary use of constraints: to specify the rules of your business directly in the database.) To express this restriction as a table constraint would be awkward at best. First, you'd have to decide whether to put the constraint on the movie_titles table or on the music_inventory table. Then you'd have to write a statement something like that shown in Example 10-16.

Example 10-16 *A Complicated Way of Using Constraints to Handle Inventory Limits*

```
CREATE TABLE movie_titles (
    title...
    ...
    CONSTRAINT maximum_inventory
      CHECK ( ( SELECT SUM ( tapes_in_stock + dvds_in_stcck )
                FROM movie_titles )
```

```
             + ( SELECT SUM ( number_cd_now_in_stock +
                                number_cassette_now_in_stock )
                  FROM music_inventory )
             < 500000 ),

        ...
    )
```

That, of course, will work—at least most of the time—but it sure doesn't feel natural to put it here. Of course, that constraint implies that the two sums have to be produced every time any of the *_in_stock values are changed, which may cause performance problems.

A more natural (if not necessarily better performing) way to express the same restriction is to state it as a *standalone* constraint—that is, as an assertion.

```
CREATE ASSERTION maximum_inventory
  CHECK ( ( SELECT SUM ( tapes_in_stock + dvds_in_stock )
              FROM movie_titles )
        + ( SELECT SUM ( number_cd_now_in_stock +
                           number_cassette_now_in_stock )
              FROM music_inventory )
        < 500000 )
```

Note that the syntax of the CHECK portion of the assertion is identical to the CHECK constraint in Example 10-16 and that we even named the constraint the same. However, as an assertion, this CHECK is *not* attached to any particular table. This has two advantages. We've already stated the first: it is more natural to express restrictions not specific to one table as standalone constraints instead of as table constraints.

Also, we're not home free with the use of assertions when their referenced table(s) are empty. In this example, in the unlikely case that either the movie_titles table or the music_inventory table happened to be empty, the corresponding SUM expression would return a null value, making the condition of the assertion Unknown.

The other advantage is due to a subtle characteristic of table constraints: because table constraints are intended to govern the restrictions on data stored in that table, they are required to be True if *and only if* there is some data stored in the table to which they are attached. This means that the constraint in our first example would *always* be satisfied if the movie_titles table were empty. Therefore, if we were to decide to no longer handle movie media, but to concentrate solely on music, we could stock as many CDs as we'd like without violating the constraint. (And the Wall Street analysts gazing through our quarterly reports might not be happy to learn that we've now stocked 2,000,000 CDs on hand in a down economy—and there goes our stock price, down by about 35% the next day!) By contrast, an assertion expresses a restriction that must always be obeyed (or satisfied) in the database, regardless of whether any particular table has data stored in it or not. (Of course, some assertions might require that a table have data stored in it, but we think you know what we mean.)

Note that some table constraints can never be violated.

```
CREATE TABLE sample (
    col1...
    ...
    CONSTRAINT table_never_empty
      CHECK ( ( SELECT COUNT(*)
                FROM sample ) > 0 ),
    ...
)
```

This constraint can never be violated, because it's satisfied when the table is empty and it's True when the table is not empty. That surprising statement—that the constraint is satisfied when the table is empty—is caused by SQL's rule that a constraint can be violated *only* by one or more rows in a table, and not by the table itself. If we were to express this as an assertion, though, the assertion would, indeed, guarantee that the table always had at least one row stored in it.

```
CREATE ASSERTION sample_table_never_empty
    CHECK ( ( SELECT COUNT(*) FROM sample ) > 0 )
```

The format of the statement to create an assertion is shown in Syntax 10-4.

Syntax 10-4 *Syntax of Assertion Definition*

```
CREATE ASSERTION constraint-name
    CHECK ( search-condition ) [ attributes ]
```

The constraint name is always required for assertions. We've already mentioned that all constraints have names, but the system will assign a name for table or column constraints that you don't name yourself (mainly to be compatible with programs written before SQL-92 was implemented). However, assertions are standalone objects in the schema, so they must have a name, and SQL:1999 requires you to give them a name of your choosing, as did SQL-92.

The `search-condition` is described in Chapter 7, "Predicates"; basically, it consists of one or more predicates (multiple predicates are connected with ANDs, ORs, and NOTs) that express the condition that must be satisfied (alternately, that must not be violated) in the database. It may reference one or more tables, but it has no inherent table context, so you'll have to provide the context by using a query expression (actually, you have to use a subquery; see discussion in Chapter 9, "Advanced SQL Query Expressions").

Ordinary constraints are checked at the end of every SQL statement unless they are deferred. See section 10.2.1 for information about constraint deferral. The attributes are the same as for any other constraint, as discussed at the very end of section 10.2.5.

Assertions, like other constraints, have some restrictions. For example, all of the values used must be literals or database values; you can't reference host variables or parameters, datetime functions, CURRENT_USER, SESSION_USER, or SYSTEM_USER. The reason for this limitation is subtle: since the value returned by those functions and special variables can change frequently, their use could cause the data in the database to violate a constraint even when the data itself is not changed. Assertion names, like any constraint names, can be qualified with a schema name. If you choose to do this and your CREATE ASSERTION statement is part of a CREATE SCHEMA, then the schema names have to match. Most assertions will reference one or more database columns; you must have REFERENCES privileges on each column that your assertions reference. If your assertion doesn't reference a particular column, but does reference a table (e.g., using COUNT(*)), then you must have REFERENCES privileges on at least one column of the table.

10.4 | PRIMARY KEY

The relational database model contains the concept of a *key,* that is, one or more columns within a table that have some unique value by which individual rows can be identified. In some cases, a single column (such as a social security number or employee ID number) is enough to uniquely identify given rows. In other cases, a combination of columns (as in the example below) is required. We showed you the syntax used to specify a primary key in Syntax 10-2.

Let's look at our `movie_stars` table. To make the explanation easier to understand, let's disregard the `year_released` and assume that all movie titles are unique. We will also, again for purposes of this example, assume that no two actors or actresses with exactly the same name appear in the same movie. And finally, another restriction for simplicity is that we'll ignore the actors' and actresses' middle names if they are used (e.g., Mary *Tyler* Moore, James *Earl* Jones).

Therefore, we initially have the following table definition (we will need to modify this, as we will see):

```
CREATE TABLE movies_stars (
    movie_title       CHARACTER (30) NOT NULL,
    actor_last_name   CHARACTER (35) NOT NULL,
    actor_first_name  CHARACTER (25) );
```

Table 10-4 *Result of CREATE TABLE*

MOVIE_TITLE	ACTOR_LAST_NAME	ACTOR_FIRST_NAME
The Way We Were	Redford	Robert
The Way We Were	Streisand	Barbra
Prince of Tides	Nolte	Nick
Prince of Tides	Streisand	Barbra

In Table 10-4, no single column is sufficient to uniquely identify given rows. Since any movie may have (and usually does have) more than one star, there will be multiple rows in which the same movie title appears. Similarly, the combination of actor_last_name and actor_first_name is also not enough to constitute a key, since actors (especially the stars, who appear in our database table) appear in many movies over the course of their careers. Only the combination of three columns—in this case, all of the columns of the table—is sufficient to constitute a key.

In some tables, there are multiple *candidate keys*. That is, there are several different options from which you can choose a column or combination of columns for the unique identification process. Assume for a moment that our MOVIE_TITLES table has a column MOVIE_NUMBER, a column that has a unique value in each row. MOVIE_NUMBER is a candidate key, as is TITLE (or in our original example, the combination of TITLE and YEAR_RELEASED).

Whichever candidate key you choose becomes your *primary key*. The primary key and its related syntax is the concept with which we are concerned. (You are free, if you wish, to use UNIQUE constraints to identify other candidate keys of interest to your applications.) Since movie titles are unique for the purposes of this example, we can designate that column as a primary key:

```
CREATE TABLE movie_titles (
    title CHARACTER (30) PRIMARY KEY,
    |
    |
    |
)
```

SQL-89 required you to say NOT NULL PRIMARY KEY. SQL-92 (in the Intermediate and Full levels) permitted you to state only PRIMARY KEY, although this means precisely the same thing. Primary keys have the inherent property that no row can have a null value for the primary key columns; this continues in SQL:1999. There can never be more than one primary key defined for a table, but a primary key can use more than one column.

Primary keys may also be designated through table constraints (discussed earlier in this chapter in conjunction with CHECK). Let's look at our alternative primary key definition.

```
CREATE TABLE movies_stars (
    movie_title          CHARACTER (30) NOT NULL,
    actor_last_name      CHARACTER (35) NOT NULL,
    actor_first_name     CHARACTER (25) NOT NULL,

    CONSTRAINT stars_pk PRIMARY KEY
       ( movie_title, actor_last_name, actor_first_name ),
)
```

The restriction prohibiting null values for primary key columns means that *no* column that forms part of a multiple column primary key is allowed to have a null value. This restriction presents somewhat of a problem for our application as currently defined. Recall from Table 10-4 that the column actor_first_name does *not* have a NOT NULL constraint applied, in order to allow for single-name actors and actresses (Sting, Cher) or for groups (the Marx Brothers). However, as we also said above, we need all three columns in the movies_stars table to uniquely identify any given row. Therefore, we have a dilemma: how to resolve these two conflicting problems.

Our view is that primary keys (and foreign keys; see section 10.5.1) are important characteristics of your database and should be implemented and maintained through your SQL syntax whenever possible. Therefore, we will add a NOT NULL constraint to the actor_first_name column definition in order to be able to create key definitions. Single-name actors and groups will then have 25 blanks in the actor_first_name column, likely placed there by some host application program. Alternatively, you could choose to not specify a PRIMARY KEY for the table, but to specify a UNIQUE constraint for all of the columns in the primary key and separately specify a CHECK constraint that prohibits the combination of all of those columns from being null:

```
CONSTRAINT stars_pk1
   UNIQUE ( movie_title, actor_last_name, actor_first_name ),
CONSTRAINT stars_pk2
   CHECK ( ( movie_title, actor_last_name, actor_first_name )
            NOT NULL )
```

This is representative of the types of tradeoff decisions you must often make when designing and implementing your SQL databases. When facets such as those discussed above conflict, you must decide which to implement and which to work around.

Most SQL implementations use the idea of an *index* (as in the typical CREATE INDEX . . . statement) to enforce uniqueness in a table. However, we feel that because uniqueness is an inherent property of data, it should not be relegated to being an implementation issue but should be designated in the standard. Therefore, whether or not a specific SQL:1999 implementation supports indices (indices also have additional uses, such as performance enhancement), the PRIMARY KEY does designate support for key fields.

Now that we've seen how to define primary keys, let's turn our attentions to FOREIGN KEYs and the concept of referential integrity.

10.5 | Referential Integrity

Referential integrity reflects the purpose of constraints whose job it is to ensure that values stored in one place in your database reference existing data in some other place in the database. That is, *references* to data must be valid. (By contrast, the kinds of constraints we've discussed up to this point in this chapter are sometimes said to enforce "semantic integrity.") Referential integrity in a database allows you to require that your sales invoices never reference a part number that is not tracked by your database, or that you never accept shipments from a supplier with whom you do not have an existing relationship. Since SQL is primarily a *value-based* system, referential integrity is not implemented by means of *pointers* (a technique that was used in some earlier data models). Instead, it is implemented by means of constraints that specify that a value in a column of a row *here* is the same as the value in the corresponding column of some row *there*.

The SQL:1999 syntax for the constraints dealing with referential integrity can be seen in Syntax 10-5. The syntax is rather lengthy and perhaps intimidating, but don't worry: we'll cover it in small bites.

Syntax 10-5 *Syntax of Referential Integrity Constraints*

```
<referential constraint definition> ::=
    FOREIGN KEY <left paren> <referencing columns> <right paren>
      <references specification>

<references specification> ::=
    REFERENCES <referenced table and columns>
      [ MATCH <match type> ]
      [ <referential triggered action> ]

<match type> ::=
      FULL
    | PARTIAL
    | SIMPLE

<referencing columns> ::=
    <reference column list>

<referenced table and columns> ::=
    <table name>
      [ <left paren> <reference column list> <right paren> ]

<reference column list> ::= <column name list>

<referential triggered action> ::=
      <update rule> [ <delete rule> ]
    | <delete rule> [ <update rule> ]

<update rule> ::= ON UPDATE <referential action>

<delete rule> ::= ON DELETE <referential action>

<referential action> ::=
      CASCADE
    | SET NULL
    | SET DEFAULT
    | RESTRICT
    | NO ACTION
```

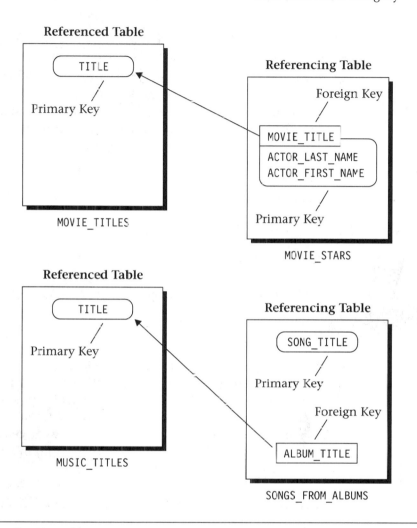

Figure 10-1   Foreign Key Usage in SQL:1999

10.5.1 FOREIGN KEY

A *foreign key* is a column or group of columns within a table that references, or relates to, some other table through its values (see Figure 10-1). The foreign key must always include enough columns in its definition to uniquely identify a row in the referenced table.

The primary reason for defining foreign keys within the data definition language is to ensure that rows in one table always have corresponding rows in another table; that is, to ensure that integrity of data is maintained. Recall, for example, the potential data integrity problem we mentioned at the beginning of this chapter: several rows exist in the MOVIES_STARS table for the movie *Man on the Moon,* but there is no corresponding row for that movie in the MOVIE_TITLES table. In this situation, there is a problem with lost linkages between data elements of one table and those of another.

To ensure that such a problem does not occur, we can define a foreign key in the MOVIES_STARS table that corresponds to our earlier defined primary key of the MOVIE_TITLES table. The syntax to accomplish this is shown in Example 10-17.

Example 10-17 *FOREIGN KEY Constraint*

```
CREATE TABLE movies_stars (
    |
    |
    |
    CONSTRAINT titles_fk FOREIGN KEY ( movie_title )
      REFERENCES movie_titles (title)
)
```

In the code segment in Example 10-17, the keywords FOREIGN KEY flag the designated column (movie_title) as the foreign key through which the table movie_titles is referenced (through the latter table's primary key column title). Note that you can use both PRIMARY KEY and FOREIGN KEY definitions within any table, as shown in Example 10-18; the primary key of a given table (in our current example, movie_stars) has no bearing on the definition of a foreign key through which another table is referenced.

Example 10-18 *Using Both PRIMARY KEY and FOREIGN KEY Constraints Together*

```
CREATE TABLE movies_stars (
    movie_title       CHARACTER (30) NOT NULL,
    actor_last_name   CHARACTER (35) NOT NULL,
    actor_first_name  CHARACTER (25) NOT NULL,

    CONSTRAINT stars_pk PRIMARY KEY
      ( movie_title, actor_last_name, actor_first_name ),

    CONSTRAINT titles_fk FOREIGN KEY ( movie_title )
      REFERENCES movie_titles ,
    |
    |
    |
)
```

As with primary keys, there are several different syntactical ways in which you can define foreign keys. You could, for example, state the following:

```
CREATE TABLE movies_stars (
    movie_title CHARACTER (30)
      CONSTRAINT title_not_null NOT NULL
      CONSTRAINT titles_fk
        REFERENCES movie_titles (title),
    |
    |
    |
)
```

If your foreign key references the primary key of the referenced table (as opposed to some candidate key that wasn't selected as the primary key; refer to our discussion earlier in this chapter), you can omit the column reference, as shown in Example 10-19.

Example 10-19 *Omitting the Column Reference in REFERENCES*

```
CREATE TABLE movies_stars (
    movie_title CHARACTER (30) NOT NULL
      REFERENCES movie_titles,
    |
    |
    |
)
```

You can also omit the primary key reference for foreign key definitions coded as table constraints (see Example 10-20), as we did in our first foreign key example (Example 10-17).

Example 10-20 *Omitting the Primary Key Reference for a FOREIGN KEY Constraint*

```
CREATE TABLE movies_stars (
    |
    |
    |
    CONSTRAINT titles_fk FOREIGN KEY
      ( movie_title ) REFERENCES movie_titles
)
```

Finally, the constraint name for the foreign key *may* be omitted, as shown in Example 10-21, although as we stated earlier in this chapter, we strongly recommend naming all of your constraints for diagnostic purposes.

Example 10-21 *Omitting the Name of the FOREIGN KEY Constraint*

```
CREATE TABLE movies_stars (
    |
    |
    |
    FOREIGN KEY ( movie_title )
      REFERENCES movie_titles ( title )
)
```

In the above example, `title` could be omitted since the primary key is being referenced rather than a nonprimary candidate key.

One more rule: If your foreign and primary or candidate keys are one-column keys, you can use the earlier "short" form (with the column definition). If they are multicolumn, you must use the later form (separate table constraint).

10.5.2 Referential Constraint Actions

When you specify a `FOREIGN KEY`, you may only wish to prohibit the execution of any SQL statement that might violate the referential integrity constraints, which is what we've demonstrated so far. This was the only referential integrity capability defined by SQL-89. However, as applications have become increasingly complex, it's been desirable to put the burden of data integrity on the database system. The feature that does this is called *referential actions*.

The following sections describe the SQL:1999 capabilities for referential actions.

Setting a Default

Suppose you have a business rule that requires that whenever you drop a distributor, you automatically switch the distributor for those movies to some specific other distributor—that is, to your default distributor. If all you wanted to do was to specify a restriction rule in your database that prohibits dropping a distributor as long as you stock movies distributed by that company, you would write something like the definition shown in Example 10-22.

Example 10-22 *REFERENCES between Movie Titles and Distributors*

```
CREATE TABLE movie_titles (
    title               CHARACTER (30) NOT NULL,
    |
    |
    |
    distributor         CHARACTER VARYING(25)
      REFERENCES distributors,
    |
    |
    |
)
```

However, to tell the database system to automatically set the distributor to the default when you delete the corresonding row in the distributor table, you would code something like that shown in Example 10-23.

Example 10-23 *Setting a Default Value*

```
CREATE TABLE movie_titles (
    title               CHARACTER (30) NOT NULL,
    |
    |
    |
    distributor         CHARACTER VARYING(25)
      DEFAULT 'Big East, Inc.'
      REFERENCES distributors
        ON DELETE SET DEFAULT,
    |
    |
    |
)
```

SET NULL

You may want to establish a business rule that if a distributor goes out of business, all of the movies available from that company have the distributor column set to null, indicating "no distributor currently available (until we get another one)." You can specify this automatic action as shown in Example 10-24.

Example 10-24 *Setting a NULL Value*

```
CREATE TABLE movie_titles (
    title              CHARACTER (30) NOT NULL,
    |
    |
    |
    distributor        CHARACTER VARYING (25)
      REFERENCES distributors
        ON DELETE SET NULL,
    |
    |
    |
)
```

CASCADE

Suppose you receive prerelease information about a movie entitled *The Certifier,* an epic starring Arnold Schwarzenegger as a postal worker (Kevin Costner has a cameo appearance—but imagine the scene where Arnie "goes postal"!). You enter information about this movie in your database, including tables MOVIE_ TITLES and MOVIES_STARS. But, before you actually receive the tapes and begin renting this blockbuster, the title is changed to *The Last Certifier.* The name change can be automatically handled in any tables (such as MOVIES_STARS), through the use of CASCADE, as shown in Example 10-25.

Example 10-25 *Using CASCADE*

```
CREATE TABLE movies_stars (
    |
    |
    |
    CONSTRAINT titles_fk
      FOREIGN KEY ( movie_title )
        REFERENCES movie_titles
          ON UPDATE CASCADE,
)
```

Likewise, referring back to our earlier example with distributors and the movies (Example 10-23), we can ensure that any company name changes among the distributors cascade through to the MOVIE_TITLES table by the syntax shown in Example 10-26.

Example 10-26 *Cascading Name Changes across Multiple Tables*

```
CREATE TABLE movie_titles (
    title              CHARACTER (30) NOT NULL,
    |
    |
    |
    distributor        CHARACTER VARYING(25)
      REFERENCES distributors
        ON UPDATE CASCADE,
    |
    |
    |
)
```

Of course, CASCADE applies equally well to the ON DELETE referential action. Suppose that our business model keeps track of DVDs that are on order from various distributors in a separate table (DVDS_ON_ORDER, perhaps). We'd probably have a business rule that says those rows must not exist if the distributor from whom the DVDs were ordered does not exist. That means that we'd undoubtedly have a referential action to delete rows from DVDS_ON_ORDER whenever the referenced rows in the DISTRIBUTORS table is deleted because the distributor from whom we'd ordered the DVDs went out of business.

NO ACTION

You can set any of the three referential actions (CASCADE, SET NULL, or SET DEFAULT) or either of the two "nonactions" (NO ACTION and RESTRICT) on each of the two activities DELETE and UPDATE as we illustrate in Figure 10-2.

The default for either activity (that is, if you don't specify the referential action syntax at all) is NO ACTION, but you can also code the defaults to say that you want the database system to ensure that you have a valid state at the end of your statement (Example 10-27).

Example 10-27 *NO ACTION*

```
CREATE TABLE movie_titles (
    title              CHARACTER (30) NOT NULL,
    |
    |
    |
```

ACTION

		CASCADE	SET NULL	SET DEFAULT	RESTRICT	NO ACTION
ACTIVITY	DELETE	✔	✔	✔	✔	✔
	UPDATE	✔	✔	✔	✔	✔

Figure 10-2 Referential Actions in SQL:1999

```
distributor        CHARACTER VARYING(25)
  REFERENCES distributors
    ON UPDATE NO ACTION
    ON DELETE NO ACTION,
  |
  |
  |
)
```

NO ACTION means just what it says: if the referential constraint remains unsatisfied at the end of the SQL statement, then no actions are performed. Actually, the phrase was chosen to indicate that no *referential* actions were performed; however, the effect is that the SQL statement making the changes is "undone" and therefore effectively performs "no action" either. Instead, the DBMS will give you a constraint violation error.

Let's consider some examples. Suppose we have our movie_titles with the PRIMARY KEY constraint on title and the movies_stars table with a FOREIGN KEY constraint on its column movie_title that specifies ON UPDATE NO ACTION. If we try to execute

```
UPDATE movie_titles
  SET title = 'One Extremely Strange Movie'
WHERE title = 'Rocky Horror Picture Show'
```

then the presence of rows in movies_stars listing Tim Curry, Susan Sarandon, Barry Bostwick, and others will cause the UPDATE statement to fail. If that FOREIGN KEY had said ON UPDATE CASCADE, then Tim, Susan, Barry, et al. would now be shown as starring in *One Extremely Strange Movie*.

On the other hand, ON UPDATE SET NULL would attempt to have them starring in no movie at all, which would violate the PRIMARY KEY of movies_stars and would thus cause the UPDATE statement to fail, too.

The action (or lack of it) doesn't have to be the same for the two activities. You can choose to SET NULL for DELETE and have CASCADE for UPDATE if you wish, as shown in Example 10-28.

Example 10-28 *Mix-and-Match Actions for ON UPDATE and ON DELETE*

```
CREATE TABLE movie_titles (
    title              CHARACTER (30) NOT NULL,
    |
    |
    |
    distributor        CHARACTER VARYING(25)
      REFERENCES distributors
      ON UPDATE CASCADE
      ON DELETE SET NULL,
    |
    |
    |
)
```

10.5.3 RESTRICT

SQL:1999 provides one more option for referential actions (SQL-92 didn't provide this option). If you use NO ACTION as your (implicit or explicit) referential action specification, then you've instructed the database system to ensure that your referential constraints are satisfied by the time the SQL statement's actions (or, for deferred constraints, the transaction's actions) have finished, including application of any other referential actions and any trigger executions (see Chapter 11, "Active Databases," for information on triggers).

The semantics of referential integrity sometimes allow changes to a table that *temporarily* (during the execution of the statement) causes a referential constraint to be violated, even though the state of the table is correct after the statement's effects are fully applied. Specifying a referential action of NO ACTION allows such temporary violations. However, your application might have a requirement that the state of a table *never* violate a specific referential constraint, even temporarily during the execution of an SQL statement. If you want to enforce this prohibition, you can use the referential action keyword RESTRICT.

10.6 | Multiple Cascades

So far, we have dealt with referential integrity between only two tables. There are probably occasions when you would want multiple levels of cascades specified in your referential integrity constraints. Let's take our MOVIE_TITLES and MOVIES_STARS example (the key data definition segments are reproduced below) and add a new table. Assume our Web site has a section through which online shoppers can browse to find out information about various awards won by movies we have in stock; perhaps it's a link to content from the online movie database at *www.imdb.com*. On Academy Awards weekend, we may want to put on sale all movies we have in stock that have won the Best Picture award. We can access our system and produce a quick list of Best Picture winners. To accomplish this, we first add a new table to our other two with awards information, as shown in Example 10-29.

Example 10-29 *A New Table for Movie Awards*

```
CREATE TABLE movie_titles (
    title                   CHARACTER (30) PRIMARY KEY,
    |
    |
    |
)

CREATE TABLE movies_stars (
    movie_title             CHARACTER (30) NOT NULL,
    actor_last_name         CHARACTER (35) NOT NULL,
    actor_first_name        CHARACTER (25) NOT NULL,

    CONSTRAINT stars_pk PRIMARY KEY
      ( movie_title, actor_last_name, actor_first_name ),
    CONSTRAINT titles_fk FOREIGN KEY ( movie_title )
      REFERENCES movie_titles
        ON DELETE CASCADE
        ON UPDATE CASCADE,
    |
    |
    |
)
```

```
CREATE TABLE movie_awards (
    movie_title            CHARACTER (30),
    first_name             CHARACTER (35),
    last_name              CHARACTER (25),
    award                  CHARACTER VARYING(10),

  FOREIGN_KEY (movie_title, first_name, last_name)
    REFERENCES movies_stars
      ON UPDATE CASCADE
      ON DELETE CASCADE,
  |
  |
  | )
```

With a structure like this, when you change the name (or just the spelling of the name) of a movie, that change is cascaded to the movie_stars table, changing the spelling of the movie's name in every row associated with that movie in the other table, too. Those changes will, in turn, be cascaded to the movie_awards table, changing the name in that table. Also, if you change the spelling of a movie star's name, that change will also be reflected in the movie_awards table. Similarly, if you delete a movie (because you no longer carry it in stock), that deletion will cause the movie_stars entries to be deleted along with the movie_awards that those stars won. Figure 10-3 illustrates the three-level cascade.

FOREIGN KEYs can even reference the table in which they're defined. For example, an employees table may have a column emp_id and another column mgr_id. Of course, you'd want all managers to also be employees; you could ensure that by specifying

```
  |
  |
  |
  emp_id                 INTEGER PRIMARY KEY,
  mgr_id                 INTEGER REFERENCES employees,
  |
  |
  |
```

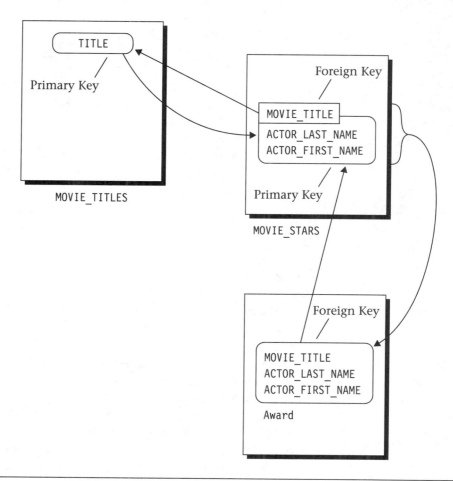

Figure 10-3   Cascading among Multiple SQL:1999 Tables

10.7 | More about Referential Integrity Constraints

To better understand how referential integrity works, we have to know a little bit more about how SQL:1999 expects statements to behave. Realize that various DBMS products might implement this in a different way, but the end result will be the same. Think of every SQL statement as having three phases: a *setup* phase, an *execution* phase, and a *cleanup* phase. During the setup phase, the DBMS first identifies every row that will be directly affected by the statement and then identifies every *matching* row for every directly affected row. (A matching row is a row in a referencing table whose foreign key values identify some directly affected row in the referenced table.)

During the execution phase, the DBMS performs the action of the statement on the directly affected rows (if the statement is a DELETE statement, then the row isn't actually deleted but is "marked for deletion"). No new matching rows are ever added to the list of matching rows as a result of any direct actions.

During the cleanup phase, the referential actions are performed. In general, when a directly affected row causes some referential action, that action is performed, and any referential actions caused by *that* action are then performed. Although this may sound like a depth-first tree walk, for those of you who stayed awake during graph theory, referential integrity actions have been very carefully designed to allow them to be performed in any order at all to arrive at a correct, consistent state of the database. (If any of those referential actions involve a row deletion, then those rows are also merely marked for deletion. The reason for this is to avoid certain anomalies that could result from actually deleting the rows before the referential actions have "died down.") At the end of the cleanup phase, any rows that are marked for deletion are actually deleted.

10.8 More about Constraints and Assertions

Let's spend just a little more time on the subject of constraints and assertions to really grasp some of the subtle issues. For example, we told you that constraint checking was done only at the end of statements and not during processing of individual rows, but we didn't tell you why it's that way. (An obvious exception to the "not during processing" policy is when you specify a referential action of RESTRICT; in that case, the referential constraint is actually checked as each row is processed to ensure no temporary violation of the referential constraint occurs.)

Consider a table that has unique ID numbers for each movie (the smarter way of doing the table definition, as you might have guessed by now, similar to what we did in the music_titles example in Chapter 8, "Working with Multiple Tables: The Relational Operators," even though there we used a CHARACTER typed unique identifier):

```
CREATE TABLE movie_titles (
    id      INTEGER constraint movie_titles_pk PRIMARY KEY,
    title   CHARACTER (30),
    |
    |
    |
)
```

After populating the table with thousands of movies and giving them ID values of 0, 1, 2, ..., we learn that we'd really rather use 1, 2, 3, ..., instead. An obvious UPDATE statement would be

```
UPDATE movie_titles
  SET id = id + 1 ;
```

If the constraint were checked during the update of each row, then the very first row that got updated (unless it happened to be the one with the highest ID value) would cause the constraint to be violated, and the statement would fail with an error. However, by waiting until the end of the UPDATE statement, after all rows have been processed, the constraint is not violated and the statement succeeds.

There are many examples of the usefulness of this characteristic. We leave as an exercise for the reader the reason why end-of-statement checking is necessary for a FOREIGN KEY constraint with ON DELETE CASCADE when the FOREIGN KEY points to the same table where it is defined.

```
CREATE TABLE employees (
    emp_id              INTEGER PRIMARY KEY,
    mgr_id              INTEGER REFERENCES employees
                            ON DELETE CASCADE )
```

10.9 | Chapter Summary

The material covered in this chapter should help you to further specify your SQL data definitions so that a great deal of the tedious processing inherent in information systems applications will be automatically handled by your underlying database management system. Each and every column may have a range of values, a list of values, a maximum or minimum value, or some other constraint designated at definition time. Further, each table may have a primary key designated through which the data from other tables may be related to the data of that table.

Through the use of foreign keys, which typically are used in conjunction with primary keys but may also be coordinated with nonprimary candidate keys if so desired, several different types of referential integrity constraints may also be specified at data definition time. These include cascading of data value modifications to related tables, automatically deleting certain logically linked rows, and setting various default or null values upon certain actions.

Chapter

11

Active Databases and Triggers

11.1 Introduction

In this chapter, we're going to discuss a feature that most SQL products have long implemented but that was not standardized until the publication of SQL:1999—triggers. In fact, the specification for triggers was complete before SQL-92 was published, but pressures to keep the size of SQL-92 from being even larger than it was caused the deferral of several features.

The definition of triggers was among the deferred features, based on the expectation that it would be several years before the feature would be widely implemented by commercial products—an obvious error in judgment! In fact, almost before the ink was dry on the SQL-92 standard, all major SQL vendors were delivering versions of their products that provided trigger support.

But the trigger specification didn't remain static in the lengthy interval between SQL-92's publication and SQL:1999's. In fact, several improvements and enhancements were made, some to align with features that vendors had added and some to simplify the specifications.

This feature arguably has an unusual name, reminding many people of weaponry. In fact, some of the terminology associated with triggers is related to the concept, including the use of the word *fire*, as in "the trigger fired." We don't believe the intent was to suggest violence against anyone or anything (not even data), but the metaphor of a dramatic action being the immediate result of another, less dramatic action is certainly appropriate. In many cases, a different term has been applied to this feature: *active database*. This term is especially relevant, since it implies that the database itself can take action on the data it contains. Nonetheless, we'll use the more familiar terminology in this book.

11.2 | Referential Actions Redux

Before we show you the syntax of defining triggers and discuss the semantics, let's briefly review a subject that we covered earlier in section 10.5.2, "Referential Constraint Actions"—namely, referential actions.

As you'll recall from that discussion, you can define certain constraints, called *referential integrity constraints*, for tables in your database. These referential integrity constraints can be written so that they prohibit programs from making certain types of changes to the data in those tables or so that they automatically keep the data in those tables synchronized in response to certain types of changes. If a constraint is written to automatically keep the data synchronized, it uses referential actions to do so.

Some people maintain that referential actions are properly included in the notion of an active database, since the database automatically updates or deletes rows of data that are not directly identified by SQL statements in response to changes to rows that are identified by those SQL statements. We don't disagree with that belief, but we do note that the changes caused by referential actions are rather closely related to the changes directly caused by an SQL statement. By contrast, the changes that can be made by a trigger in response to changes directly caused by an SQL statement may have no obvious relationship at all to those more direct changes.

As you learned in section 10.5.2, "Referential Constraint Actions," referential actions are invoked whenever the referential integrity constraint with which they are defined is violated by the actions of some SQL statement. The referential actions that you can define can take action only when row values are modified or when rows are deleted, and the actions that can be taken are limited. The referencing rows can be modified in the same way as the rows they reference, they can be deleted, or the columns containing the referencing values can be set to null or to their default values. In particular, no referential actions can be specified to address the insertion of rows into a referencing or referenced table.

11.3 | Triggers

Triggers, on the other hand, are considerably more flexible in the events that cause them to take action and in the actions that they are allowed to take.

As we will show you shortly, you can define triggers that are invoked (or fired, if you prefer) whenever you insert one or more rows into a specified table, update one or more rows in a specified table, or delete one or more rows from a specified table. These triggers can, generally speaking, take any sort of action you find appropriate for your applications. They can be fired once per INSERT, UPDATE, or DELETE statement or once per row being inserted, updated, or deleted. The table with which the trigger is defined is called the *subject table* of the trigger, and the SQL statement that causes a trigger to be fired is called the *triggering SQL statement*. When a trigger is fired, it causes another SQL statement, called the *triggered SQL statement*, to be executed.

Triggers can be fired even *before* the actions of the triggering SQL statement. Perhaps even more interesting is the fact that the trigger can have access to the values of the row or rows being inserted, updated, or deleted; and, for rows being updated, the values before the update takes place and the values after the update can both be made available.

Triggers, even though they are "schema objects" themselves, are always associated with exactly one base table. SQL:1999 does not allow them to be associated with views, although some SQL products provide extensions to allow that capability.

What uses might triggers serve? The potential uses are numerous, but we narrow them down to just a few categories:

- Logging and auditing: You can define triggers on certain tables—especially tables that have security implications, such as salary information and competitive data—to record information about changes made to those tables. That information can be recorded in other tables and might include such information as the authorization identifier under whose control the changes were made, the current time when the changes were made, and even the values being affected in the subject table. This is illustrated in Figure 11-1.

- Consistency and cleanup: Your application might benefit from allowing relatively simple sequences of SQL statements on certain tables to be supported by triggers whose responsibilities include making corresponding changes to other tables. Thus, an SQL statement that adds a line item to an order might cause a trigger to be fired that updates an inventory table by reserving the quantity of material that was ordered. We illustrate this alternative in Figure 11-2.

- Non-database operations: Your triggers are not restricted to merely performing ordinary SQL operations. Because of the power available in SQL-invoked routines, your triggers can invoke procedures that send e-mail messages, print documents, or activate robotic equipment to retrieve inventory to be shipped. You can see an illustration of this use in Figure 11-3.

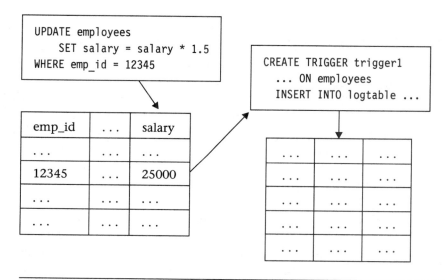

Figure 11-1 Using Triggers for Logging and Auditing

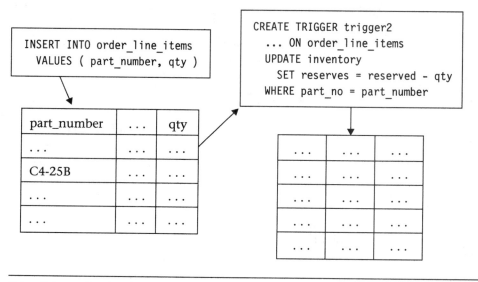

Figure 11-2 Using Triggers for Consistency and Cleanup

Having thus whetted your appetite, we're ready to show you SQL:1999's syntax for defining (and eliminating) triggers and to analyze in detail the behaviors associated with their various features.

We first consider Syntax 11-1, which specifies the syntax of a trigger definition.

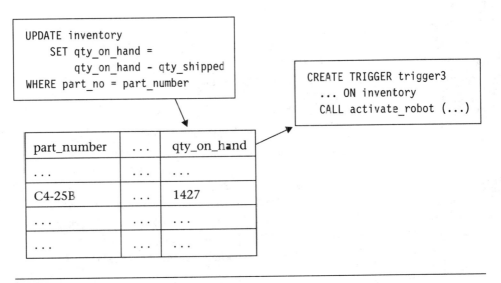

Figure 11-3 Using Triggers for Non-Database Operations

Syntax 11-1 *Syntax of <trigger definition>*

```
<trigger definition> ::=
    CREATE TRIGGER <trigger name>
      <trigger action time> <trigger event>
      ON <table name> [ REFERENCING <old or new values alias list> ]
      <triggered action>

<trigger action time> ::=
    BEFORE
  | AFTER

<trigger event> ::=
    INSERT
  | DELETE
  | UPDATE [ OF <trigger column list> ]

<trigger column list> ::= <column name list>

<triggered action> ::=
    [ FOR EACH { ROW | STATEMENT } ]
      [ WHEN <left paren> <search condition> <right paren> ]
      <triggered SQL statement>
```

```
<triggered SQL statement> ::=
    <SQL procedure statement>
  | BEGIN ATOMIC
      { <SQL procedure statement> <semicolon> }...
    END

<old or new values alias list> ::=
    <old or new values alias>...

<old or new values alias> ::=
    OLD [ROW ][AS ]<old values correlation name>
  | NEW [ROW ][AS ]<new values correlation name>
  | OLD TABLE [ AS ] <old values table alias>
  | NEW TABLE [ AS ] <new values table alias>

<old values table alias> ::= <identifier>

<new values table alias> ::= <identifier>

<old values correlation name> ::= <correlation name>

<new values correlation name> ::= <correlation name>
```

Like much of SQL's syntax, that seems complex at first glance, but we think you'll understand it pretty easily as we explain the various pieces of it.

As you will notice, one piece of syntax is the <table name> that identifies the subject table of the trigger. This <table name>, like all <table name>s, can be fully qualified, including the name of the schema in which it resides. If you specify a <schema name> as part of the <table name>, then that <schema name> must be the same as the <schema name> that (explicitly or implicitly) qualifies the <trigger name>—that is, a trigger must always reside in the same schema as its subject table.

One requirement that doesn't show in the syntax used to define a trigger is the fact that you must have a particular privilege on tables in order to define triggers on them. If you're the owner of a table, then you inherently have the TRIGGER privilege. However, if you have been granted the TRIGGER privilege on a table that you do not own, you have the ability to define triggers on that table.

We'll refer back to Syntax 11-1 a number of times in the remaining sections of this chapter, typically by using a piece of BNF as we explain a feature of triggers.

11.3.1 Types of Triggers

SQL:1999's triggers can be described, or categorized, from multiple perspectives. For example, as you can infer from <trigger action time> in Syntax 11-1, you can define a trigger to fire before the application of the effects of the triggering SQL statement or after those effects are applied. Similarly, the <trigger event> lets you decide which of three types of SQL statement will cause the trigger to be fired, and the <triggered action> lets you decide whether the trigger fires once per triggering statement or once per affected row. The <triggered action> also lets you determine whether additional conditions must be met to cause the trigger to be invoked.

As a result of applying this taxonomy to triggers, we can say that a given trigger is, for example, a *before insert statement-level trigger* or an *after update conditional row-level trigger*, depending on the choices made when the trigger was defined. (We hasten to add that those terms are our own and may or may not appear in the documentation of the SQL product you're using.)

BEFORE and AFTER Triggers

As you just read, the syntax that Syntax 11-1 calls <trigger action time> allows you to specify whether the trigger that you're defining is fired before or after the effects of the triggering SQL statement are applied to the table. The syntax, as you have observed, is trivial—merely a choice between two keywords.

The semantics are not really more complex than the syntax. In fact, the only effect of this bit of syntax is to determine whether the triggered actions are applied immediately before the effects of the triggering statement, or immediately after them.

INSERT, UPDATE, and DELETE Triggers

The <trigger event> specifies the nature of the SQL statement (or other event, such as a change caused by a referential action) that causes a trigger to fire. If you specify INSERT, then only an INSERT statement that specifies the subject table can cause the trigger to fire.

If you specify UPDATE, then there are several statements that can cause the trigger to fire. These include an UPDATE statement that specifies a search condition (that is, a searched update statement), an UPDATE statement that specifies a cursor name (a positioned update statement), and the corresponding dynamic SQL statements (see Chapter 18, "Dynamic SQL"). Similarly, if you specify DELETE, there are several statements that cause the trigger to fire, including the searched delete statement, the positioned delete statement, and the corresponding dynamic SQL statements.

We think it's worth noting that SQL:1999 does not provide SELECT as a <trigger event>. The capability to fire a trigger when information is retrieved from a table has been discussed a number of times by the designers of SQL, but it is difficult to justify for any purpose other than logging and auditing (for which there are other solutions in many products). We do not expect this capability to be added to SQL in a future revision of the standard, in spite of the fact that a few SQL products do have something corresponding to it. However, political requirements, such as the European Union's strong privacy laws, might change our expectations in the future.

As we'll see in the subsection below called "Triggering Conditions," the semantics of triggers are affected by <trigger event> more than merely by identifying which type of triggering SQL statement causes the trigger to fire.

Statement and Row Triggers

Syntax 11-1 includes a piece of syntax called the <triggered action>; that syntax has several components, one of which determines whether the trigger being defined is a *row-level trigger* or a *statement-level trigger*.

As the names imply, a row-level trigger is one whose triggered SQL statement is executed for every row that is modified by the triggering statement. Similarly, a statement-level trigger is one whose triggered SQL statement is executed only once every time a triggering SQL statement is executed.

The subsection below called "Triggered SQL Statement" has more detail about the implications of making a trigger a row-level trigger or a statement-level trigger. By the way, since the syntax with which you specify FOR EACH ROW or FOR EACH STATEMENT is optional, SQL:1999's default (if you don't specify either) is FOR EACH STATEMENT.

Triggering Conditions

Another component of a <triggered action>—this one optional—is a search condition that allows you to limit the circumstances under which a trigger will fire. You do this by specifying one or more predicates that determine whether or not your criteria have been met. If the search condition evaluates to True, then the trigger will be fired; otherwise (that is, if it evaluates either to False or Unknown), then the trigger will not be fired.

The use of triggering conditions can add considerable expressive power to your triggers. For example, you can use them to cause the trigger to fire only when the triggering SQL statement indicates the sale of more than 100 DVDs in a single operation, or when the price of a CD is lowered by more than 70%. You might also use it to cause your webstore application to issue an e-coupon that the customer can use in a future purchase.

But you must always keep in mind that the triggering conditions are never even considered except at the relevant <trigger action time>, and then only when the triggering SQL statement generates the proper <trigger event>.

Triggered SQL Statement

In Syntax 11-1, you can see that there are two alternatives for <triggered SQL statement>. It is immediately obvious why the first of these (a single SQL statement) is required: the SQL statement allows the trigger to take some action when it is fired.

The need for the other might not be as readily apparent, but a short explanation should clear it up. In SQL:1999, unless conformance to SQL/PSM (or some proprietary analog) is provided, there is no way to make a trigger's single SQL statement perform a sequence of operations, even though that is very often required. Implementation of SQL/PSM would provide your triggers with a compound statement (BEGIN...END), so SQL:1999 makes that facility available in the definition of a trigger even without the availability of SQL/PSM. Using this alternative allows you to specify triggers whose actions include multiple SQL statements executed sequentially. (If conformance to SQL/PSM is provided by your SQL product, then you can use looping, conditional statements, and the other features of computational completeness provided in SQL/PSM.)

The mandatory keyword ATOMIC is explained in section 11.3.2.

Some Examples

Before we delve into the details of how triggers are processed in an SQL implementation, let's have a look at a couple of examples of trigger definitions. You can see these, along with a few comments in SQL syntax, in Example 11-1.

Example 11-1 *Example Trigger Definitions*

```
/* We try to name our triggers meaningfully. In this example, we choose
   "short" names to respect most SQL implementations identifier limits */
CREATE TRIGGER bef_upd_inv_qty
```

```
    BEFORE UPDATE ON inventory (qty_in_stock)
    FOR EACH STATEMENT    -- We like to explicitly specify the defaults
      BEGIN ATOMIC
        CALL send_email ('ShippingManager', 'Inventory update beginning');
        INSERT INTO log_table
          VALUES ('INVENTORY', CURRENT_USER, CURRENT_TIMESTAMP);
      END;

CREATE TRIGGER limit_price_hikes
  BEFORE UPDATE ON movie_titles
  REFERENCING OLD ROW AS oldrow
              NEW ROW AS newrow
  FOR EACH ROW
    WHEN newrow.regular_dvd_sale_price >
        1.4 * oldrow. regular_dvd_sale_price
    -- Uses a PSM feature to prevent large price hikes
    SIGNAL PRICE_HIKE_TOO_LARGE;
```

11.3.2 Execution of Triggers

All triggers execute in a *trigger execution context*, and a particular SQL session might have one or more such contexts (or none) at any instant in time. The reason is probably obvious once you think about it. Execution of an SQL statement may cause one or more triggers to fire, and execution of the <triggered SQL statement>s of those triggers will probably cause other changes to various tables. The execution of those <triggered SQL statement>s is performed in a trigger execution context. But what if the tables changed by those <triggered SQL statement>s have their own triggers defined, triggers that are fired by the actions of the first set of triggers? These "secondary" triggers get their own trigger execution context to make it possible to define their actions precisely and independently of the actions taken by the first set of triggers. These secondary triggers can cause still more triggers to be fired—nested arbitrarily deep—and each level gets its own trigger execution context. (In fact, each trigger and its <triggered SQL statement> gets its own trigger execution context, but that's a detail that doesn't affect our discussion in any substantive way.)

SQL:1999 has several types of execution context, of which triggers involve just one. Some of these execution contexts are not required to be "atomic," meaning that they may complete some of their actions without all of their actions succeeding. However, trigger execution contexts are required to be atomic: either the entire triggered SQL statement completes successfully, or its effects are not allowed to become persistent in the database. In SQL/PSM, not all

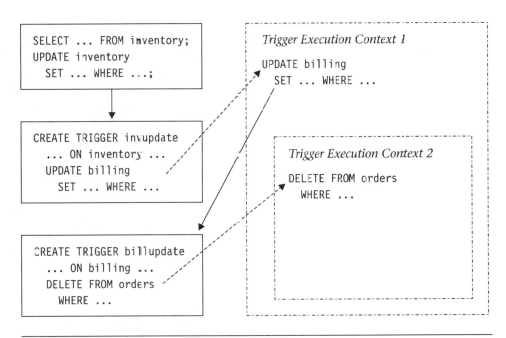

```
SELECT ... FROM inventory;
UPDATE inventory
    SET ... WHERE ...;
```

```
CREATE TRIGGER invupdate
    ... ON inventory ...
    UPDATE billing
        SET ... WHERE ...
```

```
CREATE TRIGGER billupdate
    ... ON billing ...
    DELETE FROM orders
        WHERE ...
```

Trigger Execution Context 1
```
UPDATE billing
    SET ... WHERE ...
```

Trigger Execution Context 2
```
DELETE FROM orders
    WHERE ...
```

Figure 11-4 Trigger Execution Contexts

BEGIN...END blocks are required to be atomic, so the use of BEGIN...END in a <triggered SQL statement> requires the use of the keyword ATOMIC to act as a reminder that this particular BEGIN...END block will always be handled as a unit.

Let's look at trigger execution contexts in a little more detail. If you understand how they work, you can design your triggers a little more effectively.

Trigger Execution Contexts

In Figure 11-4, we have illustrated how execution of certain SQL statements cause the creation of trigger execution contexts and how only one of those trigger execution contexts is *active* at any one time.

The UPDATE statement that updates the INVENTORY table causes trigger INVUPDATE to be fired; that trigger's triggered SQL statement is another UPDATE statement (this time, BILLING is being updated). INVUPDATE's triggered SQL statement is executed in a trigger execution context that we've labeled "Trigger Execution Context 1." (In the SQL standard, trigger execution contexts don't have names, so we've named this one just for the purposes of our discussion.) When Trigger Execution Context 1 was created, it was also made active.

When INVUPDATE's triggered SQL statement is executed, it makes changes to another table (BILLING) that is the subject table of another trigger (BILL-UPDATE). As a result of the changes made by INVUPDATE's UPDATE statement, the second trigger (BILLUPDATE) is fired. At that moment, Trigger Execution

Context 1 is "pushed onto the stack" and a second trigger execution context, Trigger Execution Context 2, is created and made active. Trigger Execution Context 1 is not destroyed or released; it is merely suspended, or made inactive, while Trigger Execution Context 2 is active.

Eventually, BILLUPDATE's DELETE statement, which is operating within Trigger Execution Context 2, completes. At this time, Trigger Execution Context 2 is no longer needed, so it is destroyed, and Trigger Execution Context 1 is "popped off the stack" and again becomes active. Only one trigger execution context at a time can be active, but there can be many such contexts "on the stack."

A trigger execution context provides the information required by the SQL system to permit a triggered SQL statement to be executed correctly. This information comprises a set of *state changes*, where each state change describes a change to the data in the target table of the trigger. A state change contains all of the following pieces of information:

- The trigger event: INSERT, UPDATE, or DELETE.

- The name of the subject table of the trigger.

- The names of the subject table's columns that are specified in the trigger definition (only for UPDATE; INSERT and DELETE triggers cannot specify a column list).

- A set of *transitions* (that is, a representation of the rows being inserted, updated, or deleted from the subject table), along with a list of all statement-level triggers that have already been executed in some existing (not necessarily active) trigger execution context and a list of all row-level triggers that have already been executed in some existing (not necessarily active) trigger execution context along with the rows for which they were executed.

The reason for tracking triggers that have already been executed is the prevention of triggers being executed multiple times for the same event, which can cause all sorts of undesirable effects, including triggers that never complete.

When a trigger execution context is first created, its set of state changes is initially empty. State changes are added to a trigger execution context's set of state changes whenever a "new" state change is encountered—one that does not duplicate any existing state change's trigger event, name of subject table, or name of subject table's columns. Each state change is initially empty of transitions, but transitions are added to a state change whenever a row is added to, updated in, or deleted from the subject table associated with the state change. That includes changes that result from the checking of referential integrity constraints and their associated referential actions.

Referencing New and Old Values

One aspect of SQL:1999's triggers that we haven't discussed yet is the optional syntax in Syntax 11-1: REFERENCING <old or new values alias list>. This syntax gives you the ability to reference values in the subject table of your trigger, either in the trigger condition or in the triggered SQL statement.

As you see in the BNF, an <old or new values alias list> is a list of phrases. Each of those phrases can be specified at most one time. They each create a new alias, or correlation name, that you can use to reference values in the trigger's subject table. If you create a correlation name for new values or an alias for new table contents, you can then reference the values that will exist in the subject table *after* an INSERT or UPDATE operation. Similarly, if you create a correlation name for old values or an alias for old table contents, you can then reference the values that existed in the subject table *before* an UPDATE or DELETE operation. Naturally, you cannot use NEW ROW or NEW TABLE for a DELETE trigger, since there are no new values being created, nor can you use OLD ROW or OLD TABLE for an INSERT trigger, since there are no old values to reference. Furthermore, you can specify OLD ROW or NEW ROW only with row-level triggers—that is, if you also specify FOR EACH ROW.

The tables that are referenced by those correlation names or aliases are called *transition tables*. Of course, they are not persistent in the database, but they are created and destroyed dynamically, as they are needed in trigger execution contexts. In a row-level trigger, you can use an old value correlation name to reference the values in a row being modified or deleted by the triggering SQL statement as it existed before the statement modified or deleted it. Analogously, you can use an old value table alias to access the values in the entire table before the triggering SQL statement's effects are applied to the row. In a statement-level trigger, the old value table alias has the same use, of course. In the same manner, you can use a new value correlation name in a row-level trigger to reference the values in a row being modified or inserted by the triggering SQL statement as it will exist after the statement's effects. You can also use a new value table alias to access the values in the entire table after the triggering SQL statement's effects are applied to the row. Finally, a new value table alias has the same use in a statement-level trigger.

You may find this restriction surprising: if you define a BEFORE trigger, you are not allowed to specify either OLD TABLE or NEW TABLE, nor may the trigger's triggered SQL statement make any changes to the database. Those are allowed only for AFTER triggers. The reason is perhaps a bit subtle. The transition tables implied by OLD TABLE and NEW TABLE are too likely to be affected by referential constraints and referential actions that are activated by the changes being caused by the triggered SQL statement; therefore, the values of the rows in that table are not stable or adequately predictable until after the triggering SQL statement has been executed.

One Subject Table: Multiple Triggers

By now, you may have recognized that Syntax 11-1 says nothing about multiple triggers on a single subject table. SQL:1999 certainly doesn't prohibit that capability; it's far too useful to omit. The way in which SQL:1999 supports multiple triggers on a single subject table is simple, if a bit subtle. If there are multiple triggers defined against a single subject table for a single <trigger action time> and a single <trigger event>, then the trigger that was defined first is the first whose <triggered SQL statement> is executed, followed by the trigger that was defined second, and so on. In other words, such triggers are fired in the same order in which they were defined. This is called the *order of execution* of a set of triggers. If, by chance, some subject table has two or more triggers that were defined "at the same time" (within the ability of the database system to measure, at least), then the order in which those triggers are executed is determined by the implementation (random, alphabetical by the definer's authorization ID, etc.).

One unfortunate implication of SQL:1999's use of the order of creation of triggers to determine their order of execution is this: if you discover late in the application development process that you need a trigger to be executed before some already existing trigger (with the same <trigger action time>, <trigger event>, and subject table), there's no standard way to insert that new trigger at the desired place in the sequence. The only standard way to deal with this is to delete all triggers that should follow your new trigger, create the new trigger, then recreate the triggers you just deleted. We certainly hope that a future revision of the SQL standard will have a more satisfactory solution to this problem.

(Your applications can find out the order of evaluation of such triggers by examining the contents of the ACTION_ORDER column of the TRIGGERS table in the Information Schema. See Chapter 22, "Information Schema," for information on the Information Schema.)

If the execution of some <triggered SQL statement> is unsuccessful, then it has no effect on the database, just like any other failed SQL statement execution. More importantly, its failure causes the triggering SQL statement to have no effect, either.

11.3.3 Triggers and Products

In the introduction to this chapter, we mentioned that SQL-92 failed to publish the specification for triggers, even though it was largely complete; we also said that most vendors have implemented triggers in spite of SQL-92's failure to specify a standard for them.

The sad result of this state of affairs is that the various products' implementations of triggers do not conform to one another. Different products (sometimes even different products from the same vendor) implement triggers slightly differently. There are syntax variations, which are relatively easy to overcome. Worse, there are behavioral variations, which cause more problems to application developers.

We find ourselves somewhat doubtful that the SQL products will be brought into conformance with SQL:1999's triggers in a mad rush, but we find reason to hope that they will gradually be migrated into compliance as user demand for standardization of this feature evolves.

11.4 Interaction between Referential Actions and Triggers

Some SQL products implement referential actions through the use of triggers that are created "under the covers." We think that is an unfortunate approach for the simple reason that referential integrity has been carefully designed to be nonprocedural in nature. That is, the SQL standard describes the effects of correct referential integrity in a way that precludes the simplistic sort of procedural code that you might embed in a trigger. (Such products may well implement much more complex code in these "referential action triggers" that give the correct semantics; we haven't evaluated them ourselves to ascertain whether they have or have not done so.)

However, even in SQL products that don't intertwine referential actions and triggers in that way, there is inevitably an interaction between referential actions that might make changes to a given table and the triggers that are defined on that table or that make changes to that table.

SQL:1999 simplifies this interaction a bit by specifying that all integrity constraints, including referential integrity constraints, be properly evaluated, and all referential actions taken, before the AFTER triggers are fired. The reason for this is undoubtedly the requirement that all constraints be satisfied before the SQL statement can be considered "successful"; that determination has to be made after all triggers have been processed, because the execution of the triggers themselves could change the contents of tables in a way that violates constraints of various sorts. While other sequences may have been just as meaningful, SQL:1999 has avoided possible different results from different products by mandating a specific sequence of application of referential actions and AFTER triggers.

11.5 Chapter Summary

In this chapter, we have discussed the need for and uses of triggers in SQL databases. We showed you SQL:1999's syntax for defining triggers and then closely examined the semantics of those triggers and how they operate.

Chapter
12

Accessing SQL from the Real World

12.1 Introduction

There are several primary models under which information *subsystems* (or logically grouped components of an organization's overall information system) operate. In one model, around which we have oriented our examples and discussion so far, the bulk of the operations are ad hoc queries, most of which can't be foreseen. ("Hey, Marty, how many of that new 'Partridge Family Reunion' CD do we have on back order?" or "Mike, check to see if we have any movies with both Stallone and Schwarzenegger.") In these circumstances, an interactive query might be the logical process through which the desired information is obtained. It is unlikely, however, that your customers or even your clerks would be interested in forming SQL queries on their own; some sort of veneer is usually required.

An alternative model is built around operations that regularly follow one another with predictable logic, branching instructions, and object (tables, views, etc.) usage. For example, your CD and movie automatic reordering systems, payroll, end-of-month reporting, and other regular functions may fall into this category. Your business operations will inevitably require more facilities than those provided solely by SQL. For these reasons, a typical environment will contain a mixture of SQL facilities (data definitions, data manipulation statements, transaction control, and others) and features from some type of host programming language: either a traditional 3GL such as COBOL or C (or one of the others that we'll discuss in this chapter), or perhaps a graphically oriented query and reporting tool through which end users might access data managed within a data warehouse or similar informationally oriented data store.

In this chapter, we explore several ways in which your SQL environments are incorporated into your overall information systems. We discuss data access methods (introduced earlier in Chapter 2, "Getting Started with SQL:1999") as well as embedded SQL and module SQL. We also briefly introduce the topic of cursors, which are discussed in detail in the next chapter.

12.2 Data Access Methods and Data Types

There are differences in the ways that conventional programming languages and SQL process data. SQL, as we have said earlier, is a set-at-a-time language. Most SQL statements operate on an arbitrary number of rows of data at one time. For example, the statement

```
UPDATE movie_titles
  SET current_tape_sale_price = regular_tape_sale_price * 0.5
```

will halve the sale price of every videotape format movie (as compared with its regular sale price), regardless of whether there are only two or three or literally hundreds of thousands of titles in our table.

Languages such as C, Fortran, COBOL, and Pascal cannot deal with such sets of data. They can only handle a finite, known number of items at a time; thus they require *loop control* logic during file processing. It is possible to store rows of data into arrays of data structures in most languages, but the maximum size of those arrays is often limited and must usually be known in advance. This creates a sort of mismatch between how SQL is used and how those other languages are used. This mismatch has sometimes been called an *impedance mismatch,* using a term from electronics. In many cases, that mismatch doesn't really matter very much, because you can decide whether you want to perform a particular operation in SQL or in your host program. In other cases, though, it may matter very much.

For example, suppose that your application is required to scan through many rows in some table and make decisions about what to do based on the contents of the rows. Perhaps you want to consider all CDs that are classified as classical music, then to display the title, artist, and price on a screen, and cut the price by some discount between 10% and 20% as determined by a (human) operator's input. It would be difficult to accomplish this purely in SQL, at least without resorting to SQL/PSM, because SQL's conditional execution capabilities are somewhat limited[1] (but see Chapter 23, "A Look to the Future"). It would also be difficult to accomplish it purely in, say, COBOL (minimally, it would require cumbersome ways of retrieving one row at a time and then processing those rows in the COBOL program as if they were records within a file). What this application requires is a mixture of SQL and a conventional programming language. However, the impedance mismatch between SQL and COBOL makes this mixture a bit awkward.

Another kind of mismatch (also sometimes called an *impedance mismatch*, but don't worry about the dual use of the term) occurs in the data types supported by SQL and by the various programming languages that interface with SQL. As we discussed in Chapter 2, "Getting Started with SQL:1999," SQL supports several data types. You know that other programming languages also support specific data types. However, what you may not have thought about is this: it is very rare for the data types supported by two different programming languages to be the same. For example, Fortran has integer and floating point data types but doesn't have a decimal data type; COBOL, on the other hand, has integer and decimal types but doesn't have a floating point type.

This mismatch makes it very difficult to write an SQL statement that can be invoked from just any language. You must know what language you plan to use when you write your SQL statements. In fact, you should have some idea of what language you plan to use when you design your database. Put another way, the kinds of data stored in your database may determine what programming languages you can use to manipulate your database. If you have floating point data (i.e., REAL, FLOAT, or DOUBLE), you shouldn't count on using COBOL to manipulate it. If you have decimal data (e.g., NUMERIC, DECIMAL), you may not want to write your applications in Fortran or C.

In fairness, we want to point out that the situations discussed in the preceding paragraph were absolutely true through SQL-89; however, SQL-92 provided the CAST facility that continues in SQL:1999 (see Chapter 6, "Advanced Value Expressions: CASE, CAST, and Row Value Expressions") that you can use specifically to avoid this type of impedance mismatch (think of CAST as a kind of "impedance-matching transformer").

---

1 There is, as we discussed in Chapter 6, "Advanced Value Expressions: CASE, CAST, and Row Value Expressions," the CASE expression, but that expression and its variou forms (CASE, NULLIF, and COALESCE) have limited capabilitiy with respect to the conditional execution as compared with the full-featured conditional processing programming constructs in SQL/PSM. For more information about SQL/PSM, we refer tyou to Jim Melton, *Understanding SQL's Stored Procedures— A Guide to SQL/PSM* (San Francisco: Morgan Kaufmann Publishers, 1998).

Applications Interface Mechanisms for SQL

There are (at least in the SQL standard) four different ways of writing your application when you want to use SQL. You can (1) directly invoke SQL statements, (2) embed SQL statements directly in your host language programs, (3) write SQL statements separately in a module and call them from your host language programs, or (4) invoke SQL statements through a functional interface. The first technique is known as *direct invocation;* the second method is called *embedded SQL;* the third is called *module language;* and the fourth uses SQL's *call-level interface* (discussed in Chapter 19, "Call-Level Interface (CLI)") .

Direct invocation is most similar to the ad hoc model we presented at the beginning of the chapter. That is, no formal program structure in the form of a host language environment is needed for the statements. There are, however, limitations on what types of SQL statements may be directly invoked. Perhaps more importantly, there is the requirement that everything be handled exclusively through a set model. We'll discuss these details in the next section.

Of the other two forms, most vendors provide only embedded SQL implementations, while a few provide both embedded SQL and module language. There are advantages and disadvantages to both approaches.

In embedded and module SQL, the SQL standard defines rules for how the SQL data types match the host language data types. Some of them are pretty obvious: for example, the SQL INTEGER data type maps pretty cleanly to a Fortran INTEGER or a C int. Other matches are not quite as obvious. For instance, SQL has a TIMESTAMP data type, but no programming language contains an analogous type (at least not in the standard for those languages). As a result, SQL cannot map the TIMESTAMP type directly to any host language type. Instead, SQL requires you to use a CAST function (see Chapter 6, "Advanced Value Expressions: CASE, CAST, and Row Value Expressions") to convert the TIMESTAMP data in the database to some other type—most often character data—in the host program (and vice versa).

Direct Invocation

There are some rules in the SQL standard[2] that state which types of SQL statements are supported. These include

---

2 ISO/IEC 9075-5:1999, *Information technology—Database languages—SQL—Part 5: Host Language Bindings (SQL/Bindings),* July, 1999.

- SQL schema statements
- SQL transaction statements
- SQL connection statements
- SQL session statements
- multiple-row SELECT statements (SELECT * FROM MOVIES_STARS WHERE...)
- INSERT statements (INSERT INTO MUSIC_TITLES...)
- searched UPDATE statements (UPDATE MOVIE_TITLES SET... WHERE...)
- searched DELETE statements (DELETE FROM MOVIE_TITLES WHERE...)
- temporary table declarations

There are many other details that aren't covered, though, and implementations vary greatly with respect to direct invocation environments. (For example, direct invocation as defined in the SQL standard doesn't allow you to use cursors, although some SQL products support this capability in their interactive SQL interfaces.) This isn't a major problem, however, since your mainstay applications will rarely be based on interactive SQL.

The impedance mismatches we discussed earlier are minimized in an interactive SQL environment. First, the output destination for your queries (a terminal or PC screen, a file, or whatever) can accept an arbitrary number of rows for output. Second, cursors and all of the related syntax (see Chapter 13, "Cursors") aren't (usually) used. Finally, the data being returned don't have to be matched with any host language variables, so the data type impedance mismatch is likewise minimized.

12.5 | Embedded SQL

One of the most important means by which SQL facilities and host language programs can interact is through the use of embedded SQL. As noted by the term, SQL statements and declarations are embedded, or directly included, in another, more traditional programming language.

12.5.1 Introduction

Virtually all vendors of SQL database systems implement embedded SQL using a preprocessor technique (in fact, we don't know of any current exceptions to this

```
host language statement
host language statement
host language statement
    embedded SQL statement
host language statement
host language statement
    embedded SQL statement
host language statement
host language statement
    embedded SQL statement
```

Figure 12-1   Embedded SQL Language Structure

statement, although it is certainly possible to design systems in other ways, and we believe that some commercial systems used other approaches in their earlier versions). Using this technique, you write your embedded SQL programs containing a mixture of SQL statements and "native" statements (statements that conform to the standard or implementor's rules for the 3GL in which you're embedding the SQL statements). You then use a preprocessor provided by the DBMS vendor to analyze the embedded SQL source code and "split" it between the SQL and the 3GL statements. The 3GL code then is compiled in the normal way with the appropriate compiler, while the SQL code is given to the DBMS in some implementation-defined way for analyzing and converting into a form that the DBMS can execute.

The SQL standard specifies the *effective* algorithm that accomplishes this split; this algorithm effectively produces an SQL *module*. (We say *effective* and *effectively* because no vendor is required to implement the processing in exactly that fashion, but they must all end up with a result that behaves the same as one that the algorithm would have produced.) The rules are really not too complicated (although we note that the SQL standard sometimes makes the rules appear more complicated than they really are). For instance, all OPEN statements for a specific cursor (see Chapter 13, "Cursors") are *effectively* converted into a single SQL procedure that contains an OPEN statement; the OPEN statement is *effectively* replaced in the resulting 3GL code by a call statement that calls that procedure.

Even though few vendors actually implement SQL's module language or follow that exact algorithm to preprocess embedded SQL programs, we find that we can better understand the behavior of the preprocessors if we keep this model in mind (Figure 12-1).

Any SQL statements so embedded begin with the words EXEC SQL (except in MUMPS, as we'll see later, and Java[3]) and are followed by the SQL statement, such as

```
EXEC SQL SELECT movie_title,....
```

As we mentioned above, the preprocessor will *effectively* replace each of those embedded statements with a *call* to the *effective* procedure in the *effective* SQL module that corresponds to the embedded program.

Correspondingly, any SQL declarations, such as those in which variables are defined, begin and end, respectively, with

```
EXEC SQL BEGIN DECLARE SECTION...
```

and

```
EXEC SQL END DECLARE SECTION...
```

Depending on the particular language syntax among the specified host languages, there may or may not be a terminator—END-EXEC, a semicolon, or a close parenthesis—following each of the above EXEC SQL statements.

There are rules about where the SQL declarations can appear. These rules are partly dependent on the host language, but the general rule is this: anywhere you can put a normal host language declaration, you can also put an SQL declaration. SQL declarations, by the way, are used to declare host language variables that the SQL statements will use (for example, to transfer data to or from the host program). There are analogous rules governing where SQL statements can be placed.

The preprocessor doesn't actually replace the embedded SQL declarations with any reference to the *effective* SQL module, but it uses the information associated with those declarations (like the variable names and data types) to do syntax checking on the other embedded SQL statements and to properly translate those other embedded SQL statements, generating the appropriate data conversions, actual parameters and formal parameters for the effective procedures, and so forth.

By the way, your implementation may very well provide an embedded SQL capability for languages other than those we've discussed. Many vendors discover that their customers want to use other languages. The standard may only provide a binding with seven languages (eight, when Java is included), but that

---

3 Jim Melton and Andrew Eisenberg, *Understanding SQL and Java Together: A Guide to SQLJ, JDBL, and Related Technologies* (San Francisco: Morgan Kaufmann Publishers, 2000).

certainly doesn't prohibit a vendor from providing others. Other languages for which we've seen bindings include BASIC, LISP, Modula-2, and even assembly languages.

If you're interested in writing Java programs that use SQL statements, then you'll be interested in a part of the SQL standard that specifies how to do just that. Object Language Bindings (SQL/OLB) and other standards related to Java and SQL are discussed in another book by one of the authors of this book.[4] The rules for embedding SQL statements in Java programs differ in some significant ways from the rules for embedding SQL in more traditional programming languages, largely because they take advantage of Java's object model and capabilities.

12.5.2 Embedded Exception Declarations

When embedded SQL is being used, we can provide exception statements for the application to use to handle program exceptions. The WHENEVER declarative statement allows you to designate what actions you would like to follow when certain situations occur. This means that you don't have to write code following every SQL statement that checks the values of the status variables and jumps to the appropriate place; you can instruct the SQL preprocessor to do it for you.

The syntax for the WHENEVER declaration is shown in Syntax 12-1.

Syntax 12-1 *WHENEVER Declaration*

```
<embedded exception declaration> ::=
    WHENEVER <condition> <condition action>

<condition> ::=
    <SQL condition>

<SQL condition> ::=
    <major category>
  | SQLSTATE ( <SQLSTATE class value>
               [ , <SQLSTATE subclass value> ] )
  | CONSTRAINT <constraint name>

<major category> ::=
    SQLEXCEPTION
```

---

4   Ibid.

```
 | SQLWARNING
 | NOT FOUND

<SQLSTATE class value> ::= !! See the Syntax Rules.
   <SQLSTATE char><SQLSTATE char>

<SQLSTATE subclass value> ::= !! See the Syntax Rules.
   <SQLSTATE char><SQLSTATE char><SQLSTATE char>

<SQLSTATE char> ::= <simple Latin upper case letter> | <digit>

<condition action> ::=
   CONTINUE
 | <go to>

<go to> ::=
   { GOTO | GO TO } <goto target>

<goto target> ::=
   <host label identifier>
 | <unsigned integer>
 | <host PL/I label variable>

<host label identifier> ::= !! See the Syntax Rules.

<host PL/I label variable> ::= !! See the Syntax Rules.
```

When you specify SQLEXCEPTION or SQLWARNING as your <condition>, you are telling the system to take the specified action when the value of SQLSTATE (see Chapter 20, "Diagnostics and Error Management") has a value that indicates an exception or warning, respectively. Correspondingly, NOT FOUND means to take the specified action when the value of SQLSTATE is 02000.

Note that in SQL:1999, the SQLERROR condition of SQL-92 has been deleted and replaced with either SQLEXCEPTION or SQLWARNING, as noted above. Provision of these two new conditions gives you more information about the database's responses to your application requests than a single condition would.

With respect to the <condition actions>, CONTINUE implies "if the specified condition occurs, then take no special action, but continue with the next statement." By contrast, GOTO (or GO TO) implies that if the specified condition occurs, then control should be transferred to the statement identified by the target specified. Depending on the host language, the target may be an integer (as in Fortran statement labels) or a label identifier (e.g., COBOL paragraph name) as required by the specific rules of that language.

The presence of a WHENEVER statement sets appropriate actions for all embedded SQL statements that physically follow it in the embedded SQL program. To choose a new course of actions, you simply code a new WHENEVER statement, which will then set the exception/not found actions for subsequent embedded SQL statements.

An example of the WHENEVER statement and various actions is as follows:

```
WHENEVER SQLEXCEPTION GO TO 100
```

If the above statement were to appear in a Fortran program, it would have the effect of placing a statement such as

```
IF SQLSTATE .GE. '03000' GO TO 100
```

following every embedded SQL statement. Since WHENEVER is actually a declarative statement (rather than a procedural one), a single WHENEVER statement such as the one presented above may apply to a number of embedded SQL statements. (In fact, many preprocessors will insert a statement exactly like our example after every embedded SQL statement affected by the WHENEVER statement.)

Correspondingly, you might have a statement like this one:

```
WHENEVER NOT FOUND CONTINUE
```

The effect of the above statement would be as if you had written a source language statement checking for an SQLSTATE indicating that the preceding SQL statement had not identified any rows of data (SQLSTATE value '02000') and executed what we might call a no operation (or do nothing) statement, like a Fortran CONTINUE statement (or even no statement at all).

To illustrate what we mean by "all embedded SQL statements that physically follow," consider this example:

```
EXEC SQL statement1;
EXEC SQL WHENEVER SQLEXCEPTION GO TO x;
EXEC SQL statement2;
EXEC SQL WHENEVER NOT FOUND GO TO y;
EXEC SQL statement3;
EXEC SQL WHENEVER SQLEXCEPTION CONTINUE;
EXEC SQL statement4;
```

In this example, the behavior is as follows:

- If statement1 had either an error or a no data condition, no special action is taken and execution continues with statement2.
- If statement2 encountered an error, the flow of control of the program continues at label x (not shown in the example). If statement2 encountered no data, execution still continues with statement3.
- If statement3 caused an error, control continues at label x; if it got the no data condition, then control continues at label y.
- If statement4 got a no data condition, then control goes to label y, but if it gets an error, then control continues with the statement that follows statement4.

One last caveat: This is called an *embedded exception declaration* because you can use it only in embedded SQL. If you choose to use module language, then you must explicitly check the value of SQLSTATE after invocations of module procedures.

12.5.3 Embedded SQL Declarations

Earlier in this chapter (in section 12.5.1), we said that an embedded SQL declaration was used to declare any host program variables used by the embedded SQL statements. For example, in the statement

```
INSERT INTO movies_stars VALUES (:hv1, :hv2, :hv3)
```

we see that the statement will insert a single row into the movies_stars table and that values for the three columns of that row come from three host variables (named hv1, hv2, and hv3). In order for the preprocessor to have any chance at all of ensuring that the host variables have the correct data type for the three columns of the movie_stars table, it has to have some access to the definitions of those host variables.

Of course, it would be *possible* for the preprocessor to simply parse the entire host program and build a symbol table (including any "include" files, should they be specified). However, that's tantamount to rebuilding the first few phases of the host language compiler! DBMS vendors are rightfully reluctant to bite that much off for a couple of reasons: first, it's redundant work, since there is already a compiler with that responsibility; second, it would consume resources that could be better applied to implementing new features or to improving performance; and third, there are better ways to resolve the problem.

The better way that SQL uses is to require that all host variable declarations (well, at least those that declare host variables that are used in embedded SQL statements) be contained between the aforementioned EXEC SQL BEGIN DECLARE SECTION and EXEC SQL END DECLARE SECTION statements (which delimit what the standard calls an *embedded SQL declare section* and which have to be completely contained on one source line with nothing except white space between the keywords). Therefore, the SQL preprocessor need only parse the host language statements that appear between those two statements. (By the way, "EXEC SQL" applies to all languages except MUMPS, which requires "&SQL(" instead.)

Because the syntax of various host languages varies so much, SQL has different rules regarding the permitted syntax of the variable declarations for each language. We note here that the SQL standard considers the statements in the embedded SQL declare section to belong to SQL and not to the host program. This distinction was unimportant in SQL-86 and SQL-89, because the contents always obeyed host language rules. However, in SQL-92, additional syntax was added that violates the host language rules and must therefore be handled by the preprocessor; this continues in SQL:1999.

For every language except MUMPS, you can optionally include a single *embedded character set declaration* in your embedded SQL declare section. This declaration tells readers (e.g., for maintenance) what character set is most likely going to be used for the variable names and character set literals in the embedded SQL program (see Chapter 21, "Internationalization Aspects of SQL:1999," for information on this aspect of SQL:1999). The embedded character set declaration is SQL NAMES ARE character-set-name.

We should point out that the designers of the language embeddings went to great lengths to make the embedded SQL declare sections feel as close as possible to the host language variable conventions. In spite of a few omissions and a few extensions, we believe that they succeeded fairly well.

Let's look at the embedded SQL declare section rules for each of the languages supported in the SQL:1999 standard. (Of course, you should feel free to skip over the sections dealing with languages that your organization doesn't use.)

Ada

An Ada variable definition is permitted to be a normal Ada host identifier (or several of them, separated by commas), followed by a colon, followed by an Ada type specification. This can optionally be followed by an Ada expression to initialize the variable (or variables) to some user-defined value. The valid Ada types specifications are as follows:

```
INTERFACES.SQL.CHAR
INTERFACES.SQL.BIT
INTERFACES.SQL.SMALLINT
INTERFACES.SQL.INT
INTERFACES.SQL.REAL
INTERFACES.SQL.DOUBLE_PRECISION
INTERFACES.SQL.BOOLEAN
INTERFACES.SQL.SQLSTATE_TYPE
INTERFACES.SQL.INDICATOR_TYPE
```

and

```
CHAR
BIT
SMALLINT
INT
REAL
DOUBLE_PRECISION
BOOLEAN
SQLSTATE_TYPE
INDICATOR_TYPE
```

In both cases, CHAR can optionally be followed by CHARACTER SET IS character-set-name (and the IS is also optional)

INTERFACES.SQL is an Ada package that is specified in the SQL:1999 standard, replacing the SQL_STANDARD package that was in SQL-92. We've included the full text of the package later in this chapter (section 12.9). The package defines each of the data types as well as a number of other symbolic values. The embedded SQL declare section has to be specified within the Ada scope of Ada with and use clauses that effectively specify:

```
with INTERFACES.SQL;
use INTERFACES.SQL;
use INTERFACES.SQL.CHARACTER_SET;
```

As you would expect, each declaration must be separated from the others with a semicolon.

Therefore, whether you specify (for example) SQL_STANDARD.REAL or simply REAL, you'll get the same effect. Each of the data types specifies an *Ada* data type (as provided in the package). Of course, they must correspond to a valid SQL data type. These correspondences are shown in Table 12-1.

Table 12-1 *Correspondence between Ada Package Type and SQL Type*

Ada Package Type	Equivalent SQL Data Type
CHAR	CHARACTER with the same length and character set
BIT	BIT with the same length
SMALLINT	SMALLINT
INT	INTEGER
REAL	REAL
DOUBLE_PRECISION	DOUBLE PRECISION
BOOLEAN	BOOLEAN
SQLSTATE_TYPE	CHARACTER(5)
INDICATOR_TYPE	any exact numeric with scale zero

Of course, the appropriate data type for the SQLSTATE definition is SQLSTATE_TYPE.

C

A C variable definition is permitted to be a normal C variable declaration, such as long, short, float, double, or char followed by the C identifier (or a sequence of C identifiers separated by commas). This may optionally be preceded by a C indication of storage class: auto, extern, or static. It may also be optionally preceded by a C class modifier: const or volatile. If char is specified, then you must follow the C identifier with an array specification to give the size of the char array; you can also optionally follow it with CHARACTER SET IS c haracter-set-name (the IS is optional). You can also optionally follow any of the variable definitions with an initial value specification.

In addition to the normal C types, you can specify VARCHAR or BIT (where VARCHAR has the same format requirements and options as char and where BIT also requires the array specification and permits the initial value). Of course, every declaration must be terminated with a semicolon.

Each of the data types that you provide specifies a C data type, which must correspond to a valid SQL data type. These correspondences are shown in Table 12-2.

Table 12-2 *Correspondence between C Type and SQL Type*

C Declared Type	Equivalent SQL Data Type
char	CHARACTER with the same length and character set
VARCHAR	CHARACTER VARYING with the same length and character set
short	SMALLINT
long	INTEGER
float	REAL
double	DOUBLE PRECISION
BIT	BIT with the same length (in C, it is a char with the length divided by the number of bits in a char)

The appropriate data type for SQLSTATE is char[6].

COBOL

A COBOL variable definition is permitted to be a normal COBOL identifier (always at level 01 or 77, though) followed by a type specification, optionally followed by other COBOL syntax to specify the initial value, a picture clause, and so forth. (Of course, like any other COBOL declaration, this must be followed by a period.)

In this case, the type specification can be one of the following (in all cases, PIC and PICTURE can be used interchangeably):

- PICTURE IS X(...); the (...) is optional, and 1 is the default value. This may be optionally preceded by CHARACTER SET IS character-set-name. Both instances of IS are optional.

- PICTURE IS B(...); the (...) is optional, and 1 is the default value. The B(...) is replaced by X(...) where the new value is the old value divided by the number of bits in a COBOL X picture (usually 8). Both instances of IS are optional.

- PICTURE IS S9(...); the (...) is optional, and 1 is the default value. This can optionally be followed by V9(...) to indicate the position of the decimal point and the precision following it. Again, the (...) is optional and defaults to 1. This can optionally be followed by USAGE IS DISPLAY SIGN LEADING SEPARATE. Both instances of IS are optional. Alternately, the first 9(...) can be eliminated and only the V9(...) be used instead.

- PICTURE IS S9(...); the (...) is optional, and 1 is the default value. This can optionally be followed by USAGE IS COMPUTATIONAL (where COMP and COMPUTATIONAL can be used interchangeably). Both instances of IS are optional.

- PICTURE IS S9(...); the (...) is optional, and 1 is the default value. This can optionally be followed by USAGE IS BINARY. Both instances of IS are optional.

As with the other languages, each COBOL data type declaration has a corresponding SQL data type. They are are shown in Table 12-3.

Table 12-3 *Correspondence between COBOL Type and SQL Type*

COBOL Declared Type (PICTURE clause only)	Equivalent SQL Data Type
PICTURE X	CHARACTER with a length equal to the number in parentheses
PICTURE B	BIT with a length equal to the number in parentheses; of course, this corresponds to a COBOL character type (X) with a number equal to the given number divided by the number of bits in an X (usually 8)
PICTURE 9 DISPLAY	NUMERIC with the same precision and scale
PICTURE 9 COMPUTATIONAL	some exact numeric type
PICTURE 9 BINARY	SMALLINT or INTEGER

NOTE: We've omitted many details of the PICTURE clause in this table, such as the "S" used by COBOL to indicate a sign and the length information that can be used to determine the precision and scale of the corresponding SQL numeric types.

The appropriate data type for SQLSTATE is PICTURE X(5).

Fortran

A Fortran variable definition is a type specification followed by a normal Fortran identifier (or multiple identifiers separated by commas). The type specification is one of the following:

- CHARACTER, optionally followed by an asterisk and an integer giving the length in characters. This can optionally be followed by CHARACTER SET IS character-set-name (the IS is optional).

- BIT, optionally followed by an asterisk and an integer giving the length in bits.

- INTEGER (note that the optional asterisk and length in bytes permitted by the Fortran standard is not permitted here).

- REAL (note that the optional asterisk and length in bytes permitted by the Fortran standard is not permitted here).

- DOUBLE PRECISION.

As with the other languages, each Fortran declaration has a corresponding SQL data type. These are shown in Table 12-4.

Table 12-4 *Correspondence between Fortran Type and SQL Type*

Fortran Declared Type	*Equivalent SQL Data Type*
CHARACTER	CHARACTER with the same length
BIT	BIT with the same length (but the Fortran equivalent is really CHARACTER with the length divided by the number of bits in a CHARACTER, usually 8)
INTEGER	INTEGER
REAL	REAL
DOUBLE PRECISION	DOUBLE PRECISION

The appropriate data type for SQLSTATE is CHARACTER*5. By the way, for use with earlier Fortran (FORTRAN) standards, you are permitted to abbreviate the status variable name to 6 characters (SQLSTA); however, we recommend that you use the full names if your compiler permits.

MUMPS

A MUMPS variable definition is a type specification followed by a MUMPS identifier (or multiple identifiers separated by commas). If the type specification VARCHAR is used, then each MUMPS identifier must be followed by an integer in parentheses giving the maximum length. For numeric variables, you can use INT, REAL, or DEC optionally followed by a parenthesized integer giving the precision (the integer may optionally be followed by a comma and another integer giving the scale). Each such declaration is terminated with a semicolon.

Readers who know the MUMPS language will immediately realize that this is a sham: MUMPS has no declarations, as all variables are automatically allocated and contain only variable-length character strings. However, to satisfy the conventions and requirements of SQL, the standard provides a way to declare variables to ensure that the preprocessor doesn't get confused. To be fair, the real reason for including the MUMPS variable declarations is so that the preprocessor can determine the proper SQL data types. Table 12-5 shows the corresponding types.

Table 12-5 *Correspondence between MUMPS Type and SQL Type*

MUMPS Declared Type	Equivalent SQL Data Type
VARCHAR	CHARACTER VARYING with the same length
INT	INTEGER
DEC	DECIMAL with the same precision and scale
REAL	REAL

The appropriate data type for SQLCODE is VARCHAR(5).

Pascal

A Pascal variable definition is permitted to be a normal Pascal identifier (or more than one separated by commas) followed by a colon, followed in turn by a type specification and a semicolon. The type specification can be one of the following:

- PACKED ARRAY (1..x) OF CHAR (where *x* is the length of the Pascal array of characters), optionally followed by CHARACTER SET IS character-set-name (the IS is optional)

- CHAR, optionally followed by CHARACTER SET IS character-set-name (the IS is optional)

- PACKED ARRAY (1..x) OF BIT (where *x* is the length of the Pascal array of bits)

- BIT

- INTEGER

- REAL

Pascal, like the other languages, has an equivalent SQL data type for each of these (see Table 12-6).

Table 12-6 *Correspondence between Pascal Type and SQL Type*

Pascal Declared Type	Equivalent SQL Data Type
PACKED ARRAY [1..N] OF CHAR	CHARACTER with the same length
CHAR	CHARACTER(1)
PACKED ARRAY [1..N] OF BIT	BIT with the same length (but the Pascal equivalent is either CHAR or PACKED ARRAY OF CHAR with a length equal to the specified length divided by the number of bits in a CHAR, usually 8)
BIT	BIT(1) (but the Pascal equivalent is CHAR)
INTEGER	INTEGER
REAL	REAL
BOOLEAN	BOOLEAN

The appropriate data type for SQLSTATE is PACKED ARRAY [1..5] OF CHAR.

PL/I

In PL/I, each PL/I variable declaration starts off with DCL or DECLARE (which are equivalent). There is then either a normal PL/I identifier, or a list of such identifiers in parentheses and separated by commas. This is followed by a type specification and a semicolon.

A type specification is one of the following:

- CHARACTER (...) (CHAR and CHARACTER are synonymous); the (...) contains the length in characters. You can optionally specify VARYING after the keyword CHARACTER, and you can also optionally specify CHARACTER SET IS character-set-name just before the semicolon (the IS is optional).

- BIT (...); the (...) contains the length in characters. You can optionally specify VARYING after the keyword CHARACTER.

- DECIMAL FIXED or FIXED DECIMAL, either one followed by an integer in parentheses giving the precision; the integer may optionally be followed by a comma and another integer giving the scale (DECIMAL and DEC are equivalent).

- BINARY FIXED or FIXED BINARY, either one optionally followed by an integer in parentheses giving the precision (BINARY and BIN are equivalent).

- BINARY FLOAT or FLOAT BINARY, either one followed by an integer in parentheses giving the precision (BINARY and BIN are equivalent).

Just as with all other languages, there are SQL equivalents for each of these (see Table 12-7).

Table 12-7 *Correspondence between PL/I Type and SQL Type*

Pascal Declared Type	Equivalent SQL Data Type
CHARACTER	CHARACTER with the same length and character set
BIT	BIT with the same length
DECIMAL FIXED	DECIMAL with the same precision and scale
BINARY FIXED	SMALLINT or INTEGER (depending on the precision)
BINARY FLOAT	FLOAT with the same precision

The appropriate data type for SQLSTATE is CHARACTER(5).

12.5.4 Embedded SQL Statements

Now that we've taken a long, lingering look at the way you define your host variables for use in embedded SQL, let's take a much briefer look at the way you actually embed your SQL statements.

The rules for embedding the actual SQL statements are really rather simple. First, every embedded statement has to be preceded by EXEC SQL, and the EXEC SQL has to appear on a single line with nothing except white space between the keywords (except in MUMPS, where you start the embedded statement with "&SQL("—with no white space at all—instead of EXEC SQL). Second, if you need to continue the embedded SQL statement across source line boundaries, you must use the conventions of the host language for such continuations; similarly, if you want to use host language comments, you must use the rules of the host language for determining where you can place those comments. Third, depending on the language into which you're embedding, you may have to end the embedded SQL statement with some sort of terminator. In Ada, C, Pascal, and PL/I, the terminator is a semicolon; in COBOL, it's END-EXEC; in Fortran, there's no terminator at all; and in MUMPS, it's a close parenthesis.

If you declare any temporary tables or cursors (including dynamic cursors; see Chapter 13, "Cursors") in your embedded SQL program, the declaration has to physically precede any references to the temporary table or the cursor. If your host language supports scoping rules (as C or Pascal does), then you can redefine variables in *nested scopes,* and the embedded SQL statements in that nested scope will use the most local definition.

The SQL standard has always defined the SQL language as though it were to be written as SQL alone, not embedded in another language. The technique for writing "pure" SQL is called *module language,* which we discuss next. We'd like to point out that SQL defines embedded SQL processing as a syntax transformation that takes an embedded program and extracts the SQL into an SQL module, replacing all SQL statements (except declarations) with a call of the corresponding procedure in that module, and leaving a pure 3GL program. Although this technique is not widely implemented (Oracle's RDB product is probably the best known), it still serves as an excellent mental model even if your implementation deals directly with embedded SQL alone.

12.6 Module Language

So far, most of the examples in this book have been presented as though we were using a form of interactive SQL—a convenient way to present new material and show immediate results. However, as we cautioned early, the standard's definition of *direct invocation of SQL* is rather loose and allows vendors to implement lots of variations. In this chapter, we've talked mostly about combining SQL with other programming languages to implement your applications; to this point, we've discussed embedded SQL, which virtually all SQL DBMS vendors provide and which is quite popular with application writers.

However, there is another paradigm for binding your SQL statements to the 3GL statements of your application, called *module language.* Module language allows you to write your SQL statements separately from your 3GL statements and combine them into an application with your linker. This has several advantages and some disadvantages.

First, you can hire SQL specialists to write the SQL code for your application without worrying about what 3GL they're trained to use; similarly, you can hire the best 3GL programmers without worrying about training them in the finer points of SQL coding. Second, you can utilize the concepts of modular programming to cleanly separate the set-at-a-time operations from the traditional data processing and similar aspects of your applications. Third, you can write the SQL in a way that permits you to choose or rechoose your 3GL at a later point in development with minimal changes to the SQL code. Finally, you can almost certainly use your favorite debuggers with full source-code facilities, at least on the 3GL parts of your application; if you use embedded SQL, you will often find that your debuggers are nearly useless on the source code.

On the other side of the coin, embedded SQL is more widely implemented than module language, which may be an important factor, especially if you want the freedom to use different DBMSs for your application. Furthermore, many people find it easier to understand and maintain an application when they can read both the 3GL and the SQL code together in a smooth flow, instead of having to look at two pieces of code simultaneously.

We should point out that the SQL standards have always used module language as the definitional technique for all of SQL. In fact, in SQL-86 and SQL-89, the definition of embedded SQL was in an appendix to the standard (which caused the USA's National Institute of Standards and Technology, or NIST, to initiate an effort to publish a new standard, X3.168, which formalized embedded SQL definitions; see Appendix F, "The SQL Standardization Process").

Okay, now that we've told you why you might want to use module language, or why you might not want to, let's have a look at what it *is*. In short, a module consists of a module header followed by a mixture of procedures and declarations. The procedures contain the actual SQL statements, and the declarations allow you to declare your cursors and temporary tables. The syntax for a module is shown below in Syntax 12-2.

Syntax 12-2   *Syntax of Module Declaration*

```
MODULE [ module-name ] [ NAMES ARE character-set-name ]
   LANGUAGE { ADA | C | COBOL | FORTRAN | MUMPS | PASCAL | PLI }
   [ SCHEMA schema-name ] [ AUTHORIZATION authID ]
   [ temporary-table-declarations... ]
   { cursor-declaration | dynamic-cursor-declaration | procedure }...
```

If you don't specify a module-name, then the module is unnamed (which isn't usually a problem, but if you have multiple modules and none of them have names, it might make it harder to debug your application). The NAMES ARE clause documents (for the benefit of readers) that the identifiers in the module are going to be expressed either in the specified character set or in the basic set of SQL characters only. The LANGUAGE clause tells the compiler how to build the calling sequences for the procedures in the module, because that can vary from language to language.

You must have either a SCHEMA clause or an AUTHORIZATION clause, or both. SQL-86 and SQL-89 permitted only the AUTHORIZATION clause, and it specified both the name of the schema that would be used as a default qualifier for table names (and view names) in SQL statements in the module *and* the authorization identifier to be used for privilege checking while executing statements in the module. SQL-92 divided these two concepts so that you could specify the default schema and the authorization identifier separately, and SQL:1999 continues to provide that valuable facility.

You can declare as many temporary tables as you need in the module (even none at all). Note that all of the temporary table declarations have to appear before any cursors or procedures but that you can mix cursor declarations and procedures in any order as long as you declare a cursor before any procedures that reference it. We'll see what cursor declarations look like in Chapter 13, "Cursors," and we'll find out about dynamic cursors in Chapter 18, "Dynamic SQL"; for now, let's look at procedures.

A procedure is, as the name suggests, a programming element that can be called from another programming element. In fact, SQL procedures are like procedures in other languages in many ways: they have parameters, they have a name, and they contain executable statements. They differ from procedures in some languages by having only a single executable SQL statement and by requiring a minimum of one parameter. The syntax for a procedure is shown in Syntax 12-3.

Syntax 12-3 *Module Language Procedure Syntax*

```
PROCEDURE proc-name
    ( parameter-declaration [ , parameter-declaration ]... )
SQL-statement ;
```

In SQL-92, it was permitted to replace the parenthesized list of comma-separated parameter declarations with

```
parameter-declaration...
```

but SQL:1999 has eliminated that rather confusing alternative. Although you may find products that continue to allow the omission of the commas, we strongly advise that you stick with their use. You should note that at least one parameter declaration is required in any case. The minimum requirement for a procedure is that it specify the status parameter, SQLSTATE (see Chapter 20, "Diagnostics and Error Messages", for more details). If you want to pass other data into the SQL statement or if you want to have the SQL statement return data to your application, you will have to declare additional parameters. A parameter declaration looks like this:

```
parameter-name data-type
```

or

```
SQLSTATE
```

Obviously, a parameter name cannot be a reserved word (especially not SQLSTATE!); in addition, SQL requires that parameter names (except the status parameter) always be preceded by a colon. Therefore, here are some valid parameter names:

```
:SERIAL_NUMBER
:"TABLE"
:param1
```

You have to use the colon both when you declare the parameter and when you use it in an SQL statement. Parameters come in four "flavors": they can be *input parameters, output parameters, input and output parameters,* or *neither input nor output parameters.* You will have already guessed that *input parameters* are those that pass data from the host program into the procedure and that *output parameters* are those that pass data back to the host program from the procedure. We're sure that you've also figured out that *input and output parameters* are parameters that serve both functions. But what about *neither input nor output parameters?* Well, SQL can tell by how a parameter is used in the SQL statement of a procedure whether it is for input, for output, or for both. If you happen to code a parameter declaration that you don't actually use in the statement, then SQL doesn't know whether you might later modify the procedure to use it for input, output, or both, so SQL declares it to be "none of the above."

Let's see some examples of procedures.

```
PROCEDURE discount_movies
    ( SQLSTATE, :title CHARACTER VARYING(25),
            :discount DECIMAL(3,2) )

  UPDATE movie_titles
    SET current_purchase_price = current_purchase_price - :discount
  WHERE movie_title = :title;

PROCEDURE drop_titles ( :star CHARACTER VARYING(25),
                        :reason CHARACTER(2), SQLSTATE )
  DELETE FROM movie_titles
    WHERE title IN ( SELECT movie_title
                     FROM movies_stars
                     WHERE :star = actor_last_name );

PROCEDURE star_name
    ( :star_last CHARACTER VARYING(25),
     :star_first CHARACTER VARYING(25),
         :title CHARACTER VARYING(25),
      SQLSTATE )
```

```
SELECT 'Starring: ' || actor_last_name
  INTO :star_last
FROM movies_stars
WHERE actor_last_name = :star_last
  AND actor_first_name = :star_first
  AND movie_title = :title;
```

In the first example, we provide the title of a movie and the amount by which its price is to be discounted and specify that the status is to be returned in SQLSTATE. In the second example, we provide for getting information back from SQLSTATE; we also provide a parameter that isn't used at all. In the third example, we use one parameter for both input and output: to retrieve a variation of the star's last name into the same parameter that we use to provide the name to the database. Useless? Probably, except that it won't perform the concatenation if SQLSTATE indicates "no data."

Let's see now what an entire module might look like using those three sample procedures.

```
MODULE demo_module NAMES ARE ascii
   LANGUAGE FORTRAN
   SCHEMA test_schema AUTHORIZATION book_authors

PROCEDURE discount_movies
    ( SQLSTATE, :title CHARACTER VARYING(25),
            :discount DECIMAL(3,2) )
   UPDATE movie_titles
     SET current_purchase_price = current_purchase_price - :discount
   WHERE movie_title = :title;

PROCEDURE drop_titles ( :star CHARACTER VARYING(25),
                       :reason CHARACTER(2), SQLSTATE )
   DELETE FROM movie_titles
   WHERE title IN ( SELECT movie_title
                    FROM movies_stars
                    WHERE :star = actor_last_name );

PROCEDURE star_name
    ( :star_last CHARACTER VARYING(25),
     :star_first CHARACTER VARYING(25),
          :title CHARACTER VARYING(25),
     SQLSTATE )
```

```
SELECT 'Starring: ' || actor_last_name
  INTO :star_last
FROM movies_stars
WHERE actor_last_name = :star_last
  AND actor_first_name = :star_first
  AND movie_title = :title;
```

It really is as simple as that. Of course, what we have not shown here is the (Fortran, in this case) code that we'd write to actually *use* the procedures in this module. You can see examples of that in Appendix B, "A Complete SQL:1999 Example."

12.6.1 Some Additional Information about Privileges

You have seen that SQL modules optionally allow you to specify AUTHORIZATION authID. We hinted that specifying the clause told the DBMS to use that authID for checking whether the SQL statements in the procedures of the module have the appropriate privileges to see and update the data they reference. However, what if you do *not* specify that clause? In this case, the DBMS will use the authID associated with your session for privilege checking.

We have heard the phrase *definer's rights* used to describe modules that do contain the AUTHORIZATION clause, because it's the privileges of the *defined* authID that determine the actions of the statements in the module. Of course, most implementations will have some sort of restrictions on what modules you can use, so you don't get super-user privileges by simply ferreting out a module with such an authID.

We've also heard the term *invoker's rights* used to refer to modules that don't have an AUTHORIZATION clause. This means that the privileges of the user who invokes procedures in the module are used to determine the actions.

In SQL-92, there was no way for an embedded SQL program to specify an explicit authorization identifier, so embedded SQL programs always behaved as if they were invoker's rights modules (unless, of course, there happened to be a vendor extension that provided a definer's rights capability).

In SQL:1999, you can now use an *embedded authorization clause*, which is aligned with the module authorization clause used in module language. This means that you can specify the authorization identifier that will be used for privilege checking when SQL statements in the embedded SQL program are executed, as well as the default schema name that will be used to qualify table names and other unqualified names appearing in those SQL statements.

12.6.2 An Implementation Note

When an SQL DBMS processes a module (whether it's an actual SQL module or merely the implied module associated with an embedded program), the results of that processing aren't really specified by the SQL standard. In some implementations, the module is compiled and converted to machine-language code that is linked with the 3GL portion of the program to be invoked at runtime. In others, the result might somehow be saved in the actual database, either in machine language for easy and fast execution or in an intermediate form that is later interpreted or even compiled into machine code at runtime. In still others, the SQL statements may simply be interpreted at runtime. All these implementation techniques are valid, even desirable, based on criteria such as implementation cost, storage facilities, and performance requirements.

12.7 | The Impedance Mismatch

Earlier in this chapter (see section 12.2), we mentioned the term *impedance mismatch*, with a couple of implications. It's worth taking a few minutes to address this poorly understood problem in a little more detail.

In electronics, the term is used to characterize circuitry in which the creator of a signal and the user of that signal are not perfectly aligned with one another. For example, a home entertainment's amplifier may have output circuits with an impedance (which is essentially a form of electrical resistance applicable only to alternating current but not to direct current) of 30Ω (ohms), while the speakers attached to that amplifier have an impedance rating of 4Ω. The effect is that the efficiency of the transfer of sound from the amplifier to the speakers is diminished, resulting in a loss of fidelity—perhaps an increase in the noise level or in the distortion of the sound being amplified. In short, the mismatch in the impedance of the amplifier with that of the speakers causes a certain loss in information.

Similarly, the fact that SQL's data types are not identical in structure and semantics to the data types of any other specific programming language means that there is a danger of information loss when data is transferred between SQL and programs written in those languages.

One of the most obvious data type mismatches arises with SQL's datetime data types DATE, TIME, and TIMESTAMP. No commonly used programming language has a data type that corresponds with SQL's datetime types. When you want to retrieve a DATE value from an SQL table into a C program, you have to CAST the value into something that C can process, often a character string. Similarly, if you want to INSERT a TIMESTAMP value into an SQL table, you have to express it in some form suitable to your C program, possibly structuring it in the form of a timestamp literal in a C character array.

The data type impedance mismatch is certainly not limited to datetime types. SQL supports DECIMAL and NUMERIC types that correspond to types in COBOL and PL/I, but to no types at all in Fortran, C, Ada, and Pascal. SQL provides support for REAL, FLOAT, and DOUBLE PRECISION types that have no analog in COBOL. Whenever you write application programs in any conventional programming language, you have to be aware of the possible presence of data type mismatches in the tables that you're accessing and take appropriate measures such as CASTing values back and forth between SQL types and host language types.

Similarly, no host language provides a native data type corresponding to SQL's BLOB and CLOB data types, so you have to use other facilities (see section 2.4.12, "Locators," for additional information) when exchanging values of those types between the database and your host language application code.

As you'll learn in the next chapter (Chapter 13, "Cursors"), another form of impedance mismatch arises from SQL's ability to process large sets of data in single operations, while most conventional programming languages can only process a single datum or a single structure of data in one operation.

These two issues—data type and data cardinality—cause the most important aspects of the impedance mismatch between SQL and other languages with which it interfaces, but there are undoubtedly other situations that could be characterized in a similar manner. Unfortunately, it is inherently unavoidable in any mixed-language programming environment that such mismatches occur and that you have to account for them as you write your applications. As we discuss features of SQL in which an impedance mismatch issue arises, we'll take pains to identify the mismatch and the steps you have to take in order to avoid loss of information that can otherwise result.

12.8 | Other Binding Styles

In this chapter, we've talked mostly about embedded SQL and module language programming. However, there are other ways of binding SQL statements to your application. We've already talked about one: direct invocation of, or interactive, SQL. Another, dynamic SQL, is a sort of binding style, but not quite. Although dynamic SQL is invoked via *normal, static* statements (that is, those statements bound "normally" in module language or embedded SQL), the actual statements that are to be executed are neither module nor embedded, but dynamic. See Chapter 18, "Dynamic SQL," for a full explanation of dynamic SQL.

A call-level interface (CLI) is another kind of binding, forming a cross between dynamic and static SQL. In general with CLI, SQL statements are passed as source text (parameters) to subroutines where they are dealt with. This means that they are given to the DBMS itself for execution, which sort of implies dynamic SQL, but without the static statements that are normally used for dynamic SQL. In 1995, SQL-92 was augmented with a new part of the SQL standard[5] that specified a standard call-level interface to SQL databases. This API was quickly made very popular through Microsoft's implementation under the name ODBC (Open DataBase Connectivity). CLI was enhanced and republished along with the other parts of SQL:1999 and is discussed further in Chapter 19, "Call-Level Interface (CLI)."

The Java programming language provides an interface to SQL database systems that has conceptual similarity to ODBC but that differs quite significantly in its detail. This interface is called JDBC[6] (Sun Microsystems states that the letters do not form an abbreviation or acronym, particularly not for "Java DataBase Connectivity"). JDBC is implemented in the style of most Java APIs—as a set of object-oriented class libraries—but takes advantage of much of the high-level architecture of SQL/CLI and of ODBC.

For the sake of completeness, we also mention that most vendors of SQL database systems have their own proprietary call-level interfaces, such as Oracle's OCI (Oracle Call Interface) that provide essentially the same function as SQL/CLI but do not technically conform to the CLI standard. These proprietary interfaces are highly customized for the underlying database engines and may well be more efficient than the standardized interfaces. Their major disadvantage, however, is that you almost certainly cannot access other vendors' database systems from your applications without rewriting them to use some other interface. Furthermore, some products don't provide clear documentation for using those proprietary call-level interfaces, sometimes because their intended use is to underlie the embedded SQL implementation. As with so many other issues, *caveat programmer*.

Another kind of binding is called *remote database access*. In fact, there is another standard called RDA or Remote Database Access (ISO/IEC 9579) that specifies an RDA facility for accessing SQL databases remotely. Of course, an application that wishes to remotely access an SQL DBMS using RDA still has to bind its 3GL statements to its SQL statements in one of the bindings we've described already; nonetheless, there are some differences in the behavior of programs using RDA. It is beyond the scope of this book to discuss RDA and remote access in general; we will say that the RDA standard has gone to great lengths to

---

5 ISO/IEC 9075-3:1995, *Information technology—Database languages—SQL—Part 3: Call-Level Interface (SQL/CLI)*.

6 See Melton and Eisenberg, *Understanding SQL and Java Together*.

be as transparent as possible, but it does include minor issues that strictly local access does not encounter. Unfortunately, RDA has not proven commercially successful, perhaps in part because the use of call-level interfaces such as ODBC have obscured the need for and benefits of standardizing remote access to SQL databases, but also likely due to the availability of vendor packages with substantially greater marketing presence, such as IBM's DRDA.

12.9 | Package Interfaces.SQL

The Ada package Interfaces.SQL that we mentioned in section 12.5.3 is listed below in its entirety. In this listing, taken directly from the SQL:1999 standard, bs, ts, bi, ti, dr, dd, bsc, and tsc are implementation-defined integer values. t is either INT or SMALLINT, corresponding with your implementation's implementation-defined exact numeric type of indicator parameters. There are other, more detailed, requirements for the Interfaces.SQL package, but they are even more tedious than the listing we present here. Your vendor's documentation will have all the information about the package that you require, or you can turn to the SQL standard itself and read the details there.

```
package Interfaces.SQL is
---The declarations of CHAR and NCHAR may be subtype declarations
  type CHAR is (See the Syntax Rules)
  type NCHAR is (See the Syntax Rules)
  type BIT is array (POSITIVE range <>) of BOOLEAN;
  type SMALLINT is range bs .. ts;
  type INT is range bi .. ti;
  type REAL is digits dr;
  type DOUBLE_PRECISION is digits dd;
  subtype INDICATOR_TYPE is t;
  type SQLSTATE_TYPE is new CHAR (1 .. 5);
  package SQLSTATE_CODES is
    AMBIGUOUS_CURSOR_NAME_NO_SUBCLASS:
      constant SQLSTATE_TYPE :="3C000";
    CARDINALITY_VIOLATION_NO_SUBCLASS:
      constant SQLSTATE_TYPE :="21000";
    CLI_SPECIFIC_CONDITION_NO_SUBCLASS:
      constant SQLSTATE_TYPE :="HY000";
    CONNECTION_EXCEPTION_NO_SUBCLASS:
      constant SQLSTATE_TYPE :="08000";
```

```
CONNECTION_EXCEPTION_CONNECTION_DOES_NOT_EXIST:
  constant SQLSTATE_TYPE :="08003";
CONNECTION_EXCEPTION_CONNECTION_FAILURE:
  constant SQLSTATE_TYPE :="08006";
CONNECTION_EXCEPTION_CONNECTION_NAME_IN_USE:
  constant SQLSTATE_TYPE :="08002";
CONNECTION_EXCEPTION_SQLCLIENT_UNABLE_TO_ESTABLISH_SQLCONNECTION:
  constant SQLSTATE_TYPE :="08001";
CONNECTION_EXCEPTION_SQLSERVER_REJECTED_ESTABLISHMENT_OF_SQLCONNECTION:
  constant SQLSTATE_TYPE :="08004";
CONNECTION_EXCEPTION_TRANSACTION_RESOLUTION_UNKNOWN:
  constant SQLSTATE_TYPE :="08007";
DATA_EXCEPTION_NO_SUBCLASS:
  constant SQLSTATE_TYPE :="22000";
DATA_EXCEPTION_ARRAY_ELEMENT_ERROR:
  constant SQLSTATE_TYPE :="2202E";
DATA_EXCEPTION_CHARACTER_NOT_IN_REPERTOIRE:
  constant SQLSTATE_TYPE :="22021";
DATA_EXCEPTION_DATETIME_FIELD_OVERFLOW:
  constant SQLSTATE_TYPE :="22008";
DATA_EXCEPTION_DIVISION_BY_ZERO:
  constant SQLSTATE_TYPE :="22012";
DATA_EXCEPTION_ERROR_IN_ASSIGNMENT:
  constant SQLSTATE_TYPE :="22005";
DATA_EXCEPTION_ESCAPE_CHARACTER_CONFLICT:
  constant SQLSTATE_TYPE :="2200B";
DATA_EXCEPTION_INDICATOR_OVERFLOW:
  constant SQLSTATE_TYPE :="22022";
DATA_EXCEPTION_INTERVAL_FIELD_OVERFLOW:
  constant SQLSTATE_TYPE :="22015";
DATA_EXCEPTION_INVALID_CHARACTER_VALUE_FOR_CAST:
  constant SQLSTATE_TYPE :="22018";
DATA_EXCEPTION_INVALID_DATETIME_FORMAT:
  constant SQLSTATE_TYPE :="22007";
DATA_EXCEPTION_INVALID_ESCAPE_CHARACTER:
  constant SQLSTATE_TYPE :="22019";
DATA_EXCEPTION_INVALID_ESCAPE_OCTET:
  constant SQLSTATE_TYPE :="2200D";
DATA_EXCEPTION_INVALID_ESCAPE_SEQUENCE:
  constant SQLSTATE_TYPE :="22025";
DATA_EXCEPTION_INVALID_INDICATOR_PARAMETER_VALUE:
  constant SQLSTATE_TYPE :="22010";
```

```
DATA_EXCEPTION_INVALID_LIMIT_VALUE:
  constant SQLSTATE_TYPE :="22020";
DATA_EXCEPTION_INVALID_PARAMETER_VALUE:
  constant SQLSTATE_TYPE :="22023";
DATA_EXCEPTION_INVALID_REGULAR_EXPRESSION:
  constant SQLSTATE_TYPE :="2201B";
DATA_EXCEPTION_INVALID_TIME_ZONE_DISPLACEMENT_VALUE:
  constant SQLSTATE_TYPE :="22009";
DATA_EXCEPTION_INVALID_USE_OF_ESCAPE_CHARACTER:
  constant SQLSTATE_TYPE :="2200C";
DATA_EXCEPTION_NULL_VALUE_NO_INDICATOR_PARAMETER:
  constant SQLSTATE_TYPE :="2200G";
DATA_EXCEPTION_MOST_SPECIFIC_TYPE_MISMATCH:
  constant SQLSTATE_TYPE :="22002";
DATA_EXCEPTION_NULL_VALUE_NOT_ALLOWED:
  constant SQLSTATE_TYPE :="22004";
DATA_EXCEPTION_NUMERIC_VALUE_OUT_OF_RANGE:
  constant SQLSTATE_TYPE :="22003";
DATA_EXCEPTION_STRING_DATA_LENGTH_MISMATCH:
  constant SQLSTATE_TYPE :="22026";
DATA_EXCEPTION_STRING_DATA_RIGHT_TRUNCATION:
  constant SQLSTATE_TYPE :="22001";
DATA_EXCEPTION_SUBSTRING_ERROR:
  constant SQLSTATE_TYPE :="22011";
DATA_EXCEPTION_TRIM_ERROR:
  constant SQLSTATE_TYPE :="22027";
DATA_EXCEPTION_UNTERMINATED_C_STRING:
  constant SQLSTATE_TYPE :="22024";
DATA_EXCEPTION_ZERO_LENGTH_CHARACTER_STRING:
  constant SQLSTATE_TYPE :="2200F";
DEPENDENT_PRIVILEGE_DESCRIPTORS_STILL_EXIST_NO_SUBCLASS:
  constant SQLSTATE_TYPE :="2B000";
EXTERNAL_ROUTINE_EXCEPTION_NO_SUBCLASS:
  constant SQLSTATE_TYPE :="38000";
EXTERNAL_ROUTINE_EXCEPTION_CONTAINING_SQL_NOT_PERMITTED:
  constant SQLSTATE_TYPE :="38001";
EXTERNAL_ROUTINE_EXCEPTION_MODIFYING_SQL_DATA_NOT_PERMITTED:
  constant SQLSTATE_TYPE :="38002";
EXTERNAL_ROUTINE_EXCEPTION_PROHIBITED_SQL_STATEMENT_ATTEMPTED:
  constant SQLSTATE_TYPE :="38003";
EXTERNAL_ROUTINE_EXCEPTION_READING_SQL_DATA_NOT_PERMITTED:
  constant SQLSTATE_TYPE :="38004";
```

```
EXTERNAL_ROUTINE_INVOCATION_EXCEPTION_NO_SUBCLASS:
  constant SQLSTATE_TYPE :="39000";
EXTERNAL_ROUTINE_INVOCATION_EXCEPTION_INVALID_SQLSTATE_RETURNED:
  constant SQLSTATE_TYPE :="39001";
EXTERNAL_ROUTINE_INVOCATION_EXCEPTION_NULL_VALUE_NOT_ALLOWED:
  constant SQLSTATE_TYPE :="39004";
FEATURE_NOT_SUPPORTED_NO_SUBCLASS:
  constant SQLSTATE_TYPE :="0A000";
FEATURE_NOT_SUPPORTED_MULTIPLE_ENVIRONMENT_TRANSACTIONS:
  constant SQLSTATE_TYPE :="0A001";
INTEGRITY_CONSTRAINT_VIOLATION_NO_SUBCLASS:
  constant SQLSTATE_TYPE :="23000";
INTEGRITY_CONSTRAINT_VIOLATION_RESTRICT_VIOLATION:
  constant SQLSTATE_TYPE :="23001";
INVALID_AUTHORIZATION_SPECIFICATION_NO_SUBCLASS:
  constant SQLSTATE_TYPE :="28000";
INVALID_CATALOG_NAME_NO_SUBCLASS:
  constant SQLSTATE_TYPE :="3D000";
INVALID_CONDITION_NUMBER_NO_SUBCLASS:
  constant SQLSTATE_TYPE :="35000";
INVALID_CONNECTION_NAME_NO_SUBCLASS:
  constant SQLSTATE_TYPE :="2E000";
INVALID_CURSOR_NAME_NO_SUBCLASS:
  constant SQLSTATE_TYPE :="34000";
INVALID_CURSOR_STATE_NO_SUBCLASS:
  constant SQLSTATE_TYPE :="24000";
INVALID_GRANTOR_STATE_NO_SUBCLASS:
  constant SQLSTATE_TYPE :="0L000";
INVALID_ROLE_SPECIFICATION:
  constant SQLSTATE_TYPE :="0P000";
INVALID_SCHEMA_NAME_NO_SUBCLASS:
  constant SQLSTATE_TYPE :="3F000";
INVALID_SQL_DESCRIPTOR_NAME_NO_SUBCLASS:
  constant SQLSTATE_TYPE :="33000";
INVALID_SQL_STATEMENT:
  constant SQLSTATE_TYPE :="30000";
INVALID_SQL_STATEMENT_NAME_NO_SUBCLASS:
  constant SQLSTATE_TYPE :="26000";
INVALID_TARGET_SPECIFICATION_VALUE:
  constant SQLSTATE_TYPE :="31000";
INVALID_TRANSACTION_STATE_NO_SUBCLASS:
  constant SQLSTATE_TYPE :="25000";
```

```
INVALID_TRANSACTION_STATE_ACTIVE_SQL_TRANSACTION:
  constant SQLSTATE_TYPE :="25001";
INVALID_TRANSACTION_STATE_BRANCH_TRANSACTION_ALREADY_ACTIVE:
  constant SQLSTATE_TYPE :="25002";
INVALID_TRANSACTION_STATE_HELD_CURSOR_REQUIRES_SAME_ISOLATION_LEVEL:
  constant SQLSTATE_TYPE :="25008";
INVALID_TRANSACTION_STATE_INAPPROPRIATE_ACCESS_MODE_FOR_BRANCH_TRANSACTION:
  constant SQLSTATE_TYPE :="25003";
INVALID_TRANSACTION_STATE_INAPPROPRIATE_ISOLATION_LEVEL_FOR_BRANCH_TRANSACTION:
  constant SQLSTATE_TYPE :="25004";
INVALID_TRANSACTION_STATE_NO_ACTIVE_SQL_TRANSACTION_FOR_BRANCH_TRANSACTION:
  constant SQLSTATE_TYPE :="25005";
INVALID_TRANSACTION_STATE_READ_ONLY_SQL_TRANSACTION:
  constant SQLSTATE_TYPE :="25006";
INVALID_TRANSACTION_STATE_SCHEMA_AND_DATA_STATEMENT_MIXING_NOT_SUPPORTED:
  constant SQLSTATE_TYPE :="25007";
INVALID_TRANSACTION_INITIATION_NO_SUBCLASS:
  constant SQLSTATE_TYPE :="0B000";
INVALID_TRANSACTION_TERMINATION_NO_SUBCLASS:
  constant SQLSTATE_TYPE :="2D000";
LOCATOR_EXCEPTION_INVALID_SPECIFICATION:
  constant SQLSTATE_TYPE :="0F001";
LOCATOR_EXCEPTION_NO_SUBCLASS:
  constant SQLSTATE_TYPE :="0F000";
NO_DATA_NO_SUBCLASS:
  constant SQLSTATE_TYPE :="02000";
NO_DATA_NO_ADDITIONAL_DYNAMIC_RESULT_SETS_RETURNED:
  constant SQLSTATE_TYPE :="02001";
REMOTE_DATABASE_ACCESS_NO_SUBCLASS:
  constant SQLSTATE_TYPE :="HZ000";
SAVEPOINT_EXCEPTION_INVALID_SPECIFICATION:
  constant SQLSTATE_TYPE :="3B001";
SAVEPOINT_EXCEPTION_NO_SUBCLASS:
  constant SQLSTATE_TYPE :="3B000";
SAVEPOINT_EXCEPTION_TOO_MANY:
  constant SQLSTATE_TYPE :="3B002";
SQL_ROUTINE_EXCEPTION_NO_SUBCLASS:
  constant SQLSTATE_TYPE :="2F000";
SQL_ROUTINE_EXCEPTION_FUNCTION_EXECUTED_NO_RETURN_STATEMENT:
  constant SQLSTATE_TYPE :="2F005";
SQL_ROUTINE_EXCEPTION_MODIFYING_SQL_DATA_NOT_PERMITTED:
  constant SQLSTATE_TYPE :="2F002";
```

```
SQL_ROUTINE_EXCEPTION_PROHIBITED_SQL_STATEMENT_ATTEMPTED:
   constant SQLSTATE_TYPE :="2F003";
SQL_ROUTINE_EXCEPTION_READING_SQL_DATA_NOT_PERMITTED:
   constant SQLSTATE_TYPE :="2F004";
SQL_STATEMENT_NOT_YET_COMPLETE_NO_SUBCLASS:
   constant SQLSTATE_TYPE :="03000";
SUCCESSFUL_COMPLETION_NO_SUBCLASS:
   constant SQLSTATE_TYPE :="00000";
SYNTAX_ERROR_OR_ACCESS_RULE_VIOLATION_NO_SUBCLASS:
   constant SQLSTATE_TYPE :="42000";
SYNTAX_ERROR_OR_ACCESS_RULE_VIOLATION_IN_DIRECT_STATEMENT_NO_SUBCLASS:
   constant SQLSTATE_TYPE :="2A000";
SYNTAX_ERROR_OR_ACCESS_RULE_VIOLATION_IN_DYNAMIC_STATEMENT_NO_SUBCLASS:
   constant SQLSTATE_TYPE :="37000";
TRANSACTION_ROLLBACK_NO_SUBCLASS:
   constant SQLSTATE_TYPE :="40000";
TRANSACTION_ROLLBACK_INTEGRITY_CONSTRAINT_VIOLATION:
   constant SQLSTATE_TYPE :="40002";
TRANSACTION_ROLLBACK_SERIALIZATION_FAILURE:
   constant SQLSTATE_TYPE :="40001";
TRANSACTION_ROLLBACK_STATEMENT_COMPLETION_UNKNOWN:
   constant SQLSTATE_TYPE :="40003";
TRIGGERED_DATA_CHANGE_VIOLATION_NO_SUBCLASS:
   constant SQLSTATE_TYPE :="27000";
WARNING_NO_SUBCLASS:
   constant SQLSTATE_TYPE :="01000";
WARNING_CURSOR_OPERATION_CONFLICT:
   constant SQLSTATE_TYPE :="01001";
WARNING_DISCONNECT_ERROR:
   constant SQLSTATE_TYPE :="01002";
WARNING_DYNAMIC_RESULT_SETS_RETURNED:
   constant SQLSTATE_TYPE :="0100C";
WARNING_IMPLICIT_ZERO_BIT_PADDING:
   constant SQLSTATE_TYPE :="01008";
WARNING_NULL_VALUE_ELIMINATED_IN_SET_FUNCTION:
   constant SQLSTATE_TYPE :="01003";
WARNING_PRIVILEGE_NOT_GRANTED:
   constant SQLSTATE_TYPE :="01007";
WARNING_PRIVILEGE_NOT_REVOKED:
   constant SQLSTATE_TYPE :="01006";
WARNING_QUERY_EXPRESSION_TOO_LONG_FOR_INFORMATION_SCHEMA:
   constant SQLSTATE_TYPE :="0100A";
```

```
     WARNING_SEARCH_CONDITION_TOO_LONG_FOR_INFORMATION_SCHEMA:
        constant SQLSTATE_TYPE :="01009";
     WARNING_STATEMENT_TOO_LONG_FOR_INFORMATION_SCHEMA:
        constant SQLSTATE_TYPE :="01005";
     WARNING_STRING_DATA_RIGHT_TRUNCATION_WARNING:
        constant SQLSTATE_TYPE :="01004";
     WITH_CHECK_OPTION_VIOLATION_NO_SUBCLASS:
        constant SQLSTATE_TYPE :="44000";
   end SQLSTATE_CODES;
end Interfaces.SQL;
```

Note that the huge bulk of that code does nothing more than assign Ada names to all of the defined SQLSTATE codes. There's a pattern being used to create those names: the SQLSTATE class followed by the SQLSTATE subclass, separated by an underscore and with all spaces replaced by underscores. Knowing that, you can always "predict" the Ada name for any new SQLSTATE values that come along, even if you don't find them in your documentation.

12.10 Chapter Summary

In this chapter, we've taken you beyond the basic—and advanced—facilities of the SQL statements themselves that we discussed in the earlier chapters. You now know about the different binding styles supported by SQL and, depending on the support of your particular implementation(s) and on what is most appropriate for your applications, can choose the module and embedded forms of SQL. The language-specific material included in this chapter should give you a thorough understanding of how SQL can be used together with the languages specified by the standard.

In the next chapter, we'll turn our attention to the subject of cursors, an important part in making embedded and module SQL work.

Chapter

13

Cursors

13.1 Introduction

We've mentioned several times that SQL processes data by sets. The primary mechanism used to permit SQL to do row-by-row access—an important facility when SQL is combined with C, COBOL, Ada, or another language—is the cursor. In this chapter, we explore cursors and how they are used within SQL. In fact, as we implied in section 12.7, "The Impedance Mismatch," the principal purpose of cursors is to act as a "transformer" to compensate for this aspect of the impedance mismatch between SQL and other programming languages.

13.2 Cursors: The Basics

Assume that you need to compute the standard deviation of the current sale cost of DVD format movies. Since there is no function to do that in SQL (well, not without the OLAP facilities discussed in Volume 2 of this book), you must retrieve that data into your application program and compute that value there. In other situations, your application may require the ability to display rows of data (formatted in some special way, perhaps) on a screen and allow a user to identify rows for deletion or modification by using a pointer of some sort, such as a cursor.

The languages in which you write your applications (that is, the languages that invoke the SQL code: C, COBOL, Ada, and the others we discussed in the previous chapter) do not support sets or multisets of data. They are capable of dealing with only one or a few pieces of data at a time. This particular difference between SQL and the host languages is part of what we have called an *impedance mismatch*. SQL has facilities to help resolve this mismatch, and the cursor is among the most important of those facilities.

The technique involves an object called a *cursor*. A cursor is something like a pointer that traverses a collection of rows. If your application has to traverse many rows of data, you cannot retrieve them all at once because your host language doesn't deal with an arbitrary number of rows. However, you can retrieve them one at a time by using a cursor.

Suppose you want to compute the standard deviation of the DVD prices of all movies whose current sales price is greater than $22.95. A SELECT statement would look something like this:

```
SELECT current_dvd_sale_price FROM movie_titles
  WHERE current_dvd_sale_price > 22.95;
```

However, as we said in Chapter 12, "Accessing SQL from the Real World," this statement cannot be executed as part of an application program because it may (and probably will) retrieve many rows of data. (It can be executed in interactive SQL because that merely displays the result on your terminal.) The way this must be handled is to declare a cursor for that expression and then use the cursor to retrieve the data. The SQL statements would look something like the statements in Example 13-1. Now, this doesn't show the complete flow of control that your application program would have to provide. We won't show that in detail here; you can deduce that yourself from your knowledge of Chapter 12, "Accessing SQL from the Real World." However, let's sketch the whole thing just to show how you would use the cursor. (Note that we're using pseudocode here instead of one of the several languages that the SQL standard specifies.)

The FETCH statement (discussed in detail later in this chapter; see section 13.4) is the SQL equivalent of a READ or GET statement.

Example 13-1 *Using a Cursor to Retrieve Multiple Rows for Processing*

```
DECLARE std_dev CURSOR FOR
  SELECT current_dvd_sale_price
  FROM movie_titles
  WHERE current_dvd_sale_price > 22.95;

OPEN std_dev;
```

```
loop:

   FETCH std_dev INTO :price;

   if no-data return, then go to finished;

   accumulate information required for standard deviation computation;

   go to loop;

finished:

   CLOSE std_dev;

   compute the standard deviation;
```

You will note that this logic permits your application to deal with only one row of data at a time but also permits it to handle all the rows, no matter how many there are. If you have written programs in COBOL, Pascal, C, or some other language in which you use loop control to cycle through one or more records in a file, you are already familiar with the fundamentals of cursor usage.

In this loop of FETCH statements, you can also perform database operations on the rows that you fetched. For example, you can update or delete the fetched rows, as we illustrate in Example 13-2.

Example 13-2 *Using a Cursor to Process Multiple Rows*

```
DECLARE std_dev CURSOR FOR
   SELECT current_dvd_sale_price FROM movie_titles;

OPEN std_dev;

loop:

   FETCH std_dev INTO :price;

   if no-data return, then go to finished;

   if :price is greater than 99.99, then
      DELETE FROM movie_titles WHERE CURRENT OF std_dev;
```

```
     if :price is greater than 22.95, but less than or equal to 99.99, then
       get the user to enter new price from terminal;
       UPDATE movie_titles
         SET current_dvd_sale_price = :newprice
       WHERE CURRENT OF std_dev;

     if :price is less than or equal to 22.95, then
       accumulate information required for standard deviation computation;

     go to loop;

finished:

   CLOSE std_dev;

   compute the standard deviation;
```

In this example, the application was able to do some maintenance on the MOVIE_TITLES table while it was accumulating the information required for the computation. The new form of the UPDATE statement shown here specifies the row to be updated by specifying WHERE CURRENT OF std_dev instead of WHERE search condition. We call this a *positioned* UPDATE statement.

13.2.1 Syntax

Let's take a closer look at all of these new statements. There are actually only four new statements, each with a set of options (shown below), plus two other statements that are variations on the UPDATE and DELETE statements we've already seen in earlier chapters (these *positioned* UPDATE and DELETE statements are discussed later in section 13.5).

The four new statements are

- DECLARE
- OPEN
- FETCH
- CLOSE

First, there is the cursor declaration. This is not an executable statement but rather a declaration. In it, you specify the name of the cursor (whose only use is in other cursor-related statements). The scope of the cursor name is the module or compilation unit in which it was declared; therefore, you cannot use modular programming techniques to split operations on one cursor among several compilation units or modules. We have adopted the convention of declaring all of our cursors and other declarable objects at the beginning of our modules and embedded SQL programs, but SQL's syntax allows you to declare cursors at any point in a module where an SQL statement is allowed, as long as it's earlier than any statement using the cursor.

The format of a cursor declaration is shown in Syntax 13-1.

Syntax 13-2 *Cursor Declaration Format*

```
<declare cursor> ::=
    DECLARE <cursor name> [ <cursor sensitivity> ]
      [ <cursor scrollability> ] CURSOR
      [ <cursor holdability> ]
      [ <cursor returnability> ]
      FOR <cursor specification>

<cursor sensitivity> ::=
      SENSITIVE
    | INSENSITIVE
    | ASENSITIVE

<cursor scrollability> ::=
      SCROLL
    | NO SCROLL

<cursor holdability> ::=
      WITH HOLD
    | WITHOUT HOLD

<cursor returnability> ::=
      WITH RETURN
    | WITHOUT RETURN

<cursor specification> ::=
      <query expression> [ <order by clause> ] [ <updatability clause> ]

<updatability clause> ::=
      FOR { READ ONLY | UPDATE [ OF <column name list> ] }
```

```
<order by clause> ::=
    ORDER BY <sort specification list>

<sort specification list> ::=
    <sort specification> [ { <comma> <sort specification> }... ]

<sort specification> ::=
    <sort key> [ <collate clause> ] [ <ordering specification> ]

<sort key> ::=
    <value expression>

<ordering specification> ::=
    ASC
  | DESC
```

The <cursor name> is an ordinary SQL identifier. You have to be sure that the <cursor name> is different from any other <cursor name> in the same module or compilation unit. The <query expression> is SQL's normal query expression that we saw in Chapter 3, "Basic Table Creation and Data Manipulation," and in Chapter 9, "Advanced SQL Query Expressions."

If we leave off all of the optional parts, then we are left with

```
DECLARE cursor-name CURSOR FOR query-expression
```

which is the most basic form of a cursor declaration. Even this limited form allows us to perform many powerful operations on our data one row at a time. The query-expression identifies the rows that we wish to retrieve (and possibly update or delete), and other statements actually manipulate that set of rows for us.

However, there are situations in which we need a bit more control over the rows we have identified. One of the most basic forms of control that we often need is to sort the rows according to some criteria. The optional <order by clause> is used for this purpose, as discussed in the next section; subsequent sections discuss the other optional portions of the cursor declaration.

13.2.2 Ordering and Column Naming

The ORDER BY is defined as shown in Syntax 13-2.

Syntax 13-2 *ORDER BY Clause*

```
<order by clause> ::= ORDER BY <sort specification list>

<sort specification list> ::=
    <sort specification> [ { <comma> <sort specification> }... ]

<sort specification> ::=
    <sort key> [ <collate clause> ] [ <ordering specification> ]

<sort key> ::=
    <value expression>

<ordering specification> ::=
    ASC
  | DESC
```

SQL:1999 goes beyond SQL-92 by permitting you to write <sort specification>s using column names that are names of columns of the table from which the cursor derives its rows, but that don't appear in the select list of the cursor. However, if you do this, then the <query expression> of the cursor is restricted to be a <query specification> (you can review Chapter 9, "Advanced SQL Query Expressions," to refresh your memory with the distinction between a query expression and a query specification). That is, SQL:1999 does not permit ordering by columns that are not selected into the cursor when the cursor has a query expression that is more complex than a query specification.

Furthermore, if your ORDER BY clauses use expressions—even if the expressions reference only those columns that otherwise appear in the select list—then there are additional restrictions placed unless those expressions are copies (think "cut-and-paste") of expressions appearing in the select list of some query specification of the cursor's query expression. (Whew!) The restrictions in this case are that the cursor's query expression cannot contain a GROUP BY clause or a HAVING clause, and no query specification contained in that query expression can specify DISTINCT or a set function. Finally, the expressions in your ORDER BY clause cannot themselves contain subqueries or set functions. (The reasons for these restrictions are rather obscure, amounting to "it becomes terribly complicated to compute the result set of the cursor if you violate them.")

There are times, however, when your select list has columns that don't have names. For example, you might declare a cursor like this:

```
DECLARE cursor1 CURSOR FOR
  SELECT current_dvd_sale_price, our_dvd_cost,
         current_dvd_sale_price - our_dvd_cost
  FROM movie_titles
```

The first column of the cursor is named current_dvd_sale_price and the second is named our_dvd_cost. However, the third column has no name (at least not a user assigned name, and therefore no name that your application can use dependably). As we saw in Chapter 9, "Advanced SQL Query Expressions," you could (and probably should) have declared your cursor like this:

```
DECLARE cursor1 CURSOR FOR
  SELECT current_dvd_sale_price, our_dvd_cost,
         current_dvd_sale_price - our_dvd_cost AS markup
  FROM movie_titles
```

which would have given the third column the name markup. In earlier versions of the SQL standard (and in some products), if you failed to give a name to your cursor's columns that otherwise don't have names, then you could identify the column using the number 3 (indicating the third column). To ORDER BY the third column and the first column of that cursor, you could have used

```
ORDER BY 3, current_dvd_sale_price
```

However, SQL:1999 has eliminated that rather archaic facility, since you always have the ability to give your cursor's columns names. Furthermore, by eliminating that capability, you can now write ORDER BY clauses that use expressions starting with an integer value:

```
ORDER BY 3 - some_value
```

You might think that you can now write an ORDER BY clause with only a single literal, such as

```
ORDER BY 3
```

but that's not the case. The designers of SQL:1999 realized that some implementations would continue to support the ability to specify ordering columns by their position, which conflicts with ordering by a literal (at least by a numeric literal). Besides which, ordering by a literal is the same as not ordering at all, so it's not a very useful feature!

Of course, the keyword ASC means "sort in ascending order," and DESC means "sort in descending order." Therefore, if you want to sort in ascending order by the markup value and in descending order by the current sales price, you would declare your cursor to look like this:

```
DECLARE cursor1 CURSOR FOR
  SELECT current_dvd_sale_price, our_dvd_cost,
         current_dvd_sale_price - our_dvd_cost AS markup
  FROM movie_titles
  ORDER BY markup, current_dvd_sale_price DESC
```

A note about ASC and DESC: They apply *only* to the column to which they are attached (ASC is the default). Whenever you want to have a specific column sorted in descending order, you have to specify DESC immediately following the name of that column. If you want the column in ascending order, you may specify ASC or specify neither ASC nor DESC. Therefore, if you specify

```
ORDER BY markup DESC, current_dvd_sale_price
```

the result is that the first column will be sorted in descending order and the second in ascending order, just as if you had specified

```
ORDER BY markup DESC, current_dvd_sale_price ASC
```

And, finally, since you know (to refresh your memory, see Chapter 7, "Predicates") that any comparison between a null value and any other value (whether null or otherwise) results in *Unknown*, you will be interested to learn how ORDER BY deals with nulls in the ordering column or columns. SQL resolves this issue by requiring that all null values be sorted either before all non-null values or after all non-null values, depending on the implementation's choice.

13.2.3 Updatability

Once in a while, you may encounter a situation that requires you to make sure your cursor is not updated, even if somebody else comes along to "maintain" your application and (perhaps without fully understanding the application) adds an UPDATE or DELETE statement. You'd like to be able to define the cursor as read-only, even though it could theoretically be updated. (Another reason for defining a cursor as read-only is to permit your DBMS implementation to perform certain performance optimizations that cannot be used for updatable cursors.) In other situations, you might want to ensure that only some columns of the cursor can be updated while some are guaranteed to be unchanged. SQL:1999 provides you with an updatability clause on your DECLARE CURSOR to allow you to control this, as you saw in Syntax 13-1.

The updatability is either FOR READ ONLY or FOR UPDATE. If you specify FOR READ ONLY, then you cannot execute UPDATE or DELETE statements on that cursor. If you specify FOR UPDATE, you can also specify a list of column names as shown in Syntax 13-3.

Syntax 13-3 *FOR UPDATE Clause*

```
FOR UPDATE [ OF column-name [ , column-name ]... ]
```

If you leave off the list of column-names (or if you don't even specify FOR UPDATE), the default is an implicit list of all the column names in the underlying table of the cursor. FOR UPDATE means that you can execute UPDATE or DELETE statements on the cursor, but you cannot update any column that was not listed. Therefore, if you define the following cursor:

```
DECLARE cursor1 CURSOR FOR
  SELECT current_dvd_sale_price, our_dvd_cost
  FROM movie_titles
  FOR READ ONLY
```

every UPDATE WHERE CURRENT or DELETE WHERE CURRENT statement that identifies that cursor will get an error. If you defined the cursor as

```
DECLARE cursor1 CURSOR FOR
  SELECT current_dvd_sale_price, our_dvd_cost
  FROM movie_titles
  FOR UPDATE OF current_dvd_sale_price
```

then a statement that said

```
UPDATE movie_titles
  SET current_dvd_sale_price = current_dvd_sale_price / 2
WHERE CURRENT OF cursor1
```

would work just fine, but

```
UPDATE movie_titles
  SET our_dvd_cost = our_dvd_cost / 2
WHERE CURRENT OF cursor1
```

would get an error.

13.2.4 Sensitivity

Cursors as defined in SQL-86 and SQL-89 had a significant problem: earlier versions of the standard simply didn't tell DBMS implementors enough about cursor characteristics. One of the characteristics that was left unspecified turned out to be pretty important for some applications and was addressed in SQL-92 and continues (with some further enhancement) in SQL:1999. We've already briefly discussed transaction semantics in Chapter 2, "Getting Started with SQL:1999" (and will do so in more detail in Chapter 15, "Transaction Management"), so you know that changes that your application makes in a transaction cannot be affected by other transactions that may be concurrently accessing the database. However, what if your *own* application executes statements that overlap with one another?

Consider the situation where you open a cursor of, say, all rows that identify DVDs costing you more than $20.00, and you are merrily fetching and updating rows but (for reasons known to yourself) you insert a searched update statement that lowers the price of all movies costing over $20.00 by $5.00. What (we ask with a straight face) happens to the rows in your cursor that you haven't processed yet? Do some of those rows "disappear" because they no longer cost more than $20.00, or do they remain in the cursor for you to process? If they remain in the cursor, does their price get lowered by $5.00 or not? Example 13-3 shows how the code might look.

Example 13-3 *Cursor and Conflicting UPDATE Statement*

```
DECLARE cursor1 CURSOR FOR
  SELECT our_dvd_cost
  FROM movie_titles
  WHERE our_dvd_cost > 20.00;

OPEN cursor1;

loop:
```

```
        FETCH cursor1 INTO :price;

        if no-data return, then go to finished;

        perform whatever action is appropriate;

        if you got interrupted by a phone call from the boss, then

          UPDATE movie_titles
            SET our_dvd_cost = our_dvd_cost - 5.00
          WHERE our_dvd_cost > 20.00;

    go to loop;

    finished:

    CLOSE cursor1;
```

Okay, so perhaps this isn't the most realistic situation, but you can picture what we're trying to evoke here: a cursor is opened using certain criteria and, while it's still open, another SQL statement that affects (some of) the same rows of the underlying table is executed.

Well, SQL:1999 allows you to protect yourself against just this sort of problem. You can declare a cursor to be *insensitive,* meaning that it will not see the effects of other statements, *not even those in the same transaction,* while it's open. Of course, if you close the cursor and then reopen it, you will see the effects of those other statements. Let's look at this in a little more detail.

Using the keyword INSENSITIVE declares the cursor to be an insensitive cursor as described above. An insensitive cursor is one that is implemented in a way that guarantees that the rows seen by the cursor will not be affected by other statements executed as part of the same transaction (transaction isolation, as discussed in Chapter 15, "Transaction Management," protects the cursor from statements executed as part of other transactions). Consider the next example shown in Example 13-4.

Example 13-4 *Cursor and Conflicting DELETE Statement*

```
DECLARE std_dev CURSOR FOR
  SELECT current_dvd_sale_price
    FROM movie_titles
    WHERE current_dvd_sale_price < 22.95;
```

```
OPEN std_dev;

loop:

  FETCH std_dev INTO :price;

  if no-data return, then go to finished;

  accumulate information required for standard deviation computation;

  DELETE FROM movie_titles
  WHERE current_dvd_sale_price < 22.95;

go to loop;

finished:

CLOSE std_dev;

compute the standard deviation;
```

After the DELETE statement (which, you will notice, deletes exactly the same set of rows that the cursor identified), what will happen on the next FETCH? Now, you can well argue that any application that does anything this dumb gets (and deserves) whatever happens, but there are more complex examples that you may find compelling. Let's go ahead and answer the question anyway.

In an ASENSITIVE cursor (that is, a cursor that is neither sensitive nor insensitive, which were the only cursors provided prior to SQL-92), the answer to the question is "I don't know" because the DBMS is free to do whatever is convenient (i.e., it's implementation-dependent). In some implementations, the cursor might happily keep on retrieving all the rows it had identified, while in others it could immediately see the no-data situation. In still others, the result would depend on many other factors, such as the presence of indices or the READ ONLY option, or even on the timing between the DELETE WHERE and the next FETCH. Note that in prior versions of SQL, this was known as an *indeterminant* cursor.

However, in an INSENSITIVE cursor, the cursor will not be affected by the DELETE...WHERE statement. As we've already said, if you close the cursor and then reopen it, the results of the DELETE...WHERE will be seen. By the way, in SQL:1999, you cannot specify FOR UPDATE and INSENSITIVE on the same cursor; INSENSITIVE forces the cursor to be read-only.

To get the full meaning of INSENSITIVE, it may help to imagine that opening an INSENSITIVE cursor causes the DBMS to immediately locate every row that the cursor identifies, copy them into some temporary table, and then make the cursor operate on the rows of that temporary table. (In fact, we happen to know that many implementations do exactly this.)

Finally, having a SENSITIVE cursor means that significant changes, such as deleting the rows in the example above, *are* made immediately visible.

SQL:1999 provides one more feature to help you avoid problems that might be caused by the interaction between an open cursor and other statements in the same transaction in your application. If you attempt to delete or update a row of an ASENSITIVE cursor that has been updated or deleted by a statement other than a statement associated with the same cursor (a searched statement or a statement associated with a different cursor), then you'll get a warning to notify you of the conflict. (Similarly, if you execute a searched update or delete statement that updates or deletes a row of an open cursor, you'll get the same warning.)

13.2.5 Scrollable Cursors

There are occasional applications where you are not able to process your cursor's rows in the default fashion, that is, fetching the next row, processing it, and then repeating. Instead, you may need to back up and revisit a row you've already processed or skipped over. You may even need to start at the end of the cursor and work backward for some reason. You may discover that you need to skip some rows or go directly to a specific row. SQL:1999 permits you to do this with *scrollable* cursors.

If you specify SCROLL, you can use additional syntax on your FETCH statements that allow you to do more than simply fetch the next row. In SQL-89, the only move that you could make when retrieving rows through a cursor was to retrieve the very next row. Even if you knew that the next row wasn't "interesting," but the one after it was, you still had to retrieve the uninteresting row in order to get to the interesting one. However, SQL-92 introduced the SCROLL option to cursors, meaning that you could skip around as needed. We'll talk more about that along with the FETCH statement below. In SQL:1999, you now can specify SCROLL and FOR UPDATE on the same cursor; previously, in SQL-92, SCROLL forced the cursor to be read-only. But, let us be clear: by default, a SCROLL cursor is read-only; you have to explicitly declare it to be FOR UPDATE if that's what you want.

13.2.6 Holdable Cursors

A cursor declared with the WITH HOLD clause is said to be a *holdable cursor* (failure to specify either WITH HOLD or WITHOUT HOLD gives the same effect as though you had specified WITHOUT HOLD—a cursor that is not a holdable cursor). But that begs the question of what a holdable cursor is; it merely tells us how one is specified.

A holdable cursor is one that is *not* automatically closed if you commit the transaction in which the cursor was opened. By contrast, if you commit a transaction without closing all of your ordinary (nonholdable) cursors, SQL will close them for you.

Recall that a transaction is a way to get atomic ("all or nothing") behavior from a sequence of SQL statements. Consider also that some of your applications might require literally thousands of SQL statements to accomplish their jobs (such as accepting into our store's inventory a very large load of DVDs arriving from the main distribution warehouse). Such huge transactions have several disadvantages, the most important of which are as follows:

- If there should be a system failure of some sort before the end of the transaction, all of the work you've accomplished so far will be lost. That could be disastrous if your system has been devoted to the transaction for some hours. You can reduce the risk of this happening if you design your application so that you can commit transactions at more frequent intervals.

- There is often significant system overhead in committing a transaction and initiating a new one, but especially in committing large transactions. A well-balanced application shouldn't commit its transactions after every row operation, because the transaction termination and initiation overhead may consume more system resources than the actual work being performed. On the other hand, deferring transaction commitment until a very large number of operations have been performed may cause the commit operation to take a very long time, during which your system may be unavailable for other transactions. Committing transactions at more optimal points helps reach a balance between the overhead of starting and finishing transactions and the delays of committing very large transactcions.

However, if your application uses a cursor to locate the rows of data that you are processing and committing a transaction closes that cursor, then it may be very difficult—even impossible—to restore conditions to precisely the state that existed when you committed the transaction. The solution to this dilemma is to permit the cursor to remain open when you commit your transactions.

SQL:1999 allows you to do this, but you have to declare each cursor that you want to be holdable. Cursors that are held open after a COMMIT statement do not lose their positions. They remain positioned in the same place where they were positioned just before the COMMIT statement. (Perhaps more accurately, if the position of the cursor was either just before some row or on some row, then it will be positioned immediately before that row when the subsequent transaction starts.) Your application is required to perform a FETCH statement on the cursor before it is allowed to issue an UPDATE or DELETE against the cursor. This ensures that the cursor is properly positioned on the row to be updated or deleted.

It is perhaps unexpected that SQL:1999 does not permit you to keep a cursor open and positioned following a ROLLBACK statement (see Chapter 15, "Transaction Management"). Some SQL implementations do permit this behavior, but SQL:1999 prohibits it on the grounds that performing a ROLLBACK causes all operations performed in the cursor to be "undone," and the results of some of those operations may well have been part of the criteria used to define the cursors opened in the transaction. As a result, the very contents of the cursor may have changed unpredictably, and so SQL:1999's designers concluded that it is safer to close all cursors, holdable and nonholdable, when a transaction is aborted.

13.2.7 Returning Result Sets from Cursors

If you specify WITH RETURN in your cursor declaration, the cursor is said to be a *result set cursor*. If you don't specify WITH RETURN or WITHOUT RETURN, then the effect is the same as having specified WITHOUT RETURN. As with holdable cursors in section 13.2.6, this definition only tells how to declare result set cursors, but gives no information about what they are.

The term *result set* refers to the virtual table that results from evaluating the query expression of a cursor. However, it has no practical consequence under normal conditions. Only when you open a result set cursor in an SQL-invoked procedure (see Chapter 17, "Routines and Routine Invocation (Functions and Procedures)," for more information about SQL-invoked procedures) does it have any effect.

If you open a result set cursor in an SQL-invoked procedure that was declared to return a result set and you leave that cursor open when the SQL-invoked procedure returns to its caller, then the cursor's result set is returned to the procedure's invoker as discussed in Chapter 17, "Routines and Routine Invocation (Functions and Procedures)."

If the SQL-invoked procedure was invoked from an SQL routine (a procedure or function written in SQL), then the result set is readily passed back to the SQL code in the form of a virtual table. If, however, the SQL-invoked procedure was invoked from 3GL code (perhaps from your application's code, but also from an external routine such as those described in Chapter 17), then the result set has to be associated with a cursor defined in that 3GL program.

We'll talk more about result set cursors and returning result sets from SQL-invoked routines in Chapter 17. We'll talk about this even more in Chapter 18, "Dynamic SQL," since you must use some of the facilities of dynamic SQL in order to effectively use result set cursors.

13.3 | OPEN and CLOSE

As we've hinted already in our examples, the first thing that you have to do to use a cursor (after declaring it, of course) is to open it. The OPEN statement is quite straightforward. It is an executable statement and its format is

```
OPEN cursor-name;
```

If the cursor is already open, then you'll get an error.

Note that the OPEN statement doesn't have any parameters or host variables associated with it. All data that must be supplied by the host program is specified in the cursor declaration, but it is actually obtained when the OPEN is executed. The cursor declaration

```
DECLARE cursor2 CURSOR FOR
  SELECT current_dvd_sale_price
  FROM movie_titles
  WHERE current_dvd_sale_price > :minprice;
```

tells the DBMS that you want to handle only those DVDs whose price is greater than some threshold that you will specify in a host variable or parameter. However, recall that the cursor declaration is a declaration that is processed by the compiler, not an executable statement. Therefore, when you execute

```
OPEN cursor2;
```

the DBMS has to obtain the value from the host variable or parameter :MINPRICE at that time and then evaluate the cursor to see what rows belong to it. If your cursor declaration has any special values like CURRENT_USER or CURRENT_TIME, they will be evaluated during the OPEN execution, too.

When you're finished with your cursors, you'll want to close them. This may free up system resources and is just generally good practice; it might also protect you against an accidental operation on the cursor that could inadvertently ruin your data.

The `CLOSE` statement merely closes the cursor. Of course, if the cursor isn't open, then you'll get an error. (A quick note on terminology: Even though we said that you'd get an error, we note that you might simply `CLOSE` all your cursors at the end of your work without regard to whether or not you'd opened them. In that case, the "error" wouldn't indicate a program bug at all, but would simply be an informational signal. That's one reason why SQL:1999 calls these notifications *exception conditions* instead of *errors*.) You cannot use the cursor again until you reopen it, at which time new values for host variables or parameters and for special values will be derived—for example,

```
CLOSE cursor2;
```

13.4 FETCH

The `FETCH` statement allows your application to retrieve data into your program space, one row at a time. The syntax of `FETCH` is shown in Syntax 13-4.

Syntax 13-4 *FETCH syntax*

```
<fetch statement> ::=
    FETCH [ [ <fetch orientation> ] FROM ]
      <cursor name> INTO <fetch target list>

<fetch orientation> ::=
    NEXT
  | PRIOR
  | FIRST
  | LAST
  | { ABSOLUTE | RELATIVE } <simple value specification>

<fetch target list> ::=
    <target specification> [ { <comma> <target specification> }... ]
```

The `<cursor name>` is obvious; it is the name of an open cursor that was declared in the same module or compilation unit that contains the `FETCH` statement. `<fetch target list>` is also pretty obvious: it is a comma-separated list of host variables or parameters that will receive the data from the row that the `FETCH` retrieves. The number of entries in the list must correspond exactly to the number of columns in the cursor. Of course, you can have data parameters and indicator parameters (or data host variables and indicator host variables; see section 5.4.1, "Types of Parameters," to refresh your memory of indicator parameters and variables) for each column.

The <fetch orientation> is associated with SCROLL cursors. The "normal" orientation is NEXT, which means "retrieve the next row associated with the cursor." This is the default behavior if you don't specify an orientation. PRIOR means "retrieve the previous row associated with the cursor." If you've done several NEXTs, then a PRIOR will retrieve a row that you've previously seen. FIRST means "retrieve the first row associated with the cursor," and LAST means (as you would expect) "retrieve the last row associated with the cursor." Finally, you can specify ABSOLUTE value or RELATIVE value (value is a literal or a host variable or parameter; it must be exact numeric with scale 0). ABSOLUTE says "retrieve the row in the position specified by value," and RELATIVE means "skip forward (or backward) the number of rows specified by value." FETCH RELATIVE 0 means "retrieve the row I just retrieved." If the row identified by RELATIVE or ABSOLUTE doesn't exist (that is, the value would require retrieving a row before the first row or after the last row in the cursor), you'll get the no-data condition and the cursor will be positioned before the first row or after the last row of the cursor.

Actually, some applications will benefit from a clever little trick put into the SQL standard. If you use the orientation ABSOLUTE 1, you will, of course, get the first row of the cursor; however, if you specify ABSOLUTE –1, you'll get the last row! In fact, if you have *n* rows in a cursor and specify ABSOLUTE –*n*, you'll get the first row. That makes ABSOLUTE orientation similar to RELATIVE orientation. Of course, if you only have, say, 15 rows in your cursor and you specify ABSOLUTE 18 or ABSOLUTE –29, you shouldn't expect to get an indication of success. (Actually, you'll get the no-data condition.) The same is true if you specify ABSOLUTE 0 or if you specify NEXT or PRIOR and you're at the end or the beginning of the cursor.

By the way, SCROLL cursors are one way that you can see the effects of specifying, or not specifying, INSENSITIVE on your cursor declarations. If you FETCH some row, then FETCH the NEXT row, and then FETCH the PRIOR row of a cursor that specified INSENSITIVE, you'd get the same row that you first FETCHed. However, if the cursor didn't specify INSENSITIVE and some DELETE statement (other than WHERE CURRENT OF that cursor) had deleted the row, it would depend on the details (and even the timing) of your implementation.

13.5 | Cursor Positioning

This is a good place to talk about the *position* of a cursor. Open cursors always have a position. That position can be before some row of the table, on some row of the table, or after the last row of the table. These are the only possibilities. If the cursor is before some row, then a FETCH NEXT will get that row and a FETCH PRIOR will get the row before that row (and FETCH RELATIVE 0 will get a no-data condition). If the cursor is on some row, then a FETCH NEXT will get the row that follows, a FETCH PRIOR will get the row preceding it, and a FETCH RELATIVE 0 will get the same row again. If the cursor is positioned after the last row, then FETCH NEXT will get the no-data condition and FETCH PRIOR will get the last row of the table. By the way, FETCH NEXT and FETCH RELATIVE 1 have the same effect; the same is true for FETCH PRIOR and FETCH RELATIVE –1.

13.5.1 Positioned DELETE

The positioned DELETE statement deletes the current row of the cursor. Its format is shown in Syntax 13-5.

Syntax 13-5 *Positioned DELETE Statement*

```
DELETE FROM table-name WHERE CURRENT OF cursor-name
```

You will recall from Chapter 9, "Advanced SQL Query Expressions," that query expressions that identify more than one table are sometimes updatable in SQL:1999, depending on a number of factors. This goes for cursors as well as for views. In spite of that fact, there's only one table-name that you can specify in the positioned DELETE statement, which naturally means that you can delete only from a single table. If your cursor involves an updatable join operation, then you can delete only from one table (of the two or more tables) that participates in the join. By using two (or more) positioned DELETE statements, you can delete from all of those tables.

If the cursor is on some row of the table, that row is deleted. If the cursor is not on some row of the table, you'll get an exception condition. Of course, the cursor has to be declared in the same module or compilation unit that contains the positioned DELETE statement.

13.5.2 Positioned UPDATE

The positioned UPDATE statement updates the current row of the cursor. Its format is shown in Syntax 13-6.

Syntax 13-6 *Positioned UPDATE Statement*

```
UPDATE table-name
  SET set-list
WHERE CURRENT OF cursor-name
```

Like the positioned DELETE, this statement requires that the cursor have an updatable query expression. And, like the positioned DELETE, you can specify only a single table-name, so the positioned UPDATE statement only updates a single table. Again, you can use multiple such statements to delete from more than one of the tables.

The set-list is a comma-separated list cf

```
column-name = source
```

where source is a value expression, the keyword NULL, or the keyword DEFAULT. Each column identified in the set-list must be part of the FOR UPDATE column-list (implicit or explicit) or the statement is syntactically invalid. If the cursor has an ORDER BY, you cannot update any column used in the ordering. You cannot update the same column more than once in a single positioned UPDATE statement. If the cursor is not positioned on a row, you'll get an error. If any error is raised during the update, the row isn't updated and the cursor remains positioned on that row.

13.6 | Chapter Summary

Remember that cursors are your primary tool in using SQL data in a row-at-a-time manner. You can retrieve from, delete from, insert into, and update in tables. There are some restrictions having to do with the updatability of cursors, but those should have little effect on your applications as long as you are aware of them.

Now that we've discussed the basic subjects of program structure and data positioning in this chapter (and the previous one), let's turn our attention to the SQL facilities through which you can protect your information. In the next chapter, we'll discuss privileges and security and how these apply to users.

Chapter

14

Privileges, Users, and Security

14.1 | Introduction

The very nature of databases—consolidating data into a logically cohesive group that many different applications and users can access—gives rise to the potential for security problems. Although the physical capability may exist, for example, for all end users throughout an organization to access all forms of organizational data through the DBMS, there are likely many cases where certain users should not have one or more types of access privileges. For example,

- Only certain employees should be able to change movie and CD prices.
- Customers using the customer assistance subsystem should never have access to our business functions (e.g., sales, payroll).
- Only managerial personnel should be able to access employee information, and only corporate management should be able to update that information.
- Customers may browse movie titles and corresponding sales and rental prices, but should not be able to see our purchase prices.

SQL provides you with the capability to *protect,* or control access to, various types of database objects, including

- tables
- columns

- views
- domains
- character sets
- collations
- translations
- triggers
- SQL-invoked routines
- user-defined types

The first three types of objects had security attributes in SQL-89, while domains, character sets, collations, and translations have security properties that were new to SQL-92. In SQL:1999, there are still more new objects with security implications, including triggers (see Chapter 11, "Active Databases"), SQL-invoked routines (see Chapter 17, "Routines and Routine Invocation (Functions and Procedures)"), and user-defined types (distinct types are discussed in Chapter 2, "Introduction to SQL:1999," while structured types are discussed in Volume 2 of this book). SQL:1999 provides this sort of protection for all schema objects defined by the language.

Security properties have evolved greatly since SQL-86 and even since SQL-92. There are nine kinds of protection in SQL:1999, which we have described in Table 14-1.

Table 14-1 *SQL:1999 Security Properties*

Kinds of Protection	Privilege	Applies To
Seeing	SELECT	Tables, columns, SQL-invoked methods*
Creating	INSERT	Tables, columns
Modifying	UPDATE	Tables, columns
Deleting	DELETE	Tables
Referencing	REFERENCES	Tables, columns
Using	USAGE	Domains, user-defined types, character sets, collations, translations
Activating	TRIGGER	Tables
Executing	EXECUTE	SQL-invoked routines
*Subtyping**	UNDER	Structured types

* Subtyping is an operation applicable only to SQL:1999's structured types, and the SELECT privilege applied to SQL-invoked methods are relevant only for those structured types, which are covered in Volume 2 of this book.

In SQL-86, your databases required protections from the actions of *seeing*, *creating*, *modifying*, and *deleting*. In SQL-89, when referential integrity was added to the standard, you needed a privilege to control *referencing* (corresponding to referential integrity REFERENCES use, as well as to other constraints), and *using* (corresponding to using domains, character sets, collations, and translations—and, new to SQL:1999, user-defined types). In SQL:1999, you can also control the execution of SQL-invoked routines and the creation of triggers on your tables.

The general philosophy in SQL is to hide information about schema objects from users who don't have any privileges to use those objects. For example, if there were a table named EMPS_TO_BE_FIRED, knowledge of its existence would probably upset current employees. Therefore, you want the same error to be returned from SELECT * FROM EMPOLYEES (if no table with that misspelled name exists) as from SELECT * FROM EMPS_TO_EE_FIRED when you don't have any privileges on EMPS_TO_BE_FIRED. If you returned "No such table" from one and "No privileges on table" from the other, you will have admitted that such a table exists, which raises a security issue. Consequently, SQL:1999 says, "Either no such table exists or you have no privilege on the table" (or words to that effect).

In Chapter 5, "Values, Basic Functions, and Expressions," we introduced the idea of users and authorization identifiers (authIDs). Recall that the authIDs are a sort of surrogate for your users: it's the only way that a user is known to an SQL database system. Privileges are granted to users, represented by authIDs (and, as you will read in section 14.2.1, subsection "Roles," to roles that are in turn granted to users). Privileges, once granted, could never be revoked in SQL-89; in SQL-92 that capability was added and, naturally, SQL:1999 continues to support it. There's also the concept of PUBLIC, which is a sort of pseudo-authID that identifies every authID that is now known to the DBMS or ever will become known to the DBMS. You can grant privileges to PUBLIC just as you can to an individual user. In our earlier example, if you wanted to allow everyone interested in accessing a terminal in your video store to browse the list of movies in stock, you would probably grant the *seeing* (SELECT) privilege to PUBLIC on the appropriate table or tables. You'll learn how to grant and revoke privileges in sections 14.2.1 (subsection "Creating and Destroying Roles") and 14.7, "REVOKE" and we merely mention here that doing so requires use of the GRANT and REVOKE statements.

In the SQL model, the creator of an object is always the owner of that object (and, as we mentioned briefly in Chapter 4, "Basic Data Definition Language (DDL)," that creator/owner can be either a user identifier or a role name). The owner has every possible privilege on the object, with one exception that we'll discuss later in section 14.6, "Other Rules." (Briefly, the owner of a view has privileges that are limited by the privileges he or she has on the table(s) that underlie the view.) The owner of an object can grant some (or all) privileges on that object to other users. If the owner wishes to relinquish a certain level of control, he can grant the privilege in a way that permits his grantee to grant the privilege to still other users, either with or without the ability for *them* to pass the privilege on.

The ability to pass a privilege onto others is called the *with grant option,* which we will discuss fully in section 14.4. You may be wondering about privileges with respect to the DDL operations we discussed in Chapter 4, "Basic Data Definition Language (DDL)" (CREATE, ALTER, and DROP). The rules in SQL:1999 with respect to these are as follows:

1. You can perform any DDL operations in a schema that *you own.*
2. You cannot perform any DDL operations in a schema that you don't own.
3. No one else can perform any DDL operations in any schema that you own (just clarifying the point directly above).
4. And finally, you *cannot* override these rules.

Most SQL products do, however, provide some sort of facility by which you can override these restrictions, by giving others permission to perform DDL operations within schemas you own; but the capabilities and syntax among these products vary widely. For purposes of the standard, however, the rules stated above apply.

14.2 | Users and Roles

Now that we've introduced the notion of security in your SQL databases and briefly discussed the various components involved—authorization identifiers, privileges, and protected objects—let's delve a bit deeper into the details.

14.2.1 The SQL Security Model

SQL has always had a security model, of course. It's just that it wasn't clearly recognized and fully specified until SQL-92, and SQL:1999 has further enhanced that model with the addition of roles. One unfortunate by-product of that fact is that a number of variations on the model have been implemented.[1] Happily, though, the various products available in the marketplace don't vary from one another in this area nearly as much as in some others.

---

1   One popular interface to SQL database systems (Microsoft's ODBC, an implementation of the SQL/CLI that we discuss in Chapter 19, "Call-Level Interface") provides SQLSTATE values that specifically identify the fact that certain objects do not exist when an SQL statement attempts to access those objects. A determined application could use those exception codes to detect the existence of tables like EMPS_TO_BE_FIRED. This is widely considered to be a serious security violation, which we believe to be an artifact of the poor understanding of security models in general and SQL's in particular.

Let's look now at the major issues involved in the security model of SQL:1999.

User Identifiers

In Chapter 5, "Values, Basic Functions, and Expressions," and in section 14.1, you learned that an SQL database user is identified by an authorization identifier, which we often abbreviate as "authID." In some implementations, of course, the database authID may be identical to the operating system login ID, but that's a product decision and has nothing to do with the SQL standard.[2] SQL:1999 defines an authID to be constructed just like any other identifier, up to 128 characters in length (and limited to 18 characters in length if only Core SQL conformance is claimed). However, many products, especially those that run on some variant of Unix or Linux, further limit authIDs to 8 characters in length (because that's the length of operating system login IDs).

SQL:1999 does not specify how authIDs are created. (More precisely, SQL:1999 does not say how valid *user* identifiers are created. An authorization identifier in SQL:1999 can be either a user identifier or a role name, and role names are explicitly created, as we'll discuss in section 14.2.1, subsection "Creating and Destroying Roles.") They might be created through some nonstandard SQL statement that enters a user identifier into some system information table (similar to the Definition Schema tables that we discuss in Chapter 22, "Information Schema"), or they might be created dynamically every time some new user starts accessing the database for the first time. But SQL:1999 keeps track of every authID known to the system, meaning every authID for which some privilege exists. And there is a very standard way for those *privileges* to come into existence: they are granted by the system to a schema owner when that owner creates an object in that schema, and they are explicitly granted by an authID who has a privilege and permission to further grant that privilege.

In SQL-92, all authorization identifiers were user identifiers, so the term *authID* was unambiguous. In SQL:1999, as you'll learn in section 14.2.1, subsection "Roles," there is a second type of authorization identifier: a role name. Throughout this book, we often have no need to distinguish between the two types of authorization identifier, so the term *authID* will be used in the generic sense of "either a user identifier or a role name, whichever is appropriate." On those occasions, especially in this chapter, when we need to distinguish, we will use the term *user identifier* to describe an authorization identifier that identifies an individual user and the term *role name* to describe an authorization identifier that identifies a role.

---

2 In fact, SQL:1999 makes it quite clear that the relationship between database authorization identifiers and operation system login IDs is determined entirely by the implementations.

In section 14.2.1, subsection "Using User Authorization Identifiers and Role Names," we provide additional discussion about the use of authorization identifiers in SQL:1999.

Roles

If our music and video operation happens to be a very large one, we might have several hundred employees, and we'd expect a very high turnover rate, with employees frequently leaving and others being hired. A large number of those employees would probably be categorized as "sales clerks" and would all require precisely the same set of privileges. If we had to individually grant a complex set of privileges to each newly hired sales clerk, and individually revoke them from departing clerks, it could easily require hiring a full-time administrative employee to handle just that task—hardly the sort of efficiency that the new economy demands.

SQL:1999 enhances the SQL-92 privilege capabilities by adding the ability to create a different sort of identity, called a *role*. In essence, a role is an identifier to which you can grant privileges but that never exists by itself. Instead, you grant roles to specific authIDs, and those authIDs are then able to operate as though the role's privileges had been granted to them.

Instead, we can streamline the process by evaluating the set of privileges required by sales clerks, creating a role (SALES_CLERK, for example) and granting exactly those privileges to that role, then merely granting the role to new sales clerks and revoking only that role from departing clerks.

SQL:1999 makes administration of database security even more flexible and efficient by allowing you to grant roles to other roles. This would allow you, for example, to define several categories of sales clerk—video clerks, music clerks, register clerks—and grant each of those roles the specific privileges required by their tasks, then grant to a different role (SALES_CLERK) additional privileges required by all clerks. The SALES_CLERK role could then be granted to VIDEO_CLERK, MUSIC_CLERK, and REGISTER_CLERK.

You'll find more information about the use of roles in SQL:1999, including an example to illustrate their benefits, in the subsection "Using Roles to Simplify Security Administration."

Using User Authorization Identifiers and Role Names

At any instant, a given SQL-session is associated with a user identifier called the *SQL-session user identifier*, and with a role name called the *SQL-session role name*. Under many conditions, the privileges associated with these values are used to determine whether or not various operations are allowed during the SQL-session.

How an authID becomes the SQL-session user identifier is one of those things left unspecified by SQL:1999—unless the SQL-session was started through the use of the CONNECT statement (see Chapter 16, "Connections and Remote Database Access"). (In that case, the authID is specified as a parameter of the CONNECT statement that starts the SQL-session.) The SQL-session user identifier might be the same as the operating system login identifier of the user, or it might be a separately assigned identifier assigned by security personnel in an organization. In general, it is the authID of the user that started the SQL-session, although SQL:1999 makes provisions for implementations that permit you to change your SQL-session user identifier using the SET SESSION AUTHORIZATION statement (see section 14.5). The special value SESSION_USER, discussed in section 5.5, "Special Values," always identifies the SQL-session user identifier. (If your implementation uses your operating system login identifier as your SQL-session user identifier, then the same value is returned by the special value SYSTEM_USER.)

When your SQL-session starts, your SQL-session user identifier is also the *current user identifier*, because nothing has occurred (yet) to override the SQL-session user identifier with a different user identifier. The special value CURRENT_USER can be used to learn the value of the current user identifier.

SQL-sessions also have a *current role name*, whose value can be determined using the special value CURRENT_ROLE. When an SQL-session is created, the current role name is the null value, which implies "no current role is assigned." When an SQL-session begins, the (null) SQL-session role name is the *current role name*.

But there are several activities that can override the SQL-session user identifier and/or the SQL-session role name. When one of these activities takes place, it specifies either a user identifier or a role name. If a user identifier is specified, then there is an implicit role name that is the null value; with few exceptions, if a role name is specified, then there is an implicit user identifier that is the null value. (One of the activities that can change the SQL-session role name without setting the current user identifier to the null value is the successful execution of the SET ROLE statement, which is discussed in section 14.5 "Changing User Identifiers and Role Names.") The privileges that are available when performing various operations during the SQL-session (called the *current privileges*) are determined by combining the privileges associated with the current user identifier with the privileges associated with the current role name.

At all times, either the current user identifier or the current role name—whichever one is not null—is used as the *current authorization identifier*. (If neither one is null, then the current user identifier effectively becomes the current authorization identifier.) The current authorization identifier is used as the authorization identifier that creates and owns all schemas and schema objects created while that authorization identifier is current, which is how schemas and their contained objects can be owned by roles instead of by individual users.

Most of your SQL statements (other than those that you execute using interactive SQL) will be written in embedded SQL or in module language. In both of these environments, you may specify an authorization identifier called the *SQL-client module authorization identifier* (remember that an embedded SQL program is described in the SQL standard as though it were translated to an SQL-client module). Embedded SQL programs and SQL-client modules can specify either a user name (called the *SQL-client module user name*) or a role name (the *SQL-client module role name*). Since a given module or embedded SQL program can specify only one of these, either the SQL-client module user name has a value and the SQL-client module role name is the null value, or vice versa.

The SQL-client module authorization identifier can be omitted entirely, in which case the SQL-client module is commonly called an *invoker's rights module,* meaning that the statements in the module or embedded SQL program are executed using the privileges available to the SQL-session authorization identifier. If there is an explicit SQL-client module authorization identifier, then the privileges associated with that authID govern execution of statements in the module or embedded SQL program, and the module is called a *definer's rights module.* Analogously, the externally invoked procedures contained in an invoker's rights module are called *invoker's rights routines,* and those contained in a definer's rights module are called *definer's rights routines.*

When you invoke stored routines—more properly called *SQL-invoked routines* (discussed in Chapter 17, "Routines and Routine Invocation (Functions and Procedures)")—yet another type of authorization identifier, the *routine authorization identifier,* gets involved. For SQL routines (those written in SQL), the routine authorization identifier is always the authorization identifier that owns the schema in which the routine is stored. For external routines (those written in another programming langauge), the authorization identifier has several possible sources, depending on the syntax used when the external routine was defined:

- If EXTERNAL SECURITY DEFINER was specified, then the routine is a definer's rights routine and its routine authorization identifier is the same as the SQL-client module authorization identifier of the SQL-client module in which the external routine is defined.

- If EXTERNAL SECURITY INVOKER was specified, then the routine is an invoker's rights routine and the effective routine authorization identifier will be the current authorization identifier whenever the routine is executed.

- If EXTERNAL SECURITY IMPLEMENTATION DEFINED is specified (or if no EXTERNAL SECURITY clause is specified at all), then the implementation decides whether the routine is an invoker's rights routine or a definer's rights routine and what the routine authorization identifier is.

(In fact, the situation for SQL-invoked routines is slightly more complicated than we've shown, because invocation of an SQL-invoked routine actually creates a brand-new SQL session with a brand-new authorization stack; see the following subsection for information about authorization stacks. However, the effect on the current authorization identifiers is as we've described here, even though we've chosen not to discuss those new SQL-sessions at this point.)

Whichever of those authIDs—the SQL-session user identifier, the SQL-client module authorization identifier, or the routine authorization identifier[3]—is in control at any instant is the authID whose privileges may be used to determine whether specific operations are allowed or prohibited. Similarly, whichever of those role names is in control is the role name whose privileges may be used to determine whether those operations are allowed. The name applied to the user identifier in control is the *current user identifier*. If the current user identifier is null, then the *current role name* cannot be null and it is used to determine the privileges of operations being performed. The *current authorization identifier* is whichever—the current user identifier or the current role name—is not null. The current authorization identifier is used to determine the privileges of the operations being performed in the SQL-session.

The SQL-Session Authorization Stacks

The preceding couple of sections gave you a lot of information, which might seem a little overwhelming. In this section, though, we'll show you just how all of those facilities are used to help you make your databases more secure.

As you read at the end of the previous subsection, the privileges under which specific operations execute are determined by either the current user identifier or the current role name. Those two values are established by several possible ways:

- By implementation-defined means when an SQL-session is started without using the CONNECT statement
- By the use of a CONNECT statement that specifies an authID
- By the specification of an authID or role name in the text of your SQL-client modules or embedded SQL programs that you invoke during your SQL-session

---

3 If SQL/PSM's SQL-server modules ("stored modules") are supported, then a third level of authorization identifier must be considered, too: the *SQL-server module authorization identifier*. The SQL-server module authorization identifier is always the authorization identifier that owns the schema in which the SQL-server module resides. Therefore, all SQL routines contained in an SQL-server module are invoker's rights routines. You can learn more about SQL-server modules in Jim Melton's *Understanding SQL's Stored Procedures—A Complete Guide to SQL/PSM* (San Francisco Morgan Kaufmann Publishers, 1998).

- By the invocation of an SQL-invoked routine (an SQL routine or an external routine that is or is not contained in an SQL-server module)

With several possibilities from which to choose, you probably won't be surprised to learn that they can interact with one another. Consider the following scenario: You start an SQL-session and the system sets the current user identifier to be your operating system login ID; because there is no current role name (that is, it is the null value), the current user identifier is also the current authorization identifier. You next invoke an embedded SQL program that specifies an explicit SQL-client module authorization identifier that is a role name, which naturally becomes the current role name—and the current authorization identifier—while executing the statements in that program (overriding the previous current user identifier). One of those embedded SQL statements calls a stored procedure that is stored in a schema owned by some user identifier that thus becomes the current authorization identifier while the statements in that stored procedure are executed.

As you might imagine, when the stored procedure returns to your embedded SQL program, the SQL-client module authorization identifier (a role name) once again becomes the current authorization identifier, and the termination of that embedded SQL program restores your operating system login ID as the current authorization identifier for the SQL-session.

In Figure 14-1, you see a visual representation of the scenario we've just outlined. We've labeled the information "Authorization Stack," and most of you will recognize our description of how the current user identifier and current role name are managed using a last-in/first-out process as just that—a stack. When an SQL-session is initiated, the stack is completely empty, but the SQL-session user identifier is immediately placed onto the stack as the current user identifier, while the current role name is set to the null value. The current authorization identifier is whichever of those two at the "top" of the stack is not null. In this case, the current authorization identifier is 'Jim'.

In our scenario above, when the embedded SQL program is run, its SQL-client module authorization identifier is placed onto the stack as the current authorization identifier, temporarily hiding the original authorization identifier that we discussed in the preceding paragraph. Because the embedded SQL program in this scenario specified a role name and not a user identifier, the current role name in that new stack entry is set to the specified value and the current user identifier is set to the null value. At this point, the current authorization identifier is 'Alan'.

If the embedded SQL program had specified a user identifier and not a role name, then the new stack entry would have a non-null user identifier and a null role name. Please note that this is a new stack entry, so that null role name is not "the same" null that is already in the previous stack entry.

Authorization Stack	
AuthID	**Role Name**
—	—
Stephen	*(null)*
(null)	Alan
Jim	*(null)*

Stored Procedure

Embedded SQL

Operating System Login

Figure 14-1 SQL-Session User Identifier and Role Stacks

Our scenario's next step involves the invocation of a stored procedure stored in a schema owned by a user identifier, so that user identifier is pushed onto the stack, obscuring the most recent current user identifier, while the current role name is set to the null value. During execution of the stored procedure, the current authorization identifier is 'Stephen'. (Although it does not affect the scenario we're describing here, we feel that thoroughness demands that we remind you that invocation of the stored procedure, an SQL-invoked routine, creates a new SQL-session and thus a new authorization stack. The effect of this new SQL-session and new authorization stack would be relevant only if the stored procedure somehow caused the invocation of a SET SESSION AUTHORIZATION statement that changed the values of the entries on that stack; see section 14.5.1 for additional information.)

As we return from the stored procedure into the embedded SQL program, we merely "pop the stack" by throwing away the top entry of the stack, revealing the entry just below it. That gives us the SQL-client module authorization identifier ('Alan') as our current authorization identifier again. When the embedded SQL program completes, the stack gets popped one more time, revealing our original SQL-session user identifier, 'Jim'! Not too terribly complicated, we think, and a bit elegant.

We realize that many users of SQL database systems are accustomed to the notion of user identifiers and intuitively think about the system's behaviors as though the assigned user identifier is the sole determinant of the applicable privileges for every operation. Life isn't that simple, and neither is SQL:1999. Instead, as we've indicated in this section, the privileges applied to the operations performed during an SQL-session are either the privileges granted to the current user identifier or the privileges granted to the current role and the privileges granted to all roles granted (directly or indirectly) to the current user identifier or to the current role.

As we indicated earlier in "Using Authorization Identifiers and Role Names," every SQL-session (other than those initiated with a CONNECT statement) starts off with a current user identifier that is determined in some implementation-defined way. We believe that most implementations derive that current user identifier either from your operating system login ID or from an ID specified when you start using the database. Every SQL-session also begins with a current role name that is the null value.

How, one might well ask, can the current role name ever become non-null? Furthermore, one might ask how the current user identifier can ever become null! As you will learn in section 14.5.2, the SET ROLE statement is one way in which you can set the current user identifier to a non-null role name. But there are other ways, too, one of which was illustrated in Figure 14-1: execution of an embedded SQL program (or, equivalently, invocation of an externally invoked procedure in an SQL-client module) that specifies an AUTHORIZATION clause containing a role name instead of a user identifier. Another way is to invoke an SQL-invoked routine whose routine authorization identifier (that is, the owner of the schema in which it resides) is a role name instead of a user identifier.

Using Roles to Simplify Security Administration

Earlier we promised you an example illustrating the benefits of roles. If, as we suggested in that section, we have a large number of employees who are all sales clerks, but some of them specialize in DVD sales, some in CD sales, and some in cash register operations, there will undoubtedly be some privilege requirements in common and some differences.

One way of dealing with that situation is to simply grant and revoke all necessary privileges for every employee as they are hired, fired, and reassigned. In a large enterprise, that can be extremely time-consuming and quite error prone.

A better way of managing privileges in this sort of environment is to create SQL roles for each category of job, then assign the roles to individual employees as required. By doing so, you not only have to enter fewer SQL statements, but you have a much better chance of getting it right.

Figure 14-2 shows a collection of roles that might be useful when designing the privilege structure for our music and video shop.

Creating and Destroying Roles

Unlike user identifiers, for which SQL:1999 provides no standardized creation and destruction mechanisms, SQL does provide explicit statements for creating and destroying roles.

Syntax 14-1 provides the syntax for creating roles. As you'd expect, this statement requires that you provide the name of the role to be created. Naturally, SQL prohibits the creation of a role whose name is the same as any authorization identifier already known to the system.

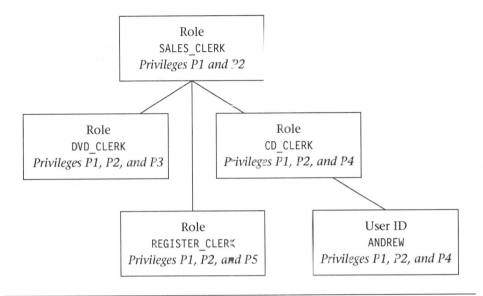

Figure 14-2 Useful Roles in Our Music and Video Store

Syntax 14-1 *CREATE ROLE Syntax*

```
CREATE ROLE role-name
  [ WITH ADMIN { CURRENT_USER | CURRENT_ROLE } ]
```

When you create a role, the system automatically grants that role to you; furthermore, you are granted that role WITH ADMIN OPTION, which means that you are allowed to administer the role by granting it to others. (We'll discuss administering roles a bit more in section 14.4.)

But just what is meant by "you"? The most obvious answer is "the user authorization identifier by which you are known to the system," but that answer isn't quite right. In fact, "you" means "the current user identifier," but even that isn't complete. After all, there might also be a (non-null) current role name, in which case "you" means "either the current user identifier or the current role name." If one of them is null, then the answer's pretty obvious: the non-null alternative. But if they're both non-null, then the CREATE ROLE statement allows you to choose which of the two alternatives will be recorded as the owner of the role.

Therefore, if you specify WITH ADMIN CURRENT_USER, then the current user identifier is granted the role WITH ADMIN OPTION; if you specify WITH ADMIN CURRENT_ROLE, then the current role name is granted the role WITH ADMIN OPTION. If you don't specify WITH ADMIN at all, then the system will grant the role to the current user identifier if it's not null; if it is null, then the system grants the role to the current role name.

The privileges necessary to be able to execute the CREATE ROLE statement are defined by the implementation. For example, an SQL:1999 product might permit only database administrators to create new roles.

When you no longer need a particular role, you can destroy it using the DROP ROLE statement seen in Syntax 14-2.

Syntax 14-2 *DROP ROLE Syntax*

```
DROP ROLE role-name
```

Obviously, if you are not the owner of a role (by which we mean "if neither the current user identifier, the current role, nor any roles assigned to the current role were the creators of the role specified"), then you cannot destroy that role. Dropping a role first causes it to be revoked from all holders of the role.

14.3 | GRANT

As we told you in Section 14.2.1, subsection "Using Roles to Simplify Security Administration," there are often advantages in granting privileges to roles and then granting those roles to users. As a result, SQL:1999 supports two forms of the GRANT statement: one form grants privileges to users or to roles, while the other form grants roles to users or to other roles. Let's first look at granting privileges.

14.3.1 Granting Privileges

In order to give a privilege on some object that you own (or for which you have a grantable privilege) to some other authID, you use the GRANT statement. The format of the GRANT statement (for granting privileges) is shown in Syntax 14-3.

Syntax 14-3 *Syntax of GRANT Statement for Privileges*

```
GRANT privilege-list
  ON privilege-object
TO user-list [ WITH GRANT OPTION ]
  [ GRANTED BY { CURRENT_USER | CURRENT_ROLE } ]
```

The SQL:1999 privilege list is shown in Syntax 14-4.

Syntax 14-4 *Privilege-List Syntax*

```
privilege [ , privilege ]...
| ALL PRIVILEGES
```

The syntax for privilege is shown in Syntax 14-5.

Syntax 14-5 *Privilege Syntax*

```
  SELECT [ ( column-name [ , column-name ]... ) ]
| SELECT ( method-designator [ , method-designator ]... )
| DELETE
| INSERT [ ( column-name [ , column-name ]... ) ]
| UPDATE [ ( column-name [ , column-name ]... ) ]
| REFERENCES [ ( column-name [ , column-name ]... ) ]
| USAGE
| TRIGGER
| UNDER
| EXECUTE
```

The syntax for privilege-object is defined in Syntax 14-6.

Syntax 14-6 *Privilege-Object Syntax*

```
  [ TABLE ] table-name
| DOMAIN domain-name
| CHARACTER SET character-set-name
| COLLATION collation-name
| TRANSLATION translation-name
| TYPE user-defined-type-name
| specific-routine-designator
```

Finally, the user-list syntax is given in Syntax 14-7.

Syntax 14-7 *User-List Syntax*

```
  authID [ , authID ]...
| PUBLIC
```

In Syntax 14-5, the alternative UNDER is applicable only for SQL:1999's structured types and is discussed in Volume 2 of this book. The same is true in Syntax 14-6 of the TYPE alternative.

We also note that the authIDs in Syntax 14-7 can be either user authorization identifiers or role names. This allows us to grant privileges not only directly to users, but also to roles.

Several rules apply to the usage of the privileges. You can only use INSERT, UPDATE, SELECT, DELETE, TRIGGER, and REFERENCES if the object is a table (if TABLE is not specified, then a table-name is assumed). Correspondingly, you can only use USAGE if the object is a domain, character set, collation, translation, or user-defined type. If you list more than one privilege, all of the privileges that you specify are granted to the user or users, but *only* if you have the privilege and the right to grant it to others (which we cover in section 14.4, "WITH GRANT OPTION and WITH ADMIN OPTION"). If you don't actually have one or more of the privileges specified or if you don't have the right to grant it to others, you'll get an error on the GRANT statement.

In a single GRANT statement, you can only grant privileges on a single object, but (if the object is a table) you can grant different privileges on the same or different columns of the table. For SELECT, INSERT, UPDATE, and REFERENCES, the statement will grant the privilege to every column in the table if you don't specify a column-name. (For the effects of granting SELECT privileges on an SQL-invoked method instead of on a column, we refer you to Volume 2 of this book.)

If you don't specify WITH GRANT OPTION, then the privilege cannot be passed on to other users by the user(s) to whom you are granting the privilege. If you do use the optional WITH GRANT OPTION, you have given permission for the user(s) to whom you are granting the privilege to pass it on to other users. You should note that you might have the right to grant the privilege to others, but not the right to give those others the right to make further grants.

Specifying the GRANTED BY clause allows you to make it explicit whether the privileges that you grant are recorded with the current user identifier as the grantor or with the current role name as the grantor.

There's also something unique about granting privileges in SQL at the table level (as opposed to the column level). Granting the privilege SELECT, INSERT, UPDATE, or REFERENCES on a table not only means "grant it on every column currently defined in the table," but it also means "grant it on every column added to the table in the future." This way, DDL modifications in the future that may add columns to a table definition don't require any overt action on your part to maintain your defined security model. Column-level SELECT privileges are new to SQL:1999 and are not yet widely implemented.

A user identifier can be granted any number of privileges and can be granted any number of roles. When that user identifier is the current user identifier of an SQL-session, then the privileges used to determine whether or not certain actions are valid are

- the user identifier's privileges
- the privileges that have been granted to the roles that have been granted to the user identifier

Actually, that second bullet is evaluated recursively, so that the system seeks out all roles that have been granted to the roles that have been granted to the user identifier, and all roles that have been granted to them, and so forth.

14.3.2 Granting Roles

Now, let's take a look at the SQL:1999 statement that lets us grant roles to users or to other roles. The syntax of this variant of the GRANT statement is seen in Syntax 14-8.

Syntax 14-8 *Syntax of GRANT ROLE Statement*

```
GRANT role-name [ { , role-name }... ]
  TO user-list
  [ WITH ADMIN OPTION ]
  [ GRANTED BY { CURRENT_USER | CURRENT_ROLE } ]
```

You will immediately notice that this statement grants any number of roles to every one of a list of grantees (this is the same user-list that appeared in Syntax 14-7). Those grantees can be user identifiers or other role names. As with granting privileges, you can grant only those roles that have been granted to you WITH ADMIN OPTION. If you have been granted a particular role, but without the ADMIN OPTION, then you cannot grant that role to any other user identifier or role name. Of course, only those roles that you grant WITH ADMIN OPTION can later be granted to others by your grantees.

Analogous to granting privileges, specifying the GRANTED BY clause when granting roles allows you to make it explicit whether the roles that you grant are recorded with the current user identifier as the grantor or with the current role name as the grantor.

A role name can be granted any number of privileges and any number of roles. When a role name is the current role name of an SQL-session, then the privileges granted to the current role name, as well as the privileges granted to all role names granted to the current role name (evaluated recursively as we explained for privileges in section 14.3.2) are used to determine the validity of various operations.

Incidentally, we're often asked why GRANT ROLE has the ADMIN OPTION, while the ordinary GRANT statement for privileges has the GRANT OPTION instead. We don't know of any compelling reason for this difference, but we believe that the designers of SQL's role capabilities merely wanted to highlight the fact that granting a role to an authID might grant a great many privileges in one operation.

14.3.3 Basic Viewing Privileges

With that theory under our belts, let's take a look at some examples of the various SQL:1999 privileges.

To GRANT viewing privileges for a table to a selected user or group of users, you would code something like this:

```
GRANT SELECT
  ON employees
TO STORE_MGR;
```

This GRANT statement will grant the SELECT privilege on the employees table to the user who has the authID STORE_MGR (or to the role named STORE_MGR).

14.3.4 Deletion Privileges with Further GRANT Permission

To GRANT deletion privileges on another table to another user or user group, you could issue this:

```
GRANT DELETE
  ON transactions
TO AUDIT_MGR
WITH GRANT OPTION;
```

This statement will allow the user AUDIT_MGR to delete rows from the transactions table; it will also allow that user to grant the same privilege to other users (by virtue of WITH GRANT OPTION).

14.3.5 Update Privileges on a Specific Column

```
GRANT UPDATE ( current_rental_price )
  ON movie_titles
TO STORE_MGR;
```

The above allows STORE_MGR to update the current_rental_price column of the movie_titles table but no other columns within that table.

14.3.6 Insertion Privileges

```
GRANT INSERT
  ON movie_titles
TO BUYER;
```

This statement gives BUYER the ability to insert new rows into the movie_titles table and to specify values for every column of that table. If the statement was written as

```
GRANT INSERT ( title, current_rental_price )
  ON movie_titles
TO ASST_MGR;
```

then the user known as ASST_MGR would be allowed to insert new rows into the movie_titles table but would be permitted to specify a value only for the title and current_rental_price columns; all other columns would be set to their default values (if they have one) or to null (if they have no default and are nullable).

14.3.7 PUBLIC Access and Privileges on VIEWS

Suppose you issue the following statement:

```
GRANT SELECT
  ON movie_titles
TO PUBLIC;
```

This statement will permit *anyone* to look at the movie_titles table, including customers using in-store Help/Browse terminals. However, the movie_titles table probably has sensitive information that you don't want the public to see. Therefore, you'd normally define a view (called, say movie_information) that selects the relevant information (perhaps the title, rating, current rental and sale prices, and a line of summary), then grant the SELECT privilege on that view rather than on the base table, as follows:

```
GRANT SELECT
  ON movie_information
TO PUBLIC;
```

Alternatively, you could use SQL:1999's ability to grant the SELECT privilege on selected columns only:

```
GRANT SELECT
  ON movie_titles ( title, year_released, part_of_series, movie_type,
                    current_tape_sale_price, current_dvd_sale_price )
TO PUBLIC;
```

thereby preventing the general public from seeing the information in columns such as our_tape_cost and our_dvd_cost.

14.3.8 REFERENCES

You'll recall the MOVIES_STARS table that we introduced in Chapter 3, "Basic Table Creation and Data Manipulation" (or take a look back at Example 3-2, "Creating the MOVIES_STARS Table"). Remember also that our MOVIE_TITLES table contains the names of movies as well as price and accounting-related information. Of course, we want the movies mentioned in the MOVIES_STARS table to be coordinated with data from the MOVIE_TITLES table, so we defined a FOREIGN KEY on the MOVIE_TITLE column (of MOVIES_STARS) to point to the MOVIE_TITLES table (see Chapter 10, "Constraints, Assertions, and Referential Integrity," for a review of FOREIGN KEYS, particularly Example 10-18, "Using Both PRIMARY KEY and FOREIGN KEY Constraints Together").

In general, you don't want just anybody defining FOREIGN KEY constraints to your tables. Why? Well, for two reasons: First, and most important, you can't modify or delete referenced rows in your own table without affecting rows in the referencing table, which a FOREIGN KEY constraint might prohibit by specifying NO ACTION or RESTRICT. Second, relevant to your ability to manage your own tables, the existence of a constraint that references one of your tables means that you will not be able to DROP that table without at the same time DROPping the FOREIGN KEY constraint in the referencing table that references the table being dropped. (See section 14.3.11, "USAGE," for additional information about this second reason for requiring such privileges.)

To control references to your tables by the definers of tables that may wish to have FOREIGN KEYs to your table, you should grant only authorized users that privilege:

```
GRANT REFERENCES (title)
  ON movie_titles
TO REVIEWER;
```

This statement will permit REVIEWER to define another table (or tables) that have FOREIGN KEY references to the movies_titles table.

Let's look at a slightly different example. Suppose your distributor provides you with advanced information about movies coming out on video over the next few months, but only on the condition that you not release the information to anyone. You honor that agreement by storing all the information about those movies in another table named UPCOMING_MOVIES and granting no privileges to anyone. You certainly wouldn't want one of your clerks, or customers, writing a table like this:

```
CREATE TABLE what_movies (
    title CHARACTER (30) REFERENCES upcoming_movies
);
```

All that clerk would then have to do is INSERT a bunch of rows into his table and wait to see which ones succeeded and which ones failed. That way, he or she would have gotten the title information just as surely as if he'd had SELECT privilege on the UPCOMING_MOVIES table. However, if a special privilege is required to define the REFERENCES (foreign key) attribute, then your clerk would be unable to ferret out that particular information.

14.3.9 Constraints and Privileges

Similarly, you have to have REFERENCES privilege to define a constraint that is based on information stored in a table. Suppose you defined a table using this CREATE TABLE statement:

```
CREATE TABLE dummy (
    low_val    INTEGER,
    high_val   INTEGER,
    CHECK ( ( SELECT salary
              FROM employees
              WHERE title = 'President' )
        BETWEEN low_val AND high_val )
)
```

By repeatedly inserting rows with different values for the `low_val` and `high_val` columns until an `INSERT` succeeded, someone could determine the salary of the company's president! A similar invasive query could determine salaries of co-workers, a supervisor, or others. To prevent this type of situation, SQL:1999 requires that you have the `REFERENCES` privilege on the `employees` table (alternatively, on the `salary` column of that table) in order to define such a constraint.

14.3.10 TRIGGER

A `TRIGGER` privilege on a table allows the owner of that privilege to create a trigger with that table as the subject table (see Chapter 11, "Active Databases," to refresh your memory of triggers). Just as you need to control the creation of `REFERENCES` to your tables, you also need to govern the creation of `triggers` on your tables.

As you will have recognized from information in section 14.1, the `TRIGGER` privilege is the key to this kind of control. Any user to whom you grant the `TRIGGER` privilege on one of your tables is then able to create a trigger using that table as the subject table. It's interesting to note that a trigger and its subject table do not have to reside in the same schema—which is just as well, because that would mean that only the owner of a table could define triggers on it (since only a schema owner can create objects, including triggers, in that schema).

14.3.11 USAGE

For one principal reason, a user has to have the `USAGE` privilege to use a domain to define a column. There aren't any security implications in using domains, but there are implications related to `DROP`ping the domain. Remember (from Chapter 4, "Basic Data Definition Language (DDL)") that you could either say

```
DROP DOMAIN domain-name CASCADE
```

or

```
DROP DOMAIN domain-name RESTRICT
```

The `RESTRICT` option, as you recall, means "if there are any columns that are based on this domain, give me an error and do not actually drop the domain." Unlike other objects, however, the `CASCADE` option on `DROP DOMAIN` means that the attributes of the domain (data type, default value, constraints, and collation) are transferred to the column directly. If the column already had a default value, however, the column default supersedes the domain's default value and is thus not transferred to the column.

This process will not drop columns or destroy data, but it could cause views to be dropped if the view definition contains a CAST that references the domain being dropped; similarly a constraint or assertion with such a CAST would be dropped. By selectively granting USAGE privilege on your domains, you can control who is allowed to use (or even see) them and therefore limit the inconvenience (to you and to others) that dropping your domain might cause. In organizations (unlike our simple video and music chain) where you have hundreds of applications developers using your SQL:1999 environment and corresponding DBMS products, such control can be invaluable during the software development and maintenance phases.

The situation is exactly the same for character sets, collations, and translations. Only those users to whom you grant USAGE privilege on those objects can see them and use them in their data definitions or in their SQL programs. For this reason, if you revoke the USAGE privilege on a character set from a user who has used that character set to define a column of a table, the column defined on that character set will automatically be dropped. While this sounds pretty harsh, if the character set no longer exists, the data in the column is meaningless—that is, it's not interpretable except as collections of bits.

14.3.12 EXECUTE

The EXECUTE privilege controls who can invoke SQL-invoked routines that you have created. You'll read about SQL-invoked routines in Chapter 17, "Routines and Routine Invocation (Functions and Procedures)," but that chapter does not discuss the privileges required to invoke such routines.

There are at least a couple of reasons for limiting the users who are allowed to invoke routines that you've written. Of course, if a view definition or constraint belonging to another user happened to invoke an SQL-invoked function you've written, then it would be more difficult for you to DROP or replace that function. In addition, you may write routines that perform operations that security demands must be prohibited from most users, such as changing sales prices of DVDs and CDs. If those routines are properly protected, then only authorized users are able to invoke them.

14.3.13 UNDER

The UNDER privilege, as we said back in section 14.1, is relevant only for SQL:1999's structured types, which are covered in Volume 2 of this book.

14.3.14 ALL PRIVILEGES

The special syntax ALL PRIVILEGES is used as a sort of shorthand. It translates to

- a list of privileges that includes . . .
- every privilege on the specified object . . .
- on which the user executing the GRANT has a grantable privilege.

For example, suppose you have SELECT privilege on movie_titles WITH GRANT OPTION and DELETE privilege on movie_titles, but without GRANT OPTION. If you execute the statement

```
GRANT ALL PRIVILEGES
  ON movie_titles
TO USER2
```

then USER2 will end up with SELECT privilege on movie_titles but will not get the DELETE privilege.

14.4 | WITH GRANT OPTION and WITH ADMIN OPTION

Several times in this chapter, we've mentioned that, when granting privileges or roles to another user or role, you can optionally choose to grant that other user or role the ability to further grant the privilege or role to yet another user or role.

If you are attempting to grant privileges, then you must have the authority to grant those privileges. That authority has two components to it:

- You must have the privilege that you are trying to grant, either because the system granted it to you when you created the object to which the privilege is relevant, or because it was granted to you by another user who had the authority to do so.
- You must have been given the privilege WITH GRANT OPTION.

When you grant a privilege for which you have the appropriate authority, you can choose to grant it without the GRANT OPTION (but SQL:1999 does not provide syntax, such as WITHOUT GRANT OPTION, for this default case). In that case, the recipient of the grant is not able to grant the privilege to anyone else.

Alternatively, you can grant the privilege WITH GRANT OPTION, which means that the grantee is able to make further grants without getting additional permission from you. (Of course, if you revoke the privilege from a grantee who has made further grants of that privilege, it is automatically revoked from everyone who received those further grants. We'll have more to say about this in sections 14.7 and 14.8.)

The analogous situation holds for granting roles. In order to grant a role, you must have the authority to grant that role. This authority also has two components:

- You must have the role that you are trying to grant, either because the system granted it to you when you created the role (using CREATE ROLE), or because it was granted to you by another user who had the authority to do so.
- You must have been given the role WITH ADMIN OPTION.

When you grant a role for which you have the appropriate authority, you can choose to grant it without the ADMIN OPTION (SQL:1999 does not provide syntax, such as WITHOUT ADMIN OPTION, for this default case, either). In that case, the recipient of the grant is not able to grant the role to anyone else. Alternatively, you can grant the role WITH ADMIN OPTION, which means that the grantee is able to make further grants without getting additional permission from you. (As with privileges, revoking the role from a grantee who has made further grants of the role means that the role is revoked from all subsequent grantees, too.)

14.5 | Changing User Identifiers and Role Names

SQL:1999 provides statements that allow you to change the current user identifier and current role name of an SQL-session.

14.5.1 SET SESSION AUTHORIZATION Statement

The statement that is used to change the current user identifier of an SQL-session is the SET SESSION AUTHORIZATION statement, whose syntax is seen in Syntax 14-9.

Syntax 14-9 *Syntax of SET SESSION AUTHORIZATION Statement*

```
SET SESSION AUTHORIZATION value-specification
```

The value-specification, like any value-specification, can be an SQL literal, a host variable or host parameter, or one of the "special values" such as CURRENT_ USER, SESSION_USER, or CURRENT_ROLE. If you use an SQL literal or a host variable or parameter, then it must have a character string type; if the specified value does not satisfy the requirements of a user identifier, then you'll get an error.

In fact, even if the value does satisfy the requirements of a user identifier, and it actually specifies a known user identifier, you may still get an error. The implementation is allowed to decide whether the current user identifier is permitted to change the SQL-session to provide a new user identifier at all; if it does permit a change, it may also limit the possible new user identifiers in whatever way it deems appropriate.

Therefore, while the DVD department supervisor might have the authority to execute a SET SESSION AUTHORIZATION to a user identifier for one of his direct reports, it's unlikely he would have the authority to execute the same statement and specify a value that identifies the user identifier for the company president. On the other hand, it's unlikely that a temporary loading dock worker would have the authority to change user identifiers to any value, for any reason.

If you (and, as before, "you" must be interpreted to mean "the SQL-session's current user identifier and/or the current role name") are allowed to successfully execute a SET SESSION AUTHORIZATION statement, then the user identifier component of every entry on the SQL-session authorization stack (see section 14.2.1, subsection "The SQL-Session Authorization Stacks") is changed to that new user identifier, eliminating all record of other user identifiers that may have been known during the SQL-session. What's more, the role name of every entry on the SQL-session authorization stack is set to the null value, effectively wiping out any known current role names for the SQL-session.

One more thing: If there's a transaction in progress, you won't be allowed to change the SQL-session's user identifier. After all, whose privileges would be used for executing triggers, evaluating deferred constraints, and so forth, if the user identifier for the SQL-session changed during the transaction?

14.5.2 SET ROLE Statement

If you want to change the current role name of your SQL-session, then you'll use the SET ROLE statement, whose syntax appears in Syntax 14-10.

Syntax 14-10 *Syntax of SET ROLE Statement*

```
SET ROLE { value-specification | NONE }
```

The restrictions on executing the SET ROLE statement are quite similar to the restrictions on executing the SET SESSION AUTHORIZATION statement. The most important difference is that you (in this case, "you" means "the current user identifier") are always allowed to execute a SET ROLE statement that specifies a role that has been granted to you or to PUBLIC; furthermore, you are always allowed to execute a SET ROLE NONE.

The primary difference in the behavior of the SET ROLE statement (compared with the SET SESSION AUTHORIZATION statement) is that the SET ROLE statement only changes the SQL-session's current role name and does not affect any other entry on the SQL-session authorization stack. Naturally, SET ROLE NONE sets the current role name to the null value.

14.6 Other Rules

If you grant a privilege to a user and then, inadvertently or on purpose, grant the identical privilege to the same user, you have defined what we call a *redundant duplicate privilege*. There is no additional effect because the redundant grant is ignored. That way, you don't have to worry about revoking several times just in case you accidentally granted several times. If you grant the privilege once with GRANT OPTION and once without (in either order but without an intervening REVOKE), the actual privilege that the user has is the one that includes the GRANT OPTION.

If you execute a GRANT statement with one or more privileges and you don't have any of those privileges (or you don't have any of them WITH GRANT OPTION), then you'll get an error. If you try to grant more than one privilege and you have at least one of them WITH GRANT OPTION but you don't have all of them (or you don't have all of them WITH GRANT OPTION), you'll get a warning and the privileges that you do have WITH GRANT OPTION are granted.

When you create a view (via the CREATE VIEW statement), special rules take care of the privileges you get on that view. For most schema objects (such as tables or domains), when you create the object, you *automatically* get every possible privilege on that object, and you get the privileges WITH GRANT OPTION. Views, however, are different. Because you may have created your view to correspond to rows in someone else's base tables (or even other views), the privileges you get on the view have to be based on the privileges that you have on those base tables or views.

For example, you will get the SELECT privilege on your view, but it will be WITH GRANT OPTION *only* if you have the SELECT privilege WITH GRANT OPTION on *each and every* table (base tables and views) that underlies the view. If you don't have the SELECT privilege on every underlying table, you can't even create the view. Similarly, you can get the INSERT, UPDATE, DELETE, and REFERENCES privileges on the view (and the columns of the view) only if you have those privileges on the underlying tables (and the corresponding underlying columns). Again, those privileges will be given to you WITH GRANT OPTION only if you hold them WITH GRANT OPTION on the underlying tables and columns.

Now, we have to consider what happens if you have created some view *V* that depends on some table *T* on which you have only some privileges but on which you are subsequently granted additional privileges. SQL:1999 carefully defines how additional privileges are granted to you on your view *V* to properly reflect your augmented privileges on the underlying table *T*. That is, the privileges are adjusted so that they end up just as they would have been if you had created your view after you were granted the additional privileges (see Figure 14-3).

14.7 | REVOKE

Like granting, revoking has two possibilities: revoking privileges and revoking roles. The two have much in common, but there are some differences that we explore in this section.

14.7.1 Revoking Privileges

After granting privileges, you sometimes have to consider revoking those privileges. For example, some user may no longer need to access data in one of your tables, so you will wish to withdraw the privilege that user had to access that table. Or perhaps some user leaves the company and must not be allowed any access at all. The REVOKE statement is used to take privileges away from users and roles, as well as to take roles away from users and roles. The format of the REVOKE statement used to revoke privileges is very similar to the GRANT statement that grants privileges, as seen in Syntax 14-11.

Syntax 14-11 *Syntax of REVOKE Privileges Statement*

```
REVOKE [ GRANT OPTION FOR ] privilege-list
  ON privilege-object
FROM user-list
[ GRANTED BY { CURRENT_USER | CURRENT_ROLE } ]
{ RESTRICT | CASCADE }
```

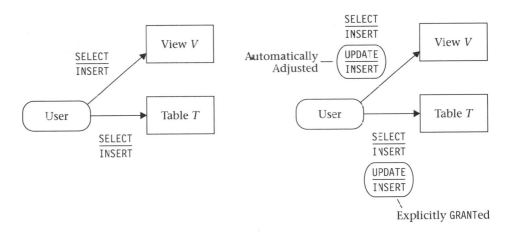

Figure 14-3   Adjusted Privileges for SQL:1999 Views

As you would expect, the various syntax components (privilege list, privilege object, and user list) have the same definitions that they have in Syntax 14-4, Syntax 14-6, and Syntax 14-7, respectively.

The major difference is the additional RESTRICT or CASCADE keyword, one of which is required (by the standard, at least; current products vary greatly in this area). If you use RESTRICT, the system will check to see if the privilege that you granted was passed on to other users (obviously, this is possible only if you granted the privilege WITH GRANT OPTION). If so, you will get an error message and the privilege will not be revoked; if not, the privilege will be revoked. If you use CASCADE, the privilege will be revoked, as will any *dependent* privileges that were granted as a result of your grant. A dependent privilege is one that could not exist if the privilege that you're trying to revoke was never granted, which is the state of events you are trying to achieve as a result of your REVOKE statement.

Another significant difference is the optional GRANT OPTION FOR clause. If you specify that clause, the actual privilege itself is not revoked but the GRANT OPTION is revoked. Of course, if the GRANT OPTION is taken away, you want the grant situation to be set to a state as though the GRANT OPTION never existed. Therefore, if you specify both GRANT OPTION FOR and CASCADE, then all grants that depend on that GRANT OPTION are revoked implicitly. If you specify GRANT OPTION FOR and RESTRICT and there are dependent privileges, you'll get an error.

The other significant difference is the optional GRANTED BY clause. If you specify that clause, you must specify either CURRENT_USER or CURRENT_ROLE. Only privileges that were granted by the current user identifier or the current role name, respectively, will be considered for revocation.

If none of the privileges that you are trying to revoke actually exists, you'll get an error; if some of them exist, but not all of them, then you'll get a warning instead. There may be situations in which you revoke a privilege from a user only to find out later that the privilege is still held by that user. This can happen when something like the following has been done:

```
(you)   GRANT SELECT ON movie_titles TO USER1 WITH GRANT OPTION;
(USER1) GRANT SELECT ON movie_titles TO USER2;
(you)   GRANT SELECT ON movie_titles TO USER2;
```

At this point, USER2 has the SELECT privilege from two sources, you and USER1. If you then execute

```
REVOKE SELECT
  ON movie_titles
FROM USER2 drop-behavior;
```

you'll find that USER2 still is able to SELECT data from movie_titles (regardless of whether we specified RESTRICT or CASCADE). Why? Simply because USER1 also granted the privilege. On the other hand, if you had executed

```
REVOKE SELECT
  ON movie_titles
FROM USER2 drop-behavior;

REVOKE SELECT
  ON movie_titles
FROM USER1 CASCADE;
```

then both USER1 and USER2 would lose their SELECT privilege on movie_titles. (That is, you have to revoke both the privilege that you granted directly to USER2 *and* the privilege that you granted to USER1 in order for USER2 to lose the ability to retrieve data from movie_titles.) This example shows that privileges can get rather complicated. In fact, graph theory (which, alas, has nothing to do with computer graphics) is used in the SQL:1999 standard to describe the effects of GRANT and REVOKE statements.

Recall that we said earlier that granting a privilege on a table implicitly grants the same privilege on every column of the table, as well as on every column that would ever be added to the table in the future. An interesting side effect of this is that you can grant some privilege, say UPDATE, on a table (thereby granting that privilege on every column of the table) and then revoke that privilege from one or more columns of the table without inhibiting the granting of that privilege to any new columns later added to the table.

However, this analogy does not apply to granting privileges to PUBLIC. While the failure to specify a column list in a GRANT (or REVOKE) statement is, in one way, the same as specifying a `column list` that contains every column of the table (and, though it's clearly impossible without a better crystal ball than we have at home, every column ever to be added to the table), a grant to PUBLIC is *not* the same as granting individually to every user and to every user that will ever be known to the system. The difference is that a sequence like

```
GRANT SELECT
  ON movie_titles
TO PUBLIC;

REVOKE SELECT
  ON movie_titles
FROM USER1 drop-behavior;
```

will get an error (unless, of course, you have also explicitly granted SELECT on movie_titles to USER1 in another statement). That's because USER1 does not have the SELECT privilege—PUBLIC does. USER1 is a member of PUBLIC, of course, and therefore can issue SELECT statements that select from the movie_titles table, but USER1 does not have the privilege himself or herself, and you cannot therefore take it away without taking it away from PUBLIC.

14.7.2 Revoking Roles

As we said in section 14.7.1, there are considerable similarities in SQL:1999's REVOKE statement used for revoking privileges and the variant used for revoking roles, but there are some differences, as you immediately notice in Syntax 14-12.

Syntax 14-12 *Syntax of REVOKE Roles Statement*

```
REVOKE [ ADMIN OPTION FOR ] role-name [ { , role-name }... ]
FROM user-list
[ GRANTED BY { CURRENT_USER | CURRENT_ROLE } ]
{ RESTRICT | CASCADE }
```

The similarities are obvious, so let's look at the differences for a moment.

First, we're dropping roles instead of privileges, so we specify a list of (one or more) role names instead of privileges. Next, role grants use WITH ADMIN OPTION instead of WITH GRANT OPTION, so we can choose to revoke the ADMIN OPTION only (instead of revoking the role itself).

Except for those two differences, the REVOKE role statement behaves very much like the REVOKE privilege statement.

14.8 | Additional Details of REVOKE

At first glance, the REVOKE statement really seems pretty straightforward. After all, it is only supposed to eliminate privileges that already exist and leave the privilege structure of the database just as it would have been if the privileges had never been granted. In fact, the entire database has to be restored to the condition it would have had if the privileges had never been granted. Unfortunately, doing that is a bit more complicated than you might think. The complications are due largely, although not wholly, to the existence of WITH GRANT OPTION (or analogously, WITH ADMIN OPTION).

Let's have a look at an example to understand what goes on. Suppose that we have only two tables in our schema: MOVIE_TITLES and MOVIES_STARS. Both of these tables are in a schema named PRODUCTION, which is owned by the authID SCREEN_TUNES. By the very act of having created these two tables, we have created the many privileges shown in Table 14-2.

Table 14-2 *Privileges Already Granted*

Grantor	*Grantee*	*Privilege*	*With Grant Option?*
_SYSTEM*	SCREEN_TUNES	SELECT ON movie_titles	Yes
_SYSTEM	SCREEN_TUNES	SELECT ON movie_titles (title)	Yes
_SYSTEM	SCREEN_TUNES	SELECT ON movie_titles (our_cost)	Yes
_SYSTEM	SCREEN_TUNES	SELECT ON movie_titles (...)†	Yes
_SYSTEM	SCREEN_TUNES	SELECT ON movie_titles (current_rental_price)	Yes
_SYSTEM	SCREEN_TUNES	INSERT ON movie_titles	Yes
_SYSTEM	SCREEN_TUNES	INSERT ON movie_titles (title)	Yes
_SYSTEM	SCREEN_TUNES	INSERT ON movie_titles (our_cost)	Yes
_SYSTEM	SCREEN_TUNES	INSERT ON movie_titles (...)	Yes
_SYSTEM	SCREEN_TUNES	INSERT ON movie_titles (current_rental_price)	Yes
_SYSTEM	SCREEN_TUNES	UPDATE ON movie_titles	Yes
_SYSTEM	SCREEN_TUNES	UPDATE ON movie_titles (title)	Yes
_SYSTEM	SCREEN_TUNES	UPDATE ON movie_titles (our_cost)	Yes
_SYSTEM	SCREEN_TUNES	UPDATE ON movie_titles (...)	Yes
_SYSTEM	SCREEN_TUNES	UPDATE ON movie_titles (current_rental_price)	Yes
_SYSTEM	SCREEN_TUNES	DELETE ON movie_titles	Yes
_SYSTEM	SCREEN_TUNES	REFERENCES ON movie_titles	Yes
_SYSTEM	SCREEN_TUNES	REFERENCES ON movie_titles (title)	Yes
_SYSTEM	SCREEN_TUNES	REFERENCES ON movie_titles (our_cost)	Yes

(Continued)

Grantor	Grantee	Privilege	With Grant Option?
_SYSTEM	SCREEN_TUNES	REFERENCES ON movie_titles (. . .)	Yes
_SYSTEM	SCREEN_TUNES	REFERENCES ON movie_titles (current_rental_price)	Yes
_SYSTEM	SCREEN_TUNES	SELECT ON movies_stars	Yes
_SYSTEM	SCREEN_TUNES	SELECT ON movies_stars (movie_title)	Yes
_SYSTEM	SCREEN_TUNES	SELECT ON movies_stars (actor_first_name)	Yes
_SYSTEM	SCREEN_TUNES	SELECT ON movies_stars (actor_last_name)	Yes
_SYSTEM	SCREEN_TUNES	INSERT ON movies_stars	Yes
_SYSTEM	SCREEN_TUNES	INSERT ON movies_stars (movie_title)	Yes
_SYSTEM	SCREEN_TUNES	INSERT ON movies_stars (actor_first_name)	Yes
_SYSTEM	SCREEN_TUNES	INSERT ON movies_stars (actor_last_name)	Yes
_SYSTEM	SCREEN_TUNES	UPDATE ON movies_stars	Yes
_SYSTEM	SCREEN_TUNES	UPDATE ON movies_stars (movie_title)	Yes
_SYSTEM	SCREEN_TUNES	UPDATE ON movies_stars (actor_first_name)	Yes
_SYSTEM	SCREEN_TUNES	UPDATE ON movies_stars (actor_last_name)	Yes
_SYSTEM	SCREEN_TUNES	DELETE ON movies_stars	Yes
_SYSTEM	SCREEN_TUNES	REFERENCES ON movies_stars	Yes
_SYSTEM	SCREEN_TUNES	REFERENCES ON movies_stars (movie_title)	Yes
_SYSTEM	SCREEN_TUNES	REFERENCES ON movies_stars (actor_first_name)	Yes
_SYSTEM	SCREEN_TUNES	REFERENCES ON movies_stars (actor_last_name)	Yes

* In SQL:1999, privileges granted by "the system" to the owner of a schema object are recorded as having been granted by the "special grantor value _SYSTEM."

† In Tables 14-2, 14-3, and 14-4, we use the notation "(. . .)" to indicate "the other columns of the table."

Now, to allow our employees the ability to execute SQL statements necessary to do their jobs, we give each of them the privileges required. Let's assume that we (under the authID SCREEN_TUNES) have granted the privileges shown in Example 14-1.

Example 14-1 *A series of GRANT statements*

```
GRANT SELECT ON movie_titles TO manager WITH GRANT OPTION ;
GRANT SELECT ON movies_stars TO manager WITH GRANT OPTION ;
GRANT UPDATE ON movie_titles TO manager ;
GRANT UPDATE ON movies_stars TO manager ;
GRANT UPDATE (current_rental_price) ON movie_titles TO asst_manager ;
GRANT DELETE ON movie_titles to manager ;
GRANT DELETE ON movies_stars to manager ;
```

Table 14-3 illustrates what the privilege list looks like after these grants.

Table 14-3 *Privileges after GRANT Statements*

Grantor	Grantee	Privilege	With Grant Option?	
_SYSTEM	SCREEN_TUNES	SELECT ON movie_titles	Yes	
_SYSTEM	SCREEN_TUNES	SELECT ON movie_titles (title)	Yes	
_SYSTEM	SCREEN_TUNES	SELECT ON movie_titles (our_cost)	Yes	→ Ⓐ
_SYSTEM	SCREEN_TUNES	SELECT ON movie_titles (…)	Yes	
_SYSTEM	SCREEN_TUNES	SELECT ON movie_titles (current_rental_price)	Yes	
_SYSTEM	SCREEN_TUNES	INSERT ON movie_titles	Yes	
_SYSTEM	SCREEN_TUNES	INSERT ON movie_titles (title)	Yes	
_SYSTEM	SCREEN_TUNES	INSERT ON movie_titles (our_cost)	Yes	
_SYSTEM	SCREEN_TUNES	INSERT ON movie_titles (…)	Yes	
_SYSTEM	SCREEN_TUNES	INSERT ON movie_titles (current_rental_price)	Yes	
_SYSTEM	SCREEN_TUNES	UPDATE ON movie_titles	Yes	
_SYSTEM	SCREEN_TUNES	UPDATE ON movie_titles (title)	Yes	
_SYSTEM	SCREEN_TUNES	UPDATE ON movie_titles (our_cost)	Yes	→ Ⓔ
_SYSTEM	SCREEN_TUNES	UPDATE ON movie_titles (…)	Yes	
_SYSTEM	SCREEN_TUNES	UPDATE ON movie_titles (current_rental_price)	Yes	→ Ⓑ
_SYSTEM	SCREEN_TUNES	DELETE ON movie_titles	Yes	→ Ⓒ
_SYSTEM	SCREEN_TUNES	REFERENCES ON movie_titles	Yes	
_SYSTEM	SCREEN_TUNES	REFERENCES ON movie_titles (title)	Yes	
_SYSTEM	SCREEN_TUNES	REFERENCES ON movie_titles (our_cost)	Yes	
_SYSTEM	SCREEN_TUNES	REFERENCES ON movie_titles (…)	Yes	
_SYSTEM	SCREEN_TUNES	REFERENCES ON movie_titles (current_rental_price)	Yes	
_SYSTEM	SCREEN_TUNES	SELECT ON movies_stars	Yes	
_SYSTEM	SCREEN_TUNES	SELECT ON movies_stars (movie_title)	Yes	→ Ⓕ
_SYSTEM	SCREEN_TUNES	SELECT ON movies_stars (actor_first_name)	Yes	
_SYSTEM	SCREEN_TUNES	SELECT ON movies_stars (actor_last_name)	Yes	
_SYSTEM	SCREEN_TUNES	INSERT ON movies_stars	Yes	
_SYSTEM	SCREEN_TUNES	INSERT ON movies_stars (movie_title)	Yes	
_SYSTEM	SCREEN_TUNES	INSERT ON movies_stars (actor_first_name)	Yes	
_SYSTEM	SCREEN_TUNES	INSERT ON movies_stars (actor_last_name)	Yes	
_SYSTEM	SCREEN_TUNES	UPDATE ON movies_stars	Yes	
_SYSTEM	SCREEN_TUNES	UPDATE ON movies_stars (movie_title)	Yes	→ Ⓖ
_SYSTEM	SCREEN_TUNES	UPDATE ON movies_stars (actor_first_name)	Yes	
_SYSTEM	SCREEN_TUNES	UPDATE ON movies_stars (actor_last_name)	Yes	
_SYSTEM	SCREEN_TUNES	DELETE ON movies_stars	Yes	→ Ⓓ
_SYSTEM	SCREEN_TUNES	REFERENCES ON movies_stars	Yes	
_SYSTEM	SCREEN_TUNES	REFERENCES ON movies_stars (movie_title)	Yes	
_SYSTEM	SCREEN_TUNES	REFERENCES ON movies_stars (actor_first_name)	Yes	
_SYSTEM	SCREEN_TUNES	REFERENCES ON movies_stars (actor_last_name)	Yes	

(Continued)

	Grantor	Grantee	Privilege	With Grant Option?
	SCREEN_TUNES	manager	SELECT ON movie_titles	Yes
	SCREEN_TUNES	manager	SELECT ON movie_titles (title)	Yes
(A)	SCREEN_TUNES	manager	SELECT ON movie_titles (our_cost)	Yes
	SCREEN_TUNES	manager	SELECT ON movie_titles (...)	Yes
	SCREEN_TUNES	manager	SELECT ON movie_titles (current_rental_price)	Yes
	SCREEN_TUNES	manager	SELECT ON movies_stars	Yes
(F)	SCREEN_TUNES	manager	SELECT ON movies_stars (movie_title)	Yes
	SCREEN_TUNES	manager	SELECT ON movies_stars (actor_first_name)	Yes
	SCREEN_TUNES	manager	SELECT ON movies_stars (actor_last_name)	Yes
	SCREEN_TUNES	manager	UPDATE ON movie_titles	No
	SCREEN_TUNES	manager	UPDATE ON movie_titles (title)	No
(E)	SCREEN_TUNES	manager	UPDATE ON movie_titles (our_cost)	No
	SCREEN_TUNES	manager	UPDATE ON movie_titles (...)	No
	SCREEN_TUNES	manager	UPDATE ON movie_titles (current_rental_price)	No
	SCREEN_TUNES	manager	UPDATE ON movies_stars	No
(G)	SCREEN_TUNES	manager	UPDATE ON movies_stars (movie_title)	No
	SCREEN_TUNES	manager	UPDATE ON movies_stars (actor_first_name)	No
	SCREEN_TUNES	manager	UPDATE ON movies_stars (actor_last_name)	No
(B)	SCREEN_TUNES	asst_manager	UPDATE ON movie_titles (current_rental_price)	No
(C)	SCREEN_TUNES	manager	DELETE ON movie_titles	No
(D)	SCREEN_TUNES	manager	DELETE ON movies_stars	No

About now, our store manager discovers that she'd like to allow customers to browse the MOVIE_TITLES table, but only to see the titles, the current rental price, and the current sales price. To do this, she creates a view in the MANAGER schema:

```
CREATE VIEW customer_movies AS
SELECT title, current_rental_price, current_sales_price
FROM movie_titles
```

and then grants a privilege that makes this view usable by the general public:

```
GRANT SELECT ON customer_movies TO PUBLIC ;
```

Let's further assume that our manager decides to pass on the ability to SELECT from the MOVIE_TITLES table to the assistant manager and to the sales clerks.

```
GRANT SELECT ON movie_titles TO asst_manager, sales_clerk ;
```

At this point, the privilege graph (remember, we warned you that this involved graph theory!) has expanded to look like Table 14-4.

Table 14-4 *Final Privilege Graph (continued on next page)*

Grantor	Grantee	Privilege	With Grant Option?	
_SYSTEM	SCREEN_TUNES	SELECT ON movie_titles	Yes	
_SYSTEM	SCREEN_TUNES	SELECT ON movie_titles (title)	Yes	
_SYSTEM	SCREEN_TUNES	SELECT ON movie_titles (our_cost)	Yes	→(A)
_SYSTEM	SCREEN_TUNES	SELECT ON movie_titles (. . .)	Yes	
_SYSTEM	SCREEN_TUNES	SELECT ON movie_titles (current_rental_price)	Yes	
_SYSTEM	SCREEN_TUNES	INSERT ON movie_titles	Yes	
_SYSTEM	SCREEN_TUNES	INSERT ON movie_titles (title)	Yes	
_SYSTEM	SCREEN_TUNES	INSERT ON movie_titles (our_cost)	Yes	
_SYSTEM	SCREEN_TUNES	INSERT ON movie_titles (...)	Yes	
_SYSTEM	SCREEN_TUNES	INSERT ON movie_titles (current_rental_price)	Yes	
_SYSTEM	SCREEN_TUNES	UPDATE ON movie_titles	Yes	
_SYSTEM	SCREEN_TUNES	UPDATE ON movie_titles (title)	Yes	
_SYSTEM	SCREEN_TUNES	UPDATE ON movie_titles (our_cost)	Yes	→(E)
_SYSTEM	SCREEN_TUNES	UPDATE ON movie_titles (...)	Yes	
_SYSTEM	SCREEN_TUNES	UPDATE ON movie_titles (current_rental_price)	Yes	→(B)
_SYSTEM	SCREEN_TUNES	DELETE ON movie_titles	Yes	→(C)
_SYSTEM	SCREEN_TUNES	REFERENCES ON movie_titles	Yes	
_SYSTEM	SCREEN_TUNES	REFERENCES ON movie_titles (title)	Yes	
_SYSTEM	SCREEN_TUNES	REFERENCES ON movie_titles (our_cost)	Yes	
_SYSTEM	SCREEN_TUNES	REFERENCES ON movie_titles (...)	Yes	
_SYSTEM	SCREEN_TUNES	REFERENCES ON movie_titles (current_rental_price)	Yes	
_SYSTEM	SCREEN_TUNES	SELECT ON movies_stars	Yes	
_SYSTEM	SCREEN_TUNES	SELECT ON movies_stars (movie_title)	Yes	
_SYSTEM	SCREEN_TUNES	SELECT ON movies_stars (actor_first_name)	Yes	→(F)
_SYSTEM	SCREEN_TUNES	SELECT ON movies_stars (actor_last_name)	Yes	
_SYSTEM	SCREEN_TUNES	INSERT ON movies_stars	Yes	
_SYSTEM	SCREEN_TUNES	INSERT ON movies_stars (movie_title)	Yes	
_SYSTEM	SCREEN_TUNES	INSERT ON movies_stars (actor_first_name)	Yes	
_SYSTEM	SCREEN_TUNES	INSERT ON movies_stars (actor_last_name)	Yes	
_SYSTEM	SCREEN_TUNES	UPDATE ON movies_stars	Yes	
_SYSTEM	SCREEN_TUNES	UPDATE ON movies_stars (movie_title)	Yes	
_SYSTEM	SCREEN_TUNES	UPDATE ON movies_stars (actor_first_name)	Yes	→(G)
_SYSTEM	SCREEN_TUNES	UPDATE ON movies_stars (actor_last_name)	Yes	
_SYSTEM	SCREEN_TUNES	DELETE ON movies_stars	Yes	→(D)
_SYSTEM	SCREEN_TUNES	REFERENCES ON movies_stars	Yes	
_SYSTEM	SCREEN_TUNES	REFERENCES ON movies_stars (movie_title)	Yes	
_SYSTEM	SCREEN_TUNES	REFERENCES ON movies_stars (actor_first_name)	Yes	
_SYSTEM	SCREEN_TUNES	REFERENCES ON movies_stars (actor_last_name)	Yes	

(Continued)

SCREEN_TUNES	manager	SELECT ON movie_titles	Yes
SCREEN_TUNES	manager	SELECT ON movie_titles (title)	Yes
(A) SCREEN_TUNES	manager	SELECT ON movie_titles (our_cost)	Yes → (J)
SCREEN_TUNES	manager	SELECT ON movie_titles (...)	Yes → (I)
SCREEN_TUNES	manager	SELECT ON movie_titles (current_rental_price)	Yes
SCREEN_TUNES	manager	SELECT ON movies_stars	Yes
SCREEN_TUNES	manager	SELECT ON movies_stars (movie_title)	Yes
(F) SCREEN_TUNES	manager	SELECT ON movies_stars (actor_first_name)	Yes
SCREEN_TUNES	manager	SELECT ON movies_stars (actor_last_name)	Yes
SCREEN_TUNES	manager	UPDATE ON movie_titles	No
SCREEN_TUNES	manager	UPDATE ON movie_titles (title)	No
(E) SCREEN_TUNES	manager	UPDATE ON movie_titles (our_cost)	No
SCREEN_TUNES	manager	UPDATE ON movie_titles (...)	No
SCREEN_TUNES	manager	UPDATE ON movie_titles (current_rental_price)	No
SCREEN_TUNES	manager	UPDATE ON movies_stars	No
SCREEN_TUNES	manager	UPDATE ON movies_stars (movie_title)	No
(G) SCREEN_TUNES	manager	UPDATE ON movies_stars (actor_first_name)	No
SCREEN_TUNES	manager	UPDATE ON movies_stars (actor_last_name)	No
(B) SCREEN_TUNES	asst_manager	UPDATE ON movie_titles (current_rental_price)	No
(C) SCREEN_TUNES	manager	DELETE ON movie_titles	No
(D) SCREEN_TUNES	manager	DELETE ON movies_stars	No
_SYSTEM	manager	SELECT ON customer_movies	Yes
_SYSTEM	manager	SELECT ON customer_movies (title)	Yes → (H)
_SYSTEM	manager	SELECT ON customer_movies (current_rental_price)	Yes
_SYSTEM	manager	SELECT ON customer_movies (current_sale_price)	Yes
_SYSTEM	manager	UPDATE ON customer_movies	No
_SYSTEM	manager	UPDATE ON customer_movies (title)	No
_SYSTEM	manager	UPDATE ON customer_movies (current_rental_price)	No
_SYSTEM	manager	UPDATE ON customer_movies (current_sale_price)	No
_SYSTEM	manager	DELETE ON customer_movies	No
manager	PUBLIC	SELECT ON customer_movies	No
manager	PUBLIC	SELECT ON customer_movies (title)	No
(H) manager	PUBLIC	SELECT ON customer_movies (current_rental_price)	No
manager	PUBLIC	SELECT ON customer_movies (current_sale_price)	No
manager	asst_manager	SELECT ON movie_titles	No
manager	asst_manager	SELECT ON movie_titles (title)	No
(I) manager	asst_manager	SELECT ON movie_titles (our_cost)	No
manager	asst_manager	SELECT ON movie_titles (...)	No
manager	asst_manager	SELECT ON movie_titles (current_rental_price)	No
manager	sales_clerk	SELECT ON movie_titles	No
manager	sales_clerk	SELECT ON movie_titles (title)	No
(J) manager	sales_clerk	SELECT ON movie_titles (our_cost)	No
manager	sales_clerk	SELECT ON movie_titles (...)	No

You'll admit that this is a startlingly large number of privileges for such a small database environment (two tables, one view, three users, plus PUBLIC). Anyway, the arrows that are drawn between some of the privileges indicate *dependencies* in the privilege graph. Many of the privileges don't connect to any others, so they form isolated nodes in the graph; others form chains of privileges, as you see.

Now, let's see what happens when we issue the statement, using the authID SCREEN_TUNES.

```
REVOKE SELECT ON movie_titles FROM manager CASCADE;
```

We first determine a set of *identified* privileges. These will be those SELECT privileges granted by SCREEN_TUNES to MANAGER on MOVIE_TITLES (see Table 14-5). If the privilege were INSERT, UPDATE, or REFERENCES, we would include any privileges on the columns of MOVIE_TITLES as well. Clearly, this process identifies only the privilege shown in Table 14-5.

Table 14-5 *Identified Privileges*

Grantor	Grantee	Privilege	With Grant Option?
SCREEN_TUNES	manager	SELECT ON movie_titles	Yes

Next, we identify all privileges that were allowed to be created as a result of the identified privilege (or privileges). This means that the identified privilege had to have been granted WITH GRANT OPTION. It also means that we're looking for privileges whose grantor is the same as the grantee of any privilege in our identified list; furthermore, the privileges for which we're looking will be on the same object (the MOVIE_TITLES table in this case; it could also be on some column of the table) and will be for the same action (SELECT, in this case). This set of rules locates the two rows shown in Table 14-6.

Table 14-6 *Additional Privileges*

Grantor	Grantee	Privilege	With Grant Option?
manager	asst_manager	SELECT ON movie_titles	No
manager	sales_clerk	SELECT ON movie_titles	No

But this represents only *some* of the privileges that were allowed to be created by the identified descriptor. The others are view privileges (granted by the system to the owner of the view) that couldn't exist if we hadn't granted privileges to the view's owner. These privileges will have the system as a grantor and the same grantee as the identified privilege (MANAGER, in this case); they will also have the same action (SELECT) on some view (or a column of a view) owned by that grantor. These privileges are shown in Table 14-7.

Table 14-7 *View Privileges*

Grantor	Grantee	Privilege	With Grant Option?
_SYSTEM	manager	SELECT ON customer_movies	Yes

Now, we further identify any privileges that were allowed to be created by the existence of *this* privilege, which turns up the one shown in Table 14-8.

Table 14-8 *Additional Permitted Privileges*

Grantor	Grantee	Privilege	With Grant Option?
manager	PUBLIC	SELECT ON customer_movies	No

Next we find all privileges that were allowed to be created by this last one. In our case, there are none, so we can move on to the next step.

We say that all of those privileges that were allowed to be created by an identified privilege are *directly dependent on* the identified privilege. At this point, we can construct a *privilege dependency graph* where we draw arrows from any privilege that allows another privilege to exist (that is, to any directly dependent privileges). We don't care about any nodes (privileges) that aren't connected to anything else, unless they're one of our identified privileges. Such unconnected and unidentified privileges (call them *independent nodes*) will be unaffected by the statement, so we can ignore them (but not delete them from the privileges graph, because we're not revoking them!). Table 14-9 shows the results.

Table 14-9 *Dependent Privileges*

Grantor	Grantee	Privilege	With Grant Option?
SCREEN_TUNES	manager	SELECT ON movie_titles	Yes
manager	asst_manager	SELECT ON movie_titles	No
manager	sales_clerk	SELECT ON movie_titles	No
_SYSTEM	manager	SELECT ON customer_movies	Yes
manager	PUBLIC	SELECT ON customer_movies	No

Now, we finally have to check if any of those privileges were created in more than one way—that is, if they were granted once as a result of the privilege being revoked and another time by some other privilege still in effect. This is done by examining each node of the graph and seeing if it has two or more incoming arrows (*arcs* in graph theory). In our case, none of them does, so they're all okay. If any did, we'd drop them (and *their* dependent privileges) from our area of concern. In addition, we check to see if there are any privileges that are not independent nodes and that cannot be reached from any independent node except through one of the identified privilege descriptors or descriptors allowed to be created by them. If we had any of these (we don't), we'd call them *abandoned* descriptors.

Now that we've collected all this data, we can start getting rid of the privileges. We get rid of all abandoned privileges, all identified privileges, and all views that are named in an abandoned SELECT privilege.

Unfortunately, as complicated as this description is, it's not the whole story. In the interest of not terminally boring you, we've omitted details related to revoking only the GRANT OPTION FOR capability (as opposed to the actual privilege) and revocations that affect constraints, assertions, and domains. If you really want to know how revocation of privileges works in all its gory detail, we urge you to review the SQL:1999 standard itself (see Appendix D, "Relevant Standards Bodies," for information about ordering standards). However, the GRANT OPTION FOR capabilities are not widely implemented (yet, although we continue to hope for wider implementation), so our failure to provide this detailed information is unlikely to have significant effects on your ability to perform the tasks you need.

Before summarizing this chapter, we must emphasize something that might have gotten lost in the details above. Revoking privileges can cause data to be deleted, because tables (or character sets) that no longer have privileges to be accessed are considered by SQL to be meaningless and they are dropped, even though you may have planned to grant new privileges later. Be careful out there.

14.9 | Chapter Summary

On the surface, the SQL:1999 privilege model appears somewhat simplistic, with two basic statements (GRANT and REVOKE) and a minimal list of privileges. In reality, the combination of these facets with the WITH GRANT OPTION and the WITH ADMIN OPTION clause and other aspects give you a fair degree of power with respect to specifying and controlling access to your tables and their data. There are some limitations we mentioned with respect to DDL operations, but most SQL products feature extensions to overcome these restrictions.

Another consideration is that in real-life, complex information systems, there are other aspects of security and privileges that must be coordinated with those of your database. These include network security (e.g., distributed access control, authentication), operating system security, and the various permissions that deal with your CASE environments, along with other areas of your information systems. As you design and implement the security model for your SQL databases, you should also keep in mind how these facets relate to the similar security models elsewhere in your environment.

Chapter

15

Transaction Management

Introduction

We first discussed the concept of transactions in Chapter 2, "Getting Started with SQL:1999." In that chapter, we discovered what a transaction was and learned about some of the characteristics of transactions, such as the ACID properties:

- *Atomicity:* The "all-or-nothing" illusion that all operations within a transaction are performed, or none takes place

- *Consistency:* The transaction concept that permits programmers to declare consistency points and validate the correctness of incorporated transformations through application-supplied checks

- *Isolation:* The regulation that concurrent transactions have no effect on one another (except in some implementations, where some of the concurrent transactions may be "blocked" and therefore delayed or even forced to abort and restart)

- *Durability:* The condition that all updates of a transaction—that is, the new states of all objects—must be preserved, even in case of hardware or software failures

  In this chapter, we discuss how transactions are constructed and managed within SQL. We look at applicable statements, as well as at various phenomena and respective SQL:1999 isolation levels under which your database transactions may be managed.

15.2 SQL:1999 Transaction Syntax

In SQL-92, there was no explicit statement that starts a transaction as there is in SQL:1999 and in some database management systems. In SQL, you *explicitly* end a transaction by executing a COMMIT or ROLLBACK statement (SQL-89 required you to write COMMIT WORK and ROLLBACK WORK, but SQL-92 made the keyword WORK optional). Transactions are started *implicitly* whenever you execute a statement that needs the context of a transaction and no transaction is active. For example, a SELECT statement, an UPDATE statement, and a CREATE TABLE statement all require the context of a transaction. However, a CONNECT statement (see Chapter 16, "Connections and Remote Database Access") doesn't require that context and therefore doesn't implicitly start a transaction. And, of course, you can *explicitly* start a transaction using SQL:1999's START TRANSACTION statement, which we discuss in section 15.2.2.

15.2.1 SET TRANSACTION Statement

If you don't tell SQL anything different, a *default transaction* will be started. That default transaction has several important characteristics (see Figure 15-1). First, it will permit both read and update (including insert and delete) operations. Second, it will have the maximum possible isolation from other concurrent transactions. Finally, it will set up a diagnostics area (see Chapter 20, "Diagnostics and Error Management") with a default size.

If you don't like the defaults, or if you just want to use good programming practice and write your applications to be self-documenting so there are no questions later, you can use the SET TRANSACTION statement before you execute a transaction-initiating statement. This statement allows you to set attributes to different settings.

The syntax for the SET TRANSACTION statement is shown in Syntax 15-1.

Syntax 15-1 *Syntax of SET TRANSACTION Statement*

```
<set transaction statement> ::=
    SET [ LOCAL ] TRANSACTION <mode> [ , <mode> ]...
```

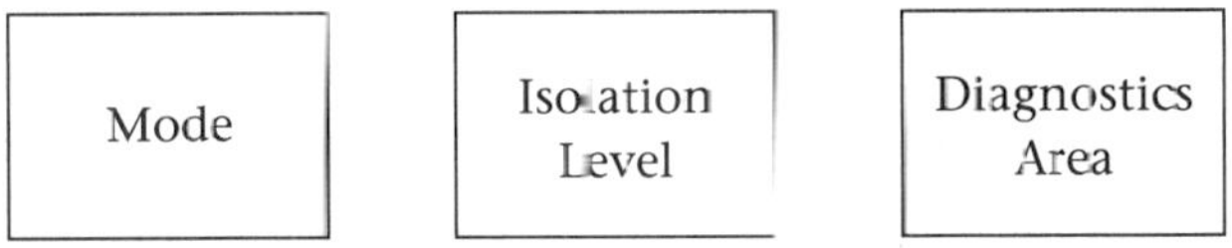

```
┌─────────────┐   ┌─────────────┐   ┌─────────────┐
│             │   │             │   │             │
│    Mode     │   │  Isolation  │   │ Diagnostics │
│             │   │    Level    │   │    Area     │
│             │   │             │   │             │
└─────────────┘   └─────────────┘   └─────────────┘
```

Figure 15-1   SQL Transaction Characteristics

```
<mode> ::=
    <isolation level>
  | <access mode>
  | <diagnostics size>

<isolation level> ::=
    READ UNCOMMITTED
  | READ COMMITTED
  | REPEATABLE READ
  | SERIALIZABLE

<access mode> ::=
    READ ONLY
  | READ WRITE

<diagnostics size> ::=
    DIAGNOSTICS SIZE <simple value specification>
```

The SET TRANSACTION statement cannot be executed when there is a transaction active; it is used only to set the modes for the *next* transaction that is initiated and therefore must be executed only "between" transactions (or before the first transaction is started in your SQL session). You are prohibited from specifying any of the three <mode> choices more than once in a single SET TRANSACTION statement, but you can execute multiple SET TRANSACTION statements at any time that there is no transaction active. As you see in Syntax 15-1, the <access mode> is either READ ONLY or READ WRITE. If you set READ ONLY, then you cannot execute any statements that will change the database (this includes UPDATE, INSERT, DELETE, and the schema definition and manipulation statements). If you specify DIAGNOSTICS SIZE, then you follow the keywords with an integer value (either a literal or a host variable or parameter) that specifies the size of the diagnostics area that you want (the value indicates the number of exception, warning, no data, and successful completion conditions that the diagnostics area can store for each SQL statement that you execute). If you don't specify <access

mode>, then the default is READ WRITE, unless you also specify an <isolation level> of READ UNCOMMITTED, in which case, the default <access mode> is READ ONLY. If you don't specify DIAGNOSTICS SIZE, then the implementation decides how large a diagnostics area to create.

The diagnostics area is populated when each SQL statement is executed. If that statement raised more conditions than the diagnostics area is configured to capture (because DIAGNOSTICS SIZE is smaller than the number of conditions raised), you should not assume that the diagnostics area will contain information about any specific set of those conditions. If, for example, you specified DIAGNOSTICS SIZE 10, but one of your SQL statements raised 15 conditions, you shouldn't assume that the diagnostics area will report the first 10 conditions reported—or the last 10. It's most likely that the 10 "most severe" will be reported; in fact, exception conditions have priority over completion conditions, warnings have priority over no data, which has priority over successful completion.

We'll discuss isolation levels in section 15.3, "START TRANSACTION Statement," but we'll tell you here that the default <isolation level>, if you don't specify one, is SERIALIZABLE; furthermore, you cannot specify an <isolation level> of READ UNCOMMITTED if you also specify an <access mode> of READ WRITE.

For example, we may issue the following statement:

```
SET TRANSACTION
  READ ONLY,
  ISOLATION LEVEL READ UNCOMMITTED,
  DIAGNOSTICS SIZE 4
```

This statement indicates that no updates will be permitted by SQL statements executed as part of this transaction (of course, other concurrent, independent transactions might make updates, which is a different issue); that the lowest level of isolation, READ UNCOMMITTED, will be present in the transaction; and that the diagnostics area will be of size 4.

Alternatively, you may issue the following:

```
SET TRANSACTION
  READ WRITE,
  ISOLATION LEVEL SERIALIZABLE,
  DIAGNOSTICS SIZE 10
```

This statement will permit updates during the transaction as well as inquiries, the highest level of isolation under SQL:1999, and a diagnostics area of size 10.

The SET TRANSACTION statement has one characteristic that is quite unexpected and traps many an unwary programmer: when you execute the SET TRANSACTION statement and specify only one or two of the <mode> choices, the values of the <mode> choice or choices that you didn't specify are automatically set to their default values, regardless of any previous SET TRANSACTION mode statement that you might have executed.

You probably noticed the optional keyword LOCAL in Syntax 15-1. That keyword was not available in SQL-92 but is supported in SQL:1999. SQL-92 allowed for the possibility of transactions that encompassed more than a single SQL database system; for example, multiple SQL database systems might participate in a single transaction, or some other transactional entity, such as a non-SQL database system, might participate in a transaction along with an SQL database system. It was presumed in SQL-92 that all participants in such "encompassing transactions" would have the same characteristics. SQL:1999 provides the ability to control the characteristics of a particular SQL database system's portion of such an encompassing transaction. As you have by now deduced, the LOCAL keyword allows you to specify the characteristics of the "local" SQL database system's transaction in an encompassing transaction. Of course, that means that the encompassing transaction in which your LOCAL transaction is to be a part must have already been initiated elsewhere (not at the SQL server on which the LOCAL branch is being started). Furthermore, the <mode>s that you use for the LOCAL branch must be compatible with the corresponding <mode>s of that encompassing transaction.

Unfortunately, that's about the only support that SQL:1999 provides for encompassing transactions. Everything else about them, including how you cause multiple transactional entities to participate in an encompassing transaction, is left to implementation-defined mechanisms. However, most SQL database systems use a specific interface, called the *XA* interface,[1] to support such participation.

15.2.2 START TRANSACTION Statement

Like the SET TRANSACTION statement, you cannot execute START TRANSACTION when a transaction is active. However, unlike SET TRANSACTION, START TRANSACTION actually initiates a transaction with the mode values that you specify, or that you allow to be defaulted by omitting them. Regardless of any SET TRANSACTION statement that you might have executed, the execution of a START TRANSACTION statement uses the mode value specified, or defaulted, in this statement alone.

---

1   ISO/IEC 14834:1996, *Information Technology—Distributed Transaction Processing—The XA Specification.*

You can see the syntax of START TRANSACTION in Syntax 15-2.

Syntax 15-2 *Syntax of START TRANSACTION Statement*

```
<start transaction statement> ::=
    START TRANSACTION <mode> [ , <mode> ]...
```

The values of <mode> are exactly the same as you saw in Syntax 15-1 and have the same meanings here that they do for SET TRANSACTION.

15.3 | SQL:1999 Isolation Levels

In SQL:1999, transaction isolation levels are defined in terms of several possible phenomena, or weird, hard-to-explain occurrences (not entirely unlike Bermuda Triangle events or Elvis sightings).

15.3.1 Transaction Phenomena and Isolation Levels

The first of these phenomena is called the *dirty read* phenomenon. A transaction exhibiting this phenomenon has a very minimal isolation from concurrent transactions; in fact, it will be able to see changes made by those concurrent transactions even before they commit.

For example, let's say we have two transactions running in our system at the same time:

- T1, the video checkout/point of sale transaction
- T2, the inventory management transaction

If the checkout transaction (T1) modifies a row in the MOVIE_TITLES table—say a customer is buying a VHS copy of the *Gilligan's Island Anthology*—the number of VHS tapes on hand is decremented by one (from three to two). While that transaction is performing the credit card authorization operation (remember that transactions can comprise many different operations), the back office manager starts running the inventory management transaction (T2), a function that will produce an inventory report and initiate automatic economic order quantity (EOQ) inventory reordering functions. When dirty reads are permitted, transaction T2 will read the newly decremented quantity on hand column for *Gilligan's Island Anthology* and determine that we now have two copies on hand, the point at which four more copies of the tape are ordered.

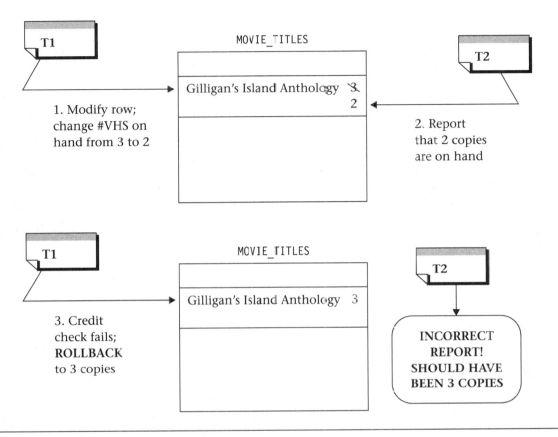

Figure 15-2 Dirty Read Phenomenon

Meanwhile, at the checkout counter, transaction T1 determines that the customer's credit limit on his or her charge card has been exceeded. The customer decides to postpone the purchase, and transaction T1 is rolled back; that is, all objects (including data values) are restored to the appropriate state as if the transaction had never begun in the first place. We now, once again, have three copies of *Gilligan's Island Anthology* in stock, and the database correctly reflects this.

However, transaction T2 has already accomplished the reordering, and we will *incorrectly* order four more copies of the tape, giving us seven in stock (Oh, boy, Mr. Howell!). The permissibility of the dirty read phenomenon has caused this situation to occur (see Figure 15-2).

Because of the possibility of making incorrect decisions based on uncommitted changes to the database, we recommend that you use an isolation level that permits this phenomenon only for transactions that do statistical functions, such as computing the average cost of movies sold in a month, where small imperfections won't have serious consequences.

The second phenomenon is called the *nonrepeatable read.* If a transaction exhibits this phenomenon, it is possible that it may read a row once and, if it attempts to read that row again later in the course of the same transaction, the row might have been changed or even deleted by another concurrent transaction; therefore, the read is not (necessarily) repeatable. Let's go back to our checkout/inventory clashing transactions.

Let's say that the university store manager calls us and says, "We had a tremendous rental run on *Road Trip;* how many do you have, and how many can you spare?" Our back office manager starts the interstore transfer transaction (T1), the first operation of which is to determine how many copies of a specific tape are currently in stock and what the recent activity has been. She discovers that we have four copies in stock and that the tape hasn't been rented in our store in two years. Figuring that we should keep one copy around, the back office manager replies that we have four, and can spare three.

In the course of this transaction, while the university store manager puts our store on hold to take care of some pressing business, the checkout transaction (now T2) swings into action. Representatives from four different fraternities come into our store, each one checking out, yup, *Road Trip.*

The university store manager comes back on the phone and tells us that sure, he'll take three copies. Transaction T1 then attempts to reread the row for the tape, but *the value has been modified.* That is, the initial read during the transaction is nonrepeatable. Figure 15-3 illustrates this phenomenon.

Finally, there is the *phantom* phenomenon. When a transaction exhibits this phenomenon, a set of rows that it reads once might be a different set of rows if the transaction attempts to read them again. It's now Sunday night, a time when we run a number of weekly reports and database maintenance functions. Clerk number 1 is running the statistical transaction (T1), one in which a number of operations are used to provide a large number of reports based on movie prices and/or quantities. One of the operations is to calculate some quantity averages based on a given price range (minimum and maximum sales prices), while another operation performs some other calculations for the same price range.

Clerk number 2 is running the price modification transaction, in which sales prices are modified based on special sales and other factors. Assume transaction T1 performs the first operation mentioned above (price averages) in which some search condition (probably SELECT... WHERE...BETWEEN...) is used. Following completion of this operation—remember that transaction T1 is still active— transaction T2 causes some price changes to movies which in turn (1) cause some movies that hadn't met the original search condition to now meet the BETWEEN clause, and (2) cause some movies that were in the original result to now be out of the desired range. However, transaction T1 then issues the same statement for its second operation, with *a different set of rows* satisfying the search conditions. Figure 15-4 illustrates how this phenomenon occurs.

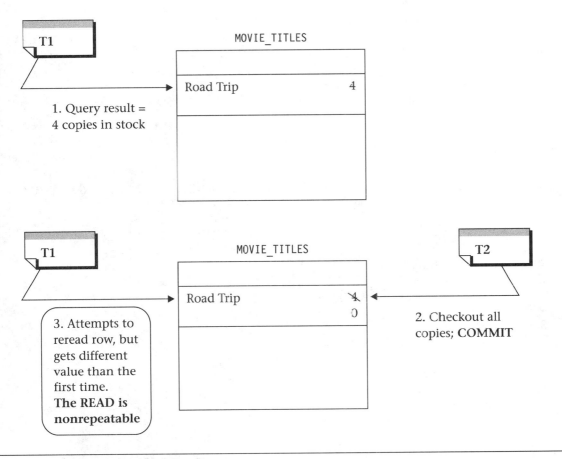

Figure 15-3   Nonrepeatable Read Phenomenon

A transaction with an isolation level of READ UNCOMMITTED means that your transaction may exhibit any or all of these phenomena. This is normally very undesirable, and SQL prohibits you from performing any database updates of your own in this sort of transaction (that is, your implicit access mode is READ ONLY, and you aren't even allowed to specify an access mode of READ WRITE if you specify ISOLATION LEVEL READ UNCOMMITTED).

An isolation level of READ COMMITTED means that your transaction will not exhibit the dirty read phenomenon, but may exhibit the other two.

A transaction level specified as REPEATABLE READ guarantees that your transaction will not exhibit either the dirty read or the nonrepeatable read phenomenon, but may exhibit the phantom phenomenon. (The possibility of the phantom phenomenon has led to the ironic possibility that, as some wags have suggested, "repeatable read isn't"!)

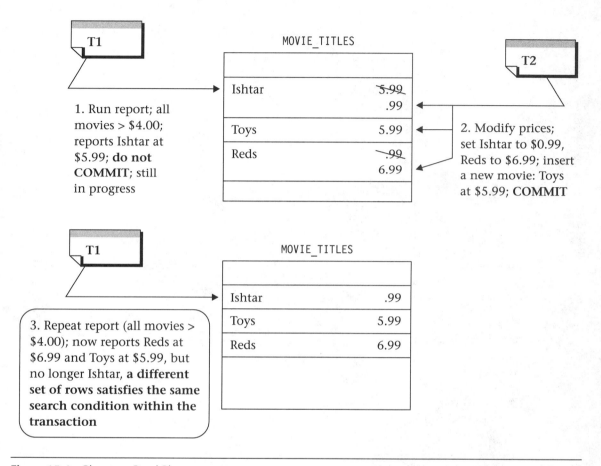

Figure 15-4 Phantom Read Phenomenon

Finally, SERIALIZABLE means that your transaction will exhibit none of these three phenomena and also means that your transaction is *serializable;* that is, it and all concurrent transactions interact only in ways that guarantee there is some serial ordering of the transactions that will return the same result. (Actually, that's true only of concurrent transactions whose isolation is also set to be serializable; concurrent transactions with reduced isolation might not interact serializably with your serializable transactions. It is beyond the scope of this book to delve into the reasons for that, so we encourage you to consult other sources.[2])

This concept is important enough for us to say it in a slightly different way to be sure we're understood. If you managed your application so that a single program runs (that is, starts a transaction, performs its operations, terminates the

---

2   Jim Gray and Andreas Reuter, *Transaction Processing: Concepts and Techniques* (San Francisco: Morgan Kaufmann Publishers, 1993).

transaction, and exits) to completion before the next program runs, then we could say that your application operates serially. A set of transactions is said to be serializable if the result of their operations is identical to *some* sequence of individual transactions that were performed serially. Specifically, this means that none of the actions of one transaction can have any influence on the actions of a different (concurrent) transaction other than the effects that would have resulted from executing one transaction to completion and then executing the other transaction.

Table 15-1 lists all SQL isolation levels and phenomena, and the relationships among them.

Table 15-1 *SQL-Transaction Isolation Levels and Phenomena*

Level	Dirty Read	Nonrepeatable Read	Phantom
READ UNCOMMITTED	Possible	Possible	Possible
READ COMMITTED	Not possible	Possible	Possible
REPEATABLE READ	Not possible	Not possible	Possible
SERIALIZABLE	Not possible	Not possible	Not possible

NOTE: From ISO/IEC 9075-2:1999, *Information Technology—Database Languages—SQL—Part 2: Foundation (SQL/Foundation)*, Subclause 4.32, "SQL-transactions."

Not all SQL DBMS products will necessarily provide all four levels of isolation. However, your SQL DBMS is required to provide you with an isolation level that is *at least* as secure as the one you request (that is, it cannot exhibit any phenomena prohibited by the level you specified), but it is free to set a higher degree of isolation if it needs to do so. For example, some DBMSs don't implement all four levels of isolation, but might implement only READ COMMITTED and SERIALIZABLE. In that case, when you request REPEATABLE READ, the implementation must give you SERIALIZABLE rather than READ COMMITTED because the latter isolation level exhibits more phenomena than the level you requested.

15.3.2 Other Phenomena and Possible Isolation Levels

Transaction theory and practice is unfortunately not as simple as the SQL standard tries to make it. In fact, there are several more phenomena than the three recognized in SQL:1999 and several additional forms of isolation that you can express using SQL:1999 language. Some SQL products allow your applications to use additional forms of isolation, but there is little consistency among vendors in what extensions they provide.

If you find yourself particularly interested in this subject, or if your vendor provides additional isolation options that you'd like to understand, there are many resources available, including the classic text by Jim Gray and Andreas Reuter,[3] as well as an interesting paper presented at an ACM SIGMOD conference.[4]

The latter reference particularly recommended that the SQL standard be enhanced to recognize additional phenomena and support more forms of transaction isolation. However, the designers of SQL:1999 felt that there was too little chance of having additional isolation types supported by multiple products and thus decided not to add these facilities to the standard.

15.3.3   Intra-Transaction and Inter-Transaction Interactions

There is enough confusion among database users about the ways in which transaction facilities protect your program's operations from interference that we feel compelled to say a few words on the subject.

As we discussed in section 15.3.1, a database system uses the *isolation* component of its transactional capabilities to protect the operations that an application performs in the context of one transaction from operations performed in the context of a different transaction. In most situations—at least in programs of modest complexity—an application program will have no more than one transaction in progress at a time. In fact, SQL:1999 provides no mechanism that would allow a single program to initiate a transaction while it has another transaction active. (Many SQL implementations have the same limitation, although we are aware of a few implementations that provide ways for a single program to operate using multiple concurrent transactions.) Transaction isolation can be quite complete when SERIALIZABLE mode is used, or very minimal when READ UNCOMMITTED mode is in effect. But the "isolation" is always isolation of one transaction's actions from those of another transaction.

It is quite easy, especially if your applications use cursors, for you to write a program having some actions that interfere with other of its actions. For example, you might write a program that opens an updatable cursor that identifies all DVDs with a sales price less than $10.00 (rare, indeed, but possible). While this cursor is open, the same program might execute an UPDATE statement that lowers the price of all DVDs starring Adam Sandler by 50%, which might well cause additional stock to satisfy the conditions of the cursor. Should the cursor "see" those Adam Sandler DVDs, even though it was opened before the UPDATE statement did its work? More importantly, should the fact that you're operating in the context of a (single) transaction have any influence on the answer to that question?

---

3   Ibid.

4   Hall Berenson, Phil Bernstein, Jim Gray, Jim Melton, Elizabeth O'Neil, and Pat O'Neil, "A Critique of ANSI SQL Isolation Levels," *SIGMOD Record*, 24, no. 2: 1–10.

In fact, the existence of a transaction has no effect, and should not have an effect, on the relationship between the open cursor and the UPDATE statement. As you learned in Chapter 13, "Cursors," the *sensitivity* of a cursor determines whether or not it is affected by concurrent operations in the same transaction that don't use the cursor. Only if that UPDATE statement were performed in the context of a different transaction would the semantics of transactions have any bearing on the question, and then the answer would depend on the isolation characteristics of both transactions.

15.4 | Mixed DML and DDL

Some SQL implementations (but not all) allow your application to execute both DML and DDL statements during the course of a single transaction. On the surface, this appears to be a relatively trivial task, such as having several UPDATE statements intertwined with some CREATE TABLE and ALTER TABLE statements. In reality, the interactions between DML and DDL statements within a DBMS can be very complicated, so it is left up to the implementation as to whether mixed DDL and DML support within a single transaction is provided. If your implementation prohibits that mixing, any attempt to execute a DDL statement in a transaction whose first (transaction-initiating) statement is a DML statement, or vice versa, will give you an error.

Many SQL implementations do allow you to mix DDL and DML within a single transaction, but we've found that few products do so without any limitations. The limitations that products put on this sort of mixing vary widely among implementations, and we have often found them to seem rather arbitrary. It seems very likely that a specific product allows certain mixtures of DDL and DML because the particular implementation technologies used by that product make those mixtures "safe," but other mixtures are prohibited because they are likely to cause problems. We suggest that you use great caution when mixing the two types of statements within single transactions, even if your implementation allows it.

15.5 | Transaction Termination

When you have executed all of the statements required to make a logical, consistent set of changes to your database, you must terminate the transaction. If you want the changes that you made to become permanent in the database, you terminate the transaction with a COMMIT statement (or COMMIT WORK, if you prefer to use the optional keyword WORK). If you want to undo all of your changes—if you made an error somewhere or simply changed your mind—then you terminate the transaction with a ROLLBACK (ROLLBACK WORK) statement, which aborts the transaction (that is, causes all actions taken by the transaction to be undone).

In some environments (for example, if your system runs under the control of a transaction monitor), transactions may be started or terminated by agents other than your actual application program. In this case, if the transaction was started via this external mechanism (that is, other than because you executed a transaction-initiating SQL statement or used the START TRANSACTION statement), then the transaction must *not* be terminated with a COMMIT or ROLLBACK statement. Instead, it must be terminated by that same external agent. If the transaction was started implicitly by an SQL statement or explicitly by a START TRANSACTION statement, then it must be terminated by a COMMIT or ROLLBACK statement. Any other combination will give you an error.

Keep in mind that it is possible for a ROLLBACK to be interrupted by a system crash, but the ROLLBACK *can never fail*. That is, it must always be possible to abort a transaction. Contrast this with COMMIT, which can fail for several reasons (such as a system crash). A ROLLBACK can be interrupted by a crash or a downed communications line, but the transaction *will* be aborted by those factors—you just won't get control back from the statement. The *only* exception is if you start the transaction from the external agent and try to ROLLBACK in SQL, or vice versa.

The syntax of the COMMIT and ROLLBACK statements is shown in Syntax 15-3.

Syntax 15-3 *COMMIT and ROLLBACK Syntax*

```
<commit statement> ::=
    COMMIT [ WORK ] [ AND [ NO ] CHAIN ]

<rollback statement> ::=
    ROLLBACK [ WORK ] [ AND [ NO ] CHAIN ]
    [ TO SAVEPOINT <savepoint name> ]
```

(We'll discuss the TO SAVEPOINT option of <rollback statement> in section 15.7 and the optional CHAIN clauses in section 15.8.2.)

15.6 Transactions and Constraints

In Chapter 10, "Constraints, Assertions, and Referential Integrity," we described constraints and assertions. One of the things that we talked about was the fact that specific constraints have a couple of constraint attributes. Let's quickly refresh our memories: A given constraint is either DEFERRABLE or NOT DEFERRABLE. If it is DEFERRABLE, then it is either INITIALLY DEFERRED or INITIALLY IMMEDIATE. In either case, the constraint is, at any given time, set to *deferred* or *immediate*. If a constraint is INITIALLY DEFERRED, then (surprise) its initial mode at the start of a transaction is *deferred*. Likewise, INITIALLY IMMEDIATE is as stated.

A constraint that is NOT DEFERRABLE is always checked at the end of every SQL statement (well, it is "effectively checked," which means that a smart implementation can often tell whether a check actually needs to be made or not). A constraint that is DEFERRABLE and is set to *immediate* mode is also checked at the end of every SQL statement. However, a constraint that is DEFERRABLE and is set to *deferred* mode is not checked at the end of every SQL statement; instead, it is checked only when its mode is set back to *immediate*, either implicitly by a COMMIT statement or explicitly by the execution of a SET CONSTRAINTS statement.

The SET CONSTRAINTS statement is shown in Syntax 15-4.

Syntax 15-4 *Syntax of SET CONSTRAINTS Statement*

```
SET CONSTRAINTS constraint-list { DEFERRED | IMMEDIATE }
```

The constraint-list is either a list of constraint names or the keyword ALL. Only DEFERRABLE constraints can be named in the constraint list; ALL implies only those constraints that are DEFERRABLE.

If you attempt to commit a transaction while you have one or more constraints in *deferred* mode, the DBMS will set the mode of those constraints to *immediate* and check them. (Put more bluntly, you can set constraints DEFERRED as much as you'd like, but they will *always* be set IMMEDIATE *and checked* immediately before each transaction commits.) If any of those constraints are violated, the DBMS automatically rolls back your transaction and gives you an error to tell you that's what it did. To avoid this inconvenient situation, we recommend that you explicitly execute a SET CONSTRAINTS ALL IMMEDIATE statement before you commit any transaction that has DEFERRABLE constraints that have been in *deferred* mode. (To help you out a little, NOT DEFERRABLE is the default for all constraints; if you specify a constraint as DEFERRABLE, but don't specify an initial mode, then INITIALLY IMMEDIATE is the default. This will minimize the surprises, because you have to explicitly set your constraint(s) to *deferred* for this to be a problem.)

Why might you need the capability to defer constraints? Consider two tables:

```
CREATE TABLE employees (
    emp_id    INTEGER  PRIMARY KEY,
    emp_name  CHARACTER VARYING (30),
    dept      INTEGER NOT NULL REFERENCES department ) ;
```

```
CREATE TABLE department (
    dept_id   INTEGER PRIMARY KEY,
    dept_name CHARACTER (10),
    manager   INTEGER NOT NULL REFERENCES employees ) ;
```

With this arrangement, you cannot create a new DEPARTMENT unless it's managed by an existing employee, but you can't hire a new employee unless he or she is assigned to work for an existing department. How do you start populating the tables? The only way is to *defer* either or both of the NOT NULL constraints. As long as you've got the appropriate combinations of DEPARTMENTs and EMPLOYEEs in place before you COMMIT (or SET CONSTRAINTS ALL IMMEDIATE), this will allow you to populate the tables.

15.7 | Savepoints—Establishment and Removal

We suggested in section 15.5 that it's possible for your programs to have very long transactions (transactions that perform a great many operations), and we offered some reasons that could justify not programming this way. One risk that we did not mention involves transactions in which you perform operations that are purposefully tentative, operations that you might wish to undo or to keep, based on the results.

Of course, you might be able to design your application so that one set of tentative operations is performed in one transaction, the next in a new transaction, and so forth. But not all applications allow that separation, perhaps because you still require that several such sets of operations succeed or fail as a unit.

If any of your applications fall into this category, you'll be interested to learn that SQL:1999 provides a facility to help reduce the risks associated with transactions that have such tentative operations. The facility depends on the use of *savepoints*, which are a bit like "markers" that you can put into a sequence of transaction operations and then decide later on to undo all operations taken since a specific marker was placed without affecting the status of operations within the transaction that were performed before that marker was placed. Figure 15-5 shows how we visualize this process.

After performing some "safe" operations, our application is ready to begin a sequence of tentative database changes—changes that we might wish to abandon without affecting the status of the safe operations. At that point, we establish a savepoint to mark the beginning of the "risky" changes. A bit later, we decide (for whatever reasons our application deems appropriate) that we must abandon those risky operations, so we instruct SQL to undo all database changes

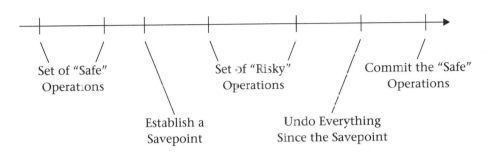

Figure 15-5   Illustration of Savepoint Use

performed since the savepoint was established. After that, we can make additional operations, if we wish, then commit the transaction to make our satisfactory changes permanent. When you instruct SQL to undo all operations performed since the establishment of a savepoint, the savepoint itself is also "forgotten," which means that, if you wish to start another set of tentative operations, you'll have to establish a new savepoint.

SQL:1999 allows you to have multiple savepoints in existence concurrently. Each savepoint has an identifier associated with it, so you can choose the savepoint to which you wish your tentative operations to be undone. If you establish two savepoints—let's call them SAVEPOINT_A and SAVEPOINT_B, established in that order—then instructing the system to undo everything performed since SAVEPOINT_A was established will also naturally undo everything performed since SAVEPOINT_B was established as a direct consequence. In fact, both savepoints are forgotten as a result of this instruction.

Of course, we could also roll back the entire transaction, whether or not we undid the risky operations made after establishing the savepoint. In addition, we could have concluded that our risky operations were worth keeping and instructed the database system to *release* the savepoint. Releasing a savepoint simply removes it from the transaction context so that it is no longer possible to undo operations made after the savepoint without rolling back the entire transaction (or undoing operations made following the establishment of an earlier savepoint).

To establish a savepoint, you must use the SAVEPOINT statement shown in Syntax 15-5. You can release a savepoint using the syntax seen in Syntax 15-6. In Syntax 15-3, the optional TO SAVEPOINT clause of the <rollback statement> provides the syntax for instructing the system to undo all operations performed since a particular savepoint.

Syntax 15-5 *SAVEPOINT Statement Syntax*

```
<savepoint statement> ::=
    SAVEPOINT <savepoint name>
```

Syntax 15-6 *RELEASE SAVEPOINT Statement Syntax*

```
<release savepoint statement> ::=
    RELEASE SAVEPOINT <savepoint name>
```

A <savepoint name> is an identifier that you choose; the identifier you specify is used to name the savepoint, to identify which savepoint you want to release, and to identify the savepoint back to which you want to undo operations.

Perhaps this is obvious, but we state it for the sake of completeness: Whenever you terminate a transaction, either with a COMMIT statement or a ROLLBACK statement, all savepoints created during the course of that transaction are forgotten.

We note, for the benefit of our readers who enjoy a deeper understanding of transaction theory and behaviors, that SQL:1999's savepoints were carefully designed so that they can be implemented as simply nested subtransactions. Some transaction managers provide subtransaction capabilities, and an SQL product associated with such a transaction manager might choose to implement savepoints using the transaction manager's subtransactions instead of implementing them internally. The interaction between savepoints and the encompassing transactions that we mentioned earlier in this chapter is not clearly specified by SQL:1999, probably because encompassing transactions are not fully addressed.

15.8 | Additional Transaction Termination Actions

When you terminate a transaction, any open cursors other than holdable cursors (see Chapter 13, "Cursors") are automatically closed. If you have any prepared dynamic statements (see Chapter 18, "Dynamic SQL"), these statements may or may not be destroyed, depending on the implementation. Finally, while COMMIT statements may fail, owing to any one of a number of causes, a ROLLBACK statement can never fail unless your transaction was started by that mysterious external agent.

Terminating a transaction can have effects other than those we've discussed so far (making the changes to your database's schema and data persistent, or undoing those changes). There might be effects on certain cursors and even on the transaction status of your application.

15.8.1 Holdable Cursors and Holdable Locators

In section 13.2.6, "Holdable Cursors," we told you about cursors that could be held open after you commit the transaction in which the cursors were opened. You'll recall that holdable cursors are always closed (using SQL:1999's semantics) when the transaction in which they were opened is rolled back. The reason for this is subtle and even controversial. In some situations, actions taken during the course of a transaction affect the conditions governing the rows of a cursor opened later in that transaction; if you roll back the transaction, those conditions no longer hold and therefore the cursor would probably identify a different set of rows if it were to be opened in a new transaction.

Consider the following code fragment:

```
/* Declare a cursor for all movies that are not discounted */
DECLARE CURSOR c1 WITH HOLD FOR
  SELECT title, current_dvd_sale_price
  FROM movie_titles
  WHERE current_dvd_sale_price = regular_dvd_sale_price;

START TRANSACTION;

/* Put all Horror movies on sale at a 10% discount */
UPDATE movie_titles
  SET current_dvd_sale_price = regular_dvd_sale_price * 0.9
WHERE movie_type = 'Horror';

/* Now, let's examine all movies that are not discounted */
OPEN c1;
FETCH c1
  INTO :title_var, :price_var;

/* Let's roll back the transaction, but assume that the cursor
   stays open (against SQL:1999 semantics) */
ROLLBACK;

/* Should this FETCH have the possibility of retrieving a row
   corresponding to the film 'The Haunting', or not? */
FETCH c1
  INTO :title_var, :price_var;
```

When the `ROLLBACK` statement executes, the effects of our `UPDATE` statement (to discount all of our horror movies by 10%) are undone—that is, the horror movies are not actually discounted. However, there's an open cursor that has selected all discounted movies. When the next transaction begins, are the horror movies still part of that cursor or not? According to SQL:1999 rules, the cursor is closed by the `ROLLBACK` statement, but some implementations allow holdable cursors to remain open after a `ROLLBACK` statement, so the question has to be asked. Unfortunately, the documentation associated with such implementations makes it impossible for us to answer the question generically. You'll have to experiment with your implementation if it supports the ability to keep holdable cursors open after a `ROLLBACK` statement to determine precisely how it behaves.

In section 2.4.12, "Locators," we described the `LOCATOR` data type of SQL:1999, including holdable locators. We mentioned then that holdable locators remain valid after the transactions in which they attained their values are committed. Holdable locators are always released (that is, their values become invalid) when the transactions in which their values are assigned are rolled back.

15.8.2 Chained Transactions

As you'd expect, supporting transaction semantics consumes resources (such as CPU time, memory, and even network communications) in a database system and its environment. Some implementations have been built so that starting a transaction is relatively inexpensive, but committing one is relatively costly; others have opposite characteristics.

In any case, if your application programs tend to start and terminate several transactions, one after the other, there is inevitably overhead associated with doing so. Of course, you could choose to write your programs so that they use a single, possibly enormous transaction. But that approach has its own problems. Long transactions may take dramatically longer to commit on some implementations than multiple shorter transactions. Long transactions have higher risks, such as losing many database changes if the system crashes or a communications link is lost. Or, your programs simply might require the different transaction contexts for application reasons.

To respond to the conflicting demands of "use multiple shorter transactions" versus "don't start and terminate transactions too often," several SQL products provide the ability to automatically initiate a new transaction as soon as a previous transaction is terminated. SQL:1999 supports this capability through the use of new syntax, seen in Syntax 15-3.

If you don't specify AND CHAIN in either statement, then the default is AND NO CHAIN, which gives exactly the same results that the corresponding SQL-92 statements gave. If you do specify AND CHAIN, then a new transaction is started as soon as the COMMIT or ROLLBACK statement has done its job. This new transaction has exactly the same characteristics (that is, modes) as the transaction just terminated. Of course, this means that you cannot execute a SET TRANSACTION or START TRANSACTION statement after such a COMMIT or ROLLBACK statement, since a transaction has already been initiated.

15.9 | Chapter Summary

Transactions can be very complex, particularly those that are distributed. A number of issues must be addressed: commit protocols (such as two-phase commit, local commitment, nonblocking), specific product interactions (such as with transaction processing monitors and repositories), and others. It is beyond the scope of this book to delve too deeply into transaction theory, although a number of reference sources are available.[5] SQL:1999 transaction management facilities aren't overly complex, but care should be taken when designating isolation levels, constraint handling, and other aspects of this subject. It's sometimes tempting, for example, to define the highest level of isolation (SERIALIZABLE) for each and every transaction specification, but this may be inefficient based on the characteristics of *your specific environment.*

---

5 See footnotes 2 and 4.

Chapter

16

Connections and Remote Database Access

16.1 Introduction

In this chapter, we discuss the relationship of *sessions* and *connections* to your applications. SQL-86 and SQL-89 did not have an explicit notion of a session in which your application ran, nor did they have the notion of a connection from your application to a session. However, modern database technology requires recognition of certain concepts that lead to these terms, which resulted in capabilities being added to SQL-92 that continue today in SQL:1999.

In the client/server environment that has become so prevalent since the early 1990s, one program (your application, perhaps) is a *client* for a service provided by another program (the database system, in our case), called the *server*. Client/server environments might be relatively simple *two-tier* architectures like those illustrated in Figure 16-1, or more complex n-*tier* architectures involving Web servers, database servers, and other types of servers. More detailed discussion is beyond the scope of this book, but we will acknowledge that different contexts might draw the boundaries differently; for example, in some situations, your application program might invoke or call the *client software,* which communicates with the *server software,* which then invokes or calls the database system (see Figure 16-1).

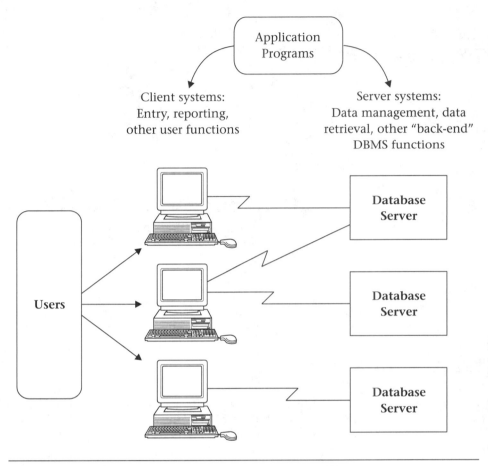

Figure 16-1   Client/Server Database Environment

16.2 | Establishing Connections

Back in SQL-89, when your program attempted to execute the first SQL state-ment, the DBMS was expected simply to accept the statement and start executing it. However, SQL:1999 recognizes (as did SQL-92) that other actions may have to take place before the DBMS can even be aware that it has been given a task to do. For example, a *context* for database execution has to be established. In some implementations, the context exists because the DBMS runtime code was linked with your application. In others, the context is established by execution of implementation-defined statements to connect the application program with the DBMS. In still others, system variables set up the context. SQL:1999 resolves this issue by defining several statements that application programs use to control connections to DBMSs and by specifying the default behavior much more thoroughly than SQL-89 did.

First, for compatibility with pre-SQL-92 and pre-SQL:1999 programs, there is always a default behavior. Second, for newer programs, SQL:1999 allows complete control over the association between your application and the DBMS or DBMSs that it uses. Here is an outline of the behavior.

- Almost all SQL statements (there are a *few* exceptions, which we'll get to shortly) can execute only when there is a *connection* between the application program (client) and the DBMS (server).

- When your application tries to execute one of these statements and a connection has been established, the DBMS to which your application is connected executes the statement.

- When your application tries to execute one of these statements and a connection has not been established, the first thing that must happen is that a connection must be established. SQL:1999 specifies that this connection is to a default server (or environment, or DBMS). How that default is determined remains implementation-defined, but it may involve environment variables or something similar. After the connection is established, the DBMS to which you are now connected executes the statement.

- If your first statement is a CONNECT statement (this is one of the exceptions), no default connection is established, but the requested server is contacted and a current connection is established to it (subject to normal security and so forth).

- You can execute a CONNECT statement to establish a connection to a second (or third . . .) server without disconnecting the earlier connection (or connections). The earlier connections are suspended and called *dormant connections,* and the new one is called the *current connection.*

- Every connection has a session associated with it. The session associated with the current connection is the *current session,* and sessions associated with any dormant connections are *dormant sessions*. As shown in Figure 16-2, there is a one-to-one relationship between sessions and connections. Many SQL standards participants use the terms interchangeably, since there are no compelling ways to distinguish between them. However, other participants observe that the word *connection* evokes the communication path (network or otherwise) between a client and an SQL server, while *session* implies the context in which the SQL server does its work.

- If you have more than one connection in existence, then you can switch among them by using the SET CONNECTION statement.

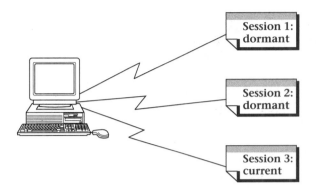

Figure 16-2   Multiple SQL Connections and Sessions

- Because connections often occupy system resources, you may sometimes wish to explicitly get rid of connections; you can do this by using the DISCONNECT statement. If you fail to disconnect any (or all) of your sessions before your program terminates, then it will be done for you. If you try to disconnect *explicitly* while you have a transaction in progress, you'll get an error.

- Your implementation may either permit or prohibit changing connections while transactions are active. If yours prohibits that behavior, you'll get an error if you try. Otherwise, all statements executed during the transaction through all connections (on all sessions) are part of the same transaction (review Chapter 15, "Transaction Management," for information about ordinary transactions and encompassing transactions).

16.3 | Connection Statements

Let's take a closer look at these three statements: CONNECT, SET CONNECTION, and DISCONNECT.

16.3.1 CONNECT

The format of the CONNECT statement is shown in Syntax 16-1.

Syntax 16-1 *CONNECT Statement*

```
<connect statement> ::=
    CONNECT TO <connection target>
```

```
<connection target> ::=
    <SQL-server name>
        [ AS <connection name> ]
        [ USER <connection user name> ]
  | DEFAULT
```

The <SQL-server name> of the <connection target> is a simple value specification (character string literal or a host variable or parameter) that identifies the server to which you wish to connect. The meaning of the value of <SQL-server name> is implementation-defined.

The <connection name> is an identifier that you can use as a sort of alias for the connection. This can be used in the SET CONNECTION and DISCONNECT statements (discussed later in this chapter); it is also reported along with any errors at that connection. If you don't specify AS <connection name>, then the default is to give you a connection-name identical to <SQL-server name>.

The <connection user name> is a value specification that you can use to identify yourself to the server. If you don't specify it, the default for <connection user name> is your current authID. Your implementation may require that <connection user name> be equal to your current authID, or it may restrict the values that you can use for <connection user name> in other ways. If you violate these restrictions, you will get an error. If you specify a <connection user name>, any leading or trailing blanks will be stripped off before it is used.

If you try to connect to a server and specify a <connection name> that's already in use by your application, you'll get an error. If you try to CONNECT TO DEFAULT and your application already has a default connection established, you'll get that same error.

If you use CONNECT TO DEFAULT, the effect is almost the same as not issuing a CONNECT at all. (That is, when you execute the next SQL statement that requires a connection, it will execute on the default connection.) However, we do recommend that you use CONNECT TO DEFAULT in this case so that your programs will be self-documenting and thus easier to maintain. There is one difference, however. If your application never issues a CONNECT statement but always uses the (implicit) default connection, any error that breaks the connection will be essentially transparent to you: the very next statement that you execute will go to the same default connection (although there are problems with maintaining your transaction, so you will have to reexecute all of the statements in that transaction).

Once you use a CONNECT statement, you will never be implicitly connected to the default connection in that application run. If your connection is broken, the next statement that you try to execute will get an error instead of making a default connection for you.

If the CONNECT statement cannot reach the server, you'll get an error. If it reaches the server, but the server refuses the connection (because, for example, it has insufficient resources or it doesn't accept your user name, or perhaps it's the deodorant you wore this morning), then you'll get a different error. Once connected, though, your authID will be set to the <connection user name> you specified (or implied).

16.3.2 SET CONNECTION

The SET CONNECTION statement is shown in Syntax 16-2.

Syntax 16-2 *SET CONNECTION Statement*

```
<set connection statement> ::=
    SET CONNECTION <connection object>

<connection object> ::=
    DEFAULT
  | <connection name>
```

Of course, there has to be a dormant connection named <connection name> or a dormant default connection (depending on which option you specify); otherwise, you'll get an error. If there is a dormant connection, your current connection is made dormant and the specified connection becomes the current (and thus no longer dormant) connection. If the new connection cannot become current for any reason (for example, a network link may have gone down), you'll get an error to signal this.

16.3.3 DISCONNECT

The DISCONNECT statement is shown in Syntax 16-3.

Syntax 16-3 *DISCONNECT Statement*

```
<disconnect statement> ::=
    DISCONNECT <disconnect object>

<disconnect object> ::=
    <connection object>
  | ALL
  | CURRENT
```

If you use <connection object>, there has to be a connection (current or dormant) by that name; if you use CURRENT, there has to be a current connection (that is, you cannot execute DISCONNECT CURRENT immediately followed by DISCONNECT CURRENT). If your current connection is identified by <connection object> or if you use CURRENT, your current connection is destroyed and you have no current connection; you must use a CONNECT or SET CONNECTION statement to establish a new current connection if you want to continue executing SQL statements.

If you execute DISCONNECT ALL, your current connection is destroyed, as are all other connections.

If you have a transaction active on a connection that you are disconnecting, you'll get an error and the disconnect will fail. If any other sort of error is encountered during a DISCONNECT, the disconnect will succeed, but you'll get a warning message.

What are the practical implications of all this? Well, the notions of connections and sessions were created to support remote database access and client/server environments. In spite of that, they work perfectly well in "one box" situations, too. It's just that the number of meaningful connections is probably more limited (perhaps just to DEFAULT... but perhaps not).

16.4 | RDA (Remote Database Access)

There is another ISO standard, called *Remote Database Access* (RDA for short), related to connections to SQL database systems. This standard defines protocols and services for accessing databases over network connections (initially, over Open Systems Interconnect, or OSI, connections, although the technology was not practically limited to OSI; more recent versions of RDA are specified to layer onto the Internet's protocol, TCP/IP). It is beyond the scope of this book to delve into RDA (and, perhaps more importantly, RDA is not widely implemented), but we do want to chat about it briefly.

RDA allows you to execute a significant fraction of the available SQL statements, but not all of them. The limitation is caused mostly by the fact that the RDA standard is inherently dynamic in nature (see Chapter 18, "Dynamic SQL"), so some statements are not supported because of the obvious redundancy, such as the dynamic SQL statements themselves.

When you use RDA to access an SQL DBMS, the RDA client software intercepts the SQL statements that your application is executing and decides how they should be handled. Most of the SQL statements are sent to the server for execution and the behavior is otherwise normal. The CONNECT, SET CONNECTION, and DISCONNECT statements are not sent to a server, but they're executed by the client software—that's how this whole thing works in the first place (with or without RDA involved). The GET DIAGNOSTICS statement (see Chapter 20, "Diagnostics and Error Management") is also executed by the client software so that information about all statements, including the CONNECT statements, can be captured.

The original RDA standard was based strictly on the OSI protocol stack developed by the International Organization for Standardization (ISO), but work on later versions of the standard altered the assumptions so that TCP/IP is assumed instead. Development of RDA continues in the ISO arena, but we observe that the RDA development committee in ISO is increasingly attentive to development of infrastructure (protocols and security paradigms) that are required by the SQL standard and is spending less energy on the RDA standard itself. This reduction of effort spent on RDA is undoubtedly influenced by the fact that RDA has not achieved significant commercial success.

16.5 | Termination Statements and Connections

Finally, your COMMIT and ROLLBACK statements (which are allowed only for non-encompassing transactions in any case; see Chapter 15, "Transaction Management") are intercepted and handled differently than by pure SQL, without the use of a connection facility like RDA. In fact, they are dealt with by other network services that handle commitment of transactions. Now, these services will notify the server to commit or rollback the transaction, but it's not done with a COMMIT or ROLLBACK statement. These services are designed to handle both single-server (single connection) transactions, using a one-phase commit protocol, and multi-server (multiple connection) transactions, using a two-phase (more generally, a multiphase) commit protocol.

16.6 | Chapter Summary

As distributed database environments become increasingly prominent among information systems, connections will become more and more important to your SQL applications. The SQL:1999 connection facilities, combined with standards such as RDA, will give your applications a great deal of flexibility with respect to distribution of data among resources. Keep in mind, however, that there is far more to truly distributed database environments, particularly heterogeneous ones (i.e., those running under multiple DBMS products), than simple connections. When coupled with distribution frameworks or front-end tools, though, the basic facilities of SQL:1999 will help you avoid the patchworked workaround environments that were formerly necessary to achieve most database distribution.

Chapter

17

Routines and Routine Invocation (Functions and Procedures)

17.1 | Introduction

In earlier editions of the SQL standard, the only sort of "procedure" available was the sort that a client program would invoke containing a single SQL statement. (As you have seen earlier in this book—section 5.4.2, "Relationship to Host Variables," for example—these are now more properly known as *externally-invoked procedures*.) Publication of the SQL/PSM standard in 1996[1] (often called *PSM-96*, "PSM" standing for "Persistent Stored Modules") added functions and procedures written in SQL, and in a choice of several host languages, that could be invoked from your SQL statements. These routines are formally called *SQL-invoked routines* but are commonly called *stored procedures* (even when they are actually functions instead of procedures).

In this chapter, we will give you a fairly brief look at SQL-invoked routines. This material partly recapitulates a lengthier treatment of the subject in an earlier book,[2] but brings the discussion up to date with SQL:1999. If you need in-depth details for SQL-invoked routines, computational completeness in SQL, and stored modules, you may wish to consult that earlier book. (A language is said to

---

1 ISO/IEC 9075-4:1996, *Information Technology—Database Languages—SQL—Part 4: Persistent Stored Modules (SQL/PSM)*, International Organization for Standardization, 1996.

2 Jim Melton, *Understanding SQL's Stored Procedures: A Complete Guide to SQL/PSM* (San Francisco: Morgan Kaufmann Publishers, 1998).

be *computationally complete* if programs can be written only in that language to compute arbitrary algorithms. The phrase is generally used to mean that the language supports flow-of-control statements such as looping constructs, conditional statements, and so forth.)

Before we proceed, however, we think that you should know that many SQL systems provide proprietary extensions that are analogous to SQL/PSM. Such extensions serve much the same purposes, including provision of SQL-invoked procedures and functions, as well as statements to make the product's dialect of SQL computationally complete. In fact, SQL/PSM was published after many of those extended products had demonstrated market demand. However, the legacy of those proprietary analogs meant that only a few SQL products have implemented SQL/PSM itself.

17.2 | Relationship of SQL:1999's Routines to SQL/PSM

When SQL/PSM was first published in 1996, it extended SQL-92, then the latest edition of the SQL standard. SQL-92 had no notion of routines (procedures or functions) that could be invoked from SQL statements, but that capability was precisely the point of SQL/PSM. As a result, this new part of the SQL standard (SQL/PSM) specified several different technologies: the ability to store and manage modules of SQL routines in your databases, a set of new SQL statements that makes SQL computationally complete, and the capability of defining and managing routines written in SQL or in one of several host languages and then invoking them from SQL statements.

The publication of a new edition of the SQL standard in 1999[3] altered SQL/PSM by removing the specifications of defining, managing, and invoking SQL-invoked routines. Those specifications were moved to SQL/Foundation largely because they were necessary infrastructure for SQL:1999's user-defined types, discussed in detail in the second volume of this book. In the course of moving the specifications from part 4 to part 2 of the standard, several enhancements were made, most of which relate to user-defined types and thus are not

---

3   ISO/IEC 9075-1:1999, *Information Technology—Database Languages—SQL—Part 1: Framework (SQL/Framework)*; ISO/IEC 9075-2:1999, *Information Technology—Database Languages—SQL—Part 2: Foundation (SQL/Foundation)*; ISO/IEC 9075-3:1999, *Information Technology—Database Languages—SQL—Part 3: Call-Level Interface (SQL/CLI)*; ISO/IEC 9075-4:1999, *Information Technology—Database Languages—SQL—Part 4: Persistent Stored Modules (SQL/PSM)*; and ISO/IEC 9075-5:1999, *Information Technology—Database Languages—SQL—Part 5: Host Language Bindings (SQL/Bindings)*, International Organization for Standardization, 1999.

discussed in this volume. Those enhancements that are independent of user-defined types are covered in this chapter.

SQL-Invoked Routines

The most concise definition of an SQL-invoked routine is "a routine that is invoked from SQL code." While that may sound circular to some ears, it's really the most accurate definition we can give. As we'll see in this section, SQL-invoked routines have several characteristics that can vary among such routines and that allows us to categorize them in rather useful ways.

17.3.1 SQL Parameters

Since SQL's externally invoked procedures are invoked from a client program (written in a traditional 3GL, at least from the SQL standard's perspective), the parameters of those externally invoked procedures are known as *host parameters*—that is, they correspond to arguments of the statements in host programs that call these externally invoked procedures.

By contrast, SQL-invoked routines are invoked from SQL code, and the parameters of SQL-invoked routines correspond to arguments in the SQL code that invokes the routines. Consequently, the parameters of SQL-invoked routines are called *SQL parameters*.

In Chapter 12, "Accessing SQL from the Real World," you learned about the impedance mismatch between SQL and most programming languages, a mismatch caused in part by the fact that SQL's data types don't have perfect correspondence to the data types of any other programming language. Perhaps obviously, if you invoke a routine written in SQL—an *SQL routine*— from SQL code, the impedance mismatch doesn't exist. (As we'll see in section 17.4, "External Routines," not all SQL-invoked routines are written in SQL; invoking an *external routine*, which is a routine written in a language other than SQL, from SQL code still creates an impedance mismatch.)

However, if you invoke an SQL routine from SQL code, then you can pass any SQL value between the two components. That is, SQL parameters (and arguments) can be declared to be any SQL data type. As you saw in Chapter 13, "Cursors," it's possible under some circumstances to pass the result set of certain cursors—a virtual table, that is—as the value of a parameter. Try doing that in your C programs!

17.3.2 Distinction between Procedures and Functions

SQL-invoked routines come in two flavors: *procedures* and *functions*. (Actually, there's a third flavor, known as *methods*; methods are relevant only in the context of user-defined types and are thus not discussed in this volume.) There are several important differences between these flavors, as well as some significant similarities. Let's look at the similarities before focusing on the differences.

First of all, both can be invoked only from SQL statements, and not directly from an application program written in some other programming language. (Remember? They're called *SQL-invoked* routines!) Second, they can both be written either in SQL or in some external language. No surprises, right? Let's look now at the differences.

The first, and most obvious, difference is that SQL-invoked procedures are invoked exclusively by means of a specific SQL statement: the CALL statement; by contrast, SQL-invoked functions are treated as "values" in an expression of some sort and are invoked exclusively as a means of evaluating that value. A little sample SQL code might make this a bit more clear:

```
-- This statement invokes a procedure, BALANCE,
--    passing it the store identification, the desired
--    date of inventory, returning the amount separately
CALL balance (store, DATE '1997-06-01', amount);

-- This statement computes sales amounts for a given
--    date at two different stores
SET total =
  sales ('Store 1', DATE '1997-01-01') +
  sales ('Store 2', DATE '1997-01-01');
```

The CALL statement invokes an SQL-invoked procedure named BALANCE. The SET statement, by contrast, invokes the SALES function twice, passing data in each of the two arguments and receiving the result back as the "value" of the function. (Both of those SQL statements belong to SQL's computational-completeness feature.)

A second difference is closely related to the first: SQL-invoked procedures are allowed to have both input and output parameters, while SQL-invoked functions are permitted to have only input parameters. SQL-invoked procedures are not *required* to have both input parameters and output parameters—it's permissible to have procedures with only input parameters or only output parameters—and, for that matter, they're not required to have any parameters at all. Therefore, you can write procedures that have no parameters at all but still carry out some important function. SQL-invoked functions are also not required to have any parameters, but any that they do have must be input parameters. All output from SQL-invoked functions is supplied as the return value of the function and not through an explicit parameter. (If you're more comfortable thinking about it this way—and you wouldn't be alone—you can think of functions as having one parameter more than specified in the function's definition, and you can even call it the *return parameter*. It's never referenced explicitly in any way; it's set through the use of the RETURN statement in the function's code.)

The third difference is a bit more subtle. SQL's routine resolution algorithm, which we address in section 17.8 "Routine Resolution Outline," is more heavily biased toward supporting multiple functions with the same name than it is toward dealing with multiple procedures with the same name. Therefore, if you plan to take advantage of the ability to write SQL-invoked routines with "overloaded" names, you'll almost certainly focus on SQL-invoked functions. Because of the effects caused by the output parameters that are possible with SQL-invoked procedures, the overloading is much more limited. (You can read more about the reason why we say that SQL-invoked procedure overloading is much more limited in a reference devoted to SQL/PSM.[4])

17.3.3 How—and Why—to Store SQL-Invoked Routines

SQL:1999, including SQL/PSM, allows you to store your SQL-invoked routines either as *schema-level routines* or as *SQL-server module routines*. An SQL-server module routine is an SQL-invoked routine that is specified as part of an SQL-server module. SQL-server modules, specified only in SQL/PSM (and now you see why it's called PSM—because of the SQL-server *modules*), are nothing more than an SQL-server analog to the SQL-client modules used to contain externally invoked procedures. That is, they are collections of SQL-invoked modules, along with declarations of associated objects (such as cursors and temporary tables). SQL-server modules are inherently *stored modules*, because they are stored in some schema in an SQL database. Unfortunately, however, SQL-server modules aren't widely implemented.

Which brings us to schema-level routines. A *schema-level routine* is one that is stored directly in one of your database's schemas, without the arguable benefits of a containing SQL-server module. And that's the only interesting difference between these two types of routine. One implication of this difference is this:

---

4 Melton, *Understanding SQL's Stored Procedures*.

schema-level routines must be entirely self-contained; they must include the definitions of any non–schema objects, such as cursors or temporary tables, that they use.

Schema-level routines (the only type of SQL-invoked routine we discuss in the remainder of this chapter) that are written in SQL are *definer's rights routines*, because the privileges used to execute their SQL statements are the privileges of the routine's definer—that is, the owner of the schema in which the routine is stored. (External routines can be either definer's rights routines or *invoker's rights routines* since the syntax for defining external routines includes syntax for specifying EXTERNAL SECURITY DEFINER or EXTERNAL SECURITY INVOKER, as discussed in section 17.4.4.) To be permitted to invoke an SQL-invoked routine, you must have been granted the EXECUTE privilege on that routine. Naturally, if you're the definer of the routine, the system granted you that privilege; otherwise, it has to be given to you by some authorization identifier that has the privilege WITH GRANT OPTION, as we discussed in Chapter 14, "Privileges, Users, and Security."

17.3.4   SQL Statements to Store, Modify, and Delete Stored Routines

The SQL statements used to create SQL routines are very similar to those used to create external routines, but there are small differences. In Syntax 17-1, we provide the syntax of SQL:1999's statement for creating SQL-invoked routines. We agree: it's long and intimidating. But we'll take it one bit at a time, explaining each component. (We've left out a few components of this syntax that deal only with methods, since methods aren't otherwise covered in this volume.)

There are a few modifications you're allowed to make to a routine once it's been created; you can see the syntax of the <alter routine statement> in Syntax 17-2. When an SQL-invoked routine is no longer needed, you can destroy it with the <drop routine statement> shown in Syntax 17-3.

Syntax 17-3 *SQL-Invoked Routine Definition Syntax*

```
<SQL-invoked routine> ::=
    CREATE <SQL-invoked procedure>
  | CREATE <SQL-invoked function>

<SQL-invoked procedure> ::=
    PROCEDURE <schema qualified routine name>
      ( [ <SQL parameter declaration list> ] )
      [ <routine characteristic>... ]
      <routine body>
```

```
<SQL-invoked function> ::=
    FUNCTION <schema qualified routine name>
      ( [ <SQL parameter declaration list> ] )
      <returns clause>
      [ <routine characteristic>... ]
      [ <dispatch clause> ]
      <routine body>

<schema qualified routine name> ::=
    3-part-name (See section 4.2.1, "Schema Concepts")

<SQL parameter declaration list> ::=
    <SQL parameter declaration> [ { , <SQL parameter declaration> }... ]

<SQL parameter declaration> ::=
    [ <parameter mode> ] [ <SQL parameter name> ]
    <parameter type>

<parameter mode> ::=
      IN
    | OUT
    | INOUT

<SQL parameter name> ::= <identifier>

<parameter type> ::= <data type> [ AS LOCATOR ]

<returns clause> ::= RETURNS <returns data type> [ <result cast> ]

<returns data type> ::= <data type> [ AS LOCATOR ]

<result cast> ::= CAST FROM <data type> [ AS LOCATOR ]

<routine characteristic> ::=
      <language clause>
    | PARAMETER STYLE <parameter style>
    | SPECIFIC <specific name>
    | <deterministic characteristic>
    | <SQL-data access indication>
    | <null-call clause>
    | <dynamic result sets characteristic>
```

```
<language clause> ::=
    SQL
  | ADA | C | COBOL | FORTRAN | MUMPS | PASCAL | PLI


<parameter style> ::=
    SQL
  | GENERAL


<specific name> ::= 3-part-name (See section 4.2.1, "Schema Concepts")


<deterministic characteristic> ::=
    DETERMINISTIC
  | NOT DETERMINISTIC


<SQL-data access indication> ::=
    NO SQL
  | CONTAINS SQL
  | READS SQL DATA
  | MODIFIES SQL DATA


<null-call clause> ::=
    RETURNS NULL ON NULL INPUT
  | CALLED ON NULL INPUT


<dynamic result sets characteristic> ::=
    DYNAMIC RESULT SETS <maximum dynamic result sets>


<maximum dynamic result sets> ::= <unsigned integer>


<dispatch clause> ::= STATIC DISPATCH


<routine body> ::=
    <SQL routine body>
  | <external body reference>


<SQL routine body> ::= <SQL procedure statement>


<external body reference> ::=
    EXTERNAL [ NAME <external routine name> ]
    [ PARAMETER STYLE <parameter style > ]
    [ <external security clause> ]
```

```
<external routine name> ::=
    <identifier>
  | <character string literal>


<external security clause> ::=
    EXTERNAL SECURITY DEFINER
  | EXTERNAL SECURITY INVOKER
  | EXTERNAL SECURITY IMPLEMENTATION DEFINED
```

One of the first things you should observe in Suntax 17-1 is the separation between <SQL-invoked procedure> and <SQL-invoked function>. The two statements have a lot in common, but defining a function involves a couple of additional clauses, one required and one optional.

When you define an SQL-invoked function, you must specify a <returns clause>. This clause provides the data type of the value that the function returns. SQL-invoked procedures don't return a value in the same way that functions do (they return values only through explicit parameters) and thus don't have a <returns clause>. The <returns clause> requires that you specify the data type of the returned value that the invoker of the function receives. When you're defining an external function, the <returns clause> also permits you to specify a <result cast>; this clause is not allowed for SQL functions. This allows you to instruct the system to convert from one of the host language types that can be returned from an external function into a preferred SQL type that is then returned to the function's invoker.

An SQL-invoked function definition also allows you to specify a <dispatch clause>, which relates to the algorithm that SQL:1999 uses for determining which routine among several with the same routine name is actually invoked at runtime. We discuss routine resolution in more detail in section 17.8, "Routine Resolution Outline"; for now, we'll simply note that this clause is required for SQL-invoked functions (but not SQL-invoked methods) for which the data type of one or more parameters is a user-defined type, a reference type, an array type whose element type is a user-defined type, or an array type whose element type is a reference type. That is, if any parameter of an SQL-invoked function fits the given description, then the definition of that function must specify STATIC DISPATCH. The definitions of functions without parameters that fit the given description are prohibited from specifying STATIC DISPATCH, because the concept is irrelevant in the absence of user-defined types. Some future version of the SQL standard might support DYNAMIC DISPATCH for SQL-invoked functions; by requiring STATIC DISPATCH to be specified now, even though that's the only alternative, the designers of SQL:1999 preserved the ability to add DYNAMIC DISPATCH—possibly (but probably not) as the default behavior—in the future without causing problems for applications that assumed STATIC DISPATCH without stating the assumption. Don't forget that user-defined types are discussed extensively in Volume 2 of this book.

You may be surprised to learn that every SQL-invoked routine has two names. One name, given in Syntax 17-1 as <schema qualified routine name>, is the name that you use when you invoke the routine. It's a normal three-part name, just like a <table name>. However, SQL permits you to have multiple routines with the same name—in section 17.7, you'll see that this capability is called *polymorphism*—so there has to be some way to distinguish between the possibly several routines with the same name. SQL's solution is to give each routine a second name, one that must be unique. This second name is called the *specific name* of the routine and is never used to invoke the routine. However, it is used to manage the routine—to alter its definition or to drop it. The specific name of a routine is provided as one of the <routine characteristic> alternatives and is completely optional. If you don't provide a specific name for a routine that you define, the system will assign one on your behalf. Of course, you have to somehow figure out that name if you ever want to drop or alter the routine. Consequently, we strongly recommend that you always assign specific names yourself; that way, you have more control over the names and don't have to depend on browsing the Information Schema (see Chapter 22, "Information Schema") to discover the names. If you do specify a specific name for a routine, and you explicitly provide a schema name as part of that specific name, then that schema name must match the explicit or implicit schema name that is part of the <schema qualified routine name>.

As we mentioned earlier, SQL-invoked routines can be defined to have no parameters. If you define routines with parameters, you must limit yourself strictly to input parameters for SQL-invoked functions, although SQL-invoked procedures can have both input and output parameters (as well as parameters that are both input and output). The parameter mode is optional, as you see in Syntax 17-1. In spite of this, you are not permitted to specify a parameter mode when you declare the parameters for an SQL-invoked function; the mode can never be anything other than input, and SQL:1999 doesn't allow you to specify the default in this case. (We think this is inconsistent with SQL's policy in other areas, where we encourage you to explicitly specify defaults, but that's the syntax chosen by SQL:1999's designers.) For SQL-invoked procedures, you can specify the parameter mode for each parameter as part of its parameter declaration. The mode is optional, and the default is IN, meaning "input."

Among the several alternatives for <routine characteristic>, we have already discussed the SPECIFIC clause, which allows you to specify a specific name for a routine being defined. Let's look at each of the other characteristics in turn (although not strictly in the order in which they appear in Syntax 17-1).

The <language clause> determines whether the routine you're defining is an SQL routine or an external routine. If you leave this clause out of your routine definition, then it's presumed to be an SQL routine, and you must provide an <SQL routine body> and not an <external routine body>. If you specify this clause and provide any value other than SQL, then the routine is an external routine and you must provide an <external routine body> rather than an <SQL routine body>.

The <deterministic characteristic> allows you to tell the SQL system whether the routine being defined is DETERMINISTIC or NOT DETERMINISTIC (the latter is the default, if you don't specify this clause). If a routine being invoked is a DETERMINISTIC routine that has been previously invoked with the same argument values, then the system may choose to retrieve the previous return value(s) from the routine and return it without bothering to invoke the routine again (of course, the system is free to invoke the routine again if it failed to cache the return values). NOT DETERMINISTIC routines, of course, have to be invoked each time. However, if you tell the system that the routine is DETERMINISTIC and it's really not (a RANDOM_NUMBER function probably isn't deterministic), then you're on your own, and your applications will probably get some unexpected results.

The <SQL-data access indication> gives you the ability to indicate whether the routine you're defining includes any SQL statements at all and, if so, what relationship they have to the data in your database. Since SQL routines inherently contain SQL, the use of CONTAINS SQL is redundant (but permitted); in fact, you cannot specify NO SQL on SQL routines. At runtime, the system will check the characteristics of the routine to ensure that it's compatible with the environment from which it was invoked. A routine that specifies MODIFIES SQL DATA cannot be invoked from a routine that does not specify that facility, and a routine that specifies READS SQL DATA cannot be invoked from one that does not specify that facility. If the routine passes these checks, then the new SQL session context is set to indicate the appropriate attributes of this routine. (By the way, if you lie to the system when you're defining a routine and fail to specify READ SQL DATA or MODIFIES SQL DATA while including SQL statements that perform those operations, that'll be caught at runtime and an exception condition will be raised then.)

The <null-call clause> was not available in PSM-96 but is new to SQL:1999. The clause is prohibited when you're defining an SQL-invoked procedure. You use this clause to inform the SQL system whether or not it should actually invoke the SQL-invoked function you're defining in response to an invocation for which any argument values are null. If you specify CALLED ON NULL INPUT, or don't specify the clause at all, then the system will invoke the function even when all arguments are null. If you specify RETURNS NULL ON NULL INPUT, then the system will simply provide the null value as the value of the function every time an invocation is made in which any (one or more) of the arguments are null.

We discussed cursors in Chapter 13, "Cursors," including the fact that you can declare cursors to be result set cursors. Leaving a result set cursor open at the time you return from the SQL-invoked procedure in which the cursor was opened allows you to return the rows of the cursor's result set back from the procedure to the SQL code that called that procedure. In order to allow this behavior to take place, the SQL-invoked procedure (this clause is prohibited on SQL-function definitions) must have been created with a DYNAMIC RESULT SETS clause that specifies some value greater than zero. The value is the maximum number of dynamic result sets that can be returned from the procedure.

If you leave more result set cursors open when the SQL-invoked procedure returns than were allowed in the DYNAMIC RESULT SETS clause, the system will raise a warning condition to let you know that you didn't allow for as many result sets as the procedure was written to return and you might be losing relevant information. If the DYNAMIC RESULT SETS clause allows more than one open result set cursor, then the result sets are returned in the order in which the cursors were opened in the procedure. All such cursors that are not scrollable cursors return only the rows of the result set that have not already been visited by FETCH statements that specify the cursor. Scrollable result set cursors left open return all of the rows of the cursors' result sets, and the position of the cursor is left positioned immediately before the most recent row that was FETCHed.

Incidentally, we still have not told you enough about result set cursors and the use of DYNAMIC RESULT SETS for you to use them effectively. Of course, if your SQL code that invokes the SQL-invoked procedure containing a result set cursor knows, a priori, the definition of the cursor, then it can use the result set returned from the SQL-invoked procedure by leaving the cursor open when the procedure returns. However, effective use of this feature requires the facilities of dynamic SQL, discussed in Chapter 18, "Dynamic SQL."

The remaining routine characteristic not yet discussed is the PARAMETER STYLE clause. Before we address that clause, however, you need to know about the difference between defining an SQL routine and defining an external routine.

An SQL routine is defined using an SQL routine body, and an SQL routine body is trivial (from a syntactic viewpoint, at least); it is simply a single SQL statement. Of course, if SQL/PSM (or a proprietary analog) is supported in your implementation, then that SQL statement can be a compound statement: BEGIN...END.

An external routine is defined by providing an external body reference. The use of the word *reference* in that phrase implies that the actual code of the external routine is not provided at this point. Unlike an SQL routine, it doesn't make sense to provide an SQL processor with, say, your C code. Instead, you provide the name of the routine, and the system locates the routine in some manner specified by your implementation. If you leave off the external routine name clause, then the name is presumed to be the same as the third part of the three-part <schema qualified routine name>. You can specify either an identifier or a character string literal as the name. Although SQL:1999 isn't specific about this, we presume that the character string literal should specify a fully qualified file-name identifying the object code for your external routine. And, lest you forget, an external routine is one that is written in one of several host languages (which you must specify in the <language clause>).

Part of an external body reference is the <external security clause>, which was discussed (in terms of its keywords, not in terms of the BNF symbol) in section 14.2.1, subsection "Using User Authorization Identifiers and Role Names." We won't repeat that discussion here, but you might wish to take a quick look at that section now to refresh your memory of the three alternatives and their meanings. It would also be beneficial for you to quickly refresh your memory of the discussion of SQL-session authorization stacks that you saw in section 14.2.1, subsection "The SQL-Session Authorization Stacks."

Now, from Chapter 12, "Accessing SQL from the Real World," you'll recall that none of the host languages support SQL's null values (this is one of the contributors to that impedance mismatch we've discussed in several places). Therefore, if you want your external routines, written in a host language, to deal with null values, you have to use the appropriate style of parameter for that external routine. You can specify PARAMETER STYLE SQL or PARAMETER STYLE GENERAL; if you don't specify, then the default is PARAMETER STYLE SQL. (Incidentally, you are not allowed to specify this clause at all for SQL routines, since their parameters are inherently PARAMETER STYLE SQL.)

PARAMETER STYLE GENERAL means that each parameter in the routine declaration corresponds to one argument in invocations of the routine. That's it. You write your external routine with one parameter for each argument that you want your users to code in their routine invocations. Each parameter has the data type that you specify in the declaration (well, to be completely honest, you must ensure that the host language type of the parameter is compatible, according to SQL's rules, with the SQL data type that you declared in the parameter declarations). When the routine is invoked, the input arguments provided in the routine invocation are simply passed to the routine as the values of the corresponding parameters, and any output arguments are returned from the routine as the values of the corresponding parameters. Of course, you cannot ever pass null values in either direction when you use PARAMETER STYLE GENERAL, because the host language's types do not support that concept. (Naturally, if you're writing both the routines and the code invoking them, you could invent a convention to signal that you're passing a null value, such as using the character string '**null value**' or using a numeric −1 if that's not a normally valid value for a parameter, to avoid using PARAMETER STYLE SQL. However, we don't recommend this approach because it is likely to cause confusion among the programmers who maintain your code in the future.) If you want to use external routines that were not written specifically to be used in SQL code, such as routines written for a different purpose that you already happen to own, then PARAMETER STYLE GENERAL is your choice. While this choice doesn't allow you to exchange SQL-specific information, such as null values, between your SQL code and your external routines, it does allow the use of routines that know nothing about SQL's conventions.

PARAMETER STYLE SQL is a little more complicated, primarily because it allows—actually, it requires—you to account for null values. If you're writing external routines specifically for use with your SQL code, this is a better choice. For every argument, input or output (or both), that you declare in the definition of an external routine, the external routine itself must be coded to have two parameters, one to exchange non-null values and the other to exchange an indicator parameter (see Chapter 12, "Accessing SQL from the Real World" for a discussion of indicators). If the external routine is an SQL-invoked function, then you must provide two additional parameters: one is for the value returned from the function, and the other is the indicator parameter for that return value (in case it's a null value). Finally, you must provide either four or six additional parameters (six only if you're defining a function that is an *array-returning external function*, discussed in section 17.4.2). The parameter meanings are given in Table 17-1 for external procedures and in Table 17-2 for external functions.

Table 17-1 *PARAMETER STYLE SQL Parameter Meanings for External Procedures*

Effective Parameter Number	Meaning or Use
1 – N	Values of actual parameters 1 – N from invoker to routine
N + 1 – 2N	Values of indicator parameters for parameters 1 – N to routine
2N + 1	SQLSTATE value returned to invoker
2N + 2	Routine's "invokable" name
2N + 3	Routine's specific name
2N + 4	Message text from routine returned to invoker

Table 17-2 *PARAMETER STYLE SQL Parameter Meanings for External Functions*

Effective Parameter Number	Meaning or Use
1 – N	Values of actual parameters 1 – N from invoker to routine
N + 1	Value of function result returned to invoker
N + 2 – 2N + 1	Values of indicator parameters for parameters 1 – N to routine
2N + 2	Indicator for function result returned to invoker
2N + 3	SQLSTATE value returned to invoker
2N + 4	Routine's "invokable" name
2N + 5	Routine's specific name
2N + 6	Message text from routine returned to invoker
2N + 5 – 2N + 6	Used only for array-returning external functions (and not present for other external functions)

Therefore, if you're writing an external function in, say, C or PL/I that has three input parameters (from SQL's viewpoint), and you want this function to deal with null values, then the actual C or PL/I code requires a function definition with 12 parameters: $((3 + 1) * 2) + 4$. We draw your attention to the fact that Table 17-2 states that some parameters are used to return information to the invoker. This does not invalidate our earlier statement that SQL-invoked procedures have only input parameters. From SQL's point of view, that remains true even in Table 17-2, since all of the external function's parameters that correspond directly to an SQL argument are input-only. Only the "supplementary" parameters return values.

Now that we know how to create and invoke SQL-invoked routines, let's take a look at the ways in which such routines can be modified after they've been created.

Syntax 17-2 *Syntax for Altering SQL-Invoked Routine Definitions*

```
ALTER <specific routine designator>
    <alter routine characteristic>... RESTRICT

<specific routine designator> ::=
    SPECIFIC { ROUTINE | FUNCTION | PROCEDURE } <specific name>
  | { ROUTINE | FUNCTION | PROCEDURE } <schema qualified routine name>
    [ ( <data type> { , <data type> }... ) ]
```

```
<alter routine characteristic> ::=
    <language clause>
  | <parameter style clause>
  | <SQL-data access indication>
  | <null-call clause>
  | <dynamic result sets characteristic>
  | NAME <external routine name>
```

You will quickly observe in Syntax 17-2 that you identify an SQL-invoked routine whose definition you want to alter by specifying something called a `<specific routine designator>`, which you also see defined in Syntax 17-2. The `<specific routine designator>` gives you two alternatives for identifying the routine whose definition you plan to alter. One alternative is simply specifying the `<specific name>` of the routine. If you use this alternative with the keyword `ROUTINE`, then the routine being altered can be either a function or a procedure. If you use `SPECIFIC FUNCTION`, then the routine identified by the `<specific name>` must be a function; naturally, if you use `SPECIFIC PROCEDURE`, the routine identified by the `<specific name>` must be a procedure.

The other alternative allows you to identify a routine by its invokable name. Since there might be multiple routines with the same invokable name, you may have to provide a list of the data types of the parameters to identify the specific routine that you wish to alter. Section 17.7 contains a discussion of the ability to have multiple routines with the same invokable name, and section 17.8 indicates how such routines are distinguished from one another.

Syntax 17-2 also provides a list of alternatives by which you identify the characteristic of the SQL-invoked routine that you want altered. This list is similar to the list of `<routine characteristic>`s that you could define (see Syntax 17-1), but there are differences. You cannot alter the `<specific name>` of a routine, nor can you alter the deterministic characteristics of a routine. But you can change the `<external routine name>` of an external routine, which will allow you to associate the SQL routine name with a different bit of object code—handy for changing to a new version of an external function or procedure.

The use of the keyword `RESTRICT` means simply this: you are not allowed to alter the definition of any SQL-invoked routine in your database if the routine is currently in use anywhere in the database—that is, if it is invoked from another routine, invoked in a view definition, and so on.

Syntax 17-3 *Syntax for Dropping SQL-Invoked Routines*

```
DROP <specific routine designator> { RESTRICT | CASCADE }
```

As with altering a routine definition as indicated in Syntax 17-2, when you want to drop a routine from your database, you identify the routine to be dropped by using either its specific name or its invokable name, possibly accompanied by a list of its parameters' data types. If you specify RESTRICT, then the drop will fail if there are any dependencies on the routine in the database. By contrast, if you specify CASCADE, dropping the routine implies dropping all objects that depend on it. CASCADE should always be used with great care.

17.4 | External Routines

So far, we've talked about SQL-invoked routines in general: SQL routines and external routines. Some of the syntax used for creating SQL-invoked routines varies depending on which of these two kinds of routine you're defining, but most of it is the same for both sorts. There are some important differences in the way the two types of routine are used and we examine them in this section.

17.4.1 Use and Need for External Routines

There are, in our opinion, three compelling reasons to consider the use of external routines. You may already own a number of routines written in some host language—a statistical package, for example. If you find that you need the capabilities provided by routines that you already own, then SQL's ability to provide access to those external routines saves you development time and other resources.

In addition, we observe that few SQL products implement SQL/PSM's procedural language, and the proprietary analogs of PSM (e.g., Oracle's PL/SQL and Sybase's Transact-SQL) aren't very portable among products. If you spend the resources to build a number of routines that require computational completeness, writing the routines in a host language may well mean that you can use them on several SQL database products. By contrast, if you develop them in the Microsoft SQL Server dialect of TSQL, you can't easily run them on an Informix database product.

Finally, you might discover that you have a need for certain functionality that is computationally intensive, such as time-series analysis of daily, weekly, monthly, and quarterly sales of DVD sales versus VHS tape sales. Writing such routines in SQL might not give you the performance that you need; after all, SQL is usually highly optimized for set-oriented database operations, not for computation-intensive math. Another language, such as Fortran or C, might offer significant computation performance advantages for uses like this one.

17.4.2 Array-Returning External Functions

You learned about SQL:1999's ARRAY data type in section 2.4.8, "Collection (or Array) Types." It's true that most, if not all, host languages support an ARRAY data type of one sort or another. One might conclude that it would be fairly easy to define a way to exchange arrays between a host program and a bit of SQL code or, conversely, between a bit of SQL code and an external function.

Unfortunately, that's not the case. Fortran programs can exchange arrays with Fortran subprograms, but that's because both sides of that interface are Fortran and the Fortran calling conventions support the exchange of arrays. An analogous statement can be made about other languages. But exchanging arrays between SQL code and code written in another language raises additional problems.

SQL:1999 defines an *array-returning external function* as a function that returns an array as the "value" of the function. That is, the function does not return an array as the value of any of its parameters, but as the value of the function itself.

SQL:1999 does this "behind the scenes" by invoking the function multiple times. That is, your SQL code only invokes the function once, but the SQL implementation takes a number of steps designed to retrieve the contents of the array one element at a time and return the entire array to you when it's ready. The first (behind-the-scenes) invocation acts as a sort of "open" that initializes the routine to return array elements. Each subsequent invocation behaves like a "fetch" that retrieves a single array element, until all elements have been retrieved (or the function's invoker no longer wants additional elements). One final call is then made to "close" the array retrieval.

In Table 17-2, the last entry indicated that two parameters deal with array-returning functions:

2N + 5 – 2N + 6	Used only for array-returning external functions (and not present for other external functions)

Parameter 2N + 5 is called the *save area data item,* and parameter 2N + 6 is called the *call type data item*. These two parameters are used to maintain the state, or the history, of the function invocation. The array-returning external function must be written to examine these parameters and respond appropriately. When you invoke an array-returning external function, SQL's routine invocation code sets the save area data item to zero and the call type data item to –1. That call type data item value, –1, tells the array-returning external function that this invocation is meant to "open" the array. In other words, the function should retrieve the values of all of its parameters and perform whatever processing it needs to perform in order to be ready to return the elements of the array.

When the function returns, the SQL system intercepts that return instead of handing control back to your SQL code. The SQL system checks the value of parameter 2N + 3 (the exception data item) that the function set. If the value indicates successful completion ('00000') or warning (in which the first two characters are 'C1'), then the system sets the value of the call type data item to zero, indicating "fetch," and invokes the function again. If the value of the exception data item indicates "no data" ('02000'), then the system sets the value of the call type data item to one, indicating "close," and invokes the function again.

When the function is invoked with the call type data item set to zero, it returns the value of a single array element ("the next" element, based on the history of invocations) to the SQL system, which places the returned value into "the next" element of the array that will be returned to your SQL code.

When the function is invoked with the call type data item set to one, it does its housekeeping and returns to the SQL system, which then returns the newly populated array to your SQL code.

This means that every external function that you write to return an array to your SQL code has to have three separate processing sections: one to initiate processing, one to retrieve and return a single array element, and one to close up shop and release any resources used. One artifact of this three-step process is that your external function doesn't have to "materialize" the array value all at once; in fact, the array doesn't have to be completely materialized as an array. Instead, your external function can generate the values corresponding to the array elements as it is requested to return those values.

That's a moderately complex process, but it does solve—rather nicely, we think—the problem of passing an array between a host language function and your SQL code.

17.4.3 Where Are External Routines Actually Stored?

One question that we are sometimes asked is this: Where, exactly, are external routines stored? Are they stored in the SQL database, right there in the schema along with the tables? Or are they stored elsewhere in the computer's file system—or, indeed, on another computer system—and just "pointed to" by the database?

The SQL standard takes no position on this, nor should it. Decisions about such matters are strictly implementation decisions. The SQL standard can only specify what the semantics must be regardless of how any particular product chooses to implement it.

In fact, the *definition* of every external routine—the metadata that provides its invokable name, its specific name, and the rest of its characteristics—does appear in the Information Schema of the database. But, as we told you in section 17.3.3, that metadata includes the external name of the routine, which might well be a file specification, including all device and directory information. The SQL standard provides the flexibility that individual products use to develop conforming implementations based on the vendors' perception of customer requirements.

17.4.4 External Routine Execution Context

In section 14.2.1, subsections "Using User Authorization Identifiers and Role Names," and "The SQL-Session Authorization Stacks," we described SQL:1999's algorithm for determining the appropriate privileges to use when executing SQL statements in various circumstances. One of those circumstances is the execution of an external routine. As you learned in those sections, the privileges used during the execution of an external routine depend on how the routine was created—that is, whether its <external security clause> specified DEFINER, INVOKER, or IMPLEMENTATION DEFINED. That, of course, is part of the context in which an external routine is executed.

However, the context is more than just the authorization identifier (user identifier and/or role name) that is chosen. It includes other obvious items such as the temporary tables and cursors that are defined in the external routine.

But that raises an important question: Does the external routine itself contain SQL code in the form of embedded SQL statements? (Analogously, does it invoke SQL statements that are contained in externally invoked procedures collected into SQL-client modules?)

Obviously, not all external routines will themselves execute SQL statements. If you've purchased a package of statistical routines, it may be very unlikely that the routines in that package use SQL at all. On the other hand, your organization may have a large collection of routines that do use SQL code and that you are able to reuse for your applications.

External routines that do not contain SQL code or invocations of SQL code should be created using an <SQL-data access indication> that specifies NO SQL. Such routines can be treated generally as though they execute in the same process space as the SQL code that invokes them. (However, we note that *process space* is a term highly dependent on specific implementation technologies and may not even apply to your environment. Furthermore, some implementations allow you to "bring in" such external routines into the database's process space for the performance advantages that ability offers, while others may force you to keep such external routines "firewalled" off into a different process space for a variety of reasons, including the security of your database data or the stability of the database environment.)

External routines that do contain embedded SQL, or invocations of externally invoked procedures, are always given their own SQL-session context in which to operate. This context includes all characteristics that any SQL-session context includes (see Chapter 16, "Connections and Remote Database Access," for additional information). Perhaps the only important difference between this context and the one created when you first initiate an SQL session is how the authorization identifiers are determined; you read about that in Chapter 14, "Privileges, Users, and Security."

17.4.5 External Routine Advantages and Disadvantages

Like any other technology, the external routines come with advantages and disadvantages. We mentioned several advantages earlier:

- You may already own routines written in a host language that were created for a different purpose.
- External routines may perform computationally intensive tasks more efficiently than SQL routines.
- External routines may be more portable among SQL database systems from different vendors.
- External routines provide the ability to invoke identical program code within the database and in other parts of your application.
- External routines support invokers' rights, which SQL routines do not support (in SQL:1999, at least).

However, there are disadvantages to be considered, too:

- Moving data between an external routine and your SQL code involves the famous impedance mismatch, both with data types and with set orientation versus single-datum orientation.
- Creation of new SQL sessions for the execution of external routines that contain SQL code may be quite expensive, and changing between various session contexts is very likely to have a negative impact on your performance.
- Your application development process may suffer from having to consider development in yet another programming language. (This is somewhat offset by the fact that SQL's computational completeness capabilities require learning the procedural statements, block structuring conventions, etc.)

In short, don't be afraid of external routines, but think about the implications before you make the choice to use them in your database applications.

17.5 | SQL Routines

By contrast, using SQL routines might be considered a "no-brainer." After all, you're already using SQL, so why not use it for everything that your applications do, at least within the database server.

17.5.1 Use and Need for SQL Routines

But the situation isn't quite that simple. Sure, using SQL for all of your application components (at least the components that reside at the database server) has these advantages:

- no impedance mismatch
- no context switching overhead
- no "special parameter lists" to be handled (see section 17.4.2)
- reduced training and debugging costs, as your database developers work only in SQL

In many situations, those advantages will prove to be persuasive, and you would be right to make the choice to use SQL for your stored routines. But, even in an environment where that choice is appropriate for most stored routines, there may be cases where the disadvantages outweigh the advantages:

- If you already own a routine that performs a specific function, rewriting it in SQL costs you valuable development resources, especially if you expect the routine to be invoked relatively infrequently and it doesn't require the use of any SQL statements to do its job.
- If the routine must make extensive computations, SQL routines might not perform as well as your application requires.
- If the routine is expected to contain complex logic and you need the ability to run the routine on different database systems, you might not wish to lock yourself into either SQL/PSM's computationally complete statements or any one vendor's equivalent proprietary language.

In spite of these tradeoffs, we believe that using SQL routines offers enough advantages in many, possibly a majority of, situations that you should only rarely reject the SQL routine approach in favor of external routines. The principal exception to this recommendation arises when your database system supports the use of Java as a programming language in which external routines can be written. The availability to Java changes the situation sufficiently to cause us to react much more favorably to the use of external routines, largely because of its ability to run in a variety of environments without change.[5]

17.5.2 Storing and Managing SQL Routines

SQL routines are created, altered, and dropped using the same SQL statements that perform those operations for external routines.

The primary differences exist because of the additional requirements that external routines have, such as the external routine name and the external security clause.

Of course, your SQL engine is likely to do a better job of discovering the dependencies that various database objects (views, for example) have on other objects that are accessed through SQL routines than on other objects that are accessed through external routines. We suspect that SQL implementations that track such dependencies closely may place more restrictions on altering and dropping SQL routines than on external reasons because of the relative ease of tracking the dependencies through SQL routines. (Certainly, SQL:1999 mandates better tracking of SQL routine dependencies.)

17.6 | Limitations of SQL for Stored Routines

In Chapter 11, "Active Databases," we told you that "because of the power available in SQL-invoked routines, your triggers can invoke procedures that send e-mail messages, print documents, or activate robotic equipment to retrieve inventory to be shipped." Indeed, an external routine can do anything supported by the language in which it's written, as long as your database implementation supports the capability. (This caveat is important, because some implementations may prohibit external routines from performing nondatabase input/output operations in the interests of security or performance.) We know that some

---

5 For additional information on the use of Java in your database system, see Jim Melton and Andrew Eisenberg, *Understanding SQL and Java Together—A Guide to SQLJ, JDBC, and Related Technologies* (San Francisco: Morgan Kaufmann Publishers, 2000).

implementations allow external routines to invoke arbitrary system services to send e-mail, broadcast messages to all users, or initiate other processes.

By contrast, an SQL routine is limited to SQL statements and the operations that they provide—that is, they're pretty much restricted to database operations. If you need an SQL-invoked routine to send e-mail, that routine's going to have to be an external routine written in C, COBOL, or some other host language.

17.7 | Polymorphism

The SQL-invoked routine facility was designed so that those routines are *polymorphic*, meaning that they have the characteristic of *polymorphism*. The word *polymorphism* comes from the Greek word πολιμορφοσ (in Latin characters, that's *polimorphos*), meaning "many forms." Webster's *Third New International Dictionary* defines the related word *polymorphic* to mean "having or assuming various forms, characters, styles, or functions."

We particularly like Webster's use of "various . . . functions," since that is extremely appropriate for SQL's purposes. After all, the word here is used to indicate that multiple SQL-invoked routines share a routine name. If we're to be strict in our use of the term, it's really the *routine name* that's polymorphic. After all, the routine name is what we would see as "having . . . various . . . functions" associated with it. And, as we saw earlier in this chapter, SQL-invoked routines each have unique (nonpolymorphic—or is that monomorphic? or unimorphic?) "specific names" that can be used to identify the routines when, for example, you want to drop them.

In this context, then, the word implies that a single name, the <schema qualified routine name>, can be applied to more than one routine. The actual behavior that occurs in response to a routine invocation using that name is determined by other factors, such as the number of arguments provided in the routine invocation, the data types of those arguments, and the path that governs which schemas are "searched" to locate routines to be considered.

17.8 | Routine Resolution Outline

Because the algorithm that SQL uses to determine the exact, single routine to invoke in response to a routine invocation is somewhat complex, we first briefly review the criteria used by the algorithm. After that, we provide a numbered list that identifies the principal steps that are involved.

Because SQL:1999 permits you to define multiple routines having the same routine name, the obvious goal of the routine resolution algorithm is to determine the routine that provides the *best match* for a given routine invocation. Please note that we said "the best match"; that phrase implies that there could well be more than one routine that provides a *possible* match for the routine invocation.

Of course, the primary criterion that the algorithm uses is the routine name: no routine named *Y* would even be considered as a candidate routine for a routine invocation that specifies a routine named *X*. In addition, the algorithm distinguishes between functions and procedures, so that function invocations are matched only with functions and procedure calls only with procedures. The next most important criterion is the number of arguments in the routine invocation; SQL:1999 won't consider any routine that has fewer or more parameters than the number of arguments specified in the routine invocation.

So far, that seems simple enough, doesn't it? Unfortunately, there's a complication: in spite of the fact that SQL is in many ways "strongly typed" (meaning that it discourages you from mixing data types in expressions and so forth), there are a number of areas where the language provides you with friendlier support for using "nearly the same" data type. One place you will find this relaxation of strong typing is in arithmetic operators such as +; SQL allows you to add an INTEGER value and a REAL value instead of requiring you to first convert the INTEGER value to REAL and then performing the addition. Similarly, SQL:1999 allows you to code a routine invocation with an INTEGER argument when the routine you want to use defines the corresponding parameter as REAL. Because you might also have a routine with the same name and same number of parameters, but with that corresponding parameter defined as INTEGER, the routine resolution algorithm has to consider a *precedence* relationship between data types in order to determine the best match.

Finally, there's one more important criterion to be applied: Only those routines for which you have the required EXECUTE privilege are considered. This is also a little more complex than it sounds at first glance, since the definition of "you" (as you learned in Chapter 14, "Privileges, Users, and Security") isn't what might be intuitively assumed. The context of the routine invocation might be any of several possibilities: the routine invocation might appear in an embedded SQL statement; it might be contained in another stored routine; it might even occur in a statement being executed dynamically. Each of these could produce a different "current user" whose privileges determine which actual routines are considered to have a possible match for the routine invocation.

Given those criteria, here's the list of the steps that the algorithm takes. Let us be clear: this is a *naive* look at the algorithm; the real thing is more complex, and we refer you to another reference for the gory details.

1. We start with a routine invocation for some routine whose routine name is R with arguments $A_1, A_2, \ldots, A_n$.

2. The algorithm then identifies all routines whose name is R that are stored in schemas (regardless of whether the routines are schema-level routines or are contained in SQL-server modules) that are part of the current path.

3. If the routine invocation is a function invocation, then all procedures named R are eliminated; if the routine invocation is a call of a procedure, then all functions named R are eliminated.

4. All routines for which the current user does not hold EXECUTE privilege are eliminated.

5. All routines that do not have the right number of parameters (in this case, *n*) are eliminated.

At this point, we have identified the routines that are reasonable candidates for invocation and can start determining the best match based on the specific data types of the arguments.

6. For each argument $(A_1, A_2, \ldots, A_n)$, eliminate any routine for which any corresponding parameter's data type is not in the *type precedence list* of the data type of the argument. The type precedence list of a data type is a list of data types to which the subject data type can be converted, in order of preference. For example, the type precedence list for the SMALLINT data type includes both INTEGER and DOUBLE PRECISION; however, converting to INTEGER is obviously more direct than converting to DOUBLE PRECISION, so INTEGER appears earlier in the type precedence list for SMALLINT.

You should note that the functions' return data types are *not* taken into consideration. It might have been possible to design this algorithm to consider each function's return data type as though it were a sort of parameter, but that would raise questions about what data type is associated with the "argument" corresponding to that return value, and that could be determined only by analysis of the context in which the function invocation appears, which is rarely completely unambiguous (a variety of data types is often appropriate because of, for example, SQL's casting rules). SQL's designers chose not to take this approach; instead, the algorithm selects the best function based on matches between actual arguments and parameters and gives a syntax error if that function's return data type is inappropriate for the context in which the function invocation appears.

7. If there is more than one routine left after all this elimination, then the algorithm makes the seemingly arbitrary decision of choosing the routine contained in the schema appearing earlier in the path than any other schema containing a remaining, competing routine. (Yes, it's arbitrary, but the assumption is made that you can reorder the names of schemas in your path to exercise some control over the selection of routines in this situation.)

8. Arguments with data type that doesn't exactly match the data type of the corresponding parameter have to be implicitly converted to the right data type using SQL's rules for assignment, and the same might be true of the return value from a function as well.

The details of the algorithm are rather more extensive; in fact, the PSM book to which we referred you earlier,[6] spends no less than four full pages on it. Since the details have not changed in SQL:1999 (other than the effects caused by user-defined types, to which we must refer you to Volume 2 of this book), we have not reproduced the minutiae here.

17.9 | Chapter Summary

In this chapter, we introduced SQL-invoked routines, including routines written in SQL and those written in a host language. These routines can be procedures invoked with an SQL CALL statement, or they can be functions that are invoked as part of an expression. We showed you the SQL statements used for creating, altering, and dropping SQL-invoked routines and discussed in some detail the various syntax components of those statements. In addition, we compared and contrasted the capabilities of SQL routines and external routines. Finally, we reviewed, at a fairly high level, the algorithm that SQL uses for resolving SQL-invoked routine invocations.

---

6   Melton, *Understanding SQL's Stored Procedures.*

Chapter
18

Dynamic SQL

Introduction

Dynamic SQL is the name usually applied to the facility that allows you to execute SQL statements whose complete text you don't know until you're ready to execute them. This has a number of different aspects, and we cover all of them (well, at least all of the important ones) in this chapter.

18.2 What Is Dynamic SQL?

Under many (perhaps even most) circumstances, you know in complete detail all of the SQL statements that you need to execute during your application, and you know them well in advance (when you are writing your application, normally). This knowledge allows you to write SQL modules or embedded SQL programs that contain those SQL statements and to write application program code to invoke those SQL statements in the sequence that they are needed. Whether you are writing an SQL module to do your online company's payroll, or you are writing C language programs with embedded SQL to do movie title lookups, you usually have a pretty good idea in advance of the SQL statements you'll need.

However, you will occasionally encounter situations in which the full text of the SQL statements aren't fully known while you are writing your application.

It's even possible that you won't know *any* of the text of the statements. For example, you may sometimes allow an end user to enter an SQL statement, or part of one. Or, more likely, that person might be using a tool for querying and reporting to perform data analysis or other "business intelligence" types of functionality that he or she might be performing against a data warehouse (see Appendix A, "Designing SQL:1999 Databases," for a brief discussion of data warehousing).

Of course, that user may use interactive SQL sometimes—to run standard "canned" reports, for example—but let's consider the case where the user is really running your application and you only want him or her to enter a single SQL statement just for the purposes of your application. Well, you couldn't have coded that statement in advance, because you hadn't a clue about what the user might choose to enter. SQL:1999 (and almost all SQL products of any level) allows you to use dynamic SQL facilities to execute that statement.

Another example involves a spreadsheet package that stores all of its data in an SQL database. As the user enters formulae into the cells of the spreadsheet, the package can convert those formulae into SQL statements that retrieve the appropriate data and compute the desired results. These SQL statements are generated in real time and therefore couldn't possibly be coded in advance. However, dynamic SQL comes to the rescue again, allowing the spreadsheet package to "invent" statements as it requires them.

When you code your statements in an SQL module or in an embedded SQL program, you will process those statements through some sort of compiler—possibly a precompiler and then one or more compilers (see Chapter 12, "Accessing SQL from the Real World," for more information). That process gives the DBMS the opportunity to process the SQL statements and perhaps to optimize them. The compilers perform the required lexical and syntactic analysis on the SQL statements and then convert them to a form that the DBMS can use to further process them. Your DBMS then determines the most efficient ways to execute the statement in the context of the database (including use of indices, sequential scans, join algorithms, and so forth) and somehow saves the result of that analysis. As we saw in Chapter 12, "Accessing SQL from the Real World," this can take many forms, ranging from storing actual machine code somewhere in the database itself to building in-memory structures that are released as soon as the application has finished running one time. In any case, use of *static SQL* (a useful term for SQL coded into modules or embedded SQL programs) often has much or most of its processing overhead done long before application execution time.

By contrast, when you use dynamic SQL, none of that processing can be done in advance; it must all be done at application execution time. This often (but not always) results in reduced execution performance. As a consequence, you have to make careful decisions about when to use static SQL and when to use dynamic

SQL. Normally, we believe that the appropriate choice is to use static whenever you know the whole text of your statements in advance and dynamic only when that's not the case. The decision can sometimes be slightly more complex, though. Often, the text of the SQL statements isn't completely known, but there are only a few choices. In such a case, you might choose to code each alternative into a module or embedded SQL program and then select which alternative to execute based on user input. This may be more effective than using dynamic SQL, but not if there are hundreds of alternatives. Furthermore, in today's environment of Web browsers, multitier applications, and network access to unpredictable databases, a popular choice for connecting to many database systems is SQL's call-level interface—discussed in Chapter 19, "Call-Level Interface (CLI)"—which is inherently a dynamic SQL environment.

SQL:1999 does not allow you to execute *every* possible SQL statement dynamically. For some statements, it makes no sense at all to execute them dynamically. Other statements are used only to set up conditions for dynamic statements, so they must be handled as static SQL statements. In still other cases, static statements are provided explicitly to support dynamic SQL and are used in lieu of (potential, but nonexistent) dynamic alternatives. We cover all of this later in this chapter.

The philosophy of dynamic SQL is fairly simple; the realities are a bit more complicated. Let's look at it in this order: the overall philosophy first, followed by an outline of how it works, finishing up with the details.

18.3 | The Philosophy of Dynamic SQL

SQL statements can be executed in dynamic SQL in two ways. They can be prepared for execution and then executed as often and as many times as required by the application. Alternatively, they can be prepared and executed in one step (called *execute immediate*). If you PREPARE an SQL statement for execution, the results of that preparation are preserved for the remainder of your session; you can execute the statement as many times as required by your application during that session without incurring the overhead of the preparation a second time. (Think of the PREPARE step as doing the same work that would be done by the compiler/DBMS combination for static SQL.) If you use EXECUTE IMMEDIATE to execute an SQL statement, the results of the preparation are not preserved. If you want to execute the same statement again, you must incur the preparation overhead another time. Consequently, you will normally choose to use the separate PREPARE and EXECUTE steps for statements that you expect to be executed more than once, and the `EXECUTE IMMEDIATE` statement for statements that will be executed only a single time.

Why wouldn't you want to *always* use `PREPARE`/`EXECUTE` just in case? Simply because preserving the results of the preparation occupies system resources (e.g., dynamic memory), and you could overload a small system if you did that for all transient statements. And just to make things balance out, if you know you're done with an SQL statement that you `PREPARE`d, you can `DEALLOCATE PREPARE` to get rid of it and release those scarce resources.

Now, when you use static SQL, you (typically) write both the SQL statements and the host language statements (if you don't actually write them both yourself, you probably have a good design document that is used by writers of both types of statements—don't you?). That allows you to write your host language statements and SQL statements to mesh seamlessly (or as seamlessly as the impedance mismatches allow). You use the proper number of parameters or host variables for every SQL statement and always know whether you're `FETCH`ing, `UPDATE`ing, or `DELETE`ing.

However, when you're using dynamic SQL, you sometimes don't know these details, which makes it pretty difficult to write the host language statements to support those SQL statements. You may not even know whether the dynamic SQL statement will retrieve data from the database or store data into it. Worse, you may not have a clue about the numbers and types of parameters or host variables to use.

SQL:1999 solves this problem by allowing you to request the DBMS to *describe* the dynamic SQL statements. This description will tell you in great detail all of the information about the parameters used by the dynamic SQL statement. SQL:1999 even allows you to describe the dynamic SQL statement once to get information about the *input parameters* (those that give data from the host program to the SQL statement) and again to get information about the *output parameters* (those that return data retrieved by the SQL statement to the host program). When you `DESCRIBE` a dynamic SQL statement, the results are put into an *SQL item descriptor area* (we'll just call them *descriptor areas* from now on). These descriptor areas are defined in detail later in this chapter.

One particularly useful component of SQL's descriptor areas is the field named `DYNAMIC_FUNCTION` and its companion, `DYNAMIC_FUNCTION_CODE`. These two fields provide a character string and an integer code, respectively, that tells you just what sort of dynamic SQL statement you're dealing with. For example, if your application has just prepared for execution a positioned `UPDATE` statement that was provided by some other application, you can "describe" the statement (see section 18.7) and then examine the contents of `DYNAMIC_FUNCTION` and/or `DYNAMIC_FUNCTION_CODE`, which will be 'UPDATE WHERE' and 82, respectively.

Not at all incidentally, these are exactly the same values that are used in the COMMAND_FUNCTION and COMMAND_FUNCTION_CODE fields of the SQL diagnostics area (see Chapter 20, "Diagnostics and Error Management") to identify the SQL statement that caused an exception condition to be raised. By inspecting DYNAMIC_FUNCTION and/or DYNAMIC_FUNCTION_CODE after preparing and describing a statement, you know right away whether you've just prepared a statement that can generate output values (such as a SELECT statement) or not. As we'll see later in this chapter, you can also readily determine how many parameters the statement uses for input values.

18.3.1 Parameters

This talk of parameters brings us to look at the way information is passed to and from dynamic SQL statements. In static SQL statements, of course, you use a parameter or host variable (of the form *:name*). However, in dynamic SQL, there are no procedures to give meaning to parameters, and there's no host language context to give meaning to host variables. Consequently, dynamic SQL uses a convention known as a *dynamic parameter specification* (or *dynamic parameter* for short, although they are often called *parameter markers* as well), which is manifested by a question mark. Therefore, you will see dynamic SQL statements like this:

```
UPDATE movie_titles
  SET current_dvd_sale_price = ? WHERE title = ?
```

This statement has two dynamic parameters, both of them used to transmit data from the application program to the SQL statement. In static SQL, the data types of the host variables or parameters are declared and are available to the application program. In dynamic SQL, the data types of dynamic parameters must be inferred from the context. As a result, there are some limitations (covered later in this chapter) on exactly where you can use dynamic parameters.

When you have a dynamic SQL statement that contains names that aren't fully qualified (as in the preceding example, where the table name isn't qualified with a catalog and schema name), the system has to apply some default qualifications (just like the compilers do for static SQL). It's pretty simple to do that for static SQL, because you have the context of a module or an embedded program to use. For dynamic, there's not as much context, so SQL:1999 provides several statements to set the appropriate defaults for dynamic SQL statements.

18.3.2 Normal and Extended Dynamic

Some dynamic SQL objects (dynamic SQL statement names and dynamic SQL cursor names) come in two "flavors." One flavor may be thought of as normal dynamic statement names and cursor names. The other type is called *extended dynamic* statement names and cursor names. The primary difference is the *time* at which the name is known. Normal dynamic names are actual identifiers that you code in the statements that provide the dynamic SQL facilities. Extended dynamic names are represented in the dynamic-providing statements by parameters or host identifiers (:name); the *real* name of the dynamic name is provided at runtime by the application.

Normal dynamic names have the advantages of being self-documenting (that is, you or someone else can read your program and have a ghost of a chance of figuring out what's going on) and of allowing the DBMS to preallocate all resources necessary to operate on them. On the other hand, they also require that you know, *when you write your application,* the exact number (or at least the maximum number) of concurrently prepared statements and concurrently open cursors that your application will use.

By contrast, extended dynamic names allow your application to decide at runtime that it needs another prepared statement (without deallocating any existing prepared statements) or another dynamic cursor (without closing any existing open dynamic cursors) and to create one by assigning a new name to it. The disadvantage is that the DBMS must do additional work to deal with objects whose names or even whose existence aren't known until runtime. Because of these complications, SQL:1999 doesn't mandate implementation of extended dynamic statement names and cursors names; the feature is optional (and, we are disappointed to have to say, not widely implemented).

18.4 | Outline of Dynamic SQL Processing

When you want to process a dynamic SQL statement, you store the text of that statement into a character string host variable and execute either a PREPARE statement or an EXECUTE IMMEDIATE statement. (Equivalently, you call the module procedure that contains the PREPARE or EXECUTE IMMEDIATE statement and pass the dynamic SQL statement as a character string parameter.) Let's look at the normal path of PREPARE/EXECUTE first; then we'll have a look at the EXECUTE IMMEDIATE alternative.

The PREPARE statement analyzes the dynamic SQL statement for appropriate syntax, to determine the data types of the dynamic parameters (if any) and to optimize the execution of the statement. The results of the preparation are associated with a statement name that you'll use in later statements when you want to identify that prepared statement.

If you need to, you can DESCRIBE the dynamic SQL statement, using the statement name associated with it. If you choose to DESCRIBE, then you must also ALLOCATE a descriptor area. Based on the information put into the descriptor area by DESCRIBE, you can then EXECUTE the statement (again, using the associated statement name). You can EXECUTE the statement using two alternatives: retrieve and store information into the descriptor area, or retrieve and store information directly from and into the host program (using host variables or parameters). If you don't DESCRIBE, you can still ALLOCATE a descriptor area and EXECUTE using that descriptor area, or you can bypass the descriptor area and EXECUTE using host variables or parameters.

As an alternative to all that, you can simply execute the dynamic SQL statement using EXECUTE IMMEDIATE. However, because EXECUTE IMMEDIATE does not allow the use either of descriptor areas or of host variables or parameters, the dynamic SQL statement cannot contain any dynamic parameters.

Different actions are taken when you need to deal with cursors dynamically. These will be covered in the following detailed sections.

18.4.1 Parameters and Codes

In virtually all SQL DBMS products, you can use dynamic SQL. Most of these products use a data structure called an *SQL Descriptor Area,* or SQLDA, to deal with the information that must be exchanged in the use of dynamic SQL. The SQLDA is a data structure allocated in the 3GL program, and its details (structure, codes, etc.) vary, sometimes widely, from product to product, making it exceedingly difficult to write a truly portable application. To make matters worse, the SQLDA in all products include fields that are *pointers* (i.e., memory addresses) of other data. The standards for several languages (such as COBOL and Fortran) have no support for pointers or for dynamic storage allocation, so it was impossible in the SQL standard to provide a standardized specification for dynamic SQL that uses the SQLDA approach.

SQL-92 resolved this problem in a rather elegant way: by giving the DBMS the responsibility of allocating and managing the data necessary for dynamic SQL operation. This technique encapsulates the structure so that the implementation details are hidden from, and irrelevant to, the application program; it also lets the DBMS worry about storage allocation and deallocation and about handling pointer problems. Not only did this solve the problems that 3GLs such as COBOL and Fortran had with the SQLDA, but it also solved the portability problem (without requiring any existing DBMS or application program to change the existing SQLDA mechanisms—the products could simply *add* the new technique

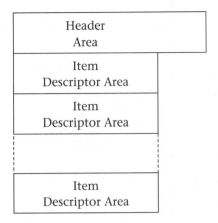

Figure 18-1   SQL Descriptor Area

and allow both to coexist). Unfortunately, by the time SQL:1999 was published, few commercial products had augmented their SQLDA implementations with SQL descriptor areas. We are uncertain whether this technique will ever be universally implemented, in spite of its advantages. The principal reason behind our doubts on this point is the fact that most vendors' compilers for various programming languages contain extensions (to the languages' standards) to support memory address pointers. These extensions overcome the problem that caused the creation of the SQL descriptor area approach in SQL-92.

The solution provided in SQL-92 and SQL:1999 requires the use of an *SQL descriptor area*, which is a DBMS-managed data structure made up of two components: a *header area* and an *item descriptor area*. Our mental image of this data structure is shown in Figure 18-1.

The header area is used to store information about the entire dynamic SQL statement that is being described. Table 18-1 contains information about the fields of the header area.

Table 18-1 *SQL Descriptor Area Header Fields*

<key word>	*Data Type*
COUNT	Exact numeric with scale 0 (zero)
DYNAMIC_FUNCTION	Character string with character set SQL_IDENTIFIER and length not less than 128 characters
DYNAMIC_FUNCTION_CODE	Exact numeric with scale 0 (zero)
KEY_TYPE	Exact numeric with scale 0 (zero)
TOP_LEVEL_COUNT	Exact numeric with scale 0 (zero)

An *item descriptor* area is used to store information about dynamic parameters in your dynamic SQL statements and about columns returned by dynamic SQL statements that retrieve data. A descriptor area must have enough room to store information about as many parameters or columns as you have in your dynamic SQL statement. Each dynamic parameter or column is represented in the descriptor area after execution of a DESCRIBE statement. The information recorded for each parameter or column is shown in Table 18-2.

Table 18-2 *Recorded Parameter Information*

<key word>	*Data Type*
CARDINALITY	Exact numeric with scale 0 (zero)
CHARACTER_SET_CATALOG	Character string with character set SQL_IDENTIFIER and length not less than 128 characters
CHARACTER_SET_NAME	Character string with character set SQL_IDENTIFIER and length not less than 128 characters
CHARACTER_SET_SCHEMA	Character string with character set SQL_IDENTIFIER and length not less than 128 characters
COLLATION_CATALOG	Character string with character set SQL_IDENTIFIER and length not less than 128 characters
COLLATION_NAME	Character string with character set SQL_IDENTIFIER and length not less than 128 characters
COLLATION_SCHEMA	Character string with character set SQL_IDENTIFIER and length not less than 128 characters
DATA	Matches the data type represented by the SQL item descriptor area
DATETIME_INTERVAL_CODE	Exact numeric with scale 0 (zero)
DATETIME_INTERVAL_PRECISION	Exact numeric with scale 0 (zero)
DEGREE	Exact numeric with scale 0 (zero)
INDICATOR	Exact numeric with scale 0 (zero)
KEY_MEMBER	Exact numeric with scale 0 (zero)
LENGTH	Exact numeric with scale 0 (zero)
LEVEL	Exact numeric with scale 0 (zero)
NAME	Character string with character set SQL_IDENTIFIER and length not less than 128 characters
NULLABLE	Exact numeric with scale 0 (zero)
OCTET_LENGTH	Exact numeric with scale 0 (zero)
PARAMETER_MODE	Exact numeric with scale 0 (zero)
PARAMETER_ORDINAL_POSITION	Exact numeric with scale 0 (zero)

(Continued)

Table 18-2 *Continued*

<key word>	*Data Type*
PARAMETER_SPECIFIC_CATALOG	Character string with character set SQL_IDENTIFIER and length not less than 128 characters
PARAMETER_SPECIFIC_NAME	Character string with character set SQL_IDENTIFIER and length not less than 128 characters
PARAMETER_SPECIFIC_SCHEMA	Character string with character set SQL_IDENTIFIER and length not less than 128 characters
PRECISION	Exact numeric with scale 0 (zero)
RETURNED_CARDINALITY	Exact numeric with scale 0 (zero)
RETURNED_LENGTH	Exact numeric with scale 0 (zero)
RETURNED_OCTET_LENGTH	Exact numeric with scale 0 (zero)
SCALE	Exact numeric with scale 0 (zero)
SCOPE_CATALOG	Character string with character set SQL_IDENTIFIER and length not less than 128 characters
SCOPE_NAME	Character string with character set SQL_IDENTIFIER and length not less than 128 characters
SCOPE_SCHEMA	Character string with character set SQL_IDENTIFIER and length not less than 128 characters
TYPE	Exact numeric with scale 0 (zero)
UNNAMED	Exact numeric with scale 0 (zero)
USER_DEFINED_TYPE_CATALOG	Character string with character set SQL_IDENTIFIER and length not less than 128 characters
USER_DEFINED_TYPE_NAME	Character string with character set SQL_IDENTIFIER and length not less than 128 characters
USER_DEFINED_TYPE_SCHEMA	Character string with character set SQL_IDENTIFIER and length not less than 128 characters

In Table 18-2, many fields are described as "character string with character set SQL_IDENTIFIER and length not less than 128 characters." The reason for requiring that the length be at least 128 characters is simple: SQL identifiers are allowed (by the standard, if not by all products) to be up to 128 characters in length, so the item descriptor area must be able to accommodate any valid identifier.

The data type description for the DATA field does not specify a particular data type, but requires that the data type "match" the data type represented by the other fields in the item descriptor area. This could have complicated the use of the SQL descriptor area slightly, but the potential complication is resolved by the use of special SQL statements (GET DESCRIPTOR and SET DESCRIPTOR, described later in this section) to access that field, as well as all other fields.

Some of the fields in the descriptor area contain codes instead of actual values. (Of course, these are only the codes seen by the application program; an implementation may use different codes internally or in the SQLDA.) One of those fields, TYPE, contains a code that indicates the data type of the dynamic parameter or the database column being described. These values are shown in Table 18-3. (We have sorted this table by the numeric code values, even though the SQL:1999 standard sorts it alphabetically by type name. We suspect that you will more often want to learn what data type is indicated by a code value that you've encountered than the other way around.)

Table 18-3 *TYPE Information*

Code	Data Type
< 0	Implementation-defined data types
1	CHARACTER
2	NUMERIC
3	DECIMAL
4	INTEGER
5	SMALLINT
6	FLOAT
7	REAL
8	DOUBLE PRECISION
9	DATE, TIME WITHOUT TIME ZONE, TIME WITH TIME ZONE, TIMESTAMP WITHOUT TIME ZONE, or TIMESTAMP WITH TIME ZONE
10	INTERVAL
12	CHARACTER VARYING
14	BIT
15	BIT VARYING
16	BOOLEAN
17	User-defined types
18	User-defined type LOCATOR
19	ROW
20	REF
30	BLOB
31	BLOB LOCATOR
40	CLOB
41	CLOB LOCATOR
50	ARRAY
51	ARRAY LOCATOR

Another code field is DATETIME_INTERVAL_CODE. Table 18-4 shows what the DATETIME_INTERVAL_CODE will be if TYPE contains 9 (DATE, TIME, or TIMESTAMP), and Table 18-5 shows the codes for cases where TYPE contains 10 (INTERVAL).

Table 18-4 *DATETIME_INTERVAL_CODE Information for DATE, TIME, or TIMESTAMP*

Value	Specific Data Type
1	DATE
2	TIME WITHOUT TIME ZONE
3	TIMESTAMP WITHOUT TIME ZONE
4	TIME WITH TIME ZONE
5	TIMESTAMP WITH TIME ZONE

Table 18-5 *DATETIME_INTERVAL_CODE Information for INTERVAL*

Value	Interval Code
1	YEAR
2	MONTH
3	DAY
4	HOUR
5	MINUTE
6	SECOND
7	YEAR TO MONTH
8	DAY TO HOUR
9	DAY TO MINUTE
10	DAY TO SECOND
11	HOUR TO MINUTE
12	HOUR TO SECOND
13	MINUTE TO SECOND

When you DESCRIBE (for input) a dynamic SQL statement that contains a dynamic parameter, the information about that parameter is put into a descriptor area (which you specify). The DBMS infers the data type information about the dynamic parameter from its context and fills in the relevant fields (other fields are ignored). When you DESCRIBE (for output) a dynamic SQL statement that contains references to database columns, the information about those columns will be put into an item descriptor area.

Let's look at an example of how these are used. First, let's assume that we have a simple table, with only a few columns, defined as follows:

```
CREATE TABLE movie_title (
    title                 CHARACTER (30),
    current_dvd_sale_price DECIMAL (5,2) NOT NULL,
    duration              INTERVAL HOUR(1) TO MINUTE,
    PRIMARY KEY (title)
)
```

Let's describe the following dynamic SQL statement,

```
SELECT title, current_dvd_sale_price, duration
FROM movie_titles INTO ?, ?, ?
```

to get the information about the database columns. First, we have to PREPARE the statement. (Assume that the host variable :stmt contains a character string representing the statement.)

```
PREPARE dynstmt FROM :stmt
```

This step causes the name DYNSTMT to be associated with the prepared (compiled) statement. Next, let's DESCRIBE the statement we've just prepared.

```
DESCRIBE OUTPUT dynstmt USING SQL DESCRIPTOR 'my_descr' ;
```

The information we get from this is shown in Tables 18-6, 18-7, 18-8, and 18-9.

Table 18-6 *Header Area Contents*

Field	Value
COUNT	3
DYNAMIC_FUNCTION	SELECT
DYNAMIC_FUNCTION_CODE	65
KEY_TYPE	1
TOP_LEVEL_COUNT	3

DESCRIBE OUTPUT is the operation we perform to determine the number of columns that the statement will return. The value of COUNT is 3 because that is the number of columns being retrieved in the SELECT statement that we just prepared and described. The value of TOP_LEVEL_COUNT is also 3 because none of those columns have data types that are composite, such as ROW. (In section 18.8, we'll discuss the descriptor area contents when composite and collections types are included.) DYNAMIC_FUNCTION indicates that the statement we've prepared is a SELECT statement, and 65 is the corresponding DYNAMIC_FUNCTION_CODE value. KEY_TYPE is 1 because a subset of the columns we're retrieving is the PRIMARY KEY of the table—in this case, that subset is the TITLE column.

Table 18-7 *Descriptor Area #1 Contents*

Field	Value
CARDINALITY	Doesn't matter
CHARACTER_SET_CATALOG	Catalog name for default character set
CHARACTER_SET_NAME	Schema name for default character set
CHARACTER_SET_SCHEMA	Name of default character set
COLLATION_CATALOG	Catalog name for default collation of default character set
COLLATION_NAME	Schema name for default collation of default character set
COLLATION_SCHEMA	Name of default collation of default character set
DATA	Set only when data is retrieved into descriptor area
DATETIME_INTERVAL_CODE	Doesn't matter
DATETIME_INTERVAL_PRECISION	Doesn't matter
DEGREE	Doesn't matter
INDICATOR	Set only when data is retrieved into descriptor area
KEY_MEMBER	1 (indicates that the column is part of a primary key)
LENGTH	30
LEVEL	0
NAME	TITLE
NULLABLE	0 (indicates that the column is not nullable)
OCTET_LENGTH	30, assuming normal ASCII is implementor-default
PARAMETER_MODE	Doesn't matter
PARAMETER_ORDINAL_POSITION	Doesn't matter
PARAMETER_SPECIFIC_CATALOG	Doesn't matter
PARAMETER_SPECIFIC_NAME	Doesn't matter
PARAMETER_SPECIFIC_SCHEMA	Doesn't matter
PRECISION	Doesn't matter
RETURNED_CARDINALITY	Doesn't matter
RETURNED_LENGTH	30
RETURNED_OCTET_LENGTH	30

(Continued)

Table 18-7 *Continued*

Field	Value
SCALE	Doesn't matter
SCOPE_CATALOG	Doesn't matter
SCOPE_NAME	Doesn't matter
SCOPE_SCHEMA	Doesn't matter
TYPE	1 (indicates the CHARACTER data type)
UNNAMED	0 (indicates that the column has a name)
USER_DEFINED_TYPE_CATALOG	Doesn't matter
USER_DEFINED_TYPE_NAME	Doesn't matter
USER_DEFINED_TYPE_SCHEMA	Doesn't matter

Table 18-8 *Descriptor Area #2 Contents*

Field	Value
CARDINALITY	Doesn't matter
CHARACTER_SET_CATALOG	Doesn't matter
CHARACTER_SET_NAME	Doesn't matter
CHARACTER_SET_SCHEMA	Doesn't matter
COLLATION_CATALOG	Doesn't matter
COLLATION_NAME	Doesn't matter
COLLATION_SCHEMA	Doesn't matter
DATA	Set only when data is retrieved into descriptor area
DATETIME_INTERVAL_CODE	Doesn't matter
DATETIME_INTERVAL_PRECISION	Doesn't matter
DEGREE	Doesn't matter
INDICATOR	Set only when data is retrieved into descriptor area
KEY_MEMBER	0 (indicates that the column is not part of a key)
LENGTH	Doesn't matter
LEVEL	0
NAME	CURRENT_DVD_SALE_PRICE
NULLABLE	0 (indicates that the column is not nullable)
OCTET_LENGTH	Doesn't matter
PARAMETER_MODE	Doesn't matter
PARAMETER_ORDINAL_POSITION	Doesn't matter
PARAMETER_SPECIFIC_CATALOG	Doesn't matter
PARAMETER_SPECIFIC_NAME	Doesn't matter

(Continued)

Table 18-8 *Continued*

Field	Value
PARAMETER_SPECIFIC_SCHEMA	Doesn't matter
PRECISION	5
RETURNED_CARDINALITY	Doesn't matter
RETURNED_LENGTH	Doesn't matter
RETURNED_OCTET_LENGTH	Doesn't matter
SCALE	2
SCOPE_CATALOG	Doesn't matter
SCOPE_NAME	Doesn't matter
SCOPE_SCHEMA	Doesn't matter
TYPE	3 (indicates the DECIMAL data type)
UNNAMED	0 (indicates that the column has a name)
USER_DEFINED_TYPE_CATALOG	Doesn't matter
USER_DEFINED_TYPE_NAME	Doesn't matter
USER_DEFINED_TYPE_SCHEMA	Doesn't matter

Table 18-9 *Descriptor Area #3 Contents*

Field	Value
CARDINALITY	Doesn't matter
CHARACTER_SET_CATALOG	Doesn't matter
CHARACTER_SET_NAME	Doesn't matter
CHARACTER_SET_SCHEMA	Doesn't matter
COLLATION_CATALOG	Doesn't matter
COLLATION_NAME	Doesn't matter
COLLATION_SCHEMA	Doesn't matter
DATA	Set only when data is retrieved into descriptor area
DATETIME_INTERVAL_CODE	11 (indicates precision of HOUR TO MINUTE)
DATETIME_INTERVAL_PRECISION	1
DEGREE	Doesn't matter
INDICATOR	Set only when data is retrieved into descriptor area
KEY_MEMBER	0 (indicates that the column is not part of a key)
LENGTH	Doesn't matter
LEVEL	0
NAME	DURATION
NULLABLE	1 (indicates that the column is nullable)

(Continued)

Table 18-9 *Continued*

Field	*Value*
OCTET_LENGTH	Doesn't matter
PARAMETER_MODE	Doesn't matter
PARAMETER_ORDINAL_POSITION	Doesn't matter
PARAMETER_SPECIFIC_CATALOG	Doesn't matter
PARAMETER_SPECIFIC_NAME	Doesn't matter
PARAMETER_SPECIFIC_SCHEMA	Doesn't matter
PRECISION	Doesn't matter
RETURNED_CARDINALITY	Doesn't matter
RETURNED_LENGTH	Doesn't matter
RETURNED_OCTET_LENGTH	Doesn't matter
SCALE	Doesn't matter
SCOPE_CATALOG	Doesn't matter
SCOPE_NAME	Doesn't matter
SCOPE_SCHEMA	Doesn't matter
TYPE	10 (indicates the INTERVAL data type)
UNNAMED	0 (indicates that the column has a name)
USER_DEFINED_TYPE_CATALOG	Doesn't matter
USER_DEFINED_TYPE_NAME	Doesn't matter
USER_DEFINED_TYPE_SCHEMA	Doesn't matter

Now, recall that we said earlier that you have to allocate the descriptor areas. You can also deallocate them when you no longer need them (to recapture system resources), but they will automatically be deallocated for you when your session ends.

To allocate a descriptor area, you use the ALLOCATE DESCRIPTOR statement (bet you saw that coming, didn't you?):

```
ALLOCATE DESCRIPTOR desc-name [ WITH MAX occurrences ]
```

The desc-name is either a literal or a host variable or parameter (remember that we called this category of things *simple value specifications*); obviously, it has to be a character string that follows the rules of an identifier. Actually, you can precede the simple value specification with the keyword LOCAL or the keyword GLOBAL (if you don't specify either one, then LOCAL is assumed). LOCAL means that the descriptor is available only to the module or compilation unit in which you allocated it, while GLOBAL means that all of your modules or compilation units can share it during your session. occurrences is an integer simple value specification that tells the DBMS how many descriptor area items to make room for. If you leave it off, then you'll get whatever your vendor wants to give you. All values in all items of the descriptor area are initially undefined, so you either have to use a DESCRIBE to get the DBMS to fill them in, or you have to do it yourself with a SET DESCRIPTOR statement (coming right up).

When you're finished using a descriptor area and want to recover those scarce system resources, you can deallocate it:

```
DEALLOCATE DESCRIPTOR desc-name
```

Of course, if you give an incorrect name, you'll get an error. If you give a correct name (that is, the name of a descriptor that you've allocated with the same GLOBAL or LOCAL scope during the session), it will be deallocated, and everything currently stored in it will be lost forever!

If you want to retrieve information from a descriptor area, you use the GET DESCRIPTOR statement. This statement has two variations, one to get the number of filled-in items, and the other to get information from a specific item.

To get the number of filled-in items, the format is as follows:

```
GET DESCRIPTOR desc-name
  target = COUNT
```

As you saw in Table 18-6, COUNT is a keyword that indicates a field in the header area. The COUNT field identifies the number of item descriptors that are filled in for the statement that is described.

The desc-name is the name of a descriptor area that you have allocated with the same GLOBAL or LOCAL scope during the session. (We're getting tired of writing that phrase, and you're probably tired of reading it. How about if we just say *valid descriptor area* from now on, and you'll understand that we mean all that other stuff? Okay?) target is a host variable or a parameter that you specify to receive the integer that tells you the number of items that are in use in this descriptor area.

You can get the values of each field of the header area by using the appropriate keyword; we've already seen the use of COUNT. The remaining header area fields keywords are KEY_TYPE, DYNAMIC_FUNCTION, DYNAMIC_FUNCTION_CODE, and TOP_LEVEL_COUNT.

To get information from a specific item, the format is as follows:

```
GET DESCRIPTOR desc-name
  VALUE item-number
  target = item-name [ , target = item-name ]...
```

As before, desc-name is the name of a valid descriptor area. item-number is an integer simple value specification that identifies the specific item in the descriptor area. It must be no greater than the value you got (or could have gotten) from COUNT, or you'll get a no-data return; if it's greater than the number of occurrences allocated for the descriptor area, you'll get an error. target is a parameter or host variable of the appropriate data type to get the value stored in the item field identified by item-name (actually, these are *simple targets* because they can never be null; therefore, no indicator parameter or variable is needed or permitted). And item-name is one of the names in that table earlier in this chapter.

If the value of the INDICATOR field is negative (meaning that the item describes a null value) and you use GET DESCRIPTOR to get a value for DATA without also GETting a value for INDICATOR, you'll get an error. To be safe, you might test NULLABLE to see if the item can ever have a null value before attempting to retrieve DATA. Alternatively, you can always retrieve INDICATOR every time you retrieve DATA.

To put all of this in context, let's look at an example.

```
ALLOCATE DESCRIPTOR 'MYDESCRIPTOR' WITH MAX 20;

DESCRIBE...

GET DESCRIPTOR 'MYDESCRIPTOR' :number = COUNT;

GET DESCRIPTOR 'MYDESCRIPTOR' VALUE 1
   :datatype = TYPE,
   :length = LENGTH,
   :name = NAME,
   :nullable = NULLABLE

if nullable = 0 then
   GET DESCRIPTOR 'MYDESCRIPTOR' VALUE 1
     :data = DATA ;

else
   GET DESCRIPTOR 'MYDESCRIPTOR' VALUE 1
     :data = DATA ,
     :ind  = INDICATOR ;

DEALLOCATE DESCRIPTOR 'MYDESCRIPTOR';
```

Occasionally, you may find yourself wanting to change the values of certain fields in some items of a descriptor area. One reason that you may want to do this is to specify that your host language variable or your parameter has a slightly different data type than the DBMS hoped you'd use. Consider this example: If you're writing your application in the C programming language, but the database that you're using contains DECIMAL data, you will often find yourself in the position of needing to access data that your programming language doesn't support. SQL:1999 comes to the rescue again! In this case, if you DESCRIBE a statement and learn that one of the columns is DECIMAL with scale 0, then you can simply set the TYPE for that item to 4 (for INTEGER) and let the database system do automatic data type conversions for you. We'll cover this a bit more later on.

The format of the SET DESCRIPTOR statement is very close to that for GET DESCRIPTOR and has the same two variations:

```
SET DESCRIPTOR desc-name
  COUNT = value
```

where desc-name is the name of a valid descriptor area and value is an integer simple value specification. This variation allows you to set the total number of items that you plan to use; if value is greater than the number of occurrences in the descriptor area, you'll get an error. As with GET DESCRIPTOR, you can set the value of the other fields in the header area by using the appropriate keywords (which are the same for GET and SET DESCRIPTOR).

Your other alternative is as follows:

```
SET DESCRIPTOR desc-name
  VALUE item-number
  item-name = value [ , item-name = value ]...
```

Of course, desc-name is the name of a valid descriptor area, and item-number is the number of the item that you're setting or changing. item-name is the name of one of the fields of an item as shown in the table earlier in this chapter. value is a simple value specification of the appropriate data type.

When you set fields in an item of a descriptor area, they are effectively set in the following order: LEVEL, TYPE, DATETIME_INTERVAL_CODE, DATETIME_INTERVAL_PRECISION, PRECISION, SCALE, CHARACTER_SET_CATALOG, CHARACTER_SET_SCHEMA, CHARACTER_SET_NAME, USER_DEFINED_TYPE_CATALOG, USER_DEFINED_TYPE_SCHEMA, USER_DEFINED_TYPE_NAME, SCOPE_CATALOG, SCOPE_SCHEMA, SCOPE_NAME, LENGTH, INDICATOR, DEGREE, CARDINALITY, and DATA, regardless of the order that you wrote them in the SET DESCRIPTOR statement. (Of course, this applies only for a single SET DESCRIPTOR statement; if you had two or more SET DESCRIPTOR statements, the second one might foul up the results of the first.) If you specify fields that are meaningless for the TYPE value, then your instructions will be ignored for those fields, and they'll be set to whatever your implementor wants. Every time you set the value of any field of the item descriptor area other than the DATA field, the value of the DATA field becomes undefined; therefore, you must be careful that you always set the DATA field last.

Well, that covers the statements that deal directly with the descriptor areas. As we shall see, other statements use them in various ways. But before we get into the more complicated statements, let's have a look at the simplest way to dynamically execute SQL statements.

18.5 | The EXECUTE IMMEDIATE Statement

The format of the EXECUTE IMMEDIATE statement is

```
EXECUTE IMMEDIATE statement-variable
```

The statement variable is a simple target (a parameter or host variable without an indicator) that contains a character string that is the dynamic statement that you want to execute. As we said earlier, a dynamic SQL statement that you're going to execute using EXECUTE IMMEDIATE can't have any dynamic parameters in it. Also, remember that the statement is executed on a one-shot basis; if you want to execute it again, you'll have to go through all the overhead again. Therefore, if you think you'll want to execute the statement more than once, consider the PREPARE/EXECUTE alternative.

The effect of EXECUTE IMMEDIATE is the same as the PREPARE, EXECUTE, and DEALLOCATE PREPARE sequence. Here's a typical example, increasing the current sale prices of all DVDs by 10%:

```
EXECUTE IMMEDIATE 'UPDATE movie_titles
                SET current_dvd_sale_price =
                    current_dvd_sale_price * 1.1'
```

Of course, if you knew while you were writing your application that you'd want to do that, you'd be better off coding the statement into your module or embedded SQL program. But if you don't know that you're going to have to execute this statement, say because the pricing of your Web site's DVDs (as well as other media merchandise) is extremely volatile because of trying to keep your pricing below that of your competition, then this is one way to do it dynamically.

If the contents of the `statement variable` don't follow the proper syntax of a valid preparable SQL statement, or if you don't have the proper privileges to execute the statement, you'll get the appropriate error. You'll also get an error if you try to execute a statement that has an SQL comment or that has any dynamic parameters.

As long as the statement is properly constructed and you have the required privileges to execute it, the effect is the same as if you had written the statement into a module and executed it—except, of course, for performance.

18.6 | PREPARE and EXECUTE Statements

If you find yourself with the need to execute an SQL statement dynamically and you expect to have to execute the statement more than once, or if the statement needs to use dynamic parameters, you will use the PREPARE statement to prepare the dynamic statement for execution and then use the EXECUTE statement to execute it as the need arises (that is, within the same session at most; many implementations only permit you to execute the dynamic statement in the same *transaction* in which it was prepared).

The format of the PREPARE statement is shown in Syntax 18-1.

Syntax 18-1 *PREPARE Statement Syntax*

```
PREPARE statement-name
  FROM statement-variable
```

The `statement-name` is either an identifier that you use to identify the prepared statement in other statements (such as the EXECUTE statement), or it's a simple value specification that you can optionally precede with GLOBAL or LOCAL (LOCAL is the default). Of course, the identifier option is a normal dynamic statement name, while the simple value specification alternative is an extended dynamic statement name.

Let's look at a couple of examples.

```
PREPARE DYN1 FROM 'DELETE FROM MOVIE_TITLES
                   WHERE TITLE LIKE ''%Dead%'''
```

Note the doubled apostrophes that stand for a single apostrophe within the character string literal. Another way to write this same statement might look something like this in C:

```
temp = "DELETE FROM MOVIE_TITLES WHERE TITLE LIKE '%Dead% ";
EXEC SQL PREPARE DYN1 FROM :temp;
```

If you didn't want to use a preknown statement name for this statement, but to invent one on the fly, you could use something like this:

```
dynstmt = "DYN1";
temp = 'DELETE FROM MOVIE_TITLES WHERE TITLE LIKE '%Dead%'";
EXEC SQL PREPARE :dynstmt FROM :temp;
```

This last example illustrates the ability of the host program to provide both the name of a dynamic prepared statement and the text of the statement itself from host variables. Using module language, the C code would look like this:

```
dynstmt = "DYN1";
temp = 'DELETE FROM MOVIE_TITLES WHERE TITLE LIKE '%Dead%'";
PREPSTMT ( status, dynstmt, temp );
```

and the procedure (in module language) would be something like this:

```
PROCEDURE PREPSTMT ( SQLSTATE, :DYN_NAME CHARACTER(128),
                     :STATEMENT CHARACTER(128) )

PREPARE :DYN_NAME FROM :STATEMENT;
```

Once you have prepared a dynamic SQL statement, you can use it repeatedly during the same transaction. Your implementation may allow you to use the same prepared statement in other transactions in the same SQL session. And presto, there go *The Dead Zone, The Quick and the Dead, I See Dead People* (the sequel to *The Sixth Sense* perhaps?), and so forth.

The statements that you can prepare and execute dynamically (including EXECUTE IMMEDIATE) are as follows: any schema definition or modification statement; any transaction statement (COMMIT, ROLLBACK, SET TRANSACTION, SET CONSTRAINTS); any session statement (SET CATALOG, SET SCHEMA, SET NAMES, SET SESSION AUTHORIZATION, and SET TIME ZONE); and several data manipulation statements (searched DELETE, searched UPDATE, single row SELECT, INSERT, and special versions of positioned DELETE and positioned UPDATE). You can also prepare a dynamic cursor specification, as we'll see a bit later in this chapter (section 18.11).

Once you have prepared a dynamic SQL statement, you're probably going to want to execute it. The format of the EXECUTE statement is given in Syntax 18-2.

Syntax 18-2 *EXECUTE Statement Syntax*

```
EXECUTE statement-name
  [ result-using ] [ parameter-using ]
```

As before, `statement-name` is either an identifier you use to identify the prepared statement in other statements (such as the `EXECUTE` statement), or it's a simple value specification that you can optionally precede with `GLOBAL` or `LOCAL` (`LOCAL` is the default). Also as before, the identifier option is a normal dynamic statement name, while the simple value specification alternative is an extended dynamic statement name.

The `result-using` is an optional `USING` clause that specifies where the results of the dynamically executed statement (for example, the results of a `FETCH` statement) are supposed to go. If the statement doesn't return any results (for example, a `DELETE` statement), then you don't use a `result-using`. The `parameter-using` is also an optional `USING` clause; it specifies where the dynamically executed statement gets the values for the dynamic parameters in the statement. If the statement doesn't have any dynamic parameters, you don't use a `parameter-using`. Each of them can be either a `using-arguments` or a `using-descriptor`. A `using-arguments` specifies host variables or values that will be the target for results or the source for dynamic parameters. A `using descriptor` specifies a descriptor area that will be used as the target for results or as the source for dynamic parameters.

When a `result-using` or a `parameter-using` is a `using-arguments`, the format is

```
USING arg [ , arg ]...
```

or

```
INTO arg [ , arg ]...
```

You use the `USING` alternative for a `parameter-using` and the `INTO` alternative for a `result-using`. (The way to remember this is that results go *into* the targets, and the dynamic parameters *use* the source.) Actually, you can use `USING` in either place (for backward compatibility with many existing products), but you cannot use `INTO` except in a `result-using`; in spite of that, we recommend using `USING` only for a `parameter-using`. The number of `args` must be equal to the number of results returned by the dynamic statement or the number of dynamic parameters in the dynamic statement.

When you execute the dynamic statement, if there are any dynamic parameters, the DBMS will retrieve the values to be associated with those dynamic parameters from the locations specified in the appropriate arg. These arg values can have indicators as well. Therefore, you can have something like this:

```
EXECUTE DYN1
   USING :arg1, :arg2 INDICATOR :argind2, :arg3
```

or

```
EXECUTE DYN1
   INTO :arg1, :arg2 INDICATOR :argind2, :arg3
```

or even

```
EXECUTE DYN1
   USING :arg1, :arg2 INDICATOR :argind2, :arg3
   INTO  :arg4, :arg5 INDICATOR :argind6, :arg6
```

Incidentally, the same arg name can be used in both the USING and the INTO clauses. The value is retrieved at the beginning of the statement (for USING), and a new value is set at the end of the statement (for INTO).

When a result-using or parameter-using is a using-descriptor, the format is

```
USING SQL DESCRIPTOR descriptor-name
```

or

```
INTO SQL DESCRIPTOR descriptor-name
```

As with the using-arguments, you use USING for a parameter-using and INTO for a result-using (but see the discussion for using-arguments). And the descriptor-name is, of course, the name of a descriptor area that has enough items to account for all of the results or dynamic parameters (as appropriate) in the dynamic statement.

In this case, when you execute the dynamic SQL statement, the DBMS doesn't go to host variables or parameters to get the dynamic parameter values, and it doesn't try to store the results into host variables or parameters. Instead, it gets values from and stores results into a descriptor area.

Of course, the descriptor area has to have appropriate descriptions (data type, etc.) for the appropriate columns, so you must either initialize all of the items and fields or use DESCRIBE to let the DBMS do the initialization for you.

Let's next take a look at the DESCRIBE statement, and then we'll examine some more details about the USING (and INTO) clause.

18.7 | The DESCRIBE Statement

As we've already mentioned, the purpose of the DESCRIBE statement is to provide you with information about the columns that you're retrieving with a dynamic SQL statement or about the dynamic parameters in your dynamic SQL statement. It comes in two forms: a *describe input statement* and a *describe output statement*. We show the format of the describe output statement in Syntax 18-3.

Syntax 18-3 *DESCRIBE OUTPUT Statement Syntax.*

```
DESCRIBE [ OUTPUT ] statement-name using-descriptor [ nesting ]
```

The keyword OUTPUT is optional, and the statement means the same thing with or without it. The statement-name is still either an identifier that you use to identify the prepared statement in other statements (such as the EXECUTE statement), or it's a simple value specification that you can optionally precede with GLOBAL or LOCAL (LOCAL is the default). Also as before, the identifier option is a normal dynamic statement name, while the simple value specification alternative is an extended dynamic statement name. As before, the using-descriptor format is

```
USING SQL DESCRIPTOR descriptor-name
```

The nesting option can be specified as WITH NESTING or WITHOUT NESTING. In addition, it can naturally be omitted, in which case you'll get the same effects as though you had specified WITHOUT NESTING. If you specify WITH NESTING, the system will include the descriptions of the fields of rows and the elements of arrays that are among the columns or parameters being described. See section 18.8, "Rows, Collections, and the DESCRIBE Statement," for a discussion of this capability.

Similarly, a describe input statement has the format shown in Syntax 18-4.

Syntax 18-4 *DESCRIBE INPUT Statement Syntax*

```
DESCRIBE INPUT statement-name using-descriptor [ nesting ]
```

In addition, statement-name, using-descriptor, and nesting are as for a DESCRIBE OUTPUT statement. Note that INPUT is mandatory in this statement.

There's one more variation of the DESCRIBE statement. We show the syntax of this third variant, called the *describe dynamic result set statement*, in Syntax 18-5.

Syntax 18-5 *DESCRIBE Dynamic Result Set Statement Syntax*

```
DESCRIBE [ OUTPUT ] CURSOR extended-name STRUCTURE
    using-descriptor [ nesting ]
```

We'll discuss each of these variations in separate sections below.

When you execute a DESCRIBE statement (either the input variety or the output variety) and the statement-name doesn't identify a dynamic SQL statement that has been PREPARED (and not deallocated) in the scope of the statement-name (including in the same session or transaction), you'll get an error.

18.7.1 DESCRIBE OUTPUT Statement Execution

When you execute a DESCRIBE OUTPUT statement, it stores into the descriptor area a description of the columns that make up the select list of the prepared statement. (Here's an exception to that rule: You'll recall from Chapter 17, "Routines and Routine Invocation (Functions and Procedures)," that SQL-invoked procedures can have output parameters. Therefore, you can execute a DESCRIBE OUTPUT to describe the output parameters of a CALL statement that invokes such an SQL-invoked procedure. If you do so, then the descriptor area receives a description of those output parameters. In this discussion, although we use the word *column*, you should understand that we also mean "output parameter" unless we explicitly say otherwise.) One implication of this is that the statement has an effect only when there is a select list in the prepared statement or output parameters of the SQL-invoked procedure invoked by a prepared CALL statement, and it must therefore be a dynamic single-row SELECT statement, a dynamic cursor, or a CALL statement. Actually, you can execute a DESCRIBE OUTPUT statement on any prepared statement without getting an error, but it will affect the descriptor area only if it is a dynamic single-row SELECT statement, a dynamic cursor, or a CALL statement. Here is how the descriptor area is set:

- If the prepared statement is a dynamic single-row SELECT statement, a dynamic cursor, or a CALL statement that has output parameters, then COUNT is set to the number of select list columns or output parameters in the statement; otherwise, COUNT is set to 0.

- If COUNT is greater than the number of occurrences specified when the descriptor area was allocated, you get a warning condition and no items in the descriptor area are set. (Obviously, if COUNT is 0, no items are set then, either.)

- Only the NULLABLE, NAME, UNNAMED, KEY_MEMBER, LEVEL, PARAMETER_MODE, PARAMETER_ORDINAL_POSITION, PARAMETER_SPECIFIC_CATALOG, PARAMETER_SPECIFIC_SCHEMA, PARAMETER_SPECIFIC_NAME, TYPE, and various other fields related to TYPE are set. In particular, the DATA and INDICATOR fields are not relevant to DESCRIBE, so they are not set. (DATA and INDICATOR are not relevant to DESCRIBE because they are used only when the prepared statement is actually executed.)

- If the column being described is possibly nullable, the NULLABLE field is set to 1; otherwise, NULLABLE is set to 0.

- If the column has a user-defined name, NAME is set to that name and UNNAMED is set to 0. If the column has an implementation-defined name, UNNAMED is set to 1, and NAME is set to the implementation-defined name of the column.

- If the prepared statement is a dynamic single-row SELECT statement or a dynamic cursor, and the column being described participates in the PRIMARY KEY of the table that results from the statement, then KEY_MEMBER is set to 1. If the column participates in the preferred candidate key of that table, then KEY_MEMBER is set to 2. Otherwise, KEY_MEMBER is set to 0.

- LEVEL is set to 0 unless the item descriptor area is a *subordinate descriptor area*. We discuss this topic in section 18.8.

- If the prepared statement is a CALL statement, then PARAMETER_ORDINAL_POSITION is set to the ordinal position of the called procedure's parameter that is being described; PARAMETER_MODE is set to a code indicating the mode (IN, OUT, or INOUT—1, 4, or 2, respectively) of the parameter; and PARAMETER_SPECIFIC_CATALOG, PARAMETER_SPECIFIC_SCHEMA, and PARAMETER_SPECIFIC_NAME are set to the catalog name, schema name, and routine name of the called procedure.

- If the column is a character string column, TYPE is set to 1, 12, or 40 (CHARACTER, CHARACTER VARYING, or CHARACTER LARGE OBJECT, respectively); LENGTH is set to the length (or maximum length) in characters of the column; OCTET_LENGTH is set to the maximum possible length (in octets) of the column; CHARACTER_SET_CATALOG, CHARACTER_SET_SCHEMA, and CHARACTER_SET_NAME are set to the components of the fully qualified name of the character set associated with the column; and COLLATION_CATALOG, COLLATION_SCHEMA, and `COLLATION_NAME` are set to the components of the fully qualified name of the collation for the column.

- If the column is a bit string column, `TYPE` is set to 14 or 15 (`BIT` or `BIT VARYING`, respectively), `LENGTH` is set to the length (or maximum length) in bits of the column, and `OCTET_LENGTH` is set to the maximum possible length in octets of the column.

- If the column is an exact numeric column, `TYPE` is set to 2, 3, 4, or 5 (`NUMERIC`, `DECIMAL`, `INTEGER`, or `SMALLINT`, respectively); `PRECISION` is set to the precision of the column; and `SCALE` is set to the scale of the column.

- If the column is an approximate numeric column, `TYPE` is set to 6, 7, or 8 (`FLOAT`, `REAL`, or `DOUBLE PRECISION`, respectively) and `PRECISION` is set to the precision of the column.

- If the column is a datetime column, `TYPE` is set to 9; `LENGTH` is set to the length in positions of the column; `DATETIME_INTERVAL_CODE` is set to 1, 2, 3, 4, or 5 (for `DATE`, `TIME WITHOUT TIME ZONE`, `TIMESTAMP WITHOUT TIME ZONE`, `TIME WITH TIME ZONE`, or `TIMESTAMP WITH TIME ZONE`, respectively); and `PRECISION` is set to the fractional seconds precision of the column.

- If the column is an interval column, `TYPE` is set to 10, `DATETIME_INTERVAL_CODE` is set to a number between 1 and 13 (see the earlier table) to indicate the interval qualifier of the column, `DATETIME_INTERVAL_PRECISION` is set to the precision of the column's leading field precision, and `PRECISION` is set to the column's trailing field precision.

- If the column is a `BLOB` column, `TYPE` is set to 30, and `LENGTH` and `OCTET_LENGTH` are both set to the maximum length in octets of the `BLOB` column.

- If the column is an array column, `TYPE` is set to 50, and `CARDINALITY` is set to the cardinality of the `ARRAY` type. See section 18.8 for additional details.

- If the column is a `ROW` type column, `TYPE` is set to 19, and `DEGREE` is set to the number of fields making up the `ROW` type. See section 18.8 for additional details.

- If the column is a REF column, `TYPE` is set to 20; `LENGTH` and `OCTET_LENGTH` are set to the implementation-defined length of a reference type; `USER_DEFINED_TYPE_CATALOG`, `USER_DEFINED_TYPE_SCHEMA`, and `USER_DEFINED_TYPE_NAME` are set to the name of the referenced user-defined type; and `SCOPE_CATALOG`, `SCOPE_SCHEMA`, and `SCOPE_NAME` are set to the name of the referenceable typed table. Volume 2 of this book discusses structured types and typed tables.

- If the column is a user-defined type column, `TYPE` is set to 17, and `USER_DEFINED_TYPE_CATALOG`, `USER_DEFINED_TYPE_SCHEMA`, and `USER_DEFINED_TYPE_`

NAME are set to the name of the user-defined type. Volume 2 of this book discusses structured user-defined types.

- The column cannot be a user-defined type locator, an array locator, or a large object locator, since those types are never the types of database data.

When all of the columns have been described, the DESCRIBE statement is finished and a description of every column in the dynamic SQL statement's select list can be found in the descriptor area.

At this time, your application can use the GET DESCRIPTOR statement to inquire about the column descriptions and to take appropriate action based on that information. We'll illustrate this a little later in this chapter. Your application can also use SET DESCRIPTOR to change the values of items in the descriptor area, but we'll cover how and why later on.

18.7.2 DESCRIBE INPUT Statement Execution

When you execute a DESCRIBE INPUT statement, it stores into the descriptor area a description of the dynamic parameters that are in the prepared statement. One implication of this is that the statement has an effect only when there are dynamic parameters in the prepared statement. Actually, you can execute a DESCRIBE INPUT statement on any prepared statement without getting an error, but it will affect the descriptor area only if there are dynamic parameters. Here is how the descriptor area is set:

- If the prepared statement has at least one input dynamic parameter, COUNT is set to the number of input dynamic parameters in the statement; otherwise, COUNT is set to 0.

- If COUNT is greater than the number of occurrences specified when the descriptor area was allocated, you get a warning condition and no items in the descriptor area are set. (Obviously, if COUNT is 0, no items are set then, either.)

- Only the NULLABLE, NAME, UNNAMED, KEY_MEMBER, LEVEL, PARAMETER_MODE, PARAMETER_ORDINAL_POSITION, PARAMETER_SPECIFIC_CATALOG, PARAMETER_SPECIFIC_SCHEMA, PARAMETER_SPECIFIC_NAME, TYPE, and various other fields related to TYPE are set. In particular, the DATA and INDICATOR fields are not relevant to DESCRIBE, so they are not set. (DATA and INDICATOR are not relevant to DESCRIBE because they are used only when the prepared statement is actually executed.)

- The NULLABLE field is set to 1 (all dynamic parameters are potentially nullable).

- NAME and UNNAMED are both set to implementation-defined values. That is, the dynamic parameters don't have column names, so these fields are irrelevant.

- The other fields are set just like those in the DESCRIBE OUTPUT statement above (except you should read *dynamic parameter* wherever the earlier list contains *column*).

When all of the dynamic parameters have been described, the DESCRIBE statement is finished and a description of every dynamic parameter in the dynamic SQL statement is stored in the descriptor area.

At this time, your application can use the GET DESCRIPTOR statement to inquire about the dynamic parameter descriptions and to take appropriate action based on that information. We'll illustrate this a little later in this chapter. Your application can also use SET DESCRIPTOR to change the values of items in the descriptor area, but we'll cover how and why later on.

18.7.3 DESCRIBE Dynamic Result Set Statement Execution

In Chapter 17, "Routines and Routine Invocation (Functions and Procedures)," we told you that you can write and use SQL-invoked procedures that return dynamic result sets from their invocations. This is done, we told you, by defining one or more cursors to be result set cursors (using the WITH RETURN clause, as you saw in Chapter 13, "Cursors") and defining the SQL-invoked procedure with the DYNAMIC RESULT SETS clause, then leaving one or more result set cursors open when the procedure returns to its invoker. (As the use of the key words DYNAMIC RESULT SETS implies, the result sets returned using this mechanism are *dynamic result sets*. It is possible in some SQL implementations to return *preplanned result sets* as well, but SQL:1999 does not support that capability. Some future version of the SQL standard might support preplanned result sets.)

As we said in Chapter 17, "Routines and Routine Invocation (Functions and Procedures)," to make good use of dynamic result sets, you must use the facilities of dynamic SQL. (Otherwise, you must know in advance the precise structure of the result set cursors.) You have no doubt deduced by now that the dynamic SQL capabilities required involve the DESCRIBE dynamic result sets statement whose syntax is shown in Syntax 18-5. In this section, we're going to bring all the pieces together and show you how to use SQL:1999's dynamic result set capabilities.

Of course, the first component we require is a result set cursor that is declared in an SQL-invoked procedure. Example 18-1 illustrates such a procedure. In the procedure, we've defined a cursor that returns a result set containing all DVDs starring Jamie Lee Curtis that are not in the category passed as an argument. Note that the procedure does *not* have a parameter corresponding to the result set that it might return. While we are aware of SQL products that permit result sets to be returned from routines as the value of parameters, SQL:1999 does not use that approach. We have sometimes heard the SQL:1999 approach called *side-channel result sets*, since they are returned outside of the normal parameter mechanism associated with SQL-invoked routines.

Example 18-1   *SQL-Invoked Procedure with Result Set Cursor*

```
CREATE PROCEDURE jlc_films ( IN category CHARACTER(10) )
  LANGUAGE SQL
  READS SQL DATA
  DYNAMIC RESULT SETS 1
  /* The single statement in this procedure is a compound stmt */
  BEGIN
    /* First, declare the cursor */
    DECLARE jlc CURSOR WITH RETURN FOR
      SELECT title
      FROM movie_titles AS mt, movies_stars AS ms
      WHERE mt.title = ms.movie_title
        AND ms.actor_last_name = 'Curtis'
        AND ms.actor_first_name = 'Jamie Lee'
        AND mt.movie_type <> category
      ORDER BY mt.year_released ASC;
    /* Next, open the cursor */
    OPEN jlc;
    /* Finally, return from the procedure with the cursor
       left open */
    RETURN;
  END;
```

The other thing required is some SQL code that invokes that SQL-invoked procedure and processes the result set that it returned. A code fragment that does just that is illustrated in Example 18-2. (While the code fragment undoubtedly resembles code written in C, we have not attempted to make it completely accurate; the goal is simply to show you the techniques that must be used to deal with dynamic result sets returned from SQL-invoked procedures.)

Example 18-2 *Code Fragment Using a Dynamic Result Set*

```
...
/* Invoke the procedure */
EXEC SQL CALL jlc_films ( 'Horror' );
...
/* Check returned SQLSTATE to see if a result set was returned */
if SQLSTATE != "0100C"
  /* If not, then just exit */
  return 1;
else {
  /* Otherwise, process the result set */
  /* First, we need an SQL descriptor area, allowing 20 columns */
  EXEC SQL ALLOCATE SQL DESCRIPTOR descr1 WITH MAX 20;
  /* The next step is to allocate a dynamic cursor to use */
  EXEC SQL ALLOCATE jamie CURSOR FOR PROCEDURE jlc_films;
  /* There is no need to explicitly OPEN this type of dynamic
     cursor, as the ALLOCATE automatically opens it. */
  /* Get a description of the result set */
  EXEC SQL DESCRIBE CURSOR jamie STRUCTURE USING descr1;
  /* Now, loop through FETCH statements until all rows processed */
  while SQLSTATE != "02000" {
    /* Fetch the row of the result set into the descriptor area */
    EXEC SQL FETCH jamie INTO descr1;
    /* Check for 'NO DATA' return */
    if SQLSTATE != "02000" {
      /* Now, process that row (not shown here) */
      ...
    }
  }
  /* Close the dynamic cursor; this automatically checks to see
     if there is another result set to be processed */
  CLOSE jamie;
  if SQLSTATE != "02001"
    /* If not, then just exit */
    return 1;
  else {
    /* Otherwise, process it, too... */
    ...
  }
}
...
```

That's it! It's not terribly complicated, and most of the steps are fairly obvious. The two aspects that we think are perhaps unexpected, and thus deserving of more explanation, are these:

- You must use a dynamic cursor in your code that will handle the dynamic result sets returned from an SQL-invoked procedure. Dynamic cursors are not declared but are allocated with the ALLOCATE CURSOR statement, specifying that the cursor is associated with an SQL-invoked procedure. The ALLOCATE CURSOR statement automatically opens cursors that are associated with SQL-invoked procedures. It is probably easiest to retrieve the values into an SQL descriptor area and use GET DESCRIPTOR statements to retrieve the values from the descriptor area. However, you can also retrieve values directly into your application code if you prefer, although this approach requires more complex use of the data type information placed into the descriptor area by the DESCRIBE statement.

- When you close the dynamic cursor, if there are additional result sets returned from the SQL-invoked procedure with which the cursor is associated, then the next result set is automatically opened and a special SQLSTATE value is returned. If there are no additional result sets, then the cursor is closed and a different SQLSTATE value is returned.

18.8 | Rows, Collections, and the DESCRIBE Statement

Several times earlier in this chapter, we've indicated that dynamic SQL handling of columns or dynamic parameters whose data types are ROW types or ARRAY types is more complex than the handling of SQL's more primitive types (such as INTEGER, CHARACTER, or even TIMESTAMP).

A few moments of reflection will bring the realization that ROW and ARRAY are different from most other SQL types in a significant way: they are more accurately described as "data type constructors," since they require additional data type information before their definitions are complete. ARRAY, for example, defines an array of some other data type; in order to describe a row type, we must also be able to describe its elements. ROW defines a row type with one or more fields, each of which must have a data type. In order to describe a row type, we must be able to describe each of the fields of that row. To make matters a bit more complex, the data type of a field of a row can itself be an array type or another row type, so the "nesting" of the descriptions can be arbitrarily deep.

SQL:1999 addresses this issue by using the concept of *subordinate descriptor areas*. As the name implies, a subordinate descriptor area is one that is a subsidiary of another descriptor area. To illustrate this concept, let's create a new table to contain some critical information about the DVDs that we stock for our e-store. See Example 18-3 for this table definition.

Example 18-3 *New Table That Illustrates Nested Data Types*

```
CREATE TABLE studios_and_movies (
  studio     CHARACTER VARYING(50),
  movie      ROW ( title    CHARACTER(30),
                   director ROW (fname  CHARACTER(25),
                                 lname  CHARACTER(35) )
                   grosses  DECIMAL(10) ARRAY[52] )
  distributor CHARACTER VARYING(100),
  PRIMARY KEY ( studio, movie ) )
```

Note particularly that the movie column has a ROW data type, one field of which (director) has another ROW data type, and another field of which (grosses) is an array of numbers.

If we then write an SQL statement like the one shown in Example 18-4, we have to be able to deal with the nested fields of the movie column's ROW type, as well as the nested fields of the director field of the movie column's type. We also have to deal with the ARRAY type of the grosses field.

Example 18-4 *Selecting Rows from Example Table*

```
SELECT studio, movie, distributor
FROM   studios_and_movies
WHERE  distributor = 'Disney'
```

In Syntax 18-3, 18-4, and 18-5, you saw that you may optionally specify WITH NESTING whenever you execute a DESCRIBE statement. The default, as we told you, is WITHOUT NESTING, protecting existing programs that are unaware of subordinate descriptors.

If you describe the SELECT statement in Example 18-4 WITHOUT NESTING, the SQL descriptor area into which the DESCRIBE places information will have three of its item descriptor areas populated (one each for columns studio, movie, and distributor) and its header area's COUNT field will contain the value 3. This is very much like the situation that you saw in Tables 18-6 through 18-9 (although some details, such as the names and data types of the described columns, are different).

However, if you describe Example 18-4's SELECT statement and specify WITH NESTING, the situation gets a bit more complex. Consider the contents shown in Table 18-10, which is abbreviated to show only the descriptor area fields of interest for this discussion.

Table 18-10 *Nested Descriptors*

Field	Value
	Header
COUNT	9 (indicates a total of 9 item descriptor areas)
DYNAMIC_FUNCTION	SELECT
DYNAMIC_FUNCTION_CODE	65
TOP_LEVEL_COUNT	3 (indicates only 3 "top-level" item descriptor areas)
	Item Descriptor #1
CARDINALITY	Doesn't matter
DEGREE	Doesn't matter
LEVEL	0 (indicates "top-level" item descriptor area
NAME	STUDIO
RETURNED_CARDINALITY	Doesn't matter
TYPE	1 (indicates CHARACTER)
UNNAMED	0 (indicates that the column is named)
	Item Descriptor #2
CARDINALITY	Doesn't matter
DEGREE	5 (number of fields in this row type)
LEVEL	0 (indicates "top-level" item descriptor area)
NAME	MOVIE
RETURNED_CARDINALITY	Doesn't matter
TYPE	19 (indicates ROW)
UNNAMED	0 (indicates that the column is named)
	Item Descriptor #3
CARDINALITY	Doesn't matter
DEGREE	Doesn't matter
LEVEL	1 (indicates "first-level" subordinate descriptor area)
NAME	TITLE
RETURNED_CARDINALITY	Doesn't matter
TYPE	1 (indicates CHARACTER)
UNNAMED	0 (indicates that the field is named)

(Continued)

Table 8-10 *Continued*

Field	*Value*
	Item Descriptor #4
CARDINALITY	Doesn't matter
DEGREE	2 (number of fields in this row type)
LEVEL	1 (indicates "first-level" subordinate descriptor area)
NAME	DIRECTOR
RETURNED_CARDINALITY	Doesn't matter
TYPE	19 (indicates ROW)
UNNAMED	0 (indicates that the field is named)
	Item Descriptor #5
CARDINALITY	Doesn't matter
DEGREE	Doesn't matter
LEVEL	2 (indicates "second-level" subordinate descriptor area)
NAME	FNAME
RETURNED_CARDINALITY	Doesn't matter
TYPE	1 (indicates CHARACTER)
UNNAMED	0 (indicates that the field is named)
	Item Descriptor #6
CARDINALITY	Doesn't matter
DEGREE	Doesn't matter
LEVEL	2 (indicates "second-level" subordinate descriptor area)
NAME	LNAME
RETURNED_CARDINALITY	Doesn't matter
TYPE	1 (indicates CHARACTER)
UNNAMED	0 (indicates that the field is named)
	Item Descriptor #7
CARDINALITY	52 (the maximum cardinality of this ARRAY type)
DEGREE	Doesn't matter
LEVEL	1 (indicates "first-level" subordinate descriptor area)
NAME	GROSSES
RETURNED_CARDINALITY	Set only when data is retrieved into descriptor area
TYPE	50 (indicates ARRAY)
UNNAMED	0 (indicates that the field is named)

(Continued)

Table 8-10 *Continued*

Field	Value
	Item Descriptor #8
CARDINALITY	Doesn't matter
DEGREE	Doesn't matter
LEVEL	2 (indicates "second-level" subordinate descriptor area)
NAME	*(null)*
RETURNED_CARDINALITY	Doesn't matter
TYPE	3 (indicates DECIMAL)
UNNAMED	1 (indicates that no name is associated with the element type subordinate descriptor)
	Item Descriptor #9
CARDINALITY	Doesn't matter
DEGREE	Doesn't matter
LEVEL	0 (indicates "top-level" item descriptor area)
NAME	DISTRIBUTOR
RETURNED_CARDINALITY	Doesn't matter
TYPE	1 (indicates CHARACTER)
UNNAMED	0 (indicates that the column is named)

You should particularly note that an ARRAY column or field is described using two item descriptor areas. The first describes the column or field whose data type is the ARRAY type, and the second describes the element data type of the ARRAY type. The LEVEL value for the second of those item descriptor areas is always one greater than the LEVEL value for the first. The CARDINALITY value in the first of those two item descriptor areas provides the maximum cardinality of the ARRAY type.

In addition, please observe that a ROW column or field is described using one item descriptor area to describe the column or field, plus one item descriptor area to describe each field of the row type. Each field will be described by "one or more item descriptor areas," since the data type of a field might be another ROW type or an ARRAY type. The values of LEVEL in the item descriptor areas describing the fields of the ROW type are always one greater than the value of LEVEL in the item descriptor area that describes the column or field whose data type is the ROW type.

If, like us, you would like to see a visual representation of subordinate descriptor areas, you'll appreciate Figure 18-2.

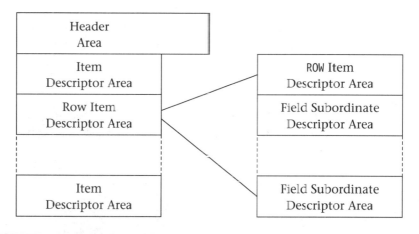

Figure 18-2   Subordinate Descriptor Areas

18.9 | The EXECUTE Statement Revisited

Now that we've got the DESCRIBE statement under our belts, let's reconsider the EXECUTE statement in light of DESCRIBE's behavior.

Suppose that you've prepared a dynamic SQL statement that has some dynamic parameters. Recall that the data types of the dynamic parameters are determined by their context, so the only way you can determine the appropriate data types to provide when the statement is executed is to describe the prepared statement with a DESCRIBE INPUT statement (unless, of course, you have intimate knowledge about the statement even before you've prepared it—for example, if you created the statement in your application program using knowledge about the data types to write the statement). Having described the statement, the information about the dynamic parameters is stored in the descriptor area that you specified.

At this point, you can execute the prepared statement (using EXECUTE, of course). You must provide input values for each of the dynamic parameters, and you can choose to provide them directly from your host variables or parameters, or you can provide them in the descriptor area itself. If you had so little information about the statement before getting to the point of executing it that you have to describe it, then you probably have not written your application in a way that would make it easy to provide input values in host variables or parameters, so you will probably choose to provide input values in the descriptor areas.

If you *do* choose to provide the dynamic parameter input values from host variables or parameters, the format of the EXECUTE statement will be

```
EXECUTE statement-name USING arg [ , arg ]...
```

In this case, the number of args provided to the EXECUTE statement must *exactly* match the number of dynamic parameters in the prepared statement; otherwise, you'll get an error.

If you choose to go the descriptor area route, the format of the EXECUTE statement will be

```
EXECUTE statement-name
  USING SQL DESCRIPTOR descriptor-name
```

Of course, the description of and restrictions on statement-name and descriptor-name are still as specified above in the earlier discussion of EXECUTE. But let's talk about the restrictions on the *contents* of the descriptor.

Recall that this option is meaningful *only* if the descriptor area has been appropriately set up for the prepared statement. The most direct way to do this is to DESCRIBE the prepared statement into the descriptor area. An alternative is to manually set up the fields of each required item in the descriptor area (using SET DESCRIPTOR). Let's assume that you decided to use DESCRIBE to do it, although it doesn't really matter for the purposes of this discussion.

When you execute the EXECUTE statement with USING SQL DESCRIPTOR, if the value of COUNT is greater than the number of occurrences in the descriptor, you'll get an error. Similarly, if the value of COUNT is not equal to the number of dynamic parameters in the prepared statement, you'll get a different error. If items 1 through COUNT are not valid (that is, all relevant fields having appropriate values corresponding to the TYPE field), you'll get yet a different error. If the value of INDICATOR for any item is not negative and the value for DATA isn't a valid value for the data type indicated by TYPE (and the other fields), you'll get an error for that, too. (If INDICATOR is negative, it means that you want the dynamic parameter to have the null value, so the value of DATA is irrelevant and isn't even verified.)

At this point, we could simply say that the value of DATA in each item of the descriptor is assigned to the corresponding dynamic parameter and the dynamic statement can be executed. We could say that, but it wouldn't be quite accurate. There's really a little more to it. (You were beginning to suspect that it wasn't quite that simple, weren't you?)

What really happens is that the DBMS first determines the data type of each dynamic parameter, by its context; this is the data type that would be represented by the information that a DESCRIBE INPUT statement would have put into the appropriate item in the descriptor area. Then the DBMS determines the data type specified by the actual information in the appropriate item in the descriptor area. Most of the time, these will be identical and our simple scenario in the preceding paragraph will be correct. However, you may have chosen to use a SET DESCRIPTOR to change the information in one or more items in the descriptor area to something different from the information that DESCRIBE put (or would have put) in there. In that case, the DBMS does a CAST from the DATA field (using the information actually in the item) to the data type of the dynamic parameter. Of course, this means that the information actually in the descriptor area has to specify a data type for which there is a valid CAST to the data type of the dynamic parameter; otherwise, you'll get an error of one sort or another (depending on whether the data type itself is improper for such a CAST, or whether the data type is all right but the actual value in DATA is inappropriate).

The last couple of paragraphs assume that you used the using-descriptor alternative. What if you used the using-arguments alternative? The same rules apply, including the implicit CAST. However, in this case, the data type of the arg is the relevant data type, and the value stored in the arg is CAST from the arg's data type to the data type of the dynamic parameter. Everything else behaves as described.

Now, we need to consider the other direction: data returned by the dynamic SQL statement. In this case, we can describe the prepared statement using a DESCRIBE OUTPUT statement, which will load up the descriptor area with a description of each select-list column in the statement. Our EXECUTE statement will look like this:

```
EXECUTE statement-name INTO arg [ , arg ]...
```

or

```
EXECUTE statement-name INTO SQL DESCRIPTOR descriptor-name
```

You can guess (and you'd be right) that the rules for statement-name and descriptor-name are the same as before. You'd also be right to guess that the rule requiring, for the using-arguments variant, the number of args to be identical to the number of select-list columns is also present (otherwise, you'll get an error). If you use the SQL DESCRIPTOR alternative, the value of COUNT must (you guessed it!) be equal to the number of select-list columns and must not be greater than the number of item occurrences created when the descriptor area was allocated. Also, items 1 through COUNT must be valid for the data type indicated by TYPE.

The same sort of CAST is done here as was done for the input case above. This time, the data from the select-list columns is CAST (from the actual data type of the select-list columns) to the data type indicated by the contents of the corresponding item in the descriptor area (or, for the using-arguments variant, to the data type of the corresponding arg). If that CAST is invalid, either because of an improper data type or because of data problems, you'll get an appropriate error.

If you choose the using-descriptor variant and the select-column has the null value, INDICATOR is set to −1 and DATA isn't set at all. If the select-list column is not null, INDICATOR is set to 0 and DATA is set to the value of the column. If the data is CAST to a character or bit string (or is already a character or bit string), RETURNED_LENGTH and RETURNED_OCTET_LENGTH are set to the length in characters or bits and the length in octets, respectively, of the value stored in DATA (or the actual select-list column).

In summary, if you know a lot about the dynamic parameters and select-list columns for your prepared statement, you are safe using the using-arguments forms of the USING (or INTO) clauses. However, if you don't know all the important aspects of the dynamic parameters or select-list columns, you'd probably be better off using the using-descriptor variants.

Now, we promised that we'd explain why you might want to use SET DESCRIPTOR after you've done a DESCRIBE. Okay, it's time.

Suppose you're writing your application in C (which, you will recall, has no decimal data type), and the prepared statement that you describe turns out, upon executing DESCRIBE, to have a select-list column (or dynamic parameter, or both) whose data type is DECIMAL. It would be most unfortunate if SQL simply said, "Sorry, people, but you can't write this application in C." Well, the standards committees thought of that problem. That's why the CAST rules were put in for the EXECUTE statement. In this case, you can simply use SET DESCRIPTOR to change the TYPE (and PRECISION and SCALE, if required) columns of the appropriate item in the descriptor area to represent INTEGER or SMALLINT, or even REAL, FLOAT, or DOUBLE PRECISION, and force the DBMS to CAST the DECIMAL data into a data type that you can handle in your application program.

Of course, you could also explicitly code the CASTs into the SQL statement being executed dynamically, but sometimes that means that your end user has to code more than he or she really needs to. By using SET DESCRIPTOR to do the CASTs for you, the end user (who may be composing partial SQL statements) can focus on the job at hand and not on grubby details of data conversion.

18.10 Dynamic SQL and Cursors

So far, we've talked only about using dynamic SQL to deal with *set-oriented* statements. But real applications need to use cursors to deal with that annoying impedance mismatch between SQL and the conventional programming languages. That fact remains true whether you're using static SQL or dynamic SQL. So, SQL:1999 has defined statements that will let you use cursors in dynamic SQL.

18.10.1 Dynamic Cursors

Logically enough, the most central statement here is the dynamic declare cursor (see Syntax 18-6). It is a very close analog to the DECLARE CURSOR for static SQL but has a somewhat different syntax, for reasons that will become immediately obvious when we show you.

Syntax 18-6 *Dynamic Cursor Declaration*

```
<dynamic declare cursor> ::=
    DECLARE <cursor name> [ <cursor sensitivity> ]
      [ <cursor scrollability> ] CURSOR
      [ <cursor holdability> ]
      [ <cursor returnability> ]
      FOR <statement name>
```

Recall that the static DECLARE CURSOR ended up with a cursor-specification, which was a query-expression and a few other things (see Chapter 13, "Cursors," for a review of these terms).

However, in dynamic SQL, you simply don't know the query expression (or the "few other things") in advance—that's why you're using dynamic SQL. Therefore, you declare a dynamic cursor that identifies a simple value specification (literal, host variable, or parameter) instead of a cursor specification. Then, at runtime, the simple value specification is set up to be a character string representation of a cursor specification. (Of course, if you choose to use a literal, then you still have to know the details when you write the application, but the more general case will allow you to plug in the values at runtime.)

The dynamic DECLARE CURSOR is a declarative statement, just like the static one. This means that the scope of the cursor name is the same as the scope of the cursor name of static cursors; you can't have a static cursor and a dynamic cursor with the same name in the same module or compilation unit. There's also a requirement that the module or compilation unit must have a PREPARE statement that references the same statement-name as the one in the dynamic DECLARE CURSOR.

There's a variation on dynamic cursors that we mentioned briefly earlier: *extended* dynamic cursors. An extended dynamic cursor is one whose *name* isn't known until runtime. This allows you to invent new cursors as you need them instead of limiting yourself to the dynamic cursors that you code in your application programs. Instead of declaring an extended dynamic cursor, you *allocate* it. The format of the ALLOCATE CURSOR statement is shown in Syntax 18-7.

Syntax 18-7   *Dynamic ALLOCATE CURSOR Statement*

```
<allocate cursor statement> ::=
    ALLOCATE <extended cursor name> <cursor intent>

<cursor intent> ::=
    <statement cursor>
  | <result set cursor>

<statement cursor> ::=
    [ <cursor sensitivity> ] [ SCROLL ] CURSOR
    [ WITH HOLD ]
    [ WITH RETURN ]
    FOR <extended statement name>

<result set cursor> ::=
    FOR PROCEDURE <specific routine designator>
```

In this case, both <extended cursor name> and <extended statement name> are host variables or parameters and can be optionally preceded by GLOBAL or LOCAL (the default is still LOCAL). You cannot have more than one cursor concurrently allocated with the same actual name. However, <extended cursor name> isn't the name of the cursor. Rather, it is the *contents* of <extended cursor name> when you execute the ALLOCATE CURSOR statement that gives the name of the cursor. Therefore, the statements in Example 18-5 are valid:

Example 18-5   *ALLOCATE CURSOR Example*

```
ext1 = "CURS1";
EXEC SQL ALLOCATE :ext1 CURSOR FOR :stmt;
ext1 = "CURS2";
EXEC SQL ALLOCATE :ext1 CURSOR FOR :stmt;
```

These statements allocate two extended dynamic cursors, named CURS1 and CURS2. By contrast, the statements in Example 18-6 are *invalid*:

Example 18-6 *Invalid Statements for ALLOCATE CURSOR*

```
ext1 = "CURS1";
EXEC SQL ALLOCATE :ext1 CURSOR FOR :stmt;
ext2 = "CURS1";
EXEC SQL ALLOCATE :ext2 CURSOR FOR :stmt;
```

The last statement attempts to allocate a second cursor named CURS1, which is invalid and will get an error.

Before you can open the cursor, the statement name for a normal dynamic cursor must identify a prepared statement, and that prepared statement must be a cursor specification (see below).

An extended dynamic cursor is even more restrictive. You must have prepared a statement (again, a cursor specification) and associated it with the ext-stmt-name *before* you execute the ALLOCATE CURSOR statement, or you'll get an error. If the ALLOCATE CURSOR statement succeeds, the extended cursor name is associated with the prepared cursor specification.

Once you have a dynamic cursor name (regular or extended) and have a valid prepared cursor specification associated with it, then you can use the cursor. As with static cursors, you must open the cursor before you do anything else. The format of a dynamic OPEN statement is very similar to the format of the static OPEN, but with one important difference:

```
OPEN cursor-name [ using-clause ]
```

The cursor name is, of course, either a regular cursor name, or an ext-cursor-name. If the cursor name isn't associated with a prepared cursor specification, you'll get an error. If it is an ext-cursor-name and it doesn't properly identify an allocated cursor in the appropriate scope, you'll get another error.

Note the using-clause. Obviously, this is either a using-arguments or a using-descriptor. If the cursor specification associated with the cursor name doesn't have any dynamic parameters in it, it doesn't matter whether or not you specify the using-clause (if you do, it won't be used). On the other hand, if the cursor specification does have dynamic parameters, you must specify a using-clause; otherwise, you'll get an error. If you properly specify the using-clause, the effects are exactly the same as described earlier for the EXECUTE statement when you have dynamic parameters in the prepared statement and you specify a using-clause to provide the values to be given to those dynamic parameters. Note that you do not specify an INTO clause; that comes later, with the dynamic FETCH statement.

When you're finished using your dynamic cursor, you will normally close it (although, as with static cursors, terminating the transaction will tell the DBMS to close any open dynamic cursors for you). The format of the dynamic CLOSE statement is almost identical to the static version:

```
CLOSE cursor-name
```

The only difference is that cursor name can be either a normal dynamic cursor name or an ext-cursor-name. The usual and expected restrictions apply, and the usual and expected errors will result from violations of those restrictions.

While the cursor is open, you will normally want to FETCH data through the cursor. The format of the dynamic FETCH statement is close to that for the static version:

```
FETCH [ [ orientation ] FROM ] cursor-name
    using-clause
```

The rules for the orientation and FROM are the same as for the static FETCH. The cursor name can, of course, be either a normal dynamic cursor name or an ext-cursor-name, with the usual restrictions and errors. The using-clause is required here, though (not optional as in the dynamic OPEN statement). A valid cursor specification will always have at least one select-list column, which means that every dynamic FETCH will retrieve at least one value. The using-clause tells the DBMS where to put those results.

Of course, the using-clause can be either a using-arguments or a using-descriptor, and the behavior is exactly as specified earlier for the EXECUTE statement when specifying the behavior for select-list column retrievals. As in that case, you may specify either USING or INTO, and we recommend INTO in this case, because you're FETCHing INTO the arguments or descriptor area.

Note that the dynamic OPEN, dynamic FETCH, and dynamic CLOSE statements are *not* preparable statements. They are static statements because you code them directly into your application program. However, they *operate* on dynamic cursors, so the only details that you have to know when you're writing your application is whether you want to declare (or allocate) the cursor to be INSENSITIVE or SCROLL. All other attributes are determined strictly at runtime based on the cursor specification that you PREPARE.

18.10.2   Dynamic Positioned Statements

Similarly, there are static statements for deleting from and updating through a dynamic cursor. These statements are generally called the *dynamic positioned*

DELETE and UPDATE statements. The format for the dynamic positioned DELETE statement is shown in Syntax 18-8.

Syntax 18-8 *Dynamic Positioned DELETE*

```
DELETE FROM table-name
WHERE CURRENT OF cursor-name
```

This is identical to the static positioned DELETE statement except that the cursor name can be either a normal cursor name or an ext-cursor-name. The behavior of the statement is precisely the same as the static positioned DELETE statement.

By the same token, the format for the dynamic positioned UPDATE statement is shown in Syntax 18-9.

Syntax 18-9 *Dynamic Positioned UPDATE*

```
UPDATE table-name
SET column-name = value [ , column-name = value ]...
WHERE CURRENT OF cursor-name
```

The only difference is that the cursor name can be a normal cursor name or an ext-cursor-name. The behavior here is also identical to the static positioned UPDATE statement.

However, life isn't always this simple. The problem with the dynamic positioned UPDATE statement is that you must know the column names when you write your application! This is sometimes practical but frequently impossible. Therefore, you really need to be able to PREPARE a positioned DELETE statement so that you can include different set-clauses (column-name = value) based on the actual cursor that you're dealing with.

The format of the *preparable* positioned UPDATE statement is shown in Syntax 18-10:

Syntax 18-10 *Preparable Positioned UPDATE*

```
UPDATE [ table-name ]
  SET column-name = value [ , column-name = value ]...
WHERE CURRENT OF cursor-name
```

The table-name is optional here because it's not really needed. Updatable cursors in SQL-92 can have only one table anyway. The other reason is that it may sometimes be difficult to determine the table name without a detailed analysis of the cursor specification. Except for that fact, the behavior is identical to the dynamic positioned UPDATE statement that we just discussed.

For symmetry, SQL:1999 also includes a preparable positioned DELETE statement, whose format is shown in Syntax 18-11.

Syntax 18-11 *Preparable Positioned DELETE*

```
DELETE [ FROM table-name ]
WHERE CURRENT OF cursor-name
```

Technically, this statement isn't actually required, although the optionality of the table-name means that you may not have to analyze your cursor specification just to delete a row via the cursor. The main reason this statement was included in SQL-92 was for symmetry with the preparable positioned UPDATE statement.

The more astute readers will have noticed that SQL:1999 has an ALLOCATE CURSOR statement, but no DEALLOCATE CURSOR statement. It's not clear why this wasn't included, since such a statement would serve to free up those scarce system resources that statements such as DEALLOCATE PREPARE and DEALLOCATE DESCRIPTOR are supposed to free up. Still, it's not there. Perhaps it will be in a future version of the standard.

18.11 A Dynamic SQL Example

Let's take a look at an example of a dynamic SQL program, which we've chosen to write using module language for the SQL code and C for the 3GL code:[1]

```
MODULE sql_1999_dyn
LANGUAGE C
AUTHORIZATION bryan

  DECLARE mycursor CURSOR FOR stmt_id

  PROCEDURE allocate_desc(SQLSTATE, :desc_name  CHAR(255));
    ALLOCATE DESCRIPTOR :desc_name;
```

---

[1] Adapted from Jim Melton and Bryan Higgs, "Details of SQL-92: Towards a Portable Dynamic SQL," *DB Programming and Design* (Nov.–Dec. 1992).

```
PROCEDURE deallocate_desc(SQLSTATE, :desc_name  CHAR(255));
  DEALLOCATE DESCRIPTOR :desc_name;

PROCEDURE prepare_statement(SQLSTATE, :stmt_string  CHAR(255));
  PREPARE stmt_id FROM :stmt_string;

PROCEDURE describe_input(SQLSTATE, :desc_name  CHAR(255));
  DESCRIBE INPUT stmt_id USING SQL DESCRIPTOR :desc_name;

PROCEDURE describe_output(SQLSTATE, :desc_name  CHAR(255));
  DESCRIBE OUTPUT stmt_id USING SQL DESCRIPTOR :desc_name;

PROCEDURE execute_statement(SQLSTATE, :in_desc_name CHAR(255));
  EXECUTE stmt_id USING SQL DESCRIPTOR :in_desc_name;

PROCEDURE open_cursor(SQLSTATE, :in_desc_name  CHAR(255));
  OPEN mycursor USING SQL DESCRIPTOR :in_desc_name;

PROCEDURE fetch_cursor(SQLSTATE, :out_desc_name  CHAR(255));
  FETCH mycursor USING SQL DESCRIPTOR :out_desc_name;

PROCEDURE close_cursor(SQLSTATE);
  CLOSE mycursor;

PROCEDURE deprepare_statement(SQLSTATE);
  DEALLOCATE PREPARE stmt_id;

PROCEDURE get_count(SQLSTATE, :desc_name CHAR(255),
                    :item_count  INTEGER);
  GET DESCRIPTOR :desc_name :item_count = COUNT;

PROCEDURE get_item_info(SQLSTATE, :desc_name  CHAR(255),
                        :item_no    INTEGER,
                        :name       CHAR(128),
                        :type       INTEGER,
                        :len        INTEGER,
                        :data       CHAR(4000),
                        :indicator  INTEGER);
  GET DESCRIPTOR :desc_name VALUE :item_no
                :name = NAME, :type = TYPE, :len = LENGTH,
                :data = DATA, :indicator = INDICATOR;
```

```
PROCEDURE set_count(SQLSTATE,
                    :desc_name   CHAR(255),
                    :item_count  INTEGER);
  SET DESCRIPTOR :desc_name COUNT = :item_count;

PROCEDURE set_item_info(SQLSTATE,
                        :desc_name   CHAR(255),
                        :item_no     INTEGER,
                        :type        INTEGER,
                        :len         INTEGER,
                        :data        CHAR(4000),
                        :indicator   INTEGER);
  SET DESCRIPTOR :desc_name VALUE :item_no
              TYPE = :type, LENGTH = :len,
              DATA = :data, INDICATOR = :indicator;
```

And here is the corresponding C code that uses it:

```
/******************************************************************
 *  Simple interactive SQL program using SQL:1999 style dynamic SQL.
 ******************************************************************/
#include <stdio.h>
#include <stdlib.h>
#include "sql_1999_dyn.h"          /* Interface to SQL_1999_DYN SQL
                                       module procedures */

/* extern function declarations */
extern int get_command(char *command_buffer,
                    size_t command_buffer_size);
extern int prompt_for_data(char *markers_desc_name);
extern void display_heading(char *select_list_desc_name);
extern void display_row(char *select_list_desc_name);

/* static, module-level data */
static char sqlstate[6];
#define SQL_UNSUCCESSFUL    (sqlstate > "02ZZZ")
#define SQL_END_OF_DATA     (sqlstate == "02000")

static char select_list_desc_name[256] = "SELECT_LIST_DESCRIPTOR";
static char markers_desc_name[256]      = "PARAMETERS_DESCRIPTOR";
```

```
#define MAX_CMD_LENGTH  4095
static char command_buffer[MAX_CMD_LENGTH + 1];

/***********************************************************
 * Function to allocate the system SQL descriptor areas.
 ***********************************************************/
static int allocate_sqldas(void)
{
  /* Allocate the two system SQL descriptor areas */
  ALLOCATE_DESC(sqlstate, select_list_desc_name);
  if (SQL_UNSUCCESSFUL)
      return 0;
  ALLOCATE_DESC(sqlstate, markers_desc_name);
  if (SQL_UNSUCCESSFUL)
     {
       DEALLOCATE_DESC(sqlstate, select_list_desc_name);
       return 0;
     }
  /* Succeeded in allocating both system SQL descriptor areas */
  return 1;
  .
  .
/***********************************************************
 *   * Function to report an error.
 ***********************************************************/
static void report_error(char *message)
{
  fprintf(stderr, "\n%s\nSQLSTATE = %s\n\n",
          message, sqlcode);
}


/***************************************************************
 * Function to prepare the command entered by the user,
 * and then to describe the select list for the prepared command.
 *
 * Any command entered by the user that is to be executed by SQL
 * must first be PREPAREd. This function calls the SQL PREPARE
 * function and checks for success or failure.
 ***************************************************************/
static int prepare_command(void)
{
```

```
      PREPARE_STATEMENT(sqlstate, command_buffer);
      if (SQL_UNSUCCESSFUL)
        {
          report_error("Failed to prepare statement");
          return 0;
        }
      DESCRIBE_OUTPUT(sqlstate, select_list_desc_name);
      if (SQL_UNSUCCESSFUL)
        {
          report_error("Failed to describe output");
          return 0;
        }
      return 1;
}


/****************************************************************
 *  Function to execute a select statement entered by the user
 *  and display the resulting row data on the screen.
 ****************************************************************/
static int execute_select(void)
{
  unsigned int count;

  /* Open the cursor. */
  OPEN_CURSOR(sqlstate, markers_desc_name);
  if (SQL_UNSUCCESSFUL)
    {
      report_error("Failed to open cursor");
      return 0;
    }
  display_heading(select_list_desc_name);

  /* Then, loop, fetching the data. */
  count = 0;
  while (1)
    {
      FETCH_CURSOR(sqlstate, select_list_desc_name);
      if (SQL_END_OF_DATA)
        break;          /* End of data */
```

```
      i= (SQL_UNSUCCESSFUL)
        {
          report_error("Failed to fetch from cursor");
          break;
        }
      /* If we get here, we have a real row. */
      count++;
      display_row(select_list_desc_name);
    }
  printf("%u rows retrieved\n", count);

  /* Finally, close the cursor. */
  CLOSE_CURSOR(sqlstate);
  if (SQL_UNSUCCESSFUL)
    {
      report_error("Failed to close cursor");
      return 0;
    }
  return 1;
}

/***************************************************************
 *  Function to execute a nonselect statement entered by the user.
 ***************************************************************/
static int execute(void)
{
  EXECUTE_STATEMENT(sqlstate, markers_desc_name);
  if (SQL_UNSUCCESSFUL)
    report_error("Failed to execute statement");
}

/***************************************************************
 *  Function to execute the command entered by the user.
 ***************************************************************/
static int execute_command(void)
{
  long count;
```

```
      /* Get information about markers. */
      DESCRIBE_INPUT(sqlstate, markers_desc_name);
      if (SQL_UNSUCCESSFUL)
        {
          report_error("Failed to describe statement");
          return 0;
        }
      /* If there are any markers, we need the data placed */
      /* into the SQL descriptor area. */
      if (prompt_for_data(markers_desc_name))
        {
          GET_COUNT(sqlstate, select_list_desc_name, &count);
          if (count > 0)
            execute_select();
          else
            execute();
        }
    return 1;
}


/*************************************************************
 *   Function to clean up the space allocated by the prepare.
 *************************************************************/
static int release_command(void)
{
  DEPREPARE_STATEMENT(sqlstate);
  if (SQL_UNSUCCESSFUL)
    report_error("Failed to release statement");
}


/*************************************************************
 *   Main entry point for program.
 *************************************************************/
main()
{
  printf("Welcome to the dynamic SQL executor...\n");
  /* Allocate and initialize the two system SQL descriptor areas. */
  if (allocate_sqldas() != 0)
    {
```

```
    /* Loop, getting commands and executing them */
    while (1)
      {
        if (get_command(command_buffer, sizeof(command_buffer))
            == 0)
          break;
        if (prepare_command())
          {
            execute_command();
            release_command();
          }
      }
    }
  printf("Bye!\n");
}
```

18.12 Chapter Summary

As you can tell from this chapter, there is a great deal more to *knowing* SQL than just a cursory familiarity with the various data definition and data manipulation statements. Intelligent use of SQL facilities requires you to know, for example, when to use dynamic SQL and when to use a static model. Those of you who develop applications that utilize database-stored data in conjunction with other software systems—such as spreadsheets and decision support packages—are likely to find yourselves making heavy use of dynamic SQL.

Chapter

19

Call-Level Interface (CLI)

19.1 | Introduction

Throughout this book, we've discussed the SQL language and given examples of its use in applications. Most of our examples have been written in "pure SQL"—that is, SQL statements illustrated in isolation from the context in which you would normally write them. If you wanted to describe it as "interactive SQL," it would be difficult to demonstrate that you are wrong.

The most notable exceptions to the practice of writing isolated SQL statements occurred in Chapter 12, "Accessing SQL from the Real World," and Chapter 18, "Dynamic SQL." In those chapters, we showed SQL statements in the context of embedded SQL programs and SQL statements written in module language. In fact, for most of SQL's history, SQL statements were most often "hard-coded" in embedded SQL programs. Dynamic SQL has also been very important to SQL applications, but the use of dynamic SQL (as you saw in Chapter 18, "Dynamic SQL") requires the use of several hard-coded SQL statements—statements such as PREPARE, DESCRIBE, and EXECUTE. Using statements like this always requires the use of a preprocessor or other language compiler capability, which is not always practical or desirable.

In recent years, applications developers have increasingly depended on an even more dynamic facility for invoking SQL statements, generally known as a *call-level interface*. Programs that use a call-level interface to access their SQL databases usually contain no hard-coded SQL statements at all. The embedded SQL notation "EXEC SQL" simply doesn't appear anywhere in such programs. Therefore, no preprocessor is required. More importantly, such programs can often be executed with any of several SQL database systems, instead of with only the single database system for which they were compiled.

In this chapter, we present the SQL standard's Call-Level Interface, including a review of its underlying assumptions, the programming model on which it is based, and the various routines that make up this interface.

19.2 | A Brief History of SQL/CLI and ODBC

A proposal by Oracle's Ken Jacobs in mid-1991 asserted a requirement for an interface to SQL systems that could support "shrink-wrapped" software—programs that could be run against any database system without recompilation. In 1992, shortly after SQL-92 was published, a number of database vendors came together to define a new API (application programming interface) for SQL database access. They recognized the requirement for an API that would allow an application program to be written without having to specify, or know, the database system that it would use when executed.

The interface developed by this group was initially called Open Database Connectivity. One of those vendors was (you've probably already guess this) Microsoft, who quickly adopted the interface for use by their applications in the form of the very popular ODBC. Of course, the initial specification of the API was not completely satisfactory to everybody involved, but the groundwork had been laid.

At about the same time, a formal consortium of database vendors, known as the SQL Access Group (sometimes called by its initials, SAG), had formed to help complete and test a new ISO standard for remote database access (RDA). While the work on RDA was never to achieve commercial success, SAG recognized the high value of Open Database Connectivity and volunteered to take over its development. Since Microsoft had by then trademarked the obvious initials (ODBC), SAG changed the name of the API to CLI, standing for "Call-Level Interface." SAG completed the development of CLI and submitted it to X/Open (a consortium of hardware vendors) for publication as part of the X/Open Portability Guide.

X/Open, in turn, submitted the specification to ISO for publication as an international standard. The ISO group given responsibility for the specification (see Appendix F, "The SQL Standardization Process") spent some months cleaning up the specification and formalizing it a bit, then published it in 1995 as a new part of the SQL-92 standard (even though it was called "CLI-95").

Some unsung heroes deserve mention for their especially important contributions to this process. Tony Gordon from the U.K. (first with ICL, then an independent consultant) was largely responsible for rewriting the specification from its X/Open style of language to the ISO style. Mike Pizzo of Microsoft was very instrumental in keeping the CLI work and the ODBC product aligned and vividly aware of each other. Kyle Geiger, also of Microsoft, contributed many technical proposals and actually chaired the specification's development group for many months. Frank Pellow, first with IBM and later with Microsoft, contributed significant technical enhancements and participated in the ANSI standards organization to help shepherd CLI through the formal standardization process. Paul Cotton of Canada (starting off with Fulcrum Technologies, moving to IBM, and now at Microsoft) spent the years between CLI's initial 1995 publication and the 1999 republication ensuring that all SQL:1999 facilities were accessible through SQL/CLI.

Over the ensuing years, Microsoft naturally enhanced its proprietary ODBC interface and ISO enhanced the CLI specification. Happily, the two organizations cooperated with each other so that the CLI part of SQL:1999[1] is quite compatible with ODBC 3.0. Because ODBC is intended to leverage the Windows environment, it contains a number of facilities that are not relevant to other environments and thus don't appear in SQL/CLI. Similarly, SQL/CLI supports new features of SQL:1999, such as its structured types (see Volume 2 of this book), that Microsoft does not support in its database products and thus are not fully supported in ODBC.

19.3 | Brief Comparison of SQL/CLI and Dynamic SQL

A call-level interface to an SQL database system is inherently a dynamic interface. By *dynamic* we mean that SQL statements to be executed using this interface are not precompiled and preoptimized as they are in embedded SQL and module language environments. Instead, the source text of SQL statements are transmitted as argument values to certain routines, after which they are processed ("compiled" and "optimized") and then executed.

The process has much in common—at least on a conceptual level—with dynamic SQL (see Chapter 18, "Dynamic SQL"), but there are also some important differences. We've summarized the most significant differences in Table 19-1.

---

1   ISO/IEC 9075-3:1999, *Information Technology—Database Languages—SQL—Part 3: Call-Level Interface (SQL/CLI)*, International Organization for Standardization, 1999.

Table 19-1 *Contrasts between Dynamic SQL and Call-Level Interface*

Characteristic	Dynamic SQL	Call-Level Interface
Connections	CONNECT, SET CONNECTION, and DISCONNECT statements	AllocConnect()*, FreeConnect(), GetConnectAttr(), and SetConnectAttr() routines used to manage resources; Connect() and Disconnect() routines; implicit connection changes based on handles supplied to other routines
Transactions	START TRANSACTION, COMMIT, and ROLLBACK statements	StartTran() and EndTran() routines
Statement preparation and execution	PREPARE and EXECUTE statements, or EXECUTE IMMEDIATE statement	Prepare() and Execute() routines, or ExecDirect() routine
Descriptor areas	SQL descriptor areas referenced by name, managed by ALLOCATE DESCRIPTOR and DEALLOCATE DESCRIPTOR statements	CLI descriptor areas referenced by handle, managed by AllocHandle() and FreeHandle()
Descriptor fields	Referenced by GET DESCRIPTOR and SET DESCRIPTOR statements	Referenced by GetDescField(), GetDescRec(), SetDescField(), SetDescRec(), and CopyDesc() routines
Cursors	DECLARE CURSOR, OPEN, FETCH, UPDATE positioned, DELETE positioned, CLOSE statements	Implicit cursor created when SELECT statement prepared, implicitly opened when that statement is executed; CloseCursor() routine, various routines to retrieve data and to update or delete rows
Metadata information	Information Schema views	Several "helper" routines implicitly retrieve information from the Information Schema
Parameter and column data exchange	Explicit USING clauses	Implicit USING clauses

* We use the notation identifier() to specify the name of, or an invocation of, a particular routine without having to specify the particular arguments for that routine.

Of course, Table 19-1 doesn't detail all of the differences between the two models, but it does indicate the nature of the differences. In section 19.4, we describe the SQL/CLI model at a fairly high level to set the context for additional details that appear in subsequent sections of this chapter.

19.4 **The SQL/CLI Model**

CLI is nothing more than a set of routines—a *database library*, as some vendors describe it—that can be called by ordinary applications using normal language mechanisms for invoking routines.[2] The routines provide capabilities that are analogous to those of dynamic SQL, but they also provide additional important capabilities such as connecting to SQL servers, accessing metadata, and retrieving status information.

Since the applications invoke the routines directly, there is no precompilation phase to separate SQL code from host language code, no compilation of the SQL code in advance of execution, and greater ease in debugging because of the much closer relationship between object code and source code. More importantly, software vendors can build applications that can be run on many vendors' database systems without delivering their (proprietary) source code for users to recompile.

The SQL/CLI model is one that

- Uses handles to reference environments, connections, statements, and descriptors.

- Specifies a number of ordinary routines (functions, in fact) that application programs invoke to execute database operations.

- Processes SQL statements using a dynamic approach, including the ability to pass dynamic arguments to those statements when they are executed.

- Automatically describes a statement's dynamic parameters (see section 18.3.1, "Parameters," for a refresher on this concept), columns of data returned by the statement, or both, at the time that the statement is prepared.

- Allows applications to retrieve descriptive information about a statement's dynamic parameters, returned columns of data, or both. The descriptive information can be retrieved for an entire dynamic parameter or column in one operation, or specific attributes of the information for a dynamic parameter or column can be retrieved individually.

- Permits applications to *bind* the dynamic parameters of a statement, its returned columns, or both to variables in the host program. Binding

---

2 The description in this section is based on a discussion contained in the change proposal (X3H2-92-208 and DBL:CBR-053), written by Tony Gordon in September, 1992, providing the initial text that eventually became the SQL/CLI standard.

dynamic parameters and returned columns in this way causes operations to transfer data directly from the host program to the database and vice versa. Dynamic parameters and returned columns that are not bound to host variables are handled through the CLI descriptors.

- Does not require the explicit creation of cursors but implicitly creates them when retrieval statements are provided by an application.

- Provides a number of *helper routines* that give applications convenient shortcuts for a number of common operations.

- Implements a CLI diagnostics area and several routines used to retrieve information about the status of statement execution.

- Requires that both connections and transactions be managed through provided CLI routines instead of through ordinary SQL statements.

19.5 | Handles

An application that uses SQL/CLI to access an SQL database system must first create an *environment* in which its operations are to be performed. Environments are created by the invocation of the CLI routine AllocHandle(), specifying that an *environment handle* is required. Alternatively, the application can use the AllocEnv() routine, a "shortcut" routine that performs the same function by invoking AllocHandle() behind the scenes, implicitly providing the appropriate arguments. The routine also sets up any additional data structures or context required for SQL database access.

Once an environment has been established, the application must allocate the resources that will be required to create a *connection* to a specific SQL database system. Connections are allocated by invoking the AllocHandle() routine, specifying that a *connection handle* is required; as with environment creation, there is an alternative approach: AllocConnect(). Connections are allocated only in the context of a specific environment, so the environment handle that was returned when the environment was created is required for allocating the connection. Allocation of a connection allocates whatever resources are required for connection management, but it does not actually establish the connection to a specific database.

Once the connection has been allocated, the application can then connect to the SQL system on which it wishes its operations to be performed. Connections are established by using Connect(), supplying the connection handle provided when the connection was allocated.

When the application wishes to execute an SQL statement, it must first allocate a statement handle, using either `AllocHandle()` or `AllocStmt()`. In order to acquire information about the dynamic parameters that the statement might contain or the columns of data that the statement might return, the application must allocate a CLI descriptor using `AllocHandle()` (there is no shortcut routine for this purpose).

This partial scenario illustrates the central role that handles play in the use of SQL/CLI. Let's take a slightly closer look at the various handle types.

19.5.1 Environment Handles

As you saw in our little scenario, CLI applications must allocate an environment before any other CLI activities can take place.

An environment is represented by, or referenced by, an environment handle. Your applications can allocate an environment by using either of two routines. If you choose to use the `AllocHandle()` routine, then you must provide three arguments: the first is a code to indicate which type of handle (environment, of course) that you want allocated; the second is the value 0 (indicating that the environment handle does not depend on any existing handle); the third is an output argument containing the address of the host variable into which you want the routine to place the actual environment handle that it allocates. If you choose to use the `AllocEnv()` routine, then you provide only a single argument: the address of the host variable.

Environment handles are used for allocating connections and for a few administrative purposes (for example, to get information about error conditions that have been raised). Of course, you have to provide a valid environment handle when you deallocate an environment, by invoking either the `FreeEnv()` routine or the `FreeHandle()` routine.

In section 19.14, "CLI Routines Summary," we show you the signatures of all SQL/CLI routines and give a brief description of their arguments.

19.5.2 Connection Handles

The scenario we sketched out in section 19.5 showed that the step that ordinarily follows environment allocation is connection allocation and establishment.

A connection is referenced by a connection handle, which is allocated by the use of either of two routines. As with environment allocation, you can use `AllocHandle()`, specifying the code representing connection handles in the first argument, or you can use AllocConnect(). In either case, you must provide a valid environment handle that identifies an allocated environment, because connections are "contained within" or "dependent on" environments. You can allocate as many connections within a single environment as you need; in general, you need to have one connection handle for each database to which you will be concurrently connected.

Connection handles are used in a variety of CLI routines to specify the particular database (among the concurrently connected databases) on which a given operation is to be performed. Unlike ordinary SQL language, CLI provides no statement or function to explicitly change from one connected database to another (see section 16.3.2, "SET CONNECTION"). Instead, CLI uses the notion of an *implicit* SET CONNECTION statement, meaning that two consecutive CLI routine invocations that specify different connection handles behave as though a SET CONNECTION statement was executed after the earlier of the two routine invocations and before the later. Merely specifying different connection handles is sufficient to change the application's database connection from one database to another.

CLI connections are fairly flexible. For example, you can establish multiple concurrent connections to a single database system, using different connection handles for each such connection. Each connection behaves as though it represented a different "user" at the database system, however; there is no standardized way for two or more of your concurrent connections to a single database system to be aware of one another or to collaborate in any way.

When you have completed the work you need to do on a given connection, you should release the resources associated with it by invoking either FreeConnect() or FreeHandle().

19.5.3   Statement Handles

All CLI operations that involve dealing with SQL statements—such as preparing them for execution, executing them, and managing them—require the use of a statement handle. Statements handles are allocated in the context of a database connection; the reason for this relationship is simple: when a statement is prepared (implicitly, compiled and optimized), the preparation is valid only for a specific database. If you want to use the statement on another database, it must be prepared (that is, compiled and optimized) for that database as a separate operation.

Statement handles are allocated using either AllocStmt() or AllocHandle(). In both cases, you must provide a valid connection handle to the routine; in fact, that connection handle has to identify an established connection.

When you allocate a statement handle, CLI automatically allocates four descriptors and associates them with the statement handle. These descriptors are used to describe the dynamic parameters that might be contained in an SQL statement associated with the statement handle, and to describe the columns that might be returned by such a statement. The four types of descriptors are *implementation parameter descriptor* (IPD), *implementation row descriptor* (IRD), *application parameter descriptor* (APD), and *application row descriptor* (ARD). See section 19.8, "CLI Descriptor Areas Versus Dynamic Descriptor Areas," for more information about these four different sorts of descriptors. The four descriptors that are automatically allocated when you allocate a statement handle are called *automatic* descriptors, and that information is indicated in the descriptor itself by setting one of the fields, ALLOC_TYPE, to contain the value 'AUTOMATIC'.

You associate an SQL statement with a statement handle by using the Prepare() routine, specifying the statement handle and the text string of the SQL statement as arguments. One effect of the Prepare() invocation is that two of the automatic descriptors (the implementation parameter descriptor and implementation row descriptor) are populated with descriptions of the statement's dynamic parameters (if any) and of the statement's returned columns (if any).

You can also associate an SQL statement with a statement handle by using the ExecDirect() routine, but the association created in this way does not permit you to execute the statement a second time. Instead, the association is relevant only because of the fact that the automatic descriptors are available only through the statement handle.

Naturally, you can free the resources associated with a statement handle when you're done with its use. Either FreeStmt() or FreeHandle() can be used to release those resources and deallocate the statement handle.

19.5.4 Descriptor Handles

By contrast with the automatic descriptors that are allocated whenever you allocate a statement handle, CLI also supports descriptors that you can allocate yourself, using the AllocHandle() routine. Unlike allocation of environment handles, connection handles, and statement handles, there is no descriptor-specific shortcut allocation routine (a routine that you might expect to be named AllocDescr(), for example) in SQL/CLI.

When you allocate a descriptor in this way, the ALLOC_TYPE field of the descriptor is set to the value 'USER' to indicate that it is a user-allocated descriptor and not an automatically allocated descriptor. All user-allocated descriptors are either application row descriptors (ARDs) or application parameter descriptors (APDs). As you'll see in section 19.8, ARDs are used by your applications to transfer the data contained in columns returned by your SQL statements into your host language variables, while APDs are used to transfer values from your host language variables into the database system for use as dynamic parameters.

Of course, user-allocated descriptors consume resources that your applications may wish to free when they no longer have need for those descriptors. The FreeHandle() routine is used to release user-allocated descriptors.

19.6 | Null Pointers

Some application programming languages support *pointers:* values that identify specific memory addresses, usually the address of some host variable or buffer. Among those languages are C and PL/I. By contrast, there are other programming languages, such as COBOL and Fortran, that do not support such pointers.

SQL/CLI is defined such that both sorts of languages can be used to write programs that use CLI to access SQL databases. When you write applications in a language that supports pointers, you will encounter situations in which a CLI routine has a parameter for which a pointer is the appropriate argument, but for which you do not wish to provide a pointer. For example, you may wish not to receive the length of a string value that is returned in another parameter, or you might not want to provide a particular input argument. In those cases, CLI often allows you to provide a *null pointer*—that is, give the memory address value 0—instead of an actual pointer to some host variable. If you provide a null pointer in a situation that CLI prohibits, then you'll be rewarded with an error.

19.7 | Database Connections and Implicit Connections

Now that we've learned about the various sorts of handles, including connection handles, let's take a look at some sample code that demonstrates the use of some of these handles, especially connection handles. Example 19-1 contains this sample code. We've chosen to write most of our code fragments, including this one, in C, since our experience suggests that a large fraction of CLI applications are written in C. (In fact, the most popular implementation of CLI—ODBC—is very strongly biased toward C.)

Example 19-1 *Allocating and Using Environments and Connections*

```
/*****************************************************
* In this example, we illustrate typical "include" files
* and other relevant declarations.  For brevity's sake,
* we do not make this part of every example.
*****************************************************/


#include <stddef.h>   /* Necessary for many C programs */
#include <string.h>   /* Necessary for many C programs */
#include <sqlcli.h>   /* Definitions used in CLI programs */


#define NAMELEN 50    /* Length of char string bfr for names */


/* The signature of a routine to print errors when we get them */
int print_err ( SQLSMALLINT handletype, SQLINTEGER handle ) ;


/* Show our example routine's header information this time. */
int example1 ( SQLCHAR *server1, SQLCHAR *uid1, SQLCHAR *auth1,
               SQLCHAR *server2, SQLCHAR *uid2, SQLCHAR *auth2 )
{
/* Declare some variables that we'll use in various examples. */
SQLHENV henv1;          /* SQLHENV is a type defined in sqlcli.h */
SQLHDBC hdbc1;
SQLHDBC hdbc2;
SQLHDESC hdesc;
SQLHDESC hdesc1;
SQLHDESC hdesc2;
SQLHSTMT hsmt1;
SQLHSTMT hsmt2;
SQLINTEGER salepct;
SQLREAL profit
SQLINTEGER profitind;
SQLCHAR name[NAMELEN+1];
SQLINTEGER namelen;
SQLINTEGER nameind;


/*****************************************************
*  The CLI code corresponding to the SQL statement:
*    EXEC SQL CONNECT TO :server USER :userid;
*  is shown here.
*****************************************************/
```

```
/* First, allocate an environment handle */
/* SQL_HANDLE_ENV is a manifest constant = 1 ==> "environment handle" */
/* SQL_NULL_HANDLE = 0 */
/* SQLAllocHandle is the "proper name" for the AllocHandle() routine */
SQLAllocHandle ( SQL_HANDLE_ENV, SQL_NULL_HANDLE, &henv ) ;

/* Allocate a connection handle associated with the new environment */
SQLAllocHandle ( SQL_HANDLE_DBC, henv, &hdbc1 ) ;

/* Connect to the first database and test for success */
if ( SQLConnect ( hdbc1, server1, SQL_NTS, uid1, SQL_NTS, auth1, SQL_NTS )
    != SQL_SUCCESS )
  return ( print_err ( SQL_HANDLE_DBC, hdbc1 ) ) ;

/* Allocate another connection handle associated with the environment */
SQLAllocHandle ( SQL_HANDLE_DBC, henv, &hdbc2 ) ;

/* Connect to the second database and test for success. */
if ( SQLConnect ( hdbc2, server2, SQL_NTS, uid2, SQL_NTS, auth2, SQL_NTS )
    != SQL_SUCCESS )
  return ( print_err ( SQL_HANDLE_DBC, hdbc2 ) ) ;

/* Allocate a statement handle associated with the first connection. */
SQLAllocStmt ( hdbc1, &hstmt1 );

/* Implicitly change connection to allocate another statement handle. */
SQLAllocStmt ( hdbc2, &hstmt2 );


...


}
```

In Example 19-1, we demonstrated a number of ideas that we think worth explaining, which we do in the next couple of paragraphs.

In the SQL/CLI standard,[3] Appendix A, "Typical Header Files," contains a sample C header file with a complete specification of all "manifest constants" used in C programs that will use CLI, as well as a corresponding COBOL library item for analogous COBOL programs. That appendix doesn't contain the corre-

---

3 ISO/IEC 9075-3:1999.

sponding definitions for other programming languages, but we expect that CLI implementations will provide such definitions for all languages that they support. In Example 19-1, we brought these definitions into our code through the use of a #include statement that identified sqlcli.h as the file to be included.

You should also note that the routines that we invoked have all had a prefix ("SQL") added to their names. We like to say that the "canonical names" of the routines are unadorned with any such prefix, so we normally speak of the AllocHandle() routine without a prefix. However, the actual name of the routine that is invoked in a C program has the prefix SQL added, making the proper name of the routine SQLAllocHandle. All CLI routines come in two variants. The variant with the CLI prefix can be invoked from languages like C in which all arguments are passed by value. (It is beyond the scope of this book to explain programming languages' argument-passing mechanisms.) By contrast, languages such as Fortran or COBOL, in which arguments are passed by reference, invoke CLI routines using a different prefix, SQLR; as a result, the routine whose canonical name is AllocHandle() would be invoked from COBOL using the actual name SQLRAllocHandle.

Finally, we point out that the last two statements in Example 19-1 are AllocStmt() routine invocations that use different connection handles. There is no explicit SET CONNECTION statement involved, but the effects of that statement are implicitly invoked when the second AllocStmt() invocation occurs with a different connection handle. (Of course it is not relevant that we used a different host variable in the second invocation of AllocStmt(); it is the contents of the host variables provided as arguments that are the determining factors.)

19.8 | CLI Descriptor Areas Versus Dynamic Descriptor Areas

In Figure 18-1 in Chapter 18, "Dynamic SQL," we illustrated the mental model we use when thinking about the SQL descriptor area. An identical figure could be used to show you the mental model we have of the CLI descriptor area. For most purposes, a CLI descriptor is nothing more than an SQL descriptor area. However, as with many other facets of life, the differences show up when we examine the details. Most significantly, CLI descriptor areas have additional fields in both the header area and the item descriptor area, compared with SQL descriptor areas. You can read about these additional fields in section 19.8.2, "CLI Descriptor Area Fields."

19.8.1 Types of CLI Descriptor Area

As you read in Chapter 18, "Dynamic SQL," there is only one sort of SQL descriptor area. Of course, you can allocate as many SQL descriptor areas as you need, and each SQL descriptor area has one header area and as many item descriptor areas as you specify when you allocate it.

CLI's descriptor areas are used somewhat differently than ordinary SQL descriptor areas; there's a tighter relationship between CLI and application programs in many ways, and the descriptor areas reflect that close relationship. In particular, there are four different types of CLI descriptor area:

- *Application Parameter Descriptor (APD):* Describes the values in the application program that will be used to resolve dynamic parameter references in a prepared SQL statement when it is executed

- *Application Row Descriptor (ARD):* Describes the application program host variables (*targets*) into which values are stored when they are retrieved from the columns returned by executing a prepared SQL statement

- *Implementation Parameter Descriptor (IPD):* Describes the dynamic parameter references in a prepared SQL statement

- *Implementation Row Descriptor (IRD):* Describes the columns that will be returned by a prepared SQL statement

There are several CLI routines that allow you to retrieve and set the values of fields in CLI descriptor areas. These routines are roughly analogous to the SQL statements GET DESCRIPTOR and SET DESCRIPTOR. The routines that retrieve CLI descriptor area field values are GetDescRec() and GetDescField(); the routines that set field values are SetDescRec() and SetDescField(). However, there are restrictions placed by CLI on your ability to set fields in some types of descriptors. For example, you cannot use SetDescRec() or SetDescField() to set the values of any field in an IRD; only the database system is permitted to set those fields. As we'll see in section 19.9, "Statement Preparation and Execution," there are several other routines that set the values of certain fields in one or more descriptor area types; these routines usually do so in conjunction with getting ready to execute a prepared SQL statement.

Figure 19-1 illustrates the relationships among the four types of CLI descriptor areas, the CLI client, and the database system. As you will notice, data being transferred from the application to the database system is conceptually processed using information in the APD and then using information in the IPD. Similarly, data being transferred from the database to the application is conceptually processed first using information in the IRD and then using information in the ARD.

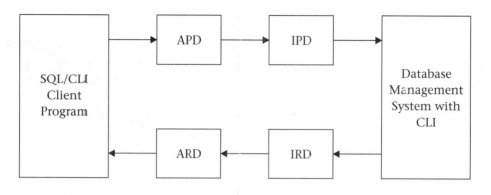

Figure 19-1   Relationships among Various Types of CLI Descriptor Areas

Each type of CLI descriptor area is used in one or more situations. For example, whenever you execute a prepared SQL statement that contains dynamic parameters, CLI will use the IPD and APD associated with the statement handle that you specify to assist in transferring the host program values corresponding to those dynamic parameters into the database. Similarly, when you retrieve data using Fetch() or FetchScroll(), CLI uses the IRD and ARD associated with the statement handle used by those two routines to assist in transferring retrieved column values from the database into your host program variables.

In the preceding paragraph, we twice used the phrase "assist in transferring," which deserves a word of explanation. In general, CLI is quite willing to transfer the value of an INTEGER column in a row retrieved via a call to Fetch(), merely moving the integer value into the integer variable to which the DATA field points. But integers are simple, and it's fairly likely that an INTEGER value in your SQL database has exactly the same format, including range of values, as an int variable in your C program. However, that level of confidence doesn't apply to all of SQL's data types: C has no native type corresponding to SQL's DECIMAL and NUMERIC types, and none of the programming languages for which SQL has a defined relationship supports SQL's DATE, TIME, TIMESTAMP, and INTERVAL types.

Consequently, if you are retrieving, say, a DATE column from the database into a C program, you must make sure that the value is retrieved using a format with which C can deal, such as character string. In embedded SQL and module language, you would have to use a CAST expression in the select list of your query to force the DATE values to be converted to character strings—something like this:

```
CAST (birthdate TO CHARACTER VARYING(10))
```

CLI makes life a little easier, though. Instead of having to ensure that the SQL statements you're executing through CLI have the CAST expressions coded into them, you can set up the ARDs for those statements to cause those conversions to be done automatically. If the IRD for an SQL statement you've just described contains an item descriptor area for a DATE column, then the TYPE field of that item descriptor area contains the code for DATE (9). If you set the TYPE field of the corresponding ARD item descriptor area to 1, which is the code for CHARACTER, then CLI will automatically perform a CAST from DATE to CHARACTER for you. (Of course, there are other fields that have to be properly set in the ARD, such as the LENGTH field.)

19.8.2 CLI Descriptor Area Fields

As you will see in Table 19-2 and Table 19-3, some fields in the CLI descriptor area have names ending in "_POINTER." These fields are intended to contain memory addresses of host variables that will be given values (usually lengths or counters) resulting from the execution of some SQL statement through the CLI. The SQL descriptor areas have no other fields that are not also in the CLI descriptor area. Therefore, the CLI descriptor area could be considered to be a superset of the SQL descriptor area. In fact, we believe that SQL implementations could implement only a single set of descriptor areas (the CLI descriptor areas, enhanced by the nonpointer fields corresponding to some of the "_POINTER" fields used by CLI) and use syntax restrictions to prohibit ordinary dynamic SQL programs from accessing some of the fields. Similarly, CLI programs would have to obey some syntax restrictions and access the "_POINTER" fields where appropriate.

The additional header area fields are shown in Table 19-2, and the additional item descriptor area fields are shown in Table 19-3.

Table 19-2 *CLI Descriptor Area Header Fields Not in the SQL Descriptor Area*

<key word>	*Data Type*
ALLOC_TYPE	SMALLINT
ARRAY_SIZE	INTEGER
ARRAY_STATUS_POINTER	Host variable address of INTEGER
ROWS_PROCESSED_POINTER	Host variable address of INTEGER
Implementation-defined header field <key word>	Implementation-defined

We've already mentioned the ALLOC_TYPE field in section 19.5.3 and section 19.5.4, so we don't need to cover that field again. The names of the ARRAY_SIZE and ARRAY_STATUS_POINTER fields seem to imply that they have something to do with handling columns whose data type is ARRAY, but that's the wrong conclusion. Instead, the two fields, along with ROWS_PROCESSED_POINTER, support a CLI capability that is not available in ordinary dynamic SQL. CLI allows you to retrieve multiple rows, called a *rowset,* with a single invocation of the Fetch() or FetchScroll() routines. By contrast, dynamic SQL's use of the FETCH statement only allows retrieval of one row at a time.

The ARRAY_SIZE field allows the CLI application to specify the number of rows that the application is able to process as a result of a single fetch operation. The ARRAY_STATUS_POINTER field must contain the address of a host variable that is an array of INTEGERs. The cardinality of that array must be at least as large as the value specified in ARRAY_SIZE. When a call to Fetch() or FetchScroll() returns a rowset, elements of the host variable to which ARRAY_STATUS_POINTER points are set to integer values indicating the status of the corresponding row (that is, the first element in the array corresponds to the first row in the rowset, and so forth.) The status values are as follows:

0   Indicates that the row was retrieved successfully

6   Indicates that the row was retrieved successfully, but that warnings were raised during the retrieval

3   Indicates that there is no row at the corresponding position in the rowset, usually because the rowset has ended and a partial rowset was retrieved

5   Indicates that an exception condition was raised during the retrieval of the row

Each array element whose value is either 5 or 6 (meaning that an exception or a warning was raised for the corresponding row) implies that there are one or more status records available in the CLI diagnostics area (see section 19.12, "Diagnostics Facilities").

The ROWS_PROCESSED_POINTER field must contain the address of a host variable that is an INTEGER, or it must be a null pointer. When the Fetch() or FetchScroll() routines complete, if ROWS_PROCESSED_POINTER is not a null pointer, then the host variable to which it points is set to the number of rows in the rowset that has just been fetched.

Finally, you should note that the CLI descriptor area allows "implementation-defined header fields." Even though the SQL standard doesn't address that concept for the SQL descriptor area, we don't believe that it was deliberately excluded. As a result, we think you're just as likely to find implementation extensions in the SQL descriptor area as you are in the CLI descriptor area. Naturally, the data types and meanings of those extensions' fields are defined solely by the implementation.

Table 19-3 *CLI Descriptor Area Item Descriptor Fields Not in the SQL Descriptor Areas*

<key word>	*Data Type*
CURRENT_TRANSFORM_GROUP	Character string with character set SQL_IDENTIFIER and length not less than the maximum number of characters supported for the value CURRENT_TRANSFORM_GROUP_FOR_TYPE
DATA_POINTER	Host variable address of appropriate data type
DATA_POINTER serves the same purpose as DATA in the SQL descriptor area	
INDICATOR_POINTER	Host variable address of INTEGER
INDICATOR_POINTER serves the same purpose as INDICATOR in the SQL descriptor area	
OCTET_LENGTH_POINTER	Host variable address of INTEGER
OCTET_LENGTH_POINTER serves the same purpose as OCTET_LENGTH in the SQL descriptor area, when used to return a value to the application	
RETURNED_CARDINALITY_POINTER	Host variable address of INTEGER
RETURNED_CARDINALITY _POINTER serves the same purpose as RETURNED_CARDINALITY in the SQL descriptor area	
SPECIFIC_TYPE_CATALOG	Character string with character set SQL_IDENTIFIER and length not less than 128 characters
SPECIFIC_TYPE_SCHEMA	Character string with character set SQL_IDENTIFIER and length not less than 128 characterss
SPECIFIC_TYPE_NAME	Character string with character set SQL_IDENTIFIER and length not less than 128 characters
Implementation-defined item field <key word>	Implementation-defined

Let's first consider those fields whose names end with "_POINTER." Each of those fields corresponds to a field in the SQL descriptor area whose name excludes "_POINTER" but is otherwise the same as the CLI descriptor area field. For example, in the SQL descriptor area, the field INDICATOR is used to return a value that indicates whether the corresponding column is, or is not, the null value. Similarly, RETURNED_CARDINALITY_POINTER serves the same purpose in the CLI descriptor area that RETURNED_CARDINALITY serves in the SQL descriptor area. In the CLI descriptor area, some (but not all) fields in which values are returned to the application are pointers, so that the values are actually returned in host variables to which the fields point. The designers of CLI chose the pointer approach for fields that are likely to be used by almost all CLI applications for practically every exchange of data between the application and the database system. Other fields used to return information to the application, such as the three components of the character set name of character string values, are not specified as pointers, so the values returned are simply placed into the descriptor field itself.

The CLI descriptor area has both a field named OCTET_LENGTH and a field named OCTET_LENGTH_POINTER. The former is used for supplying the length (in octets) of values being transferred from the application to the database system or the maximum length that the application is willing to tolerate for values being returned. The latter is used only to return to the application the length of some value being transferred from the database to the application.

DATA_POINTER requires a little more explanation. Observe in Table 19-3 that its data type is specified as "Host variable address of appropriate data type"—which you might reasonably think not terribly helpful. The reason for the deliberate vagueness may be obvious once explained: DATA_POINTER contains the address of a host variable into which CLI will place the value of the column retrieved (or, conversely, from which CLI takes the value of a dynamic parameter used in an SQL statement), and the data type of that variable has to match the data type specified in the TYPE column. That data type varies from column to column, and from dynamic parameter to dynamic parameter. Therefore, the CLI descriptor area cannot prescribe a single data type for the host variable to which DATA_POINTER points.

The remaining four fields—CURRENT_TRANSFORM_GROUP, SPECIFIC_TYPE_CATALOG, SPECIFIC_TYPE_SCHEMA, and SPECIFIC_TYPE_NAME—are all used with structured types, which are discussed in Volume 2 of this book.

19.9 | Statement Preparation and Execution

To this point in this chapter, we've described several of the central components of SQL's Call-Level Interface. It's time to put that knowledge to use and to begin addressing some of the more subtle points of CLI. In this section, we'll describe how you prepare an SQL statement for execution using CLI, how you execute that prepared statement, and how you can alter the details of its execution (e.g., by supplying different values to correspond to dynamic parameters).

19.9.1 Simple Statements That Do Not Retrieve Data

Let's consider a fairly simple SQL statement, one that we might use to put all of the DVDs that are in stock on sale—but the sale percentage will be provided dynamically when the statement is executed. The statement itself probably looks something like this:

```
UPDATE movie_titles
SET    current_dvd_sale_price
     = regular_dvd_sale_price * ( ( 100 - percentage_discount ) / 100 )
WHERE  dvds_in_stock > 0
```

Of course, we must have some way to pass in the value represented by *percentage_ discount*. If we were using ordinary embedded SQL, we'd use a host variable. If we were using dynamic SQL, we'd use a dynamic parameter (the question mark, ?), and that's what we do in CLI, too. To prepare this statement for execution, there are a number of steps we must take. As you already know, the first steps are allocation of an environment, followed by allocation and establishment of a connection, and then allocation of a statement handle. You saw those steps in Example 19-1, so we don't need to repeat them here in Example 19-2. For clarity, though, we do repeat the statement handle allocation. (Again, we have chosen to illustrate the concepts using program fragments written in C.)

Example 19-2 *Preparing an SQL Statement for Execution*

```
/* Allocate a statement handle associated with the first connection */
SQLAllocStmt ( hdbc1, &hstmt1 );

{
  /******************************************************************
   * Construct a string containing the SQL statement.  Notice that we
   * used a dynamic parameter (?) instead of a host variable name.
   ******************************************************************/
  SQLCHAR updstmt =
    "UPDATE movie_titles
     SET    current_dvd_sale_price
          = regular_dvd_sale_price * ( ( 100 - ? ) / 100 )
     WHERE  dvds_in_stock > 0";

  /******************************************************************
   * Prepare the statement for execution. We use the statement handle
   * allocated above and the string we just created containing the
   * UPDATE statement.  We used "SQL_NTS" to indicate that the string
   * containing the statement is passed using the C convention of
   * null termination.
```

```
**********************************************************/
if ( SQLPrepare ( hstmt1, updstmt, SQL_NTS ) != SQL_SUCCESS )
  return ( print_err ( SQL_HANDLE_STMT, hstmt1 ) );


...


}
```

With this, we have a prepared statement that we can use as long as we like—well, at least until its statement handle is deallocated or another statement is prepared using the same statement handle.

Once we have prepared the statement, we have to get ready to execute it. This process requires that we consider the APD and IPD, since the statement has one dynamic parameter. In order to get a handle to the automatically allocated APD associated with the statement handle we're using, we have to use a CLI routine we haven't mentioned yet: GetStmtAttr(). Statement handles have a number of attributes that can be retrieved, some of which can also be set using SetStmtAttr(). Example 19-3 continues the example by getting the APD and IPD ready for executing our UPDATE statement.

Example 19-3 *Readying the CLI Descriptor Areas for Statement Execution*

```
{
    ...  /* Construct the string and invoke SQLPrepare() */


    /****************************************************************
    * Get the application parameter descriptor ready.  The first step
    * is to get a handle to the APD from the statement handle. Then
    * we set certain fields of the first item descriptor in the APD
    * to state that we're using a C int variable named 'salepct'.
    ****************************************************************/
    SQLGetStmtAttr ( hstmt1, SQL_ATTR_APP_PARAM_DESC, &hdesc1, 0L,
                (SQLINTEGER *)NULL ) ;
    SQLSetDescRec ( hdesc1, 1, SQL_INTEGER, 0, 0L, 0, 0,
                (SQLPOINTER)&salepct, (SQLINTEGER *)NULL,
                (SQLINTEGER *)NULL);

    /* Get the implementation parameter descriptor ready. */
    SQLGetStmtAttr ( hstmt1, SQL_ATTR_IMP_PARAM_DESC, &hdesc2, 0L,
                (SQLINTEGER *)NULL ) ;
    SQLSetDescRec ( hdesc2, 1, SQL_INTEGER, 0, 0L, 0, 0,
```

```
                    (SQLPOINTER)NULL, (SQLINTEGER *)NULL,
                    (SQLINTEGER *)NULL);


        ...


    }
```

At this point, the statement has been prepared and we've set up the two CLI descriptor areas dealing with dynamic parameters—the ADP and the IPD—to indicate that we're transferring one integer value that will be available in a C variable named salepct and that the dynamic parameter itself is to be considered an INTEGER. The other fields of the descriptor area are not relevant for our purposes, so the arguments we pass to SetDescRec() are either 0 or null values (as appropriate). (Don't forget that the signatures of all CLI routines, including the ones we're using in these examples, are shown in section 19.14, "CLI Routines Summary.")

The next step is really easy and straightforward. As you see in Example 19-4, we ensure that the host variable we're using (salepct) has a value representing the percentage discount we're offering, and then we execute the statement.

Example 19-4 *Executing a Prepared Statement Having a Dynamic Parameter*

```
{
  ... /* Construct the string, invoke SQLPrepare(), and set up IPD/APD. */

  /* Assign an appropriate value to salepct. */
  salepct = 10;  /* Times are tight for us -- only give a 10% discount. */

  /* Execute the statement...let's have a sale! */
  if ( SQLExecute ( hstmt1 ) != SQL_SUCCESS )
    return ( print_err ( SQL_HANDLE_STMT, hstmt1 ) ) ;


  ...


}
```

Naturally, there are subsequent steps that must be taken, such as committing the transaction (otherwise, our statement's changes won't be persistent and we've wasted our time) and releasing resources allocated during the course of the example. We defer those until later in the chapter, particularly until section

19.15, "Annotated CLI Example," where you can see the entire example in one piece.

If our SQL statement had not required the use of a dynamic parameter (we could have chosen to hard-code the 10% discount, for example), we could have avoided many of the statements above and simply used ExecDirect(), as shown in Example 19-5.

Example 19-5 *Even Simpler Statement Execution*

```
{
  /* Set up the UPDATE statement. */
  SQLCHAR updstmt =
    "UPDATE movie_titles
    SET    current_dvd_sale_price
         = regular_dvd_sale_price * 0.90
    WHERE  dvds_in_stock > 0";

  /* Execute the statement...let's have a sale! */
  if ( SQLExecDirect ( hstmt1, updstmt, SQL_NTS ) != SQL_SUCCESS )
    return ( print_err ( SQL_HANDLE_STMT, hstmt ) ) ;
}
```

19.9.2 Implicit Cursors

The situation gets slightly more complex when we consider SQL statements that return values—namely, the so-called SELECT statements. But CLI's facilities make this easier than you might expect.

In fact, we think CLI makes it a bit easier than dynamic SQL does. In dynamic SQL, as in embedded SQL and module language, you have to explicitly declare or (in dynamic SQL only) allocate a cursor, open it, fetch from it and perhaps update or delete through it, and then close it. In CLI, you simply execute the query expression (that "SELECT statement") that you would otherwise use in your cursor declaration. The process of executing the query expression implicitly creates a cursor on your behalf and even opens it for you.

If your query expression doesn't require the use of any dynamic parameters— that is, if the query expression has all the information hard-coded into it—then you can use ExecDirect() as we illustrated in Example 19-5. On the other hand, you'll find that many, if not most, of your query expressions require the use of one or more dynamic parameters, in which case you will have to prepare the "statement," set up the APD and IPD, and finally execute it as we did in Examples 19-2, 19-3, and 19-4.

Let's see how we'd retrieve information telling us how much profit we *could* make if we sold every one of our in-stock DVDs at the new sales price. The query expression we need looks like this:

```
SELECT title, dvds_in_stock * ( current_dvd_sale_price - our_dvd_cost )
FROM   movie_titles
WHERE  dvds_in_stock > 0
```

To keep things simple, we've chosen a query expression that doesn't require the use of dynamic parameters. Also, let's take advantage of the facilities we've already set up in Example 19-1, such as the declarations, environment, and connection.

Example 19-6 *Retrieving Database Data with CLI*

```
{
  ...


/***********************************************************************
* Construct a character string containing our query expression, then
* execute it using ExecDirect(), since we're not using dynamic params.
***********************************************************************/
  {
    SQLCHAR selstmt [ ] =
      "SELECT title,
              dvds_in_stock * ( current_dvd_sale_price -  our_dvd_cost )
       FROM   movie_titles
       WHERE  dvds_in_stock > 0" ;
   if ( SQLExecDirect ( hstmt1, selstmt, SQL_NTS) != SQL_SUCCESS)
      return ( print_err ( SQL_HANDLE_STMT, hstmt ) ) ;
  }


/***********************************************************************
* This time, let's explicitly allocate an application row descriptor.
* After allocating the ARD, we have to set some fields in each of
* two item descriptor areas (one per column returned from our query).
***********************************************************************/
  SQLAllocHandle ( SQL_HANDLE_DESC, hdbc1, &hdesc );
```

```
SQLSetDescRec ( hdesc, 1, SQL_CHAR, 0, NAMELEN,
                0, 0, (SQLPOINTER)&name, (SQLINTEGER *)&namelen,
                (SQLINTEGER *)&nameind ) ;

SQLSetDescRec ( hdesc, 2, SQL_REAL, 0, 0L, 0, 0,
                (SQLPOINTER)&profit, (SQLINTEGER *)NULL,
                (SQLINTEGER *)&profitind ) ;

/* Now, we have to associate this descriptor with the statement handle. */
  SQLSetStmtAttr ( hstmt1, SQL_ATTR_APP_ROW_DESC, &hdesc, 0 ) ;


/***********************************************************************
 * Fetch one row only, just to show how easy it is. When Fetch() executes,
 * it retrieves one row from the (implicit) cursor, placing column
 * values into host variables whose addresses are in the descriptor.
 ***********************************************************************/
  SQLFetch ( hstmt1 ) ;

/* Close the cursor -- just a good habit! */
  SQLCloseCursor ( hstmt1 ) ;


}
```

As we said following Example 19-4, there are some housekeeping tasks that need doing. but we'll defer them just a little bit longer, until the complete example in section 19.15.

19.9.3 Implicit Dynamic Operations

In Chapter 18, "Dynamic SQL," you learned about the USING clause that is applied to other statements (such as DESCRIBE and EXECUTE) to govern where those statements get and place values they use and produce. CLI doesn't have any syntax corresponding to dynamic SQL's USING clause. Instead, an *implicit USING clause* is specified in the CLI standard.

In particular, whenever you invoke either ExecDirect() or Prepare(), CLI implicitly invokes the effects of a USING SQL DESCRIPTOR clause so that the descriptions of the dynamic parameters and/or retrieved columns of the statement that you're executing or preparing are placed into the appropriate CLI descriptor area. In addition to ExecDirect() and Prepare(), CLI invokes the

effects of USING SQL DESCRIPTOR clauses when you invoke MoreResults() to see if
there are additional result sets to process and, if there are, get ready to process the
next one (see section 18.7.3, "DESCRIBE Dynamic Result Set Statement Execution") and NextResult() to see if there are additional result sets to process and, if
there are, get ready to process the next one using a different statement handle. In
the CLI standard, this variation is called an *implicit DESCRIBE USING clause*
because it serves the same purpose as the USING SQL DESCRIPTOR clause when it
appears in dynamic SQL's DESCRIBE statement.

CLI also implicitly invokes the effects of a USING SQL DESCRIPTOR whenever you
invoke ExecDirect() or Execute() to execute a query expression (that is, to create
and open an implicit cursor), as well as when you invoke ExecDirect() or
Execute() to execute an SQL statement other than a query expression (or, as
you'll learn in the next paragraph, a CALL statement). The CLI standard refers to
this use as an *implicit EXECUTE USING and OPEN USING clause*, because it
addresses the same issues that are addressed by the USING SQL DESCRIPTOR clauses
applied to dynamic SQL's EXECUTE statement and dynamic OPEN statement.

A third alternative, called an *implicit FETCH using clause*, is applied to invocations of Fetch() and FetchScroll(). Naturally, it mimics the behavior of the
USING SQL DESCRIPTOR clause applied to the FETCH statement in dynamic SQL. A
final variant, called an *implicit CALL USING clause*, is invoked whenever the SQL
statement that you're executing with an invocation to Execute() or ExecDirect()
is an SQL CALL statement. CALL statements are treated separately in SQL/CLI, but
the differences between the implicit CALL USING clause and the implicit EXECUTE
USING and OPEN USING clause are quite small and occur only because of minor
details.

19.10   Deferred Parameters

In section 19.9, you saw examples in which SQL statements were prepared and
executed through CLI's facilities, some of which involved dynamic parameters
whose values were provided before the Execute() or ExecDirect() routine was
invoked. If a dynamic parameter's value is established before execution of the
SQL statement is initiated, it's called an *immediate parameter value*.

Sometimes, however, it is not appropriate to specify the value to be assigned
to a dynamic parameter before the statement's execution. The most common
such situation is when the value of a dynamic parameter is a LARGE OBJECT value
(BLOB or CLOB); such values may be extremely large, and specifying them as immediate parameter values is awkward at best. It would mean that your application must define a host variable sufficiently large to contain the entire LOB

value, which can potentially be gigabytes of data. In such situations, CLI allows you to use a *deferred parameter value* to provide the value to be assigned to a dynamic parameter value. CLI allows you to provide the value of a deferred parameter during statement execution, either all at once or in as many pieces as the situation requires.

To cause a dynamic parameter to be treated as a deferred parameter instead of as an immediate parameter, there are several steps that you must take.

- First, set the value of the host variable to which the LENGTH_POINTER field in the prepared statement's associated item descriptor area (either an application parameter descriptor or an implementation parameter descriptor) points to the special value –2.

- If the prepared statement contains more than one deferred parameter, your application may set the value of the host variable to which the DATA_POINTER field in the prepared statement's associated item descriptor points to some unique value that your application associates with each specific deferred parameter. For example, you might use the value 1 for a deferred parameter that is the first dynamic parameter and 6 for a deferred parameter that is the sixth dynamic parameter (in which case dynamic parameters two through five would be immediate parameters).

- When you execute the prepared statement, Execute() or ExecDirect() (whichever your application uses) returns a special status value, 99, which means "data needed." It is at this point that your application must supply the value of a deferred parameter.

- To supply the value of a deferred parameter, your application first invokes ParamData(). When ParamData() is invoked the first time, it retrieves the value in the host variable to which the DATA_POINTER field points (which your application may have set to help distinguish among multiple deferred parameters) and returns that value in an OUT parameter; it also returns that special status value, 99, continuing to indicate "data needed."

- Your application then invokes PutData() to supply data for use by ParamData() in assigning the deferred parameter value to the correct dynamic parameter. If the data type of the deferred parameter is not a character type, then only a single invocation of PutData() is permitted, which must be followed by another invocation of ParamData() to cause the deferred parameter value to be assigned to the dynamic parameter. If the data type of the deferred parameter is a character type (including LOB types), then multiple invocations of PutData() can be used to transfer the deferred parameter value in multiple chunks. Your application invokes ParamData() one more

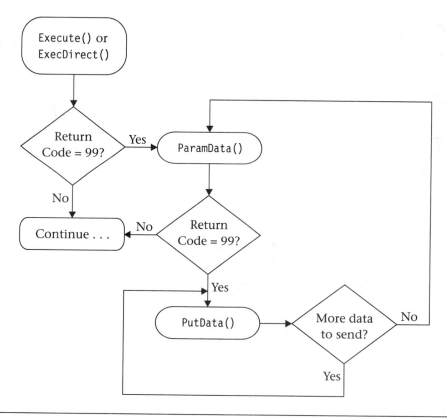

Figure 19-2   Using Deferred Parameter Values

time to cause the deferred parameter value to be assigned to the dynamic parameter.

- If the second invocation of ParamData() returns that special status value, 99, then there is at least one more deferred parameter and your application must process it like it did the first one. When ParamData() returns success (a value of 1), there are no more deferred parameters and execution of the prepared statement has completed.

A visual representation of this process[4] can be seen in Figure 19-2, and an example demonstrating its use is shown in Example 19-7.

In Example 19-7, we've assumed that the movie_title table has a new column, trailer, whose data type is a BINARY LARGE OBJECT and whose content is an MPEG film clip containing a trailer (preview) of the movie. This example,

---

4 Adapted from a change proposal, DBL:SOU-158, written by Tony Gordon.

adapted from an example in an Annex of the SQL/CLI standard, is more complete than the ones we've shown you earlier in this chapter.

Example 19-7 *Sample Code to Illustrate Use of Deferred Parameter Values*

```
/*************************************************************************
* Demonstrate the use of ParamData() and PutData() to handle deferred
* parameter values.
*************************************************************************/

/* Standard #include files used with CLI programs. */
#include <stddef.h>
#include <stdio.h>
#include <string.h>
#include <sqlcli.h>

/* Some global declarations we will use. */
#define TITLE_LENGTH          30    /* Length of MOVIE_TITLES.TITLE */
#define MAX_FILE_NAME_LENGTH  256
#define MAX_VIDEO_LENGTH  16000000   /* Allow film clips up to 16MB */
#define MAX_DATA_LENGTH     100000   /* But transfer no more than 100KB */

/*Declare signatures of some routine we will use. */
int print_err ( SQLSMALLINT handletype, SQLINTEGER handle ) ;

void InitUserData ( SQLSMALLINT sParam, SQLPOINTER InitValue ) ;

SQLSMALLINT GetUserData ( SQLPOINTER InitValue, SQLSMALLINT sParam,
                          SQLCHAR *Data, SQLINTEGER *StrLen_or_Ind ) ;


/*************************************************************************
* Now, let's get started with the example. We assume that the
* information required to find and connect to a database is provided.
*************************************************************************/
AddFilmClip ( SQLCHAR *server, SQLCHAR *uid, SQLCHAR* pwd )
{
/* Some local declarations we will use. */
SQLHENV     henv;
SQLHDBC     hdbc;
SQLHSTMT    hstmt;
SQLRETURN   rc;
```

```
SQLINTEGER   TitleParamLength, VideoParamLength, StrLen_or_Ind;
SQLSMALLINT  Param1=1, Param2=2;
SQLPOINTER   pToken, InitValue;
SQLCHAR      Data[MAX_DATA_LENGTH];

/* Allocate an environment handle. */
SQLAllocHandle ( SQL_HANDLE_ENV, SQL_NULL_HANDLE, &henv ) ;

/* Allocate a connection handle. */
SQLAllocHandle ( SQL_HANDLE_DBC, henv, &hdbc ) ;

/* Connect to the database. */
rc = SQLConnect ( hdbc, server, SQL_NTS, uid, SQL_NTS, pwd, SQL_NTS ) ;
if (rc != SQL_SUCCESS && rc != SQL_SUCCESS_WITH_INFO)
  return ( print_err ( SQL_HANDLE_DBC, hdbc ) ) ;

/* Allocate a statement handle. */
SQLAllocHandle ( SQL_HANDLE_STMT, hdbc, &hstmt ) ;

/* Prepare the UPDATE statement to add the film clip. */
rc = SQLPrepare ( hstmt, "UPDATE movie_titles
                         SET trailer = ?
                         WHERE title = ?",
                 SQL_NTS ) ;

/* If the Prepare() invocation was successful, we can proceed. */
if (rc == SQL_SUCCESS) {

  /***********************************************************************
   * Bind the parameters. For the first (video) parameter and second
   * (movie title) parameters, pass the parameter number in ParameterValue
   * instead of a buffer address.
   ***********************************************************************/
  SQLBindParameter ( hstmt, 1, SQL_PARAM_MODE_IN, SQL_CHAR, SQL_BLOB,
                     MAX_VIDEO_LENGTH, 0, &Param1, MAX_DATA_LENGTH,
                     &VideoParamLength ) ;
  SQLBindParameter ( hstmt, 2, SQL_PARAM_MODE_IN, SQL_CHAR, SQL_CHAR,
                     TITLE_LENGTH, 0, &Param2, TITLE_LENGTH,
                     &TitleParamLength ) ;
```

```
/******************************************************************
* Set values so that the data for both parameters will be passed
* at execution time.
******************************************************************/
TitleParamLength = VideoParamLength = SQL_DATA_AT_EXEC;

/* Execute the UPDATE statement. */
rc = SQLExecute ( hstmt ) ;

/******************************************************************
* For data-at-execution parameters, invoke SQLParamData to get the
* parameter number set by SQLBindParameter(). Call InitUserData to
* initialize the process of getting the video film clip to be stored.
* Call GetUserData and SQLPutData() repeatedly to get and put all
* data for the parameters.  Invoke SQLParamData() to finish
* processing this parameter and proceed to the next parameter.
******************************************************************/

/******************************************************************
* This is the key part of the example!
******************************************************************/
while (rc == SQL_NEED_DATA) {
  rc = SQLParamData ( hstmt, &pToken ) ;
  if (rc == SQL_NEED_DATA) {
    InitUserData ( pToken, InitValue ) ;
    while ( GetUserData ( InitValue, pToken, Data, &StrLen_or_Ind ) )
      SQLPutData ( hstmt, Data, StrLen_or_Ind ) ;
  }
}

/* Commit the transaction. */
SQLEndTran ( SQL_HANDLE_ENV, henv, SQL_COMMIT ) ;

/* Free the statement handle. */
SQLFreeHandle ( SQL_HANDLE_STMT, hstmt ) ;

/* Disconnect from the database. */
SQLDisconnect ( hdbc ) ;
```

```
        /* Free the connection handle. */
        SQLFreeHandle ( SQL_HANDLE_DBC, hdbc ) ;

        /* Free the environment handle. */
        SQLFreeEnv ( SQL_HANDLE_ENV, henv ) ;

        return(0);
    }


    /*********************************************************************
    * The following functions are given for completeness but are not
    * relevant for understanding the database processing nature of CLI.
    *********************************************************************/

    /* InitUserData returns a handle to the file with the film clip. */
    void InitUserData ( SQLSMALLINT sParam, SQLPOINTER InitValue )
    {
        SQLCHAR szFilmFile[MAX_FILE_NAME_LENGTH];

        /* This routine really does its work only for the video parameter. */
        switch sParam {
          case 1:

            /* Prompt user for bitmap file containing film clip video. */
            /* OpenVideoFile opens the file and returns the file handle. */
            PromptVideoFileName ( szFilmFile ) ;
            OpenVideoFile ( szFilmFile, (FILE *)InitValue ) ;
            break;
        }
    }

    /* GetUserData returns a piece of the film clip. */
    SQLSMALLINT GetUserData ( SQLPOINTER InitValue, SQLSMALLINT sParam,
                              SQLCHAR *Data, SQLINTEGER *StrLen_or_Ind )
    {
        switch sParam {
          case 1:
```

```
    /* Prompt user for movie title. */
    PromptMovieTitle ( Data ) ;
    /* And indicate null-terminated string convention in use. */
    *StrLen_or_Ind = SQL_NTS;
    return (1);

  case 2:

    /* GetNextVideoData returns the next piece of video data and */
    /* the number of octets of data returned (up to MAX_DATA_LENGTH).*/
    Done = GetNextVideoData ( (FILE *)InitValue, Data,
                              MAX_DATA_LENGTH, StrLen_or_Ind ) ;
    if (Done) {
      CloseVodeoFile ( (FILE *)InitValue ) ;
      return(1);
    }
    return(0);
  }
  return(0);
}
```

19.11 Transaction Management

In Table 19-1, you saw that CLI has a single routine that corresponds to embedded SQL's COMMIT and ROLLBACK statements (including ROLLBACK TO SAVEPOINT). That routine, EndTran(), also performs the functions that in embedded SQL are performed by the RELEASE SAVEPOINT statement. Another routine, StartTran(), serves the function that the START TRANSACTION statement serves in embedded SQL. It is important that you realize that CLI prohibits the execution of START TRANSACTION, COMMIT, ROLLBACK, and RELEASE SAVEPOINT statements using Execute() or ExecDirect(). On the other hand, you establish savepoints by invoking Execute() or ExecDirect() to execute a SAVEPOINT statement. While this seems inconsistent, it does avoid a number of tricky problems in environments where transaction management is done by an agent other than the SQL database system (such as a transaction manager).

Example 19-8 contains a code fragment that demonstrates starting and terminating transactions using the CLI routines.

Example 19-8 *Starting and Ending Transactions*

```
...

/***********************************************************************
 * Start a transaction, specifying the connection handle (hdbc1) that
 * identifies the connection where we want the transaction, and set the
 * access mode to READ WRITE and the isolation level to SERIALIZABLE.
 ***********************************************************************/
SQLStartTran ( SQLHDBC, hdbc1,
               SQL_TRANSACTION_READ_WRITE,
               SQL_TRANSACTION_SERIALIZABLE ) ;

...   /* Do whatever it is that needs doing. */

/***********************************************************************
 * Commit the transaction, specifying the connection handle (hdbc1)
 * identifying the connection on which the transaction is active.
 ***********************************************************************/
SQLEndTran ( SQLHDBC, hdbc1, SQL_COMMIT ) ;

...
```

We chose in this example to use a connection handle to identify the database where we wanted to execute the statements that are part of the transaction. StartTran() and EndTran() also accept an environment handle, in which case all active connections in that environment may participate in the transaction. However, not all implementations allow transactions to be active on more than one connection in an environment. Check your product's documentation before trying this!

19.12 | Diagnostics Facilities

In Chapter 20, "Diagnostics and Error Management," we'll discuss the facilities that SQL:1999 provides for dealing with the various sorts of conditions that can arise as a result of executing SQL statements. If you haven't had previous exposure to SQL's GET DIAGNOSTICS statement and the diagnostics area used to report those conditions, we urge you to pause right now and have a look at Chapter 20.

You will better understand the material in this section if you have a grasp of the SQL language facilities that address the same subject.

Like the SQL language, CLI provides a diagnostics area in which information is placed to inform your application about various conditions that may arise as a result of invoking CLI routines. There are many similarities between the two types of diagnostics areas; for example, both contain a header area and zero or more status records. There are, however, some important differences between the SQL diagnostics area and the CLI diagnostics area:

- There is a separate CLI diagnostics area associated with each environment handle, each connection handle, each statement handle, and each descriptor handle. Conditions arising from invocation of CLI routines that use a handle are reported in the diagnostics area associated with that handle. By contrast, there is one SQL diagnostics area per connection, shared among all SQL statements.

- Only one condition is reported in a CLI diagnostics area for a single routine invocation, unless the routine invocation returns a rowset; when the routine returns a rowset, one condition is reported for each row in the rowset and the status records appear in the same order as the rows appear in the rowset. In contrast, SQL diagnostics areas may receive any number of entries as a result of executing a single SQL statement.

- The CLI diagnostics areas contain different fields than the SQL diagnostics area. Table 19-4 and Table 19-5 contain information about the fields in the CLI diagnostics areas.

Table 19-4 *CLI Diagnostics Area Header Fields*

Field	Data Type
DYNAMIC_FUNCTION	CHARACTER VARYING(254)
DYNAMIC_FUNCTION_CODE	INTEGER
MORE	INTEGER
NUMBER	INTEGER
RETURNCODE	SMALLINT
ROW_COUNT	INTEGER
TRANSACTIONS_COMMITTED	INTEGER
TRANSACTIONS_ROLLED_BACK	INTEGER
TRANSACTIONS_ACTIVE	INTEGER
Implementation-defined header field	Implementation-defined data type

Those header fields for which the SQL diagnostics area has a corresponding field with the same name have the same semantics that they have in the SQL diagnostics area, even though the data types (and thus the precise values that they contain) may differ.

The CLI diagnostics area header field named RETURNCODE contains the value returned as the status of each CLI routine invocation. The values of RETURNCODE and their meanings are as follows:

0	*Success:* The CLI routine executed successfully.
1	*Success with information:* The CLI routine executed successfully, but a warning was raised.
100	*No data found:* The CLI routine executed successfully, but a no-data condition was raised.
99	*Data needed:* The CLI routine did not complete its execution because additional data was needed.
−1	*Error:* The CLI routine did not execute successfully, and an exception condition was raised (but not for an invalid handle).
−2	*Invalid handle:* The CLI routine did not execute successfully, and an exception condition was raised for an invalid handle.

Table 19-5 *CLI Diagnostics Area Status Record Fields*

Field	Data Type
CATALOG_NAME	CHARACTER VARYING (128)
CLASS_ORIGIN	CHARACTER VARYING (254)
COLUMN_NAME	CHARACTER VARYING (128)
COLUMN_NUMBER	INTEGER
CONDITION_IDENTIFIER	CHARACTER VARYING (128)
CONDITION_NUMBER	INTEGER
CONNECTION_NAME	CHARACTER VARYING (128)
CONSTRAINT_CATALOG	CHARACTER VARYING (128)
CONSTRAINT_NAME	CHARACTER VARYING (128)
CONSTRAINT_SCHEMA	CHARACTER VARYING (128)
CURSOR_NAME	CHARACTER VARYING (128)
MESSAGE_LENGTH	INTEGER
MESSAGE_OCTET_LENGTH	INTEGER
MESSAGE_TEXT	CHARACTER VARYING (254)
NATIVE_CODE	INTEGER
PARAMETER_MODE	CHARACTER VARYING (128)

(Continued)

Table 19-5 *Continued*

Field	Data Type
PARAMETER_NAME	CHARACTER VARYING (128)
PARAMETER_ORDINAL_POSITION	INTEGER
ROUTINE_CATALOG	CHARACTER VARYING (128)
ROUTINE_NAME	CHARACTER VARYING (128)
ROUTINE_SCHEMA	CHARACTER VARYING (128)
ROW_NUMBER	INTEGER
SCHEMA_NAME	CHARACTER VARYING (128)
SERVER_NAME	CHARACTER VARYING (128)
SPECIFIC_NAME	CHARACTER VARYING (128)
SQLSTATE	CHARACTER (5)
SUBCLASS_ORIGIN	CHARACTER VARYING (254)
TABLE_NAME	CHARACTER VARYING (128)
TRIGGER_CATALOG	CHARACTER VARYING (128)
TRIGGER_NAME	CHARACTER VARYING (128)
TRIGGER_SCHEMA	CHARACTER VARYING (128)
Implementation-defined status field	Implementation-defined data type

As with the header area fields, the CLI diagnostics area status record fields for which the SQL diagnostics area has a corresponding field with the same name have the same semantics that they have in the SQL diagnostics area, even though the data types (and thus the precise values that they contain) may differ. There are four fields in the CLI diagnostics area status record that do not have corresponding fields in the SQL diagnostics area.

The SQL diagnostics area named RETURNED_SQLSTATE corresponds to the CLI diagnostics area named SQLSTATE. Even though the names are different, the semantics are essentially the same. The only difference is that the SQLSTATE field in the CLI diagnostics area reports the SQLSTATE values that result from invocation of a CLI routine, while the RETURNED_SQLSTATE field in the SQL diagnostics area report the SQLSTATE values resulting from SQL statement execution.

The ROW_NUMBER field in the CLI diagnostics area status record is the same as the number of the corresponding row in the rowset with which the diagnostics area is associated.

The CLI diagnostics area field named CONDITION_IDENTIFIER is usually an empty string (that is, no characters, length 0). If the value of the SQLSTATE field in a status record is the code for "unhandled user-defined exception," then the CONDITION_IDENTIFIER field will contain a text string corresponding to the condition name of that user-defined exception.

19.13 | Metadata Access and Catalog Routines

Every SQL database system keeps metadata describing the database contents. Metadata is required for the database system's use—for example, in analyzing SQL statements for correctness and then compiling and optimizing them. Applications often find beneficial uses for knowledge about the tables, views, columns, and other objects contained in an SQL database.

In Chapter 22, "Information Schema," we present information about the mechanisms that SQL:1999 provides for making metadata knowledge available to application programs. However, CLI takes a slightly different approach to providing metadata information to applications.

Of course, an application using CLI to access an SQL database system that implements the views of the Information Schema as discussed in Chapter 22, "Information Schema," is able to formulate SELECT statements that retrieve the information they need and then execute those statements using either the ExecDirect() routine or the Prepare() routine followed by the Execute() routine. Applications that choose this approach must be sure that the implementation to which they make such queries either provides a conforming Information Schema or is able to translate a query against a conforming Information Schema into something that the implementation is able to process successfully. Alternatively, such applications may contain queries that are written to retrieve information from a vendor's proprietary "system tables" that serve essentially the same purpose as the Information Schema.

Neither approach is completely satisfactory, because there are (at the time we write this chapter) few conforming implementations of the Information Schema and a great many analogous proprietary facilities implemented by various vendors.

CLI, because its major purpose is to improve support for truly portable applications, provides a number of *catalog routines* that retrieve some of the most commonly required information from a database system's system tables. While the definitions of these catalog routines are written in terms of a conforming Information Schema, products that don't support a conforming Information Schema will implement the catalog routines to retrieve the data from the products' proprietary system tables, giving the same result in a standard-conforming manner. Table 19-6 contains the signatures and a brief description of each such routine and each of their parameters. Here is a list of those routines, so you can more easily ferret them out from the table:

- ColumnPrivileges()
- Columns()

- ForeignKeys()
- PrimaryKeys()
- SpecialColumns()
- TableFrivileges()
- Tables()

If you need metadata information other than the information provided by these seven routines, you must formulate queries against the Information Schema or against the proprietary system tables that your implementation provides.

19.14 CLI Routines Summary

Before we conclude this chapter with a complete example of CLI use, we show you the signatures of every CLI routine, along with a (brief) explanation of any parameters whose meaning is not obvious. To this end, we offer Table 19-6. In this table, we've presented the routine signatures in the form of C function prototypes; since they're all functions, they return a value, indicated by the use of SQLRETURN. The value they return is a status indicating the success or failure of the function execution. In a few cases (e.g., Execute()), the return value indicates that more information is required before the requested operation can complete.

Table 19-6 *CLI Routine Signatures*

Routine Signature	Routine and Parameter Description
SQLRETURN SQLAllocConnect (	Allocates a connection handle.
SQLHENV EnvironmentHandle,	The environment handle providing the context for the connection.
SQLHDBC *ConnectionHandle)	The returned handle identifying the connection being allocated.
SQLRETURN SQLAllocEnv (	Allocates an environment and environment handle.
SQLHENV *EnvironmentHandle)	The returned handle identifying the environment being allocated.
SQLRETURN SQLAllocHandle (	Allocates one of four types of handles.
SQLSMALLINT HandleType,	A code specifying what sort of handle to allocate.
SQLINTEGER InputHandle,	An existing handle providing the context for the new handle; 0 otherwise.
SQLINTEGER *OutputHandle)	The returned handle that was allocated.

(Continued)

Table 19-6 *Continued*

Routine Signature	Routine and Parameter Description
SQLRETURN SQLAllocStmt (	Allocates a statement handle.
SQLHDBC ConnectionHandle,	The connection handle providing the context for the statement.
SQLHSTMT *StatementHandle)	The returned handle identifying the statement resources.
SQLRETURN SQLBindCol (	Sets information in the current ARD for use in retrievals.
SQLHSTMT StatementHandle,	Identifies a prepared "SELECT statement."
SQLSMALLINT ColumnNumber,	Specifies which column is to be bound.
SQLSMALLINT BufferType,	The data type of the host variable into which the column is to be retrieved.
SQLPOINTER Data,	The address of that host variable.
SQLINTEGER BufferLength,	The length in octets of that host variable.
SQLINTEGER *StrLen_or_Ind)	The address of the indicator variable associated with that host variable.
SQLRETURN SQLBindParameter (	Sets information in the current APD and current IPD for dynamic parameters.
SQLHSTMT StatementHandle,	Identifies a prepared statement.
SQLSMALLINT ParamNumber,	Specifies which dynamic parameter is to be found.
SQLSMALLINT InputOutputMode,	Specifies whether the parameter is an IN, OUT, or INOUT parameter.
SQLSMALLINT ValueType,	The data type of the value to be supplied to replace the dynamic parameter.
SQLSMALLINT ParameterType,	The data type required by the dynamic parameter's context.
SQLINTEGER ColumnSize,	The length (in units appropriate for the data type) required by the parameter.
SQLSMALLINT DecimalDigits,	The precision (in appropriate units) required by the parameter.
SQLPOINTER ParameterValue,	The address of the host variable that will contain the value for the parameter.
SQLINTEGER BufferLength,	The length in octets of the host variable.
SQLINTEGER *StrLen_or_Ind)	The address of the indicator variable associated with that host variable.
SQLRETURN SQLCancel (SQLHSTMT StatementHandle)	Cancels a statement execution, if possible.
SQLRETURN SQLCloseCursor (SQLHSTMT StatementHandle)	Closes the implicit cursor associated with a prepared statement.

Table 19-6 *Continued*

Routine Signature	Routine and Parameter Description
SQLRETURN SQLColAttribute (	Retrieves the attribute of a column described when a statement was prepared.
SQLHSTMT StatementHandle,	Identifies a prepared statement.
SQLSMALLINT ColumnNumber,	Specifies the column for which attributes are desired.
SQLSMALLINT FieldIdentifier,	Specifies the field (of the associated IRD) that is to be retrieved.
SQLCHAR *CharacterAttribute,	Address of host variable where attribute value is stored (if character string).
SQLSMALLINT BufferLength,	Length in octets of that host variable.
SQLSMALLINT *StringLength,	Length in octets of the attribute value stored into the host variable.
SQLINTEGER *NumericAttribute)	Address of host variable where attribute value is stored (if numeric).
SQLRETURN SQLColumnPrivileges (	Retrieves result set describing privileges on selected columns of a table.
SQLHSTMT StatementHandle,	Statement handle to use for implicit query on Information Schema.
SQLCHAR *CatalogName,	First part of 3-part table name.
SQLSMALLINT NameLength1,	Length of first part of 3-part table name.
SQLCHAR *SchemaName,	Second part of 3-part table name.
SQLSMALLINT NameLength2,	Length of second part of 3-part table name.
SQLCHAR *TableName,	Third part of 3-part table name.
SQLSMALLINT NameLength3,	Length of third part of 3-part table name.
SQLCHAR *ColumnName,	String suitable for use in LIKE predicate to match column names.
SQLSMALLINT NameLength4)	Length of that string.
SQLRETURN SQLColumns (	Retrieves result set describing columns of selected tables.
SQLHSTMT StatementHandle,	
SQLCHAR *CatalogName,	
SQLSMALLINT NameLength1,	
SQLCHAR *SchemaName,	
SQLSMALLINT NameLength2,	
SQLCHAR *TableName,	String suitable for use in LIKE predicate to match table names.
SQLSMALLINT NameLength3,	Length of that string.
SQLCHAR *ColumnName,	Column name or empty string.
SQLSMALLINT NameLength4)	Length of column name or 0.

(Continued)

Table 19-6 *Continued*

Routine Signature	*Routine and Parameter Description*
`SQLRETURN SQLConnect (`	Establishes a connection to an SQL database system.
`  SQLHDBC ConnectionHandle,`	Connection handle previously allocated.
`  SQLCHAR *ServerName,`	String containing name of server or null pointer.
`  SQLSMALLINT NameLength1,`	Length of server name string, or 0.
`  SQLCHAR *UserName,`	String containing user name to be used for connecting to server or null pointer.
`  SQLSMALLINT NameLength2,`	Length of user name string, or 0.
`  SQLCHAR *Authentication,`	String containing other authentication value (e.g., password) or null pointer.
`  SQLSMALLINT NameLength3 )`	Length of other authentication value, or 0.
`SQLRETURN SQLCopyDesc (`	Copies contents of one CLI descriptor area to another.
`  SQLHDESC SourceDescHandle,`	Handle for source CLI descriptor area.
`  SQLHDESC TargetDescHandle )`	Handle for target CLI descriptor area.
`SQLRETURN SQLDataSources (`	Retrieves server names to which the application can connect, plus other info.
`  SQLHENV EnvironmentHandle,`	Environment handle previously allocated.
`  SQLSMALLINT Direction,`	A code (`FIRST` or `NEXT`) indicating which server in list is wanted.
`  SQLCHAR *ServerName,`	Address of host variable where name of server is placed.
`  SQLSMALLINT BufferLength1,`	Length of that host variable.
`  SQLSMALLINT *NameLength1,`	Length of returned server name.
`  SQLCHAR *Description,`	Address of host variable where information about server is placed.
`  SQLSMALLINT BufferLength2,`	Length of that host variable.
`  SQLSMALLINT *NameLength2 )`	Length of returned server information.
`SQLRETURN SQLDescribeCol (`	Describes a column of a prepared "`SELECT` statement."
`  SQLHSTMT StatementHandle,`	Statement handle associated with prepared statement.
`  SQLSMALLINT ColumnNumber,`	Ordinal number of column in statement's virtual table.
`  SQLCHAR *ColumnName,`	Address of host variable where the column's name is placed.
`  SQLSMALLINT BufferLength,`	Length of that host variable.
`  SQLSMALLINT *NameLength,`	Length of the returned column name.
`  SQLSMALLINT *DataType,`	Address of host variable where code for column's data type is placed.
`  SQLINTEGER *ColumnSize,`	Address of host variable where column's length in appropriate units is placed.

Table 19-6 *Continued*

Routine Signature	*Routine and Parameter Description*
SQLSMALLINT *DecimalDigits,	Address of host variable where column's precision in such units is placed.
SQLSMALLINT *Nullable)	Address of host variable where code indication column's nullability is placed.
SQLRETURN SQLDisconnect (	Disconnects from an existing connection.
SQLHDBC ConnectionHandle)	Handle representing an existing connection.
SQLRETURN SQLEndTran (	Terminates a transaction or a savepoint.
SQLSMALLINT HandleType,	Code indicating the type of handle (environment or connection).
SQLINTEGER Handle,	Environment handle or connection handle.
SQLSMALLINT CompletionType)	Code for type of completion (e.g., commit, rollback, release savepoint, etc.)
SQLRETURN SQLError (	Retrieves diagnostics information.
SQLHENV EnvironmentHandle,	If ConnectionHandle and StatementHandle are null pointers, use this.
SQLHDBC ConnectionHandle,	If StatementHandle is a null pointer and ConnectionHandle is not, use this.
SQLHSTMT StatementHandle,	If StatementHandle is not a null pointer, get diagnostics info about this handle.
SQLCHAR *Sqlstate,	Address of host variable where SQLSTATE string is placed.
SQLINTEGER *NativeError,	Address of host variable where implementation-defined code can be placed.
SQLCHAR *MessageText,	Address of host variable where implementation-defined string can be placed.
SQLSMALLINT BufferLength,	Length of that host variable.
SQLSMALLINT *TextLength)	Length of returned string.
SQLRETURN SQLExecDirect (	Executes a statement without prior preparation.
SQLHSTMT StatementHandle,	Statement handle to associate with that statement.
SQLCHAR *StatementText,	Address of host variable containing string of statement to be executed.
SQLINTEGER TextLength)	Length of the string.
SQLRETURN SQLExecute (	Executes a previously prepared statement.
SQLHSTMT StatementHandle)	Statement handle associated with prepared statement.

(Continued)

Table 19-6 *Continued*

Routine Signature	Routine and Parameter Description
SQLRETURN SQLFetch (	Fetches next row of implicit cursor associated with prepared SELECT statement.
SQLHSTMT StatementHandle)	Statement handle associated with prepared SELECT statement.
SQLRETURN SQLFetchScroll (	Fetches specified row of implicit scrollable cursor.
SQLHSTMT StatementHandle,	Statement handle associated with prepared SELECT statement.
SQLSMALLINT FetchOrientation,	Code representing fetch orientation (e.g., first, last, next, prior, etc.).
SQLINTEGER FetchOffset)	Number of row (for absolute orientation) or number to skip (relative).
SQLRETURN SQLForeignKeys (	Retrieves result set identifying primary and associated foreign keys of a table.
SQLHSTMT StatementHandle,	Statement handle used for implicit query.
SQLCHAR *PKCatalogName,	First part of 3-part name for table whose PRIMARY KEY is reported.
SQLSMALLINT NameLength1,	Length of the first part of 3-part name.
SQLCHAR *PKSchemaName,	Second part of 3-part name for table whose PRIMARY KEY is reported.
SQLSMALLINT NameLength2,	Length of the second part of 3-part name.
SQLCHAR *PKTableName,	Third part of 3-part name for table whose PRIMARY KEY is reported.
SQLSMALLINT NameLength3,	Length of the third part of 3-part name.
SQLCHAR *FKCatalogName,	First part of 3-part name for table whose FOREIGN KEY is reported.
SQLSMALLINT NameLength4,	Length of the first part of 3-part name.
SQLCHAR *FKSchemaName,	Second part of 3-part name for table whose FOREIGN KEY is reported.
SQLSMALLINT NameLength5,	Length of the second part of 3-part name.
SQLCHAR *FKTableName,	Third part of 3-part name for table whose FOREIGN KEY is reported.
SQLSMALLINT NameLength6)	Length of the third part of 3-part name.
SQLRETURN SQLFreeConnect (	Deallocates a connection handle.
SQLHDBC ConnectionHandle)	The connection handle to be deallocated.
SQLRETURN SQLFreeEnv (	Deallocates an environment handle.
SQLHENV EnvironmentHandle)	The environment handle to be deallocated.
SQLRETURN SQLFreeHandle (	Deallocates a handle of specified type.
SQLSMALLINT HandleType,	Code indicating handle type.
SQLINTEGER Handle)	Handle to be deallocated.

Table 19-6 *Continued*

Routine Signature	Routine and Parameter Description
SQLRETURN SQLFreeStmt (	Deallocates a statement handle.
SQLHSTMT StatementHandle,	The statement handle to be deallocated.
SQLSMALLINT Option)	Code indicating specific actions to take (e.g., close cursor, unbind columns).
SQLRETURN SQLGetConnectAttr (	Gets the value of a connection attribute.
SQLHDBC ConnectionHandle,	The connection handle identifying the desired connection.
SQLINTEGER Attribute,	A code indicating the attribute whose value is desired.
SQLPOINTER Value,	Address of host variable where the attribute's value is placed.
SQLINTEGER BufferLength,	Length of that host variable.
SQLINTEGER *StringLength)	Length of returned value.
SQLRETURN SQLGetCursorName (	Retrieves the name of the cursor associated with prepared SELECT statement.
SQLHSTMT StatementHandle,	Statement handle identifying prepared SELECT statement.
SQLCHAR *CursorName,	Address of host variable where cursor name is placed.
SQLSMALLINT BufferLength,	Length of that host variable.
SQLSMALLINT *NameLength)	Length of returned cursor name.
SQLRETURN SQLGetData (	Retrieves the value of a column of a row in a retrieved rowset.
SQLHSTMT StatementHandle,	Statement handle identifying prepared SELECT statement.
SQLSMALLINT ColumnNumber,	Ordinal number of the column whose value is desired.
SQLSMALLINT TargetType,	The data type of the host variable where the column's value is placed.
SQLPOINTER TargetValue,	Address of the host variable where the column's value is placed.
SQLINTEGER BufferLength,	The length of that host variable.
SQLINTEGER *StrLen_or_Ind)	The length of the column's value.
SQLRETURN SQLGetDescField (	Retrieves the value of a field from a descriptor area.
SQLHDESC DescriptorHandle,	The descriptor handle identifying the desired descriptor area.
SQLSMALLINT RecordNumber,	Ignored for header fields; otherwise, ordinal position of item descriptor area.
SQLSMALLINT FieldIdentifier,	Code indicating which field's value is to be retrieved.
SQLPOINTER Value,	Address of the host variable where that field's value is placed.
SQLINTEGER BufferLength,	Length of that host variable.
SQLINTEGER *StringLength)	Length of the field's value.

(Continued)

Table 19-6 *Continued*

Routine Signature	*Routine and Parameter Description*
SQLRETURN SQLGetDescRec (	Retrieves values of commonly used fields from a descriptor area.
SQLHDESC DescriptorHandle,	The descriptor handle identifying the desired descriptor area.
SQLSMALLINT RecordNumber,	Ordinal position of item descriptor area whose field values are desired.
SQLCHAR *Name,	Address of the host variable where the parameter or column name is placed.
SQLSMALLINT BufferLength,	Length of that host variable.
SQLSMALLINT *NameLength,	Length of parameter or column name.
SQLSMALLINT *Type,	Address of host variable where data type code is placed.
SQLSMALLINT *SubType,	Address of host variable where data subtype code is placed.
SQLINTEGER *Length,	Address of host variable where length value is placed.
SQLSMALLINT *Precision,	Address of host variable where precision value is placed.
SQLSMALLINT *Scale,	Address of host variable where scale value is placed.
SQLSMALLINT *Nullable)	Address of host variable where code identifying nullability is placed.
SQLRETURN SQLGetDiagField (	Retrieves value of specific field in specific diagnostics area record.
SQLSMALLINT HandleType,	Code indicating type of handle to use (e.g., environment, connection, etc.).
SQLINTEGER Handle,	Handle to use.
SQLSMALLINT RecordNumber,	Ordinal number of diagnostics area record (most common = 1).
SQLSMALLINT DiagIdentifier,	Code identifying specific field in that record to retrieve.
SQLPOINTER DiagInfo,	Address of host variable where diagnostics information is placed.
SQLSMALLINT BufferLength, SQLSMALLINT *StringLength)	
SQLRETURN SQLGetDiagRec (	Retrieves commonly used information from specific diagnostics area record.
SQLSMALLINT HandleType,	Code indicating type of handle to use (e.g., environment, connection, etc.).
SQLINTEGER Handle,	Handle to use.
SQLSMALLINT RecordNumber,	Ordinal number of diagnostics area record (most common = 1).
SQLCHAR *Sqlstate,	Address of host variable where SQLSTATE value is placed.

Table 19-6 *Continued*

Routine Signature	Routine and Parameter Description
SQLINTEGER *NativeError,	Address of host variable where implementation-defined code is placed.
SQLCHAR *MessageText,	Address of host variable where implementation-defined text is placed.
SQLSMALLINT BufferLength,	
SQLSMALLINT *TextLength)	
SQLRETURN SQLGetEnvAttr (	Retrieves the value of an environment attribute.
SQLHENV EnvironmentHandle,	Handle identifying the environment whose attribute value is desired.
SQLINTEGER Attribute,	Code identifying the attribute whose value is desired.
SQLPOINTER Value,	Address of host variable where attribute value is placed.
SQLINTEGER BufferLength,	
SQLINTEGER *StringLength)	
SQLRETURN SQLGetFeatureInfo (	Retrieves information about features supported by the SQL implementation.
SQLHDBC ConnectionHandle,	Connection handle identifying valid connection to an SQL database system.
SQLCHAR *FeatureType,	'FEATURE', 'SUBFEATURE', or 'PACKAGE'.
SQLSMALLINT FeatureTypeLength,	
SQLCHAR *FeatureId,	String indicating the specific feature or package for which information is wanted.
SQLSMALLINT FeatureIdLength,	
SQLCHAR *SubFeatureId,	String indicating the specific subfeature for which information is wanted.
SQLSMALLINT SubFeatureIdLength,	
SQLSMALLINT *Supported)	Address of host variable where supported code (1 = Yes, 0 = No) is placed.
SQLRETURN SQLGetFunctions (	Determines whether a specific CLI routine is supported.
SQLHDBC ConnectionHandle,	Connection handle identifying valid connection to an SQL database system.
SQLSMALLINT FunctionId,	Code identifying function about which information is wanted.
SQLSMALLINT *Supported)	Address of host variable where supported code (1 = Yes, 0 = No) is placed.

(Continued)

Table 19-6 *Continued*

Routine Signature	*Routine and Parameter Description*
SQLRETURN SQLGetInfo (	Retrieves information about a connected SQL implementation.
SQLHDBC ConnectionHandle,	Connection handle identifying valid connection to an SQL database system.
SQLSMALLINT InfoType,	Code identifying specific information requested.
SQLPOINTER InfoValue,	Address of host variable where requested information is placed.
SQLSMALLINT BufferLength, SQLSMALLINT *StringLength)	
SQLRETURN SQLGetLength (	Retrieves the actual length of a LARGE OBJECT represented by a locator value.
SQLHSTMT StatementHandle,	Handle to be used for implicit query.
SQLSMALLINT LocatorType,	Code indicating CLOB or BLOB.
SQLINTEGER Locator,	Locator value, previously retrieved in some query.
SQLINTEGER *StringLength,	Address of host variable where actual length of CLOB or BLOB is placed.
SQLINTEGER *IndicatorValue)	Address of host variable used as indicator in case CLOB/BLOB is null.
SQLRETURN SQLGetParamData (	Retrieves the value of a dynamic parameter.
SQLHSTMT StatementHandle,	Statement handle identifying prepared statement using dynamic parameters.
SQLSMALLINT ParameterNumber,	Ordinal number of dynamic parameter whose value is desired.
SQLSMALLINT TargetType,	Data type of host variable into which dynamic parameter value is placed.
SQLPOINTER TargetValue,	Address of host variable into which dynamic parameter value is placed.
SQLINTEGER BufferLength, SQLINTEGER *StrLen_or_Ind)	
SQLRETURN SQLGetPosition (	Retrieves starting position of string within CLOB or BLOB identified by locator.
SQLHSTMT StatementHandle,	Statement handle used for implicit query.
SQLSMALLINT LocatorType,	Code indicating CLOB or BLOB.
SQLINTEGER SourceLocator,	Locator value of LOB to be searched, previously retrieved in some query.
SQLINTEGER SearchLocator,	Optional locator value of LOB to be matched, previously retrieved.

Table 19-6 *Continued*

Routine Signature	Routine and Parameter Description
SQLCHAR *SearchLiteral,	Optional literal string to be matched.
SQLINTEGER SearchLiteralLength,	Length of literal string, or 0.
SQLINTEGER FromPosition,	Starting offset in LOB to be searched, 0 = start at beginning of LOB.
SQLINTEGER *LocatedAt,	Address of host variable where offset is placed if match found; otherwise, 0.
SQLINTEGER *IndicatorValue)	Address of host variable used as indicator in case either CLOB/BLOB is null.
SQLRETURN SQLGetSessionInfo (	Retrieves value of a "special value" at connected database.
SQLHDBC ConnectionHandle,	Connection handle identifying a connected database.
SQLSMALLINT InfoType,	Code indicating which "special value" (e.g., CURRENT_USER, etc.) is wanted.
SQLPOINTER InfoValue,	Address of host variable where retrieved value is placed.
SQLSMALLINT BufferLength,	
SQLSMALLINT *StringLength)	
SQLRETURN SQLGetStmtAttr (	Gets the value of a statement attribute.
SQLHSTMT StatementHandle,	The statement handle identifying the desired statement.
SQLINTEGER Attribute,	A code indicating the attribute whose value is desired.
SQLPOINTER Value,	Address of host variable where the attribute's value is placed.
SQLINTEGER BufferLength,	
SQLINTEGER *StringLength)	
SQLRETURN SQLGetSubString (	Retrieves portion of LOB or creates LOB values and return a locator.
SQLHSTMT StatementHandle,	Statement handle used for implicit query.
SQLSMALLINT LocatorType,	Code indicating CLOB or BLOB.
SQLINTEGER SourceLocator,	Locator value, previously retrieved, for LOB from which substring is wanted.
SQLINTEGER FromPosition,	Starting position of substring.
SQLINTEGER ForLength,	Length of substring.
SQLSMALLINT TargetType,	Data type of host variable where result is placed.
SQLPOINTER TargetValue,	Address of host variable where result is placed.
SQLINTEGER BufferLength,	
SQLINTEGER *StringLength,	
SQLINTEGER *IndicatorValue)	Address of host variable used as indicator in case LOB is null.

(Continued)

Table 19-6 *Continued*

Routine Signature	Routine and Parameter Description
SQLRETURN SQLGetTypeInfo (	Retrieves information about one or all data types supported by SQL database.
SQLHSTMT StatementHandle,	Statement handle to use for implicit query.
SQLSMALLINT DataType)	Code indicating ALL TYPES or specific data type.
SQLRETURN SQLMoreResults (	Determines whether more result sets are available on query; initiate processing.
SQLHSTMT StatementHandle)	Statement handle identifying prepared SELECT statement.
SQLRETURN SQLNextResult (	Determines whether more result sets are available on query; initiate processing.
SQLHSTMT StatementHandle1,	Statement handle identifying prepared SELECT statement.
SQLHSTMT *StatementHandle2)	Statement handle on which next result set will be processed.
SQLRETURN SQLNumResultCols (	Retrieves the number of result columns of a query.
SQLHSTMT StatementHandle,	Statement handle identifying prepared SELECT statement.
SQLSMALLINT *ColumnCount)	Address of host variable where the number of result columns is placed.
SQLRETURN SQLParamData (	Cycles through and processes a deferred input and input/output parameter values.
SQLHSTMT StatementHandle,	Statement handle identifying prepared statement having deferred a parameter.
SQLPOINTER *Value)	Address of host variable where ordinal number of deferred parameter is placed.
SQLRETURN SQLPrepare (	Prepares a statement for subsequent execution.
SQLHSTMT StatementHandle,	Statement handle to associate with statement when it is prepared.
SQLCHAR *StatementText,	Text of SQL statement to prepare.
SQLINTEGER TextLength)	Length of that SQL statement.
SQLRETURN SQLPrimaryKeys (	Retrieves a result set with column names of PRIMARY KEY of specified table.
SQLHSTMT StatementHandle,	Statement handle to use for implicit query.
SQLCHAR *CatalogName,	
SQLSMALLINT NameLength1,	
SQLCHAR *SchemaName,	
SQLSMALLINT NameLength2,	
SQLCHAR *TableName,	
SQLSMALLINT NameLength3)	

Table 19-6 *Continued*

Routine Signature	*Routine and Parameter Description*
SQLRETURN SQLPutData (	Provides value for deferred parameters.
SQLHSTMT StatementHandle,	Statement handle identifying prepared statement having deferred a parameter.
SQLPOINTER Data,	Address of host variable containing data to associate with deferred parameter.
SQLINTEGER StrLen_or_Ind)	Address of host variable to act as indicator for that data.
SQLRETURN SQLRowCount (	Retrieves the number of rows in the result set derived from a prepared query.
SQLHSTMT StatementHandle,	Statement handle identifying the prepared SELECT statement.
SQLINTEGER *RowCount)	Address of host variable where the number of rows is placed.
SQLRETURN SQLSetConnectAttr (	Sets the value of a connection attribute.
SQLHDBC ConnectionHandle,	Connection handle identifying connection whose attribute is to be set.
SQLINTEGER Attribute,	Code indicating which attribute of the connection is to be set.
SQLPOINTER Value,	The value to be set.
SQLINTEGER StringLength)	The length of that value.
SQLRETURN SQLSetCursorName (	Sets the cursor name of the implicit cursor associated with a prepared query
SQLHSTMT StatementHandle,	Statement handle identifying the prepared SELECT statement.
SQLCHAR *CursorName,	The name to be applied to the cursor.
SQLSMALLINT NameLength)	The length of that name.
SQLRETURN SQLSetDescField (	Sets the value of a field in a descriptor area.
SQLHDESC DescriptorHandle,	The descriptor handle identifying the desired descriptor area.
SQLSMALLINT RecordNumber,	Ignored for header fields; otherwise, ordinal position of item descriptor area.
SQLSMALLINT FieldIdentifier,	Code indicating which field's value is to be set.
SQLPOINTER Value,	Value to be set into the field.
SQLINTEGER BufferLength)	Length of that value.
SQLRETURN SQLSetDescRec (	Sets commonly used fields in a descriptor area.
SQLHDESC DescriptorHandle,	The descriptor handle identifying the desired descriptor area.
SQLSMALLINT RecordNumber,	Ordinal position of item descriptor area whose field values are to be set.
SQLSMALLINT Type,	Code for data type to be set in descriptor field.

(Continued)

Table 19-6 *Continued*

Routine Signature	Routine and Parameter Description
SQLSMALLINT SubType,	Code for data subtype to be set in descriptor field.
SQLINTEGER Length,	Length value to be set in descriptor field.
SQLSMALLINT Precision,	Precision value to be set in descriptor field.
SQLSMALLINT Scale,	Scales value to be set in descriptor field.
SQLPOINTER Data,	Data value to be set in descriptor field.
SQLINTEGER *StringLength,	Length of that data value.
SQLINTEGER *Indicator)	Indicator associated with that data value.
SQLRETURN SQLSetEnvAttr (	Sets the value of an environment attribute.
SQLHENV EnvironmentHandle,	Environment handle identifying the environment whose attribute is to be set.
SQLINTEGER Attribute,	Code indicating which attribute of the environment is to be set.
SQLPOINTER Value,	The value to be set.
SQLINTEGER StringLength)	The length of that value.
SQLRETURN SQLSetStmtAttr (	Sets the value of a statement attribute.
SQLHSTMT StatementHandle,	Statement handle identifying statement whose attribute is to be set.
SQLINTEGER Attribute,	Code indicating which attribute of the statement is to be set.
SQLPOINTER Value,	The value to be set.
SQLINTEGER StringLength)	The length of that value.
SQLRETURN SQLSpecialColumns (	Retrieves a result set listing the columns of a UNIQUE key of the specified table.
SQLHSTMT StatementHandle,	Statement handle to use for implicit query.
SQLSMALLINT IdentifierType,	Code identifying query type (must be BEST ROWID or product extension).
SQLCHAR *CatalogName,	
SQLSMALLINT NameLength1,	
SQLCHAR *SchemaName,	
SQLSMALLINT NameLength2,	
SQLCHAR *TableName,	
SQLSMALLINT NameLength3,	
SQLSMALLINT Scope,	Code indicating scope of query (current row, transaction, or session).
SQLSMALLINT Nullable)	Code to indicate whether to retrieve column names if the columns are nullable.

Table 19-6 *Continued*

Routine Signature	*Routine and Parameter Description*

SQLRETURN SQLStartTran (
  SQLSMALLINT HandleType,
  SQLINTEGER Handle,
  SQLINTEGER AccessMode,
  SQLINTEGER IsolationLevel)
	Starts a transaction with specified characteristics.
	Type of handle (environment or connection only).
	Handle identifying where transaction is to be started.
	Code indicating desired access mode.
	Code indicating desired isolation level

SQLRETURN SQLTablePrivileges (
  SQLHSTMT StatementHandle,
 	
  SQLCHAR *CatalogName,
  SQLSMALLINT NameLength1,
  SQLCHAR *SchemaName,
  SQLSMALLINT NameLength2,
  SQLCHAR *TableName,
 	
  SQLSMALLINT NameLength3)
	Retrieves result set describing privileges on selected table.
	Statement handle to use for implicit query on Information Schema.
	First part of 3-part table name.
	Length of first part of 3-part table name.
	Second part of 3-part table name.
	Length of second part of 3-part table name.
	String suitable for use in LIKE predicate to match third part of table names.
	Length of that string.

SQLRETURN SQLTables (
  SQLHSTMT StatementHandle,
  SQLCHAR *CatalogName,
  SQLSMALLINT NameLength1,
  SQLCHAR *SchemaName,
  SQLSMALLINT NameLength2,
  SQLCHAR *TableName,
  SQLSMALLINT NameLength3,
  SQLCHAR *TableType,
  SQLSMALLINT NameLength4)
	Retrieves result set describing selected tables.
	
	String suitable for use in LIKE predicate to match table names.
	Length of that string.
	String indicating the type of table (e.g., TABLE, VIEW, etc.).
	Length of table type string or 0.

19.15 | Annotated CLI Example

In this section, we present a complete example of CLI's use, based on the code fragments seen in Examples 19-1 through 19-4.

Example 19-9 *Complete CLI Example*

```
/*******************************************************
* In this example, we illustrate typical "include" files
* and other relevant declarations.  For brevity's sake,
* we do not make this part of every example.
*******************************************************/

#include <stddef.h>  /* Necessary for many C programs */
#include <string.h>  /* Necessary for many C programs */
#include <sqlcli.h>  /* Definitions used in CLI programs */

#define NAMELEN 50    /* Length of char string bfr for names */

/* The signature of a routine to print errors when we get them */
int print_err ( SQLSMALLINT handletype, SQLINTEGER handle ) ;

/* Show our example routine's header information this time */
int example1 ( SQLCHAR *server1, SQLCHAR *uid1, SQLCHAR *auth1,
               SQLCHAR *server2, SQLCHAR *uid2, SQLCHAR *auth2 )
{
/* Declare some variables that we'll use in various examples */
SQLHENV henv1;        /* SQLHENV is a type defined in sqlcli.h */
SQLHDBC hdbc;
SQLHDESC hdesc;
SQLHDESC hdesc1;
SQLHDESC hdesc2;
SQLHSTMT hstmt1;
SQLHSTMT hstmt2;
SQLINTEGER salepct;
SQLREAL profit
SQLINTEGER profitind;
SQLCHAR name[NAMELEN+1];
SQLINTEGER namelen;
SQLINTEGER nameind;

/*******************************************************
*  The CLI code corresponding to the SQL statement:
*     EXEC SQL CONNECT TO :server USER :userid;
*  is shown here.
*******************************************************/
```

```
/* First, allocate an environment handle. */
/* SQL_HANDLE_ENV is a manifest constant = 1 ==> "environment handle" */
/* SQL_NULL_HANDLE = 0 */
/* SQLAllocHandle is the "proper name' for the AllocHandle() routine. */
SQLAllocHandle ( SQL_HANDLE_ENV, SQL_NULL_HANDLE, &henv ) ;

/* Allocate a connection handle associated with the new environment. */
SQLAllocHandle ( SQL_HANDLE_DBC, henv, &hdbc ) ;

/* Connect to the database and test for success. */
if ( SQLConnect ( hdbc, server1, SQL_NTS, uid, SQL_NTS, auth, SQL_NTS )
     != SQL_SUCCESS )
  return ( print_err ( SQL_HANDLE_DBC, hdbc ) ) ;

/* Allocate a statement handle associated with the database connection. */
SQLAllocStmt ( hdbc1, &hstmt );

{
  /***********************************************************************
   * Construct a string containing the SQL statement.  Notice that we
   * used a dynamic parameter (?) instead of a host variable name.
   ***********************************************************************/
  SQLCHAR updstmt =
    "UPDATE movie_titles
     SET    current_dvd_sale_price
          = regular_dvd_sale_price * ( ( 100 - ? ) / 100 )
     WHERE  dvds_in_stock > 0";

  /***********************************************************************
   * Prepare the statement for execution. We use the statement handle
   * allocated above and the string we just created containing the
   * UPDATE statement.  We used "SQL_NTS" to indicate that the string
   * containing the statement is passed using the C convention of
   * null termination.
   ***********************************************************************/
  if ( SQLPrepare ( hstmt, updstmt, SQL_NTS ) != SQL_SUCCESS )
    return ( print_err ( SQL_HANDLE_STMT, hstmt ) );
```

```
/***************************************************************
 * Get the application parameter descriptor ready.  The first step
 * is to get a handle to the APD from the statement handle. Then
 * we set certain fields of the first item descriptor in the APD
 * to state that we're using a C int variable named 'salepct'.
 ***************************************************************/
SQLGetStmtAttr ( hstmt, SQL_ATTR_APP_PARAM_DESC, &hdesc1, 0L,
                 (SQLINTEGER *)NULL ) ;
SQLSetDescRec ( hdesc1, 1, SQL_INTEGER, 0, 0L, 0, 0,
                 (SQLPOINTER)&salepct, (SQLINTEGER *)NULL,
                 (SQLINTEGER *)NULL);

/* Get the implementation parameter descriptor ready. */
SQLGetStmtAttr ( hstmt, SQL_ATTR_IMP_PARAM_DESC, &hdesc2, 0L,
                 (SQLINTEGER *)NULL ) ;
SQLSetDescRec ( hdesc2, 1, SQL_INTEGER, 0, 0L, 0, 0,
                 (SQLPOINTER)NULL, (SQLINTEGER *)NULL,
                 (SQLINTEGER *)NULL);

/* Assign an appropriate value to salepct. */
salepct = 10;  /* Times are tight for us -- only give a 10% discount. */

/* Execute the statement...let's have a sale! */
if ( SQLExecute ( hstmt ) != SQL_SUCCESS )
   return ( print_err ( SQL_HANDLE_STMT, hstmt ) ) ;

}

/* Finally, do the housekeeping. */

/* Commit the transaction. */
SQLEndTran ( SQL_HANDLE_ENV, henv, SQL_COMMIT ) ;

/* Free the statement handle. */
SQLFreeHandle ( SQL_HANDLE_STMT, hstmt ) ;

/* Disconnect from the database. */
SQLDisconnect ( hdbc ) ;

/* Free the connection handle. */
SQLFreeHandle ( SQL_HANDLE_DBC, hdbc ) ;
```

```
/* Free the environment handle. */
SQLFreeEnv ( SQL_HANDLE_ENV, henv ) ;

return(0);

}
```

19.16 | Chapter Summary

In this chapter, we've given you a fairy good overview of SQL/CLI, SQL:1999's Call-Level Interface. CLI, as you learned, provides a greater ability for application programs to be truly portable among a variety of SQL database systems—more so than embedded SQL (at least until more vendors are able to claim conformance to SQL:1999).

CLI is an interface of moderate complexity, and we could have written an entire book—not just one chapter—on the subject. If you plan to use CLI when writing your applications, we urge you to use the many resources available to address the details of CLI's most popular implementation: Microsoft's ODBC interface.

Chapter

20

Diagnostics and Error Management

20.1 | Introduction

Throughout this book so far, we've been telling you things such as "you'll get an error" or "you'll get a warning" as we've described the requirements and actions of SQL statements. Now it's time to clarify what we mean by those phrases. We'll discuss a special status indicator named SQLSTATE, and the errors and conditions that get reported through that status indicator.

20.2 | SQLSTATE

SQL-89 was a bit casual about the idea of errors, but it did distinguish among three situations: genuine errors, the no-data condition, and successful completion. SQL-92 enhanced that taxonomy somewhat by distinguishing among those three and adding warnings to the mix. SQL:1999 doesn't add any new categories of condition, but there are several new facilities that your applications can use.

In SQL-89 and most SQL products available today, the primary way of reporting errors is by a status parameter (or host variable) called SQLCODE. The earlier standard (SQL-86 and SQL-89) really defined only two values for SQLCODE plus one range of values. The value 0 was returned by the DBMS to indicate *successful completion,* meaning that your statement executed completely successfully and actually did something. The value 100 was defined to indicate *no data,* which meant that the statement didn't incur any errors, but found no rows on which to operate (for example, if the statement that you executed was a FETCH statement, but there were no more rows in the cursor). Finally, *all negative values* were defined to mean *error,* but the specific negative values associated with any specific error were left up to the implementations. As a result, SQL products differed wildly in the values returned for a given situation. If your applications were to be portable across SQL DBMS products, the error handling by specific values had to be recoded for each target product.

SQL-92 was intended to fix problems like this, but the need not to obsolete many existing applications made it impossible to simply start defining values for SQLCODE. Instead, SQL-92 added a second status parameter, called SQLSTATE, which has many predefined values and still leaves lots of room for implementor-defined values where needed. SQLCODE was defined to be an integer parameter. By contrast, SQLSTATE is defined to be a five-character string (using only the upper-case letters *A* through *Z* and the digits 0 through 9). This five-character string is divided into two components. The first two characters are called the *class code,* and the last three characters are called the *subclass code.* Any class code that begins with the characters *A* through *H* or 0 through 4 indicates an SQLSTATE value that is defined by the SQL standard (or by another standard related to SQL, such as SQL/MM). For those class codes, any subclass code starting with the same character is also defined by the standard. Any class code starting with the characters *I* through *Z* or 5 through 9 is implementor-defined, and *all* their subclass codes (with one exception) are also implementor-defined. The exception is subclass code 000, which *always* means *no subclass code defined.*

Because the SQL standard specifies so little about SQLCODE, it has been dropped from SQL:1999 entirely; it was *deprecated* in SQL-92 (meaning that SQL's developers were considering eliminating it and wanted to warn potential users of the standard not to depend too much on SQLCODE). Of course, SQLCODE is still supported by SQL products, but it is not required for products to claim conformance to the standard. In fact, we believe that products will continue to implement it for years to come simply because of customers' requirements for support of existing applications. However, SQLSTATE is definitely the recommended way to go for future applications, especially if you're concerned with issues such as portability of your applications.

Let's look at how you use SQLSTATE in your applications. First, let's look at an example using module language. A procedure in a module must include a parameter that specifies SQLSTATE, so you might write the following:

```
PROCEDURE MYPROC (SQLSTATE, :param1 DECIMAL (5,2),
                  :param2 SMALLINT, :param3 CHARACTER (50))

UPDATE movie_titles
  SET current_rental_price = :param1 INDICATOR :param2
WHERE title = :param3;
```

Then, to invoke that procedure from C, you would write something like this:

```
title = "Gone With The Wind";
price = 1.95;
/* Except, of course, C does not have DEC */
notnull = 0;
MYPROC (state, price, notnull, title);
```

To check on the result, you have to examine the returned value of SQLSTATE, as found in the state variable. You can check for successful completion, which has the code '00000', like this:

```
if (strcmp (state, "00000"))
  whatever-you-do-in-C;
```

If you're writing in embedded SQL, the actions aren't all that different. Your program might look like this:

```
title = "Gone With The Wind";
price = 1.95;
/* DECIMAL not supported in C */
notnull = 0;
EXEC SQL UPDATE movie_titles
         SET current_rental_price = :price INDICATOR :notnull
       WHERE title = :title;
if (strcmp (SQLSTATE, "00000"))
  whatever-you-do-in-C;
```

Note that we used the host variable names directly in the SQL statement instead of parameter names (there aren't any parameters, after all), but we had to use the status parameter name (SQLSTATE) in the if statement, because there must be a host variable named SQLSTATE. Note, too, that the SQL statement didn't actually use SQLSTATE. The DBMS automatically set the status return value into the status parameter.

Recall from Chapter 12, "Accessing SQL from the Real World," that SQL provides a DECLARE SECTION where you declare all host variables that you plan to use in your embedded programs. The rules for declaring SQLSTATE are simple:

- If you have explicitly declared a host variable named SQLSTATE as a five-character string, then that will be used *automatically* for all of your embedded SQL statements.

- If your implementation allows you to INCLUDE a definition file (for example, a .h file in C programs), those definition files may include a declaration for SQLSTATE. If it does, then it's your responsibility to ensure that you don't specify a conflicting declaration.

- If you don't declare SQLSTATE (and it's not provided for you in some other way), then your embedded SQL program has a syntax error and probably won't compile successfully

People who write embedded SQL programs are usually far more interested in writing the *real* semantics of their applications than in the details of SQL error handling. In Chapter 12, we told you about the WHENEVER declarative statement that allows you to instruct your precompiler to do most of the work for you. What we didn't talk about in Chapter 12 is what sort of code you have to write to handle errors once the WHENEVER statement has caused a GOTO to be invoked.

Recall that you can write either

```
WHENEVER error-type CONTINUE
```

which says that you are willing to ignore that error category and just continue executing the next statement in your program, or

```
WHENEVER error-type GOTO target-label
```

If you choose the GOTO alternative, any errors of the specified type (SQLERROR or NOT FOUND, as you will recall) will cause the flow of control for your program to change to the specified target-label. Now you have to worry about what to do once this happens.

In general, you will either terminate processing of your application and record some sort of error (for example, printing an error message on a terminal or console, recording an entry in a log somewhere, or setting off an alarm), or you will take action to correct the problem in the application and continue processing after that. Knowing which decision to take, knowing how to correct the problem, and knowing what sort of error to record usually requires that you know more about the situation than merely the overall nature of the problem. The rest of this chapter tells you how to get more information about the errors that you encounter. With this knowledge, your error processing can be more intelligent and discriminating, and your applications can be more useful to your clients.

Once you start using an SQL product, it won't take you long to figure out that SQLSTATE often doesn't give you enough information about the results of your statements. There are several reasons for this:

- There may actually be several errors that occur during the execution of a single SQL statement. For example, the statement

```
SELECT C1/C2, C3
      INTO :param1, :param2
   FROM TA
```

  could get one error because of a division by zero (if C2 has the value 0) and a second error because C3 is null and no indicator parameter was specified; it could also get a third error if the cardinality of TA is greater than 1. Which error gets reported in SQLSTATE or SQLCODE?

- A complex application may have hundreds of SQL statements in it. When the application suddenly announces that it's encountered an error, locating the specific statement may be tedious and uncertain.

- Applications that operate concurrently on many databases may actually reuse the same SQL statements over and over at multiple databases. When an error occurs, it may be difficult to determine the specific context of the error.

SQL:1999 comes to the rescue with the *diagnostics area* and the accompanying GET DIAGNOSTICS statement. The diagnostics area is a DBMS-managed data structure (but more on that shortly) that captures specific information about the results of each SQL statement (except one—be patient!). The GET DIAGNOSTICS statement (that's the one) is then used to extract the information from the diagnostics area. To protect you against the loss of the diagnostics area contents because of errors in the GET DIAGNOSTICS statement itself, SQL:1999 prescribes that the GET DIAGNOSTICS statement status is reported only in SQLSTATE, but that the statement never changes the contents of the diagnostics area.

The diagnostics area actually has two components. One component is the *header* and contains information about the last SQL statement as a whole. The other area is a *detail* area that contains information about each error, warning, or success code that resulted from the statement. Conceptually, it looks like the diagram in Figure 20-1.

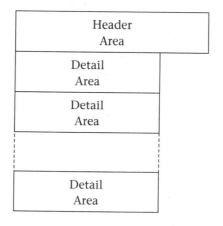

Figure 20-1   Diagnostics Area

When each transaction starts, the diagnostics area is set up to contain the number of detail records that is the default for the implementation or that you specified in the SET TRANSACTION statement (see Chapter 15, "Transaction Management," for a review of these terms). A DBMS is *required* to put information corresponding to the status reported in SQLSTATE into Detail 1. The DBMS *may* put additional information into subsequent detail areas, but there is no presumption of precedence or importance. (Contrast this with CLI's diagnostics area usage, as we discussed in Chapter 19, "Call-Level Interface (CLI)," in which multiple detail areas are populated with information about the status of multiple rows in a rowset.) In general, if the SQL standard specifies a particular error for a given situation and the implementation has another error for precisely the same problem, then the error defined by the standard must be reported in SQLSTATE and also recorded in Detail 1. However, the DBMS may detect a more serious error (such as a disk head crash) and choose to report *that* error in preference to, say, a divide-by-zero error.

A DBMS is also free to put information only into Detail 1 and not into any other detail area, even if there are potentially many more errors resulting from the SQL statement. Although this may superficially sound irresponsible, consider a DBMS that is designed to be extremely fast and efficient. As soon as it detects one error while executing an SQL statement, it reports the results and returns control to the application program, thus freeing up system resources for other users. Imagine, then, a different implementation that has been designed to have outstanding support for debugging, so it exhaustively pursues the entire statement to detect as many errors as possible. Both alternatives (and many in between) are valid, so you may find them on the market. Read your product's documentation to see how it behaves.

The contents of the header area are shown in Table 20-1.

Table 20-1 *Contents of Diagnostics Header Area*

Contents	Data Type
NUMBER	Exact numeric, scale 0
MORE	Character string, length 1
COMMAND_FUNCTION	Character varying, length ≥ 128
COMMAND_FUNCTION_CODE	Exact numeric, scale 0
DYNAMIC_FUNCTION	Character varying, length ≥ 128
DYNAMIC_FUNCTION_CODE	Exact numeric, scale 0
ROW_COUNT	Exact numeric, scale 0
TRANSACTION_ACTIVE	Exact numeric, scale 0
TRANSACTIONS_COMMITTED	Exact numeric, scale 0
TRANSACTIONS_ROLLED_BACK	Exact numeric, scale 0

By using this information, you can identify the specific type of SQL statement that encountered the error, warning, or success condition. The value of NUMBER is the number of detail entries filled in as a result of the SQL statement. MORE will contain the character 'Y' if all conditions detected by the DBMS were recorded in the diagnostics area, and N' if additional conditions were detected but not recorded (for example, if there were too many conditions for the size of the diagnostics area created). If the statement being reported is a static SQL statement, COMMAND_FUNCTION will contain a character string that represents the SQL statement and COMMAND_FUNCTION_CODE will contain a corresponding numeric value. See Table 20-3 for a list of the codes that represent each SQL statement. If the problem occurred during a dynamic SQL statement, COMMAND_FUNCTION will have 'EXECUTE' or 'EXECUTE IMMEDIATE' in it (and COMMAND_FUNCTION_CODE the corresponding numeric value), and DYNAMIC_FUNCTION will have the character string code for the dynamic SQL statement itself, while DYNAMIC_FUNCTION_CODE will have the numeric code corresponding to that dynamic SQL statement.

ROW_COUNT contains the number of rows that were affected by the SQL statement. In some SQL implementations, another host language data structure, called the SQLCA, is used to capture this information. However, the same sort of problems applied to the use of SQLCA as to the SQLDA (for example, too much variance between implementations), so it was replaced by other facilities, including the ROW_COUNT field in the diagnostics area header.

TRANSACTION_ACTIVE will contain the value 1 if a transaction is active when you retrieve that field using GET DIAGNOSTICS and the value 0 if there is no transaction active. (GET DIAGNOSTICS does not require the context of a transaction to execute.) TRANSACTIONS_COMMITTED contains a number specifying the number of transactions that have been committed since the diagnostics area was last initialized, which is normally at the beginning of every SQL statement. Similarly, TRANSACTIONS_ROLLED_BACK specifies the number of transactions that have been rolled back since the diagnostics area was last initialized.

The detail areas are a bit longer, as you can see in Table 20-2. There is, as we've said, one detail area for each error, warning, or success condition the DBMS reports, with a minimum of one that corresponds to the condition reported in SQLSTATE. In each filled-in detail area, the value of CONDITION_NUMBER is the sequence number of the detail area. This value ranges from 1 to NUMBER and corresponds to the value that you use in the GET DIAGNOSTICS statement to retrieve the information from the detail areas.

Table 20-2 *Contents of Diagnostics Detail Area*

Contents	*Data Type*
CONDITION_NUMBER	Exact numeric, scale 0
RETURNED_SQLSTATE	Character string, length 5
CLASS_ORIGIN	Character varying, length ≥ max. length of an identifier
SUBCLASS_ORIGIN	Character varying, length ≥ max. length of an identifier
CONSTRAINT_CATALOG	Character varying, length ≥ max. length of an identifier
CONSTRAINT_SCHEMA	Character varying, length ≥ max. length of an identifier
CONSTRAINT_NAME	Character varying, length ≥ max. length of an identifier
CONNECTION_NAME	Character varying, length ≥ max. length of an identifier
SERVER_NAME	Character varying, length ≥ max. length of an identifier
CATALOG_NAME	Character varying, length ≥ max. length of an identifier
SCHEMA_NAME	Character varying, length ≥ max. length of an identifier
TABLE_NAME	Character varying, length ≥ max. length of an identifier
COLUMN_NAME	Character varying, length ≥ max. length of an identifier

Table 20-2 *Continued*

Contents	Data Type
CURSOR_NAME	Character varying, length ≥ max. length of an identifier
TRIGGER_CATALOG	Character varying, length ≥ max. length of an identifier
TRIGGER_SCHEMA	Character varying, length ≥ max. length of an identifier
TRIGGER_NAME	Character varying, length ≥ max. length of an identifier
ROUTINE_CATALOG	Character varying, length ≥ max. length of an identifier
ROUTINE_SCHEMA	Character varying, length ≥ max. length of an identifier
ROUTINE_NAME	Character varying, length ≥ max. length of an identifier
SPECIFIC_NAME	Character varying, length ≥ max. length of an identifier
PARAMETER_ORDINAL_POSITION	Exact numeric, scale 0
PARAMETER_NAME	Character varying, length ≥ max. length of an identifier
PARAMETER_MODE	Exact numeric, scale 0
MESSAGE_TEXT	Character varying, length ≥ max. length of an identifier
MESSAGE_LENGTH	Exact numeric, scale 0
MESSAGE_OCTET_LENGTH	Exact numeric, scale 0

RETURNED_SQLSTATE contains the SQLSTATE value that corresponds to the condition reported in the detail area. Because SQLSTATE values have both a class code and a subclass code, either of which can be defined by the standard or by an implementation, the diagnostics area separately tells you the source of the value returned. CLASS_ORIGIN will be 'ISO 9075' if the class code value is defined in the SQL standard; otherwise, it will depend on your implementation (for example, an Oracle Corporation implementation might return 'Oracle9i' in this field for an implementor-defined class code). Similarly, SUBCLASS_ORIGIN will be 'ISO 9075' if the subclass code value is defined in the SQL standard and will otherwise depend on the implementation.

If the detail area reports a constraint violation, the fields CONSTRANT_CATALOG, CONSTRAINT_SCHEMA, and CONSTRAINT_NAME will contain the fully qualified name of the constraint that was violated.

The CONNECTION_NAME and SERVER_NAME fields contain the name of the connection and the environment to which you are connected when you executed the SQL statement that is being reported.

If the reported situation involves a table, CATALOG_NAME, SCHEMA_NAME, and TABLE_NAME will contain the fully qualified name of the table. If the situation involves a column, the table information will be completed and COLUMN_NAME will contain the name of the column.

If the situation involves a cursor, CURSOR_NAME will contain the name of the cursor.

If the condition was related to a trigger, then TRIGGER_CATALOG, TRIGGER_SCHEMA, and TRIGGER_NAME will contain the fully qualified name of the trigger.

If the condition was raised in conjunction with an SQL-invoked routine, then ROUTINE_CATALOG, ROUTINE_SCHEMA, and ROUTINE_NAME will hold the fully qualified name of the routine, and SPECIFIC_NAME will have the specific name of the routine. (See Chapter 17, "Routines and Routine Invocation (Functions and Procedures).") If a parameter of that routine was involved, then PARAMETER_NAME contains the name of the parameter and PARAMETER_ORDINAL_POSITION contains the ordinal position of the parameter; PARAMETER_MODE contains a code indicating the mode (IN, OUT, or INOUT) of the parameter.

The implementation may also record a character string that contains natural-language error text (or anything else the implementation chooses to record). The standard does not prescribe the contents of this string, partly because the standard couldn't possibly specify the contents in every natural language that people may use. Therefore, the implementation can choose whether or not to record anything in the MESSAGE_TEXT field; if it records something, the details are left to the implementor. However, we expect that most implementors will record a printable text string that describes the error in the user's selected natural language. The length, in characters, of this message is recorded in MESSAGE_LENGTH and the octet length in MESSAGE_OCTET_LENGTH.

After each SQL statement has been executed (except, as we noted, the GET DIAGNOSTICS statement itself), information is recorded in the diagnostics area. To avoid confusion among multiple statements, the diagnostics area is emptied (erased, if you prefer) at the beginning of each SQL statement (except GET DIAGNOSTICS). You can then use GET DIAGNOSTICS to retrieve any information available in it. If your statement completes with SQLSTATE '00000', meaning "successful completion," you would normally expect only a single detail area to be filled in. However, your implementation may report all sorts of other information at the same time, taking up other detail areas.

The format of the GET DIAGNOSTICS statement is

```
GET DIAGNOSTICS target = item [ , target = item ]...
```

or

```
GET DIAGNOSTICS EXCEPTION number
  target = item [ , target = item ]...
```

If you use the first alternative, you will get information about the header of the diagnostics area. In that case, item can be one of these keywords: NUMBER, MORE, COMMAND_FUNCTION, COMMAND_FUNCTION_CODE, DYNAMIC_FUNCTION, DYNAMIC_FUNCTION_CODE, TRANSACTION_ACTIVE, TRANSACTIONS_COMMITTED, TRANSACTIONS_ROLLED_BACK, or ROW_COUNT. Anything else will cause an error. target is a host variable or a parameter; no indicator is needed or permitted.

If you use the second alternative, you'll get information from the detail areas of the diagnostics area. Here, the value of number cannot be greater than the value you'd get from NUMBER in the header. The value of number will always be the same as that returned in CONDITION_NUMBER for the detail area. target is as before, and item must be one of the following:

- CONDITION_NUMBER
- RETURNED_SQLSTATE
- CLASS_ORIGIN
- SUBCLASS_ORIGIN
- SERVER_NAME
- CONNECTION_NAME
- CONSTRAINT_CATALOG
- CONSTRAINT_SCHEMA
- CONSTRAINT_NAME
- CATALOG_NAME
- SCHEMA_NAME
- TABLE_NAME
- COLUMN_NAME
- CURSOR_NAME
- TRIGGER_CATALOG
- TRIGGER_SCHEMA
- TRIGGER_NAME
- ROUTINE_CATALOG

- ROUTINE_SCHEMA

- ROUTINE_NAME

- SPECIFIC_NAME

- PARAMETER_ORDINAL_POSITION

- PARAMETER_NAME

- PARAMETER_MODE

- MESSAGE_TEXT

- MESSAGE_LENGTH

- MESSAGE_OCTET_LENGTH

Of course you can request any number of these items in a single GET DIAGNOSTICS statement. Also, because GET DIAGNOSTICS does not affect the contents of the diagnostics area, you can execute it multiple times to get different information, even about the same detail area. Therefore, you might do something like this in Fortran:

```
      EXEC SQL BEGIN DECLARE
      CHARACTER*128 CMDFNC, CONTMP, CURTMP
      CHARACTER*128 CONNAM(10), CURNAM(10)
      CHARACTER*5 SQLSTA
      INTEGER NUM
      EXEC SQL END DECLARE
      EXEC SQL DECLARE CUR1 CURSOR FOR some-expression
      EXEC SQL ON SQLERROR GOTO 1000
      EXEC SQL OPEN CUR1
         .
         .
         .
1000  CONTINUE
      PRINT (5.1010) SQLSTATE
1010  FORMAT (' SQLSTATE was ', A)

      EXEC SQL GET DIAGNOSTICS :NUM = NUMBER,
     x                        :CMDFNC = COMMAND_FUNCTION

      IF (NUM .GT. 10) NUM = 10
```

```
      DO 1100 I = 1, NUM
      EXEC SQL GET DIAGNOSTICS EXCEPTION :NUM
    x     :CONTMP = CONNECTION_NAME, :CURTMP = CURSOR_NAME
      CONNAM(NUM) = CONTMP
      CURNAM(NUM) = CURTMP
1100  CONTINUE
```

This example uses an embedded exception declaration to cause the flow of control to pass to the error-handling code whenever an SQL error is encountered. That code gets some header information and then gets up to 10 detail information items. We don't know what was done with it afterward, but you can be sure that . . . it was no picnic.

20.3 | Whatever Happened to SQLCODE?

One question we're frequently asked is this: What happened to SQLCODE? As we mentioned early in section 20.2, SQLCODE was the only status parameter (and variable) supported by SQL-86 and SQL-89. SQL-92 was enhanced by the addition of SQLSTATE. To some, it may seem that SQL:1999 has taken a step backward by the removal of SQLCODE.

However, the truth is that SQLCODE was not very useful as a component of a standard. While all vendors agreed that SQLCODE was an integer value, the only values of SQLCODE that were universally agreed upon were 1 and 100, indicating *successful completion* and *no data*, respectively.

It simply wasn't very helpful to application programmers who need to solve complex problems to be informed that "all negative values mean errors." The great majority of programs need to discover what errors arise and attempt to take some sort of corrective action. Even when the only "action" they take is informing a user or making a log entry, reporting "an error occurred" serves more to frustrate than anything else.

Eventually, the SQL standards community realized that no vendor would ever be able to change its products' SQLCODE values to correspond to a standard or to some other products' choices. Too many customers and too many applications would have to be changed correspondingly, and the last thing a vendor wants to tell customers is "OK, all of your applications have to be edited"! Without any hope of standardizing the correspondence between specific errors and SQLCODE values, there remained no reason to continue pretending that SQLCODE was a useful part of the SQL standard. Thus it was deleted from SQL:1999 in favor of SQLSTATE.

If you have existing applications that use SQLCODE, we certainly do not recommend that you rewrite those applications to use SQLSTATE. If you're committed to a particular SQL product, then continuing to use SQLCODE in new applications may be appropriate. But we strongly suggest that you at least consider writing new applications to use SQLSTATE whenever possible, since it may offer you more possibilities if and when you choose other SQL database products in the future.

20.4 | SQL Statement Codes

Table 20-3 contains the SQL statement character codes that are used in the diagnostics area.

Table 20-3 *SQL Statement Codes for Diagnostics Area*

SQLStatement	Identifier	Code
<allocate cursor statement>	ALLOCATE CURSOR	1
<allocate descriptor statement>	ALLOCATE DESCRIPTOR	2
<alter domain statement>	ALTER DOMAIN	3
<alter routine statement>	ALTER ROUTINE	17
<alter table statement>	ALTER TABLE	4
<alter type statement>	ALTER TYPE	60
<assertion definition>	CREATE ASSERTION	6
<assignment statement>	ASSIGNMENT	5
<call statement>	CALL	7
<case statement>	CASE	86
<character set definition>	CREATE CHARACTER SET	8
<close statement>	CLOSE CURSOR	9
<collation definition>	CREATE COLLATION	10
<commit statement>	COMMIT WORK	11
<compound statement>	BEGIN END	12
<connect statement>	CONNECT	13
<deallocate descriptor statement>	DEALLOCATE DESCRIPTOR	15
<deallocate prepared statement>	DEALLOCATE PREPARE	16
<declare cursor>	DECLARE CURSOR	101
<delete statement: positioned>	DELETE CURSOR	18
<delete statement: searched>	DELETE WHERE	19

Table 20-3 *Continued*

SQLStatement	Identifier	Code
<describe statement>	DESCRIBE	20
<direct select statement: multiple rows>	SELECT	21
<disconnect statement>	DISCONNECT	22
<domain definition>	CREATE DOMAIN	23
<drop assertion statement>	DROP ASSERTION	24
<drop character set statement>	DROP CHARACTER SET	25
<drop collation statement>	DROP COLLATION	26
<drop data type statement>	DROP TYPE	35
<drop domain statement>	DROP DOMAIN	27
<drop module statement>	DROP MODULE	28
<drop role statement>	DROP ROLE	29
<drop routine statement>	DROP ROUTINE	30
<drop schema statement>	DROP SCHEMA	31
<drop table statemert>	DROP TABLE	32
<drop transform statement>	DROP TRANSFORM	116
<drop translation statement>	DROP TRANSLATION	33
<drop trigger statement>	DROP TRIGGER	34
<drop user-defined cast definition>	DROP CAST	78
<drop user-defined ordering statement>	DROP ORDERING	115
<drop view statement>	DROP VIEW	36
<dynamic close statement>	DYNAMIC CLOSE	37
<dynamic delete statement: positioned>	DYNAMIC DELETE CURSOR	38
<dynamic fetch statement>	DYNAMIC FETCH	39
<dynamic open statement>	DYNAMIC OPEN	40
<dynamic select statement>	SELECT CURSOR	85
<dynamic single row select statement>	SELECT	41
<dynamic update statement: positioned>	DYNAMIC UPDATE CURSOR	42
<execute immediate statement>	EXECUTE IMMEDIATE	43
<execute statement>	EXECUTE	44
<fetch statement>	FETCH	45
<for statement>	FOR	46
<free locator statement>	FREE LOCATOR	98
<get descriptor statement>	GET DESCRIPTOR	47
<grant privilege statement>	GRANT	48

(Continued)

Table 20-3 *Continued*

SQLStatement	Identifier	Code
<grant role statement>	GRANT ROLE	49
<handler declaration>	HANDLER	87
<hold locator statement>	HOLD LOCATOR	99
<if statement>	IF	88
<insert statement>	INSERT	50
<iterate statement>	ITERATE	102
<leave statement>	LEAVE	89
<loop statement>	LOOP	90
<open statement>	OPEN	53
<preparable dynamic delete statement: positioned>	DYNAMIC DELETE CURSOR	54
<preparable dynamic update statement: positioned>	DYNAMIC UPDATE CURSOR	55
<prepare statement>	PREPARE	56
<release savepoint statement>	RELEASE SAVEPOINT	57
<repeat statement>	REPEAT	95
<resignal statement>	RESIGNAL	91
<return statement>	RETURN	58
<revoke statement>	REVOKE	59
<role definition>	CREATE ROLE	61
<rollback statement>	ROLLBACK WORK	62
<savepoint statement>	SAVEPOINT	63
<schema definition>	CREATE SCHEMA	64
<schema routine>	CREATE ROUTINE	14
<select statement: single row>	SELECT	65
<set catalog statement>	SET CATALOG	66
<set connection statement>	SET CONNECTION	67
<set constraints mode statement>	SET CONSTRAINT	68
<set descriptor statement>	SET DESCRIPTOR	70
<set local time zone statement>	SET TIME ZONE	71
<set names statement>	SET NAMES	72
<set path statement>	SET CURRENT_PATH	69
<set role statement>	SET ROLE	73
<set schema statement>	SET SCHEMA	74
<set session characteristics statement>	SET SESSION CHARACTERISTICS	109
<set session user identifier statement>	SET SESSION AUTHORIZATION	76
<set transaction statement>	SET TRANSACTION	75

Table 20-3 *Continued*

SQLStatement	Identifier	Code
<set transform group statement>	SET TRANSFORM GROUP	118
<signal statement>	SIGNAL	92
<SQL variable declaration>	DECLARE VARIABLE	96
<SQL-server module definition>	CREATE MODULE	51
<start transaction statement>	START TRANSACTION	111
<table definition>	CREATE TABLE	77
<temporary table declaration>	TEMPORARY TABLE	93
<transform definition>	CREATE TRANSFORM	117
<translation definition>	CREATE TRANSLATION	79
<trigger definition>	CREATE TRIGGER	80
<update statement: positioned>	UPDATE CURSOR	81
<update statement: searched>	UPDATE WHERE	82
<user-defined cast definition>	CREATE CAST	52
<user-defined ordering definition>	CREATE ORDERING	114
<user-defined type definition>	CREATE TYPE	83
<view definition>	CREATE VIEW	84
<while statement>	WHILE	97

20.5 | Chapter Summary

In this chapter, we've discussed SQLSTATE and the various aspects of SQL exception handling. With the facilities presented, you should be able to include robust exception handling in all of your SQL applications.

Remember that we discussed the program structure relative to exception handling in Chapter 12, "Accessing SQL from the Real World." In Appendix E, "Status Codes," we provide the complete list of SQLSTATE values.

Chapter

21

Internationalization Aspects of SQL:1999

Introduction

Until SQL-92, programming and database language standards simply did not provide any reasonable support for languages other than English. In fact, most programming language and database *products* provided no such support. Everybody "knew" that 7-bit or 8-bit characters were all that were supported, and there was an implicit assertion that these were all that were needed. As a result, most computer hardware and software systems support ASCII (or its IBM analog, EBCDIC) or, occasionally, an 8-bit extension of ASCII (perhaps the ISO Latin-1 set).

Unfortunately, an 8-bit character set can support a maximum of 256 characters. Because of the way character sets are set up, such sets actually support about 192 characters. Similarly, a 7-bit set usually supports either 95 or 96 characters. It is quite possible to use such a set to support English, French, German, Arabic, Hebrew, or even Hindi. However, it is *not* possible to support all of these at the same time because the total number of characters far exceeds the number that an 8-bit character set can support.

Worse, it is impossible to support Japanese, Chinese, or Korean with an 8-bit character set. These languages routinely use thousands of characters, which require more bits per character for encoding. Several database system vendors

701

have produced localized versions of their products that support a 16-bit character set (or even character sets in which some characters require 8 bits and some require 16 bits) for use in countries such as Japan, China, or Korea, but it has not been until fairly recently that any DBMS vendor supplied an internationalized product that could simultaneously support multiple languages.

As SQL-92 was being developed, it became obvious, largely because of the international participation, that an important factor would be support of character sets other than that required for English or Western European languages. Several facilities were provided by SQL-92 to support various character set internationalization requirements. (By the way, we say *character set internationalization* because it really is the character facilities that are affected and not such things as datetime formats, decimal points, or currency formats. SQL's architects made the decision to use canonical forms for such items and to depend on user interface tools to generate localized forms for such data.)

The situation in SQL:1999 has not changed dramatically from that in SQL-92. The most important differences are the elimination from SQL:1999 of several facilities that SQL-92 included solely because there were no other standards in place to provide them. Those standards have arisen (or, at least, they have begun to appear), and thus the facilities are no longer required within the SQL standard. For example, SQL-92 included a feature that allowed a user, such as a database administrator, to create a collation from scratch. SQL required the ability to meet user requirements, but there were at that time no standards for defining collations. In recent years, though, an international standard for a customizable collation facility has been published, and the SQL standard no longer needs to provide that capability.

21.2 | Character Sets and Collations

In any computer language, whether a conventional programming language or a database language, every character string has a character set associated with it. Most languages do not allow the user to control the character set that is used for any given character string. (Some implementations of some languages permit the user to specify the character set to be used for *all* character strings in a specific program, but even this is uncommon.) As a result, the character set associated with a character string is whatever the vendor chose when the product you're using was designed. Because of the history of the development of computer systems, the most likely choice is an 8-bit character set such as 8-bit ASCII or 8-bit EBCDIC, or their 7-bit predecessors. Many computer users, implementors, designers, and vendors have thus come to accept implicitly the false premise that one byte equals one character. In fact, most computer hardware makes the same assumption (look at the IBM 370 MVCL and DEC VAX MOVC5 instructions for examples).

However, a *character* is really a text element that is used to write a natural language (or perhaps an artificial display element used in writing, such as punctuation marks, bullet characters, and logos). Therefore, we have to accept that the one-character-equals-one-byte premise is artificial and undependable. Some character sets require two (or more) bytes per character; others have been designed to use one byte for some characters and two bytes for others. The specific mechanism used to encode characters for a computer is called an *encoding*, and a character set so encoded is called a *coded character set*. The way that character *strings* are represented (e.g., one byte per character, two bytes per character, or even variable number of bytes per character) is called (in the SQL standard, at least) the *form-of-use* of the character set. The actual collection of characters that can be represented is called the *repertoire* of the character set. Finally, character strings expressed in a character set must have rules that control how those strings compare with one another; such a set of rules is called a *collation*. Every character set has a default collation (there may be many possible collations for a character set).

Therefore, a character set has three attributes that we will discuss here:

1. the repertoire of characters
2. the form-of-use
3. the default collation

Each of these attributes has an important effect on character strings that have a specific character set. The repertoire determines the characters that can be expressed. In a purist sense, character sets that have only 96 characters should never permit a character string with a 97th encoding to be expressed, and some implementations provide this integrity service to applications. However, many implementations allow any encoding of the appropriate number of bits to be expressed (effectively defining a full 256 characters, even though many of them have no printed representation). There are positive aspects to both alternatives: the laissez-faire approach may provide higher performance, while the more restrictive approach may help applications avoid the semantic problems associated with uncontrolled input.

Two character strings can be compared with each other only if they have the same character repertoire (more properly, if their character sets have the same character repertoire). If you think about this for a few moments, the reason becomes obvious: if one string's character set contains, say, the character "double dagger" (‡) and the other string's character set doesn't, how can you compare a double dagger in the first string with any other character in the other string? Sure, we can determine that the double dagger is not equal to, say, the letter *A*, but is it less than or greater than the *A*?

The form-of-use determines how character strings are represented to the hardware and software. It has nothing to do with high-level issues like comparisons, but it has a great deal to do with how data is stored and manipulated by the underlying computer system. In an ideal world, we'd never have to worry about the form-of-use of a character string. But this isn't an ideal world. Although SQL doesn't care about the form-of-use in its operations, when your SQL code exchanges data with your host language code, your host language program must know (or be able to find out) the form-of-use of character data so that it can invoke the appropriate routines to process that data.

Each character string has a collation associated with it; normally, it's the default collation of the character set, but it is possible to override the default and assign a specific collation to a specific string. However, collations affect *operations* and are really relevant only when you are comparing (or sorting, which is really nothing but a form of comparison) strings. Therefore, certain operations in SQL can be given specific collations, too.

21.2.1 Unicode and UCS

In the early 1990s, work was begun in earnest to develop a true multinational character set. A committee affiliated with ISO began working on a character set that was to become known as UCS, the Universal Character Set. When this standard was published,[1] it quickly became both controversial and welcomed.

At about the same time, a large group of language and computer experts formed an organization called the Unicode Consortium. The purpose of the Unicode Consortium was to develop a—you guessed it—universal character set that would be widely implemented.

The competing efforts could have caused the creation of two "universal" character sets, resulting in even more confusion and chaos in the software industry. Happily, the groups decided to work together instead of separately. The most significant difficulty they faced, however, dealt with the fact that many experts believe that there are more—many more—than 65,536 characters used in natural languages today. That number is significant because the Unicode Consortium's participants believed that a commercially successful character set could require the use of no more than 16 bits per character, while the ISO group felt just as pas-

---

[1] ISO/IEC 10646-1:1993, *Universal Multiple-Octet Coded Character Set (UCS)*, International Organization for Standardization, 1993.

sionately that every character used by every language in use on the planet had to be included. The ISO group initially specified four bytes, 32 bits, per character, which resulted in many observers predicting that it would never be economic to implement that standard.

The Unicode Consortium's approach required the use in some cases of multiple *codepoints* (16-bit character encodings) to represent a single written language element (a *glyph*). Therefore, a language element that, say, a Spanish speaker would view as a single character (ñ, for example) would be encoded using two codepoints. The first codepoint would be the encoding for the ordinary letter *n*, and the second one would be the encoding for the "combining tilde," represented as ~. (Of course, Unicode supports the enyay—ñ—as a single encoded character, but there are many examples of language elements in, say, Vietnamese, for which there are no single encoded characters in Unicode.)

The ISO committee's approach was to allow a number of "compression" formats in which character strings would be represented using fewer than four times the number of characters.

Eventually, the groups merged the two approaches. As a result, both UCS and Unicode now specify a way for all characters to be encoded in 16-bit units, with some characters requiring multiple units. Furthermore, both allow the use of compressed encodings. For example, an encoding named UTF-8 (Unicode Transformation Format for 8 bits) encodes some characters (128 of the Latin-based characters) using only 8 bits, many more using 16 bits, still more using 24 bits, and so on, up to a maximum of 48 bits for the most uncommon characters. There is also an encoding known as UTF-16, a fixed-length encoding called UCS-2 (2 bytes per character), and a canonical form called UCS-4 (4 bytes per character).

While you no doubt find all this character set discussion fascinating, you are probably wondering just what it has to do with SQL:1999. SQL-92 was written without a clear character model available; therefore, its character internationalization facilities were a bit muddled and very difficult to understand. It was also widely accepted that no vendor was likely to invest the resources to implement all of those capabilities.

SQL:1999, however, was able to depend on the Unicode model for characters. In fact, the standard explicitly refers to Unicode[2] and takes advantage of certain Unicode definitions (e.g., the definition of *whitespace* includes about 20 different Unicode characters). All "special characters" that SQL:1999 uses (such as the space character) are specified in terms of an equivalence to a particular Unicode character, regardless of the actual coded character set that the database system, or the application, chooses to use.

---

2 *The Unicode Standard,* the Unicode Consortium (Reading, MA: Addison-Wesley, 2000).

21.2.2 Character Set Use in SQL

Let's take a look at where all this is actually used in SQL. In Chapter 2, "Getting Started with SQL:1999," we told you that one of the data types supported by SQL:1999 is CHARACTER, another is NATIONAL CHARACTER, and yet another is CHARACTER LARGE OBJECT. As we said then, NATIONAL CHARACTER is exactly the same as CHARACTER except that an implementation-defined character set is implied. Well, the full syntax to specify the data type CHARACTER is

```
CHARACTER [ VARYING ] [ length ] [ CHARACTER SET charset-name ]
```

The list of charset-names that your implementation supports is specified in the product documentation. For purposes of discussion, let's assume that we have access to an implementation that supports ASCII, LATIN1, KANJI, and SQL_TEXT. Therefore, we could write the following table definition:

```
CREATE TABLE t1 (
    col1  CHARACTER (10),
    col2  CHARACTER VARYING (50) CHARACTER SET KANJI,
    col3  CHARACTER (25)         CHARACTER SET LATIN1,
    col4  CHARACTER              CHARACTER SET ASCII,
    col5  NATIONAL CHARACTER (30)
)
```

In this example, the character set of col1 is whatever the implementation has defined as the default for CHARACTER without a character set. The character set of col2 is KANJI; col3 has LATIN1, col4 has ASCII, and col5 has whatever the implementation has defined as the character set for NATIONAL CHARACTER. In all cases, the collation of the columns is the default collation for the character set.

If we want a different collation for these columns, we may write the following:

```
CREATE TABLE t2 (
    cola CHARACTER (10)          COLLATE FRENCH,
    colb CHARACTER VARYING (50)  CHARACTER SET KANJI COLLATE JIS_X0212,
    colc CHARACTER (25)          CHARACTER SET LATIN1 COLLATE ISO8859_1,
    cold CHARACTER               CHARACTER SET ASCII COLLATE EBCDIC,
    cole NATIONAL CHARACTER (30) COLLATE RUSSIAN_GEORGIAN
)
```

In these column definitions, the collations specified also have to be supported by the implementation, and your product's documentation will tell you which collations it supports.

You can make the same sort of character string specifications when you define parameters for your SQL procedures (in SQL modules). There are similar facilities provided in SQL:1999 for host variable declarations. However, you must recall that most host languages do not currently provide any support for internationalized character strings but support only that old, incorrect assumption of one byte equals one character. (A notable exception is the Java programming language, which uses Unicode as its internal character set.) As a result, the specification of character set for SQL parameters or for host variables merely allows you to assist in providing the appropriate interface between your SQL code and your host language code.

21.2.3 Coercibility

SQL:1999 has a set of rules that determines the collation of the result of a character string operation (such as concatenation or substring) based on the collations of the participating character strings. To cover all possible cases, SQL:1999 has also defined another attribute of character strings (but this attribute is associated with specific strings and their specific appearance in an SQL expression; it is not associated with the character set at all). The attribute is called the *coercibility* of the character string, and it determines whether a specific character string has a rigid collation, whether it can be *coerced* to have a collation from another source, or whether it automatically picks up a collation from another source. The rules are defined for monadic operators (that is, operations that have only one character string operand, like SUBSTRING), dyadic operators (operations with two character string operands, like concatenation), and comparisons (see Tables 21-1, 21-2, and 21-3).

Table 21-1 *Collating Coercibility Rules for Monadic Operators*

Operand		Result	
Coercibility	*Collating Sequence*	*Coercibility*	*Collating Sequence*
Coercible	Default	Coercible	Default
Implicit	X	Implicit	X
Explicit	X	Explicit	X
No collating sequence		No collating sequence	

Table 21-2 *Collating Coercibility Rules for Dyadic Operators*

Operand 1		Operand 2		Result	
Coercibility	*Collating Sequence*	*Coercibility*	*Collating Sequence*	*Coercibility*	*Collating Sequence*
Coercible	Default	Coercible	Default	Coercible	Default
Coercible	Default	Implicit	Y	Implicit	Y
Coercible	Default	No collating sequence		No collating sequence	
Coercible	Default	Explicit	Y	Explicit	Y
Implicit	X	Coercible	Default	Implicit	X
Implicit	X	Implicit	X	Implicit	X
Implicit	X	Implicit	Y ≠ X	No collating sequence	
Implicit	X	No collating sequence		No collating sequence	
Implicit	X	Explicit	Y	Explicit	Y
No collating sequence		Any, except Explicit	Any X	No collating sequence	
No collating sequence		Explicit	X	Explicit	X
Explicit	X	Coercible	Default	Explicit	X
Explicit	X	Implicit	Y	Explicit	X
Explicit	X	No collating sequence		Explicit	X
Explicit	X	Explicit	X	Explicit	X
Explicit	X	Explicit	Y ≠ X	Not permitted: *invalid syntax*	

Table 21-3 *Sequence Usage for Comparisons*

Comperand 1		Comperand 2		Collating Sequence Used for This Comparison
Coercibility	*Collating Sequence*	*Coercibility*	*Collating Sequence*	
Coercible	Default	Coercible	Default	Default
Coercible	Default	Implicit	Y	Y
Coercible	Default	No collating sequence		Not permitted: *invalid syntax*
Coercible	Default	Explicit	Y	Y
Implicit	X	Coercible	Default	X
Implicit	X	Implicit	X	X
Implicit	X	Implicit	Y ≠ X	Not permitted: *invalid syntax*
Implicit	X	No collating sequence		Not permitted: *invalid syntax*
Implicit	X	Explicit	Y	Y
No collating sequence		Any, except Explicit	X	Not permitted: *invalid syntax*

Table 21-3 *Continued*

Comperand 1		Comperand 2		Collating Sequence Used for This Comparison
Coercibility	Collating Sequence	Coercibility	Collating Sequence	
No collating sequence		Explicit	X	X
Explicit	X	Coercible	Default	X
Explicit	X	Implicit	Y	X
Explicit	X	No collating sequence		X
Explicit	X	Explicit	X	X
Explicit	X	Explicit	Y ≠ X	Not permitted: *invalid syntax*

To use Tables 21-1, 21-2, and 21-3, you have to know how to determine the coercibility attribute and collation of any specific character string. Once you know these two characteristics of the character string or strings that participate in an operation or comparison, you can determine the outcome of that operation or comparison.

21.2.4 Coercibility Attributes

Individual character strings acquire their coercibility attribute of *explicit, implicit,* or *coercible* as follows:

1. If the character string is a column reference, the coercibility attribute is *implicit* (because the referenced column was defined by a column definition that provided, implicitly or explicitly, a collation). The default collation is the collation provided by the column definition.

2. If the character string is a value other than a column reference (a parameter, a host variable, or a literal), the coercibility attribute is *coercible* and also has the default collation for its character set.

3. In any case, if you provide an explicit collate-clause along with the character string, the coercibility attribute is *explicit* and the collation is the one specified in the collate-clause.

Here are some examples of character string operations that are affected by character sets. Let's assume that we have the table definition we've been using above:

```
col1 || col3
```

Because the character set for col3 is LATIN1 and the character set for col1 is unspecified (and hence is the default), this would be valid if and only if the default character set for CHARACTER columns is LATIN1 *or* some other character set that has the exact same repertoire as LATIN1 (and, in our example, there is no other such set).

```
t1.col1 = t2.cola
```

This comparison is invalid as stated even though t1.col1 and t2.cola have the same character repertoire, because t1.col1 has the default collation and t2.cola has the (presumably different) collation FRENCH. An inspection of Tables 18-1 through 18-3 shows that this is invalid syntax. However, we can remedy that by writing

```
t1.col1 = t2.cola COLLATE FRENCH
```

or

```
t1.col1 COLLATE FRENCH = t2.cola
```

because either way introduces an *explicit* collation.

21.2.5   ORDER BY

As you recall from Chapter 13, "Cursors," DECLARE CURSOR allows you to specify an ORDER BY clause that tells the DBMS how to sort the rows that the cursor references. When you specify an ORDER BY clause, you identify one or more columns of the retrieved rows (either by column name or by ordinal position of the column in the row). You can also specify whether the DBMS is to do an ascending sort or a descending sort (using the keywords ASC or DESC). All this was discussed in Chapter 13. What we didn't discuss in Chapter 13 was the fact that you can also specify a collation to be used for ordering a particular column.

As with other uses of specifying an explicit collation, you have to use a collation that is appropriate and permitted for the character set of the column where you specify it. For example, you could declare a cursor with this ORDER BY clause,

```
ORDER BY movie_title COLLATE FRENCH
```

to specify that you want the movies sorted by their titles according to French conventions. (Obviously, we're assuming that your database designer was reasonable and used the collation name FRENCH to identify a French collating sequence. If that's true, then it's reasonable to assume that FRENCH was defined to be valid on LATIN-1 characters. which our mcvie_title could well be.)

21.2.6 GROUP BY

Another place where you can use an explicit collate-clause is in the GROUP BY clause. Recall from Chapter 9, "Advanced SQL Query Expressions," that the purpose of the GROUP BY clause is to break a table into groups in which every row has an equal value in the grouping column or columns. If the grouping columns include one or more character string columns, then the collation of those columns must be well defined. You can always use the default collation, of course, but there may be times when you want to use an alternative collation for a GROUP BY operation. In this case, you simply use

```
GROUP BY column-name collate-clause [ , column-name collate-clause ]...
```

For example, you might say

```
GROUP BY col1 COLLATE ITALIAN, col2 COLLATE JIS_X0208
```

To do grouping without regard for case, you might be able to write

```
GROUP BY col3 COLLATE all_upper_case
```

21.3 | Translations and Conversions

SQL:1999 also provides you with the ability to translate character strings from one character set to another. Translations are defined by implementations or by standards (alas, we know of no widely recognized standards for character set translations), and the set of translations that are available in your implementation are all documented by the product's documentation. For example, your product may support translation from one encoding to another (such as ASCII to EBCDIC), from a character set with characters that you can't print or display on your hardware into characters that you can (for example, you could translate the German sharp S—ß—to two lowercase s characters), from lowercase characters to uppercase equivalents, or even from one alphabet into another (such as Hebrew into Latin characters).

The format of a translation is

```
TRANSLATE ( source USING conversion )
```

The character set of the translation is defined by the conversion function.

In other cases, you may want to change the form-of-use of a character string for some reason. For example, you may know that internally you have been using a form-of-use with a variable number of bytes per character, but you want to have two bytes per character when you transfer your character data to your host program. A conversion will allow you to specify this operation. The format is

```
CONVERT ( source USING conversion )
```

As with translations, your product's documentation will tell you which conversions it supports and what those conversions actually do.

21.4 | Mapping Host Language Capabilities to SQL's Character Set Facilities

In general, the host languages with which SQL has a defined relationship do not offer very much in the way of character internationalization support.

While we anticipated that the standards for at least COBOL and C would be upgraded to have significant internationalization capabilities, we have not seen that happen. The standards for those languages, and several others, do offer new character data types that allow applications to specify (sometimes indirectly) a character set. But there is rarely any support for collations other than "binary ordering."

Whether this situation will improve over time is difficult to predict, but we are generally hopeful that user demand will present enough opportunities that compiler developers and computer system builders will find it economically attractive. (Incidentally, we believe that the continuing growth of the World Wide Web will add encouragement to product developers; after all, the vast majority of the consuming public in the world doesn't speak English as their first language, if at all.)

21.5 | Equal, Distinct, Identical

We believe it's important that you understand that in SQL:1999 there are three ways of determining whether or not two values are "the same" or "different." All three of these ways apply to all data types, including character strings; when they are applied to character strings, then the character set and collation of those character strings must be considered.

You can compare two values of "comparable types" (that is, two data types for which SQL permits comparisons between values of the types) in several ways, but the most obvious is the <comparison predicate> that we discussed in section 7.4.1, "The Big Six Comparison Types." If you wish to compare two character string values, then they must have the same character repertoire, which merely prohibits the possibility that one string might contain a character that does not appear in the character set of the other string. If you compare two character strings, you might learn that they are equal or that they are unequal; if they are unequal, then you can learn which is greater than the other. Comparing character strings is *always* done in the context of a collation, even if that collation happens to be based purely on the numerical value of the character encodings. Your SQL code might not ever explicitly acknowledge the existence of a collation, but character string comparisons (including ORDER BY, DISTINCT, GROUP BY, etc.) always use a collation.

SQL provides another facility to determine whether two values are "the same" or "different," called *distinct*. Two values (of comparable types, of course) are distinct if

1. they are both not null and they are unequal;
2. one is null and the other is not null.

By contrast, if two values of comparable type are either equal or are both the null value, then they are not distinct.

The third such facility is called *identical*. Two values are identical if there is no way in the context of the SQL language to distinguish between then. Therefore, the character strings 'weisse' and 'weiße' are equal if compared using a German collation, but their string lengths are different, and they are thus not identical. More particularly, however, character strings are converted to bit strings (using their underlying encodings) to determine whether or not they are identical. If the encodings are different (e.g., they have different coded character sets), then they cannot be identical.

21.6 | Chapter Summary

We've briefly discussed the internationalization aspects of SQL:1999. Unlike the early versions of SQL, and most DBMS products in general, a great deal of effort has gone into allowing for international-class database applications. (However, we don't wish to leave you with the wrong impression: many database vendors are rapidly providing facilities to use Unicode and other internationalization facilities in their products.) When you think about the direction in which database applications are headed—distributed, multinational environments that encompass products from vendors in different companies and data in many different character sets—it becomes obvious that built-in internationalization characteristics are needed within the database framework.

SQL:1999's features such as multiple character sets and collations help you to achieve international applications in your database environments. Why would these facilities be important to you? Consider our sample application. Assume that our video and music stores become so successful that we begin offering franchises in other countries. In keeping with the spirit of distributed, international computing, we will likely allow individual stores (regional headquarters) to handle the information systems processing tasks, including SQL database management. If we have stores in Japan, the United States, Germany, and a number of other countries, we want each store or region to use appropriate character sets and other local aspects as applicable. By using SQL's internationalization facilities, your applications may be easily adapted to whatever countries in which your business operations occur.

Chapter

22

Information Schema

22.1 | Introduction

In each catalog in an SQL environment, there is a schema named INFORMATION_
SCHEMA that is accessible to your application programs. In this chapter, we discuss
this schema and its contents, as well as the associated privileges. We also take a
brief look at the DEFINITION_SCHEMA, in which base tables are defined to support
the INFORMATION_SCHEMA.

Before we introduce the various schemas, let's briefly review the topic of
metadata.

22.2 | Metadata, Repositories, and the INFORMATION_SCHEMA

We discussed the concept of metadata in Chapter 2, "Getting Started with
SQL:1999." As a reminder, metadata is "data about data." That is, it is a description of the data (and, for that matter, the metadata itself) contained within a
database.

In many information system environments, a dictionary or repository functions as the primary storage mechanism for an organization's metadata. While
this is an implementation-dependent situation, there are two general rules in the
SQL standard.

- Metadata that applies primarily to the runtime database environment is managed through the INFORMATION_SCHEMA.

- Metadata that applies to the information system environment as a whole is managed through a *data dictionary* or *metadata repository.*

When this type of "dual metadata" environment is present, the INFORMATION_SCHEMA metadata must be coordinated with that of the overall dictionary/repository (let's just call it a *repository,* since that is the term that seems to be most nearly politically correct) environment.

Why do we mention this? Simply so you realize that your particular SQL implementation may be doing a great deal of behind-the-scenes action to manage this coordination. It is to your benefit to know as much as possible about your particular implementation, and in many organizations there may be multiple SQL:1999 DBMS implementations, each with its own different technology for metadata management. In distributed database environments, the metadata management must often be coordinated, or at least known, among implementations. Therefore, you should understand

- what views are provided within the respective INFORMATION_SCHEMAs, particularly with respect to extensions

- how the metadata of each INFORMATION_SCHEMA interacts with various repositories across the environment

By the way, the INFORMATION_SCHEMA and DEFINITION_SCHEMA contain information about tables, privileges, and other SQL entities within a single catalog. Each catalog contains its own INFORMATION_SCHEMA and DEFINITION_SCHEMA.

22.3 DEFINITION_SCHEMA and Base Tables

In Chapter 4, "Basic Data Definition Language (DDL)," we discussed how all SQL views are defined in terms of one or more base tables. The same is true for the views of the INFORMATION_SCHEMA. The base tables are defined as being in a schema called DEFINITION_SCHEMA. However, these base tables are *not* accessible from any of your SQL statements; the sole purpose of the DEFINITION_SCHEMA is to define a set of (perhaps hypothetical) base tables that are used in SQL:1999 to provide a standard definition of the INFORMATION_SCHEMA views. An implementation can define the INFORMATION_SCHEMA views exactly as specified in SQL:1999 and can actually supply the DEFINITION_SCHEMA base tables, or it can define the INFORMATION_SCHEMA views based on other implementation-specific catalog tables or any other source of information. We suspect that some SQL products actually implement the INFORMATION_SCHEMA views by means of stored procedures that operate behind the scenes to aggregate information that is provided in various ways into a unified view as specified in SQL:1999.

22.4 | Self-Description

The INFORMATION_SCHEMA also describes itself. By that, we mean that the views of INFORMATION_SCHEMA—such as TABLE_CONSTRAINTS, TABLES, VIEWS, VIEW_COLUMN_USAGE, and the others we discuss in this chapter—have appropriate entries in the base tables of DEFINITION_SCHEMA and, consequently, in the INFORMATION_SCHEMA views.

For example, there is an INFORMATION_SCHEMA view called VIEWS (the VIEWS view—now stay with us!). In addition, there is a VIEWS base table in DEFINITION_SCHEMA (the VIEWS table. . . . Still following?).

To make it simple, let's see them as defined by their qualified names, shown in Table 22-1.

Table 22-1 *The VIEWS Table and the VIEWS View*

DEFINITION_SCHEMA.VIEWS	The base table
INFORMATION_SCHEMA.VIEWS	The view

Self-description means that there will be an entry for INFORMATION_SCHEMA.VIEWS in (1) the DEFINITION_SCHEMA.VIEWS base table (though, as we mentioned above, it may not be a "real" entry since the base tables don't really have to exist); and (2) the INFORMATION_SCHEMA.VIEWS view.

The concept of self-description does *not* apply to the DEFINITION_SCHEMA, however. That is, there won't be an entry in DEFINITION_SCHEMA.VIEWS nor in INFORMATION_SCHEMA.VIEWS that describes DEFINITION_SCHEMA.VIEWS.

So what does this mean? Simply that your programs or SQL statements may access information about the numerous views of the INFORMATION_SCHEMA but cannot access any information about the tables of DEFINITION_SCHEMA. In nearly every circumstance, this is not a problem because any metadata information you could possibly want is accessible through the INFORMATION_SCHEMA views. Now, let's discuss how privileges apply to the INFORMATION_SCHEMA.

22.5 | INFORMATION_SCHEMA and Privileges

The INFORMATION_SCHEMA views all have identical privilege assignments: SELECT is granted to PUBLIC WITH GRANT OPTION. This means (refer to Chapter 14, "Privileges, Users, and Security," if you're fuzzy on PUBLIC privileges) that the views may be queried by any user, and that the SELECT privileges can be further granted to user-defined views that may reference the INFORMATION_SCHEMA views.

There are *no* other privileges granted on INFORMATION_SCHEMA; therefore, the views are not updatable (at least not through ordinary SQL UPDATE, INSERT, or DELETE statements). To understand why, let's look at the following situation. Let's say that a particular SQL:1999 DBMS implementation controls its metadata, and therefore definitions of all its database objects, through the INFORMATION_SCHEMA. Application requests to access a particular user table or column may first be validated against the INFORMATION_SCHEMA to see if the object exists before physical access is actually attempted (for efficiency reasons). This action is similar to an operating system that checks a directory on a disk in order to find out if a requested file exists before actually seeking out the file.

Now let's say that the INFORMATION_SCHEMA tables were updatable; an application or user could come along and delete one or more entries from the INFORMATION_SCHEMA. The physical tables, columns, or the like might still exist, but an implementation would likely return an error to the next requestor of the lost objects. Maybe all accesses to MOVIE_TITLES would now be invalidated because of lost metadata for the table. For the sake of security and consistency, therefore, the INFORMATION_SCHEMA views aren't updatable. Of course, the DDL statements such as CREATE TABLE and DROP TABLE implicitly cause updates to the INFORMATION_SCHEMA views while they perform their data definition operations.

22.6 | INFORMATION_SCHEMA Extensions

SQL:1999 implementations are permitted to add viewed tables to the INFORMATION_SCHEMA above and beyond the definitions supplied in the standard, as well as to add columns to the views that SQL:1999 specifies in the INFORMATION_SCHEMA. If, for example, a particular SQL implementation has data mining extensions that require special database contents, the metadata of those objects may be stored in the INFORMATION_SCHEMA.

Correspondingly, additional DEFINITION_SCHEMA base tables are created (or simulated) as necessary to support the INFORMATION_SCHEMA extensions.

22.7 | Identifier Representation

When you create a schema object, such as a table, view, column, character set, or domain, that object is represented by a row in one or more of the DEFINITION_SCHEMA tables and one or more of the INFORMATION_SCHEMA views. In order for you to retrieve information from the INFORMATION_SCHEMA views about one of those objects, you must know how to code a character string literal that represents the name of the object. That, in turn, means that you have to understand how the object is represented in the view.

Consider the TABLES view. It has a column called TABLE_NAME; that column contains the names of all tables in the catalog to which you have access (that is, for which you have some privilege). The TABLE_NAME column, of course, has a character string data type. As you see in our samples later in this chapter, the specific data type is CHARACTER VARYING (*L*) CHARACTER SET SQL_TEXT. *L* represents a number that is the maximum length of an identifier for your implementation; in most cases, that number will be something like 18, 31, 32, or 128 (18 is the Core SQL limit, 31 and 32 are popular implementors' choices, and 128 is specified for eventual implementation; we recommend that you assume the number is 128 so that your applications will be portable and upwardly compatible with later implementations).

The character set named SQL_TEXT is a special character set that contains every character supported by your implementation. Unfortunately, this means that different implementations will probably support different sets of characters and different definitions of SQL_TEXT. While this will undoubtedly reduce portability of your applications, it also reflects the fact that different vendors have different views of the market's requirements. As you learned in Chapter 21, "Internationalization Aspects of SQL:1999," SQL:1999's character set model is based on the Unicode standard. That makes it more probable that SQL_TEXT will actually be Unicode in various SQL products, improving the possibility of application portability.

Let's assume that SQL_TEXT for some particular DBMS is, in fact, Unicode, which is being fairly widely implemented by database vendors. Unicode (as we told you in Chapter 21, "Internationalization Aspects of SQL:1999") is a character set in which each character is encoded into 16 bits, so potentially it can represent up to 65,536 characters. Therefore, programs written for that DBMS must reserve 2 "bytes" (octets) for each character that they wish to retrieve from the TABLE_NAME column. Since that column is potentially 128 characters in length, your application should set aside 128 2-byte positions (or 256 bytes) for TABLE_NAME retrieval.

More important to this discussion is the question of what the actual characters are (as opposed to their bit encodings). Suppose we execute the following CREATE TABLE statement:

```
CREATE TABLE music_lovers (
    ...
)
```

What are the resulting contents of the TABLE_NAME column of the TABLES view? Actually, the results are

```
MUSIC_LOVERS
```

because SQL:1999 has a rule that requires that normal identifiers *always* be treated *in every respect* as though they had been entered in uppercase letters. Therefore, all of the following have the same effect.

```
CREATE TABLE MUSIC_LOVERS (
    ...
)
```

```
CREATE TABLE MuSiC_LoVeRs (
    ...
)
```

```
CREATE TABLE Music_Lovers (
    ...
)
```

Each of these (done independently) would create the row in TABLES shown in Table 22-2.

Table 22-2 *TABLES Contents for MUSIC_LOVERS Table*

CATALOG_NAME	SCHEMA_NAME	TABLE_NAME	TABLE_TYPE
whatever	*whatever*	MUSIC_LOVERS	BASE TABLE

If you tried to execute two or more of these statements (without an intervening DROP TABLE, of course), the second and subsequent ones would give you an error, because a table with that name already exists.

This is done for two reasons: first, so that you can use your favorite case conventions (uppercase only, lowercase only, mixed-case, etc.) when coding your SQL statements, and, second, so you always know how to retrieve data from the INFORMATION_SCHEMA. Therefore, you can retrieve information about this table only as follows:

```
SELECT table_name, table_type
FROM information_schema.tables
WHERE table_name = 'MUSIC_LOVERS'
```

You can *always* use this statement, regardless of which of the previous four alternatives (or quite a few others) were used for creating the table. This means that you can retrieve information from the INFORMATION_SCHEMA without knowing in intimate detail how the information there was created.

However, you will recall that SQL:1999 also provides something called a *delimited identifier*. The initial purpose of this was to allow you to specify identifiers that are otherwise identical to SQL's reserved keywords (such as TABLE or USAGE). Specifically, it allows you to protect yourself against future product (or standard) versions that introduce new reserved keywords that you've already used in your applications. SQL:1999 also makes delimited identifiers case *sensitive*, so that C, C++, Java, and UNIX programmers can obtain behavior that is more comfortable in their environment. That means that you can execute

```
CREATE TABLE "Music_Lovers" (
    ...
)
```

and get a *different* table than any of the previous examples. In this case, you'd better know that the table was created with a delimited identifier with mixed case and precisely what characters were used with which case, because that's how you'll have to retrieve it:

```
SELECT table_name, table_type
FROM information_schema.tables
WHERE table_name = 'Music_Lovers'
```

This example retrieves only information about the table created using a delimited identifier.

Now the TABLES view will contain both of these rows, as seen in Table 22-3.

Table 22-3 *TABLES Contents for Two Tables*

CATALOG_NAME	SCHEMA_NAME	TABLE_NAME	TABLE_TYPE
whatever	*whatever*	MUSIC_LOVERS	BASE TABLE
whatever	*whatever*	Music_Lovers	BASE TABLE

You can, of course, retrieve information about either one of them by using the appropriate character string literal in your WHERE clause:

```
SELECT table_name, table_type
FROM information_schema.tables
WHERE table_name = 'Music_Lovers'
```

or

```
SELECT table_name, table_type
FROM information_schema.tables
WHERE table_name = 'MUSIC_LOVERS'
```

Note that SQL:1999 does not provide any obvious way to express the semantics of "ignore the case of the literal and/or the column values when making the comparison." Many SQL implemetntations offer such extensions, but the SQL standard's approach to providing that facility is to require the use of a specific collation for which case is ignored:

```
SELECT table_name, table_type
FROM information_schema.tables
WHERE table_name = 'MUSIC_LOVERS'
      COLLATE my_case_insensitive_collation
```

22.8 | The DEFINITION_SCHEMA

Although it may seem a bit backward, given the emphasis placed on INFORMATION_SCHEMA as compared with DEFINITION_SCHEMA, let's take a look at the DEFINITION_SCHEMA first. The reason is that, as we look at the view definitions of the INFORMATION_SCHEMA, the references to the DEFINITION_SCHEMA base tables won't be as hard to follow.

22.8.1 Schema Definition

The DEFINITION_SCHEMA schema is defined through a simple statement:

```
CREATE SCHEMA DEFINITION_SCHEMA
AUTHORIZATION DEFINITION_SCHEMA
```

22.8.2 The Base Tables

The following base tables are defined for the DEFINITION_SCHEMA. Note that the complete CREATE TABLE definitions may be found in the SQL:1999 standard. In this list, we include only those base tables that are associated with the nonobject features of SQL:1999. For the remaining base tables, please refer to Volume 2 of this book.

1. USERS: There is one row for each authorization identifier referenced in the INFORMATION_SCHEMA of the catalog. These rows represent the aggregate of all authorization identifiers that may grant or receive privileges as well as those that may create a schema or currently own a schema. The means by which rows are inserted into and deleted from the USERS table are implementation-defined.

2. SCHEMATA: This table has one row for each schema in the catalog. Additionally, a foreign key (see Chapter 10, "Constraints, Assertions, and Referential Integrity") references the USERS table (item 1 above) to provide a constraint between these two objects.

3. DATA_TYPE_DESCRIPTOR: This table contains (1) one row for each domain and (2) one row for each column in each table that is defined as having a data type in lieu of a domain. That is, if you have a very small database with five domains plus a total of fifteen columns across four tables that had data types (example: CHARACTER (20) or INTEGER) rather than domains, this table will have 20 rows. It also has (3) one row for each distinct type used in the catalog, (4) one row for each SQL parameter of each SQL-invoked routine, (5) one row for the result type of each SQL-invoked method, and (6) one row for each structured type whose associated reference type has a user-defined representation.

4. DOMAINS: One row for each domain exists in this table.

5. DOMAIN_CONSTRAINTS: One row for each domain constraint exists in this table.

6. TABLES: This table contains one row for each table, including views. Temporary tables are also included. A quick note: By viewing the primary key definition of this table,

```
CREATE TABLE TABLES (
    TABLE_CATALOG...
    TABLE_SCHEMA...
    TABLE_NAME...
    TABLE_TYPE...

    CONSTRAINT TABLES_PK PRIMARY KEY
      ( TABLE_CATALOG, TABLE_SCHEMA, TABLE_NAME )...
)
```

you can see how the namespace management occurs in SQL:1999.

7. VIEWS: This table contains one row for each row in the TABLES table (see item 6 above) that has a TABLE_TYPE of VIEW. Additionally, the rows describe the respective query expressions and characteristics that define the various views, including whether the view is updatable.

8. COLUMNS: This table contains one row for each column of each table. Note that the PRIMARY KEY definition is the same as that of TABLES, with one additional column: COLUMN_NAME:

```
PRIMARY KEY (TABLE_CATALOG, TABLE_SCHEMA, TABLE_NAME, COLUMN_NAME)
```

We mention this as a reminder that your seemingly simple column references, such as SELECT TITLE, MOVIE_TYPE, OUR_COST, are in actuality qualified within the database according to the catalog, schema, and table. Another point worth noting, for your general information: there is a column within the COLUMNS table called ORDINAL_POSITION, which is the ordinal position of the column within the table. Therefore, DDL changes that add one or more columns to a table or delete one or more columns from a table frequently cause adjustments to the ORDINAL_POSITION values for the columns in the table.

9. VIEW_TABLE_USAGE: This table has one row for each table referenced in the query expression of a view. A CHECK constraint ensures that the referenced tables actually exist within the TABLES table, and a FOREIGN KEY constraint maintains the linkage to the VIEWS table.

10. VIEW_COLUMN_USAGE: This table is similar to VIEW_TABLE_USAGE, except that one row exists for each column referenced by a view. A similar CHECK constraint to that discussed in item 9 ensures that the column name really exists.

11. TABLE_CONSTRAINTS: This table contains one row for each table constraint associated with a table. Constraints are defined, using a CHECK constraint on the column CONSTRAINT_TYPE, as being one of the following: UNIQUE, PRIMARY KEY, FOREIGN KEY, and CHECK. Deferrability of the constraint is also specified.

12. KEY_COLUMN_USAGE: This table contains one or more rows for each row in the TABLE_CONSTRAINTS table (see item 11) that has a CONSTRAINT_TYPE of UNIQUE, PRIMARY KEY, or FOREIGN KEY (that is, all except for CHECK constraints).

13. REFERENTIAL_CONSTRAINTS: This table contains one row for each row of the TABLE_CONSTRAINTS table that has been inserted by a referential constraint definition. A variety of update rules—CASCADE, SET NULL, SET DEFAULT, and NO ACTION, all of which we discussed in Chapter 10—may be specified for each constraint.

14. CHECK_CONSTRAINTS: As contrasted with KEY_COLUMN_USAGE, this table has one row for each domain CHECK constraint, table CHECK constraint, or assertion.

15. CHECK_TABLE_USAGE: This table has one row for each table referenced by the search condition of a domain CHECK constraint, table CHECK constraint, or assertion (and, therefore, has a FOREIGN KEY constraint of its own on the CHECK_CONSTRAINTS table discussed in item 14).

16. CHECK_COLUMN_USAGE: This table contains one row for each column referenced by the search condition of a domain CHECK constraint, table CHECK constraint, or assertion. It is the same as CHECK_TABLE_USAGE, except for columns instead of tables.

Authors' interjection: By now, you should be getting an idea of the type of metadata that SQL maintains and manages. We've found that by looking at the DEFINITION_SCHEMA base table definitions, as well as the views of INFORMATION_SCHEMA, you can actually learn a great deal about how SQL works with respect to the various language features. Even if you will have little to do with metadata when you develop your applications, you can still learn a lot by looking at the various constraints and search conditions, as well as at the column values and even the table names, of the metadata tables. It's probably accurate to say that the DEFINITION_SCHEMA contains a representation of the SQL data model. Now, back to the rest of the base tables.

17. ASSERTIONS: This table contains one row for each assertion, including whether the assertion is deferrable or not.

18. TABLE_PRIVILEGES: One row exists for each table privilege descriptor. The various privilege types are specified in a CHECK constraint, as is whether or not the privilege is grantable. Additionally, FOREIGN KEYS exist between the GRANTOR and GRANTEE columns to the USERS table (base table 1).

19. COLUMN_PRIVILEGES: Remember that we said privileges may be granted on columns as well as tables (see Chapter 14, "Privileges, Users, and Security"). This table contains the privilege descriptors for all column-specific privileges.

20. USAGE_PRIVILEGES: One row exists for each usage privilege descriptor, which applies to domains, character sets, collations, and translations.

21. CHARACTER_SETS: This table contains one row for each character set description.

22. COLLATIONS: By now, you should be able to figure out that this table contains one row for each character collation descriptor.

23. TRANSLATION: Of course, this table contains one row for each character translation descriptor.

24. TRIGGERS: There is one row for each trigger in the catalog.

25. TRIGGER_TABLE_USAGE: One row is provided for each table identified by a table name contained in the search condition of a triggered action, or referenced in the triggered SQL statement of a trigger.

26. TRIGGER_COLUMN_USAGE: One row is provided for each column identified by a column name contained in the search condition of a triggered action, or referenced in the triggered SQL statement of a trigger.

27. TRIGGERED_UPDATE_COLUMNS: One row is provided for each column identified by a column name contained in the trigger column list of a trigger.

28. ELEMENT_TYPES: One row exists for each ARRAY type; the row describes the array's associated element type.

29. FIELDS: One row exists for each field of a ROW type.

30. ROUTINES: There is a row for each SQL-invoked routine.

31. ROUTINE_PRIVILEGES: Each row describes an EXECUTE privilege that has been granted on an SQL-invoked routine.

32. ROUTINE_TABLE_USAGE: A row exists for each table that is referenced in an SQL-invoked routine.

33. ROUTINE_COLUMN_USAGE: A row exists for each column that is referenced in an SQL-invoked routine.

34. PARAMETERS: One row is provided for each SQL parameter of each SQL-invoked routine.

35. ROLES: This view contains one row for each role known to the system.

36. ROLE_AUTHORIZATION_DESCRIPTORS: There is one row for each role authorization descriptor.

37. SQL_FEATURES: This table contains one row for each package, each feature, and each subfeature identified in the SQL:1999 standard, specifying whether or not the SQL product implements that feature.

38. SQL_IMPLEMENTATION_INFO: There is one row for each SQL implementation information item specified by SQL:1999, documenting the value of that item as provided by the implementation.

39. SQL_SIZING: One row exists for each SQL sizing item (e.g., maximum length of identifiers, maximum number of columns in a table) specified by SQL:1999.

40. SQL_LANGUAGES: One row exists for each binding style per host language. Note the complete table description; you can learn a lot about the history, background, and supported languages just from reading the CHECK constraint.

```
CREATE TABLE SQL_LANGUAGES (
    SQL_LANGUAGE_SOURCE           INFORMATION_SCHEMA.CHARACTER_DATA
      CONSTRAINT SQL_LANGUAGES_SOURCE_NCT_NULL NOT NULL,
    SQL_LANGUAGE_YEAR             INFORMATION_SCHEMA.CHARACTER_DATA
      CONSTRAINT SQL_LANGUAGES_YEAR_ISO
        CHECK ( SQL_LANGUAGE_SOURCE <> 'ISO 9075'
            OR
              ( SQL_LANGUAGE_YEAR IS NOT NULL
            AND
              SQL_LANGUAGE_YEAR IN
              ( '1987', '1989', '1992', '1999' ))),
    SQL_LANGUAGE_CONFORMANCE      INFORMATION_SCHEMA.CHARACTER_DATA
      CONSTRAINT SQL_LANGUAGE_CONFORMANCE_ISO_1987
        CHECK ( SQL_LANGUAGE_SOURCE <> 'ISO 9075'
            OR
              ( SQL_LANGUAGE_YEAR <> '1987'
            OR
              ( SQL_LANGUAGE_CONFORMANCE IS NOT NULL
            AND
              SQL_LANGUAGE_CONFORMANCE IN
              ( '1', '2' ) ) ) )
```

```
                    CONSTRAINT SQL_LANGUAGE_CONFORMANCE_ISO_1989
                      CHECK ( SQL_LANGUAGE_SOURCE <> 'ISO 9075'
                            OR
                               ( SQL_LANGUAGE_YEAR <> '1989'
                             OR
                               ( SQL_LANGUAGE_CONFORMANCE IS NOT NULL
                               AND
                                 SQL_LANGUAGE_CONFORMANCE IN
                                 ( '1', '2' ) ) ) )
                    CONSTRAINT SQL_LANGUAGE_CONFORMANCE_ISO_1992
                      CHECK ( SQL_LANGUAGE_SOURCE <> 'ISO 9075'
                            OR
                               ( SQL_LANGUAGE_YEAR <> '1992'
                             OR
                               ( SQL_LANGUAGE_CONFORMANCE IS NOT NULL
                               AND
                                 SQL_LANGUAGE_CONFORMANCE IN
                                 ( 'ENTRY', 'INTERMEDIATE', 'FULL' ) ) ) )
                    CONSTRAINT SQL_LANGUAGE_CONFORMANCE_ISO_1999
                      CHECK ( SQL_LANGUAGE_SOURCE <> 'ISO 9075'
                            OR
                               ( SQL_LANGUAGE_YEAR <> '1999'
                             OR
                               ( SQL_LANGUAGE_CONFORMANCE IS NOT NULL
                               AND
                                 SQL_LANGUAGE_CONFORMANCE IN
                                 ( 'CORE' ) ) ) ),
          SQL_LANGUAGE_INTEGRITY INFORMATION_SCHEMA.CHARACTER_DATA
                    CONSTRAINT SQL_LANGUAGE_INTEGRITY_ISO_1989
                      CHECK ( SQL_LANGUAGE_SOURCE <> 'ISO 9075'
                            OR
                               ( SQL_LANGUAGE_INTEGRITY IS NULL
                             OR
                               ( SQL_LANGUAGE_YEAR = '1989'
                               AND
                                 SQL_LANGUAGE_INTEGRITY IS NOT NULL
                               AND
                                 SQL_LANGUAGE_INTEGRITY IN
                                 ( 'NO', 'YES' ) ) ) ),
```

22.8 The DEFINITION_SCHEMA

SQL_LANGUAGE_IMPLEMENTATION INFORMATION_SCHEMA.CHARACTER_DATA
CONSTRAINT SQL_LANGUAGE_IMPLEMENTATION_ISO
CHECK (SQL_LANGUAGE_SOURCE <> 'ISO 9075'
OR
SQL_LANGUAGE_IMPLEMENTATION IS NULL),
SQL_LANGUAGE_BINDING_STYLE INFORMATION_SCHEMA.CHARACTER_DATA
CONSTRAINT SQL_LANGUAGE_BINDING_STYLE_ISO_1987
CHECK (SQL_LANGUAGE_SOURCE <> 'ISO 9075'
OR
(SQL_LANGUAGE_YEAR <> '1987'
OR
(SQL_LANGUAGE_BINDING_STYLE IS NOT NULL
AND
SQL_LANGUAGE_BINDING_STYLE IN
('DIRECT', 'EMBEDDED', 'MODULE'))))
CONSTRAINT SQL_LANGUAGE_BINDING_STYLE_ISO_1989
CHECK (SQL_LANGUAGE_SOURCE <> 'ISO 9075'
OR
(SQL_LANGUAGE_YEAR <> '1989'
OR
(SQL_LANGUAGE_BINDING_STYLE IS NOT NULL
AND
SQL_LANGUAGE_BINDING_STYLE IN
('DIRECT', 'EMBEDDED', 'MODULE'))))
CONSTRAINT SQL_LANGUAGE_BINDING_STYLE_ISO_1992
CHECK (SQL_LANGUAGE_SOURCE <> 'ISO 9075'
OR
(SQL_LANGUAGE_YEAR <> '1992'
OR
(SQL_LANGUAGE_BINDING_STYLE IS NOT NULL
AND
SQL_LANGUAGE_BINDING_STYLE IN
('DIRECT', 'EMBEDDED', 'MODULE')))),
SQL_LANGUAGE_PROGRAMMING_LANGUAGE INFORMATION_SCHEMA.CHARACTER_DATA
CONSTRAINT SQL_LANGUAGES_STANDARD_VALID_CHECK_ISO_1987
CHECK (SQL_LANGUAGE_SOURCE <> 'ISO 9075'
OR
(SQL_LANGUAGE_YEAR <> '1987'
OR
(SQL_LANGUAGE_BINDING_STYLE = 'DIRECT'

```
                            AND
                              SQL_LANGUAGE_PROGRAMMING_LANGUAGE IS NULL )
                        OR
                          ( SQL_LANGUAGE_BINDING_STYLE IN
                            ( 'EMBEDDED', 'MODULE' )
                          AND
                            SQL_LANGUAGE_PROGRAMMING_LANGUAGE IN
                            ( 'COBOL', 'FORTRAN', 'PASCAL', 'PLI' ) ) ) )
        CONSTRAINT SQL_LANGUAGES_STANDARD_VALID_CHECK_ISO_1989
          CHECK ( SQL_LANGUAGE_SOURCE <> 'ISO 9075'
                OR
                    ( SQL_LANGUAGE_YEAR <> '1989'
                OR
                        ( SQL_LANGUAGE_BINDING_STYLE = 'DIRECT'
                        AND
                          SQL_LANGUAGE_PROGRAMMING_LANGUAGE IS NULL )
                OR
                        ( SQL_LANGUAGE_BINDING_STYLE IN
                          ( 'EMBEDDED', 'MODULE' )
                        AND
                          SQL_LANGUAGE_PROGRAMMING_LANGUAGE IN
                          ( 'COBOL', 'FORTRAN', 'PASCAL', 'PLI' ) ) ) )
        CONSTRAINT SQL_LANGUAGES_STANDARD_VALID_CHECK_ISO_1992
          CHECK ( SQL_LANGUAGE_SOURCE <> 'ISO 9075'
                OR
                    ( SQL_LANGUAGE_YEAR <> '1992'
                OR
                        ( SQL_LANGUAGE_BINDING_STYLE = 'DIRECT'
                        AND
                          SQL_LANGUAGE_PROGRAMMING_LANGUAGE IS NULL )
                OR
                        ( SQL_LANGUAGE_BINDING_STYLE IN
                          ( 'EMBEDDED', 'MODULE' )
                        AND
                          SQL_LANGUAGE_PROGRAMMING_LANGUAGE IN
                          ( 'ADA', 'C', 'COBOL', 'FORTRAN',
                            'MUMPS', 'PASCAL', 'PLI' ) ) ) )

          )
```

BASE TABLES	CHECK_TABLE_USAGE
USERS	CHECK_COLUMN_USAGE
SCHEMATA	ASSERTIONS
DATA_TYPE DESCRIPTOR	TABLE_PRIVILEGES
DOMAINS	COLUMN_PRIVILEGES
DOMAIN_CONSTRAINTS	USAGE_PRIVILEGES
TABLES	CHARACTER_SETS
VIEWS	COLLATIONS
COLUMNS	TRANSLATION
VIEW_TABLE_USAGE	SQL_LANGUAGES
VIEW_COLUMN_USAGE	
TABLE_CONSTRAINTS	**ASSERTIONS**
KEY_COLUMN_USAGE	UNIQUE_CONSTRAINT_NAME
REFERENTIAL_CONSTRAINTS	EQUAL_KEY_DEGREES
CHECK_CONSTRAINTS	KEY_DEGREE_GREATER_THAN_OR_EQUAL_TO_1

Figure 22-1   Summary of DEFINITION_SCHEMA

22.8.3 Assertions on the Base Tables

There are three assertions defined on the base tables. These are as follows:

1. UNIQUE_CONSTRAINT_NAME: This ensures that the same combination of a schema name and a constraint name is not used by more than one constraint. By using an assertion, separate checks on the DOMAINS, TABLE_CONSTRAINTS, and ASSERTIONS tables aren't needed.

2. EQUAL_KEY_DEGREES: This assertion ensures that every FOREIGN KEY is of the same degree as the corresponding UNIQUE or PRIMARY KEY constraint.

3. KEY_DEGREE_GREATER_THAN_OR_EQUAL_TO_1 (whew!): This assertion ensures that every UNIQUE constraint has at least one unique column, and that every referential constraint has at least one referencing column.

22.9 | The INFORMATION_SCHEMA

Let's take a look now at the INFORMATION_SCHEMA.

22.9.1 Schema Definition

The schema is defined, as was DEFINITION_SCHEMA, by a simple statement:

```
CREATE SCHEMA INFORMATION_SCHEMA
    AUTHORIZATION INFORMATION_SCHEMA
```

Additionally, there is a single base table definition in the INFORMATION_ SCHEMA along with the views we'll see.

```
CREATE TABLE INFORMATION_SCHEMA_CATALOG_NAME (
    CATALOG_NAME    SQL_IDENTIFIER,

    CONSTRAINT INFORMATION_SCHEMA_CATALOG_NAME_PRIMARY_KEY
      PRIMARY KEY ( CATALOG_NAME )

    CONSTRAINT INFORMATION_SCHEMA_CATALOG_NAME_CHECK
      CHECK ( 1 = ( SELECT COUNT(*)
                    FROM INFORMATION_SCHEMA_CATALOG_NAME ) )

)
```

This table identifies the name of the catalog in which the particular information schema resides. The CHECK constraint ensures that there is exactly one row in the INFORMATION_SCHEMA_CATALOG_NAME table.

22.9.2 Domains

There are four domains in the INFORMATION_SCHEMA.

1. SQL_IDENTIFIER: This defines a domain that allows all valid identifiers of CHARACTER SET SQL_TEXT.
2. CHARACTER_DATA: This domain contains specifications for any character data.

3. CARDINAL_NUMBER: This domain is defined for nonnegative numbers.

4. TIME_STAMP: This last domain defines timestamp values used in the INFORMATION_SCHEMA.

22.9.3 Views

There are 61 views defined within the INFORMATION_SCHEMA (compared with only 23 defined in SQL-92). Let's take a look at a selection of them. Note that most of these views have special code that allows you to see information about objects for which you have some privilege but prevents you from even seeing a row that concerns an object for which you have no privileges. Several more INFORMATION_SCHEMA views are used only with structured types, which are discussed in Volume 2 of this book.

1. SCHEMATA: This view identifies the schemas that are owned by the current user. It uses columns from DEFINITION_SCHEMA.SCHEMATA and uses a subquery to match the CATALOG_NAME against the INFORMATION_ SCHEMA_ CATA_OG_NAME base table that resides in this schema.

2. ADMINISTRABLE_ROLE_AUTHORIZATIONS: This view identifies the role authorizations that the current user has with the ability to grant them to others.

3. APPLICABLE_ROLES: This view identifies the roles that are applicable for the current user.

4. ENABLED_ROLES: This view identifies the enabled roles for the current SQL-session.

5. ROLE_COLUMN_GRANTS: This view identifies the privileges on columns that are available to or granted by the currently enabled roles.

6. ROLE_TABLE_GRANTS: This view identifies the privileges on tables that are available to or granted by the currently enabled roles.

7. ROLE_ROUTINE_GRANTS: This view identifies the privileges on SQL-invoked routines that are available to or granted by the currently enabled roles.

8. ROLE_USAGE_GRANTS: This view identifies the privileges on schema objects that are available to or granted by the currently enabled roles.

9. DOMAINS: This view identifies the domains defined in the catalog that are accessible to the current user. The view definition uses a complex JOIN definition to match several base tables, including DEFINITION_SCHEMA. DOMAINS.

10. DOMAIN_CONSTRAINTS: This view identifies the domain constraints, of the domains in the catalog, that are accessible to the current user.

11. TABLES: This view identifies the *persistent* tables, defined in the catalog, that are accessible to the current user.

12. VIEWS: This view identifies the views in the catalog that are accessible to the current user.

13. COLUMNS: This view identifies the columns of persistent tables that are accessible to the current user. The actual CREATE VIEW statement and the usage of a number of SQL:1999 language constructs, including COALESCE, LEFT JOINs, subqueries, and others, is educational. As a general point of interest, this particular view definition is the longest of those in the INFORMATION_SCHEMA.

14. TABLE_PRIVILEGES: The privileges on persistent tables which are available to or granted by the current user are identified in this view.

15. COLUMN_PRIVILEGES: This view identifies the privileges on columns of persistent tables that are defined in the catalog and are available to or granted by the current user.

16. USAGE_PRIVILEGES: This view identifies USAGE privileges on catalog objects that are available to or owned by the current user.

17. DATA_TYPE_PRIVILEGES: This view identifies schema objects whose data type descriptors are accessible to the current user.

18. TABLE_CONSTRAINTS: This view identifies table constraints that are owned by the current user.

19. REFERENTIAL_CONSTRAINTS: This view identifies referential constraints that are owned by the current user.

20. CHECK_CONSTRAINTS: In keeping with the current trend, this view identifies CHECK constraints that are owned by the current user.

21. KEY_COLUMN_USAGE: This view identifies columns defined in the catalog that are constrained as keys by the current user.

22. ASSERTIONS: This view identifies the catalog's assertions that are owned by the current user.

23. CHARACTER_SETS: This view identifies the catalog's character sets that are accessible to the current user.

24. COLLATIONS: This view identifies character collations for the catalog that are accessible to the current user.

25. TRANSLATIONS: This view identifies character translations for the catalog that are acessible to the current user.

26. TRIGGERS: This view identifies the triggers owned by the current user.

27. TRIGGER_COLUMN_USAGE: This view identifies the columns on which triggers owned by the current user are dependent, either because of their reference in the trigger's search condition or their appearance in the SQL statement of a trigger.

28. TRIGGER_TABLE_USAGE: This view identifies the tables on which triggers owned by the current user are dependent, either because of their reference in the trigger's search condition or their appearance in the SQL statement of a trigger.

29. TRIGGERED_UPDATE_COLUMNS: This view identifies the columns that are identified in an explicit UPDATE trigger event of triggers owned by the current user.

30. VIEW_TABLE_USAGE: This view identifies the tables on which the catalog's views that are owned by the current user are dependent.

31. VIEW_COLUMN_USAGE: This view identifies the columns on which the catalog's views that are owned by the current user are dependent.

32. CONSTRAINT_TABLE_USAGE: This view identifies tables that are used by constraints—referential, unique, and assertions—and owned by the current user.

33. CONSTRAINT_COLUMN_USAGE: Similar to the view in item 20, columns are identified for the various constraints that are owned by the current user.

34. COLUMN_DOMAIN_USAGE: This view identifies columns for the catalog that are dependent on domains defined in the catalog and owned by the current user.

35. ELEMENT_TYPES: This view identifies the array element types that are accessible to the current user.

36. FIELDS: This view identifies the field types that are accessible to the current user.

37. PARAMETERS: This view identifies the SQL parameters of SQL-invoked routines for which the current user has EXECUTE privileges.

38. ROUTINES: This view identifies the SQL-invoked routines for which the current user has EXECUTE privileges.

39. ROUTINE_PRIVILEGES: This view identifies the privileges on SQL-invoked routines that are available to the current user.

VIEWS	COLLATIONS
SCHEMATA	TRANSLATIONS
DOMAINS	VIEW_TABLE_USAGE
DOMAIN_CONSTRAINTS	VIEW_COLUMN_USAGE
TABLES	CONSTRAINT_TABLE_USAGE
VIEWS	COLUMN_DOMAIN_USAGE
COLUMNS	SQL_LANGUAGES
TABLE_PRIVILEGES	
USAGE_PRIVILEGES	**DOMAINS**
TABLE_CONSTRAINTS	SQL_IDENTIFIER
REFERENTIAL_CONSTRAINTS	CHARACTER_DATA
CHECK_CONSTRAINTS	CARDINAL_NUMBER
KEY_COLUMN_USAGE	
ASSERTIONS	**ASSERTION**
CHARACTER_SETS	INFORMATION_SCHEMA_CATALOG_NAME_ CARDINALITY

Figure 22-2   Summary of INFORMATION_SCHEMA

40. `ROUTINE_COLUMN_USAGE`: This view identifies the columns owned by the current user on which SQL-invoked routines are dependent.

41. `ROUTINE_TABLE_USAGE`: This view identifies the tables owned by the current user on which SQL-invoked routines are dependent.

42. `SQL_FEATURES`: This lists the features and subfeatures of SQL:1999 and indicates which are supported by the implementation.

43. `SQL_IMPLEMENTATION_INFO`: This view lists the implementation information items defined by SQL:1999 and indicates for each one the value supported by the implementation.

44. `SQL_PACKAGES`: This view lists the packages of SQL:1999 and indicates which ones the implementation supports.

45. `SQL_SIZING`: This view lists the sizing items defined by SQL:1999 and indicates for each one the value supported by the implementation.

46. `SQL_SIZING_PROFILES`: This view lists the sizing items defined by SQL:1999 and indicates for each one the value required by a specific profile of SQL:1999.

47. SQL_LANGUAGES: This view identifies the conformance levels, options, and dialects supported by a given SQL implementation. Earlier, we showed you the base table definition for SQL_LANGUAGES. Let's take a look at the view definition defined on top of that base table.

```
CREATE VIEW SQL_LANGUAGES AS
    SELECT SQL_LANGUAGE_SOURCE, SQL_LANGUAGE_YEAR,
           SQL_LANGUAGE_CONFORMANCE, SQL_LANGUAGE_INTEGRITY,
           SQL_LANGUAGE_IMPLEMENTATION, SQL_LANGUAGE_BINDING_STYLE,
           SQL_LANGUAGE_PROGRAMMING_LANGUAGE
    FROM DEFINITION_SCHEMA.SQL_LANGUAGES
```

22.10 | Short-Name Views

In section 14.2.1, subsection "User Identifiers," we told you that SQL:1999 provides for identifiers (that is, names) up to 128 characters in length. We also told you that Core SQL:1999 only requires that implementations support identifiers with a maximum of 18 characters.

As you will have seen earlier in this chapter, the INFORMATION_SCHEMA contains views whose names exceed 18 characters in length, which leads to an interesting dilemma: how can a Core SQL implementation support Information Schema views whose names exceed 18 characters?

The answer is probably rather obvious, but it is also controversial among those members of the SQL standards community most interested in persuading vendors to provide advanced conformance capabilities in their products. A second set of views was defined in the Information Schema, one for each "primary" view whose view name exceeded 18 characters or any of whose select-list columns had names exceeding 18 characters. This second set of views is called *short-name views* because it contains views whose names—and the names of whose select-list columns—never exceed 18 characters. Table 22-4 contains the names of all of SQL:1999's short-name views (including those relevant only to Volume 2 of this book). You will quickly see a couple of patterns in the view names. If the view name doesn't exceed 16 characters (that is, 18 – 2), then it's kept as is with "_S" appended. If the view name does exceed 16 characters, then portions of the name are abbreviated, and specific abbreviations are always used (e.g., COL for COLUMN).

Table 22-4 *Short-Name Views*

Short-Name View	Corresponding View
CATALOG_NAME	INFORMATION_SCHEMA_CATALOG_NAME
ADMIN_ROLE_AUTHS	ADMINISTRABLE_ROLE_AUTHORIZATIONS
ATTRIBUTES_S	ATTRIBUTES
CHARACTER_SETS_S	CHARACTER_SETS
COLLATIONS_S	COLLATIONS
COL_DOMAIN_USAGE	COLUMN_DOMAIN_USAGE
COLUMNS_S	COLUMNS
CONSTR_COL_USAGE	CONSTRAINT_COLUMN_USAGE
CONSTR_TABLE_USAGE	CONSTRAINT_TABLE_USAGE
DOMAINS_S	DOMAINS
ELEMENT_TYPES_S	ELEMENT_TYPES
FIELDS_S	FIELDS
METHOD_SPECS	METHOD_SPECIFICATIONS
METHOD_SPEC_PARAMS	METHOD_SPECIFICATION_PARAMETERS
PARAMETERS_S	PARAMETERS
REFERENCED_TYPES_S	REFERENCED_TYPES
REF_CONSTRAINTS	REFERENTIAL_CONSTRAINTS
ROLE_ROUT_GRANTS	ROLE_ROUTINE_GRANTS
ROL_TAB_METH_GRANTS	ROLE_TABLE_METHOD_GRANTS
ROUTINE_COL_USAGE	ROUTINE_COLUMN_USAGE
ROUT_TABLE_USAGE	ROUTINE_TABLE_USAGE
ROUTINES_S	ROUTINES
SCHEMATA_S	SCHEMATA
SQL_IMPL_INFO	SQL_IMPLEMENTATION_INFO
SQL_SIZING_PROFS	SQL_SIZING_PROFILES
SQL_LANGUAGES_S	SQL_LANGUAGES
TABLE_METHOD_PRIVS	TABLE_METHOD_PRIVILEGES
TABLES_S	TABLES
TRANSLATIONS_S	TRANSLATIONS
TRIG_UPDATE_COLS	TRIGGERED_UPDATE_COLUMNS
TRIG_COLUMN_USAGE	TRIGGER_COLUMN_USAGE
TRIG_TABLE_USAGE	TRIGGER_TABLE_USAGE
TRIGGERS_S	TRIGGERS
UDT_S	USER_DEFINED_TYPES

You might be interested to see just how one of these short-name views is defined, so we've included Example 22-1 to satisfy your curiosity.

Example 22-1 *The TABLES_S Short-Name View*

```
CREATE VIEW TABLES_S
  ( TABLE_CATALOG, TABLE_SCHEMA,    TABLE_NAME,
    TABLE_TYPE,    SELF_REF_COLUMN, REF_GENERATION,
    UDT_CATALOG,   UDT_SCHEMA,      UDT_NAME ) AS
  SELECT TABLE_CATALOG, TABLE_SCHEMA, TABLE_NAME,
         TABLE_TYPE, SELF_REFERENCING_COLUMN, REFERENCE_GENERATION,
         USER_DEFINED_TYPE_CATALOG, USER_DEFINED_TYPE_SCHEMA,
         USER_DEFINED_TYPE_NAME
  FROM INFORMATION_SCHEMA.TABLES;
```

22.11 | Chapter Summary

We've spent some time discussing the INFORMATION_SCHEMA for several reasons. First, if you are developing system programs using an SQL DBMS, you will likely find yourself with the need to access metadata. It's important that you understand not only how SQL manages metadata, but also how your own particular environment's dictionary, repository, or other metadata storage mechanism handles metadata.

Second, as we mentioned earlier, the base table and view definitions themselves provide a learning tool about SQL:1999. Think of a metadata management environment as a more or less complete subsystem. There are defined functions and missions of that subsystem. By looking at base table definitions and, more importantly, the views created on top of those tables, the "what do I have to do" aspect of table creation starts to become somewhat second nature. As you create your own tables, you will find yourself instinctively thinking questions such as, "What constraints do I have to apply to this table or view to make it useful?" and "What accessibility should this view have?"

In the final chapter, we'll discuss some of the anticipated characteristics and features of future versions of SQL. Stay tuned.

Chapter

23

A Look to the Future

Introduction

Now that we've examined most of the contents of SQL:1999 in detail, you may be wondering what the future of SQL is likely to bring. In this chapter, we take a brief look at the progress currently being made to develop the next generation of the language.

The standardization process makes it impossible to predict exactly what the future of the standard will be, but we can make some fairly reasonable guesses based on our participation in the various committees that are involved in this effort. Work has been in progress on the next generation of the SQL standard, which has the working title SQL:200n, for several months (at publication), so it's really far too soon to be certain what will and what will not become part of the next SQL standard. The name "SQL:200n" was chosen to help encourage republication of the standard in about three or four years after SQL:1999 (thus avoiding the extremely long seven-year cycle between SQL-92 and SQL:1999). In other words, the standards organizations have a goal of becoming more schedule-driven and less feature-driven.

SQL:200*n* Overview

It appears that SQL:200*n* will have three primary foci: correcting a fairly large number of errata, enhanced relational capabilities, and support for the object paradigm. Let's look at these separately. Please keep in mind that this discussion reflects the current work on SQL:200*n* at the time of publication, but that significant changes may be made (indeed, are quite likely for some features) before SQL:200*n* becomes a standard. We also want to warn you that our predictions for SQL:200*n* are less confident (in spite of the relatively short time between SQL:1999's publication and the expected publication of SQL:200*n*) than we would like. We think that the SQL:1999 development effort was so intense, and took so long, that a fatigue factor is having an effect on the people who will have to do the design work for SQL:200*n*. Another factor is that the vendor community must first focus on implementing SQL:1999, and the user community must evaluate its requirements for the next generation.

23.2.1 New Data Types

One of the most significant additions being considered for SQL:200*n* (at least in terms of the amount of text in the documents that will have to be changed and/or inserted) is a group of additional collection data types.

You learned in Section 2.4.8, "Collection (or Array) Types," that SQL:1999 has a single collection type: ARRAY. While most participants in the SQL standardization process believe that ARRAY is powerful enough to address a wide range of application requirements, it is also felt that there are other application demands that are not met by ARRAY. It seems quite likely that other collection types will be added in SQL:200*n*, possibly including SET, MULTISET (sometimes called *bag*), and perhaps even LIST.

As database products respond to market requirements that SQL and XML (eXtended Markup Language) be used together, the inability for SQL to effectively model XML document contents will become a liability. The nature of XML is that it is a language for building *tree* structures; in fact, XML documents are treated as tree structures by XML itself. Trees are, of course, collections of other trees and of atomic values. Therefore, in order for SQL to reasonably model—that is, capture, process, and store—XML documents in a reasonable way, SQL must have powerful and flexible collection capabilities. In fact, nested collections (such as SETs of MULTISETs of ARRAYs) are likely to be found to have significant uses and will be supported in SQL:200*n*.

23.2.2 Enhancements to Triggers

As you learned in Chapter 11, "Active Databases," triggers in SQL:1999 can be associated only with base tables—that is, only INSERT, UPDATE, and DELETE operations on base tables can cause triggers to be fired.

As SQL's view update capabilities improve (see section 9.3, "Functional Dependencies: Rules for Updatability"), database administrators will start defining views that will be manipulated by applications more than the underlying base tables. When this starts happening, the distinction between views and base tables will begin to blur, and we think it's going to be more and more useful to allow users to define triggers that are associated with views.

We have heard some SQL standardization participants state their desire to add to SQL:200*n* the capability of defining triggers that are associated with views, and we believe that several SQL vendors will be willing to participate in the effort to do so.

23.2.3 SQL-Invoked Routines

In SQL:1999, it is not possible for SQL-invoked routines to return a value whose data type is more complex than a user-defined type, an ARRAY type, or a ROW type.

In particular, routines cannot return *tables* to their invokers. While returning a table to a host application obviously has significant difficulties associated with it, returning a table to SQL code as (for example) the result of a function should pose no major problems.

We think it modestly likely that the ability to return a table (possibly in the form of a MULTISET of ROWs) as the value of a function will be added to SQL:200*n*.

23.2.4 Improved Security Features

In section 12.6.1, "Some Additional Information about Privileges," we told you about *invoker's rights* and *definer's rights* and about the value that each approach offers. In section 17.3.3, "How—and Why—to Store SQL-Invoked Routines," you learned that SQL's stored routines written in SQL (schema-level routines, in particular) are always definer's rights routines in SQL:1999.

However, the architects of SQL/PSM recognize the value of invoker's rights routines and have indicated plans to add that capability to schema-level routines in SQL:200*n*. We believe that the proposals to allow schema-level routines to execute using the rights of the invoker's authorization identifier (or perhaps the roles granted to that authID) will be controversial and may not succeed. A few SQL vendors' products do not support the notion of invoker's rights, and it may be difficult to persuade those vendors' representatives to the SQL standards process that enough benefit will arise from providing a standard for the facility. As with all other predictions, time will tell.

23.2.5 Object Capabilities

SQL:1999's support for user-defined types and the object paradigm is discussed extensively in Volume 2 of this book, but we felt that the interests of completeness demanded that we mention here a likely SQL:200n enhancement in this technology.

The SQL:1999 model of subtyping (that is, of inheritance) is a single-inheritance model, which was more than a little controversial during its development: several participants asserted the need for a multiple-inheritance capability to address certain types of applications. However, the implementation difficulties associated with multiple inheritance are known to be severe, especially in a persistent-metadata environment like SQL, particularly when the possibility of data distribution exists. Therefore, the single-inheritance model carried the day. Nonetheless, the knowledge remains that some applications can be adequately addressed only with the use of multiple inheritance.

Happily, a path forward is available, a path that provides (at least) most of the advantages of multiple inheritance without the implementation difficulties associated with it. The Java programming language, with which many of our readers will be familiar, clearly distinguishes between *implementation* and *interface*. (In brief summary: *implementation* includes actual stored data of user-defined types and the code associated with methods that operate on instances of the types; by contrast, *interface* is nothing more than the signatures of the methods themselves.)

Java provides for single inheritance of implementation, but multiple inheritance of interface. Most participants in the SQL standards process believe that following the example of Java will give SQL programmers (at least most of) the advantages of multiple inheritance without imposing on the vendors the rather significant implementation burdens usually associated with multiple inheritance.

We predict that adding this capability to SQL will be a high priority as SQL:200n is developed.

23.3 | XML and SQL

As XML continues to capture the attention of the business world, it has become obvious to many observers that SQL and XML must interoperate as closely as possible. After all, a tremendous and ever increasing amount of the world's business data is stored in SQL database systems, while XML is rapidly becoming the lingua franca of the Web and a vital tool for exchanging data between applications that are otherwise unaware of each other.

Many of our readers will know that the World-Wide Web Consortium (W3C) develops standards (called "Recommendations" by the W3C) for and related to XML, and that one such standard is a language (currently being called "XQuery") for querying XML documents and collections of such documents. The emergence of XQuery will make it possible for applications to retrieve documents based on their contents, just as SQL makes it possible to retrieve data based on values stored in rows of tables. XQuery will not eliminate the need for SQL, since XQuery's focus is XML-encoded documents, while SQL retains its object-relational emphasis. However, the user community will find increasing requirements to manage document-oriented data and object-relational data in a single application. Those of us involved in SQL's standardization are actively pursuing the ability to intermingle SQL and XML facilities in applications.

At the time these words are being written, work is just beginning in the SQL standards arena on a new part of the SQL standard, called SQL/XML. This document is planned to contain specifications related to the interactions between the two languages. It is far too soon to predict exactly what will be published in even the first version of SQL/XML, never mind subsequent versions, but we think you'll benefit from knowing some of the possibilities that have been discussed.

- Mapping (in both directions) between SQL data types and XML data types, as well as between SQL data values and XML values.

- Mapping (in both directions) between SQL identifiers and XML names.

- Inclusion of XPath (a W3C language used for locating XML documents and identifying specific locations within those documents) as part of SQL queries to aid in managing XML data stored in SQL databases.

- An SQL-based syntax for querying (repositories of) XML documents.

- XML syntax corresponding to (probably limited) SQL statements and components.

The first version of SQL/XML may be published as early as late 2001 or early 2002 (thus making it technically part of SQL:1999), with a subsequent version entering development immediately.

23.4 | Chapter Summary

Standards evolve over time. While there is no way to know exactly what features and aspects will wind up in SQL:200n a couple of years from now, this chapter gives you a few clues. We do *not*, however, believe that any of our predictions are so assured, especially not in any detail, that you should take the risks now to start designing applications that use the features we're predicting will appear in SQL:200n. The amount of time that the SQL standards folks have allowed for the development of this next generation of the language is pretty short—only three years or so—and it is becoming increasingly difficult to add new features (probably because most "easy" features have been considered and either adopted or deliberately excluded).

Again, remember that certain DBMS products may jump the gun and introduce tentative SQL:200n features into their products. While this may give you a head start with these features, keep in mind that syntax, behavior, and other aspects may vary from those eventually adopted into the next iteration of the standard. In these cases, the usual good programming practices—specifically, isolation and modularization of system-specific features, documentation, and the like—will help ease any subsequent transformations that you must make.

Appendix A

Designing SQL:1999 Databases

A.1 | Introduction

In Appendix A of the previous edition of this book,[1] we presented a brief, fairly standard discourse about the state of the art of database design at that time. Well, a lot has changed in the (almost) decade since that book was published with regard to designing SQL databases. Perhaps the most significant change that occurred during the 1990s in this area was the advent of *data warehousing* for purposes of reporting, data analysis, and other types of *informational* database usage (as contrasted with transactional database usage).

Therefore, we feel it's important to take a totally fresh look at the topic of designing SQL:1999 databases, encompassing both transactional and informational environments and discussing both the similarities and differences between the two. Additionally, as we'll discuss shortly, some of the feature enhancements to SQL:1999 (as compared with SQL-92) have opened up new possibilities in how your SQL databases are implemented, and this has also impacted some of the database design steps and processes you should perform.

---

1   J. Melton and A. Simon, *Understanding the New SQL: A Complete Guide* (San Francisco: Morgan Kaufmann Publishers, 1992), Appendix A.

A.2 | Overview of Database Design

The classical approach to database design is illustrated in Figure A-1. *Conceptual* database design—that is, concentrating on information concepts and the semantics of the proposed contents of your database, rather than worrying about implementation details or performance—should be the first set of activities you accomplish. A technique such as *entity-relationship modeling* (see Figure A-2) is used to help keep you focused at the conceptual level.

This is then followed by *logical* database design, in which you map your conceptual database model into a sort of "product-neutral" design in which the general, high-level rules and structures of your database management system begin to come into play. In the case of a traditional SQL database, your conceptual model's constructs (e.g., entities, attributes, and relationships) are mapped into tables, columns, and, to represent relationships, some basic primary and foreign key constraints.

Finally, the logical model is "physicalized" to take advantage of the capabilities and strengths (and to avoid the weaknesses of) your specific DBMS product. This *physical design* (or *implementation-specific design*) is the design model from which your database schema is actually generated.[2]

Let's take a look at the mapping from a conceptual model to a logical model as an example of how SQL:1999 features have changed the face of database design. Figure A-3 illustrates a segment of a conceptual database model, one that contains a *multivalued attribute* within the design. A multivalued attribute is just what it sounds like: an attribute that can have more than one underlying data value in an instance (e.g., a row in a relational database), as contrasted with an "ordinary" attribute that has only one underlying data value. A simple example commonly used to explain a multivalued attribute is the one illustrated here: a person who has more than one telephone number. (Contrast this with the other attributes illustrated in Figure A-3, such as a person having only one social security number, name, address, city, state, and zip code.)

While the concept of a multivalued attribute is a powerful one in terms of being able to accurately represent the "real world," multivalued attributes have long been a thorn in the side of relational database designers and modelers. Why? Because a multivalued attribute is a direct violation of the relational

---

2   We realize that a scant three paragraphs is woefully inadequate with respect to discussing database design; this brief discussion is intended primarily as "context setting" material for experienced database professionals as an introduction for the rest of Appendix A. Readers who are less experienced in the practice and concepts of database design are directed to a text such as Toby J. Teorey, *Database Modeling and Design: The Entity-Relationship Approach* (San Francisco: Morgan Kaufmann Publishers, 1990), for a much more complete discussion that is beyond our scope here.

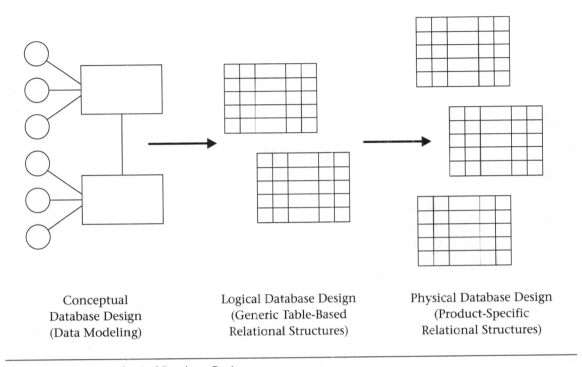

| Conceptual Database Design (Data Modeling) | Logical Database Design (Generic Table-Based Relational Structures) | Physical Database Design (Product-Specific Relational Structures) |

Figure A-1   Steps in Classical Database Design

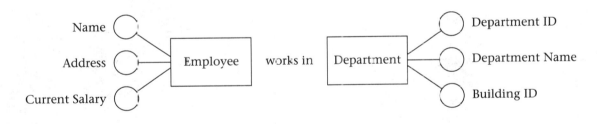

Figure A-2   Entity-Relationship Conceptual Database Modeling

model's first normal form rule ("no repeating groups"; see section 1.2.3, subsection "Normal Forms") and therefore cannot be represented in the "pure" relational model. The classical approach to representing multivalued attributes within the relational model is to do something like that shown in Figure A-4 when mapping your conceptual model to a logical model: create another table that can be joined via the same primary key (social security number in this example) to its "parent table" when you want to "reconstruct" the semantics of your conceptual model entity (e.g., PERSON).

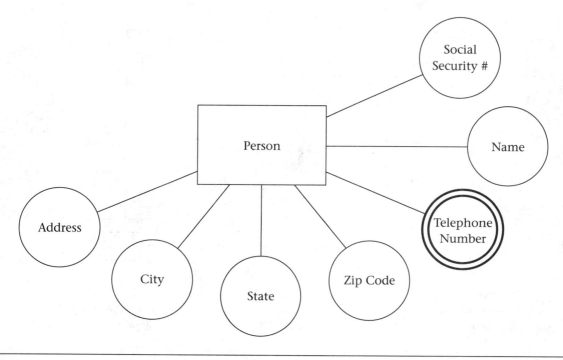

Figure A-3   Multivalued Attribute as Part of a Database Design

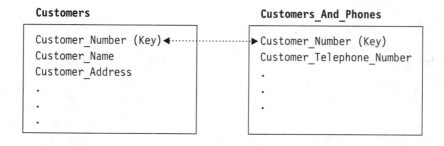

Figure A-4   Mapping a Conceptual Multivalued Attribute to a Logical Relational Model

However, with SQL:1999, we now have an ARRAY data type. While relational model purists might cringe at the idea of arrays as a violation of first normal form of the relational model, the reality is that real-world applications can greatly benefit from this construct and, with its inclusion in the SQL:1999 standard, it's here to stay. (In point of fact, several relational model purists we know have said that they have no objection to the inclusion of an ARRAY type in SQL, since it can be treated as a single data item—that is, a single ARRAY—for relational modeling purposes.)

And that means that the conceptual-to-logical mapping shown in Figure A-3 and Figure A-4 to "get around" multivalued attributes is no longer necessary, and indeed the construct of a multivalued attribute can be carried all the way through to the physical (or implementation-specific) database design that will eventually be instantiated in the RDBMS's schema. Thus, one of the most significant (even if not necessarily problematic) database design challenges of the relational era, one that results in *semantic loss* in the physical database as compared with the originating conceptual model, is no longer an issue and, indeed, should now be handled in a different manner.[3]

A.3 | Impact of Data Warehousing on Designing SQL:1999 Databases

The discussion in section A.2 is applicable to transactionally oriented databases, but as discussed at the outset of this appendix, the advent of informational-oriented databases through data warehousing has caused complications, or at least challenges, in relational database design.

Consider for a moment the following brief history of relational databases. Unlike earlier approaches to database management such as hierarchical and network models (as was briefly discussed in Chapter 1, "Introduction to SQL:1999"), which contained physical pointers linking pieces of data with one another, relational databases relied on the query planning and optimization capabilities of their respective DBMS products to determine the most appropriate and efficient paths and mechanisms to traverse through a database's contents.

Basically, it took about 15 years from the earliest days of relational database research in the 1970s until the late 1980s until relational databases were considered "ready for prime time" in terms of acceptable high-performance throughput in real-world, mission-critical transactions. All this time, the query planning, optimization, and transaction management facilities of commercial RDBMS products continually got "smarter" to the point where transactionally focused execution *that typically involved only a single table or a small number of tables within the database* could execute quickly and efficiently. (This focus is widely known as OLTP, or On-Line Transaction Processing.)

---

3 Some database design tool products, recognizing the dominance of relational databases, prohibit the creation of multivalued attributes, instead forcing the database designer to create constructs such as those shown in Figure A-4 from the outset of the design process. It is hoped that tools with that particular limitation will evolve to include multivalued attributes within their repertoire of design constructs to better map to modern RDBMS capabilities and features.

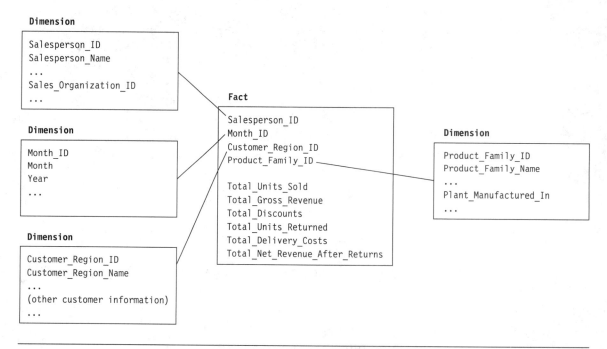

Figure A-5   A Simple Data Warehouse Structure with Fact and Dimension Tables

But then, in the early 1990s, along came the idea of data warehousing, or creating database structures oriented toward reporting and analysis that had to be radically different from those used for transactional purposes. Instead of normalized or "lightly denormalized" database structures, data warehouses were typically structured around heavily denormalized *fact tables* and *dimension tables*, as illustrated in Figure A-5.

While data warehouse database structures such as those illustrated in Figure A-5 tend to be easy to understand and have a high degree of synergy with how the underlying data will be analyzed and used for analytically oriented business functions, significant problems were created for relational DBMSs with regard to these highly denormalized structures and the need to perform many complex JOIN operations that often involve five, six, seven, or more tables. The problem wasn't in the tools' ability to generate the SQL to perform these JOIN operations, but rather in the underlying infrastructure facilities of the DBMSs themselves (e.g., the query optimizers and planners) that had, after years, finally been successfully tuned for the structures of transactionally oriented databases.

Typically, data warehouse users don't execute SQL statements directly, but instead use a graphically oriented tool for querying, reporting, and analysis.

Early generations of these tools usually interpreted the database request that the user specified using the tool's graphical interface and then simply generated the most complex, multitable SQL JOIN operation possible, which usually resulted in abysmal performance when large volumes of data (typical in a data warehouse containing historical data for analysis and trending) were present in the database. What would often happen is that the DBMS's query planning facility would look at the number of tables involved in the query and, unable to confidently create an efficient query plan, would do the electronic equivalent of throwing its hands up in the air, saying, "I have no idea!," and create a Cartesian product from the underlying data of all the tables, requiring enormous amounts of disk and main memory space, and time, to execute the desired SQL statement.

Subsequent generations of tools, recognizing the performance limitation described above, took a different approach. Instead of creating a single SQL statement that would likely execute very inefficiently, query planners *within the tools themselves* (not the underlying DBMS) would decompose the data access plan into a *series* of SQL statements that would create and use temporary tables to store partial results from pieces of the overall query, thus limiting the amounts of data needed for various portions of the overall query.

By the mid-1990s, however, the leading relational DBMS vendors took notice of the tremendous growth in informationally focused data warehousing environments and began focusing their product engineering efforts on more efficient query execution of dimensionally structured databases requiring many tables to participate in a join. Though different product vendors have taken different approaches, most have incorporated some form of a *star join* operation, which first appeared commercially in Red Brick's (now part of Informix Corporation) data warehouse–oriented relational DBMS product in the early 1990s.

Why is this important for you to understand? The steps you take in designing your SQL:1999 database *will* vary depending on whether you're designing and implementing an informational database (e.g., a data warehouse) or a transactional one. In the case of a transactional database, you will likely follow the same sequence of activities that you would have 10, 15, or 20 years ago, beginning with an entity-relationship conceptual model (or a semantically equivalent model using a different technique, such as binary-relationship modeling) that evolves to a logical relational model and then, as we'll discuss in section A.4, a physical database design. Alternatively, if your intention is to design and build a data warehouse, then you should *not* proceed with traditional database design and modeling steps (as was discussed in section A.2); instead, you need to focus your efforts on a more dimensionally oriented approach to database design, following the best practices from that discipline.

A.4 | Physical Database Design

To this point in the relational database design process—that is, during conceptual and logical design—the steps you accomplish will be product-independent. That is, whether your underlying SQL DBMS product comes from Oracle, IBM, Microsoft, or some other vendor, we *strongly* recommend that you do conceptually focused data modeling during the conceptual design phase, and then logical (i.e., product-independent) relational modeling during the logical phase, as indicated by the titles of those respective design phases. The tasks you accomplish during these first two phases will vary little, if at all, depending on your underlying DBMS.

At some point, though, there must be a translation from product-independent models into something that can actually be implemented, a translation that (1) takes advantage of the features and capabilities of the specific DBMS product you're using, and (2) at the same time avoids problematic aspects (e.g., known performance problems) of your DBMS product.

This physical—or implementation-specific, as we noted earlier—design actually has two different levels upon which you will need to focus your energies. First, there is (for lack of a better term) the *logical* SQL level. That is, you will take advantage of nonstandard SQL language extensions provided by your DBMS: additional constraints, enhanced GRANT/REVOKE security, and so on. You would also, as necessary and if applicable, take specific aspects of your logical design and, should your planned application have complexities that are *not* supported within basic SQL:1999 or within your product's extensions, design workarounds.

Two common pre-SQL:1999 examples with which you might be familiar are as follows:

- Specifying a Boolean data type if your DBMS supported that construct for Yes/No or True/False columns (recall that SQL-92 and earlier versions of the SQL language didn't have a Boolean data type)

- Specifying triggers (through a CREATE TRIGGER statement) and their relationship to product-specific stored procedures

The second part of your implementation-specific design might be termed the *physical* SQL level. Here, you would use product-specific SQL statements that are provided as a mechanism for you to specify as much as you possibly can about the physical storage of data within your database, as well as planned (or preplanned) access patterns. Perhaps the most familiar portion to most readers is the ever-popular CREATE INDEX statement through which you would create physical indices on one or more columns in a table (and, in most products, the ability to specify a particular type of index, such as a B-tree or bit-mapped index). Another example includes statements such as CREATE TABLESPACE.

A.5 | Use of CASE and Data Modeling Tools

Ideally, you should use some type of computer-aided software engineering (CASE) or data modeling–specific tool as the online mechanism through which you would perform your conceptual and logical database modeling (whether transactional or informational/data warehouse), and then generate the product-specific SQL through which your database will actually be implemented. Our thoughts about the necessity of using a tool have changed somewhat from a decade ago, though, given what has happened (or, more accurately, what has *not* happened) within the CASE tool arena.

In the mid- and late 1980s and into the early 1990s, the operating premise within the software development world was that some type of overall CASE framework would provide full life-cycle support (conceptual modeling through implementation-specific design and code generation), not only for initial development but also for subsequent system maintenance and enhancement. The reality is that, for reasons too numerous to discuss, CASE technology and its use never came close to approaching the whole life-cycle support described above, and for the most part, data modeling tools have been used primarily as a vehicle through which an initial database design can be graphically drawn with some degree of semantics enforcement (e.g., the cardinality of relationships between two entities), but then, following initial database generation and population, the modeling-implementation relationship would break down and the machine-readable design would be frozen in time as representative of the initial state of the database, and nothing more.

Our belief these days is that data modeling tool usage should be very much a matter of personal preference. Some database designers love to use data modeling–specific tools, while others (and one of the authors, Mr. Simon, admits to belonging to this latter category) prefer using a graphical drawing package such as Microsoft PowerPoint or Visio that does *not* contain any underlying semantics or rules enforcement.

So it's your call. If you have a preferred CASE or data modeling tool, then by all means use it to design your SQL:1999 databases. If, however, you find these products to be more cumbersome than helpful, then a simple drawing package—or even pencil and paper, for that matter—may well be the tools you use instead.

But either way, CASE or not, the best practices discussed briefly in this appendix should guide the actual steps and tasks you perform as you navigate your way from the earliest, most conceptual stages of database modeling to the actual physical design choices you make with the product in which your SQL:1999 database will be implemented.

A.6 | Appendix Summary

There are many, many texts that discuss data modeling and database design, both for transactional as well as for informational (e.g., data warehouses) databases. The very brief discussion we've provided in this appendix is only intended as an "advanced introduction" for those readers who have not had a great deal of experience designing real-world databases and applications, and our objective was to briefly walk you through two major topics: (1) the flow from conceptual to logical to physical design, focusing on a specific new feature of SQL:1999 (ARRAY data types) as an example of how the rules of this process are now changing, and (2) the importance of understanding whether your database will be transactional or informational in nature, as the design constructs and guidelines you use will vary between these two different types of database usage.

Appendix

B

An SQL:1999 Application Example

B.1 Introduction

In this appendix we present an application example of an SQL:1999-based information system, built around the video and music sales model that we've used throughout this book. Many real-life systems can be built around the sample queries and other facets included in this example. Most information systems share many of the same characteristics: data must be entered, modified, and removed; queries must be processed against the database; and so on. Even though you may not operate a retail video and music Web site or retail store, the example in this appendix may be used as a reference around which you can design and develop your own customized information systems.

B.2 The Schema Definition

The following schema definition creates the application schema and the domains that are used throughout.

```
CREATE SCHEMA video_and_music
    AUTHORIZATION m_s_enterprises
    DEFAULT CHARACTER SET "Latin-1"

-- The definition of the schema for the company includes definitions
--   of base tables, views, privileges, referential constraints,
--   integrity constraints, assertions, and domains.
-- Next, we create the base tables required for the application.


CREATE TABLE movie_titles (
    title                       CHARACTER ( 30 )
        CONSTRAINT movie_titles_title_not_null NOT NULL,
    year_released               DATE,
    our_tape_cost               DECIMAL ( 5,2 ),
    our_dvd_cost                DECIMAL ( 5,2 ),
    regular_tape_sale_price     DECIMAL ( 5,2 ),
    current_tape_sale_price     DECIMAL ( 5,2 ),
    regular_dvd_sale_price      DECIMAL ( 5,2 ),
    current_dvd_sale_price      DECIMAL ( 5,2 ),
    part_of_series              CHARACTER ( 3 ),
    movie_type                  CHARACTER ( 10 ),
    tapes_owned                 INTEGER,
    dvds_owned                  INTEGER,
    tapes_in_stock              INTEGER,
    dvds_in_stock               INTEGER,
    total_tape_units_sold       INTEGER,
    total_dvd_units_sold        INTEGER,
    total_tape_sales_revenue    DECIMAL ( 9,2 ),
    total_dvd_sales_revenue     DECIMAL ( 9,2 ),
    CONSTRAINT movie_titles_primary_key
    PRIMARY KEY ( title, year_released )
) ;

CREATE TABLE movies_stars (
    movie_title                 CHARACTER ( 30 ),
        CONSTRAINT movies_stars_movie_title_not_null NOT NULL,
    year_released               DATE,
    actor_last_name             CHARACTER ( 35 ),
        CONSTRAINT movies_stars_actor_last_name_not_null NOT NULL,
    actor_first_name            CHARACTER ( 25 ),
```

```
        actor_middle_name           CHARACTER ( 25 ),
        CONSTRAINT movies_stars_unique
            UNIQUE ( movie_title, actor_last_name, actor_first_name
                        actor_middle_name )
                NOT DEFERRABLE,
        CONSTRAINT movies_stars_fk_movie_titles
            FOREIGN KEY ( movie_title, year_released )
                REFERENCES movie_titles ( movies, year_released )
                    ON DELETE CASCADE
                    ON UPDATE CASCADE
) ;

CREATE TABLE music_titles (
    music_id                    CHARACTER ( 12 )
        CONSTRAINT music_titles_music_id_not_null NOT NULL,
    title                       CHARACTER ( 30 )
        CONSTRAINT music_titles_title_not_null NOT NULL,
    artist                      CHARACTER ( 40 ),
    artist_more                 CHARACTER ( 50 ),
    record_label                CHARACTER ( 20 ),
    type                        CHARACTER ( 10 ),
    greatest_hits_collection    BOOLEAN,
    category                    CHARACTER ( 10 ),
    date_released               DATE,
    cd_list_price               DECIMAL ( 9, 2 ),
    cd_current_price            DECIMAL ( 9, 2 ),
    cassette_list_price         DECIMAL ( 9, 2 ),
    cassette_current_price      DECIMAL ( 9, 2 )
) ;

CREATE TABLE music_distributors (
    distributor_id              CHARACTER ( 15 )
        CONSTRAINT music_distributors_distributor_id_not_null NOT NULL,
    distributor_name            CHARACTER ( 25 )
        CONSTRAINT music_distributors_distributor_name_not_null NOT NULL,
    distributor_address         CHARACTER ( 40 ),
    distributor_city            CHARACTER ( 30 ),
    distributor_state           CHARACTER ( 2 ),
    distributor_zip_code_full   CHARACTER ( 10 ),
    distributor_phone_1         CHARACTER ( 10 ),
    distributor_phone_2         CHARACTER ( 10 ),
```

```
    distributor_fax_number_1     CHARACTER ( 10 ),
    distributor_fax_number_2     CHARACTER ( 10 ),
    distributor_web_site_addr    CHARACTER ( 40 )
) ;

CREATE TABLE music_inventory (
    music_id                     CHARACTER ( 12 )
      CONSTRAINT music_inventory_music_id NOT NULL,
    number_cd_now_in_stock       INTEGER,
    number_cassette_now_in_stock INTEGER,
    total_cd_sold                INTEGER,
    total_cassette_sold          INTEGER,
    total_cd_returned            INTEGER,
    total_cassette_returned      INTEGER
) ;


CREATE TABLE current_distributor_costs (
    music_id                     CHARACTER ( 12 )
      CONSTRAINT current_distributor_costs_music_id_not_null NOT NULL,
    distributor_id               CHARACTER ( 15 )
      CONSTRAINT current_distributor_costs_distributor_id_not_null
        NOT NULL,
    our_cd_cost                  DECIMAL ( 9, 2 ),
    our_cassette_cost            DECIMAL ( 9, 2 )
) ;

CREATE TABLE customers (
    cust_last_name               CHARACTER ( 35 )
        CONSTRAINT customers_cust_last_name_not_null NOT NULL,
    cust_first_name              name
        CONSTRAINT customers_cust_first_name_not_null NOT NULL,
    cust_address                 CHARACTER VARYING ( 30 ),
    cust_city                    CHARACTER VARYING ( 15 ),
    cust_state                   CHARACTER ( 2 ),
    cust_zip                     CHARACTER VARYING ( 9 ),
    cust_phone                   CHARACTER ( 10 ),
    cust_fax                     CHARACTER ( 10 ),
    cust_e_mail_address          CHARACTER ( 30 ),
    cust_credit_card             CHARACTER VARYING ( 20 )
      CONSTRAINT customers_cust_credit_card_not_null NOT NULL,
```

```
    cust_current_charges     DECIMAL ( 9, 2 ),
    cust_total_charges       DECIMAL ( 10, 2 ),
    number_of_problems       SMALLINT,
    last_access              TIMESTAMP
) ;

CREATE TABLE employees (
    emp_id                   INTEGER
        CONSTRAINT employees_emp_id_pk PRIMARY KEY,
    emp_last_name            CHARACTER ( 35 ),
        CONSTRAINT employees_emp_last_name_not_null NOT NULL,
    emp_first_name           CHARACTER ( 25 ),
        CONSTRAINT employees_emp_first_name_not_null NOT NULL,
    emp_address              CHARACTER VARYING ( 30 ),
    emp_city                 CHARACTER VARYING ( 15 ),
    emp_state                CHARACTER ( 2 ),
    emp_zip                  CHARACTER VARYING ( 9 ),
    emp_phone                CHARACTER ( 10 ),
    emp_start_date           DATE,
    emp_hourly_rate          DECIMAL ( 7, 2 )
) ;

-- Third, we create a couple of views that help us manage some aspects
-- of our business.

CREATE VIEW problem_customers ( last, first, addr, city, state, email )
  AS
    SELECT cust_last_name, cust_first_name, cust_address, cust_city,
           cust_state, cust_e_mail_address
      FROM customers
WHERE number_of_problems
    > 0.8 * ( SELECT MAX ( number_of_problems )
            FROM customers)
      GROUP BY cust_zip ;

CREATE VIEW employee_customers AS
    SELECT emp_id, cust_current_charges
    FROM customers INNER JOIN employees
      ON cust_last_name = emp_last_name AND
         cust_first_name = emp_first_name AND
         cust_address = emp_address AND
```

```
            cust_city = emp_city AND
            cust_state = emp_state AND
            cust_zip = emp_zip AND
            cust_phone = emp_phone
    WHERE cust_total_charges > 1000.00 AND
            emp_hourly_rate < 5.00 ;

CREATE VIEW emp_view AS
    SELECT emp_id, emp_last_name, emp_first_name, emp_address,
            emp_city, emp_state, emp_zip, emp_phone, emp_start_date,
            emp_hourly_rate
    FROM employees
    WHERE emp_id = SESSION_USER ;

-- The next thing we do is define the various privileges required
--  by our employees, managers, auditors, etc., to do their jobs.

GRANT ALL PRIVILEGES ON names TO store_manager WITH GRANT OPTION ;

GRANT ALL PRIVILEGES ON price TO store_manager WITH GRANT OPTION ;

GRANT ALL PRIVILEGES ON revenue TO store_manager WITH GRANT OPTION ;

GRANT ALL PRIVILEGES ON movie_titles TO store_manager WITH GRANT OPTION ;

GRANT ALL PRIVILEGES ON movies_stars TO store_manager WITH GRANT OPTION ;

GRANT ALL PRIVILEGES ON music_titles TO store_manager WITH GRANT OPTION ;

GRANT ALL PRIVILEGES ON music_distributors TO store_manager WITH GRANT OPTION ;

GRANT ALL PRIVILEGES ON music_inventory TO store_manager WITH GRANT OPTION ;

GRANT ALL PRIVILEGES ON current_distributor_costs TO store_manager WITH GRANT OPTION ;

GRANT ALL PRIVILEGES ON customers TO store_manager WITH GRANT OPTION ;

GRANT ALL PRIVILEGES ON employees TO store_manager WITH GRANT OPTION ;

GRANT ALL PRIVILEGES ON problem_customers TO store_manager WITH GRANT OPTION ;

GRANT ALL PRIVILEGES ON employee_customers TO store_manager WITH GRANT OPTION ;
```

```
GRANT SELECT ( title, year_released, regular_rental_price,
               regular_tape_sale_price, current_tape_sale_price,
               regular_dvd_sale_price, current_dvd_sale_price,
               part_of_series, movie_type) ON movie_titles TO PUBLIC ;

GRANT SELECT ON movie_titles TO movie_clerk ;

GRANT UPDATE (tapes_owned, dvds_owned, tapes_in_stock, cvds_in_stock,
              total_tape_urits_sold, total_dvd_units_sold,
              total_tape_sales_revenue, total_dvd_sales_revenue)
         ON movie_titles TO movie_clerk ;

GRANT INSERT ON movie_titles TO movie_clerk ;

GRANT DELETE ON movie_titles TO movie_clerk ;

GRANT INSERT ON movies_stars TO movie_clerk ;

GRANT SELECT ON movies_stars TO PUBLIC ;

GRANT SELECT ( title, artist, artist_more, record_label, type,
               greatest_hits_collection, category, date_released,
               cd_list_price, cd_current_price, cassette_list_price,
               cassette_current_price)
         ON music_titles TO PUBLIC ;

GRANT SELECT ON music_titles TO music_clerk ;

GRANT UPDATE (number_cd_now_in_stock, number_cassette_now_in_stock,
              total_cd_sold, total_cassette_sold,
              total_cd_returned, total_cassette_returned)
         ON music_inventory TO music_clerk ;

GRANT INSERT ON music_titles TO music_clerk ;

GRANT DELETE ON music_titles TO music_clerk ;

GRANT SELECT ON song_titles TO PUBLIC ;

GRANT INSERT ON song_titles TO music_clerk ;
```

```
GRANT REFERENCES ON music_titles TO music_clerk ;

GRANT DELETE ON song_titles TO music_clerk ;

GRANT SELECT ( cust_last_name, cust_first_name, cust_address, cust_city,
               cust_state, cust_zip, cust_phone, cust_fax,
               cust_e_mail_address, cust_credit_card )
    ON customers TO register_clerk ;

GRANT UPDATE ( cust_current_charges, cust_total_charges,
               number_of_problems, last_access )
    ON customers TO register_clerk ;

GRANT INSERT ON customers TO register_clerk ;

-- Finally, we create a couple of assertions that will implement
--   rules placed on us by our bank.

CREATE ASSERTION limit_total_movie_stock_value
    CHECK ( ( SELECT SUM ( ( our_tape_cost * tapes_owned ) +
                           ( our_dvd_cost * dvds_owned ) )
              FROM movie_titles )
        < 1000000.00 ) ;

CREATE ASSERTION do_not_sell_to_many_problem_customers
    CHECK ( ( SELECT COUNT(*)
              FROM customers
              WHERE cust_total_charges > 150.00 AND
                    cust_total_charges < 1000.00 AND
                    number_of_problems > 5 )
        < 10 ) ;
```

B.3 | Application Code

The various functions that we need to perform for our video and music site can be executed in many ways. We have chosen to illustrate a few of these as SQL modules. The remainder are presented as standalone SQL statements, and the binding of these SQL statements to application programs is left as an exercise for you to perform.

There is no attempt to present the application code in any sequence that may conform to the order in which operations are performed during a business day in the store. Instead, we have attempted to group SQL statements according to their function, with related operations grouped together. This is closer to how you would write a real application system.

B.3.1 Data Input

```
MODULE data_input
    NAMES ARE "Latin-1"
    LANGUAGE COBOL
    SCHEMA video_and_music


-- By not specifying AUTHORIZATION, we're requiring that the authID
--  of the user executing the procedures in the module be the one used
--  for privilege checking.


-- Insert a new movie title into MOVIE_TITLES and star information into
-- MOVIES_STARS.


-- First, insert into MOVIE_TITLES

PROCEDURE insert_movie_titles
    ( SQLSTATE,
        :title                      CHARACTER (50),
        :year                       CHARACTER (10),
        :our_tape_cost              DECIMAL (5,2),
        :our_dvd_cost               DECIMAL (5,2),
        :reg_tape_sale_price        DECIMAL (5,2),
        :current_tape_sale_price    DECIMAL (5,2),
        :reg_dvd_sale_price         DECIMAL (5,2),
        :current_dvd_sale_price     DECIMAL (5,2),
        :part_of_series             CHARACTER (3),
        :ser_ind                    INTEGER,
        :movie_type                 CHARACTER (10),
        :tapes_owned                INTEGER,
        :dvds_owned                 INTEGER,
        :tapes_in_stock             INTEGER,
        :dvds_in_stock              INTEGER );
```

```
INSERT INTO movie_titles
    VALUES (:title, CAST(:year AS DATE), :our_tape_cost,
            :our_dvd_cost, :reg_tape_sale_price, :cur_tape_sale_price,
            :reg_dvd_sale_price, :cur_dvd_sale_price,
            :part_of_series INDICATOR :ser_ind, :movie_type,
            :tapes_owned, :dvds_owned, :tapes_in_stock, :dvds_in_stock,
            :0, 0, 0, 0, 0.00, 0.00, 0.00, 0.00);


-- Insert corresponding information into MOVIES_STARS.

PROCEDURE insert_movies_stars
    ( SQLSTATE,
        :title      CHARACTER (30),
        :"date"     CHARACTER (10),
        :first      CHARACTER (35),
        :middle     CHARACTER (25),
        :last       CHARACTER (25),
        :last_ind   INTEGER );

INSERT INTO movies_stars
    VALUE (:title, CAST(:"date" AS DATE),
        :first, :middle, :last INDICATOR :last_ind);


-- Insert a new customer into the CUSTOMERS table.

PROCEDURE insert_customers
    ( SQLSTATE,
        :last       CHARACTER (50),
        :first      CHARACTER (50),
        :addr       CHARACTER (30),
        :addr_ind   INTEGER,
        :city       CHARACTER (15),
        :city_ind   INTEGER,
        :state      CHARACTER (2),
        :st_ind     INTEGER,
        :zip        CHARACTER (9),
        :zip_ind    INTEGER,
        :phone      CHARACTER (10),
        :phone_ind  INTEGER,
```

```
            :fax        CHARACTER (10),
            :fax_ind    INTEGER,
            :e_mail     CHARACTER (30),
            :e_mail_ind INTEGER,
            :credit     CHARACTER (20),
            :credit_ind INTEGER );

INSERT INTO customers
    VALUES (:last, :first, :addr INDICATOR :addr_ind,
            :city INDICATOR :city_ind, :state INDICATOR :st_ind,
            :zip INDICATOR :zip_ind, :phone INDICATOR :phone_ind,
            :fax INDICATOR :fax_ind, e_mail INDICATOR :e_mail_ind,
            :credit, 0.00, 0.00, 0, CURRENT_TIMESTAMP);


-- Insert a group of new CD and tape titles from an "input source table"
--  into the MUSIC_TITLES table.

PROCEDURE insert_new_titles_from_temp_titles
    ( SQLSTATE );

INSERT INTO music_titles SELECT * FROM temp_titles;

-- We need a procedure to COMMIT a transaction in any module.

PROCEDURE commit_transaction
    ( SQLSTATE );

COMMIT;

-- We also need a procedure for GET DIAGNOSTICS.

PROCEDURE get_diagnostics
    ( SQLSTATE,
      message     CHARACTER(128) );

GET DIAGNOSTICS EXCEPTION 1 MESSAGE;
```

B.3.2   Data Modification

```
MODULE data_modification
    NAMES ARE "Latin-1"
    LANGUAGE C
    SCHEMA video_and_music

-- By not specifying AUTHORIZATION, we're requiring that the authID
--   of the user executing the procedures in the module be the one used
--   for privilege checking.


-- Put a DVD title on sale.

PROCEDURE movie_on_sale
    ( SQLSTATE,
      :title CHARACTER VARYING (50) );

UPDATE movie_titles
    SET current_dvd_sale_price = regular_dvd_sale_price - 2.00
    WHERE title = :title;

-- We need a procedure to COMMIT a transaction in any module.

PROCEDURE commit_transaction
    ( SQLSTATE );

COMMIT WORK;

-- Put all cassettes (but not CDs) by a specific artist or group on
--   sale (mark down by 10% from list price).

PROCEDURE artist_music_on_sale
    ( SQLSTATE,
      :artist        CHARACTER VARYING (40),
      :artist_more   CHARACTER VARYING (50),
      :other_ind     INTEGER );

UPDATE music_titles
        SET cassette_current_price = casette_list_price * 0.9
WHERE artist = :artist AND
        ( ( :artist_more INDICATOR other_ind IS NOT NULL AND
```

```
                     artist_more = :artist_more INDICATOR other_ind ) OR
                ( artist_more IS NULL AND
                  :artist_more INDICATOR other_ind IS NULL ) );
```

B.3.3 Table Structure Modification

We decide to streamline inventory by getting rid of all cassette tapes; from now on we'll only handle CDs. The tables must be updated to delete unneeded columns and their data.

```
ALTER TABLE music_titles DROP COLUMN cassette_list_price;

ALTER TABLE music_titles DROP COLUMN cassette_current_price;

ALTER TABLE music_inventory DROP COLUMN total_cassette_sold;

ALTER TABLE music_inventory DROP COLUMN total_cassette_returned;

ALTER TABLE current_distributor_costs DROP COLUMN our_cassette_cost;

COMMIT;
```

B.3.4 Data Removal

1. We need to delete an employee who has left the company.

   ```
   DELETE FROM employees
   WHERE emp_id = :id;
   ```

2. We decide to remove some movies from inventory. This requires deletion from multiple tables, with referential integrity control enforced.

   ```
   DELETE FROM movie_titles
   WHERE title = :title AND
   year_released = :year;
   ```

3. We decide to automatically remove all customers who have had more than four problem reports.

   ```
   DELETE FROM customers
   WHERE number_of_problems > 4;
   ```

B.3.5 Data Access and Management

The Customer Assistance Subsystem

1. Produce a comprehensive listing of all movie titles and the stars for that movie.

```
int cust_assist ()

{

    char    title[51], year[11], result[102], star_name[51]

    EXEC SQL DECLARE CURSOR movie_cursor FOR
        SELECT title, CAST (year_released AS CHARACTER(10))
            FROM movie_titles;

    EXEC SQL DECLARE CURSOR star_cursor FOR
        SELECT TRIM (BOTH ' ' FROM actor_last_name) || ',' ||
                TRIM (BOTH ' ' FROM actor_first_name ||
                        TRIM (BOTH ' ' FROM actor_middle_name)
            FROM movies_stars
            WHERE movie_title = :title AND
                year_released = CAST (:year AS DATE);

    EXEC SQL OPEN movie_cursor;

    if ( SQLSTATE != "00000" )
        { /* Print, display, or otherwise record SQLSTATE value */
            EXEC SQL GET DIAGNOSTICS EXCEPTION 1 MESSAGE;
            /* Print, display, or otherwise record MESSAGE text */
    }

    while (1==1) {

    EXEC SQL FETCH NEXT FROM movie_cursor
        INTO :title, :year;

    if ( SQLSTATE != "00000" )
        { /* Print, display, or otherwise record SQLSTATE value */
```

```
      EXEC SQL GET DIAGNOSTICS EXCEPTION 1 MESSAGE;
      /* Print, display, or otherwise record MESSAGE text */
      }

/* Check SQLSTATE for '02000'; if so, then skip to abc */

if (SQLSTATE != "02000")

    { /* Print, display, or otherwise output movie title */

    EXEC SQL OPEN star_cursor;

    if ( SQLSTATE != "00000" )
        { /* Print, display, or otherwise record
             SQLSTATE value */
        EXEC SQL GET DIAGNOSTICS EXCEPTION 1 MESSAGE;
        /* Print, display, or otherwise record MESSAGE text */
        }

while (1==1)

    { EXEC SQL FETCH NEXT FROM star_cursor
        INTO :name;

if ( SQLSTATE != "00000" )
    { /* Print, display, or otherwise record SQLSTATE value */
    EXEC SQL GET DIAGNOSTICS EXCEPTION 1 MESSAGE;
    /* Print, display, or otherwise record MESSAGE text */
    }

/* Check SQLSTATE for '02000'; if so, then get out of loop
Otherwise, print and then loop to FETCH star_cursor */

if ( SQLSTATE == '02000' ) break;

}

EXEC SQL CLOSE star_cursor;
```

```
    if ( SQLSTATE != "00000" )
    { /* Print, display, or otherwise record SQLSTATE value */
        EXEC SQL GET DIAGNOSTICS EXCEPTION 1 MESSAGE;
        /* Print, display, or otherwise record MESSAGE text */
    }


} \* Loop to FETCH movie_cursor */

EXEC SQL CLOSE movie_cursor;

if ( SQLSTATE != "00000" )
    { /* Print, display, or otherwise record SQLSTATE value */
        EXEC SQL GET DIAGNOSTICS EXCEPTION 1 MESSAGE;
        /* Print, display, or otherwise record MESSAGE text */
    }


}
```

2. Produce a list of all movies starring Barbra Streisand.

```
SELECT m.title
    FROM movie_titles m, movies_stars s
    WHERE s.actor_first_name = 'Barbra' AND
        s.actor_last_name = 'Streisand';
```

3. Produce a list of all movies starring both Nick Nolte and Eddie Murphy.

```
SELECT m.title
    FROM movie_titles m, movies_stars s
    WHERE (s.actor_first_name, s.actor_last_name )
        IN ( ('Nick', 'Nolte'), ('Eddie', 'Murphy') );
```

4. List all soundtrack CD and tape titles for which the movies are in stock.

5. List all music titles where the CD and tape title is the same as that of the singer or group.

```
SELECT title
    FROM music_titles
    WHERE title = artist AND artist_more IS NULL;
```

6. List all CDs and tapes where the group's or artist's name is part of the music title.

```
SELECT title
    FROM music_titles
    WHERE ( title LIKE '%'||artist||'%' OR
        title LIKE '%'||artist_more||'%' );
```

7. List all artists that have greatest hits collections.

```
SELECT artist, artist_more
    FROM music_titles
    WHERE greatest_hits_collection IS NOT NULL;
```

8. Does the store have a soundtrack for the movie *Titantic*?

```
SELECT CASE COUNT(*) WHEN 0 THEN 'No' ELSE 'Yes' END
    FROM music_titles
    WHERE title = 'Titantic' AND
        category = 'Soundtrack';
```

Appendix
C

The SQL:1999 Annexes

C.1 Introduction

The SQL:1999 standard contains several Annexes. These Annexes are not normative, or enforceable, parts of the standard, but are purely informative in nature. In fact, four of the six Annexes merely summarize information that is available in other places in the standard; the other two offer material that would be difficult to ascertain without carefully reading the standard and perhaps comparing it with the previous edition. In this chapter, we capture the essence of the Annexes, without actually going into the detail that is inevitably present in the standard. We'll discuss the differences between SQL-92 and SQL:1999 (including incompatibilities as well as additions), implementation-defined and implementation-dependent features, deprecated features, and a summary of conformance requirements.

C.2 Differences between SQL-92 and SQL:1999

Most SQL programmers, especially those familiar with SQL-92, will want to know all the differences between the new standard and the earlier one. There really are quite a few differences, and we can divide them into two broad categories: incompatible differences and compatible differences.

C.2.1   Incompatible Differences

The incompatible differences are very few in number; the standards process is heavily biased against introducing incompatibilities between versions of a standard, and it is generally done only with great debate and reluctance. Here are all of the incompatibilities between SQL-92 and SQL:1999.

1. In SQL-92, the parameter declaration list associated with a module language procedure had a second alternative: a parameter list not surrounded by parentheses and with the individual component parameter declarations not separated by commas. This option was deprecated in SQL-92. SQL:1999 does not provide this option. SQL-client modules that used this deprecated feature may be converted to conforming SQL by inserting a comma between each pair of parameter declarations and placing a left parenthesis before and a right parenthesis after the entire parameter list.

2. In SQL-92, if one or more rows deleted or updated through some cursor C1 are later updated or deleted in the same transaction through some other cursor C2, by a DELETE...WHERE, by an UPDATE...WHERE, or by some update rule or delete rule of some referential constraint, no exception condition is raised and no completion condition other than *successful completion* is raised. In SQL:1999, a completion (warning) condition is raised—*warning—cursor operation conflict*—to warn your applications of the possible conflict.

3. In SQL-92, there were two status parameters provided: SQLCODE and SQLSTATE. In SQL-92, SQLCODE was listed as a deprecated feature in deference to SQLSTATE. In SQL:1999, SQLCODE has been removed, and "SQLCODE" has been removed from the list of reserved words.

4. In SQL-92, it was permitted to omit the semicolon at the end of the contents of a module language module, but this was listed as a deprecated feature. In SQL:1999, the use of the semicolon at the end of the module contents is mandatory.

5. In SQL-92, it was possible for applications to define new character sets, collations, and translations from scratch. In SQL:1999, those capabilities have been limited to defining new character sets, collations, and translations that are identical to existing character sets, collations, and translations, respectively, except for their names and other minor details.

6. In SQL-92, it was possible for applications to specify a character set to be associated with an identifier using the notation "_charsetname". In

SQL:1999, that capability has been removed. (It was never widely implemented and was finally understood to serve no truly useful purpose.)

7. In SQL-92, it was permitted to have the start field and end field of an interval qualifier be the same. In SQL:1999, the start field must be *more significant than* the end field. The case of identical start field and end field was equivalent in SQL-92 to an interval qualifier that is a single datetime field; this latter construct has been retained in SQL:1999.

8. In SQL-92, it was permitted to order a cursor by a column specified by an unsigned integer that specified its ordinal position in the cursor. In SQL:1999, that capability has been eliminated.

9. In PSM-96, the character set for the SQL parameter list entry used to return a message from an SQL-invoked routine was SQL_TEXT. In SQL:1999, the character set for that SQL parameter list entry is the character set specified for SQLSTATE values.

10. In PSM-96, the Syntax Rules for routine invocation would never select a subject routine that was an SQL-invoked function if the SQL-invoked function had one or more SQL parameters whose declared type was a character string type whose character set was not the same as the character set of the corresponding SQL argument. In SQL:1999, the Syntax Rules for routine invocation allow the selection of such a subject routine and a syntax error would then be raised if the SQL argument is not assignable to the SQL parameter.

11. In PSM-96, the value of the IS_DETERMINISTIC column of the ROUTINES base table indicated whether DETERMINISTIC was specified when the SQL-invoked routine was defined, regardless of whether that routine was an external routine or an SQL routine. In SQL:1999, the value of IS_DETERMINISTIC is the null value if the routine is an SQL routine.

12. In SQL-92, if the value of a character value expression was a zero-length string or if a zero-length character string was assigned to a target, there were no exception conditions permitted. In SQL:1999, it is implementation-defined whether in these circumstances an exception condition is raised: *data exception—zero-length character string*. (This rule provides support for some SQL implementations that do not distinguish between zero-length character strings and the null value.)

13. In SQL-92, CREATE SCHEMA without an explicit CHARACTER SET specification was assumed to associate with the created schema a schema character set specification containing an implementation-defined character set specification. In SQL:1999, such a schema definition is assumed to have

associated with it a schema character set specification that specifies an implementation-defined character set that contains at least every character that is required for implementing SQL statements. Similarly, in SQL-92, a character string type that is not contained in a domain definition or a column definition and for which CHARACTER SET is not specified is assumed to be associated with an implementation-defined character set specification. In SQL:1999, such a character string type is assumed to be associated with an implementation-defined character set specification that specifies an implementation-defined character set that contains at least every character that is required for implementation of SQL statements. These comprise slight restrictions on the choice of character sets to be used in such cases.

14. In CLI-95, the SetDescField() routine raised an exception condition *CLI-specific condition—cannot modify an implementation row descriptor* whenever the allocated CLI descriptor area identified by the DescriptorHandle parameter was an implementation row descriptor. In SQL:1999, that exception condition is no longer raised under this circumstance; instead, the exception condition *CLI-specific condition—invalid descriptor field identifier* is raised.

15. In CLI-95, in the definition of the GetInfo() routine, the data types of the BufferLength and StringLength parameters were specified to be INTEGER. In SQL:1999, the data types of those two parameters have been changed to SMALLINT to correspond to popular implementations.

16. In CLI-95, the descriptor area field DATETIME_INTERVAL_PRECISION was assigned the code 1014. In SQL:1999, this code has been changed to 26 to correspond to popular implementations.

17. Finally, SQL:1999 has defined a large number of additional reserved keywords:

ABS	CALL	DICTIONARY
ACTION	CARDINALITY	EACH
AFTER	CLOB	EQUALS
AGGREGATE	COMPLETION	EVERY
ALIAS	CUBE	FACTOR
ARRAY	CURRENT_PATH	FREE
BEFORE	CYCLE	GENERAL
BINARY	DATA	GROUPING
BLOB	DEPTH	HOLD
BOOLEAN	DEREF	HOST
BREADTH	DESTROY	IGNORE

INITIALIZE	PARAMETERS	SIMILAR
ITERATE	PATH	SPACE
LARGE	PREORDER	SPECIFIC
LESS	READS	SPECIFICTYPE
LIMIT	RECURSIVE	SQLEXCEPTION
LOCATOR	REF	SQLWARNING
MAP	REFERENCING	START
MOD	RELATIVE	STATE
MODIFIES	REPLACE	STATIC
MODIFY	RESULT	STRUCTURE
NCLOB	RETURN	SUBLIST
NEW	RETURNS	SYMBOL
NO	ROLE	TERM
NONE	ROLLUP	TERMINATE
OBJECT	ROUTINE	THE
OFF	ROW	TREAT
OLD	SAVEPOINT	TRIGGER
OPERATION	SEARCH	TYPE
OPERATOR	SENSITIVE	UNDER
ORDINALITY	SEQUENCE	VARIABLE
OVERLAY	SESSION	WITHOUT
PARAMETER	SETS	

Whew! That probably seems like a lot of incompatibilities, but most of them are pretty trivial and address really unusual situations. The lengthy list of new reserved words is clearly the most problematic for most users, but we note that (just as in SQL-92) you can use the delimited identifiers (identifiers in double quotes) to get around that problem. Therefore, if you happened to name one of your columns ACTION, you can modify your programs to now refer to it as "ACTION".

C.2.2 Compatible Differences

Now, let's look at the compatible differences—the new features.

- Object orientation (not addressed in this volume; see Volume 2 of this book for details on this feature)
- Triggers

- Referential action NO ACTION
- Recursive queries
- New data types: BOOLEAN, ARRAY, ROW, CHARACTER LARGE OBJECT, and BINARY LARGE OBJECT, as well as the use of LOCATOR types to reference the LARGE OBJECT types
- Distinct types
- Use of Unicode as the character model, accompanied by several new named character sets: UCS2, UTF8, UTF16, and ISO10646
- User of functional dependencies to permit updating of more views
- The addition of the keyword ASENSITIVE for cursors that are neither SENSITIVE nor INSENSITIVE
- Holdable cursors
- Roles
- Savepoints
- START TRANSACTION statement
- The AND CHAIN option on COMMIT and ROLLBACK
- SET SESSION CHARACTERISTICS statement
- Bracketed comments (/*...*/)
- Additional built-in functions (CARDINALITY, ABS, MOD, OVERLAY, LOCALTIME, LOCALTIMESTAMP)
- Additional grouping options (ROLLUP, CUBE, GROUPING SETS)
- SIMILAR and DISTINCT predicates
- Additional views in the Information Schema
- Short-name views in the Information Schema
- Representation of SQL's built-in functions in the Information Schema
- A new conformance model for the SQL standard

C.3 | Implementation-Defined and Implementation-Dependent

It would have been very nice, indeed, if the SQL standard had completely defined every aspect of every element. However, there are a number of elements that the standard did not define for one reason or another. The precise definition of these aspects of the language will, of course, be determined in one way or another by each implementation.

The standard uses the phrase *implementation-defined* to indicate one of these areas. This is meant to imply that the implementation *must* document the syntax, value, or behavior of the element. For example, the standard leaves the exact precision of the INTEGER data type as implementation-defined, and in order to claim conformance to the standard, the implementation *must* document the precision.

The other phrase the standard uses is *implementation-dependent*. This phrase means that the implementation need not document the syntax, value, or behavior of some element and that application programs certainly must never depend on it. (In fact, interpretations of the SQL standard have indicated that implementors are actually *discouraged* from documenting items that are specified to be implementation-dependent, thus reducing the temptation for application writers to depend on that information.) For example, the physical representation of a value of any given data type is implementation-dependent. Implementation-dependent information is typically the sort that may change from version to version of a product, that is unusually difficult to describe, or is of no (logical) use to applications.

SQL:1999 identifies no fewer than 381 items that are implementation-defined (17 in SQL/Framework, 131 in SQL/Foundation, 200 in SQL/CLI, 5 in SQL/PSM, and 28 in SQL/Bindings) and 137 that are implementation-dependent (11 in SQL/Framework, 50 in SQL/Foundation, 50 in SQL/CLI, 11 in SQL/PSM, and 15 in SQL/Bindings). While that may sound like the standard is left wide open for almost anything, many of these items are closely related to others, many are so obvious that they may be overlooked by a more casual specification, and others are descriptive of realistic behaviors in any situation. Let's try to summarize at least the more important of them. Readers should note that SQL:1999 specifies more implementation-defined and implementation-dependent items than summarized in this appendix; the contents of this appendix are intended to be illustrative and not comprehensive.

C.3.1   Implementation-Defined

The following lists contain a large selection of the implementation-defined items of SQL:1999.

Data Types

1. The specific character set associated with the subtype of character string represented by the key words NATIONAL CHARACTER is implementation-defined.

2. When trailing digits are removed from a numeric value, the choice of whether to truncate or to round is implementation-defined.

3. When an approximation is obtained by truncation or rounding and there are two or more approximations, which approximation is chosen is implementation-defined.

4. It is implementation-defined which numerical values have approximations obtained by rounding or truncation for a given approximate numeric type.

5. The boundaries within which the normal rules of arithmetic apply are implementation-defined.

6. When converting between numeric data types, if least significant digits are lost, it is implementation-defined whether rounding or truncation occurs.

7. If a precision is omitted, an implementation-defined precision is implicit.

8. The decimal precision of a data type defined as DECIMAL for each value specified by an explicit precision is implementation-defined.

9. The precision of a data type defined as INTEGER is implementation-defined but has the same radix as that for SMALLINT.

10. The precision of a data type defined as SMALLINT is implementation-defined but has the same radix as that for INTEGER.

11. The binary precision of a data type defined as FLOAT for each value specified by an explicit precision is implementation-defined.

12. The precision of a data type defined as REAL is implementation-defined.

13. The precision of a data type defined as DOUBLE PRECISION is implementation-defined but greater than that for REAL.

14. For every data type, the limits of the data type are implementation-defined.

15. The maximum lengths for character string types, variable-length character string types, bit string types, and variable-length bit string types are implementation-defined.

16. If CHARACTER SET is not specified for a character string type, the character set is implementation-defined.

17. The character set named SQL_TEXT is an implementation-defined character set that contains every character in the basic set of characters necessary to represent SQL language and all characters that are in other character sets supported by the implementation.

18. For the exact numeric types DECIMAL and NUMERIC, the maximum values of precision and of scale are implementation-defined.

19. For the approximate numeric type FLOAT, the maximum value of precision is implementation-defined.

20. For the approximate numeric types FLOAT, REAL, and DOUBLE PRECISION, the maximum and minimum values of the exponent are implementation-defined.

21. The maximum number of digits in a fractional seconds precision is implementation-defined but shall not be less than 6.

22. Interval arithmetic that involves leap seconds or discontinuities in calendars will produce implementation-defined results.

Metadata

1. The default schema for preparable statements that are dynamically prepared in your session through the execution of PREPARE statements and EXECUTE IMMEDIATE statements is initially implementation-defined but may be changed by the use of SET SCHEMA statements.

2. The creation and destruction of catalogs is accomplished by implementation-defined means.

3. The set of catalogs that can be referenced in any SQL statement, during any particular transaction, or during the course of a session is implementation-defined.

4. The default catalog for modules whose module authorization clause does not specify an explicit catalog name to qualify a schema name and the default catalog name substitution value for execution of preparable statements that are dynamically prepared in your session through the execution of PREPARE statements and EXECUTE IMMEDIATE statements are implementation-defined.

5. The constituents of an SQL-environment beyond those specified in the standard are implementation-defined.

6. The rules determining whether a module is within the environment are implementation-defined.

7. The mechanisms by which modules are created or destroyed are implementation-defined.

8. The manner in which an association is made between a module and an SQL agent is implementation-defined.

9. Whether a compilation unit may invoke or transfer control to other compilation units, written in the same or a different programming language, is implementation-defined.

10. The names of character sets that are implementation-defined or defined by national or international standards that are supported by your implementation are implementation-defined.

11. The names of collations that are implementation-defined or defined by national or international standards that are supported by your implementation are implementation-defined.

12. The names of translations that are implementation-defined or defined by national or international standards that are supported by your implementation are implementation-defined.

Sessions, Transactions, and Connections

1. It is implementation-defined whether or not the nondynamic or dynamic execution of a data manipulation statement is permitted to occur within the same SQL transaction as the nondynamic or dynamic execution of a schema definition or manipulation statement. If it does occur, the effect on any open cursor, prepared dynamic statement, or deferred constraint is also implementation-defined.

2. If an implementation detects unrecoverable errors and implicitly initiates the execution of a ROLLBACK statement, an error is returned.

3. It is implementation-defined how an implementation uses an SQL-server name to determine the location, identity, and communication protocol required to access the environment and create a session.

4. When a session is initiated other than through the use of an explicit CONNECT statement, a session associated with an implementation-defined environment is initiated. The default environment is implementation-defined.

5. The mechanism and rules by which an environment determines whether a call to a procedure is the last call within the last active module are implementation-defined.

6. A session uses one or more implementation-defined schemas that contain the instances of any global temporary tables, created local temporary tables, or declared local temporary tables within the session.

7. When a session is initiated other than through the use of an explicit CONNECT statement, there is an implementation-defined default authorization identifier that is used for privilege checking the execution of statements contained in modules not having an explicit module authorization identifier.

8. When a session is initiated, there is an implementation-defined default catalog whose name is used to effectively qualify all unqualified schema names contained in preparable statements that are dynamically prepared in the current session through the execution of PREPARE statements and EXECUTE IMMEDIATE statements or are contained in direct SQL statements when those statements are invoked directly.

9. When a session is initiated, there is an implementation-defined default schema whose name is used to effectively qualify all unqualified names contained in preparable statements that are dynamically prepared in the current session through the execution of PREPARE statements and EXECUTE IMMEDIATE statements or are contained in direct SQL statements when those statements are invoked directly.

10. When a session is initiated, there is an implementation-defined default time zone displacement that is used as the current default time zone displacement of the SQL session.

11. When an agent is active, it is bound in some implementation-defined manner to a single client.

12. If the module that contains a procedure is associated with an agent that is associated with another module that contains a procedure with the same procedure name, the effect is implementation-defined.

13. The isolation level that is set for a transaction is an implementation-defined isolation level that will not exhibit any of the phenomena that the explicit or implicit level of isolation would not exhibit.

14. If any error has occurred other than one specified in the General Rules preventing commitment of the transaction, then any changes to data or schemas that were made by the current transaction are canceled and an error is returned.

15. It is implementation-defined whether or not an SQL implementation may support transactions that affect more than one server. If it does so, then the effects are implementation-defined.

16. If a user name is not specified in a CONNECT statement, an implementation-defined user name for the connection is implicit.

17. The restrictions on whether or not the user name in a CONNECT statement shall be identical to the module authorization identifier for the module that contains the procedure that contains the CONNECT statement are implementation-defined.

18. If DEFAULT is specified, the method by which the default environment is determined is implementation-defined.

19. The method by which an SQL-server name is used in a CONNECT statement to determine the appropriate environment is implementation-defined.

20. Whether or not the authorization identifier for the session can be set to an authorization identifier other than the authorization identifier of the session when the session is started is implementation-defined, as are any restrictions pertaining to such changes.

SQL Statements

1. Implementations are allowed to provide additional, implementation-defined statements; the classification of such statements is also implementation-defined.

2. If a value V is approximate numeric and a target T is exact numeric, then whether the approximation of V retrieved into T is obtained by rounding or by truncation is implementation-defined.

3. If a value V is approximate numeric and a target T is exact numeric, then whether the approximation of V stored into T is obtained by rounding or by truncation is implementation-defined.

4. If all of the data types in a set of values are exact numeric, then the result data type for the purposes of UNION or other similar requirements is exact numeric with implementation-defined precision.

5. If any data type in a set of values is approximate numeric, then each data type in the set of values shall be numeric and the result data type is approximate numeric with implementation-defined precision.

6. If character set specification is not specified on a CREATE SCHEMA, a character set specification containing an implementation-defined character set specification is implicit.

7. The privileges necessary to execute CREATE SCHEMA are implementation-defined.

8. Whether null values shall be considered greater than or less than all non-null values in determining the order of rows in a table associated with a DECLARE CURSOR is implementation-defined.

9. If WITH MAX is not specified, an implementation-defined default value that is greater than 0 is implicit.

10. The maximum number of SQL descriptor areas and the maximum number of item descriptor areas for a single SQL descriptor area are implementation-defined.

11. Restrictions on changing TYPE, LENGTH, PRECISION, DATETIME_INTERVAL_CODE, DATETIME_INTERVAL_PRECISION, SCALE, CHARACTER_SET_CATALOG, CHARACTER_SET_SCHEMA, and CHARACTER_SET_NAME values resulting from the execution of a DESCRIBE statement before the execution of an EXECUTE statement, a dynamic OPEN statement, or a dynamic FETCH statement are implementation-defined, except as specified in specific rules for the USING clause.

12. The format and syntax rules for a preparable implementation-defined statement are implementation-defined.

13. The method of invoking direct SQL statements, the method of raising conditions as a result of direct SQL statements, the method of accessing diagnostic information, and the method of returning the results are all implementation-defined.

14. The value specification that represents the null value in direct invocation of SQL is implementation-defined.

15. The format, syntax rules, and access rules for direct implementation-defined statements are implementation-defined.

16. Whether a direct implementation-defined statement may be associated with an active transaction is implementation-defined.

17. Whether a direct implementation-defined statement initiates a transaction is implementation-defined.

18. The methods of raising a condition and of accessing diagnostics information are implementation-defined.

19. The method of returning the results from multirow SELECT statements in direct invocation is implementation-defined.

Literals, Names, and Identifiers

1. The end-of-line indicator *(newline)* is implementation-defined.

2. The character set name of the character set used to represent national characters is implementation-defined.

3. If a schema name contained in a schema name clause that is not contained in a module does not contain a catalog name, an implementation-defined catalog name is implicit.

4. If a schema name contained in a module authorization clause does not contain a catalog name, an implementation-defined catalog name is implicit.

5. The data type of the simple value specification of an extended statement name shall be character string with an implementation-defined character set.

6. The data type of the simple value specification of an extended cursor name shall be character string with an implementation-defined character set.

7. Those identifiers that are valid authorization identifiers are implementation-defined.

8. Those identifiers that are valid catalog names are implementation-defined.

9. All form-of-use conversion names are implementation-defined.

Value Expressions and Functions

1. Whether the character string of the value specifications CURRENT_USER, SESSION_USER, and SYSTEM_USER is variable-length or fixed-length, and its maximum length if it is variable-length or its length if it is fixed-length, are implementation-defined.

2. The value specified by SYSTEM_USER is an implementation-defined string that represents the operating system user who executed the module that contains the SQL statement whose execution caused the SYSTEM_USER value specification to be evaluated.

3. The precision of the value derived from application of the COUNT function is implementation-defined.

4. The precision of the value derived from application of the SUM function to a data type of exact numeric is implementation-defined.

5. The precision and scale of the value derived from application of the AVG function to a data type of exact numeric is implementation-defined.

6. The precision of the value derived from application of the SUM function or AVG function to a data type of approximate numeric is implementation-defined.

7. The precision of the POSITION expression is implementation-defined.

8. The precision of the EXTRACT expression is implementation-defined. If a datetime field specifies SECOND, the scale is also implementation-defined.

9. The precision of the various LENGTH expressions is implementation-defined.

10. The maximum length of a character translation or form-of-use conversion is implementation-defined.

11. Whether to round or truncate when casting to exact or approximate numeric data types is implementation-defined.

12. When the data type of both operands of the addition, subtraction, multiplication, or division operator is exact numeric, the precision of the result is implementation-defined.

13. When the data type of both operands of the division operator is exact numeric, the scale of the result is implementation-defined.

14. When the data type of either operand of an arithmetic operator is approximate numeric, the precision of the result is implementation-defined.

15. Whether to round or truncate when performing division is implementation-defined.

16. When an interval is produced from the difference of two datetimes, the choice of whether to round or truncate is implementation-defined.

17. The maximum value of an interval leading field precision is implementation-defined but shall not be less than 2.

18. The maximum value of an interval fractional seconds precision is implementation-defined but shall not be less than 6.

Diagnostics

1. The actual length of variable-length character items in the diagnostics area is implementation-defined but shall not be less than 128.

2. The character string value set for CLASS_ORIGIN and SUBCLASS_ORIGIN for an implementation-defined class code or subclass code is implementation-defined but shall not be 'ISO 9075.'

3. The value of MESSAGE_TEXT is an implementation-defined character string.

4. The character set associated with the class value and subclass value of the SQLSTATE parameter is implementation-defined.

5. The values and meanings for classes and subclasses that begin with one of the digits 5, 6, 7, 8, or 9 or one of the uppercase letters *I, J, K, L, M, N, O, P, Q, R, S, T, U, V, W, X, Y,* or *Z* are implementation-defined. The values and meanings for all subclasses that are associated with implementation-defined class values are implementation-defined.

Information Schema

1. If the containing ADD TABLE CONSTRAINT definition does not specify a constraint name definition, the values of CONSTRAINT_CATALOG, CONSTRAINT_SCHEMA, and CONSTRAINT_NAME are implementation-defined.

2. The values of FORM_OF_USE and NUMBER_OF_CHARACTERS, in the row for the character set INFORMATION_SCHEMA.SQL_TEXT, are implementation-defined.

3. The value of PAD_ATTRIBUTE for the collation SQL_TEXT is implementation-defined.

4. The value of SQL_LANGUAGE_IMPLEMENTATION is implementation-defined. If the value of SQL_LANGUAGE_SOURCE is not 'ISO 9075,' the value of all other columns is implementation-defined.

Embedded SQL and Modules

1. Whether a portion of the namespace is reserved by an implementation for the names of procedures, subroutines, program variables, branch labels, modules, or procedures is implementation-defined; if a portion of the namespace is so reserved, the portion reserved is also implementation-defined.

2. If the explicit or implicit schema name does not specify a catalog name, an implementation-defined catalog name is implicit.

3. If a module character set specification is not specified, a module character set specification that specifies the implementation-defined character set that contains every character that is in SQL language is implicit.

4. Whether or not a given authID can invoke procedures in a module with an explicit module authorization identifier is implementation-defined, as are any restrictions pertaining to such invocation.

5. If the value of any input parameter provided by the SQL agent falls outside the set of allowed values of the data type of the parameter, or if the

value of any output parameter resulting from the execution of the procedure falls outside the set of values supported by the SQL agent for that parameter, the effect is implementation-defined.

6. There is an implementation-defined package and character type for use in Ada bindings. The precisions and scales of the Ada types for SQL data types and the exact numeric type of indicator parameters are implementation-defined.

7. The null character that defines the end of a C character string is implementation-defined.

8. The number of bits in a C character is implementation-defined.

9. The number of bits contained in a COBOL character is implementation-defined.

10. The precision of a COBOL data type corresponding to SQL INTEGER or SMALLINT is implementation-defined.

11. The number of bits contained in a Fortran character is implementation-defined.

12. The number of bits contained in a Pascal character is implementation-defined.

13. The precision of an SQLCODE parameter in an embedded PL/I program is implementation-defined.

14. The precision of a PL/I data type corresponding to SQL INTEGER or SMALLINT is implementation-defined.

15. If an embedded character set declaration is not specified, then an embedded character set declaration containing an implementation-defined character set specification is implicit.

16. If character set specification is not specified when CHAR is specified, an implementation-defined character set specification is implicit.

17. If character set specification is not specified when a C character variable or C VARCHAR variable is specified, an implementation-defined character set specification is implicit.

18. The COBOL data description clauses, in addition to the PICTURE, SIGN, USAGE, and VALUE clauses, that may appear in a COBOL variable definition are implementation-defined.

19. If character set specification is not specified when a COBOL character type is specified, an implementation-defined character set specification is implicit.

20. If character set specification is not specified when CHARACTER is specified in Fortran, then an implementation-defined character set specification is implicit.

21. In a MUMPS character variable, an implementation-defined character set specification is implicit.

22. If character set specification is not specified when PACKED ARRAY OF CHAR is specified in Pascal, an implementation-defined character set specification is implicit.

23. The PL/I data description clauses, in addition to the PL/I type specification and the INITIAL clause, that may appear in a PL/I variable definition are implementation-defined.

24. If character set specification is not specified when CHARACTER is specified in PL/I, an implementation-defined character set specification is implicit.

Call-Level Interface

1. If a CLI routine provides a return code indicating No Data, then there may be one or more diagnostics records generated with an implementation-defined subclass code.

2. The null character used to terminate C strings is implementation-defined (and, as we all know, every implementation defines it to be a character all of whose bits are zero).

3. The validity of a CLI handle in any compilation unit other than the one in which it was allocated is implementation-defined.

4. It is implementation-defined whether a given CLI implementation is provided using CLI procedures or CLI functions.

5. An implementation that has additional, implementation-defined CLI functions must give them unique, implementation-defined names.

6. A CLI implementation may provide additional, implementation-defined data conversions in addition to those required by the standard.

7. When a handle is allocated, if there are insufficient resources for the handle or the object that it identifies, then an implementation-defined exception is raised.

8. The mechanism used to identify the names of SQL servers to which a CLI application can connect is implementation-defined, as is the mechanism used to provide the strings that describe those servers.

9. A CLI implementation may support additional types of handles, as well as additional attributes associated with standardized handle types; such additions are implementation-defined.

Miscellaneous

1. If an SQL implementation provides user options to process conforming SQL language in a nonconforming manner, it is required that the implementation also provide a flagger option, or some other implementation-defined means, to detect SQL conforming language that may be processed differently under the various user options.

2. The default collating sequence of the character repertoire specified by an implementation-defined character repertoire name or by an implementation-defined universal character form-of-use name is implementation-defined. Whether that collating sequence has the NO PAD attribute or the PAD SPACE attribute is also implementation-defined.

3. The collating sequence resulting from the specification of EXTERNAL in a collation definition is implementation-defined.

4. The method of flagging nonconforming SQL language or of processing conforming SQL language is implementation-defined, as is the list of additional keywords that may be required by the implementation.

C.3.2 Implementation-Dependent

The following lists contain some of the implementation-dependent features of SQL:1999.

Information Schema

1. The actual objects on which the Information Schema views are based are implementation-dependent.

2. The values of DEFAULT_COLLATE_SCHEMA, DEFAULT_COLLATE_CATALOG, and DEFAULT_COLLATE_NAME for default collations specifying the order of characters in a repertoire are implementation-dependent.

Miscellaneous

1. The treatment of language that does not conform to the SQL formats and syntax rules is implementation-dependent.

2. It is implementation-dependent whether expressions are actually evaluated left-to-right when the precedence is not otherwise determined by the formats or by parentheses.

3. If evaluation of the *inessential parts* of an expression or search condition would cause an exception condition to be raised, it is implementation-dependent whether or not that condition is raised.

4. Because global temporary table contents are distinct within SQL sessions, and created local temporary tables are distinct within modules within SQL sessions, the effective schema name of the schema in which the global temporary table or the created local temporary table is instantiated is an implementation-dependent schema name that may be thought of as having been effectively derived from the schema name of the schema in which the global temporary table or created local temporary table is defined and from the implementation-dependent SQL-session identifier associated with the SQL-session.

5. The effective schema name of the schema in which the created local temporary table is instantiated may be thought of as being further qualified by a unique implementation-dependent name associated with the module in which the created local temporary table is referenced.

6. Whether or not a temporary viewed table is materialized is implementation-dependent.

7. The mapping of authorization identifiers to operating system users is implementation-dependent.

8. When a session is initiated, the current authorization identifier for the session is determined in an implementation-dependent manner, unless the session is initiated using a CONNECT statement.

9. An SQL agent is an implementation-dependent entity that causes the execution of SQL statements.

10. The schema definitions that are implicitly read on behalf of executing an SQL statement are implementation-dependent.

11. The session module contains a module authorization clause that specifies SCHEMA schema-name, where the value of schema-name is implementation-dependent.

12. A unique implementation-dependent session identifier is associated with each session.

13. The module name of the module that is effectively materialized on an SQL server is implementation-dependent.

14. Diagnostic information passed to the diagnostics area in the client is passed in an implementation-dependent manner.

15. If the number of conditions is not specified in a SET TRANSACTION statement or a START TRANSACTION statement, an implementation-dependent value not less than 1 is implicit.

16. If ALL is specified in a DISCONNECT statement, then L is a list representing every active connection that has been established by a CONNECT statement by the current SQL agent and that has not yet been disconnected by a DISCONNECT statement, in an implementation-dependent order.

Diagnostics

1. The effect on diagnostic information of incompatibilities between the character repertoires supported by the SQL client and SQL server environments is implementation-dependent.

2. The effect on target specifications and SQL descriptor areas of an SQL statement that terminates with an exception condition, unless explicitly defined by the standard, is implementation-dependent.

3. If more than one condition could have occurred as a result of execution of a statement, then it is implementation-dependent whether diagnostic information pertaining to more than one condition is made available.

4. The actual size of the diagnostics area is implementation-dependent when the SQL agent does not specify the size.

5. The ordering of the information about conditions placed into the diagnostics area is implementation-dependent, except that the first condition in the diagnostics area always corresponds to the condition corresponding to the SQLCODE value.

6. The value of ROW_COUNT following the execution of an SQL statement that does not directly result in the execution of a searched DELETE statement, an INSERT statement, or a searched UPDATE statement is implementation-dependent.

7. If the condition number in a GET DIAGNOSTICS statement has a value other than 1, the association between condition number values and specific

conditions raised during evaluation of the general rules for that SQL statement is implementation-dependent.

SQL Statements

1. If the DECLARE CURSOR does not include an ORDER BY clause, or includes an ORDER BY clause that does not specify the order of the rows completely, then the rows of the table have an order that is defined only to the extent that the ORDER BY clause specifies an order and is otherwise implementation-dependent.

2. When the ordering of a cursor is not defined by an ORDER BY clause, the relative position of two rows is implementation-dependent.

3. The effect on the position and state of an open cursor when an error occurs during the execution of an SQL statement that identifies the cursor is implementation-dependent.

4. If a cursor is open and a change is made to SQL data from within the same transaction other than through that cursor, then whether or not that change will be visible through that cursor before it is closed is implementation-dependent.

5. The specific character set chosen is implementation-dependent but shall be the character set of one of the data types in the set of values being evaluated for UNION compatibility.

6. The order of assignment to targets in the fetch target list of values returned by a FETCH statement, other than status parameters, is implementation-dependent.

7. If an error occurs during assignment of a value to a target during the execution of a FETCH statement, the values of targets other than status parameters are implementation-dependent.

8. If the cardinality of the query expression in a single-row SELECT statement is greater than 1, it is implementation-dependent whether or not values are assigned to the targets identified by the select target list.

9. The order of assignment to targets in the select target list of values returned by a single-row SELECT statement, other than status parameters, is implementation-dependent.

10. If an error occurs during assignment of a value to a target during the execution of a single-row SELECT statement, the values of targets other than status parameters are implementation-dependent.

11. If an exception condition is raised in a GET DESCRIPTOR statement, the values of all targets are implementation-dependent.

12. For a select list column described by a DESCRIBE statement, if the column name is implementation-dependent, then NAME is the implementation-dependent name for the column and UNNAMED is set to 1.

13. For a dynamic parameter specification described by a DESCRIBE statement, the values of NAME and UNNAMED are implementation-dependent.

14. Item descriptor area fields not relevant to the data type of the item being described are set to implementation-dependent values.

15. If an exception condition is raised in a SET DESCRIPTOR statement, the values of all elements of the descriptor specified in the SET DESCRIPTOR statement are implementation-dependent.

16. The validity of an extended statement name value or a statement name in a transaction different from the one in which the statement was prepared is implementation-dependent.

17. When a DESCRIBE OUTPUT statement is executed, the values of DATA and INDICATOR, as well as the value of other fields not relevant to the data type of the described item, are implementation-dependent. If the column name is implementation-dependent, then NAME is set to that implementation-dependent name.

18. When a DESCRIBE INPUT statement is used, the values for NAME, DATA, and INDICATOR, as well as the value of other fields not relevant to the data type of the described item, in the SQL dynamic descriptor area structure are implementation-dependent.

19. If an unrecoverable error has occurred, or if the direct invocation of SQL terminated unexpectedly, or if any constraint is not satisfied, a ROLLBACK statement is performed. Otherwise, the choice of ROLLBACK or COMMIT is implementation-dependent. The determination of whether a direct invocation of SQL has terminated unexpectedly is implementation-dependent.

Literals, Other Value Expressions, Functions, Predicates, and Queries

1. The implicit qualifier of a column reference for which there is more than one possible qualifier with most local scope is implementation-dependent.

2. The time of evaluation of the CURRENT_DATE, CURRENT_TIME, and CURRENT_TIMESTAMP functions during the execution of an SQL statement is implementation-dependent.

3. The start datetime used for converting intervals to scalars for subtraction purposes is implementation-dependent.

4. The names of the columns of a row value constructor that specifies a row value constructor list are implementation-dependent.

5. When a column is not named by an AS clause and is not derived from a single column reference, the name of the column is implementation-dependent.

6. If a simple table is not a query specification, the name of each column of the simple table is implementation-dependent.

7. If a non-join query term is not a non-join query primary and the column name of the corresponding columns of both tables participating in the non-join query term are not the same, then the result column has an implementation-dependent column name.

8. If a non-join query expression is not a non-join query term and the column name of the corresponding columns of both tables participating in the non-join query expression are not the same, then the result column has an implementation-dependent column name.

9. If a collation has the NO PAD attribute, the pad character is an implementation-dependent character different from any character in the character set associated with the collation that collates less than any string under that collation.

10. When the operations MAX, MIN, DISTINCT, references to a grouping column, and the UNION, EXCEPT, and INTERSECT operators refer to character strings, the specific value selected by these operations from a set of such equal values is implementation-dependent.

Data Types and Metadata

1. The constraint name of a constraint that does not specify a constraint name definition is implementation-dependent.

2. The specific value to use for cascading among various values that are not distinct is implementation-dependent.

3. The physical representation of a value of a data type is implementation-dependent.

4. The null value for each data type is implementation-dependent.

Embedded SQL and Modules

1. If the SQL agent that performs a call of a procedure in a module is not a standard program in the language specified in the language clause of the module, the results are implementation-dependent.

2. The procedure name should be a standard-conforming procedure, function, or routine name of the language specified by the subject language clause. Failure to observe this recommendation will have implementation-dependent effects.

3. After the execution of the last procedure, if an unrecoverable error has not occurred, and the SQL agent did not terminate unexpectedly, and there aren't any unsatisfied constraints, then the choice of whether to perform a COMMIT statement or a ROLLBACK statement is implementation-dependent. The determination of whether an SQL agent has terminated unexpectedly is implementation-dependent.

4. If there are two or more status parameters, the order in which values are assigned to these status parameters is implementation-dependent.

5. The module name of the implied module derived from an embedded SQL program is implementation-dependent.

6. The module authorization identifier of the implied module derived from an embedded SQL program is implementation-dependent.

7. In each DECLARE CURSOR in the implied module derived from an embedded SQL program, each embedded variable name has been replaced consistently with a distinct parameter name that is implementation-dependent.

8. The procedure name of each procedure in the implied module derived from an embedded SQL program is implementation-dependent.

9. In each procedure in the implied module derived from an embedded SQL program, each embedded variable name has been replaced consistently with a distinct parameter name that is implementation-dependent.

10. For SQL statements other than OPEN statements, whether one procedure in the implied module derived from an embedded SQL program can correspond to more than one SQL statement in the embedded SQL program is implementation-dependent.

11. In each procedure in the implied module derived from an embedded SQL program, the order of the instances of parameter declaration is implementation-dependent.

Call-Level Interface

1. When a dynamic SELECT statement is executed, an implicit cursor is created whose name is implementation-dependent.

2. After the execution of a CLI routine, the values of all arguments whose values are not expressly specified in the standard are implementation-dependent.

3. The order in which multiple diagnostics area records appear is implementation-dependent.

4. When a character string value is retrieved into a host program, the value of all characters in the receiving buffer following the last character of the source value is implementation-dependent.

C.4 | Deprecated Features

A very few features in SQL:1999, although retained in this version to permit continued use of programs written against the SQL-92 standard, will likely be removed from later versions of the standard. These features are *deprecated,* meaning that application programs should not use the feature and existing applications should remove their use of the feature whenever they are updated. These are listed below.

1. The UNION JOIN has been deprecated and will probably be removed from the next generation of the SQL standard.

2. The ability to specify certain GetInfo items in SQL/CLI has been deprecated and may be removed from the next generation of the SQL standard; these items are ALTER TABLE, CURSOR SENSITIVITY, DATA SOURCE READ ONLY, DESCRIBE PARAMETER, GETDATA EXTENSIONS, FETCH DIRECTION, INTEGRITY, OUTER JOIN CAPABILITIES, SCROLL CONCURRENCY, and USER NAME.

3. Even though domains have not been deprecated in SQL:1999, the SQL standards community has agreed that no further enhancement of that feature—even to align it with other new features of the language—will be done. This should be construed as an effort to discourage new applications from using the feature.

SQL:1999 Conformance Claims

In several places in this book, we've briefly referenced the notion of conformance to SQL:1999, and in Chapter 2, "Introduction to SQL:1999," section 2.9.1, subsection "Core SQL", we mentioned Core SQL and told you that it was essentially all of Entry SQL-92 plus a number of additional features.

When SQL-92 was published, the designers believed that a staged approach to conformance—first Entry SQL, followed by Intermediate SQL, and finally ending up with Full SQL—would provide targets for the vendors of SQL products that would lead in a very few years to fully standardized implementations of the language. Unfortunately, the marketplace had different ideas. Some of the features that were specified in Intermediate SQL-92 ended up with little market demand, while features put off to the next generation of SQL (such as triggers) were urgently required by applications builders.

As a result, no vendor of which we are aware formally claimed conformance even to Intermediate SQL-92, much less Full SQL-92. Naturally, there were plenty of disappointed members of the user community, since they would have benefited from having multiple, compatible implementations of a larger set of language features.

The designers of SQL:1999 took a different approach. Instead of having several levels of conformance, there is only one major collection of features in SQL:1999 to which a vendor might claim conformance: Core SQL. In fact, no vendor can claim conformance to the SQL standard at all (since the publication of SQL:1999) without implementing all of Core SQL. Core SQL was carefully designed to be a set of features to which all known SQL vendors could conform in a reasonable period of time (we estimate that most vendors will require one or two minor product cycles, or "dot releases," to conform), but which no known vendor had fully implemented at the time the standard was released. In other words, all vendors would have to do *some* new work, but none would be locked out of the conformance game.

Whether or not this tactic will be successful will be revealed only as vendors release their products. We observe that several vendors appear to be moving in the direction of Core SQL conformance, notably Microsoft, Oracle, and IBM. Others may also be moving in that direction without it having come to our attention.

However, Core SQL is far from all of SQL:1999. In fact, there are dozens, even scores, of features that are not in Core SQL. SQL:1999 places a few of those features into *packages*—collections of features that are related to one another—to which vendors may (or may not) claim conformance. Vendors will choose which packages, if any, to implement based on their perceptions of their marketplaces.

But the SQL standards community explicitly disclaimed the sole ability to define packages. In fact, it is hoped that applications communities will publish *profiles* of the SQL standard that define new packages and provide specific conformance claims of the standard. For example, the financial community (e.g., banks, stock brokerages, insurance companies) could choose to define several new packages of SQL:1999 features and specify a way in which an SQL database system can claim conformance to the "financial database" requirements. Similarly, the petrochemical industry or the energy distribution industry might create packages and conformance requirements for their markets. Again, only time will tell.

C.5.1   The Features of Core SQL:1999

The features of Core SQL:1999 are listed in Table C-1, along with their subfeatures. Features are identified by a letter and a three-digit number. (The letter originally had some meaning to the SQL:1999 designers, so it is not quite an arbitrary choice; however, that meaning has lost its value and we don't even attempt to explain it here.)

Subfeatures are nothing more than breakdowns of features to help explain a feature's content. They are identifiable by the presence of a hyphen and a two-digit subfeature number following the feature identification. For example, Feature E011 ("Numeric data types") contains six subfeatures, which gives a pretty good picture of what the features includes.

Table C-1 *Core SQL:1999 Features*

Feature ID	Feature Description
B011	Embedded Ada
B012	Embedded C
B013	Embedded COBOL
B014	Embedded Fortran
B015	Embedded MUMPS
B016	Embedded Pascal
B017	Embedded PL/I
E011	Numeric data types
E011-01	INTEGER and SMALLINT data types (including all spellings)
E011-02	REAL, DOUBLE PRECISON, and FLOAT data types
E011-03	DECIMAL and NUMERIC data types
E011-04	Arithmetic operators

Table C-1 *Continued*

Feature ID	Feature Description
E011-05	Numeric comparison
E011-06	Implicit casting among the numeric data types
E021	Character data types
E021-01	CHARACTER data type (including all its spellings)
E021-02	CHARACTER VARYING data type (including all its spellings)
E021-03	Character literals
E021-04	CHARACTER_LENGTH function
E021-05	OCTET_LENGTH function
E021-06	SUBSTRING function
E021-07	Character concatenation
E021-08	UPPER and LOWER functions
E021-09	TRIM function
E021-10	Implicit casting among the character data types
E021-11	POSITION function
E021-12	Character comparison
E031	Identifiers
E031-01	Delimited identifiers
E031-02	Lowercase identifiers
E031-03	Trailing underscore
E051	Basic query specification
E051-01	SELECT DISTINCT
E051-02	GROUP BY clause
E051-04	GROUP BY can contain columns not in select list
E051-05	Select list items can be renamed
E051-06	HAVING clause
E051-07	Qualified * in select list
E051-08	Correlation names in the FROM clause
E051-09	Rename columns in the FROM clause
E061	Basic predicates and search conditions
E061-01	Comparison predicate
E061-02	BETWEEN predicate
E061-03	IN predicate with list of values
E061-04	LIKE predicate
E061-05	LIKE predicate: ESCAPE clause
E061-06	NULL predicate

(Continued)

Table C-1 *Continued*

Feature ID	Feature Description
E061-07	Quantified comparison predicate
E061-08	EXISTS predicate
E061-09	Subqueries in comparison predicate
E061-11	Subqueries in IN predicate
E061-12	Subqueries in quantified comparison predicate
E061-13	Correlated subqueries
E061-14	Search condition
E071	Basic query expressions
E071-01	UNION DISTINCT table operator
E071-02	UNION ALL table operator
E071-03	EXCEPT DISTINCT table operator
E071-05	Columns combined via table operators need not have exactly the same data type
E071-06	Table operators in subqueries
E081	Basic privileges
E081-01	SELECT privilege
E081-02	DELETE privilege
E081-03	INSERT privilege at the table level
E081-04	UPDATE privilege at the table level
E081-05	UPDATE privilege at the column level
E081-06	REFERENCES privilege at the table level
E081-07	REFERENCES privilege at the column level
E081-08	WITH GRANT OPTION
E091	Set functions
E091-01	AVG
E091-02	COUNT
E091-03	MAX
E091-04	MIN
E091-05	SUM
E091-06	ALL quantifier
E091-07	DISTINCT quantifier
E101	Basic data manipulation
E101-01	INSERT statement
E101-03	Searched UPDATE statement
E101-04	Searched DELETE statement

Table C-1 *Continued*

Feature ID	Feature Description
E111	Single-row SELECT statement
E121	Basic cursor support
E121-01	DECLARE CURSOR
E121-02	ORDER BY columns need not be in select list
E121-03	Value expressions in ORDER BY clause
E121-04	OPEN statement
E121-06	Positioned UPDATE statement
E121-07	Positioned DELETE statement
E121-08	CLOSE statement
E121-10	FETCH statement: implicit NEXT
E121-17	WITH HOLD cursors
E131	Null value support (nulls in lieu of values)
E141	Basic integrity constraints
E141-01	NOT NULL constraints
E141-02	UNIQUE constraints of NOT NULL columns
E141-03	PRIMARY KEY constraints
E141-04	Basic FOREIGN KEY constraint with the NO ACTION default for both referential delete action and referential update action
E141-06	CHECK constraints
E141-07	Column defaults
E141-08	NOT NULL inferred on PRIMARY KEY
E141-10	Names in a foreign key can be specified in any order
E151	Transaction support
E151-01	COMMIT statement
E151-02	ROLLBACK statement
E152	Basic SET TRANSACTION statement
E152-01	SET TRANSACTION statement: ISOLATION LEVEL SERIALIZABLE clause
E152-02	SET TRANSACTION statement: READ ONLY and READ WRITE clauses
E153	Updatable queries with subqueries
E161	SQL comments using leading double minus
E171	SQLSTATE support
E182	Module language
F021	Basic information schema
F021-01	COLUMNS view
F021-02	TABLES view

(Continued)

Table C-1 *Continued*

Feature ID	Feature Description
F021-03	VIEWS view
F021-04	TABLE_CONSTRAINTS view
F021-05	REFERENTIAL_CONSTRAINTS view
F021-06	CHECK_CONSTRAINTS view
F031	Basic schema manipulation
F031-01	CREATE TABLE statement to create persistent base tables
F031-02	CREATE VIEW statement
F031-03	GRANT statement
F031-04	ALTER TABLE statement: ADD COLUMN clause
F031-13	DROP TABLE statement: RESTRICT clause
F031-16	DROP VIEW statement: RESTRICT clause
F031-19	REVOKE statement: RESTRICT clause
F041	Basic joined table
F041-01	INNER JOIN (but not necessarily the INNER keyword)
F041-02	INNER keyword
F041-03	LEFT OUTER JOIN
F041-04	RIGHT OUTER JOIN
F041-05	Outer joins can be nested
F041-07	The inner table in a left or right outer join can also be used in an inner join
F041-08	All comparison operators are supported (rather than just =)
F051	Basic date and time
F051-01	DATE data type (including support of DATE literal)
F051-02	TIME data type (including support of TIME literal) with fractional seconds precision of at least 0
F051-03	TIMESTAMP data type (including support of TIMESTAMP literal) with fractional seconds precision of at least 0 and 6
F051-04	Comparison predicate on DATE, TIME, and TIMESTAMP data types
F051-05	Explicit CAST between datetime types and character types
F051-06	CURRENT_DATE
F051-07	LOCALTIME
F051-08	LOCALTIMESTAMP
F081	UNION and EXCEPT in views
F131	Grouped operations
F131-01	WHERE, GROUP BY, and HAVING clauses supported in queries with grouped views

Table C-1 *Continued*

Feature ID	Feature Description
F131-02	Multiple tables supported in queries with grouped views
F131-03	Set functions supported in queries with grouped views
F131-04	Subqueries with GROUP BY and HAVING clauses and grouped views
F131-05	Single-row SELECT with GROUP BY and HAVING clauses and grouped views
F181	Multiple module support
F201	CAST function
F221	Explicit defaults
F261	CASE expression
F261-01	Simple CASE
F261-02	Searched CASE
F261-03	NULLIF
F261-04	COALESCE
F311	Schema definition statement
F311-01	CREATE SCHEMA
F311-02	CREATE TABLE for persistent base tables
F311-03	CREATE VIEW
F311-04	CREATE VIEW: WITH CHECK OPTION
F311-05	GRANT statement
F471	Scalar subquery values
F481	Expanded NULL predicate
F501	Features and conformance views
F501-01	SQL_FEATURES view
F501-02	SQL_SIZING view
F501-03	SQL_LANGUAGES view
F812	Basic flagging
S011	Distinct data types
S011-01	USER_DEFINED_TYPES view
T321	Basic SQL-invoked routines
T321-01	User-defined functions with no overloading
T321-02	User-defined stored procedures with no overloading
T321-03	Function invocation
T321-04	CALL statement
T321-05	RETURN statement
T321-06	ROUTINES view
T321-07	PARAMETERS view

C.5.2   The Features of SQL:1999 Not in Core SQL

The features of SQL:1999 that are not in Core SQL are listed in Table C-2, along with their subfeatures.

Table C-2   *Features Not in Core SQL:1999*

Feature ID	Feature Description
B021	Direct SQL
B031	Basic dynamic SQL
B032	Extended dynamic SQL
B032-01	DESCRIBE INPUT statement
B041	Extensions to embedded SQL exception declarations
B051	Enhanced execution rights
C011	SQL/CLI
C021	Automatic population of implementation parameter descriptor
C041	Information Schema data controlled by current privileges
C051	GetData() extensions
C051-01	GetData() on columns before the last bound column
C051-02	GetData() can be called for columns in any order
C061	GetParamData() extensions
C061-01	GetParamData() on parameters before the last bound parameter
C061-02	GetParamData() can be called for parameters in any order
C071	Scroll concurrency
C071-01	Read-only scrollable cursors
C071-02	Updatable with locking
C071-03	Updatable with optimisitic concurrency based on row identifiers or timestamps
C071-04	Updatable with optimistic concurrency based on comparing values
C081	Read-only data source
F032	CASCADE drop behavior
F033	ALTER TABLE statement: DROP COLUMN clause
F034	Extended REVOKE statement
F034-01	REVOKE statement performed by other than the owner of a schema object
F034-02	REVOKE statement: GRANT OPTION FOR clause
F034-03	REVOKE statement to revoke a privilege that the grantee has WITH GRANT OPTION
F052	Intervals and datetime arithmetic

Table C-2 *Continued*

Feature ID	Feature Description
F111	Isolation levels other than SERIALIZABLE
F111-01	READ UNCOMMITTED isolation level
F111-02	READ COMMITTED isolation level
F111-03	REPEATABLE READ isolation level
F121	Basic diagnostics management
F121-01	GET DIAGNOSTICS statement
F121-02	SET TRANSACTION statement: DIAGNOSTICS SIZE clause
F171	Multiple schemas per user
F191	Referential delete actions
F222	INSERT statement: DEFAULT VALUES clause
F231	Privilege tables
F231-01	TABLE_PRIVILEGES view
F231-02	COLUMN_PRIVILEGES view
F231-03	USAGE_PRIVILEGES view
F251	Domain support
F271	Compound character literals
F281	LIKE enhancements
F291	UNIQUE predicate
F301	CORRESPONDING in query expressions
F302	INTERSECT table operator
F302-01	INTERSECT DISTINCT table operator
F302-02	INTERSECT ALL table operator
F304	EXCEPT ALL table operator
F321	User authorization
F341	Usage tables
F361	Subprogram support
F381	Extended schema manipulation
F381-01	ALTER TABLE statement: ALTER COLUMN clause
F381-02	ALTER TABLE statement: ADD CONSTRAINT clause
F381-03	ALTER TABLE statement: DROP CONSTRAINT clause
F391	Long identifiers
F401	Extended joined table
F401-01	NATURAL JOIN
F401-02	FULL OUTER JOIN

(Continued)

Table C-2 *Continued*

Feature ID	Feature Description
F401-03	UNION JOIN
F401-04	CROSS JOIN
F411	Time zone specification
F421	National character
F431	Read-only scrollable cursors
F431-01	FETCH with explicit NEXT
F431-02	FETCH FIRST
F431-03	FETCH LAST
F431-04	FETCH PRIOR
F431-05	FETCH ABSOLUTE
F431-06	FETCH RELATIVE
F441	Extended set function support
F451	Character set definition
F461	Named character sets
F491	Constraint management
F502	Enhanced documentation tables
F502-01	SQL_SIZING_PROFILES view
F502-02	SQL_IMPLEMENTATION_INFO view
F502-03	SQL_PACKAGES view
F511	BIT data type
F521	Assertions
F531	Temporary tables
F555	Enhanced seconds precision
F561	Full value expressions
F571	Truth value tests
F591	Derived tables
F611	Indicator data types
F641	Row and table constructors
F651	Catalog name qualifiers
F661	Simple tables
F671	Subqueries in CHECK
F691	Collation and translation
F701	Referential update actions
F711	ALTER domain
F721	Deferrable constraints

Table C-2 *Continued*

Feature ID	Feature Description
F731	INSERT column privileges
F741	Referential MATCH types
F751	View CHECK enhancements
F761	Session management
F771	Connection management
F781	Self-referencing operations
F791	Insensitive cursors
F801	Full set function
F813	Extended flagging
F821	Local table references
F831	Full cursor update
F831-01	Updatable scrollable cursors
F831-02	Updatable ordered cursors
P001	Stored modules
P001-01	<SQL-server module definition>
P001-02	DROP MODULE statement
P002	Computational completeness
P002-01	<compound statement> (BEGIN...END)
P002-02	<handler declaration>
P002-03	<condition declaration>
P002-04	<SQL variable declaration>
P002-05	<assignment statement>
P002-06	<case statement>
P002-07	<if statement>
P002-08	<iterate statement>
P002-09	<leave statement>
P002-10	<loop statement>
P002-11	<repeat statement>
P002-12	<while statement>
P002-13	<for statement>
P002-14	<signal statement>
P002-15	<resignal statement>
P002-16	<control statement>s as the SQL statement of an externally invoked procedure
P003	Information Schema views

(Continued)

Table C-2 *Continued*

Feature ID	Feature Description
P003-01	MODULES view
P003-02	MODULE_TABLE_USAGE view
P003-03	MODULE_COLUMN_USAGE view
P003-04	MODULE_PRIVILEGES view
S023	Basic structured types
S024	Enhanced structured types
S041	Basic reference types
S043	Enhanced reference types
S051	Create table of type
S071	SQL paths in function and type name resolution
S081	Subtables
S091	Basic array support
S091-01	Arrays of built-in data types
S091-02	Arrays of distinct types
S091-03	Array expressions
S092	Arrays of user-defined types
S094	Arrays of reference types
S111	ONLY in query expressions
S151	Type predicate
S161	Subtype treatment
S201	SQL routines on arrays
S201-01	Array parameters
S201-02	Array as result type of functions
S211	User-defined CAST functions
S231	Structured type locators
S232	Array locators
S241	Transform functions
S251	User-defined orderings
S261	Specific type method
T011	Timestamp in Information Schema
T031	BOOLEAN data type
T041	Basic LOB data type support
T041-01	BLOB data type
T041-02	CLOB data type

Table C-2 *Continued*

Feature ID	Feature Description
T041-03	POSITION, LENGTH, LOWER, TRIM, UPPER, and SUBSTRING functions for LOB data types
T041-04	Concatenation of LOB data types
T041-05	LOB locator: non-holdable
T042	Extended LOB data type support
T051	Row types
T111	Updatable joins, unions, and columns
T121	WITH (excluding RECURSIVE) in query expression
T131	Recursive query
T141	SIMILAR predicate
T151	DISTINCT predicate
T171	LIKE clause in table definition
T191	Referential action RESTRICT
T201	Comparable data types for referential constraints
T211	Basic trigger capability
T211-01	Triggers activated on UPDATE, INSERT, or DELETE of one base table.
T211-02	BEFORE triggers
T211-03	AFTER triggers
T211-04	FOR EACH ROW triggers
T211-05	Ability to specify a search condition that must be True before the trigger is invoked
T211-06	Support for runtime rules for the interaction of triggers and constraints.
T211-07	TRIGGER privilege
T211-08	Multiple triggers for the same event are executed in the order in which they were created in the catalog
T212	Enhanced trigger capability
T231	SENSITIVE cursors
T241	START TRANSACTION statement
T251	SET TRANSACTION statement: LOCAL option
T261	Chained transactions
T271	Savepoints
T281	SELECT privilege with column granularity
T301	Functional dependencies
T312	OVERLAY function

(Continued)

Table C-2 *Continued*

Feature ID	Feature Description
T322	Overloading of SQL-invoked functions and procedures
T323	Explicit security for external routines
T331	Basic roles
T332	Extended roles
T351	Bracketed SQL comments (/*...*/ comments)
T401	INSERT into a cursor
T411	UPDATE statement: SET ROW option
T431	CUBE and ROLLUP operations
T441	ABS and MOD functions
T461	Symmetric BETWEEN predicate
T471	Result sets return value
T491	LATERAL derived table
T501	Enhanced EXISTS predicate
T511	Transaction counts
T541	Updatable table references
T551	Optional keywords for default syntax
T561	Holdable locators
T571	Array-returning external SQL-invoked functions
T581	Regular expression substring function
T591	UNIQUE constraints of possibly null columns

C.5.3   Content of SQL:1999 Packages

In Chapter 1, "Introduction to SQL:1999," we listed the packages that are defined in SQL:1999, but we didn't tell you precisely what was in each of those packages. Table C-3 contains that information.

Table C-3 *SQL:1999 Package Contents*

Package ID	Package Description
PKG001	Enhanced datetime facilities
	Feature F052
	Feature F411
	Feature F555

Table C-3 *Continued*

Package ID	Package Description
PKG002	Enhanced integrity management
	Feature F191
	Feature F491
	Feature F521
	Feature F701
	Feature F671
	Feature T191
	Feature T201
	Feature T211
	Feature T212
PKG003	OLAP facilities
	Feature F302
	Feature F304
	Feature F401
	Feature F591
	Feature F641
	Feature T431
PKG004	PSM
	Feature T322
	Feature P001
	Feature P002
	Feature P003
PKG005	CLI
	Feature C011
PKG006	Basic object support
	Feature S023
	Feature S041
	Feature S051
	Feature S151
	Feature T041
PKG007	Enhanced object support
	Feature S024
	Feature S043
	Feature S071

(Continued)

Table C-3 *Continued*

Package ID	Package Description
	Feature S081
	Feature S111
	Feature S161
	Feature S211
	Feature S231
	Feature S241
PKG008	Active database
	Feature T211
PKG009	SQL/MM support
	Feature S023
	Feature S024
	Feature S091
	Feature S092
	Feature S211
	Feature T322

C.6 | Appendix Summary

With the information in this appendix, you should now have a thorough understanding of (1) what is contained in Core SQL:1999 and what is not, (2) how SQL:1999 differs from its predecessor standard (SQL-92), and (3) how the various implementation-defined and implementation-dependent aspects of the language are defined. The topics discussed in this appendix are useful in several ways. First, you can evaluate commercial DBMS products that claim SQL:1999 compliance and support, based on the degree to which SQL:1999 is supported. Additionally, you can check product features that are implementation-specific against the lists provided here. Since these variables are likely to be among the major differentiators for DBMS products, you can concentrate on these aspects in your product-to-product comparisons. Finally, you can also use the list of deprecated features to avoid future applications-related problems with respect to potentially unsupported SQL facilities.

Appendix
D

Relevant Standards Bodies

D.1 | Introduction

If you would like to acquire a copy of the SQL:1999 standard, you should be able to do so by contacting the accredited standards body for your country. You can request a copy of the ISO SQL:1999 standard by specifying the documents listed in the "ISO Number" column of Table D-1. If you live in the United States, you can get the ANSI standard (which is identical to the ISO standard except for such trivial matters as the name of the standard) by specifying the documents listed in the "ANSI Number" column of Table D-1. Unlike SQL-92 and earlier versions of the SQL standard, SQL:1999 is *not* available in hardcopy form—that is, printed on paper—from ISO or from ANSI (although it may be from certain national bodies: we believe that BSI has published all five parts in hardcopy form, for example). Instead, it is available from ANSI and ISO only in electronic, or machine-readable, form, specifically as an Adobe Acrobat Portable Document Format (PDF) file, either for download or on CD-ROM (depending on the source).

Table D-1 *ISO and ANSI Standards Numbers for SQL:1999*

Part Name	ISO Number	ANSI Number
SQL/Framework	ISO/IEC 9075-1:1999	ANSI/ISO/IEC 9075-1:1999
SQL/Foundation	ISO/IEC 9075-2:1999	ANSI/ISO/IEC 9075-2:1999
SQL/CLI	ISO/IEC 9075-3:1999	ANSI/ISO/IEC 9075-3:1999
SQL/PSM	ISO/IEC 9075-4:1999	ANSI/ISO/IEC 9075-4:1999
SQL/Bindings	ISO/IEC 9075-5:1999	ANSI/ISO/IEC 9075-5:1999

At the time of publication, we did not know the prices for purchasing the standards documents from ISO directly or from any national body other than ANSI in the United States. We would not be surprised, based on our experience with other standards and with previous editions of the SQL standard, if the price were quite high, possibly several hundred U.S. dollars for all five parts.

However, we do know that it is possible to purchase the five parts of the SQL standard from an organization that operates in the United States under the procedures of ANSI by means of a Web transaction (using a credit card) and a file download. At the URL *http://www.cssinfo.com/ncitsgate.html*, you can purchase each part for less than U.S. $20.00 (a total of less than U.S. $100 if you want all five parts).

In this appendix, we provide the names, addresses, telephone numbers, and (where available) fax numbers and Web addresses for the national standards bodies for several countries. If we have omitted your country, we apologize, but it is not feasible to list every country, so we have focused on those countries we believe are most likely to have interested readers.

Some countries have adopted the ISO standard and put their own standard number on it. However, this practice is not widespread and often lags publication of the ISO standard by as much as two or three years, so we won't attempt to provide that information.

The information we provide here was current at the time of publication but is always subject to change.

D.2 | Contacting ISO

You can contact ISO at these addresses:

International Organization for Standardization (ISO)
1, rue de Varembé
Case postale 56
CH-1211 Genève 20
Switzerland
Telephone: +41.22.749.0111
Telefax: +41.22.733.3430
E-mail: central@iso.ch
WWW: *http://www.iso.ch*

D.3 | Selected National Standards Bodies

The information shown was correct at the time this book went to press. However, such addresses and telephone numbers are always subject to change. You may be able to determine updates to this information by means of the ISO Web site whose URL is given in section D.2.

Australia
Standards Australia International, Ltd. (SAI)
286 Sussex Street
Sydney, NSW 2000
GPO Box 5420
Sydney, N.S.W. 2001
Telephone: +.61.2.82.06.60.00
Fax: +61.2.82.06.60.01
E-mail: intsect@standards.com.au
WWW: *http://www.standards.com.au*

Austria
Österreichisches Normungsinstitut (ON)
Heinestrasse 38
Postfach 130
1021 Wien
Telephone: +43.1.213.00
Telefax: +43.1.213.00/650
E-mail: elisabeth.stampfl-blaha@on-norm.at
WWW: *http://www.on-norm.at/*

Brazil
Associação Brasileira de Normas Técnicas (ABNT)
Av. 13 de Maio, n° 13, 28° andar
20003-900—Rio de Janeiro—RJ
Telephone: +55.21.210.31.22
Fax: +55.21.220.17.62
E-mail: abnt@abnt.org.br
WWW: *http://www.abnt.org.br/*

Canada
Standards Council of Canada (SCC)
270 Albert Street, Suite 200
Ottawa, Ontario K1P 6N7
Telephone: +1.613.238.3222
Fax: +1.613.569.7808
E-mail: isosd@scc.ca
WWW: *http://www.scc.ca*

People's Republic of China
China State Bureau of Quality and Technical Supervision (CSBTS)
4, Zhichun Road, Haidian District
P.O. Box 8010
Beijing 100088
Telephone: +86.10.6.203.2424
Fax: +86.10.6.203.3737
E-mail: csbts@mail.csbts.cn.net
WWW: *http://www.csbts.cn.net*

Denmark
Dansk Standard (DS)
Kollegievej 6
DK-2920 Charlottenlund
Telephone: +45.39.96.61.01
Fax: +45.39.96.61.02
E-mail: dansk.standard@ds.dk
WWW: *http://www.ds.dk*

France

Association Française de Normalisation (AFNOR)
Tour Europe
F-92049 Paris La Défense Cedex
Telephone: +33.1.42.91.55.55
Fax: +33.1.42.91.56.56
E-mail: international@email.afnor.fr
WWW: *http://www.afnor.fr*

Germany

Deutsches Institut für Normung (DIN)
Burggrafenstrasse 6
DE-10787 Berlin
DE-10772 Berlin
Telephone: +49.30.26.01-0
Fax: +49.30.2601.1231
E-mail: directorate.international@din.de
WWW: *http://www.din.de*

Hungary

Magyar Szabványügyi Testület (MSZT)
Üllöi út 25
Pf. 24
H-1450 Budapest 9
Telephone: +36.1.218.3011
Fax: +36.1.218.5125
E-mail: isoline@mszt.hu
WWW: *http://www.mszt.hu*

India

Bureau of Indian Standards (BIS)
Manak Bhavan
9 Bahadur Shah Zafar Marg
New Delhi 110002
Telephone: +91.11.323.7991
Fax: +91.11.323.5414
E-mail: bis@vsnl.com
WWW: *http://wwwdel.vsnl.net.in/bis.org*

Ireland

National Standards Authority of Ireland (NSAI)
Glasnevin
Dublin-9
Telephone: +353.1.807.3800
Fax: +353.1.807.3838
E-mail: nsai@nsai.ie
WWW: *http://www.nsai.ie*

Israel
Standards Institution of Israel (SII)
42 Chaim Levanon Street
Tel Aviv 69977
Telephone: +972.3.646.5154
Fax: +972.3.641.9683
E-mail: iso/iecsii.org.il
WWW: *http://www.sii.org.il*

Italy
Ente Nazionale Italiano di Unificaziono (UNI)
Via Battistotti Sassi 11/b
I-20133 Milano
Telephone: +39.2.70.02.41
Fax: +39.2.70.10.61.06
E-mail: uni@uni.com
WWW: *http://www.uni.com*

Japan
Japanese Industrial Standards Committee (JISC)
c/o Standards Department
Ministry of International Trade and Industry
1-3-1, Kasumigaseki, Chiyoda-ku
Tokyo 100
Telephone: +81.3.3501.2096
Fax: +81.3.3580.8637
E-mail: jisc_iso@jsa.or.jp
WWW: *http://www.jis.org*

Republic of Korea
Korean National Institute of Technology and Quality (KATS)
Ministry of Commerce, Industry, and Energy
2 Joongang-dong
Kwachon-city
KR-Kyunggi-do 427-010
Telephone: +82.2.507.4369
Telefax: +82.2.503.7977
E-mail: standard@ats.go.kr
WWW: *http://www.ats.go.kr*

The Netherlands
Nederlands Normalisatie-instituut (NEN)
Vlinderweg 6
NL-2623 AX Delft
P.O. Box 5059
NL-2600 GB Delft
Telephone: +31.15.2.69.0390
Fax: +31.15.2.69.0190
E-mail: info@nen.nl
WWW: *http://www.nen.nl*

New Zealand
Standards New Zealand (SNZ)
Radio New Zealand House
155 The Terrace
NZ-Wellington 6001
Private Bag 2439
NZ-Wellington 6020
Telephone: +64.4.498.59.90
Telefax: +64.4.498.59.94
E-mail: snz@standards.co.nz
WWW: *http://www.standards.co.nz/*

Norway
Norges Standardiseringsforbund (NSF)
Drammensveien 145 A
Postboks 353 Skoyen
NO-0213 Oslo
Telephone: +47.22.04.92.00
Fax: +47.22.04.92.11
E-mail: firmapost@standard.no
WWW: *http://www.standard.no*

Russian Federation
State Committee of the Russian Federation for Standardization
   and Metrology (GOST R)
Leninsky Prospekt 9
Moskva 117049
Telephone: +7.95.236.4044
Fax: +7.95.237.6032
E-mail: info@gost.ru
WWW: *http://www.gost.ru*

Spain
Asociación Española de Normalización y Certificación (AENOR)
Génova, 6
E-28004 Madrid
Telephone: +34.1.432.6000
Fax: +34.1.310.4976
E-mail: aenor@aenor.es
WWW: *http://www.aenor.es*

Sweden
Standardiseringkommissionen i Sverige (SIS)
S:t Eriksgatan 115
SE-113 43 Stockholm
Box 6455
S-113 82 Stockholm
Telephone: +46.8.610.3000
Fax: +46.8.30.7757
E-mail: info@sis.se
WWW: *http://www.sis.se*

Switzerland
Swiss Association for Standardization (SNV)
Mühlebachstrasse 54
CH-8008 Zurich
Telephone: +41.1.254.5454
Fax: +41.1.254.5474
E-mail: info@snv.ch
WWW: *http://www.snv.ch*

United Kingdom
British Standards Institute (BSI)
389 Chiswick High Road
GB-London W4 4AL
Telephone: +44.208.996.9000
Fax: +44.208.996.7400
E-mail: standards.international@bsi-global.com
WWW: *http://www.bsi-global.com*

United States of America
American National Standards Institute (ANSI)
11 West 42nd Street, 13th floor
New York, NY 10036
Telephone: +1.212.642.4900
Fax: +1.212.398.0023
E-mail: info@ansi.org
WWW: *http://www.ansi.org*

Appendix

E

Status Codes

Values of SQLSTATE

In this appendix, we list the various values of SQLSTATE. We discussed this status code in Chapter 20, "Diagnostics and Error Management," and we talked about exception handling and program structure in Chapter 12, "Accessing SQL from the Real World."

In Table E-1, the column named "Category" contains a code to indicate the specific type of SQLSTATE to which the Condition and Class correspond. A value of 'X' means that the Condition and Class identify an exception condition; 'N' means the no-data completion condition; 'W' means a warning completion condition; and 'S' means a successful completion condition. As you'd expect, rows for subconditions take on the SQLSTATE type of their associated condition and class.

Table E-1 *SQLSTATE Values*

Category	Condition	Class	Subcondition	Subclass
X	Ambiguous cursor name	3C	(No subclass)	000
X	Attempt to assign to non-updatable column	0U	(No subclass)	000
X	Attempt to assign to ordering column	0V	(No subclass)	000
X	Cardinality violation	21	(No subclass)	000
X	Case not found for case statement	20	(No subclass)	000
X	CLI-specific condition	HY	(No subclass)	000
			Associated statement is not prepared	007
			Attempt to concatenate a null value	020
			Attribute cannot be set now	011
			Column type out of range	097
			Dynamic parameter value needed	*
			Function sequence error	010
			Inconsistent descriptor information	021
			Invalid attribute identifier	092
			Invalid attribute value	024
			Invalid cursor position	109
			Invalid data type	004
			Invalid data type in application descriptor	003
			Invalid descriptor field identifier	091
			Invalid fetch orientation	106
			Invalid FunctionId specified	095
			Invalid handle	†
			Invalid information type	096
			Invalid LengthPrecision value	104
			Invalid parameter mode	105
			Invalid retrieval code	103
			Invalid string length or buffer length	090
			Invalid transaction operation code	012
			Invalid use of automatically allocated descriptor handle	017
			Invalid use of null pointer	009

* No subclass value is defined for *dynamic parameter value needed,* since no diagnostic information is generated in this case.

† No subclass value is defined for *invalid handle,* since no diagnostic information can be generated in this case.

Table E-1 *Continued*

Category	Condition	Class	Subcondition	Subclass
			Limit on number of handles exceeded	014
			Memory allocation error	001
			Memory management error	013
			Non-string data cannot be sent in pieces	019
			Non-string data cannot be used with string routine	055
			Nullable type out of range	099
			Operation canceled	008
			Optional feature not implemented	C00
			Row value out of range	107
			Scope out of range	098
			Server declined the cancellation request	018
X	Connection exception	08	(No subclass)	000
			Connection does not exist	003
			Connection failure	006
			Connection name in use	002
			SQL-client unable to establish SQL-connection	001
			SQL-server rejected establishment of SQL-connection	004
			Transaction resolution unknown	007
X	Cursor sensitivity exception	36	(No subclass)	000
			Request failed	002
			Request rejected	001
X	Data exception	22	(No subclass)	000
			Array data, right truncation	02F
			Array element error	02E
			Character not in repertoire	021
			Datetime field overflow	008
			Division by zero	012
			Error in assignment	005
			Escape character conflict	00B
			Indicator overflow	022
			Interval field overflow	015
			Invalid character value for cast	018

(Continued)

Table E-1 *Continued*

Category	Condition	Class	Subcondition	Subclass
			Invalid datetime format	007
			Invalid escape character	019
X	Data exception *(Continued)*		Invalid escape octet	00D
			Invalid escape sequence	025
			Invalid indicator parameter value	010
			Invalid limit value	020
			Invalid parameter value	023
			Invalid regular expression	01B
			Invalid time zone displacement value	009
			Invalid update value	014
			Invalid use of escape character	00C
			Most specific type mismatch	00G
			Null instance used in mutator function	02D
			Null row not permitted in table	01C
			Null value in array target	00E
			Null value in reference target	00A
			Null value in field reference	006
			Null value, no indicator parameter	002
			Null value not allowed	004
			Numeric value out of range	003
			Row already exists	028
			String data, length mismatch	026
			String data, right truncation	001
			Substring error	011
			Trim error	027
			Unterminated C string	024
			Zero-length character string	00F
X	Dependent privilege descriptors still exist	2B	(No subclass)	000
X	Dynamic SQL error	07	(No subclass)	000
			Cursor specification cannot be executed	003
			Invalid descriptor count	008
			Invalid descriptor index	009
			Prepared statement not a cursor specification	005
			Restricted data type attribute violation	006
			Undefined DATA value	00C

Table E-1 *Continued*

Category	Condition	Class	Subcondition	Subclass
			Undefined DATA target	00D
			Undefined LEVEL value	00E
			Undefined DATETIME_INTERVAL_ CODE	00F
			USING clause does not match dynamic parameter specifications	001
			USING clause does not match target specifications	002
			USING clause required for dynamic parameters	004
			USING clause required for result fields	007
			Data type transform function violation	00B
			Containing SQL not permitted	001
			Modifying SQL-data not permitted	002
			Prohibited SQL-statement attempted	003
			Reading SQL-data not permitted	004
X	External routine invocation exception	39	(No subclass)	000
			Invalid SQLSTATE returned	001
			Null value not allowed	004
X	Feature not supported	0A	(No subclass)	000
			Multiple server transactions	001
X	Integrity constraint violation	23	(No subclass)	000
			Restrict violation	001
X	Invalid authorization specification	28	(No subclass)	000
X	Invalid catalog name	3D	(No subclass)	000
X	Invalid character set name	2C	(No subclass)	000
X	Invalid condition number	35	(No subclass)	000
X	Invalid connection name	2E	(No subclass)	000
X	Invalid cursor name	34	(No subclass)	000
X	Invalid cursor state	24	(No subclass)	000
X	Invalid grantor	0L	(No subclass)	000
X	Invalid role specification	0P	(No subclass)	000
X	Invalid schema name	3F	(No subclass)	000

(Continued)

Table E-1 *Continued*

Category	Condition	Class	Subcondition	Subclass
X	Invalid schema name list specification	0E	(No subclass)	000
X	Invalid SQL descriptor name	33	(No subclass)	000
X	Invalid SQL-invoked procedure reference	0M	(No subclass)	000
X	Invalid SQL statement name	26	(No subclass)	000
X	Invalid SQL statement	30	(No subclass)	000
X	Invalid target specification value	31	(No subclass)	000
X	Invalid target type specification	0D	(No subclass)	000
X	Invalid transaction initiation	0B	(No subclass)	000
X	Invalid transaction state	25	(No subclass)	000
			Active SQL-transaction	001
			Branch transaction already active	002
			Held cursor requires same isolation level	008
			Inappropriate access mode for branch transaction	003
			Inappropriate isolation level for branch transaction	004
			No active SQL-transaction for branch transaction	005
			Read-only SQL-transaction	006
			Schema and data statement mixing not supported	007
X	Invalid transaction termination	2D	(No subclass)	000
X	Invalid transform group name specification	0S	(No subclass)	000
X	Locator exception	0F	(No subclass)	000
			Invalid specification	001
N	No data	02	(No subclass)	000
			No additional dynamic result sets returned	001

Table E-1 *Continued*

Category	Condition	Class	Subcondition	Subclass
X	Prohibited statement encountered during trigger execution	0W	(No subclass)	000
X	Resignal when handler not active	0K	(No subclass)	000
X	Savepoint exception	3B	(No subclass)	000
			Invalid specification	001
			Too many	002
X	SQL routine exception	2F	(No subclass)	000
			Function executed no return statement	005
			Modifying SQL-data not permitted	002
			Prohibited SQL-statement attempted	003
			Reading SQL-data not permitted	004
X	SQL statement not yet complete	03	(No subclass)	000
S	Successful completion	00	(No subclass)	000
X	Syntax error or access rule violation	42	(No subclass)	000
X	Target table disagrees with cursor specification	0T	(No subclass)	000
X	Transaction rollback	40	(No subclass)	000
			Integrity constraint violation	002
			Serialization failure	001
			Statement completion unknown	003
			Triggered action exception	004
X	Triggered action exception	09	(No subclass)	000
X	Triggered data change violation	27	(No subclass)	000
X	Unhandled user-defined exception	45	*(No subclass)*	000
W	Warning	01	(No subclass)	000
			Additional result sets returned	00D
			Array data, right truncation	02F
			Attempt to return too many result sets	00E
			Cursor operation conflict	001

(Continued)

Table E-1 *Continued*

Category	Condition	Class	Subcondition	Subclass
			Default value too long for Information Schema	00B
			Disconnect error	002
			Dynamic result sets returned	00C
W	Warning *(Continued)*		External routine warning (the value of *xx* to be chosen by the author of the external routine)	H*xx*
			Implicit zero-bit padding	008
			Insufficient item descriptor areas	005
			Null value eliminated in set function	003
			Privilege not granted	007
			Privilege not revoked	006
			Query expression too long for Information Schema	00A
			Search condition too long for Information Schema	009
			Statement too long for Information Schema	005
			String data, right truncation	004
X	With check option violation	44	(No subclass)	000

Appendix F

The SQL Standardization Process

F.1 Introduction

In this appendix, we present an overview of the ANSI and ISO standardization processes with an emphasis on SQL. While this material isn't essential to use SQL, it will give interested readers some background about how certain facets of the language have been developed. Those who wonder why SQL doesn't have such-and-such a feature or why SQL does things in a particular way will likely understand a bit more about the standardization process from this discussion.

F.2 The Various Standards Bodies

F.2.1 National Standards

ANSI, the American National Standards Institute, is the primary formal standards-making body in the United States. Other countries (at least the developed countries, but also many developing countries) have their own standards bodies: for example, BSI (the British Standards Institute) in the UK, AFNOR (Association Française de Normalization) in France, and DIN (Deutsches Institut für Normung) in Germany. We will limit our national standards overview to ANSI, since no other national standards body has developed its own SQL standard. (However, it is not uncommon for other national standards bodies to republish ISO standards with a domestic number assigned to the republished standard.)

ANSI is really an oversight organization. The actual work of developing standards is the responsibility of ACMOs (accredited standards-making organizations). Responsibility for standards in the area of information processing has been given to an organization called NCITS (National Committee for Information Technology Standards), formerly known by the code-without-a-meaning "X3." The day-to-day affairs of NCITS are managed by an industry group called ITIC (Information Technology Industry Council), headquartered in Washington, DC.

NCITS's responsibilities are very broad and extensive, so it further delegates the actual technical work to technical committees (TCs) and to special working groups. When NCITS was still known as X3, it had created a special group called SPARC (Standards Planning and Requirements Committee), whose job it was to determine the need for standards in certain areas and to oversee the development of those standards. SPARC had its own subgroups, one of which was named DBSSG (Database Systems Study Group), which was concerned with broad issues of database standardization (as opposed to specific standards like SQL). However, with the change in name to NCITS, the special groups were also dropped, leaving NCITS as a whole responsible for reviewing proposals for new standards, progress on standards development, and so forth.

There are many NCITS technical committees. One of these is named H2, which has the title "Database." H2's responsibilities include SQL and other projects not relevant to this book. (For more information about H2's other responsibilities, please contact ITIC.)

When an interested party believes that the time is ripe to develop a standard for some area of information processing, that party writes a project proposal for submission to NCITS. This document, called an SD-3 (for "Standing Document number 3"), sets forth the details of the standards development activity proposed for the specific area. This includes information such as the proposed name, the relationship to existing standards or developing standards, the affected industry, the likely participants in the project, and so forth.

If NCITS agrees that an effort should be made to standardize the subject matter in question, it will either assign the project to an existing NCITS technical committee (which may have been the interested party that wrote the SD-3 in the first place) or recommend the formation of a new technical committee to do the work.

The TC assigned responsibility for the project then produces a working draft of the standard (indeed, many SD-3s are accompanied by a proposed working draft, which considerably accelerates the work). At some point, the committee conducts a formal ballot to decide if the working draft is ready for broader review.

This decision requires a ballot agreement of at least two-thirds of the committee. If ready, the TC asks NCITS to approve the initiation of a public review of the document. The purpose of a public review is to permit the general public, in the United States and elsewhere, to review the document and comment on it. The TC is required to respond to every comment within a relatively short period following a public review (although they are obviously not required to satisfy every request).

The document may iterate through several cycles of development and public review. At some point, though, the TC members will decide that the document is complete and will make no further changes as a result of public review comments. The document is then forwarded to BSR (the Board of Standard Review) for its review. BSR's review ensures that the ANSI and NCITS rules have been followed and that no one has been deprived of due process. Assuming that these requirements have been met, the document is then published as an ANSI standard. NCITS's standards are published with an identifying number: NCITS n, where NCITS identifies the standard as coming from NCITS, and n identifies the nth standard published by NCITS (possibly in its earlier incarnation as X3). Before X3 became NCITS, its standards were numbered "X3.n." In addition, the year of publication is attached to the number: X3.135-1986 is the number of the first version of the SQL standard, published in 1986, for example.

In recent years, some standards—recently, SQL among them—that are developed principally in the international community (that is, in ISO) are merely adopted by ANSI and given the ISO number prefixed with "ANSI/."

F.2.2 International Standards

Once upon a time, when the world was a larger and simpler place to do business, national standards were quite sufficient for most people's and organizations' purposes. In fact, one often found that ANSI developed a standard for some area of information processing technology and other national standards bodies simply adopted the ANSI standard unchanged. This process occasionally worked the other way, too: ANSI sometimes adopted other countries' standards unchanged.

However, as the world became smaller and more complex, businesses and other users of information processing systems realized that they were sometimes faced with using products that had to conform to one standard in one country and a different standard in another country. That fact cost many organizations countless millions of dollars and untold difficulties. These organizations, and others who became aware of the problems, realized that only international standards would address their requirements. The International Organization for Standardization (ISO) was formed specifically to address these concerns. Note:

ISO was (and is) not the only such organization. The International Electro-technical Commission (IEC) exists specifically to address international standards in the electrotechnical area (obvious, isn't it?); CCITT (Comité Consultatif International de Téléphone et Télégraph) exists to standardize communications issues (that's why you can place telephone calls between countries).

Some such organizations are called *treaty organizations* because they are established by treaty among various nations, and their specifications are mandatory for adoption by signatories to those treaties. Others, such as ISO, are *voluntary standards organizations*, because adoption of their standards is not mandated by a treaty (although this can be mandated within a given country, as determined by the laws of that country).

Like ANSI, ISO has far too broad a scope to permit actual work to be done at that level. Instead, ISO also assigns areas of work to technical committees (TCs). In some cases, such as information technology, the scope is still too broad, so subcommittees (SCs) are formed. In a few cases, data management among them, the work is still too extensive, so working groups (WGs) are given the responsibility.

In ISO, work on information technology was assigned in the mid-1980s to a technical committee numbered TC97. This committee was later reorganized, in cooperation with IEC, as JTC1 (where JTC1 stands for "Joint Technical Committee 1"). An area of information technology called Open Systems Interconnect (or OSI) was divided into two groups; the responsibility for "Information Processing, Transfer, and Retrieval for OSI" was given to a subcommittee numbered SC21. In turn, responsibility for database issues was given to a working group, WG3 (full title: ISO/IEC JTC1/SC21/WG3).

In the late 1990s, the failure of OSI became apparent to even the most casual observer: a different networking standard, often known as "TCP/IP," had won the day while the *de jure* standards organizations were fighting over the details of their intended new protocols. In the wake of OSI's demise, SC21 was dismantled and its projects either canceled entirely or assigned to other subcommittees. The various data management–related projects, including some that had not been part of SC21, were assigned to a new subcommittee numbered SC32. SC32 has divided itself into several working groups, of which WG3 is responsible for SQL.

F.2.3 Standards Development in ISO

As you might expect, the ISO process is quite different from the ANSI process. In the former, only countries—that is, the standards body from each country—are allowed to vote at ISO meetings, to propose projects, or to raise issues. By contrast, in ANSI, individuals who attend meetings represent their employers or may even represent themselves. Of course, individuals represent their countries at ISO meetings, but the decisions must have been previously coordinated in the national standards bodies. The United States is represented in ISO by ANSI, the UK by BSI, France by AFNOR, and so forth.

When some country believes that it's time to standardize some aspect of information technology, it raises an issue as a national position either directly with ISO/IEC JTC1 or with one of the SCs, such as SC32, who (if approved at that level) forwards the request to JTC1. A JTC1 ballot is initiated to determine if JTC1 member countries believe that such a project should be initiated and if there is likely to be sufficient resources (read "active participation") to develop a standard based on the project. If enough countries agree (at least five countries must commit to participation in the development), then the work is assigned to an existing SC or, in some situations, a new SC is formed and the project assigned to it. The SC then decides whether the work can be done by the SC as a whole or whether it should be assigned to an existing or new WG for development.

As in ANSI, a working draft is developed (and may accompany the project proposal) by the assigned group. At some point, the group believes that the document is ready for wider review, so it distributes the document as a Working Draft (note the capital letters, WD); the document still has no real formal standing at this point. However, the document may be formally registered as a Committee Draft (CD), which implies distribution at least throughout the SC's participating national bodies. It also implies the initiation of a CD ballot. A successful CD ballot means that the document (perhaps after an editing meeting, at which ballot comments are resolved) progresses to become a Final Committee Draft (FCD).

Alternatively, at some point after the document has been distributed as a working draft, it may be registered for a Final Committee Draft ballot, during which national bodies submit ballot comments, which are typically resolved at an editing meeting. After a successful FCD ballot, the document is progressed to the next stage, which may be either Draft International Standard (DIS) or Final Draft International Standard (FDIS).

If the CD or FCD ballot is unsuccessful (as a result of too many substantial changes, regardless of the actual vote), then the assigned group does more work and tries again. (Common wisdom says that a document that fails three CD and/ or FCD ballots is probably dead in the water.)

Progression to DIS or FDIS status, in turn, implies the initiation of a DIS ballot or an FDIS ballot. Once the document reaches this stage, a DIS ballot or an FDIS ballot is initiated (sometimes after doing a bit more editorial work, but not changing the document substantially). Again, if that ballot is unsuccessful, there may be more work and additional DIS or FDIS ballots; indeed, the document may be pushed back to CD status or even WD status. A successful DIS ballot means that (after an editing meeting to resolve comments) the document is advanced to FDIS status.

A successful FDIS ballot means that, without any additional editing, the document progresses to International Standard (IS) status and is forwarded to the ISO Central Secretariat (via the SC and TC or JTC responsible for it) for a review of the process used. If it passes this review, then the document is published with an ISO or ISO/IEC number. SQL, for example, was initially published as ISO 9075-1987. Later, ISO changed the convention so that a colon was used to separate the standard number from the year of publication, so that the next revision was ISO 9075:1989. Still later, when JTC1 was formed, its standards used ISO/IEC, so the title of SQL-92 was ISO/IEC 9075:1992.

Usually, this process works very well. Every generation of SQL, for example, has been published both as an ANSI and an ISO standard. Except for such obvious matters as the standard number and references to other ANSI and ISO standards, the two publications are identical. This represents an ideal model of cooperation between a national standards group and the international process. Other standards have been less fortunate, and national bodies have developed standards that are incompatibly different from the international version.

F.3 | History of the SQL Standard

In 1978, ANSI X3 SPARC recommended the formation of a new technical committee (TC) called X3H2; the project assigned to this new committee was the development of a data definition language for CODASYL databases (CODASYL = Common Data System Languages; CODASYL developed COBOL and also developed a specification for the network database model). It quickly became apparent to the participants of this TC that developing a DDL alone would not satisfy the requirements of the marketplace, so the scope of work was enlarged to include a data sublanguage for network databases. This language was called Database Language NDL (and it was broadly understood that NDL stood for "Network Database Language").

During development of NDL, it became apparent that the relational data model was increasingly important, so the DBSSG (q.v.) recommended a second project for the development of a relational database standard, and in 1982 that project was also assigned to X3H2. X3H2 decided to base the standard on the SQL database language, since it had been implemented by more than one vendor (first Oracle, and then IBM) and appeared to be gaining widespread acceptance. For a couple of years, X3H2 "improved" SQL with many changes based on 20-20 hindsight, and, since a good many of those changes made the draft standard incompatible with SQL, the working name was changed to RDL, for "Relational

Database Language." In 1984, the committee reassessed this effort and concluded that the changes it had made to the SQL specification did not in fact improve the language enough to justify the incompatibilities with the de facto SQL standard already implemented. The committee decided to revert to the original SQL specifications. These specifications were refined somewhat and then published as the initial SQL standard late in 1986 (ISO ratified the document early in 1987). Subsequently, almost all of the improvements and generalizations that had been developed for RDL were added to SQL in the SQL-92 revision; as it turned out, most of them could be accomplished in an upward compatible manner.

In about 1984, ISO TC97/SC5 (which previously had responsibility for programming languages, graphics, database languages, and various other areas) was reorganized along with TC97/SC16. Some of the projects were assigned to one new subcommittee—TC97/SC22 (programming languages)—while others were assigned to another new SC—TC97/SC21 (related to OSI). The database work went into SC21 because it was viewed as an "application" of the networking standards being developed by SC21.

In fact, TC97/SC5 was already reviewing the NDL and RDL work as early as 1982. When SC21 was formed, the actual project assigned was titled "Data Definition Language" and was only later evolved into NDL. As ANSI X3H2 began serious development on RDL and, later, on SQL, TC97/SC21 also picked up that work.

These efforts resulted in the late 1986 publication of ANSI X3.135-1986, "Database Language SQL," in the United States. Because of differences in the process, it was early in 1987 before ISO published ISO 9075-1987, "Database Language SQL." This standard was very close to the IBM implementation, but with sufficient restrictions, escape hatches, and unspecified areas that it served as a sort of least common denominator for several implementations. Unfortunately, it left users with little ability to write meaningful applications that were portable among products from different vendors (indeed, IBM's several implementations were not completely compatible even among themselves).

This standard was defined to have two levels, called (cleverly enough) Level 1 and Level 2. Level 1 was designed to be an intersection of features that were already widely implemented by most SQL vendors, while Level 2 added a few additional features and relaxed some restrictions.

One significant comment in the various public reviews and ISO ballots was that the language was missing a very important feature: referential integrity (see Chapter 10, "Constraints, Assertions, and Referential Integrity"). A compromise was reached that allowed the first version of SQL (often referred to as SQL-86 or, less often, SQL-87 because of the ISO publication date) to go forward; the compromise required the rapid turnaround of an amendment (often called "Addendum 1" by the committees) or a revised standard that included at least basic referential integrity.

Work had begun on that revision even before SQL-86 was published. However, because the TCs (and WGs) were unfamiliar with publishing revised standards and because both ANSI and ISO had undergone some reorganization, delays mounted until the so-called rapid turnaround became three years. It was thus mid-1989 when ISO published ISO 9075:1989, "Database Language SQL With Integrity Enhancement," and late 1989 when ANSI published the corresponding X3.135-1989.

Some U.S. government users were critical of SQL-86 because the specification of how to embed SQL in conventional programming languages was contained in an appendix that was explicitly "informative." These users worried that this fact might mean that portable implementations of embedded SQL wouldn't be supported because they weren't "normative" (required). These concerns caused X3H2 to develop a second standard that made the embedding specifications normative; that standard was published in 1989 as ANSI X3.168-1989, "Database Language Embedded SQL." ISO chose not to publish an analogous standard because of a lack of similar concerns in the international community. Unfortunately, this decision meant that ISO had no definition for embedding SQL into Ada or C until SQL-92 was published, while ANSI did.

SQL-89 retained the two levels of SQL-86. It also made the Integrity Enhancement Feature optional, so that vendors could claim conformance to the standard without having to implement that feature.

F.3.1   SQL2

Because of the delays in publishing SQL-89 (as it became known), work was already in full swing for a second revision of SQL by late 1987. This project, code-named "SQL2" by both X3H2 and ISO/IEC JTC1/SC21, was to define a major revision to the language, making it a more complete language instead of a least common denominator.

Work was completed on that project in late 1991 (although fine-tuning persisted into early 1992), and the document was published in late 1992 by ANSI as X3.135-1992, "Information Systems—Database Language—SQL," and by ISO as ISO/IEC 9075:1992, "Information Technology—Database Languages—SQL." SQL-92, as this standard was commonly known, was extensively addressed by an earlier work by the authors of this book.[1]

---

[1] Jim Melton and Alan R. Simon, *Understanding the New SQL: A Complete Guide* (San Francisco: Morgan Kaufmann Publishers, 1992).

F.3.2 SQL3

Even before publication of SQL-92, work had begun on the next generation of the SQL standard, which was naturally called "SQL3" in its project stage. SQL3 was planned to be a major enhancement of the language, adding object technology along with a host of more traditional relational database features (such as triggers).

The object additions proved to be vastly more difficult, both technically and politically, than anyone had anticipated. As a result, the "tradition" of publishing a revision of the SQL standard at three-year intervals fell apart, and it took a full seven years to finish this major revision of the standard.

Of course, the committees were not idly limiting themselves strictly to the major enhancement of SQL. In 1995, a new "part"—a separate document closely aligned with the rest of the standard—was published in alignment with SQL-92. This new part, called SQL/CLI or CLI-95, defined a call-level interface to SQL database systems. Then, in 1996, another new part was published to align with SQL-92; this part, called SQL/PSM or PSM-96, specified the ability to define functions and procedures written in SQL or in a host programming language and invoked from SQL programs, commonly called *stored procedures* because they are actually stored right in the database itself. It also defined a number of procedural SQL statements, thus making SQL computationally complete for the first time.

When SQL3 was finally completed in 1999, it contained five parts: SQL/Framework, SQL/Foundation, SQL/CLI, SQL/PSM, and SQL/Bindings. However, other parts were already in development and have very recently (as of the time we write these words) been completed: SQL/MED (Management of External Data) and SQL/OLB (Object Language Bindings). You can read about SQL/MED in Volume 2 of this book, while SQL/OLB is discussed in detail in another work by one of the authors of this book.[2]

F.4 | NIST and the FIPS

In the United States, the federal government is a major user of computer systems, including database systems. Agencies of the U.S. federal government depend on the National Institute of Standards and Technology (NIST, formerly known as the National Bureau of Standards, or NBS) to advise them on information technology procurements. In many cases, this advice took the form of a Federal Information Processing Standard (FIPS).

---

2 Jim Melton and Andrew Eisenberg, *Understanding SQL and Java Together: A Guide to SQLJ, JDBC, and Related Technologies* (San Francisco: Morgan Kaufmann Publishers, 2000).

A FIPS often specified a particular way to conform to an existing ANSI standard, or to an existing ISO standard, or it sometimes defined a completely independent specification itself. In the case of SQL, NIST wrote a FIPS in early 1987 that specified conformance to ANSI X3.135-1986. This FIPS was published as FIPS PUB 127 (PUB standing for "publication"). It ignored Level 1 of SQL-86 and required conformance to Level 2 of that standard.

In 1989, NIST published a revised FIPS called FIPS PUB 127-1, which specified conformance to Level 2 of X3.135-1989. Like the SQL-89 standard, FIPS PUB 127-1 specifies the Integrity Enhancement Feature as an optional feature. It also specifies the required minimum values for many elements of the language that the standard left as implementation-defined.

NIST published yet another revision in 1992, called FIPS PUB 127-2. That revision specified conformance to ANSI X3.135-1992, with the emphasis on the Entry SQL level. It also specified minimum values for additional implementation-defined elements as well as requiring additional "system tables" to document some aspects of the implementation. NIST has also developed a conformance test suite that allows it to test implementations that claim conformance to SQL-89. FIPS PUB 127-2 defined a new conformance level for SQL-92, about halfway between Entry SQL and Intermediate SQL, called Transitional SQL. Transitional SQL had the goal of giving SQL DBMS developers guidance on which features should be implemented first and which could safely be deferred. It also permitted claims of conformance to the Intermediate SQL and Full SQL levels but did not provide additional requirements or clarification.

However, changes determined by the United States Congress removed NIST's responsibilities for developing and publishing FIPS, as well as their mandate to do conformance testing for many standards, including SQL. At the time we write these words, there is no widely recognized authority doing conformance testing on SQL database systems.

F.5 | Other SQL-Related Organizations

So far, we've talked about the *de jure*, or formal, standards organizations that produce SQL standards. However, there are also several additional bodies that are concerned with SQL. These groups do not publish formal standards, but their work is sometimes referred to as a *de facto* standard because it gets widely implemented.

X/Open Company, Ltd., now known as The Open Group, is a consortium of companies (initially UNIX system vendors) that publishes Portability Guides for many computer-related areas, including operating system interfaces (UNIX), programming languages (C and COBOL), networking, security, and data management. The X/Open Data Management Working Group was responsible for producing the XPG (XPG = X/Open Portability Guide) text for SQL. The fourth generation of these guides (XPG4) was published late in 1992 and included a definition of SQL closely based on the Entry SQL level of SQL-92, but with several extensions. These extensions are based on commonly implemented vendor extensions (such as CREATE INDEX and DROP INDEX) and several features of Intermediate SQL (such as the diagnostics area, the GET DIAGNOSTICS statement, and parts of dynamic SQL).

X/Open worked closely with another consortium, called the SQL Access Group (SAG), in database-related matters. SAG was formed to prototype the (then) emerging ISO standard for Remote Database Access (RDA); that work inevitably led to SQL-related questions and issues, so X/Open and SAG joined forces to update X/Open's SQL definition to better conform to the ANSI and ISO SQL-92 standards and to "fill in the blanks" where the ANSI and ISO standards left elements implementation-defined. SAG's most important contribution, however, was development of the call-level interface that eventually became SQL/CLI.

As mentioned in the preceding paragraph, ISO produced a standard called "Remote Database Access," or "RDA" (ISO/IEC 9579-1, *Remote Database Access, Part 1: Generic*, and ISO/IEC 9579-2, *Remote Database Access, Part 2: SQL Specialization*). This standard specified the formats and protocols for accessing an SQL database system across an OSI (Open Systems Interconnect) network. The 1992 version of RDA supported Entry SQL-92; later work supported Intermediate and Full SQL-92. RDA, even after revision to remove the OSI dependencies (and replace them with a TCP/IP orientation), has not proven to have commercial support.

We should also point out that, although SQL defines language for metadata operations (CREATE, ALTER, and DROP) and a place where the metadata is "reflected" (the information and definition schemas, which we discussed in Chapter 22, "Information Schema"), you shouldn't look at SQL as the answer to all data dictionary or repository questions. ANSI NCITS H4 produced a standard called IRDS that addresses repository issues without using SQL at all. ISO/IEC JTC1/SC21/WG3 produced a *different* standard, also called IRDS, that addresses repository issues, but with a close relationship to SQL (in fact, it uses SQL language in many places for the definition). As with RDA, neither IRDS standard had commercial support. Other metadata standards continue to be pursued, none with significant commercial presence.

F.6 | Appendix Summary

As we mentioned at the outset of this appendix, you don't need to know much about the background and history of SQL, nor about the standards process, to use SQL:1999. You can, however, amaze your friends and co-workers with your in-depth knowledge about the standards process. Who knows, you may even get selected (or drafted) to participate in a standards development process.

Index

About the Authors

Jim Melton is editor of all parts of ISO/IEC 9075 (SQL) and representative for database standards at Oracle Corporation. Since 1986, he has been his company's representative to ANSI NCITS Technical Committee H2 for Database and a U.S. representative to ISO/IEC JTC1/SC32/WG3. He was the editor of SQL-92 and the recently published SQL:1999 suite of standards, and he is the author of several SQL books. Jim recently became active in the World Wide Web Consortium (W3C) process, working on development of a query language for XML.

Alan Simon is a leading authority on data warehousing and database technology. He is the author of 26 books, including the previous edition of this book and the forthcoming *Data Warehousing and Business Intelligence for E-Commerce*, available from Morgan Kaufmann Publishers in 2001. He currently provides data warehousing–related consulting services to clients.